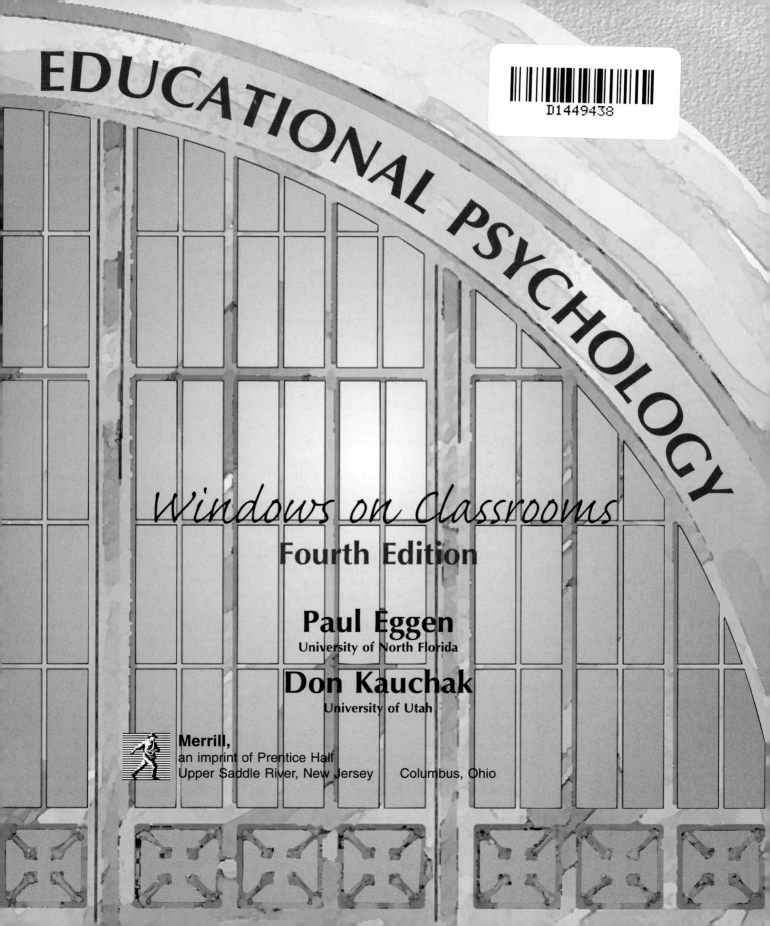

EDUCATIONAL PSYCHOLOGY

Windows on Classrooms

Fourth Edition

Paul Eggen
University of North Florida

Don Kauchak
University of Utah

Merrill,
an imprint of Prentice Hall
Upper Saddle River, New Jersey   Columbus, Ohio

Library of Congress Cataloging-in-Publication Data

Eggen, Paul D.
    Educational psychology : windows on classrooms / Paul Eggen, Don
Kauchak. —4th ed.
        p.   cm.
    Includes bibliographical references and index.
    ISBN 0-13-080091-0 (pbk.)
    1. Educational psychology—Study and teaching (Higher)—United
States.   2. Learning, Psychology of—Case studies.   I. Kauchak,
Donald P.   II. Title.
LB1051.E463   1999
370.15—dc21   98-16498
                                                             CIP

Cover Photo: © Photo Edit	Text Designer: Susan Unger
Editor: Kevin M. Davis	Cover Designer: Ceri Fitzgerald
Developmental Editor: Linda Ashe Montgomery	Production Manager: Laura Messerly
Production Editor: Sheryl Glicker Langner	Director of Marketing: Kevin Flanagan
Photo Editor: Nancy Harre Ritz	Marketing Manager: Suzanne Stanton
Design Coordinator: Karrie M. Converse	Marketing Coordinator: Krista Groshong

This book was set in Garamond by the Clarinda Company and was printed and bound by R. R. Donnelley & Sons Company. The cover was printed by R. R. Donnelley & Sons Company.

©1999, 1997, 1994 by Prentice-Hall, Inc.
Simon & Schuster/A Viacom Company
Upper Saddle River, New Jersey 07458

Earlier edition © 1992 by Merrill, an imprint of Macmillan Publishing Company.

Photo credits: pp. xx, 6, 11, 14, 15, 19, 29, 32, 52, 100, 120, 135, 173, 175, 186, 194, 218, 226, 238, 243, 261, 264, 273, 292, 315, 346, 352, 353, 356, 363, 394, 415, 418, 427, 446, 457, 530, 543, 547, 554, 578, 599, 602, 611 by Scott Cunningham/Merrill; pp. 9, 160a, 213, 309, 369, 505, 509, 524, 545, 548, 595 by James L. Shaffer; p. 24 by John Elk/Stock Boston; pp. 34, 74, 106a, 106b, 174, 200, 280, 325, 332, 335, 454, 460, 513 by Todd Yarrington/Merrill; pp. 38a, 38b, 68, 182 by Anthony Magnacca/Merrill; p. 44 by Jeff Greenberg/Photo Edit; pp. 59, 108, 378, 384, 389, 475, 496, 539, 563 by David Young-Wolff/Photo Edit; p. 73 by Gail Zucker' pp. 77, 465, 506 by Robert Finken; p. 83 by Bill Aron/Photo Edit; pp. 87, 95, 209, 246, 248, 252, 262, 358, 423, 433, 482, 516, 566, 582 by Tom Watson/Merrill; pp. 115, 221, 301, 401, 471 by KS Studios; p. 127 by Anne Vega/Merrill; pp. 138, 185, 257 by Paul Conklin/Photo Edit; pp. 150, 376 by Frank Siteman/Photo Edit; pp. 156, 559 by Tony Freeman/Photo Edit; p. 165 by Bob Daemmich/The Image Works; p. 167 by Linda Peterson/Merrill; pp. 198, 569 by Bill Bachmann/Photo Researchers, Inc.; pp. 204, 551 by Larry Hamill/Merrill; p. 231 by Barbara Schwartz; p. 282 by Bonnie Kamin/Photo Edit; p. 313 by Steve Skjold/Photo Edit; p. 412 by Blair Seitz; p. 487 by Mary Kate Denny/Photo Edit; p. 503 by David Napravnik/ Merrill

Printed in the United States of America

10 9 8 7 6 5 4 3 2 1

ISBN: 0-13-080091-0

Prentice-Hall International (UK) Limited, *London*
Prentice-Hall of Australia Pty. Limited, *Sydney*
Prentice-Hall Canada Inc., *Toronto*
Prentice-Hall Hispanoamericana, S.A., *Mexico*
Prentice-Hall of India Private Limited, *New Delhi*
Prentice-Hall of Japan, Inc., *Tokyo*
Simon & Schuster Asia Pte. Ltd., *Singapore*
Editora Prentice-Hall do Brasil, Ltda., *Rio de Janeiro*

This book is dedicated to Clifton Eggen and Martin Kauchak. They gave us their best.

Preface

Educational psychology is a growing, changing field, and we have written the fourth edition of this text to reflect this dynamic growth. In preparing this edition we have attempted to stay true to our original goals in writing the book: to introduce the exciting field of educational psychology to you, our readers, and to show you how it applies to your personal and professional lives.

The students and professors who have used our book tell us that the connection to actual classrooms is what has made the content understandable, meaningful, relevant, and, consequently, more motivating for them. The links between educational psychology and the "real world," and the implications these links have for learning and teaching, are the core of our text and are reflected in its subtitle "Windows on Classrooms."

In the fourth edition we expand on our original goals, strengthen the application focus, and open our window even wider. We attempt to do so in three ways:

- We have expanded the *use* and *integration* of written and video case studies. We present case studies in a way that is unique in the field of educational psychology. Instead of "layering" case studies onto the content of the text, our case studies—both written and video—are truly *integrated* with each topic presented. As topics are discussed, frequent references to the cases are made, which help readers understand how the content is applied in classrooms. In several instances actual dialogue from the case is inserted into the discussion of a topic. This integration capitalizes on research in important areas related to learning, such as **anchored instruction** and **situated cognition.** The number and integration of cases have been expanded in this edition.

- We have broadened the learner-centered orientation of the text. This is a book that focuses on learners and learning, and each chapter examines influences on learning and ways that learning can be increased.

- We have increased the application of prominent theories of learning, motivation, and development. The theories and their application in both classrooms and the outside world are presented in detailed, yet clear and succinct ways. The same approach was used in presenting research on instruction, assessment, and learner differences.

We believe this emphasis—**an integrated, learner-centered focus** grounded in accurate frameworks of theory and research—will result in a thorough understanding of educational psychology that you can apply in your growth as a professional.

New to This Edition

In our attempt to provide you with coverage of educational psychology that is the most up-to-date and applied in the field, we have added three new elements to this edition:

- New chapters that reflect the most recent advances in theory and research

- New, learner-focused, integrated video cases
- A new section on technology and learning

New Chapters

In our commitment to being the most up-to-date text on the market, we have added four new chapters. They are:

Chapter 9: Cognition in the Content Areas.   Research suggests that learning different kinds of content presents unique challenges to both students and teachers. In this chapter we examine learning in reading, writing, math, and science, first describing how cognitive learning theories help us understand the unique aspects of learning in each of these areas, and second, examining instructional strategies that support student growth in each. We close the chapter by considering the aspects of learning that are common to the four areas.

Chapter 11: Creating Productive Learning Environments.   Emphasis in this chapter is on the interdependence of effective instruction and orderly classrooms, and how this interdependence increases learning. The chapter first examines the skills all teachers must have to promote learning and then considers the role of classroom management in developing learner responsibility. The chapter also describes ways that learning environments can be adapted to accommodate diverse learner needs.

Chapter 12: Teacher-Centered Approaches to Instruction.   This chapter considers instruction from a teacher-centered perspective. It begins by examining content that is most effectively taught from a teacher-centered orientation, considers planning and the importance of instructional alignment, and then describes strategies in detail. The chapter analyzes the advantages and disadvantages of lectures, lecture discussions, and direct instruction, and describes ways that classroom interaction can be adapted to meet the needs of diverse learners.

Chapter 13: Learner-Centered Approaches to Instruction.   Using APA's Learner-Centered Psychological Principles as a foundation, this chapter describes a number of different learner-centered instructional strategies. Guided discovery, inquiry, discussions, cooperative learning, and individualization are analyzed in terms of their ability to promote learning.

Insights-into-Learning Video Cases

The success of the third edition's **integrated** cases—*classroom case studies that exist in both video and written form*—has prompted us to create a new generation of integrated video cases that truly "get into learners' heads." By examining learners' thinking in both classroom learning activities and follow-up interviews, these videos provide **insights into learning** by illustrating learners' thinking and demonstrating the complexities of learning and the sophistication of teaching that promotes that learning. The three, hour-long videos include the actual lesson, an interview with four students, and an interview with the teacher. The focus in each case is on learning and learners' thinking.

The written transcripts of these lessons introduce Constructivism in Chapter 7, Complex Cognitive Processes in Chapter 8, and Learner-Centered Approaches to Instruction in Chapter 13. For the first time in the history of the field, a text includes both video and written classroom episodes that are truly learner-centered.

New Section on Technology and Learning

This new section in Chapter 13 describes how technology can be used to promote students' learning. Different applications of technology, including simulations, spreadsheets, databases, problem solving, and drill and practice are described and analyzed.

Increased Emphases

To reflect recent developments in educational psychology, emphasis on the following topics has been increased in this edition:

- Learner-centered instruction
- Authentic assessment, including performance assessment, portfolios, and grading rubrics
- Constructivism, including situated cognition, sociocultural learning, and cognitive apprenticeship
- Cognitive views of learning
- Bilingualism and English-as-a-second-language
- Self-regulated learning
- Character education and moral development
- Language and learning
- Learner diversity including language, culture and SES
- Inclusion

Features of This Text

Integrated Video Case Studies

To truly *integrate* topics presented in the text with real-world applications, seven classroom case studies—the three new *Insights-into-Learning* cases that introduce topics in Chapters 7, 8, and 13, plus the end-of-chapter cases in Chapters 2, 7, 8, and 13—exist in both written and video formats. These cases illustrate actual classroom life—real learners and real teachers involved in learning and teaching in authentic classroom contexts. No other text has this feature.

Additional Case Studies

In addition to the *integrated video case studies* described above, the text includes more than 50 additional written cases—all taken from actual classroom experiences—that illustrate the content of the chapters. Each chapter begins with a case study that provides a concrete anchor for the chapter. The case study is then woven into the chapter to illustrate the topics being discussed.

Each chapter, except Chapter 9, also ends with a case. This feature, called *Windows on Classrooms*, shows how you might apply your understanding of the chapter content. The end-of-chapter case is followed by a series of "Questions for Discussion and Analysis" that encourage you to observe and assess the learning and teaching in the case and to reflect on your own knowledge and beliefs as your understanding of learning and teaching develops. The topics within each chapter are also liberally illustrated with shorter cases taken from classrooms.

David Shelton has been preparing a unit on the solar system for his ninth-grade earth science class. From his filing cabinet, he retrieved a color transparency showing the sun throwing off globs of gases into space. He assembled a large model of the solar system to illustrate the planets in their orbital planes and their relative distances from the sun. Finally, he prepared a large matrix, made from a roll of chart paper, and taped it to the back wall of the room.

David began his unit on Monday by saying, "We're getting ready to study the solar system for the next several days, so I've prepared some things to help us get started. Take a look at the chart I made," he said, pointing to the back of the room.

"This chart is going to help us learn about the solar system. . . . But first, we need information to fill in the chart. . . . So, I want you to work in your groups to gather the in...

Windows on Classrooms

Video Case

At the beginning of the chapter, you saw how David Shelton planned and conducted his lesson in an effort to make the information meaningful for his students and help them construct their own understanding of the topic he was teaching. Then you saw how Jenny Newhall attempted to apply the characteristics of constructivism with her fourth graders.

Let's look now at another teacher as she conducts a lesson with a group of high school students studying the novel *The Scarlet Letter.* As you read the case study, consider the extent to which the teacher applied the information you have studied in this chapter in her lesson.

Sue Southam, an English teacher at Highland High School, is discussing Nathaniel Hawthorne's *The Scarlet Letter.* This novel, set in Boston in the 1600s, describes a tragic and illicit love affair between the heroine (Hester Prynne) and a minister (Arthur Dimmesdale). The novel gets its title from the letter *A* meaning "adulterer," that the Puritan community makes Hester wear as punishment for her adultery. The class has been discussing the book for several days; the focus

"Okay, anything else, any other clues?"

"The baby . . . it points at Reverend Dimmesdale."

"Good observation. That is a good clue and one of my favorite scenes from the novel," Sue adds.

After several more comments, Sue pauses and says, "Class, I'd like to read a passage to you from the text describing Dimmesdale. Listen carefully, and then I'd like you to do something with it."

After reading the paragraph, Sue continues, "In your logs, jot

his hands as if he's mopping his brow.

"What else?" Sue encourages.

"Wire-framed glasses," Tamara contributes.

"With brown, melancholy eyes," Jeremy adds.

After the class discusses additional characteristics, Sue shifts gears by asking, "What do these characteristics tell us about Dimmesdale as a person? . . . Anyone? . . . Sonya?"

"I think he's worried about getting caught."

". . . Kasha?"

"I think he feels bad about what has happened to Hester. He feels guilty," Kasha adds.

After a few additional comments, Sue says, "Let's see whether we can find out more about the Dimmesdale character through his actions. I'd like you to listen carefully while I read the speech by Reverend Dimmesdale in which he confronts Hester Prynne in front of the congregation and exhorts her to identify her secret lover and partner in sin. Think about both Dimmesdale's and Hester's thoughts while I'm reading."

Questions for Discussion and Analysis

Analyze Sue's lesson in the context of the information in this chapter. In doing your analysis, you may want to consider the following questions. Be specific and take information directly from the case study.

1. To what extent did Sue apply the information-processing model in her teaching? Explain, using the concepts of *attention, perception, working memory, encoding,* and *long-term memory,* together with information taken directly from the case study.
2. To what extent did Sue help make the information meaningful for the students? Explain, using the concepts of *elaboration, organization,* and *activity,* together with information taken from the case study.
3. To what extent did Sue apply the characteristics of constructivism in her lesson? Explain, using information taken directly from the case study.
4. Provide an overall assessment of the lesson. Provide evidence taken from the case study in making your assessment. What could Sue have done to make the lesson more effective? Be specific in your suggestions.

Cognitive Views of Learning **287**

Summary

Cognitive Views of Learning

Behaviorism and cognitive learning theories differ fundamentally in that behaviorism treats learners as passively responding to the environment, whereas cognitive theories assume that learners are mentally active and construct their own understanding of the topics they study.

Cognitive theories acknowledge the role of environmental influence but emphasize internal, mental processes in attempting to understand learning. Behavioral theories contend that mental processes are not necessary to explain learning; rather, one looks to stimuli and reinforcers in the environment. Cognitive theories were developed, in part, because behaviorism was unable to adequately explain both research results and everyday events, especially complex phenomena such as language learning and problem solving.

Information Processing

Information processing is a cognitive view of learning that compares human thinking to the way computers process information. Information stores—sensory memory, working memory, and long-term memory—hold information; cognitive processes, such as attention, perception, rehearsal, and encoding, move the information from one store to another.

Information received by sensory memory is moved to working memory through the processes of attention and perception. Working memory, with its limited capacity, can easily be overloaded and become a bottleneck to subsequent processing. The capacity of working memory can, in effect, be increased through chunking and making aspects of processing automatic.

Cognitive Views of Learning **289**

Chapters begin and end with a case study. **Chapter opening cases** are referred to throughout the chapter to bring concepts into sharper focus for the learner. Chapter-ending cases, **Windows on Classrooms,** give learners a second look at chapter content in context. **Questions for Discussion and Analysis** that follow each case guide analysis and reflection.

Each chapter contains at least three **Classroom Connections**, which review practical strategies for improving the learning of diverse student populations. Aimed at helping you see the application of teaching in real classrooms, with real learners, they provide practical suggestions for implementing the content by making connections to classroom learning.

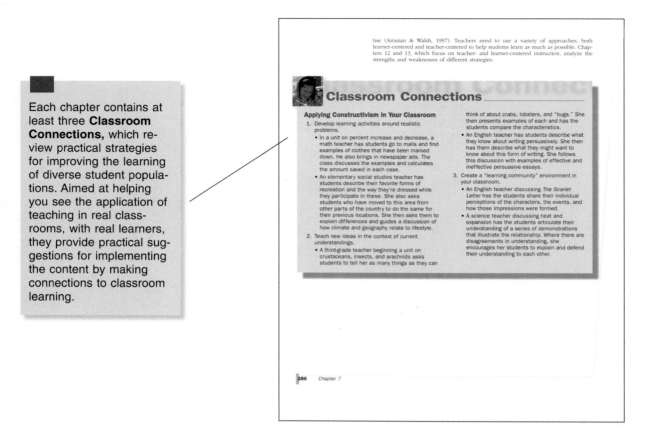

Theory into Perspective

Teachers are faced with a variety of theories that attempt to describe learning. Assessing the appropriateness of these theories for specific learning situations can be a daunting task. *Theory into Perspective* sections at the end of each major learning theory analyzes the strengths and weaknesses of these theories and their value in different learning contexts.

Classroom Connections

As in earlier editions, we have included sections throughout each chapter that offer suggestions for applying the content to specific learning and teaching situations. *Classroom Connections* describe and illustrate successful teaching practices in classrooms, from all grade levels and content areas, to provide a variety of effective applications.

Learner Diversity

To respond to the increasingly diverse student populations that we as teachers will encounter, it is critical that we capitalize on the richness that this diversity can bring to the learning and teaching environment. To reflect this emphasis, learner diversity is a theme for this text. Each chapter contains a section on diversity, with its own set of *Classroom Connections,* and Chapter 4 is devoted to this topic.

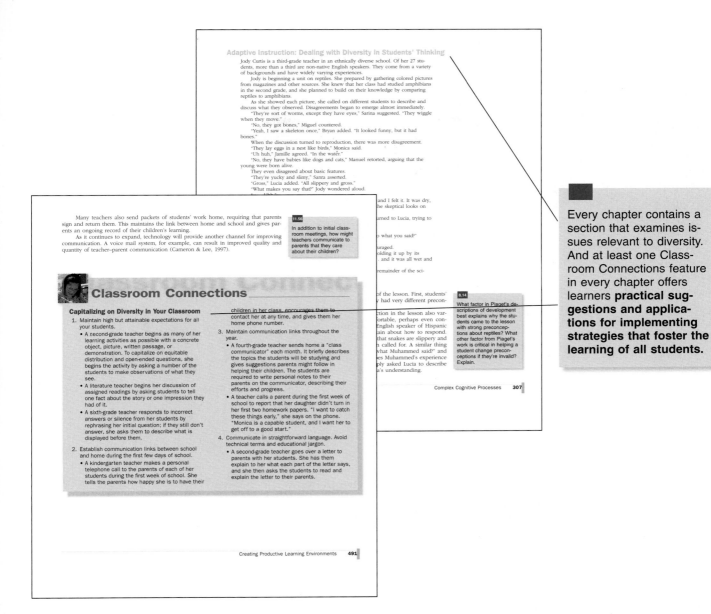

Every chapter contains a section that examines issues relevant to diversity. And at least one Classroom Connections feature in every chapter offers learners **practical suggestions and applications for implementing strategies that foster the learning of all students.**

Margin Questions

Research indicates that learning is advanced when students are actively involved in the learning process. To place you in an active learning role, we use margin questions that ask you to do one or more of three things: explain a specific aspect of the content on the basis of theory and/or research, relate the immediate topic to one you've studied in an earlier chapter, or relate a topic to a real life experience. In this regard, the margin questions are intended to help you reflect on the content, further apply your understanding of educational psychology to classrooms, integrate topics, and make the content more personal by applying it to your everyday experiences.

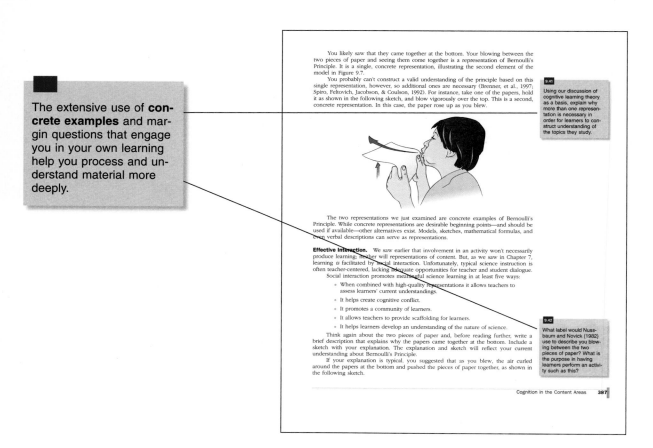

> The extensive use of **concrete examples** and margin questions that engage you in your own learning help you process and understand material more deeply.

Important Concepts

Important concepts in this book are identified in the body of the text with bold-faced type followed by an *italicized definition*. This allows you to identify these in context as you read and study the text. These important concepts also appear at the end of each chapter, identified by page number.

Figures, Tables, and Outlines

Learning is more efficient when information is organized so that connections and relationships are apparent, rather than presented in isolated segments. Figures, tables, and outlines are used frequently to summarize important information and give you additional examples of each chapter's topics.

Chapter Endings

We know that learning is enhanced by summaries and reviews of important topics. For this reason we close each chapter with a *Summary* that succinctly describes significant ideas in the chapter. The summary for each chapter is organized using the major headings and is intended to further help you integrate the ideas you've studied in earlier chapters.

End of Text

A *Reference* list provides bibliographic information for all the sources we cite. Detailed *Name* and *Subject Indexes* allow quick access to specific topics.

Text Supplements

To further aid your learning and development as a teacher, several supplements have been provided for you and your instructor's use. To maximize the opportunities for learning, the entire package—text, videocases, and supplements—are thoroughly integrated. In our attempt to provide you and your instructor with the most complete educational psychology package that exists, we have written our own supplements, making every effort to ensure that all the components complement each other.

Student Study Guide

Organized by chapter, the *Student Study Guide* includes chapter outlines, chapter overviews, chapter objectives, and application exercises. These exercises put you in an active role as you apply concepts to authentic classroom situations. Feedback is provided for the application exercises.

Each chapter also includes a self-help quiz, using the same format as the items in the test bank that accompanies the text, answers to the self-help quiz, and suggested responses to the margin questions in the chapters.

In addition to the chapter-by-chapter materials, the *Student Study Guide* includes suggestions and guidelines to enable you to better understand the value of reading and using case studies in your coursework.

Website for Students

New to this edition is a website which provides you with an interactive study guide and tutorial. Hot links to a number of key educational psychology sites on the Web can facilitate your research efforts and thus support a more thorough understanding of course concepts. Use www.prenhall.com/eggen to access the website.

Transparencies

A transparency package is available for your instructor's use. As with the figures and tables that appear throughout the text, the transparencies help organize the information you're studying to deepen and broaden your understanding. Electronic versions of the transparencies are also available on the CD-ROM for Instructors.

Video Tapes

In Chapter 1, we discuss the work of experts who suggest that teachers should think critically, practically, and artistically. They believe that teachers should meticulously examine research, their own work, and the work of other teachers. To help you develop your critical thinking, you will have the opportunity to study videotaped segments that focus on cognitive development, classroom management, cooperative learning, metacognition, whole language, and diversity. Some episodes represent "slices of classroom life" that can serve as focal points for analysis and discussion. Questions such as "What are the major strengths and weaknesses of this lesson?" and "How could this have been taught more effectively?" encourage reflection. This process of analysis will help cultivate your ability to critically examine your own work, complementing the written and video *Windows on Classrooms* that we've already described.

Test Bank

Research consistently indicates that learning is enhanced when teachers have high expectations for their students and when they ask them to think critically and analytically about the content they are learning. In line with these findings, many of the test items you'll encounter on quizzes will be case studies that require you to analyze information taken from classrooms and to make decisions based on evidence. Instead of memorizing strings of words, you'll apply what you have learned to new situations. This is a challenging and rewarding experience and, with practice, your ability to think critically and analytically will improve.

The self-help quizzes in the Student Study Guide will help you develop your analytical skills with practice items similar to those you'll encounter on quizzes and tests.

A printed test bank and computerized versions in Windows® or Macintosh software are available to your professor.

Instructor's Manual

In addition to the supplements we've already described, your instructor will be offered suggestions for learning activities, groupwork, and out-of-class assignments. While you won't encounter the content of the Instructor's Manual directly, it is an integral part of this overall package.

CD-ROM for Instructors

A flexible and user-friendly CD-ROM is also available to your instructor. All features of the printed supplements can be accessed on the CD-ROM and printed out. In addition, for professors who teach using an LDS screen or some other electronic display, all print materials including the transparencies will be accessible for editing and creating customized presentations.

All of the components in this text and the supplements are designed to be consistent with what we know about learning and motivation. We believe they reflect a realistic view of learning and teaching today and as we move into the new millennium. We wish you the best of luck in your study. We hope that you find it both exciting and meaningful.

Acknowledgments

Every book reflects the work of a team that includes the authors, the staff of editors, and the reviewers. We appreciate the input we've received from professors and students who have used previous editions of the book, and gratefully acknowledge the contributions of the reviewers who offered us constructive feedback to guide us in this new edition: Kay S. Bull, Oklahoma State University; Thomas G. Fetsco, Northern Arizona University; Newell T. Gill, Florida Atlantic University; Dov Liberman, University of Houston; Hermine H. Marshall, San Francisco State University; Luanna H. Meyer, Massey University-New Zealand; Nancy Perry, University of British Columbia; Jay Samuels, University of Minnesota; Gregory Schraw, University of Nebraska-Lincoln; Dale H. Schunk,

Purdue University; Rozanne Sparks, Pittsburg State University; and Karen M. Zabrucky, Georgia State University. In addition, we acknowledge with our thanks, the reviewers of our previous editions. They are: Patricia Barbetta, Florida International University; David Bergin, University of Toledo; Scott W. Brown, University of Connecticut; Kay S. Bull, Oklahoma State University; Barbara Collamer, Western Washington University; Betty M. Davenport, Campbell University; Charles W. Good, West Chester University; Hermine H. Marshall, San Francisco State University; Tes Mehring, Emporia State University; Evan Powell, University of Georgia; Dale H. Schunk, Purdue University; Rozanne Sparks, Pittsburg State University; Robert J. Stevens, Pennsylvania State University; and Julianne C. Turner, Notre Dame University.

We also owe special thanks to three reviewers who made significant contributions through their constructive suggestions. Patricia Barbetta of Florida International University helped shape and improve Chapter 5, "Learners with Exceptionalities." In addition, very special thanks go to Dale Schunk of Purdue University for his thoughtful reviews of Chapter 7, "Cognitive Views of Learning"; Chapter 8, "Complex Cognitive Processes"; Chapter 9, "Cognition in the Content Areas" and Chapter 10, "Increasing Learner Motivation." His expertise made an important contribution to our work. We further appreciate the insightful reviews of Chapter 11, "Creating Productive Learning Environments"; Chapter 12, "Teacher-Centered Approaches to Instruction"; and Chapter 13, "Learner-Centered Approaches to Instruction," carefully completed by Dr. Nancy Perry of the University of British Columbia.

In addition to the reviewers who guided our revisions, our team of editors gave us support in many ways. Kevin Davis, our editor, brought zeal and enthusiasm to our revision and meshed insight with knowledge of both content and market. Linda Montgomery and Linda Peterson, our developmental editors, again fulfilled their role of helping us make the book more accessible to our readers, and supplying us with doses of humor and encouragement when we needed it. A special thanks to Sheryl Langner for her conscientiousness and diligence in producing the book, in spite of often being overworked. Through many phone conversations she was supportive, flexible, and positive in every way. We want to acknowledge the professional quality of her work and her commitment to excellence.

Our appreciation goes to all these fine people who have taken our words and given them shape. We hope that their efforts—together with ours—will result in enhanced learning for students and more meaningful and pleasurable teaching for the instructor.

Finally, we would sincerely appreciate any comments or questions about anything that appears in the book or any of its supplements. Please feel free to contact either of us at any time. Our email addresses are: peggen@gw.unf.edu and kauchak@gse.utah.edu.

Good luck.

Paul Eggen
Don Kauchak

Brief Contents

Contents

1

Teaching in the Real World

CHAPTER OUTLINE

"Good morning." Jan Davis, a sixth-grade math teacher greeted Keith Jackson, a first-year teacher and colleague at Lake Park Middle School. "How're you doing? You look beat. Never realized how tired you can get teaching, huh?" Jan continued with a wry smile.

After a short pause to see how Keith reacted, she went on, "Seriously, you look deep in thought. What's up?"

"Oh, not much really. I was just sitting here thinking about my last-period math class. Sometimes I'm not sure what I'm doing. I think about it quite a bit, and then I get a little confused—well, not exactly confused—maybe uneasy, I think."

Reacting to the questioning look on Jan's face, Keith continued, "It's like this. The students are fine when we do the plain old mechanics. They do their work, seem to understand what they're doing, and even act like they sort of like it. Then . . . we get to word problems. Ugh! It's the exact opposite. I know we're supposed to try to teach the students

to solve problems. So . . . I try it. They hate it. Then I ask myself what I'm doing. They drag their feet so badly. They act as if this is the first time they've ever had to solve word problems. . . . I understand why word problems are important, but I just hate cramming them down their throats. They always try to take the easiest way out. They memorize a formula and work like robots. If a problem is written even the teeniest bit differently, they can't do it, and they cry that they don't understand this material. See what I mean?

"Then," he continued, "some of them just blow the whole thing off. They just sit like bumps on logs and barely try. . . . I thought I was going to be so great when I got out here. I have a really good math background, and I love math. I just knew the students would love it too. I'm not so sure anymore. No one prepared me for this.

"And then there's Kelly," Keith went on with a resigned shrug. "She disrupts everything I do. I can't get her to keep her mouth shut. I've

tried everything. I've ignored her talking, given her referrals, put her in detention, tried to 'catch her being good.' I even bribed her. Nothing has worked. She's not really a bad student. . . . I even took her aside after school and simply leveled with her. I asked her straight out why she was giving me such a hard time. I said, 'Kelly, you're a good girl. Why are you acting like this?' Actually, I think she's a bit better lately.

"I know that I'm in my first year and that you've been here forever," Keith continued, "but don't you ever get frustrated? Maybe I'm just having a bad day."

"I'll just ignore that 'forever' remark," Jan replied, "but yes, I get frustrated. I think everybody does.

"You're actually in the process of becoming a real teacher," she continued. "You're looking at problems for which there are no easy answers, and for the most part, the solutions—to the extent that they exist—must come from you. Very little in teaching is cut-and-dried. . .

but then, that's also part of the fun of it," she added, smiling.

"Seriously, though, I do have a few reactions," she went on. "Think about Kelly. She's not actually a rotten kid. Stay with the personal approach. You said it seemed to help when you took her aside. Make it a point to talk with her one-on-one every now and then. Talk with her about her behavior and continue to be straight with her. I don't think she has another adult she can talk to, and this may be her way of reaching out to someone. I know that sounds a little corny, but I actually think it's the case. She needs someone to be interested in her."

"I guess I'll stay with it," Keith shrugged. "I've got nothing to lose."

"No, you don't—just like with your quiet ones in the back of the room. Every class has them. They just don't seem to care, and that can be discouraging. Let me tell you what works for me. First, I move them right up to the front of the room. I tell them why: 'I want you to learn, and I want you up close where I can work with you.' Then I make it a point to call on all of them, and I do it randomly. At first, they complain that they didn't have their hands up, but after I explain that I'm trying to get everyone to participate, they actually like it. It really makes a difference."

"Hmm. . . ? Do you have any suggestions about the math part?" Keith asked, changing the subject. "I've tried explaining the stuff until I'm blue in the face. Or maybe I shouldn't worry about it. It's just that I keep thinking they don't really understand the material, and they resist all my efforts."

"As it happens, I'm taking a course to upgrade my certificate, and I wasn't too crazy about it at first, but I've really learned a lot. Anyway, the course is based on the NCTM standards . . . National Council of Teachers of Mathematics," Jan added, seeing the uncertain look on Keith's face, "and in a way they're talking about exactly the stuff you're struggling with, like problem solving and all that. . . . But the biggest thing was I actually thought I didn't have that much to learn. I've been around *forever* as you say, but this course and these new standards have opened my eyes. They're making a big deal of shifting emphasis, if that's the right way to say it. . . . What I mean is, they're trying to focus more on the student. We have to read these research articles for class, and then we're learning how to apply it with our students. . . . Anyway, they talk about putting the student in the center of the process . . . take us out of simply telling them stuff. . . . I'm not sure I'm being clear. . . . Let me give you an example.

"By the way," she interjected, "I was really skeptical at first, but I said, 'What the heck; I'll give it my best shot,' and interestingly, the students really got into it."

"Anyway, here's what I did. We've been reviewing decimals and, just as you're saying, the students don't get it and they don't like it all that well. So I went into class, and just as class started I put a shopping bag on my desk and said, 'You all drink soft drinks. Do you know which is the best buy in terms of size and number?' Then I took out a single twelve-ounce can, a 16-ounce bottle, a liter bottle, a six-pack, a twelve-pack, and a 24-can pack.

"'Which is the best buy?' I challenged them. We had a lively discussion and most agreed that bigger is better, but the skeptical ones asked how much better and is it worth the hassle?

"Then I put price tags on each of the containers, starting with the single can from the vending machine and broke them into small groups. Some of the groups struggled for a while trying to figure out whether they should do price per can or price per ounce and what to do about liters. At the end of the class we agreed to use a common format for a table and the next day the groups computed their answers, and we compared them as a whole-class activity. The bottom line is that they have to see how math relates to them and their lives."

"Maybe even more important," she continued, "although I had to guide them, a lot of what we did came from them, and it gave me some things to think about. I'll do parts of it differently next time. At times I think I jumped in too soon when they could have figured it out for themselves, and at other times I think I let them stumble around too long, and they wasted more time than necessary. But overall, I feel good about it, and I'm definitely going to do more of it."

"I hate to admit this," Keith responded almost sheepishly, "but some of my courses at the university suggested just what you did. It was fun, but I didn't think it was 'real' teaching. I thought it was all pie-in-the-sky stuff, and I didn't pay much attention to it. I guess I always thought that stuff wasn't quite real, and it didn't change my mind."

"Maybe you couldn't relate to it at that time," Jan returned. "You didn't have a real class with real students who 'didn't get it.'

"My compliments to you, and I mean that," she continued. "The fact that you're thinking about it means you really care about what you're doing. That's what we need in teaching. If you hadn't brought it up, we probably wouldn't have had this talk. For a rookie, you're okay," she added, bantering again.

Keith peered at Jan, impressed with her fervor. "Why aren't you burned out? I thought all 'old' teachers burned out."

"Watch it, kid," Jan returned in a mock threat. "But seriously," she went on, "I have my days. I get tired, and the students sometimes bother me, but I try to leave it here, go home, get a little exercise, let off some steam, and then everything is pretty good again.

"Uh-oh. There goes the bell. I'd better get moving, or my fourth-period class will be locked out."

Welcome! You're beginning what we hope will be an interesting and fascinating study: interesting because you'll be examining people, and fascinating because you'll be seeing yourself in many of the experiences described in the text. In some cases, you'll even find that ideas you hold about people, teaching, and learning aren't valid.

In this book, we focus particularly on school-age children—how they grow and develop, what makes them different, what motivates them (and what doesn't), how they learn and, particularly, what teachers can do to facilitate these processes. This study makes up the content of "educational psychology," and this is where we're headed.

After you've completed your study of this chapter, you should be able to meet the following objectives:

- Identify the implications that studying educational psychology has for classroom practice.
- Explain how research in educational psychology is applied to classroom practice.
- Describe the relationships between research and theory.
- Explain how professional decision making affects teaching.
- Explain how reflective teaching uses educational psychology to improve professional decision making.

Educational Psychology:
Teaching in the Real World

Although the focus in educational psychology is on teaching and learning, it deals with much more than the study of school-age learners. To illustrate, consider these questions:

- Have you ever listened to someone describe something to you, not quite followed their point, and said, "Give me an example"?
- Does a song, a picture, or even a smell sometimes conjure up a feeling or mood that you can't otherwise capture?
- Have you ever done one job to get it out of the way and saved a more enjoyable one for later?

- Have you ever been with someone who showered you with positive comments or flattery? Why did that person's attentions quickly lose their appeal?
- What kind of class are you most comfortable in: one in which the requirements are explicitly described, or one in which the requirements, schedule, and topics are somewhat loose?
- How do you feel when an instructor knows your name and seems to take a personal interest in you?
- For what kind of class do you usually study the most: one in which you're given weekly quizzes, or one in which you have only a midterm and final?
- Have you ever done a "double take" when something unusual or unexpected happened?
- Have you ever asked, "Why should I do that? There's nothing in it for me"?

These questions and others like them are all part of the real world. Educational psychology can help us explain your answers to these questions and even why people's answers vary. So although the primary focus in this text is on school-age learners, it's also relevant to you as a student and developing teacher.

Let's begin our study of educational psychology by examining the themes that guided us as we wrote the text.

Beginning Teachers and Learning to Teach

1.1

Research indicates that students enter teacher preparation programs with strong views about what is good teaching (Calderhead & Robson, 1991). On what basis are these views most likely formed?

As we wrote this book, several themes guided us, and many of those themes were evident in the case study at the beginning of the chapter. Keith Jackson displays characteristics typical of first-year teachers. Many are idealistic—some even unrealistically so. Most believe they will be better than teachers in the field. Many also believe that teaching is a process of transmitting knowledge, as Keith demonstrated with his comment, "I've tried explaining the stuff until I'm blue in the face" (Pajares, 1992). Further, his experience in his preservice program failed to change his beliefs, also typical of beginning teachers (Carter, 1990; Kagan, 1992b).

Misconceptions About Teaching and Learning to Teach

Evidence indicates that novices in different fields of study often have misconceptions about those fields. Misconceptions are often embedded in complex networks of knowledge and are difficult to eliminate unless they are confronted directly (Anderson & Roth, 1989; Driver, Asoko, Leach, Mortimer, & Scott, 1994; Siegler, 1991). In introducing the text, we want to confront three misconceptions about teaching and learning to teach. They are:

- Teaching is a process of transmitting knowledge to learners.
- Majoring in an academic subject provides all the knowledge needed to teach the subject.
- Learning to teach requires only experience in classrooms.

Misconception: Teaching Is a Process of Transmitting Knowledge to Learners

You saw in our opening case study that "explaining until I'm blue in the face" often doesn't work. Simply "explaining" fails to take into account students' motivation and the way they learn. Bransford (1993) describes this as "the 'wisdom can't be told' problem" (p. 6). Learners don't passively receive and record information. Instead, they (mentally) change what they receive so that it makes sense to them, while at the same time responding to their own beliefs and expectations. For example, if a car is moving along a highway at a steady speed, such as 50 mph, most people believe that the forces moving the car forward are greater than those holding the car back. This makes sense. In reality, the forces forward and backward are equal, and students in science classes are taught that they are equal. Yet most people retain the misconception.

Our study of learning in Chapters 7, 8, and 9 will help us understand why learners acquire misconceptions such as the one above, why they tend to retain the misconceptions, and what teachers must do to help eliminate them.

1.2

What is the most likely reason that preservice and beginning teachers believe teaching is the process of transmitting knowledge to learners?

Misconception: Majoring in an Academic Subject Provides All the Knowledge Needed to Teach the Subject

One of the most pervasive myths in teaching is that knowledge of subject matter is all that is necessary to teach effectively. By his own description, Keith's understanding of math was more than adequate. His problem was that he didn't know how to represent it in a way that was both understandable and engaging for his students.

This predicament is not uncommon. In a study of teacher candidates, math majors were no more able than nonmajors to effectively illustrate and represent math concepts in ways that learners could understand (National Center for Research on Teacher Learning, 1993). Both majors and nonmajors lacked **pedagogical content knowledge** (Shulman, 1986), which is *knowledge of effective ways to represent topics for learners plus an understanding of what makes topics difficult or easy to learn for students of different ages*. Acquiring pedagogical content knowledge takes time and effort. It doesn't automatically result from knowledge of content itself (Jetton & Alexander, 1997).

Knowledge of content is critical, of course, but is not sufficient by itself. Teaching is a complex process that requires different kinds of knowledge—knowledge of content, understanding of the ways people learn, information about learners' beliefs and expectations, and a repertoire of teaching strategies. Educational psychology examines learning, as well as learner beliefs and expectations in depth. As teachers study educational psychology, they acquire the different kinds of knowledge that are needed to effectively promote learning in their students.

1.3

What is the most likely reason that math majors were no more successful than nonmajors in effectively illustrating math topics?

Misconception: To Learn to Teach, Experience in Classrooms Is All That Is Necessary

Like an understanding of subject matter, experience in classrooms is important in learning to teach. It is not, however, sufficient. There are at least two problems with the "just watch and learn" approach. First, you won't always observe good teaching; second, you will see teachers who are good yet teach very differently. Which teachers or which part of their teaching provide the best model to follow?

Studies of modeling and its impact on learning indicate that unless observers are given specific guidance about which behaviors they're supposed to focus on, they're

1.4

What is the most likely reason that observers, if they don't know "what to look for" in classrooms, often imitate inappropriate or irrelevant behaviors?

uncertain and often learn inappropriate or irrelevant behaviors (Bandura, 1986, 1989). This particularly applies to preservice teachers. Unless they know what to look for, experiences in classrooms can be quite confusing, in some cases increasing rather than eliminating misconceptions (Smylie, 1989). One way to combat this problem is to have a solid, conceptual base to guide your observations and your own teaching. Studying educational psychology can help provide that base.

Goals for This Book

1.5

To what concept does knowledge of "how to represent ideas so that they're understandable" refer?

It's clear that one of the most important factors in learning to teach is knowledge—knowledge of content, of course, but also knowledge of learners and the differences among them, the way they learn and what motivates them, how ideas can be represented so that they're understandable, how classrooms can be organized to promote learning, and what teachers can do to assess learner understanding.

Our goal in writing this text is to provide some of this knowledge. You obviously won't learn everything you need to know about teaching from this book, but we believe that studying educational psychology can make an important contribution to your professional development. In addition, you will draw from your past experience and learn from other teachers, some of whom, like Jan, are more experienced. You will also learn by doing, thinking and reflecting on your successes and failures.

This book is based on the belief that a body of knowledge exists that can help beginners like Keith *and* veterans like Jan in their efforts to become better teachers. This body of knowledge is the content of educational psychology, and our goal is to describe and illustrate its application in the real world of teaching.

Concepts learned in educational psychology help teachers understand the complex events occurring in classrooms.

Themes for This Book

In writing this book, we used four themes to organize our work. The first is the *role of research* in helping teachers understand students and classrooms. Educational psychology benefits from a growing body of research that studies the ways people learn and how teachers can help in this process. We report this research throughout the book. Our second theme is the *application of this knowledge* in the classroom. Without application, research isn't useful in the real world. In applying any research, teachers need to exercise *sensitive and sound decision making,* the third theme of the text. The findings of educational psychology don't exist as simple rules to be followed without critical examination. Although teaching would be easier if they did, it would also be less rewarding. As Jan commented in our opening case study, "Very little in teaching is cut-and-dried . . . but then, that's also part of the fun of it."

Our final theme is related to each of the others and further contributes to the complexity of the process. This theme is *a focus on learners.* A focus on learners means that learners are at the center of the learning process. A body of research that expanded rapidly during the 1980s and 1990s suggests that learners don't passively receive information from teachers, books, and other materials (Alexander & Murphy, 1994; Brophy, 1992; Bruning, Schraw, & Ronning, 1995; Derry, 1992; Marshall, 1992). Instead, they rework it in the context of what they already know until it makes sense to them, and a central role for teachers is to assist them in this process. These four themes are summarized in Figure 1.1. Let's look at them in a bit more detail.

1.6

What kind of teaching method would be most common in instruction that is not learner focused?

Research on Learning and Teaching

In our opening case study, Jan offered Keith suggestions and, in making them, she drew information from research. Her idea for helping students understand decimals by posing a concrete and practical problem was drawn from research she had read in journal articles. The research served as the conceptual foundation for what she did. Let's see how this works.

Figure 1.1   Organizing themes for this book

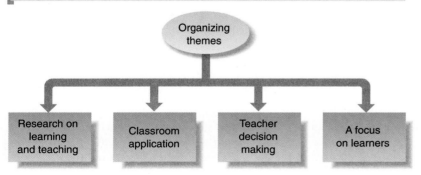

A Knowledge Base

Any academic pursuit has a **body of knowledge,** which is *the information on which the content is built.* This is the case for physics, history, anthropology, political science, engineering, and every other field. Some professions—engineering and education, for example—rely heavily on other areas, such as physics or psychology, to develop their own knowledge base. Research is the primary process used for accumulating this body of knowledge.

Research is *a systematic process of collecting information for some purpose,* and it often confirms common sense. For example, think about some of your own experiences. You study hard for a challenging test and do well. Because of the challenge and your success in meeting it, you feel a sense of exhilaration (Schunk, 1994), and you are more inclined to study hard for the next one. Both your achievement and motivation to succeed have increased. This is intuitively sensible, and these results are confirmed by systematic research; increased achievement and motivation go hand in hand (Pintrich & Schunk, 1996).

The link between intuition and research is not unique to education. For instance, a lifestyle that eliminates smoking and includes exercise and proper diet as ways of maintaining health certainly makes sense. And it doesn't take a medical degree to recognize that excessive alcohol consumption is damaging to your health. Yet much is made of medical research that confirms these notions. Similarly, educational research that confirms our intuitions is reassuring and allows us to proceed with renewed confidence.

Not all cases are common sense, however. For example, when teachers question their students, they typically call on the ones with hands raised, or those they think will be able to answer, much more often than they call on less aggressive or lower achieving students. Some even argue that a teacher shouldn't call on reluctant learners for fear of embarrassing them or putting them on the spot. Research indicates, however, that this is not effective questioning. All students need to be drawn into lessons through questioning that invites, and even requires, participation (Good & Brophy, 1997; Kerman, 1979; McDougall & Granby, 1996; Nystrand & Gamoran, 1989). When you are aware of these research findings, as Jan was, you can change your questioning patterns and call on all the students as frequently as possible. This change would be unlikely if you relied on intuition alone.

Other results are even less intuitive. For instance, retaining underachieving students in the lower grades makes sense to many people, and on the basis of this conventional wisdom, retention is still practiced in some school systems. Research indicates, however, that the practice of retention not only fails to increase achievement but also detracts from motivation and damages self-esteem (Doyle, 1989).

These examples illustrate how intuition and common sense are often not sufficient for making professional decisions. Educational research supplements intuition by providing knowledge—about learners, the learning process, and effective teaching—that allows professionals to improve and refine their practice.

Role of Theory in a Body of Knowledge

As research accumulates, results are summarized and patterns begin to emerge. After a number of related patterns are identified, general principles are formed; these in turn generate further studies. As the knowledge accumulates, theories are gradually constructed.

A **theory** is *a set of related principles based on observations that in turn are used to explain additional observations.* Simply, theories can be thought of as peo-

1.7

Which kind of research result—intuitive or nonintuitive—is more common? Why? What does this tell you about human nature?

1.8

When you learn to write, it makes sense intuitively to first learn the mechanics of grammar and spelling and then apply these skills in writing. Does research confirm this intuitively sensible approach? Explain.

1.9

What might happen if the research base in teaching were complete? How would that influence controversies in education? Are the research bases in other areas, such as medicine and economics, more or less complete than the research base in education? How do you know?

ples' descriptions of how things work. Theories help organize research findings and can provide valuable guidance for teachers.

Let's look at a brief example. One research-based principle indicates that reinforced behaviors increase in frequency, and a related principle indicates that intermittently reinforced behaviors will persist longer than those that are continuously reinforced (Alberto & Troutman, 1995; Skinner, 1957). Too much reinforcement can actually decrease behavior (satiation). A classroom application of these principles occurs in learning activities. If students are praised for their attempts to answer questions (reinforced), they are likely to increase their efforts, but they will persist longer if they are praised for some but not all of their attempts (intermittently reinforced). If they are praised too much or too effusively, they actually reduce their efforts, believing that the praise is insincere or unwarranted.

These related principles are part of the theory of behaviorism, which studies the effects of experience on observable behavior. Our illustration, of course, is only a tiny portion of the complete theory. (We examine behaviorism in depth in Chapter 6.) The key feature of any theory is that a comprehensive body of information is formed when a number of principles are related to each other.

Theories are useful in at least two ways. First, they allow us to explain behaviors and events. For instance, look at the cartoon.

The theories of child development (which we examine in Chapters 2 and 3) enable us to explain why the child in the cartoon thinks the way he does. These theories suggest that young children tend to be dominated by their perceptions: He can see only the

FAMILY CIRCUS

"How do they fit so much water in that little spigot?"

1.10

In the opening case study, how did Keith use reinforcement theory (behaviors that are reinforced will increase in frequency) to explain and predict Kelly's behavior?

Theories help teachers understand the complex world of classrooms and the connections between teacher actions and student learning.

water and the faucet, so he concludes that all the water is in it. Likewise, we can use the theory of behaviorism to explain why casino patrons persist in playing slot machines, though coins rarely fall into the trays: they are being intermittently reinforced.

Second, theories also allow us to predict behavior and events. For instance, we predict that students who believe they are the ones who control how good their grades will be try harder than those who believe their grades are due primarily to luck or the whim of the teacher. Attribution theory, a topic we present in Chapter 9, provides the basis for this prediction (Pintrich & Schunk, 1996; Weiner, 1990).

In all three instances—child development, behaviorism, and attribution theory—theories help us understand teaching and learning by allowing us to explain and predict people's actions. Whenever possible, we attempt to explain specific research results on the basis of theory as we progress in this study.

Classroom Application

This book focuses on **application**—*how the principles of educational psychology actually work in classrooms.* Our study of the theories and research that make up the content of educational psychology focuses on their implications for classroom practice. To assist you in applying research findings, we build much of the content of this book around case studies.

Case studies are *segments or samples of students' and teachers' experiences in the teaching–learning process.* Some are specific classroom scenarios illustrating students' experiences in learning activities; others, such as the one at the beginning of this chapter, deal with larger issues, such as learning to teach and professional growth. All are designed as windows to the real world of teaching and provide opportunities for you to analyze and reflect on real-world classrooms.

We have used case studies in our teaching, and the reactions of our students support the claims of experts (Doyle, 1986; Shulman, 1992): Cases help students see how theories and abstract ideas relate to real-world practice (Fernald, 1989) and they stimulate the growth of professionals (Hmelo, 1995).

We use different types of cases in this book. Each chapter begins with a case study, just as this one does. They are designed to illustrate the chapter content and provide concrete reference points for the information you study.

Shorter cases are interspersed throughout the chapters to introduce problems and further illustrate the topics, and each chapter closes with a case that we ask you to analyze on the basis of the chapter content. The cases at the beginnings of Chapters 8 and 13, and ends of Chapters 2, 7, 8, and 12 exist in two forms. A written version appears in the text. This version is based on an actual classroom lesson with a real teacher and students. A videotaped version showing the lesson as it was actually taught exists as a companion to the text. Because it illustrates the teaching episode in context, it further integrates the text content with the classrooms you'll encounter. Research indicates that the use of video cases stimulates the development of expertise in teachers (Copeland & Decker, 1995).

Cases are also embedded in applied exercises in test items to provide you with opportunities to use the information in this text in solving classroom problems. Each case study is designed to help you apply the information in the text to the real world of teaching. Let's look at an example:

> April Sumner teaches remedial English to a first-period class of inner-city high-schoolers. Students need to pass the class to graduate from high school, but motivation and attendance are major problems.

She likes the class and, because it's small, she knows all her students well. This closeness is rewarding, but the class is also frustrating: The students refuse to bring any materials to class. *Refuse* isn't exactly the right word. On students' lists of important things to do in the morning, finding a pencil and notebook paper doesn't rank high. Daily reminders don't seem to help, nor do threats of failure, because many students are repeating the class for the second or third time.

April talks with other teachers. Some say, "Let them sit"; others respond, "Lend them your own," but warn of logistical nightmares and economic disaster when the pencils disappear and she runs out of paper.

April has been hired to teach English, but first she has to solve the materials problem. What would you do?

Case studies such as this can be effective learning tools, and that's why we include them. They're powerful because they're real; they illustrate the real world of classrooms. They also stimulate your thinking, and they demonstrate the role of educational psychology in understanding and solving problems.

The problem we just presented, like all our cases, was taken from a teacher's actual experiences in working with real students. In selecting the content to be included in this book, we carefully analyzed its applicability in the real world. We continually asked ourselves, "Is this real? Can it make a difference in the real world of teaching?"

As you study this text, ask yourself, "As a teacher, what do I do differently because I understand this theory or these research results, compared with what I would have done if I didn't know about them?" Because of the importance of classroom application, try to put yourself in the place of the teacher in each case study as you study this material. Looking at the content in the chapters in this way will make the information more meaningful by helping you relate to it personally.

1.11

Case studies are concrete examples of abstract ideas. What abstract ideas are the case studies intended to illustrate?

Teacher Decision Making

In an earlier section, we examined the role of research in guiding practice. It doesn't answer all our questions, however. Just as medical research doesn't tell us exactly how many times a week people can safely eat red meat or how much exercise is necessary to maintain a healthy lifestyle, educational research doesn't answer all questions about

Case studies provide opportunities for students to analyze and reflect on real-world classrooms.

best classroom practice. For instance, research indicates that students should be taught to set personal learning goals, that the goals should be moderately difficult, and that students should monitor and assess the goals themselves (Pintrich & Schunk, 1996). It doesn't tell teachers, however, exactly how to approach the process as they introduce it, what "moderately difficult" means for a particular student, or how the individual goals students set are integrated with the goals for the class. It also doesn't tell teachers who to call on at a particular time, how to assess students' verbal and nonverbal reactions, what examples will best illustrate a topic, or how to treat a shy and withdrawn student compared with an outgoing and assertive one. Research helps teachers understand patterns of student learning and effective teaching, but the specific decisions are left to them.

Throughout this text we'll make statements, such as, "A teacher's careful judgment is required . . ." "The specific decision will be left up to you," and "You must decide." Teaching includes a great deal of uncertainty and ambiguity. It is virtually impossible to overstate the importance of careful judgment and decision making.

Decision making will also be complicated by research results that appear contradictory. Shulman (1986) describes one such dilemma related to waiting after asking a question—a practice that gives students time to think and results in increased learning:

> From Rowe's (1974) research on wait-time, for example, we learn the principle that longer wait-times produce higher levels of cognitive processing. Yet Kounin's (1970) research on classroom management warns the teacher against slowing the pace of the classroom too severely lest the frequency of discipline problems increase. How can the principle of longer wait-times and that of quicker pacing both be correct? (p. 13)

Should teachers wait longer to give students time to think through a question fully, or will long pauses result in lessons that drag? Research doesn't provide a precise answer, so teachers must use their professional judgment and decide how long to wait and how quickly the lesson should be moved along.

April Sumner's experience is another example of the need for teacher decision making. Providing students with pencils reinforces their coming to class unprepared. Allowing students to sit passively, however, runs counter to the research on both learning and motivation (Blumenfeld, 1992; Bruer, 1993; Good & Brophy, 1997).

It would be easier if teachers could simply call up a research result, apply it as a rule, and get consistent, predictable results. However, neither the world nor teaching and learning work this way. So to be a successful teacher, the ability to cope with uncertainty and deal with ambiguity is necessary, and informed decision making is critical.

Informed Decision Making

How should research be used in making decisions? Gage and Berliner (1989) suggest that teachers should think *critically, practically,* and *artistically* about the results of research. If they're able to do so, they do more than simply apply research; they select, modify, and adapt the suggested applications to best meet the needs of their students.

Critical Decision Making: The Impact of Classroom Context. When using research results *critically,* teachers analyze their own situations and compare them with the settings that produced the results. For instance, one study found that students called on in predictable patterns achieved more than students called on at random (Anderson, Evertson, & Brophy, 1979). Does this mean teachers should stop the intuitively sensible prac-

1.12

Identify at least one decision that April Sumner had to make in working with her students.

1.13

Why might patterned turn-taking work with reading skills and first-graders? Why might it not be as effective in other settings?

tice of calling on students at random? Certainly not. Examining the results critically, we find that the study was conducted with first-graders in small reading groups, a context very different from whole-group instruction, in which calling on students at random is more effective.

Lesson context also helps teachers resolve the dilemma with wait-time that we mentioned earlier. For example, if a question is thought provoking, the lesson is proceeding smoothly, and the student "on the spot" is comfortable, the teacher should probably wait. However, if the question calls for a fact, the lesson is dragging, other students are fidgety, or the student appears uncomfortable, the teacher should reduce the amount of wait-time. The context in which the question is asked is different. Each situation requires a decision. Research helps in the process, but does not substitute for sound teacher judgment.

1.14

What, specifically, would you look for to determine whether students are uncomfortable when asked questions?

Practical Decision Making: The Need for Efficiency. *Practicality* is a second factor in making informed decisions. To be useful, research must be applied efficiently, with a minimum of disruption to the class or extra work for the teacher. Classrooms are complex and busy places; researchers estimate that elementary teachers have more than 500 exchanges with individual students in a day (Doyle, 1986). Many, if not most, of these require a teacher decision. To be practical, research results must be applied efficiently.

For example, research suggesting that all students should be called on equally is practical. While it requires teachers skilled in questioning and monitoring, the curriculum, classroom routines, and general patterns of instruction don't have to be changed. On the other hand, research also suggests that students taught in a one-to-one, personalized mode of instruction learn the most (Bloom, 1984a; Slavin, Madden, Karweit, Dolan, & Wasik, 1992), but, unfortunately, this isn't feasible.

1.15

Why is a one-to-one teacher-to-student ratio most effective in promoting learning? What can teachers with classes of 25 students do to approximate these benefits?

April Sumner's dilemma was strongly influenced by practical considerations. Allowing students to sit passively day after day can't be justified professionally. On the other hand, a teacher can spend a lot of money handing pencils to students who consider the whole process a game.

At least two practical solutions to the problem exist. One teacher kept a box of short pencil stubs in his desk (Shulman, 1986). When a student forgot a pencil, the teacher would give the student the shortest stub he could find, require the student to complete the work with it, and return it after class. Another teacher required a personal article, such as an earring, bracelet, or belt, as collateral, which she exchanged for the pencil at the end of class. These were simple, practical solutions that worked.

Artistic Decision Making: Creativity in Teaching. The *artistic* element, the third dimension of informed decision making, asks teachers to apply the results of research in original and creative ways. Let's look at an example of creativity in teaching.

After three separate efforts to teach the principle of exposition, development, and recapitulation in music—each of which failed—the teacher was at wit's end. Having repeatedly reminded her students that composers like Wagner depended on the listeners' remembering earlier themes so as to recognize their later elaboration, she was determined to make her students understand musical form, no matter what it took.

The class had little trouble with simple variations and could easily identify themes that were repeated in a related key, but when it came to the development sections, the students' attention focused on the new detail to such an extent that they no longer "heard" the basic motif. For a week or two, the young teacher fretted over the problem. She discarded one idea after another as either too complicated or impractical. Older teachers advised her to go on with something else, sug-

Creative teachers design
activities that motivate
students to learn.

gesting that she was overly ambitious, and that such discrimination was impossible without formal music training. Still, the teacher searched in her mind for a solution.

One afternoon during the lunch hour, she noticed a group of students clustered in a corner of the yard. Several girls were swaying their bodies in a rhythmic cadence. Curious, she drew closer and found that the students were listening to a new rock hit. A slender boy in the center of the group held a tape recorder in his hand. A few moments later, as the teacher continued on her noon duty rounds, a sudden inspiration took hold.

The following day, when her music appreciation class arrived, she asked how many students had tape recorders. A dozen or so students immediately said, "I do." The teacher looked at her students pensively. "I have an idea," she said with sudden animation. "Maybe machines have better memories than people. What would you think," she said, "about trying an experiment? We could play Beethoven's `Eroica' again, and one of you can record the theme of the second movement when it's first introduced. Then, later, when Beethoven gets into the development section, someone else can record that segment. Finally, when he comes to the recapitulation—the restatement—we'll have a third person record again. Of course," she added, "technically, it won't be a real recapitulation because we'll select passages in the same key. If," she finished triumphantly, "we can synchronize the timing, and start all three recorders at exactly the same instant, we'll play the three recordings together and see if they fit. What do you think?"

Her students looked at her in surprise. Suddenly, however, delight appeared on their faces.

"Neat," one boy exclaimed.

"We'll have to get three recorders with the same speed," another exclaimed. "I'll bring a timer."

And so it was arranged. They had difficulty starting the recorders simultaneously; there were slight variations in their pitch; and the tempo of the recorded passages was a bit uneven; but the sounds blended sufficiently for the students to recognize their commonality. (L. Rubin, *Artistry in Teaching,* 1985, McGraw-Hill, Inc., pp. 32–33, reproduced with permission of McGraw-Hill)

Research indicates that actively involving students and relating abstract ideas to their personal lives increases learning; artistic decision making, such as we saw above, applies these ideas to create meaningful lessons (Brophy, 1990; Maheady, Sacca, & Harper, 1987). The teacher's instruction was artistic, but informed by research.

Reflection and Decision Making

Teaching involves making an enormous number of decisions, most of which can't be reduced to simple rules. How do teachers know whether their decisions are wise and valid? This is a tough question, because teachers receive little feedback about their performance. They are observed by administrators a few times a year at most, and receive only vague, sketchy, and uncertain feedback from students and parents. In addition, they get virtually no feedback from their colleagues, unless the school has a peer coaching or mentoring program in place (Darling-Hammond, Wise, & Pease, 1983; Glickman & Bey, 1990). To improve, teachers must be able to assess their own classroom performance.

Can the ability to conduct this self-assessment be acquired? We think so. It requires that teachers develop a disposition to critically examine what they're doing. This is the essence of a simple, yet powerful notion called **reflective teaching** (Cruickshank, 1987; Schon, 1983), which simply means *think about what you're doing.* Reflective teachers

1.16

How was the music teacher's problem similar to the one Keith faced in the opening case study, when he attempted to teach problem solving to his students? How did they both apply an idea from educational psychology?

1.17

Identify a specific example in which Jan Davis demonstrated reflection in her teaching.

Reflective teachers analyze their teaching to ensure that learning activities meet the needs of students.

Figure 1.2 Questions for reflective teaching

- Did I have a clear goal for the lesson? What specifically was the goal?
- Was the goal important? How do I know?
- Was my learning activity consistent with the goal?
- What examples or representations would have made the lesson clearer for students?
- What could I have done to make the lesson more interesting for students?
- How do I know whether students understand what I taught? What would be a better way of finding out?
- Overall, what will I do differently to improve the lesson the next time I teach it?

are thoughtful, analytical, even self-critical about their teaching. They plan lessons thoughtfully and take the time to analyze and critique them afterward.

Educational psychology supports reflection by providing a knowledge base that teachers can use in critiquing their teaching. In Keith's case, the fact that he knew, for instance, that students should be actively involved in the learning process and that problem solving is important to understanding helped him in his reflection. Had he been less well informed, he wouldn't have reacted as strongly when some of his students wanted to sit like "bumps on logs" and were unable and unwilling to go beyond "the plain old mechanics." He also recognized that the problem Jan suggested could improve both student motivation and understanding. His uneasiness about his students' progress and his openness to new ideas indicated a tendency to be reflective, and his knowledge base made the process more effective.

Teachers can acquire the tendency to reflect by continually asking questions of themselves as they teach. Although they aren't exhaustive, some possibilities are listed in Figure 1.2.

More important than the questions themselves is the inclination to ask them. If teachers keep questions such as these at the forefront of their thinking, they can avoid the trap of teaching in a certain way because they've always taught that way. Openness to change and the desire for improvement are two of the most important characteristics of professional growth, and careful reflection can have positive effects on the decisions teachers make.

A Focus on Learners

Now let's look again at Keith's experience with Kelly as a way of introducing our fourth theme. When his other efforts failed, a direct, personal appeal finally made an impact on her. Although this approach won't work in all cases, the experience is a convincing reminder that if teaching is to be effective, it must focus on learners. Effective teaching strategies don't exist for their own sake; they exist because they contribute to students' learning. Effective instruction is a means to that end.

A shift in emphasis away from the teacher and toward learners reflects a subtle but powerful turn in the direction of educational psychology. One indicator of that shift is the American Psychological Association's "Learner-Centered Psychological Principles" (Alexander & Murphy, 1994). These principles reflect our improved understanding of learning and factors that affect it. These factors include the following:

1.18

What evidence do you have that the music teacher practiced reflection in her teaching? How are reflection and artistry in teaching linked to each other?

- The importance of learners' prior knowledge in influencing new learning
- The importance of learners being able to reflect on and control their thoughts and strategies in the learning process
- The role of learners' intrinsic motivation, explanations for their performances, and personal goals in the learning process
- The influence of development, affected by both heredity and environment, on learning
- The importance of the context in which learning takes place

You can see several of these factors illustrated in Keith's and Jan's experiences. He noted that his students "act as if this is the first time they've ever had to solve word problems," and "memorize a formula and work like robots," suggesting that their prior knowledge may be limited, that their motivation to learn is less than desirable, and that they're exercising little control over their thoughts and strategies in the process. You can see that a teacher-centered or "teacher-focused" approach, such as "explaining the stuff until I'm blue in the face," isn't effective.

Guiding student learning is a complex process requiring sophisticated skills, much more complicated than simply presenting information. To effectively guide learners, a teacher must take student backgrounds, needs, beliefs, expectations, and individual differences into account. Educational psychology provides some guidance in this task.

1.19

Explain why "explaining the stuff until I'm blue in the face" is less than desirable in promoting learning.

A Focus on Learners: Developing Self-Regulation

You saw in the previous section that learners' personal goals and their control over their thoughts and behaviors are an integral part of what is meant by "a focus on learners." Goals and control over thoughts and behaviors are part of **self-regulation,** *the process of students using their own thoughts and actions to reach academic learning goals* (Bruning et al., 1995; Schunk, 1994). Jan's efforts helped her students begin to develop self-regulation, as reflected by her comments: "Although I had to guide them, a lot of what we did came from them." Students acquire self-regulation as a natural and valuable outgrowth of a focus on learners. It takes time and effort from both the teacher and the students, but its long-term benefits can be enormous.

Because of the importance of self-regulation, we reexamine it at several points in this book. Helping students take responsibility for their own learning is an essential element of learner-focused instruction.

1.20

From the description so far, are you self-regulated? Do you do any things in this class that suggest self-regulation?

A Focus on Learners: Caring

A focus on learners also means that teaching is, at its heart, a *human* activity and that the relationships between teachers and students are an essential part of the teaching–learning process. The decisions teachers make must always be made with their students in mind. Teachers don't teach algebra or reading or physical education—they teach people. To be effective, they must adopt a theme of **caring,** *the ability to empathize with and invest in the protection and development of young people* (Chaskin & Rauner, 1995). Caring teachers create supportive learning environments that help all students reach their potential. Students know when teachers care, and it makes a difference in their learning; it makes them more willing to experiment with new ideas and to take personal and academic risks (Purkey & Novak, 1984). A focus on learners is virtually impossible without caring as a foundation.

1.21

Describe specifically how Keith, in the chapter's opening case study, demonstrated caring.

A Focus on Learners: Learner Diversity

Consider these statistics:

- Caucasians are now 75% of the U.S. population. By the year 2050, experts estimate this figure will shrink to 51%, with the remainder consisting of 21% Hispanic, 16% African American, 11% Asian American, and 1.2% Native American.

- Minority enrollments now range from 70% to 96% in the nation's 15 largest school systems; 300 languages and dialects are spoken.

- One-fourth of U.S. children currently live below the poverty level. Between one-fourth and one-third of today's children have no adult at home when they return from school.

- Girls score lower than boys on the ACT and SAT, especially in math and science. In terms of the professions, females account for only 21% of lawyers, 20% of doctors, and 8% of engineers (Hakuta & Garcia, 1989; Oakes, 1990; Sadker & Sadker, 1994; U.S. Bureau of the Census, 1994).

These numbers paint a picture of diversity and challenge for today's teachers. Today's students differ in gender, ability and motivation, and cultural and economic backgrounds. They bring different experiences with them and, in some cases, their backgrounds place them "at risk" of failing to complete their education with the skills needed to survive in a modern technological society (Slavin, Karweit, & Madden, 1989). To maintain a focus on learners, teachers must be aware of this diversity and make conscious plans to accommodate it.

Dimensions of Diversity.

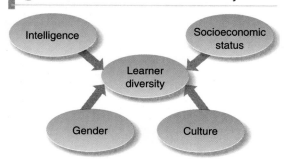

Figure 1.3   Dimensions of diversity

1.22

Describe specifically what made Jan Davis's problem-solving activity effective for working with students of diverse backgrounds

"What's wrong, Tanya? You look a little down," Clarice Hodgekins asked as she entered Tanya Redding's classroom during Friday's planning period. Tanya is a first-year teacher who has been paired with Clarice, a six-year veteran, for mentoring and help.

"I guess I am, a little. I spent the whole summer reading curriculum guides and material from the district and teachers' editions to plan for the year. I knew exactly what second-graders were supposed to learn in each of the areas, and I was so excited. I was really ready. Hah, so I thought.

"Look at these papers! Some of them can't add. A lot of them can't read.
Some of the boys are out of control and several of the girls never participate. I've got some students who are struggling to speak English, much less learn reading and math."

Clarice listened sympathetically and then sat down next to Tanya. She waited a moment until Tanya looked up, and then said with a smile, "I think I remember what it was like when I was starting out. Let's talk about it and see what we can do."

Learner diversity makes teaching both challenging and interesting. As Tanya discovered, diversity involves several factors, as illustrated in Figure 1.3.

Two of the most important are *intelligence* and *background experience*, which Tanya encountered when she discovered that some of her second-graders couldn't add and others couldn't read.

Culture is also an important dimension of diversity. Students' cultural backgrounds are becoming more and more varied. Research indicates that the teaching force is overwhelmingly Caucasian (less than 10% of U.S. teachers are members of minority groups), but many of these teachers work in schools with predominantly minority populations (Gollnick & Chinn, 1994). Understanding and capitalizing on cultural differences requires skill and sensitivity.

Socioeconomic status (SES)—the combination of parents' occupation, income, and level of schooling—also influences learning. A growing percentage of students come from environments where poverty is a fact of life. Some students come to school tired, hungry, and emotionally ill-prepared for school. Effective schools attempt to overcome these barriers with programs such as free breakfast, after-school activities, and parent involvement activities. However, nothing substitutes for caring and committed teachers who believe that all students can learn and who accept responsibility for ensuring that they do.

Gender, a final dimension of diversity, also affects learning. Enter a kindergarten class and see how students' choices of toys are influenced by gender. Walk into a junior- or senior-level math class, and you're likely to see that students are disproportionately male. Although awareness and sensitivity are changing some of these trends, some experts believe that schools still shortchange girls (Sadker & Sadker, 1994).

What can teachers do to deal with the challenges raised by these different dimensions of diversity? Fortunately, research provides some answers.

Strategies for Dealing With Diversity.   Three general strategies have been found to be effective in dealing with all types of diversity:

1. A general attitude of acceptance and caring
2. Positive expectations
3. Valuing differences in learners

To which of the four previous themes—*research, application, decision making,* and *focus on learners*—do these three strategies relate the most? Why?

Effective teachers respond to diversity by designing learning tasks that meet individual learning needs.

A general climate of acceptance and caring makes students feel safe and secure and forms a foundation for learning. Positive expectations communicate the belief that all students can learn and are expected to do so. Finally, an attitude that values diversity communicates that your classroom is a place for all students to live and grow.

Adapting Instruction to Meet Learners' Needs. In addition to general approaches, research has uncovered a number of specific strategies for working with diverse populations. These include providing experiences for students; using language-embedded instruction; combining challenge and success; using peer tutoring, cooperative learning, and individualization; and teaching in culturally responsive ways. These strategies, described in Table 1.1, are discussed in detail in later chapters.

Organization of This Book

Having discussed educational psychology in general terms, we now turn to the specific content of this book. It is organized into five parts, which are summarized in Table 1.2.

Part I: The Learner

Consistent with the theme of a focus on learners, the first part of the text examines the influence of student characteristics on learning. Chapter 2 provides an overview of cognitive development and language. Chapter 3 examines personal and social development, self-concept, self-esteem, and moral development. In Chapter 4 we investigate how differences in intelligence, culture and ethnicity, socioeconomic status, and gender influence learning. The focus on learner differences continues in Chapter 5, where we discuss teaching students with exceptionalities.

Part II: Learning

The focus changes in Part II to the process of learning. Two key questions are, What is learning? and What can teachers do to promote it? Chapter 6 begins with a discussion

Table 1.1   Strategies for accommodating diversity

Strategy	Goal	Chapters
Providing experiences	To help accommodate differences in learner backgrounds	2,5,7
Culturally responsive teaching	To match teaching strategies with student backgrounds and strengths	3,4,7,8,10,11,12,13
Language-embedded instruction	To aid the development of English as a second language	4
Combining challenge and success	To promote a sense of accomplishment	4,6,9
Peer tutoring	To increase involvement and interaction	5
Individualization	To adapt instruction to students' unique interests and needs	12
Cooperative learning	To increase achievement and improve relations among groups	12

Table 1.2 Organization of this book

Parts and Chapters	Goal
Part I: The Learner	
Chapter 2: Development of Cognition and Language	To understand how learners' intellectual capacities and language abilities develop over time
Chapter 3: Personal, Social, and Emotional Development	To understand how learners' personal characteristics, moral reasoning, and socialization develop over time
Chapter 4: Learner Differences	To understand how intelligence, culture, socioeconomic status, and gender affect learning
Chapter 5: Learners with Exceptionalities	To understand how learner exceptionalities affect learning
Part II: Learning	
Chapter 6: Behaviorism and Social Cognitive Theory	To understand learning from behaviorist and social cognitive perspectives
Chapter 7: Cognitive Views of Learning	To understand learning from cognitive perspectives
Chapter 8: Complex Cognitive Processes	To understand concept learning, problem solving, and the development of strategic learners
Chapter 9: Cognition in Content Areas	To understand differences in the ways learning occurs in reading, writing, math, and science
Part III: Classroom Processes	
Chapter 10: Increasing Learner Motivation	To understand factors that affect students' motivation to learn
Chapter 11: Creating Productive Learning Environments	To understand how instruction and classroom management are related
Chapter 12: Teacher-Centered Approaches to Instruction	To understand instruction from a teacher-centered perspective
Chapter 13: Learner-Centered Approaches to Instruction	To understand instruction from a learner-centered perspective
Chapter 14: Assessing Classroom Learning	To understand how teachers assess student learning

of behaviorism, one of the oldest and most developed theories of learning. The second part of the chapter analyzes social cognitive theory, which extends behaviorism to consider individual, internal factors such as learners' beliefs and expectations and how they influence learning.

Cognitive views of learning are the focus of Chapter 7. The chapter begins with a discussion of information processing and continues with constructivism, which is becoming increasingly influential in curriculum development, instruction, and assessment. Chapter 8 continues the discussion of cognitive learning to include concept learning, problem solving, the development of strategic learners, and the transfer of understanding. In Chapter 9 we examine learning in reading, writing, math, and science.

Part III: Classroom Processes

In Part III we consider relationships among learner motivation, classroom management, instruction, and assessment. Research indicates that the two biggest problems facing beginning teachers are classroom management and learner motivation (Veenman, 1984), and we tackle them in this section. Chapter 10 begins with a discussion of motivation from behaviorist, cognitive, and humanistic perspectives and describes their implications for classroom practice. A classroom model for promoting learner motivation, synthesized from theory and research, relates motivational theory to practice. Chapter 11 examines classroom management and the relationships between efficient management and effective instruction. Chapter 12 examines the research on teacher-centered approaches to instruction, and Chapter 13 complements Chapter 12 by describing the expanding body of research on learner-centered approaches, such as guided discovery, discussions, individualization, cooperative learning, and technology.

The section is completed by considering assessment, one of the most critical classroom processes. The gathering of data and the evaluation of student progress are ongoing processes that have a powerful impact on instruction and learning. Chapter 14 discusses the assessment process (including both traditional and authentic assessments), preparing students for assessments, and grading and reporting. The role of assessment as an integral part of the teaching–learning process is analyzed.

Using This Book

We've tried to make the information in this text not only current and accurate but also accessible to you as learners. To assist you in your study, we have included the following features in each chapter.

- **Chapter Outlines** describe the major ideas in a chapter and how they're organized.
- **Case Studies** open each chapter. The cases—all taken from actual classroom experiences—illustrate the content of the chapter, and frequent references to the case studies are made as the chapter's topics are discussed. The case studies reinforce our theme of application of educational psychology in the real world of classrooms.
- **Objectives** identify main concepts and ideas in each chapter. The objectives supplement the outlines and provide you with a picture of the chapter's directions.
- **Important Concepts** identify major ideas in each chapter. They appear in bold type and are all defined in italics in the body of the text. They are also listed by page number at the end of each chapter to help you as you review the content.
- **Margin Questions** appear throughout each chapter. They encourage you to actively work with the content as you study. The **margin questions** are designed to stimulate your thinking and to help you

form links among: (a) topics you study and your personal life, (b) topics from different chapters with each other, and (c) topics in the chapters and their classroom applications. Answers to some of the questions can be found in the chapter itself; other questions require you to relate information from previous chapters. Some ask you to hypothesize, predict, explain, or apply. These processes are the foundation for your own analysis and reflection.

- **Classroom Connections** offer suggestions for applying each chapter's topics to classrooms. They exist in two types. The first helps you bridge the gap between theory and practice by offering classroom-tested suggestions for applying the chapter content to your own teaching. The second focuses specifically on ideas for adapting your teaching to the diverse learners in your classroom.

- **Windows on Classrooms** provides each chapter with an additional case study for analysis and reflection. In many cases, the teaching described in the case could be improved, and you will be asked to make specific suggestions for improving it on the basis of chapter content. This slice of classroom life is an attempt to make the content of the text applicable to your future role in classrooms.

- **Integrated Case Studies** provides a feature that doesn't exist in any other educational psychology text. The case study that introduces our discussion of constructivism in Chapter 7, the opening case studies in Chapters 8 and 13, and the case studies at the end of Chapters 2, 7, 8, and 13 are also available on videotape. These seven cases, in both written and video form, provide authentic, concrete examples taken from actual classrooms and further integrate the content of the book with the real world of teaching and learning.

- A **Summary** which integrates the chapter's main ideas appears at the end of each chapter. You may wish to review it before reading a chapter a second time.

Again, we welcome you to your study of educational psychology. We sincerely hope our book enhances both your personal and professional growth.

Important Concepts _____

application (p. 10)	case studies (p. 10)	research (p. 8)
body of knowledge (p. 8)	pedagogical content knowledge (p. 5)	self-regulation (p. 17)
caring (p. 17)	reflective teaching (p. 15)	theory (p. 8)

2

The Development of Cognition and Language

Karen Johnson, an eighth-grade physical science teacher, walked into the teachers' workroom with a clear plastic drinking cup filled with cotton balls.

"What are you up to?" asked Ken, one of her colleagues. "Drinking cotton these days?"

"I just had the greatest class," Karen exclaimed. "You know how I told you the other day that my third-period students didn't understand 'density?' They would memorize the formula and solve problems but didn't really get it. I also found out they were confused about basic concepts such as *mass, weight, size, volume,* everything. To them, mass and weight were the same, and if something is bigger it's heavier, so it has more mass and also is more dense. It was a mess."

"I thought you said they were your low class." Ken responded. "You said they're a little slow."

"They're not that bad," Karen said, shaking her head. "Their backgrounds are weak, but then they've never really had this material other than to memorize some definitions, so what do you expect?

"Anyway," she continued, "I kept thinking they could do better, so I decided to try something a little different, even if it seemed sort of elementary. See," she went on, compressing the cotton in the cup. "Now the cotton is more dense. . . . And now it's less dense," she pointed out, releasing the cotton.

"Then yesterday I made some blocks out of wooden cubes, and we compared the densities of the large blocks with those of the small blocks. Some of them still wanted to say the density of a big block was greater, but after I went through the examples with them and we discussed each one, they started doing better.

"Now, this morning," she said with increasing animation, "I had them put water and vegetable oil in little bottles that were the same volume on our balances, and when the balance tipped down on the water side they saw that the mass of the water was greater, so water is more dense. I had asked them to predict which was more dense before we did the activity, and most of them said oil, so we talked about that and they concluded the reason they predicted oil is the fact that it's 'thicker.'

"Here's the good part," she continued, gesturing and raising her voice, "Calvin—he hates science—remembered that oil floats on water, so it made sense to him that oil is less dense. He actually got excited about what we were doing.

"So we formed a principle that less dense materials float on more dense materials. Then, even better, Donelle wanted to know what would happen if the materials mixed together, you know, like water and alcohol. You could almost see the wheels turning. So we discussed that and thought about more examples where that might be the case. We even got into population density, and how a door screen with the wires close together compared with one with the wires farther apart, and how that related to what we were studying. I loved it. It was really exciting. I really felt as if I was teaching and the students were really into learning for a change, instead of poking each other. A day like that now and then keeps you going."

As you began your study of teaching and learning, one of the first principles you probably heard was "You must begin where the learner is." This self-evident principle has important implications for teachers. If we are to be effective, we must have a clear understanding of our learners. One aspect of this understanding is knowing how students typically think, feel, and act at different ages and what factors influence their thoughts and actions.

In this chapter, we examine cognitive development—the ways students grow in thinking, reasoning, and problem solving. In this process, we cover four major topics. First, we look at the work of Jean Piaget, who described the ways children at different ages deal with information from their environments. Second, we turn to the work of Lev Vygotsky, a Russian psychologist; his work helps us understand the role that activity, language, and social interaction play in development. Third, we examine the influence of Piaget and Vygotsky on constructivism—an emerging perspective on development and learning. We introduce constructivism in this chapter and return to it throughout the text. Finally, we examine language development and analyze how it relates to learning and development.

Theories of development help teachers understand learners by describing student differences in systematic patterns. They help teachers understand the ways children's minds grow and develop, and this understanding helps teachers respond more effectively to children's individual needs.

After you've completed your study of this chapter, you should be able to meet the following objectives:

- Explain how development is influenced by learning, experience, and maturation.
- Explain the role of language, activity, and social interaction in Vygotsky's theory of development.
- Describe the implications of constructivism for teaching.
- Explain how language development reflects constructivist views of learning.

In our opening case study, Karen Johnson was describing a problem typical for many teachers. In working with her students, she found they had only a superficial understanding of an important concept. Her students' reactions were also typical; in their efforts to cope, they memorized a formula, plugged in numbers, and cranked out answers that had little meaning for them.

Why are some concepts, such as *density,* so hard for students to understand? It would be easy to think of these students as being a little slow, as Ken suggested, and let it go at that. This, however, leads nowhere. Even if these aren't the most able students, they're often capable of achieving much more than they demonstrate. Other, more useful explanations are needed.

Karen's experience and our search for explanations introduce the theme of this chapter. After we've finished, you'll see how differences in intellectual development influence learners' ability to understand the content you teach, and we'll examine factors that affect that development.

We begin with the work of Jean Piaget.

Piaget's Theory of Intellectual Development

Jean Piaget (1896–1990) was an unlikely influence on American education. His initial work was in biology, rather than psychology or education, and his writing had to be translated from French into English. He wasn't even interested in education, instead being fascinated by *genetic epistemology,* or the study of the growth of knowledge in people. He formed the beginnings of his theory by observing his own three children. His research method—intensively observing small numbers of subjects—was very different from the behaviorist tradition so dominant in the United States at the time and, as a result, it took time for his work to be accepted.

As additional research has verified and expanded his findings, however, his work has had an increasingly important impact on our views of development and learning and on education in the United States.

Development: A Definition

Mike began playing the trumpet as a sixth-grader in his middle-school band. Evenings were filled with odd sounds coming from his bedroom, and even Chews, his devoted dog, retreated to the relative sanctuary of the living room. As an eighth-grader, however, practicing his part in the piece that he and two friends were playing for a concert, he produced very different sounds. Now, after listening to his son play his last concert as a high-school senior, Mike's dad is convinced that Mike could play in a professional orchestra.

Several factors influenced Mike's success. First, he practiced and worked and practiced some more. In the process, he learned much about playing the trumpet. In addition, he simply became stronger and more physically capable as a high-schooler than he was earlier. In short, he matured. We use this example to illustrate the concept of **development,** *the orderly, durable changes in a learner resulting from a combination of learning, experience, and maturation.*

In Mike's case, his musical ability developed. Athletes develop their physical skills; all of us try to develop our social skills. In this chapter, however, our focus will be on the ways that learners' thinking, reasoning, and intellectual abilities develop. As you study, keep in mind the questions, "How is the thinking of little kids different from the thinking of older learners and adults?" and "How do learners' thinking patterns change as they get older?"

Development for all of us begins at birth and continues until we die, and this development results from the interaction of learning, maturation, and experience. Figure 2.1 illustrates this relationship.

2.1

A first-grader tries to imitate her brother shooting baskets on the basketball court, but has neither the strength nor the skill. She practices, receives tips from her brother, gets bigger and stronger, and by the fourth grade is making baskets consistently. Identify the experiential, the learning, and the maturation parts of development.

Figure 2.1 Factors influencing human intellectual development

The Drive for Equilibrium

Think about some of your everyday experiences. Are you bugged when something doesn't make sense? Do you want to world to be predictable? Are you more comfortable in your classes when the instructor specifies the requirements, schedules the classes, and outlines the grading practices? Do you tend to follow a routine when you get up in the morning? Does your life in general follow patterns more than random experiences? Most people's do.

According to Piaget (1952, 1959), people have an innate need to understand how the world works and to find order, structure, and predictability in their existence. He calls this need the drive for **equilibrium,** or *a state of balance.*

Equilibration, *the act of searching for order,* involves testing one's understanding against the real world. When learners' understandings fit with or explain the events they observe, the world makes sense, and they are at equilibrium. When they can't explain what they see on the basis of their understanding, disequilibrium occurs, which motivates them to search for better understanding. Disequilibrium is an energizing force in development.

Organization and Adaptation: The Creation of Schemes

The drive for equilibrium is the cornerstone of Piaget's theory. We are all motivated by a need to understand the world and, as we acquire experiences, we try to fit them into what we already know. For example, when you first went off to college, you probably based your expectations on your high-school experiences. When these experiences were similar, you remained at equilibrium. When your expectations weren't met, you changed your thinking.

In response to the need for equilibrium, people try to organize life's experiences into coherent patterns, which Piaget calls schemes. **Organization** is *the process of forming schemes* and **schemes** are *mental patterns or systems that describe the ways people think about the world.* Schemes are the building blocks of thinking.

Learners' schemes vary with age. Very young children work on psychomotor schemes such as reaching for and holding an object; school-age children work on more abstract schemes such as classification or proportional reasoning. As you learned to operate a car, you developed a driving scheme to start the car, shift gears, maneuver in traffic, obey traffic signals and laws, make routine decisions about your speed, and respond to warning signs.

Although Piaget used the concept of schemes to refer to a narrow range of abstract operations, such as infants' object permanence scheme (the idea that an object is still there even when we can't see it) or a conservation of number scheme (the idea that the number of objects doesn't change if they are spread out) in young children, teachers and some researchers (e.g., Wadsworth, 1996) find it useful to extend his idea to include content-related schemes as they adapt their instruction to meet the developmental needs of their students. We use this expanded view in our description of Piaget's work.

The formation of schemes abounds in school. For example, we want young learners to understand that number is something that can be applied to a variety of objects varying from cookies to toys, and the number of objects doesn't change with their spacing or arrangement. Older learners work on a classification scheme in science when they decide if crabs or snakes are vertebrates and in math if they're asked to determine if integers are rational numbers. From a content perspective, all the concepts, principles, rules, and procedures that students learn in school are organized into schemes that allow them to make sense of the world.

2.2

Before bedtime, a child requests a story her father has read to her many times. As he reads, she corrects each miscue. Why might she request such a familiar story, and why would she correct each mistake her father makes?

2.3

Identify at least one or two schemes that you should have formed to this point in your study of this chapter.

Adapting Schemes

As we acquire experiences, our existing schemes often become inadequate, and we are forced to adapt to function effectively. **Adaptation** is *the process of adjusting schemes and experiences to each other to maintain equilibrium.* For example, if we have learned to drive a car with an automatic transmission and we buy one with a stick shift, we must adjust our driving scheme to accommodate driving with a standard shift.

Adaptation consists of two reciprocal processes: accommodation and assimilation. **Accommodation** is *a form of adaptation in which an existing scheme is modified and a new one is created in response to experience,* such as learning to drive with the stick shift. The driving scheme has been modified, and a driving-with-a-stick-shift scheme is created. Accommodation functions with its counterpart process, assimilation. **Assimilation** is *a form of adaptation in which an experience in the environment is incorporated into an existing scheme.* For instance, a child who has formed a "doggy" scheme encounters a chihuahua and a German shepherd. Although the dogs are obviously very different from each other, she classifies them both as dogs. The child ignores characteristics such as size and color and focuses on the critical ones—those that make each a dog. This is adaptation through the process of assimilation. In contrast, in response to seeing a bear, the child says, "Doggy," but hears her father say, "No, that's not a dog. That's a bear. Look how big it is." The child in this case has to modify her "doggy" scheme so that bears are not included and has to form a new, "bear," scheme. Modifying her existing scheme and creating the new one is an example of accommodation. The relationship between assimilation and accommodation is illustrated in Figure 2.2.

2.4

We said that existing schemes become inadequate. What does this mean?

2.5

A young child believes that all short-haired people are male and long-haired ones are female. This classification system works until she encounters a long-haired male married to a short-haired female. This causes her to reconsider her original classification system. Describe these changes in terms of adaptation, assimilation, and accommodation.

Concrete experiences allow children to form schemes through the process of adaptation.

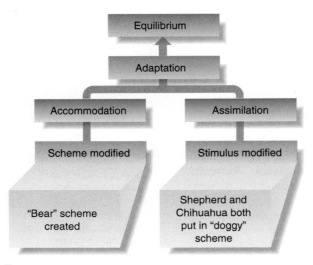

Figure 2.2 Maintaining equilibrium through the process of adaptation

Both assimilation and accommdation are required to maintain equilibrium. If new knowledge is only assimilated into existing schemes, the existing schemes wouldn't change and growth would not occur. "Flat-earthers," or people who still cling to the belief that Earth is flat, are an extreme example. On the other hand, if existing schemes never work, a person is in a constant state of disequilibrium. *Culture shock,* the uneasy feeling people have when they visit a new country and must quickly adjust to different customs, food, and language, is an example. The amount of accommodation required is often overwhelming and disconcerting.

The processes of assimilation and accommodation, together with the drive for equilibrium, combine to promote cognitive development in children. For instance, a kindergarten student playing with objects counts them over and over again and finally concludes that number doesn't depend on spacing. The student's ability to cope with the mathematical world has expanded; development has occurred.

Factors Influencing Development

Piaget suggests that the drive for equilibrium is central to the process of development. In addition, three other factors combine to influence changes in thinking (Piaget, 1970):

- maturation
- experience with the physical world
- social experience

Before we examine these factors, keep in mind an important principle: *All growth depends on existing schemes.* In other words, no information is ever added directly to memory, nor is any scheme formed in complete isolation. All new learning occurs in the context of existing understanding. For example, a math student's ability to add fractions with unlike denominators developed from an understanding of adding fractions with like denominators, which was based on an understanding of fractions themselves, which began with an understanding of numbers and numerals. This principle, one of the most important contributions of Piaget's developmental theory, is illustrated in Figure 2.3.

This principle has important implications for designing and sequencing instruction. It suggests that topics should be presented that build on learners' current understanding. Learning experiences should be designed to disrupt equilibrium enough to be motivating but not overwhelming. If new information is presented at the same level as existing information, it is merely assimilated and no growth occurs. On the other hand, if it is too different from present understanding, learners will be incapable of linking it to what they already know, and they will maintain equilibrium by discarding the experience. Let's look more closely at the factors that influence development.

Maturation

Maturation refers to *the biological changes in individuals that result from the interaction of their genetic makeup with the environment.* A child's genes provide the blueprint for development; the environment interacts with these genes to influ-ence the rate and direc-

---

2.6

A child believes that all mammals have four legs and that whales are fish. Then he learns that whales are mammals and are warm-blooded. Concluding that whales are fish illustrates what concept from Piaget's work? Learning that whales are mammals illustrates what concept?

2.7

Research consistently indicates that the best predictor of future academic achievement is past achievement. Use Piaget's ideas to explain this finding. Identify some subject matter areas in which this finding is more relevant than in others.

tion of growth. In extreme cases, such as malnutrition or severe sensory deprivation, the environment can retard normal maturation. In most cases, however, genes and the environment interact to produce normal growth. Let's see how teachers can design environments to enhance that growth.

Experience with the Physical World

Carol Barnhart is working with her students on map-reading skills in social studies. She wants them to understand how the scale on a map relates to real distances.

She began by saying, "Look at the map of Ohio in front of you. How far is it from Cleveland to Columbus? . . . Antonio?"

"I . . . er . . . I . . . I don't know . . . About four inches," Antonio shrugged.

Carol could tell from the silence and embarrassed giggles that met Antonio's answer that most of her students didn't have a clue about the scale on their map and how it worked.

She was about to launch into a mini-lecture on scale when she thought better of it. Instead, she said, "Okay everyone, let's try something different. . . . Each of you take out a sheet of paper and a ruler. We're going to make a map of our classroom."

She then organized the students into pairs and had each pair use rulers to measure the room and draw pictures of what they found. When they finished, she reconvened the class and led a discussion on the problem of scale. Some groups made larger drawings by taping their sheets together, giving Carol an opportunity to discuss different kinds of scale. During their lunch break, she paced off approximate dimensions of the outside of the school and, after lunch, the class again constructed a map and discussed the problems of scale.

The next day she returned to the map of Ohio and related the map to their activities of the day before. As they compared the map they had constructed to the map of Ohio, she could see that their understanding was much improved.

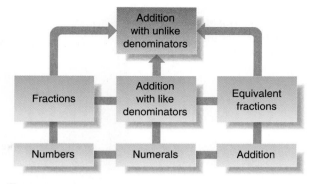

Figure 2.3 Illustration of growth in math depending on existing schemes

Children form schemes through interaction with their environment. Carol applied this principle by attempting to relate the concept of scale on the map of Ohio to something tangible and concrete that came from their own experience. This is how learners use background experiences in their development.

Piaget's emphasis on direct experience has provided the foundation for the emphasis on hands-on activities in schools. Using sticks, blocks, and shapes helps children understand how abstract math concepts and operations relate to their everyday lives. In our opening case study, Karen's eighth-graders lacked background knowledge related to density so, instead of gaining a meaningful understanding of the concept, they memorized and mechanically applied the formula. Karen attempted to address this problem by providing concrete experiences that allowed them to develop more effective schemes. This strategy—providing opportunities to interact with concrete experiences—is one of Piaget's most enduring contributions to education.

The approach Carol used in helping her students understand the concept of scale is another example. She could have merely written the words and definitions on the chalkboard and had students memorize them, which would have taken less time and effort. However, we've all been in situations where we've memorized definitions that we promptly forget; without concrete references, Carol's students would fail to understand this idea in a meaningful way.

2.8

A middle-school science teacher starts discussing the principles behind sundials and realizes that most of the class is confused because they aren't familiar with how shadows are affected by the different positions of the sun. Describe what the teacher can do to help remedy the situation.

Hands-on science activities provide opportunities for students to test their schemes through active experimentation.

Background Experience: A Source of Diversity

Celena Parker was beginning a social-studies unit on the growth of cities with her sixth-graders. She had taught the same unit the previous year, and was expecting similar results with basically the same materials. As an introduction to the first reading assignment, she was discussing concepts found in the text, such as *subway, mass transit, skyscraper, elevator,* and *escalator.* As she began discussing these terms, she could see blank looks on many faces.

"What's a subway?" Shareena finally asked.

"It's an underground train with funny writing on it," Leroy, who had recently moved here from New York, answered. "It's under the skyscrapers."

Celena was struck by the differences in the two students. Shareena had previously told Celena that she'd never been out of her neighborhood. She had never seen a subway or a skyscraper. In contrast, Leroy grew up in the canyons formed by New York's skyscrapers and had ridden on its graffiti-covered subways.

The next day, Celena brought in a series of color pictures of a New York subway and another of a subway in Washington, D.C. She also showed them skyscrapers and had the students see how small cars and people looked in comparison. She explained what mass transit meant and asked the class to offer examples of different types of mass transit.

<table>
<tr><td>**2.9**</td></tr>
</table>

Use the concepts of *scheme, adaptation, assimilation,* and *accommodation* to explain Celena's attempts to make her topics meaningful.

Students construct their understanding of the world (their schemes) on the basis of their experiences. Their schemes then determine how effectively new experiences can be assimilated and accommodated. If these experiences are lacking, the prerequisite schemes to which new learning can be attached won't exist. This was the case with Shareena, who had no schemes for *subway* or *skyscraper.* If Celena hadn't intervened with her pictures, the gap in Shareena's background would have become even wider.

Teachers often comment on how easily they can identify children whose parents have spent time and worked with them in activities that support schooling, compared with those whose backgrounds aren't as well matched to school-related activities. Children whose parents have read to them, talked with them, taken them to the zoo, the mountains, museums, and even auto parts stores, come to school with a rich array of school-related background experiences. These experiences help them find school to be meaningful, because they provide the basis for assimilating and accommodating new knowledge. As a result, cognitive development is enhanced.

Dealing with Student Diversity.   What can teachers do when learners come to them lacking the necessary experience to make the topics they're teaching meaningful? The answer is simple: *Provide it for them.* Although this can be challenging, it often isn't as difficult as it seems. For example, Karen's students lacked the experience needed to understand the concept of *density,* so she provided experience in the form of simple, easy-to-prepare examples that concretely illustrated the concept. *The examples became the experience for the learners.* Celena did the same for her students. The only thing better would have been a visit to a real mass transit system, allowing her students to experience firsthand the sights, sounds, and smells of a subway system.

Social Experience

Piaget found that social experience also influences development (Devries, 1997). Social experience allows learners to test their schemes against those of others. When their schemes are comparable, they remain at equilibrium; when they aren't, equilibrium is disrupted, learners adapt their schemes, and development occurs.

Recognizing the importance of social interaction has strongly influenced education and child-rearing practice. Parents, for example, organize play groups for their young children, cooperative learning is strongly endorsed in schools, and students are encouraged to get involved in service clubs and extracurricular activities. The positive influence of these activities illustrates the value of social interaction.

Stages of Development

Perhaps the most widely known elements of Piaget's theory are his descriptions of stages of development. Piaget's stages describe the ways children at different ages use information and think about the world. Progress from one stage to another represents qualitative changes in children's thinking, that is, changes in the *kind* of thinking rather than the *amount* (Siegler, 1991). These changes are more like the transformation of a caterpillar to a butterfly than the accumulation of bricks to make a house. For example, kindergartners' thinking is essentially limited to their perceptions, a conceptual "what you see is what you get." They typically don't reason logically. A fourth-grader, in comparison, can think logically but requires concrete objects as reference points. More advanced students can think logically and hypothetically about abstract ideas. The differences in the ways learners at different ages think have important implications for teaching.

As you study the characteristics of each stage, keep three ideas in mind.

- Development is continuous, rather than discrete. This means that children develop steadily and gradually, and experiences in one stage form the foundation for movement to the next (Berk, 1997).

2.10

Parents are encouraged to read to their children, talk to them, and take them to places such as the zoo, the grocery store, concerts, and museums. Using Piaget as a frame of reference, explain why.

2.11

Two kindergarten teachers, one from a rural and the other from an urban area, are planning for a unit on farm animals. Using the concepts of schemes, assimilation, and accommodation, explain how their planning might differ.

2.12

Child development experts consistently suggest that play is important in children's development. Explain this suggestion on the basis of Piaget's work. What implications does this have for the curriculum in a preschool or day-care environment?

Classroom Connections

Capitalizing on Diversity in Your Classroom

1. To compensate for background differences, provide clear examples of the topics you're teaching.
   - A second-grade teacher writes the numeral 34 on the chalkboard. She then has the students make three groups of ten interlocking cubes and place them alongside four unattached cubes. She then points out that the numeral 3 represents the three groups of ten and that the numeral 4 represents those unattached.

2. Have students share their diverse experiences.
   - A high-school geography teacher has a girl who grew up in Guatemala describe what life was like there. She brings in samples of clothing, food, and music to illustrate different aspects of the culture.
   - A sixth-grade class in the Midwest is studying different regions of the country. One of the students has just moved from a fishing village in the Northeast. When the class studies that region, the girl brings in photographs of her old home and explains how people in the town made a living.

3. Encourage parents to share their experiences in the classroom.
   - A fifth-grade teacher writes a personal letter to each student's parents, describing his goals and encouraging them to share their native culture with the class. He writes the letter to non-native English speakers in their native language. As the class studies different countries, the teacher invites students and their parents to come in and share their culture with the class.
   - A middle-school teacher invites parents to come in and talk about their jobs during a unit on career exploration. Parents describe their work experiences and explain how they prepared for them.

Social interaction facilitates development by allowing students to test and compare their views of the world with those of other students.

- Although approximate chronological ages are attached to the stages, the rate at which individual children pass through them differs widely, depending on maturation rates and culture (Papalia & Wendkos-Olds, 1996).

- Although rates vary, all children pass through each stage before progressing into a later one. No one skips any stage.

Piaget's stages of development are summarized in Table 2.1.

Sensorimotor Stage (0 to 2 Years)

In the **sensorimotor stage,** *children use their sensory and motor capacities to make sense of the world.* The schemes they develop are based on physical interactions and focus on goal-directed behaviors, such as using eye–hand coordination to grab objects and bring them to their mouths.

Initially, sensorimotor children don't mentally represent objects; for these children, it is "out of sight, out of mind." Later in the stage, however, they acquire **object permanence,** *the ability to represent objects in memory.* Sensorimotor children also develop the ability to imitate, an important skill that forms the basis for later observational learning.

2.13

You go up a set of steps to get to the door of a building; your friend walks up a ramp. Which path corresponds to discrete movement, and which to continuous?

Table 2.1   Piaget's stages and characteristics

Stage	Characteristics	Example
Sensorimotor (0–2)	Goal-directed behavior	Makes jack-in-the-box pop up
	Object permanence (Represents objects in memory)	Searches for object behind parent's back
Preoperational (2–7)	Rapid increase in language ability with overgeneralized language	"We goed to the store."
	Symbolic thought	Points out car window and says, "Truck!"
	Dominated by perception	Concludes that all the water in a sink came out of the faucet (our cartoon in chapter 1)
Concrete Operational (7–11)	Operates logically with concrete materials	Concludes that two objects on a "balanced" balance have the same mass even though one is larger than the other
	Classifies and serial orders	Orders containers according to decreasing volume
Formal Operational (11–Adult)	Solves abstract and hypothetical problems	Considers outcome of WW II if the Battle of Britain had been lost
	Thinks combinatorially	Systematically determines how many different sandwiches can be made from three different kinds of meat, cheese, and bread

Preoperational Stage (2 to 7 Years)

The **preoperational stage** is *characterized by perceptual dominance.* The name of this stage comes from the idea of *operation* or mental activity. A child who can classify animals as dogs, cats, and bears, for example, is performing a mental operation.

In one sense, use of the term *preoperational* is unfortunate, because it suggests an incomplete stage of development. In fact, many dramatic changes occur in children as they pass through the preoperational stage, and a child at the end of the stage is very different from one at the beginning. For example, enormous, rapid progress in language development occurs, reflecting growth in symbolic thought and conceptual ability (Miller, 1993).

Children at this stage develop an understanding of many concepts. For example, a child riding with her parents in a car will look out the window, point animatedly, and say, "Truck," "Horse," and "Tree," delighting in exercising these newly formed ideas. These concepts are concrete, however; the horse, the truck, and the tree are physically present or associated with the current situation. Children at this age have limited notions of abstract concepts such as *fairness, truth, democracy,* and *energy.*

Preoperational thinking is also characterized by five other aspects of development: egocentrism, centration, and lack of transformation, reversibility, and systematic reasoning.

Egocentrism. **Egocentrism** is *the inability to interpret an event from someone else's point of view.* For example:

> Two three-year-olds are playing in the same area. They are both talking enthusiastically but aren't the least bit concerned that each conversation is independent of the other. A toy truck is sitting between the children, and at the moment neither is playing with it. When Sean begins to play with the truck, however, Gail grabs it away from him, saying, "My truck!" Gail's mother reprimands her with an admonition to share. For Gail, however, the mother's reproof is incomprehensible, and she only reluctantly gives up the truck.

From the three-year-old's perspective, the truck is hers; she saw it and wanted it. Later, through the process of accommodation, the preoperational child's thinking expands to consider others' perspectives.

Centration. **Centration** is *the tendency to focus on one perceptual aspect of an object or event to the exclusion of all others.* For instance, suppose four- or five-year-olds are shown two rows of nickels such as the following:

When asked whether the number of coins in each row is the same, they will say it is. However, when one row is lengthened right in front of the children, like this,

2.14

A small child has not acquired object permanence. His mother takes a stuffed toy the child can see and puts it behind her back. What is the child likely to do? What will the child do after object permanence is acquired?

2.15

Children in kindergarten learn concepts such as *square, circle, triangle,* and other geometric shapes. Given what is known about cognitive development, is this appropriate practice? Explain your answer.

2.16

Which factor affecting development—experience with the physical world, social interaction, or maturation—is probably most important for reducing egocentrism? Why?

the children typically conclude that the bottom row has more coins. They center on the length of the bottom row, rather than considering the number.

Transformation.   **Transformation** is *the ability to mentally record the process of changing from one state to another.* Preoperational children, because of their preoccupation with the here and now of the physical world, have a difficult time thinking about the process of change and consequently are *unable to transform.* For instance, the children in the example with the coins are unable to mentally represent the process of change, even though they directly observe one row being lengthened; they focus instead only on the beginning and ending state. They see it as a different row, rather than as the earlier one lengthened.

2.17

Suppose you are working with a preoperational child. What might you do to help the child "de-center" in the case of the coin problem?

Reversibility.   **Reversibility** is *the ability to mentally trace a line of reasoning back to its beginning.* Again using the example with the coins, the children are mentally *unable* to "reverse" the lengthening process to determine that the two rows indeed have the same number of coins. Preoperational children don't mentally represent the process of lengthening the row, can't mentally reverse the operation, and focus on only one perceptual aspect of the event—the length—rather than on the number. It's easy to see why the children conclude that the bottom row is longer.

Systematic Reasoning.   Preoperational children also cannot systematically use inductive or deductive reasoning. For instance, a child reasoning deductively—albeit unconsciously—would conclude that the number of coins in the two rows remains the same, because the numbers were initially the same and no coin has been added or taken away. A fourth-grader given the problem would say simply, "You just made the row longer," or, "You just spread the coins apart," reflecting systematic reasoning about the event.

Conservation.

> As he's taking an order, the waiter at the pizza place asks, "Do you want that pizza cut into four or eight pieces?"
> The customer replies, "You'd better make it four; I couldn't eat eight all by myself!"

This joke illustrates a widely publicized feature of Piaget's work: his concept of conservation. **Conservation** is *the idea that the "amount" of some substance stays the same regardless of its shape or the number of pieces into which it is divided.* For instance, referring again to the example with the coins, preoperational children conclude that the number is somehow different, even though only the length of the row is changed. For them, the number can "magically" increase without disrupting their equilibrium; number for them is not "conserved." Older thinkers realize that this is impossible.

a   b

A nonconserver is influenced by appearances, believing that the flat pieces of clay have different amounts than the balls of clay even though they were initially the same size.

The ability to conserve can be determined by a number of tasks. One was illustrated in the example with the coins. A second, measuring conservation of mass, is illustrated by the following:

· A child is given two balls of clay, as shown.

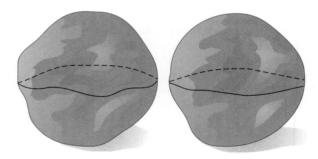

The child is asked which ball has more clay, and she concludes that they have the same amount. If she believes they are unequal, she is asked to remove clay from one and put it on the other until she says they have the same amount. The experimenter then rolls out one of the balls, as shown here:

The child is asked if she now has the same amount of clay. The nonconserver concludes that the amounts are unequal; the conserver notes that the shape has changed but that the amount of clay is the same.

Preoperational children don't think about the world in the same way adults do. Their thinking is dominated by perception, their mental representations are limited primarily to concrete objects, and they do not process abstract ideas of change. However, they have made huge strides from the sensorimotor stage. They have a greater ability to think about their world by using symbols and words to represent objects.

2.18

Use the concepts of *egocentrism, centration, transformation,* and *reversibility* to explain the lack of conservation in the clay problem.

Concrete Operational Stage (7 to 11 Years)

The concrete operational stage marks another important advance in children's thinking. The **concrete operational stage** is *characterized by the ability to think logically about concrete objects*. During this stage children acquire reversible, organized mental operations that allow them to conserve, classify, and take alternate perspectives (Flavell, Miller & Muller, 1993).

The fourth-grader who concluded that the number of coins in the two rows was the same because all the experimenter did was "spread the coins apart" was performing a logical operation. As another example, consider the following:

2.19

Describe the "logic" in the fourth-grader's thinking.

We have three sticks. We see 1 and 2 as shown:

1   2

Now we see 1 and 3, as follows (Stick 2 is no longer visible):

1   3

We're then asked, "What do we know about the relationship between Sticks 2 and 3?"

A preoperational thinker is incapable of dealing with the problem. A concrete operational thinker would conclude that 2 is longer than 3, reasoning that, since 2 is longer than 1 and 1 is longer than 3, 2 must be longer than 3. This is a logical operation.

Seriation and Classification.   Seriation and classification are two logical operations that develop during this stage (Piaget, 1977); both are critical to understanding number concepts (Siegler, 1991). **Seriation** is *the ability to order objects according to increasing or* *decreasing length, weight, or volume.* Piaget's research indicates that this ability gradually evolves until it is finally acquired at age 7 or 8.

Classification *involves grouping objects on the basis of a common characteristic.* Prior to age 5, children can group along a single dimension, such as putting white circles in one group and black ones in another. When a black square is included, however, children simply add it to the black circles, rather than form subclasses of black circles and black squares. By age seven, they can form subclasses, but they still have problems with the idea of multiple-class inclusion. For example, if children are shown ten black circles and three white circles cut from cardboard, they agree that the circles are all made of cardboard with ten black and three white. When asked whether there are more cardboard circles or more black circles, however, six-year-olds typically respond that there are more black; this finding suggests that they center on the comparison between black and white, rather than on the larger class of cardboard circles and the subclass of black cardboard circles.

Teaching the Concrete Operational Student.   Although concrete operational thinkers have made important developmental strides, their thinking is still tied to available experiences; they need to solve problems, such as the three sticks, with concrete objects. In working with concrete operational learners, the challenge for teachers is to structure learning activities that provide a concrete foundation for their thinking. Let's see how one third-grade teacher does this.

> Lucy Amato introduced the concept of *graphing* to her third-graders by having each student plant bean seeds in a pot. Each day after the seeds sprouted, the students measured them with a piece of paper and glued the actual length of paper on a graph. As the plants grew, the lines on the graph also got longer, and students could see the link between the actual plant growth and the graph.

Lucy Amato taught graphing by using concrete objects—the pieces of paper and actual plants. Her teaching demonstrates how teachers of elementary students can facilitate effective learning by using concrete materials that allow students to see abstract concepts and operations in action.

Use of manipulatives is common in elementary math, where concepts such as *place value, borrowing* in subtraction, and *carrying* in multiplication are illustrated with interlocking cubes that represent 100s, 10s, and units. As students perform these operations with the cubes, they begin to understand the abstract processes that lay the foundation for more advanced thinking. Examples with other topics can be found in Table 2.2.

Concrete Materials and Language.   Teachers often mistakenly believe that if their students are using manipulatives, then learning is taking place. This is not always the case, however (Ball, 1992). Unless links between manipulatives and symbols are specifically made, students are left uncertain about these connections and may even see the use of manipulatives and the use of symbols as two different lessons. Let's see how a second-grade teacher uses language to help students make these important connections.

> Kristen Michler is teaching her students about place value. She begins by putting the students in pairs and has them make three groups of ten interlocking cubes and then gather four separate cubes beside the groups.
>
> After the groups are finished, Kristen asks, "Look at what you've made. What do we have there? . . . Jason?"
>
> "Cubes."
>
> "What have we done with the cubes? . . . Lonnie?"

Table 2.2 Use of concrete examples in teaching

Topic	Example
Geography: Longitude and latitude	A teacher draws longitude and latitude lines around a beach ball to illustrate that latitude lines are parallel and longitude lines intersect.
Elementary Science: Air takes up space	A first-grade teacher places an inverted cup into a fishbowl of water. To demonstrate that air keeps the water out of the cup, she tips it slightly to let some bubbles escape.
Chemistry: Charles's law (when pressure is constant, an increase in temperature causes an increase in the volume of a gas.)	A teacher places one balloon into ice water, a second, equally inflated balloon, into room-temperature water, and a third into hot water. She asks the students to compare the final volumes of each.
History: Mercantilism	A teacher writes short case studies illustrating England and France trading raw materials from their colonies with manufactured products, forbidding trade with others, and requiring their ships for transport.

"Put them together."

"All of them?"

". . . No, not these" (pointing at the four separate ones).

"When we put them together, how many do we have in each group? . . . Jianna?"

". . . ten."

"How many groups of ten?"

". . . Three."

"Good," Kristen smiles. "What else do we have? . . . Trang?"

". . . These" (pointing to the four separate ones).

"Good. So, we have three groups of ten and four separate ones. Now, look up here."

Kristen then writes *34* on the chalkboard.

"Look at the number I've just written. What do you suppose the 3 is?" she asks, pointing at the 3. . . . "Yolanda?"

". . ."

"Look at your cubes. How many groups of ten do you have?"

". . . Three."

"Yes, good! So, what is this 3?"

". . . It's . . . these."

"Yes," Kristen smiles encouragingly. "Go ahead and say it."

". . ."

"It is the number of groups of . . . ," Kristen goes on, ". . . ten."

"Yes, excellent. We have made three groups of ten, and this 3," again pointing at the 3 on the chalkboard, "is the *number of groups of ten* that we have."

Kristen then continues by asking the students about the 4 on the chalkboard. Next, she has the groups make two groups of ten cubes and six separate ones, discussing that example just as she did the first one.

2.21

Think again about Karen Johnson's work with her students. Describe a series of questions that she would need to ask to help her students link the abstract formula for density (density = mass/volume) to her demonstration with the cotton.

As you can see, students don't automatically form links between concrete materials and the abstract numerals (Ball, 1992). An essential part of Kristen's lesson was her questioning, which led students to think about the relationship between the cubes and the numerals. This process is difficult for students, but it's critical if they are to understand the connection between abstractions and their experiences. If this link is missing, learning will be incomplete, with manipulatives and numerals remaining unrelated in students' minds.

Formal Operational Stage (Adolescent to Adult)

Although concrete thinkers are capable of logic, their logical operations are tied to the real and tangible. Formal thinkers, in contrast, can think logically about the hypothetical—and even the impossible—as well as the real. During the **formal operational stage,** *the learner can examine abstract problems systematically and generalize about the results*. These abilities open a whole range of possibilities for thinking about the world that were unavailable to learners at the concrete operational stage.

For instance, formal thinkers can solve the problem with the three sticks but do so by concluding that the problem is of a general type described as "If A is greater than B, and if B is greater than C, then A is greater than C." In generalizing this way, formal thinkers are thinking abstractly, an ability that allows them to use the solution for a variety of problems not tied directly to the three sticks.

Formal operational thinkers also recognize the need to isolate and control variables in forming conclusions. For example, a girl hearing her father say, "I've got to stop drinking so much coffee. I've been sleeping terribly the last few nights," responds, "But, Dad, maybe that's not it. You've also been bringing work home every night, and you didn't do that before." She recognizes that her father's sleeplessness may be caused by extra work, rather than by the coffee, and that they can't tell until they isolate each variable.

Let's look at formal operational thinking in a classroom.

2.22

Adding and subtracting are considered to be concrete operations in math, whereas finding percentages is not. Using Piaget's ideas, explain the difference.

Characteristics of Formal Thought.   Flavell (1985) identified three characteristics of formal thinking:

1. Thinking abstractly
2. Thinking systematically
3. Thinking hypothetically and deductively

Differences between concrete and formal operational thinkers on these dimensions are illustrated in Figure 2.4.

As you can see in the figure, the formal operational learner is able to consider the abstract and hypothetical, as in the question about laws. This ability makes the study of courses such as algebra, in which letters and symbols stand for numbers, meaningful on a different level. To the concrete operational child, $x + 2x = 9$ is made meaningful only by representing it as a concrete problem, such as:

> Dave ate a certain number of cookies. His sister ate twice as many. Together they ate nine. How many did each one eat?

The formal operational learner, in contrast, can think about the equation as an abstract idea that can apply to a myriad of cases. In geometry, students are asked to

Figure 2.4   A comparison of concrete and formal operational thinking

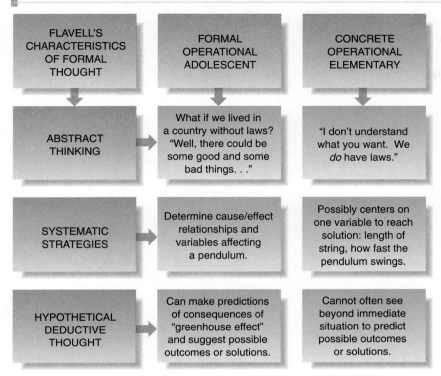

FLAVELL'S CHARACTERISTICS OF FORMAL THOUGHT	FORMAL OPERATIONAL ADOLESCENT	CONCRETE OPERATIONAL ELEMENTARY
ABSTRACT THINKING	What if we lived in a country without laws? "Well, there could be some good and some bad things. . ."	"I don't understand what you want. We *do* have laws."
SYSTEMATIC STRATEGIES	Determine cause/effect relationships and variables affecting a pendulum.	Possibly centers on one variable to reach solution: length of string, how fast the pendulum swings.
HYPOTHETICAL DEDUCTIVE THOUGHT	Can make predictions of consequences of "greenhouse effect" and suggest possible outcomes or solutions.	Cannot often see beyond immediate situation to predict possible outcomes or solutions.

consider different hypothetical arrangements; for example, "Are the interior angles of congruent triangles always identical?" The ability to use symbols to deal with abstract ideas—a characteristic of formal operational thinking—is central to thinking like a mathematician.

Because much of the content of middle, junior-high, and high-school curricula is abstract, the transition to formal thinking is very important. For instance, in American history, considering what might have happened if the British had won the Revolutionary War requires hypothetical and deductive thinking. Biology students are asked to consider the results of crossing different combinations of dominant and recessive genes. Art students must imagine multiple perspectives and light sources when they create drawings. In the study of literature, students are asked to consider the viewpoints of characters in the stories they read. Middle- and high-school curricula are filled with experiences requiring formal operational thought.

The difficulty Karen Johnson's students had in understanding the concept of *density* further illustrates the need for formal thinking. When students are unable to think abstractly and solve abstract problems, they revert to memorizing what they can or, in frustration, give up altogether.

Because of the interaction between development and learning, you can see it's important to understand that this link will affect *how* you teach your students. Let's look further at ways in which Piaget's work has influenced current conceptions of teaching and learning.

2.23

You saw earlier in our discussion that experience is critical for development. This factor has an important implication for teachers of junior-high, high-school, and even university students. Describe this implication.

Formal operational learners can think logically about abstract and hypothetical ideas.

Piaget's Theory: Classroom Applications

Influence on Instruction

The influence of Piaget's work on education is so pervasive that teachers take many of its contributions for granted, almost forgetting there was a time when curriculum and teaching were different. Historically, educators emphasized memorizing long passages to "train" mental faculties. More recently, students memorized rules and procedures, such as the algorithm for subtracting one two-digit number from another, in the hope that memorization would enable students to apply the rule. Research now suggests that the ability to transfer memorized rules is limited (Porter, 1989). Today, in part because of Piaget's work, learning is viewed as an active, constructive process in which students seek organization and meaning in their worlds (we discuss constructivism in more detail later in the chapter).

Influence on Curriculum Development

Because of Piaget's work, curriculum is designed differently than in the past. Lessons are organized with concrete experiences presented first, followed by more abstract and detailed ideas. Memorization is de-emphasized in favor of deeper understanding.

To help their students in the transition from concrete to abstract, we see elementary math teachers armed with beans glued to craft sticks, boxes filled with cubes, and wooden geometric shapes (National Council of Teachers of Mathematics, 1989). In reading and language arts, we see emphasis on "language experience" and "whole language", where reading and writing abilities are developed by building on children's experience and naturally developing language instead of memorized words and definitions (Tompkins, 1997). In social studies, the curriculum begins with a study of children's homes and families and then moves to their neighborhoods, cities, states, and finally to a study of their culture and those of other nations (Brophy, 1990). Their concrete and personal neighborhood serves as an appropriate point of departure for learning about distant and different cultures. The emphasis on hands-on science is also designed to be developmentally appropriate (American Association for the Advancement of Science, 1993).

Putting Piaget's Theory into Perspective

Research on Piaget's Theory

Research indicates that educators should use caution in applying Piaget's descriptions to individual students or even classes; the ages attached to each stage are only approximations, and considerable variation exists within age groups (Berk, 1997).

Further, although his theory implies that learners in junior high, high school, and beyond should be formal thinkers, research indicates that this usually is not the case (Karplus, Karplus, Formisano, & Paulsen, 1979; Lawson & Snitgren, 1982; Thornton & Fuller, 1981). For example, seventh-graders observed a balance with boxes on it, as shown in Figure 2.5, and were then asked to judge the accuracy of the following propositions:

1. The volume of A is greater than the volume of B.
2. The mass of A is greater than the mass of B.
3. The density of A is greater than the density of B.

The reasoning involved can be described as follows:

> We can see that the volume of A is greater than B. The balance is level, so the masses are equal. Because the masses are equal but A's volume is greater, its density is less than B's.

The problem occurs in the present and is tangible; thus, it requires concrete operational thinking. The seventh-graders, typically 12 or 13 years old, were chronologically at the formal operational stage; they should have been able to solve the problem. Researchers found, however, that more than three-fourths of the students concluded that both the mass and density of A were greater. They were still dominated by perceptions, concluding that because A is larger, it must have more mass and also be more dense (Eggen & McDonald, 1987).

Additional research indicates that older learners, too, have difficulty with formal thought. For instance, De Lisi and Straudt (1980) found that college students were unlikely to reason formally in areas outside their majors, and similar patterns have been found in adults.

. . . formal operations, like the concrete reasoning that preceded it, seems to be a gradual rather than abrupt development. And rather than emerging in all contexts at

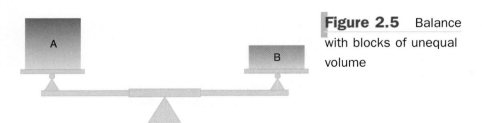

Figure 2.5 Balance with blocks of unequal volume

2.24

Using Piaget's work as a basis, explain why junior high students have difficulty solving problems requiring formal thought.

2.25

What preoperational characteristic explains why the students would conclude that the bigger box was heavier even though the balance was balanced?

once, it is specific to situation and task. All normal adults are capable of abstract thought, but they are likely to demonstrate it only in areas in which they have achieved considerable mastery. (Berk, 1996, p. 552)

These findings have critical implications for teachers, particularly those in middle and junior-high schools (and even high schools and universities). Many students come to these learning situations without the concrete experiences needed to think at the level of abstraction often required. Wise teachers realize this and provide the experiences themselves, as Karen Johnson did with her eighth-graders. Otherwise, the students will revert to whatever it takes for them to survive: in most cases, memorization without understanding.

Criticisms of Piaget's Theory

As you've seen, Piaget has had an enormous impact on teaching and curriculum development. More recent research, however, has led to criticisms of his ideas:

1. Research indicates that Piaget may have underestimated the abilities of young children. Overly abstract directions and tasks cause children to fail at tasks they can do under simpler conditions (Gelman, Meck, & Merkin, 1986).

2. A number of researchers are now questioning Piaget's idea of broad stages of development that affect all types of tasks (Siegler, 1991). For example, research indicates that progression to concrete operational thinking doesn't occur all at once; instead, it begins with conservation of mass and ends with conservation of volume (Bee, 1989). Further, researchers argue that children's logical abilities strongly depend on past experiences and are more dependent on knowledge in a specific area than Piaget suggested (Byrnes, 1988; Overton 1984; Resnick & Klopfer, 1989). For example, students who are provided appropriate experiences with proportional reasoning problems learn to master the problems, whereas students of the same age who are not provided the experiences may never learn to solve them.

3. Piaget's work is also criticized on the grounds that it fails to take cultural differences into account (Berk, 1997). The role of culture is critical in development. Culture determines the kinds of experiences children have, the values they develop, the language they use, and the way they interact with adults and each other (Rogoff & Chavajay, 1995). In the next section, we consider the contributions of Lev Vygotsky, a psychologist who placed culture at the center of his theory of development.

Classroom Connections _____

Applying an Understanding of Piaget's Views of Development in Your Classroom

1. Provide concrete and personalized examples, particularly when abstract concepts are first introduced.

• A kindergarten teacher begins her unit on animals by taking her students to the zoo. She plans for most of the time to be spent with hands-on activities in the petting zoo.

• A social-studies teacher involves his students in a simulated trial to help them understand the American court system. After the trial is over, he has participants discuss the process from their different perspectives.

2. Ask students questions and involve them in discussions to assess their present levels of development.
   - A kindergarten teacher is discussing geometric shapes with his students. Using a flannel board and shapes of different colors and sizes, he asks the students to group them in different ways. After each grouping, he asks the class, "Does that make sense? Are there other ways to group these together?" At the conclusion of his lesson, he emphasizes that there are many ways to group objects.
   - Before beginning a unit on light, reflection, and refraction, a science teacher asks students to explain different phenomena using a flashlight, mirrors, prisms, and lenses. As students explain different phenomena, such as shadows and rainbows, she asks, "Does that make sense?" and encourages other students to ask questions.

3. Use student interaction to expose students to the thought processes of more advanced students.
   - A high-school math teacher talks about problems at the chalkboard, helping students see how he solves each one. He then encourages students who have solved problems to demonstrate solutions, and asks questions that elicit their thinking in the process.
   - A junior-high science teacher gives her students a brief pretest at the beginning of the year on formal operational tasks such as controlling variables and doing proportional thinking. She uses this information to group students for cooperative learning projects, placing some formal- and some nonformal-thinking students in the same groups. She encourages students to think aloud when they solve problems and does the same herself at the chalkboard.

4. Provide practice in hypothetical reasoning for upper-elementary, middle, and junior-high school students.
   - An eighth-grade algebra teacher is working with factoring polynomials and has the students factor the expression:

$$m^2 + 2m + 1$$

   She then asks, "What if no 2 appeared in the middle term? Would it still be factorable?"
   - A history class concludes that people often emigrate for economic reasons. The teacher asks, "Consider a family named Fishwiera, who are upper-class Lebanese. What is the likelihood of their immigrating to the United States?"

A Sociocultural View of Development: The Work of Lev Vygotsky

An alternative to Piaget's view of development comes from a Russian psychologist, Lev Vygotsky (1896–1934), who emphasized the critical role of language and culture in human development. As a boy, he was instructed by private tutors who used Socratic dialogue to transmit information and to clarify ideas (Kozulin, 1990). These sessions, combined with his study of literature and experience as a teacher, convinced him of the importance of two factors in human development: language and activity in social interactions (Vygotsky, 1978, 1986). These two ideas are his most powerful contributions to the field of human development.

Language: A Vehicle for Development and a Tool for Thinking

Language is central to Vygotsky's theory of development. It allows people to learn from others and provides access to the knowledge that others already know. Language provides learners with cognitive tools that allow them to think about the world and to solve problems.

> "Okay, here we go. Let's get dressed so we can go visit Grandma. First we take off your pajamas and put on your underwear. Wow, these pajamas are tight. Next we put on your shirt. There. Then your big boys, and now your pants. Look at those little doggies on the pants."
>
> "Doggy?"
>
> "Yes, those are doggies. Aren't they cute? Ruff, ruff! Grrr! Now we put on this sock. Then your shoe. Now you do the other one."
>
> "Shoe?"
>
> "Yes, that's a shoe. Wait a minute, though. What do we have to put on before the shoe? Look over here" (pointing to the sock). "That's right, first you put on your sock, then your shoe."
>
> "Sock first?"
>
> "Yeah, that's right. Put on your sock first, then your shoe. Atta boy!"

2.26

In mainstream American culture, the concept of *snow* is a relatively simple idea, whereas for Eskimos there are many terms for the concept of *snow*. This difference illustrates what idea that was discussed in this section?

When children learn language, they aren't just learning words; they also are learning the ideas connected with those words, as in the exchange above. When children learn the word *doggie,* they don't just learn how to pronounce it, they also begin learning a wealth of other ideas connected to *doggie* (e.g., doggies are warm, they lick your hand, pictures of doggies sometimes appear on pants). In this sense, language becomes a "cultural tool kit" that children can carry around in their heads to help them make sense of the world. Language facilitates cognitive development and provides children with a vehicle to produce, test, and refine their thoughts about the world, as you saw in the example with the father teaching his son how to dress. Language provides opportunities for the sharing and refinement of ideas.

Language, Social Interaction, and Activity

Language serves another function in development. It allows a child to interact with other people and to begin the process of cultural exchange, or the trading of ideas between people. Vygotsky believed that culture plays an important role in development, and social interaction is the primary way culture is shared and transmitted. You saw earlier how language provides children with a cultural tool kit; social interaction is the way the tool kit is filled. It is the way ideas are exchanged and refined.

2.27

Some educators believe that non-native English-speaking students should be immersed in "English only" programs as soon as possible. On the basis of the information in this section, how effective are those programs likely to be? Explain.

Adults—particularly parents and other caregivers—and peers both play an important role in the process of cultural transmission. Adults explain, give directions, provide feedback, and guide communication (Rogoff, 1990). Children use conversation to collaborate when solving problems—both in play and in the classroom. This interaction allows the exchange of information and feedback about the validity of existing ideas.

The concept of *activity* is also an important element of Vygotsky's theory. Children learn by doing—by becoming involved in meaningful activities with more knowledgeable people. Activity provides a framework in which dialogue can occur. The child puts on his own sock and shoe after watching his father do it and by dialoguing with his dad about the process. Through dialogue driven by activity, ideas are naturally exchanged and development occurs.

Language: A Tool for Self-Regulation and Reflection

In addition to helping people think about the world and communicate with others, language serves a third role in development: It provides people the means to reflect on and regulate their own thinking.

All of us talk to ourselves. For example, we grumble when we're frustrated or angry: "Now where did I put those x%#* keys? I'm going to be late to work." We also talk to ourselves when we're in an uncertain situation: "Oh no, a flat tire. Now what? Let's see. I hope the jack is in the trunk. Yeah. I'd better loosen the nuts before I jack up the car." Children, too, talk to themselves; walk into a preschool or kindergarten during free play time and you'll hear muttering that appears to have no specific audience. If you listen more closely, you'll hear learners talking to themselves as they attempt challenging tasks: "Hmm, which button goes where? I'd better start at the bottom and put the first button in the first hole." Vygotsky believed that this free-floating external speech was the precursor of internalized, private speech.

Private speech is *self-talk that guides thinking and action*. Piaget (1926) observed it in young children and termed it "egocentric speech," reflecting his belief that it was a by-product of the preoperational child's inability to consider the perspectives of others. To Piaget, egocentric speech was an indication of cognitive immaturity, of not being aware of the need to target an audience.

Vygotsky interpreted private speech differently. He believed that these seemingly targetless mutterings were the beginnings of private, inner speech and that this type of language played an important role in the development of self-regulation. Private speech, first muttered aloud and then internalized, forms the foundation for complex cognitive skills such as sustaining attention ("I better pay attention now. This is important."), memorizing new information ("If I repeat the number to myself, I'll be able to remember it."), and problem solving ("Hmm, what should I do first?").

Research supports Vygotsky's functional view of private speech. Children use more of it when tasks are difficult or when they are confused about how to proceed (Berk, 1997). In addition, children who use private speech during problem-solving tasks are more attentive and goal oriented and show more improvement in performance than their less talkative peers (Behrend, Rosengren, & Perlmutter, 1992). Finally, as Vygotsky predicted, private speech becomes internalized with age, converted from overt mutterings to whispers and lip movements.

2.28

You have assigned your second-graders a series of word problems in math. As they work, you hear audible muttering about the problems. What might you infer on the basis of these mutterings? Would you expect similar mutterings if you were teaching sixth-graders?

Vygotsky's Work: Instructional Applications

Vygotsky's theory of development emphasizes the importance of language in learning that occurs in activity-oriented, social situations. By using language, more knowledgeable partners share their expertise about the world. Instructional strategies based on Vygotsky's theory place students in situations where the topics and skills discussed are within the developmental grasp of the learner, an area called the *zone of proximal development*.

Zone of Proximal Development

The **zone of proximal development** is *a range of tasks that a child cannot yet do alone but can accomplish when assisted by a more skilled partner*. For learners, there is a zone of proximal development for each task they are expected to master. When learners are in the zone, they can benefit from the teacher's assistance. Let's see what the zone of proximal development looks like in a classroom.

Jeff Malone, a student intern, was working with a small group of students on percentage problems in math. He began by presenting the three students with a sample percentage problem and observing their work. Sandra zipped through the problem in no time; Javier struggled, muttering to himself; Stewart gave up and sat with his arms folded, a frown on his face.

Instead of explaining the procedure to Javier and Stewart, as he had done in the past when students had difficulty, Jeff tried a different approach.

"Let's talk about how we compute percentages in problems like this. Sandra, why don't you explain to us how you did the first problem? The rest of us will follow along, and then I'll ask someone else to do the next one."

Sandra started, "Okay, the problem asks what percentage of the video games are on sale. Now, when I see a problem like this, I think, how can I make a fraction? After I make a fraction, then I make a decimal out of it and then make a percent. Yeah, that's what I do, so here's what I do first."

As she continued to think aloud, Stewart and Javier followed along.

On the next problem, Jeff involved the two who were having problems. "Javier and Stewart, follow along with me and help me solve this problem."

Joseph raised gerbils to sell to the pet store. He had 12 gerbils and sold 9 to the pet store. What percentage did he sell?

"The first thing," Jeff continued, "I need to find out is what fraction he sold. Now, why do I need to find a fraction? . . . Javier?"

"To . . . then . . . if . . . once we get a fraction, we can make a decimal and then a percent."

"Good," Jeff smiled. "What fraction did he sell?"

". . . Nine . . . twelfths."

"Excellent, Javier. Now, Stewart, how might we make a decimal out of the fraction?"

". . ."

"Look again at the fraction. What is it?"

". . . Nine twelfths."

"Good. So, to find a decimal, we divide the twelve into what number? Go ahead and give it a try."

As Jeff watched, he saw that Javier quickly got .75. Stewart, however, began hesitantly, appearing confused by dividing a large number into a smaller one.

2.29

You are unsuccessfully trying to learn a new word-processing program on your computer. A friend comes over. You're fine with her help, but after she leaves you again run into problems. Are you below, in, or beyond the zone of proximal development? In which of these three areas is your friend?

This lesson relates to Vygotsky's theory in several ways. First, students differed in their ability to benefit from instruction. Sandra was beyond the zone for percentage problems; she required no additional help. Stewart was below the lower limit; he was unable to perform the task even with Jeff's help. Javier was in the zone, as indicated by his ability to solve the problem with help from Jeff and Sandra. The zone represents a learning situation in which teachers, working with students, can promote development (Walsh, 1991).

Jeff also attempted to take advantage of inner speech as a developmental tool by having Sandra think aloud. This task both made her tacit problem-solving procedures observable and provided a model other students could follow.

Applying the Zone of Proximal Development to Teaching

Applying the zone of proximal development to teaching involves three tasks: *assessing, selecting learning activities,* and *providing instructional support* to help students move through the zone successfully. Let's look at them.

The first task is assessment. As Jeff worked with the students, he *gauged their ability to understand within the context of a realistic problem,* a process called **dynamic**

assessment (Spector, 1992). Reasoning ability, background knowledge, and motivation all influence a learner's zone of proximal development (Winn, 1992) and, as he worked with the students, Jeff was able to assess each.

The second task is to adapt learning tasks to the developmental levels of the students. If tasks are too easy, instruction is unnecessary; if too difficult, students become confused and frustrated. Jeff, for example, would need to simplify the task for Stewart and increase the challenge for Sandra in his next session.

In addition to selecting tasks, the teacher must design them to attain shared understanding. **Shared understanding** *occurs when the teacher and students have a common understanding of the task.* Shared understanding is important because it marks a beginning point for development through joint problem solving.

The teacher can ensure shared understanding in at least two ways. First, the task can be embedded in a meaningful context. Instead of presenting math problems in the abstract, for example, the teacher relates them to students' lives; rather than teaching writing as disengaged communication, a teacher has students write letters to friends and relatives and compose stories about their experiences. Second, shared understanding can be accomplished through dialogue that helps students analyze the problems they face. Jeff used teacher and student think-alouds and questioning to help students see how percentage problems could be solved by means of a fraction algorithm.

The third way to ensure shared understanding is to provide instructional support. This is accomplished by applying the concept of *scaffolding*.

Scaffolding: Interactive Instructional Support.

A toddler is learning to walk. As she takes her first tentative steps, her father walks behind her, holding both hands above her head as she lurches forward with uncertain steps. As she gains confidence, the father holds only one hand, walking to the side, keeping an eye out for toys and other objects that could trip her. After awhile, he lets go but continues at his daughter's side to catch her if she falls. When the child becomes tired or the terrain gets bumpy, Dad grabs her hand to make sure she doesn't fall and skin a knee. Eventually, his daughter both walks and runs on her own. (Adapted from Cazden, 1988)

The father provided scaffolding for his daughter as she learned to walk. In an educational setting, **scaffolding** is *assistance that allows students to complete tasks they are not able to complete independently* (Wood, Bruner, & Ross, 1976). Scaffolding helps learners move through the zone of proximal development by enabling them to eventually complete tasks independently. Effective scaffolding is responsive to learners' needs; it adjusts instructional requirements to the learners' level of performance (Rosenshine & Meister, 1992). When learners need more help, the teacher steps in; when less is required, the teacher steps back to allow learners to progress on their own.

Instructional scaffolding is a metaphor for the scaffolding that workers use as they construct a building. An instructional scaffold provides support to the learner. In the example of learning to walk, the father provided both literal and figurative support to his daughter. In classrooms, teachers provide scaffolding by breaking content into manageable pieces, modeling skills, providing practice and examples with prompts, and letting go when the student is ready. The scaffold functions as a tool for students, helping them learn new skills, much as an actual scaffold supports workers as they paint or plaster. The scaffold extends the range of learners, allowing them to accomplish tasks otherwise impossible. If children were faced with learning to walk with no intermediate props, such as a parent or even furniture to pull themselves up on, their development

2.30

Explain how the father accomplished the three instructional tasks—assessing, adapting, providing support—as he helped his daughter progress through the zone of proximal development.

2.31

The distinction between *scaffolding* and simply *explaining* is subtle but important. What is the key characteristic of scaffolding that makes it different from simple explaining?

Teachers provide individualized scaffolding for students through their numerous personal interactions during the day.

would be delayed because of a lack of scaffolding. Similarly, some classroom tasks are so formidable that they cannot be accomplished without a teacher's support.

Types of Instructional Scaffolding. Teachers can provide instructional scaffolding in a number of ways. Some of these are listed in Table 2.3.

One of the most common forms of scaffolding is teacher *modeling*. By demonstrating how to solve problems, teachers provide students with concrete examples of experts at work. Effective teachers also *think aloud* as they model the process. This provides students with access to their teacher's thinking as they wrestle with problems themselves. When students struggle to solve their own problems, teachers can also use *questions* to provide assistance, focus attention, and suggest alternatives.

In addition to interactive forms of scaffolding, teachers can provide support through *adapting instructional materials.* One form of adaptation is to vary the demands of the task (Rosenshine & Meister, 1992). For example, when teaching students to ask questions about the material they are reading, the teacher can first focus on generating questions about a single sentence, then paragraphs, and finally entire passages (Palincsar, 1987).

Instructional scaffolding can also occur through written or verbal *prompts* and *cues.* For example, when giving students a reading or writing assignment, the teacher might provide a list of questions to guide students to important information or remind them of important steps to follow in writing.

Table 2.3 Types of Instructional Scaffolds

Type of Scaffolding	Example
Modeling	An art teacher demonstrates drawing with two-point perspective before asking students to try a new drawing on their own.
Think aloud	A physics teacher verbalizes her thinking as she solves momentum problems at the chalkboard.
Questions	After modeling and thinking aloud, the same physics teacher "walks" students through several problems, asking them questions at critical junctures.
Adapting instructional materials	An elementary physical education teacher lowers the basket while teaching shooting techniques and then raises it as students become proficient.
Prompts and cues	Preschoolers are taught "The bunny goes around the hole and then jumps into it" as they learn to tie their shoelaces.

This concludes our discussion of Vygotsky's description of development. Having studied both Piaget and Vygotsky, we now examine constructivism, a view of learning and development based on their work.

Constructivism: A Developmentally Based View of Teaching and Learning

The study of development, learning, and teaching is going through something close to a revolution, and the learner is at the center of this change. **Constructivism** is *a view of learning and development that emphasizes the active role of the learner in building understanding and making sense of the world.*

> Constructivists believe that knowledge results from individual constructions of reality. From their perspective, learning occurs through the continual creation of rules and hypotheses to explain what is observed. The need to create new rules and formulate new hypotheses occurs when student's present conceptions of reality are thrown out of balance by disparities between those conceptions and new observations. (Brooks, 1990, p. 68)

Constructivism emphasizes active learners, the linking of new knowledge to knowledge learners already possess, and the application of understanding to authentic situations. Experience and interaction between teachers and students and students with each other are instructional tools for constructivists.

Piaget's and Vygotsky's Views of Knowledge Construction

Although they disagreed on some points, Piaget and Vygotsky were both constructivist in their orientation (Fowler, 1994). These similarities and differences are outlined in Table 2.4.

As you can see in Table 2.4, Piaget more strongly emphasized individual learners' creation of new knowledge, whereas Vygotsky focused on the transmission of the tools of knowledge—namely, culture and language (Fowler, 1994; Rogoff, 1990). Regardless of philosophical differences, however, all views of constructivism recommend that teachers go beyond lecturing and "telling" as teaching methods and move toward ". . . structuring reflective discussions of the meanings and implications of content and providing opportunities for students to use the content as they engage in inquiry, problem solving, or decision making" (Good & Brophy, 1997, p. 398–399).

2.32

Which view of constructivism provides for a more prominent role for teachers?

Applying Constructivist Ideas to Teaching

To illustrate these ideas, let's look at a teacher using constructivist concepts to guide her teaching.

> Tracey Stoddart began her unit on heat by innocently asking, "What is heat?" Her students, confident of their nine years of experience with the world, were more than willing to share their knowledge of the sun, fires, radiators, and other sources of heat.
> Everything was going smoothly until Nick shared his belief that heat came from clothes such as sweaters and coats. The rest of the class nodded in agreement.

Table 2.4 A comparison of Piaget's and Vygotsky's views of knowledge construction

	Piaget	Vygotsky
Basic question	How is new knowledge created in all cultures?	How are the tools of knowledge transmitted in a specific culture?
Role of language	Aids in developing symbolic thought; It does not qualitatively raise the level of intellectual functioning. (The level of functioning is raised by action.)	Is an essential mechanism for thinking, cultural transmission, and self-regulation. Qualitatively raises the level of intellectual functioning.
Social interaction	Provides a way to test and validate schemes.	Provides an avenue for acquiring language and the cultural exchange of ideas.
View of learners	Active in manipulating objects and ideas.	Active in social contexts and interactions.
Instructional implications	Design experiences to disrupt equilibrium.	Provide scaffolding. Guide interaction.

Tracey was momentarily at a loss for words. How should she deal with this situation? We have all had the experience of being "cold," putting on a sweater, and "warming up."

After thinking for a few moments, she set aside her plans for the day and continued by asking, "Which do you think produces more heat, a sweater or a coat?"

"A coat!" the class unanimously agreed.

"What about a sweater and a jacket? Which one makes more heat?"

Students weren't so sure about this one. Some of them had heavy wool sweaters that they said kept them warmer than jackets; others thought they felt warmer in jackets.

"How could we find out for sure?" Tracey wondered aloud.

"How about we put a thermometer in a coat," Brad suggested.

"Yeah, and we can put another one in a sweater, and see which one gets hotter," Sonja added.

"Very good ideas," Tracey smiled. After more discussion, the class divided into seven groups of three and two groups of four. Three groups dug out thermometers from the file cabinet, read and recorded the temperature, and carefully wrapped them in coats. Three other groups did the same with sweaters, and the final three with jackets. They then went to lunch.

They returned, again read the temperatures, and recorded them on the chalkboard.

		Before	After
Coat	1:	72	72
	2:	73	72
	3:	72	73
Sweater	1:	74	73
	2:	74	74
	3:	73	73
Jacket	1:	71	72
	2:	72	71
	3:	72	73

As they looked at the information, the students began mumbling and commenting that the numbers didn't seem to make sense.

"None of them got hot," Brad said with uncertainty in his voice.

"About three of them got colder," Anne added in bewilderment.

"Yeah, but the sweaters and coats weren't the same," Anthony countered.

"That doesn't matter," Greta responded. "They shoulda still got hot."

"Maybe we didn't do it long enough," Gary suggested.

"When I was up in the attic with my mom, it was terrible hot 'cause air couldn't get in there," Suzanne added. "I think we should put plastic around them."

Several additional suggestions were made, and the groups went back to work on additional experiments. To the students' amazement, the results were the same, and finally, most of the students were willing to consider the possibility that coats and sweaters don't actually generate heat.

"If that's the case, how do they keep us warm?" Tracey wondered aloud. After additional discussion, Tracey asked what the class would expect if they wrapped a book with a sweater. Would the book warm up? How about a piece of metal? A pencil?

Opinions varied. The class did additional experiments to check and confirm their ideas. Finally, Tracey asked the students for some important differences between them and the book, pencil, and piece of metal.

"We're big, and they're little."

"The book is square, sort of."

"The pencil is skinny."

"We're alive; they aren't."

After several additional comments, Sonja noted, "The iron is cold."

"Do you think that's important?" Tracey queried.

". . . Maybe. We're not cold."

". . . Maybe if we're warm, a coat just keeps us warm," Andrew added after several seconds.

They then considered and discussed the idea that clothing merely traps heat rather than generates it. As the discussion came to a close, most of the students suggested that this was probably a more sensible idea.

The process had taken more time, but the time was well spent.[1]

Let's compare Tracey's experience with Karen Johnson's at the beginning of the chapter. In both instances, they found that their students had a limited—in some cases inaccurate—understanding of the topic. For example, most of Karen's students believed, on the basis of their experience with the "thickness" of oil, that vegetable oil is more dense than water, and Tracey's students thought coats and sweaters produced heat. Both teachers adapted their lessons to learners' existing conceptions and provided the concrete experiences that Piaget stresses to help them construct more accurate and valid concepts. In addition, both teachers used the Vygotskyan idea of social interaction to assist students in evaluating old and constructing new ideas. The evolving nature of constructed understanding was illustrated as Karen's students, on the basis of the experiences she provided for them, linked population density and the "density" of a screen to their understanding of the density of cotton, water, oil, and wood. Tracey used the experiments with coats and sweaters to help them revise and refine their ideas about heat.

Constructivism is a powerful idea. It helps teachers apply Piaget's and Vygotsky's work to classroom learning and development. It suggests that teachers provide experi-

2.33

Describe one approach to teaching that would be consistent and another approach that would be inconsistent with constructivism.

[1]*Source:* "Teaching for Conceptual Change: Confronting Children's Experience" by Watson and Konicek, 1990. *Phi Delta Kappan, 71,* 680–685. Copyright 1990 by *Phi Delta Kappan.* Adapted by permission.

ences, guide discussions, and assume a supportive role in assisting students' attempts at developing understanding.

Teaching based on constructivist principles is demanding and requires a great deal of expertise (Brown, 1994). For instance, both teachers had to be alert and flexible enough in their own thinking to capitalize on students' thoughts and insights when they surfaced in discussions. Less alert teachers might have missed opportunities to help their students move through their zones of proximal development. Worse yet, less effective teachers might ignore or even disapprove of student's reactions. With effort and practice, however, teachers can learn to guide student learning and help develop both the thinking and the deep understanding of content you saw in these classrooms. We return to constructivism in later chapters to discuss specific implications for instruction, motivation, and assessment.

Classroom Connections

Applying Vygotsky's Descriptions of Development in Your Classroom

1. Use meaningful activity as an organizing theme for your curriculum.

   • A third-grade teacher structures a unit on weather around a daily recording of the weather conditions at her school. Each day, students observe the temperature, clouds, and precipitation; record the data on a calendar; graph it by using strips of paper; and compare it to the weather report in the paper.

   • A middle-school social studies teacher tries to help his students understand political polls and the election process. Prior to a national election, he has students poll their parents and peers. Students then have a class election and compare their results with national results.

2. Use scaffolding to help students progress through the zone of proximal development.

   • When her students are first learning to print, a primary teacher initially provides dotted outlines of letters for the students and half lines to help them gauge size. Gradually, these aids are removed.

   • A middle-school teacher helps her students learn to prepare lab reports by doing a lab with the whole class and writing it up as a class activity. Later, she provides only an outline with

the essential categories in it. Finally, she only reminds them to follow the proper format.

Applying an Understanding of Constructivism in Your Classroom

3. Provide experiences that allow students to construct their own understanding.

   • An art teacher begins a unit on perspective by showing slides, displaying works from other students, and sharing her own work. As students turn in their products, she shares them with the class and asks the class to discuss how perspective contributed to each drawing.

   • To help his students understand the "process" of history, a history teacher asks them to write a "history" of some local event or phenomenon. He asks the students to find primary sources, interview people, and present their findings in writing.

4. Embed important concepts in authentic learning tasks.

   • A second-grade teacher teaches graphing by having the students graph class attendance. Information is recorded for both boys and girls, the figures are kept for several weeks, and patterns are discussed.

   • Students in a high-school biology class adopt a local stream as a project for a study of ecology.

They study stream conditions and identify local polluters. They share this information by writing to local newspapers and politicians.

5. Structure classroom tasks to encourage student interaction.
   - After students complete an experiment, their fourth-grade teacher has them verbally describe their observations and conclusions.

When they disagree, she encourages detailed discussion of the differences and guides them to valid explanations.

- An English teacher uses cooperative learning groups to discuss the literature the class is studying. The teacher asks each group to respond to a list of prepared questions and to share their conclusions with the class.

Language Development

A miracle occurs in the time from birth to five years of age. Born with a limited ability to communicate, the young child enters kindergarten with an impressive command of the language spoken at home. Kindergartners have vocabularies of thousands of words and can carry on conversations in complex sentences with adults and peers.

How does this language ability develop, and why do we want to understand it? The answers to these questions are the topics of this section.

Understanding language development is important for three reasons:

- As we saw in the developmental theories of Vygotsky and Piaget, language is a catalyst for developmental change. As children interact with peers and adults they construct increasingly complex and accurate schemes and ideas about the world.
- The development of language is closely tied to learning to read and write (Adams, 1990). As we'll see in Chapter 9, these processes provide learners with essential communication tools.
- Language development facilitates learning in general (Berk, 1997). As students' develop their capacity to communicate, they also increase their ability to learn about abstract ideas and concepts.

Theories of Language Acquisition

Psychologists who study the growth and development of human language have differing views of how language is acquired. Let's look now at three of those theories.

Behaviorist Theories

Behaviorists describe language learning as the acquisition of specific behaviors that are reinforced by the environment (Moerk, 1992; Skinner, 1953, 1957). Children gurgle, parents ooh and aah, and the children figure out that the way to make their parents jump up and down and say strange things is to make funny sounds. Over time, certain sounds are reinforced, others are not, and language develops. For instance,

A 1½-year-old picks up a ball and says, "Baa."

Mom smiles broadly and says, "Good boy! Ball."

The little boy repeats, "Baa."

Mom responds, "Very good."

Interaction between child and parent provides opportunities for reinforcement that are essential components of behaviorist theories of language learning.

Social Cognitive Theory

Social cognitive theory emphasizes the role of modeling, the child's imitation of adult speech, adult reinforcement, and corrective feedback (Bandura, 1977, 1986).

"Give Daddy some cookie."

"Cookie, Dad."

"Good. Giselle gives Daddy some cookie."

Children learn language by hearing it spoken by others, trying it out themselves, and receiving praise or corrective feedback about their efforts. Social cognitive theory stresses the importance of observational learning in social interactions—seeing and hearing language used by others. (We examine social cognitive theory in detail in Chapter 6.)

Both behaviorism and social cognitive theory make intuitive sense. Children probably do learn certain aspects of language by observing and listening to others, trying it out themselves, and being reinforced. Scientists who study the development of languages in different cultures, however, believe something else is occurring.

Psycholinguistic Theories

Ms. Shin smiles as she watches the group of eager kindergartners wave their hands during show-and-tell.
"Antonio, do you want to tell us what your parents do?"
"He nurses at the hospital."
"He nurses at the hospital? Good. What does he do?"
"He band-aids sick people."
"Oh, he's a nurse who fixes sick people. He helps the doctor make people feel better. That's a good job. Who else wants to tell us what their parents do?"

Virtually all humans learn to speak and, despite diversity, all languages share basic structures, such as a subject–verb sequence at the beginning of sentences, called *language universals* (Faw & Belkin, 1989). In addition, children pass through basically the same age-related stages when learning these diverse languages.

Psycholinguistic theories assert that all humans are genetically "wired" to learn language and that exposure to language triggers this development (Chomsky, 1972). Noam Chomsky (1976), the father of psycholinguistic theories, hypothesized that an innate, genetically driven language acquisition device (LAD) predisposes children to learn a new language. According to Chomsky, the **LAD** is *a genetic set of language-processing skills that enables children to understand the rules governing others' speech and to use these in their own speech.* When children are exposed to language, this program analyzes speech patterns for the rules of grammar—such as the subject after a verb when asking a question—that govern a language. The LAD explains why children are so good at producing sentences they have never heard before. For example, Antonio said, "He nurses at the hospital" and "He band-aids sick people." Both behaviorists and social cognitive theorists have trouble explaining these original constructions.

2.34

Children who grow up in bilingual families typically learn to speak both languages. Which approach—*behaviorism* or *social cognitive theory*—better explains this phenomenon? Why?

2.35

Explain why behaviorists and social cognitive theorists have trouble explaining these original constructions.

Chomsky's position is not without its critics, however. Most developmental psychologists believe that language is learned through a combination of factors that include both an inborn predisposition, as Chomsky proposed, and environmental factors that shape the specific form of the language. These environmental factors explain how different languages and dialects are learned, as well as why some home environments are better for language growth than others (Walker, Greenwood, Hart, & Carta, 1994). In addition, increased emphasis is being placed on the child as active participant in language learning (Genishi, 1992). This constructivist view of language learning emphasizes the importance of experience and interaction with others in a child's language development. Let's look at this view.

A Constructivist View of Language Development

As you saw earlier, language is central to Vygotsky's theory of cognitive development. It allows social interaction and provides a vehicle for both the transmission of culture and the internal regulation of thinking. Vygotsky's theory also provides insights into the process of language development itself.

As we saw earlier, activity is central to Vygotsky's theory of development, and language is no exception. Children learn language by using it in their interactions with adults and peers. As they interact with others, they use and practice language. Language development appears to be effortless because it is embedded in the everyday process of communication.

In helping young children learn to speak, adults adjust their speech to operate within the children's zone of proximal development (Bruner, 1985). Baby talk and "motherese" use simple words, short sentences, and voice inflections to simplify messages and to highlight important aspects of a message (Baringa, 1997). These alterations in speech provide a form of linguistic scaffolding that facilitates communication.

Through language embedded in meaningful activity, adults transmit important ideas in the culture to children.

2.36

Describe specifically how constructivist views of language development are different from each of the other three views that have been discussed. Which of the other three views is most closely related to constructivist views?

Let's see why this linguistic scaffolding works. First, communication revolves around activities that are meaningful to participants. For example, the child wants a cookie or is unhappy about something, and language provides a medium to communicate with others. Both participants have a stake in the process. The more knowledgeable partner adapts language to fit the capabilities of the child, raising the ante by using bigger words and more complex sentences as the child becomes more capable. Children develop as they acquire more complex language skills. Teachers and other adults promote language development through interactions that encourage children's use of language and feedback that helps correct and refine language (Arnold, Lonigan, Whitehurst, & Epstein, 1994).

Stages of Language Acquisition

A parent listened one morning at breakfast while her six- and three-year-olds were discussing the relative dangers of forgetting to feed the goldfish versus overfeeding the goldfish:

six-year-old:	"It's worse to forget to feed them."
three-year-old:	"No, it's badder to feed them too much."
six-year-old:	"You don't say badder, you say worser."
three-year-old:	"But it's baddest to give them too much food."
six-year-old:	"No it's not. It's worsest to forget to feed them." (Bee, 1989, p. 276)

Children pass through a series of stages as they learn to talk. In the process, they make errors, and their speech is an imperfect version of adult language. Most important, however, are the huge strides they make. Understanding this progress helps teachers promote language growth through their interactions with learners.

Early Language: Building the Foundation

Learning to speak actually begins in the cradle when "Ooh" and "Aah" and "Such a smart baby!" are used to encourage the infant's gurgling and cooing. These interactions lay the foundation for future language development by teaching the child that communication is a reciprocal process between human beings.

The first words occur between ages one and two when the child uses holophrases to convey meaning. **Holophrases** are *one- and two-word utterances that carry as much meaning for the child as complete sentences.* For example,

"Momma car."	That's Momma's car.
"Banana."	I want a banana.
"No go!"	Don't leave me alone with this scary babysitter!

During this stage, the child also uses intonation to convey meaning. For example, the same word said differently has a very different message for the parent:

"Cookie."	That's a cookie.
"Cookie!"	I want a cookie.

This intonation is significant; it indicates that the child is beginning to use language as a functional tool.

Two patterns—overgeneralization and undergeneralization—creep into speech at this stage and stay with the child through the other stages. **Overgeneralization** occurs when *a child uses a word to refer to a broader class of objects than is appropriate*

(Naigles & Gelman, 1995). This occurs, for example, when *car* is used to refer not only to cars but also to buses and trains.

Undergeneralization is harder to detect. **Undergeneralization** occurs when *a child uses a word too narrowly,* such as *kitty* used only for a child's cat but not for cats in general. Both overgeneralization and undergeneralization are normal aspects of language development, and most instances are corrected through normal listening and talking. Sometimes a parent or teacher may intervene to clear up a misconception, such as, "No, spiders aren't really insects. See how they have eight legs instead of six?"

Notice how closely language development relates to the development of schemes or mental structures in children. Overgeneralization occurs when children inappropriately assimilate new information into an already-existing structure; undergeneralization occurs when they over-accommodate. A variety of concrete experiences plus interaction with adults and peers helps young children fine-tune their language.

2.37

Sometimes a child will call all men "Daddy." What is this an example of? How could it be remedied?

Fine-Tuning Language

During the "twos," children elaborate and fine-tune the choppy speech found earlier (Berk, 1996, 1997). The present tense is elaborated to include the following verb forms:

Present progressive:	I eating.
Past regular:	He looked.
Past irregular:	Jimmy went.
Third person irregular:	She does it.

One problem that surfaces in this stage is overgeneralization of grammatical rules, for example, "badder," "worst," and "He goed home." Piaget's work helps explain this tendency. "He goed home" uses an existing pattern, which allows the child to remain at equilibrium, whereas "He went home" requires accommodation.

Advancing Development

At about age three, a child learns to use sentences more strategically. Subject and verb are reversed to form questions, and positive statements are modified to form negative statements. For instance, "He hit him" is changed to "He didn't hit him" and "Did he hit him?" The idea that the form of language is determined by its function begins to develop more fully in this stage.

Simple declarative sentences with subject–verb–object evolve into more complex forms during this stage. Two separate but related ideas that earlier appeared as distinct sentences now become one. For example, "The boy ran too fast" and "The boy fell down" can now be combined to produce "The boy ran too fast and fell down." Notice how the increasingly complex sentence structure also reflects more complex thinking.

The introduction of more complex sentence forms happens at around age six and relates to other aspects of cognitive development. For instance, "Jackie paid the bill" and "She had asked him out" become "Jackie paid the bill, because she had asked him out." The ability to form and use more complex sentences relates to the child's developing understanding of cause-and-effect relationships.

2.38

What theory of language acquisition supports the fact that virtually all children reach school able to speak a language? What theory can explain the fact that some children have better language backgrounds than others?

Increasing Language Complexity

The picture that emerges is one of a growing language that becomes increasingly complex and allows children to describe and think about their environment. The typical child brings to school a healthy and confident grasp of the powers of language and how it can be used to communicate with others and think about the world. The importance of this language foundation for reading and writing instruction as well as learning in general is becoming increasingly apparent to educators (Adams, 1990; Berk, 1996, 1997; Hornberger, 1989). We'll return to this topic in Chapter 4 when we discuss dialects and bilingualism, and in Chapter 9 when we describe learning to read and write.

Classroom Connections

Applying an Understanding of Language Development in Your Classroom

1. Begin language development and concept learning activities with tangible experiences.
   - A fourth-grade teacher begins a unit on cities by having her inner-city students describe their neighborhoods in as much detail as possible. She then illustrates a rural neighborhood with pictures and asks the students to compare their own neighborhoods with what they see in the pictures.
   - A second-grade teacher stops whenever an unfamiliar word is used in a reading passage or discussion and asks for an example of it. He keeps a list of new words, writes them on cards, and displays them next to objects around the classroom. If the objects don't exist in the room, he gathers pictures and displays the words and pictures together.
   - A third-grade teacher begins a unit on bones and muscles by having the students feel their own legs, arms, ribs, and heads. As they do this, she identifies the bones on a life-skeleton in front of the classroom.

2. Use open-ended questions to encourage the development of language.
   - The third-grade teacher doing the unit on bones and muscles begins her discussion by having the students simply describe what they feel when they squeeze their arms and legs and poke their ribs and heads. She writes these descriptions on the chalkboard and uses them to frame her discussion.

   - A fifth-grade teacher, in a unit on fractions, has the students fold pieces of paper into halves, thirds, fourths, and eighths. She then has them shade different sections of the folded papers, describe what they've done, and compare the sections.

3. Focus on meaning, rather than on pronunciation and mechanics in reading comprehension activities. Model standard pronunciation for students.
   - A first-grade teacher asks students to discuss stories, including what they think would happen in a different situation, why the characters behaved as they did, and what a good summary of the story would be. She accepts each response without correction and paraphrases the responses by using standard English when necessary.

4. Provide for differences in language proficiency in your classroom.
   - At the beginning of the school year, a junior-high social studies teacher finds out which of his students have limited abilities in English. He pairs these students with student volunteers who sit next to the students, answer questions, and generally help with the course. The teacher has discovered that tutors not only enjoy their task, but also benefit from it cognitively.
   - A second-grade teacher enlists the aid of older students to come into her classroom to tutor her students in reading. When possible, the tutors speak the same native language as her second-graders and provide assistance in both English and the native tongue.

Windows on Classrooms

At the beginning of the chapter, you saw how Karen Johnson used her understanding of student development to help her students learn about density. In studying the chapter, you've seen how concrete and personalized examples and high levels of interaction facilitate learning and development. In addition, you've seen how an understanding of students' developmental needs can affect the effectiveness of instruction.

Let's look now at another teacher who is working with a group of first-grade students. As you read the case study, analyze the teacher's approach in terms of the ideas you've studied in the chapter.

Jenny Newhall gathered her first-graders around her on the rug in front of a small table to begin her science lesson. After they were settled, she announced, "Today, we are going to be scientists. Scientists use their senses to find out about the world."

She then reviewed what the five senses were by asking students for examples as she proceeded, and then she asked, "How do you know if something is real? . . . Jessica?"

When Jessica failed to respond, Jenny continued by holding up a spoon and asking, "Jessica, is this real?"

Jessica nodded, and Jenny continued, "How do you know?"

" . . ."

"What is it?"

" . . . A tablespoon."

"How do you know it's a spoon?" Jenny prompted.

After some thought, students agreed they could touch it, see it, and even taste it. Jenny then asked, "Is air real? . . . Anthony?"

Anthony offered, "Yes, because you can breathe it."

Jenny probed further, "Can we see it?"

Her students thought for a moment and shook their heads, indicating no.

"Let's think about air for a while," Jenny said as she turned to a large fishbowl filled with water.

"What do you see?" she asked, pointing to the fishbowl.

"A tank with water in it," one student volunteered.

"Are you sure it's water?" Jenny continued. The students weren't sure how to answer.

"How do you know it's water?" Jenny continued.

"It's moving," Devon replied.

"How else can you tell?"

Receiving no answer, Jenny went on, "If you were to drink this, would you know it's water?"

After warning them about drinking things they don't know about, she assured them the liquid was safe to test. One student came up, put his finger in it, and said, "Yep, it's water."

"What is this?" Jenny continued, holding up an empty water glass.

After spending a few minutes asking them to use their sense of sight to describe various features of the glass, Jenny said, "I'm going to put this glass in the water

Video Case

upside down. What's going to happen? What do you think? . . . Michelle?"

" . . . Water will go in the glass."

"No, it'll stay dry," Samantha countered.

To address this difference of opinion, Jenny asked, "Raise your hand if you think it will get water in it. . . . Okay," she said, surveying the room. "Raise your hand if you think it'll remain dry. . . . How many aren't sure? . . . Well, let's see if we can find out.

"First, we have to be sure it's dry. Terry, because you're not sure, I want you to help me by feeling the inside of the glass. How does it feel? Is it dry?"

"Yeah," replied Terry after putting his hand into the glass.

Then Jenny asked the students to watch carefully as she pushed the inverted glass under the water, as shown in the following drawing.

"Is the glass all the way under?" she asked, with her hand under the water.

The class agreed that it was.

Terry then offered, "There's water inside it. I can see the water inside."

"Then what will it feel like when I pull it out?" Jenny asked.

"Wet," Terry responded.

After pulling it carefully out of the water, she then asked Terry to check the inside of the glass.

"How does it feel?"

"Wet."

Jenny was momentarily taken aback. For the demonstration to work, the inside of the glass was supposed to be dry. After pausing a second, she said, "Samantha, come up here and tell us what you feel."

As Samantha placed her hand up the glass she said, "It's wet on the outside, but dry on the inside."

"It's wet!" Terry asserted.

With a look of concern, Jenny said, "Uh, oh! We have two differing opinions. We've got to find out how to solve this problem." After a short pause, she continued, "Let's dry this glass off and start again. Only this time, we're going to put a paper towel in the glass. Now if water goes in the glass,

what is the paper towel going to look like?"

The class agreed it would be wet and soggy.

Then she held up the glass for the class to see. "Okay, it's dry. The paper towel is up in there. We're going to put it in the water again and see what happens."

The class watched carefully as Jenny put the glass into the water again, and after a few moments, she pulled it out.

"Okay, Marisse, come up here and check the paper towel and tell us whether it's wet or dry."

Marisse felt the towel, thought for a moment, and said, "Dry."

"Why did it stay dry? Raise your hand if you can tell us why it stayed dry. What do you think, Jessica?"

"'Cause it's inside and the water is outside?"

"But why didn't the water go into the glass? What kept the water out? . . . Anthony?"

"A water seal."

"A water seal. Hmm, . . . There's all that water on the outside. How come it didn't go inside? How can the towel stay dry?"

A quiet voice volunteered, "Because there's air in there."

"*Air!* Is that what kept the water out?" Jenny asked with enthusiasm.

"Well, earlier Samantha said that when she was swimming in a pool and put a glass under some water, it stayed dry, but when she tipped it, it got wet inside. Now what do you think will happen if I put the glass under the water and tip it? What do you think . . . Devon?"

"It'll get wet."

"Let's see. Now watch very carefully. What is happening?" Jenny asked as she slowly tipped the inverted glass, allowing some of the bubbles to escape. ". . . Andrea?"

"There were bubbles."

"Andrea, what were those bubbles made of?"

"They're air bubbles."

"Now look at the glass. What do you see?" Jenny asked, pointing to the half empty glass upside down in the water. "In the bottom half is water. What's in the top half?"

"It's dry."

"What's up in there?"

"Air."

"*Air* is up there. Well, how can I get that air out?"

"Tip it over some more," several students responded. When Jenny did that, additional bubbles floated to the surface.

"Samantha, how does that work? When I tip it over, what's pushing the air out?"

". . . The water," Samantha offered hesitantly.

"So, when I tip it this way (tipping it until more bubbles came out), what's pushing the air out?"

"Water," several of the class answered in unison.

Jenny then changed the direction of the lesson by saying, "Now I have something else for you," showing the students a glass full of water. "What do you think will happen if I tip this glass over?"

Jenny continued by covering the glass with a card, and again asked what they thought would happen. This time there were disagreements, some suggesting that the water would spill, but others believing that the water would stay in the glass.

Jenny then held the card on the glass, tipped the glass over, and the students saw that the water didn't spill. Jenny asked for explanations, and one of the students suggested that the water acted like "super glue" to keep the card on the glass.

After some additional discussion, one of the children suggested that air kept the card next to the glass. They discussed this possibility a bit further, and Jenny then turned the lesson to small-group work.

She divided the class into groups of four or five and gave the students detailed directions about how to take turns. The students

then used tubs of water, glasses, cards, and paper towels to experiment on their own.

After each student had a chance to try the activities, Jenny again called the children together and they reviewed and summarized what they had found.

Questions for Discussion and Analysis

Analyze Jenny's lesson in the context of the information in this chapter. In doing your analysis, consider the following questions. In each case, be specific and take information directly from the case study.

1. At what level of cognitive development were Jenny's students likely to be? Was her instruction effective for that level? Explain.

2. Why was the medium of water important for Jenny's lesson? How does this relate to Piaget's levels of development?

3. How well did Jenny follow constructivist guidelines? What could she have done differently to make the lesson more constructivist?

4. When Samantha and Terry disagreed about the condition of the inside of the glass, how did Jenny respond? What other alternatives might she have pursued? What are the advantages and disadvantages of these alternatives?

5. Were Jenny's students in the zone of proximal development for the lesson she was teaching? What forms of scaffolding did Jenny provide? How effective was the scaffolding?

6. How did Jenny use social interaction in her lesson? What instructional functions did this social interaction perform?

7. On the basis of this chapter's content, what suggestions do you have to improve the instruction in this lesson?

Summary

Piaget's Theory of Cognitive Development

Piaget suggests that development results from the combination of learning, experience, and maturation. The quality of experience in the physical and social world, together with the drive for equilibrium, combine to influence development. Intellectually, developing children organize their experiences into schemes that help them understand the world. Compatible experiences are assimilated into the schemes. Incongruent experiences require an accommodation of the schemes to reestablish equilibrium.

As children develop, they progress through stages characterized by unique ways of understanding the world. During the sensorimotor stage young children develop eye–hand coordination schemes and object permanence. The preoperational stage includes the growth of symbolic thought, as evidenced by increased use of language. During the concrete operational stage children can perform basic operations such as classification and serial ordering on concrete objects. In the final stage, formal operations, students develop the ability to think abstractly, reason hypothetically, and think about thinking.

Piaget's work has influenced curriculum and instruction, as evidenced by the emphasis on manipulatives, language experience, hands-on activities, and discovery-oriented instruction.

Vygotsky's Description of Development

Lev Vygotsky offers an alternate view of development. His description focuses heavily on language and social interaction, and the role they play in helping learners acquire an understanding of the culture in which they live. Language is the tool people use for cultural transmission, communication, and reflection on their own thinking.

Vygotsky's work has begun to exert influence in classrooms. Teachers are encouraged to engage students in meaningful learning tasks that involve language and social interaction. Those learners who are able to benefit from assistance are in what Vygotsky calls the zone of proximal development. Learners within this zone can profit from instructional scaffolding in the form of modeling, questions, prompts, and cues.

Constructivism

Constructivism suggests that learners form or develop their own understanding of the way the world works, rather than have that understanding delivered to them. Piaget and Vygotsky, both constructivists, agree that active learners and social interaction are important for development, but they differ in their reasons why. Piaget focuses on active manipulation of objects and ideas, together with the validation of schemes; Vygotsky emphasizes active participation in cultural exchange.

The implications of constructivism for teaching suggest that learners should be active participants in learning activities, that learning should be guided rather than presented by teachers, and that interaction and discussion should be used in the learning process.

Language Development

All views of development are closely linked to language and its uses. Behaviorism, social cognitive theory, and psycholinguistic theories explain language development differently; each probably forms part of the explanation. Children progress from one- and two-word utterances to elaborate language that involves complex sentence structures by the time they reach school.

Important Concepts

accommodation (p. 29)

adaptation (p. 29)

assimilation (p. 29)

centration (p. 36)

classification (p. 40)

concrete operational stage (p. 39)

conservation (p. 37)

constructivism (p. 53)

development (p. 71)

dynamic assessment (p. 50)

egocentrism (p. 36)

equilibration (p. 28)

equilibrium (p. 28)

formal operational stage (p. 42)

holophrases (p. 60)

LAD (p. 58)

maturation (p. 30)

object permanence (p. 35)

organization (p. 28)

overgeneralization (p. 60)

preoperational stage (p. 36)

private speech (p. 49)

reversibility (p. 37)

scaffolding (p. 51)

schemes (p. 28)

sensorimotor stage (p. 35)

seriation (p. 39)

shared understanding (p. 51)

transformation (p. 37)

undergeneralization (p. 61)

zone of proximal development (p. 49)

3

Personal, Social, and Emotional Development

CHAPTER OUTLINE

"Ahh," Anne Dillard, an eighth-grade English teacher, sighed wearily as she slumped into a chair in the faculty lounge.

"Tough day?" her friend Beth asked.

"Yes. It's Sean again," Anne explained, straightening up. "I just can't seem to get through to him. He won't do his work, and he has a bad attitude about school in general. He can't get along with the other students, and when I try to talk with him about it, he always says they're picking on him for no reason. I don't know what's going to become of him. The funny thing is, I get the feeling that he knows he's out of line, but he just can't seem to change."

"I know what you mean," Beth responded. "I had him for English last year. He was a tough one—very distant. He lost his dad in a messy divorce; his mother got custody of him, and his father just split. Every once in a while, he'd open up to me, but then the wall would go up again."

"He's a bright boy, too," Anne continued, "but he seems to prefer avoiding work to doing it. If I could just help him get his act together, I think he'd do all right. If. . . ?"

In Chapter 2, we studied theories that describe the cognitive, or intellectual, development of students and, as a result, we know that younger students think, feel, and act in ways that are qualitatively different from those of adults. We now want to turn to an examination of the personal, social, and emotional development of students at different ages. Understanding this development can help teachers make informed decisions about ways to best meet students' emotional and interpersonal needs.

We begin the chapter with a discussion of Erikson's theory of personal and social development, followed by an analysis of research on self-concept. We then turn to the development of morality, social responsibility, and self-control by examining the contributions of Piaget and Kohlberg in these areas.

After you have completed your study of this chapter, you should be able to meet the following objectives:

- Explain the implications that Erikson's theory has for teaching.
- Explain the relationships between self-concept and academic achievement, and what teachers can do to influence each.
- Describe similarities and differences between Piaget's and Kohlberg's theories of moral development.
- Identify different stages of moral reasoning and how they apply to classroom practice.

The world that students are now experiencing is the toughest in this country's history. The news is replete with stories about drug and sexual abuse, teen pregnancy, single-parent families, and an alarming school dropout rate. Teachers can no longer effectively teach without considering the personal, social, and emotional well-being of their students. If all of us as teachers understand our students' emerging senses of self, their search for identity, and how they relate to others, we are better prepared to help them function effectively in the classroom. Erik Erikson (1902–1994) developed a theory (1968) linking these three elements, which we discuss in the next section.

Erikson's Theory of Personal and Social Development

Erik Erikson's background, like Piaget's and Vygotsky's, provides insights into his work. He dropped out of high school and spent time traveling in Europe and studying art. In the process, he met Sigmund Freud and studied under Freud's daughter, Anna. As he studied young people in different cultures, Erikson became interested in how they acquire a personal identity and how society helps shape that identity. *Because his theory integrates personal, emotional, and cultural or social development,* it is often called a **psychosocial theory.** Erikson's theory differs from Piaget's in that Piaget focused on the cognitive or intellectual development of learners, while Erikson focused on students' emotional health.

Erikson's work is based on five important ideas:

1. People in general have the same basic needs.
2. The development of the ego or self occurs in response to these needs.
3. Development proceeds in stages.
4. Each stage is characterized by a psychosocial challenge, or *crisis,* that presents opportunities for development.
5. Different stages reflect differences in the motivation of an individual.

3.1

Erikson suggests that stages reflect differences in motivation for an individual. What differences are reflected in Piaget's stages?

A **crisis** is *a time of vulnerability to a psychological challenge,* and the challenge is closely tied to social relationships. An acceptable resolution of a crisis means that a favorable ratio of positive to negative psychosocial traits emerges. Although a crisis is never permanently resolved, healthy resolution of the crisis at each stage leads to a positive view of oneself as a person, an accurate perception of self in the larger society, and an integration of the two. A negative resolution can retard development at later stages and leave the personality impaired.

Here we see a second difference between Piaget's and Erikson's theories. Piaget's stages are hierarchical, and progression to formal operations, for example, depends on development at the concrete operational stage. Erikson's stages, in contrast, are not hierarchical. They are influenced by, but don't directly depend on, development in earlier stages.

3.2

Is the statement "Motivation is an important part of Erikson's theory, but it isn't a part of Piaget's work" true or false? Explain your answer.

Erikson's Stages of Psychosocial Development

Descriptions of Erikson's developmental stages are outlined in Table 3.1. Notice how each stage involves a crisis that the person resolves through interaction with others.

Trust versus Mistrust (Birth to 1 Year)

Developing a sense of **trust,** or *confidence in the honesty and justice of others,* is the first psychological challenge facing all people, and it is especially important to infants

Table 3.1   Erikson's stages of psychosocial development

Stage	Approximate Age	Characteristics
Trust vs. Mistrust	Infancy (0–1 year)	Trust in the world is developed through consistent and continuous love and support.
Autonomy vs. Shame and Doubt	Toddler (1–3 years)	Independence is fostered by successful experiences formed by support and structure.
Initiative vs. Guilt	Early Childhood (3–6 years)	An exploratory and investigative attitude results from meeting and accepting challenges.
Industry vs. Inferiority	Middle Childhood (6–12 years)	Enjoyment of mastery and competence comes through success and recognition of accomplishment.
Identity vs. Confusion	Adolescence (12–18 years)	Personal, social, sexual, and occupational identity comes from success in school and experimentation with different roles.
Intimacy vs. Isolation	Young Adulthood	Openness to others and the development of intimate relationships result from interaction with others.
Generativity vs. Stagnation	Middle Adulthood	Productivity, creativity, and concern for the next generation are achieved through success on the job and a growing sense of social responsibilities.
Integrity vs. Despair	Old Age	Acceptance of one's life is achieved by an understanding of a person's place in the life cycle.

Source: Adapted from *Identity, Youth and Crisis* by Erik E. Erikson, by permission of W.W. Norton & Company, Inc. Copyright 1968 by W. W. Norton & Company, Inc.

because of their dependence on others. An infant who receives consistently good care from parents develops a sense of trust; an infant who is left to cry and who receives unpredictable care can develop basic mistrust that leads to fear and suspicion of other people and the world in general. These ideas are consistent with studies of *bonding,* or the social attachment between babies and their primary caregivers, usually parents (Isabella & Belsky, 1991). Although we can't evaluate the care Sean received as an infant, his behavior suggests that he didn't fully resolve the trust–mistrust crisis. His perception that the other students are "picking on him for no reason" and his inability to communicate with his teachers may be indicators of this problem.

Autonomy versus Shame and Doubt (Ages 1 to 3)

Securely attached children next face the challenge of **autonomy,** or *doing things on their own.* They learn to feed and dress themselves, and toilet training begins. As you recall from studying cognitive development, they demonstrate goal-directed behavior and begin to communicate verbally. They no longer want to depend totally on others. At this point, parents need to encourage and reassure children who try to put their shoes on, for example, and express confidence in the child's ability, even though it would be easier to do the task for them. Overly restrictive parents or those who punish minor accidents, such as bed-wetting or spills while eating, can lead children to doubt their own abilities or to have a sense of shame about their bodies. Erikson believed this leads to a lack of confidence in their power to deal with and control their world.

Initiative versus Guilt (Ages 3 to 6)

Initiative is *characterized by an exploratory and investigative attitude that results from meeting and accepting challenges.* At the beginning of this stage, children are likely to be found upside-down in the drawer with the pots and pans—"into everything." Having developed a sense of autonomy, children are now ready to explore and respond to their curiosity. This is the stage at which children make enormous cognitive leaps, and those developing abilities provide the impetus for exploration in all areas of their lives. When a child offers to "help" his mother make cookies, for example, he needs the assurance that his contributions are welcome and valued. Parents who criticize or punish initiative cause children to feel guilty about their self-initiated activities. Sean's withdrawal and lack of personal initiative at school suggest problems at this stage.

School and the Development of Initiative.   As children enter preschool and kindergarten, they are moving forward, taking on more tasks, and searching eagerly for more experiences. "I can do it!" and "Let me try," are signs of this initiative. They are interacting more with their peers, and their play is becoming more complex and interdependent. As children go through these changes, parents and teachers can do much to help them develop into happy and healthy children.

> "Good, Felipe. I see you've used a lot of colors to draw your bird. That's a very pretty bird."
>
> "Nice, Taeko. Those are really bright colors. They make me feel happy."
>
> "Look what Raymond did. He cut out his picture when he was done. That's a nice job of cutting."

Teachers play an important role in students' developing independence and initiative. Felipe and Taeko made their own decisions about coloring, and Raymond decided

3.3

Identify at least two things a preschool/kindergarten teacher might do to encourage students' initiative.

3.4

Given what you know about young children's socioemotional growth, is competition a generally healthy or generally unhealthy component of the early school curriculum? Explain.

on his own to cut out the picture when he was finished. The kind of support they receive influences their future sense of initiative and competence. Criticism of this initiative detracts from the feeling of independence and, in extreme cases, leads to guilt and dependency. Simple tasks, such as buttoning clothes and putting away toys, form the concrete challenges that children use to estimate their own competence and self-worth. A child's performance on a task isn't as important as an adult's response to it. Children at this age are taking initiative and trying to be independent, but adult assessment is still very important. Supportive and encouraging teachers play a critical role in learners' growing sense of initiative.

Industry versus Inferiority (Ages 6 to 12)

The crisis at the industry versus inferiority stage also has important implications for teachers. The challenge is to develop a sense of **industry,** *the enjoyment of mastery and competence through success and recognition of accomplishment.* Because children spend large amounts of time and energy at school, the influence of teachers and peers is very important. If challenges are too difficult and result in failure, the child may develop a sense of inferiority, or if accomplishments involve only trivial tasks, industry fails to develop.

Early childhood and elementary classrooms should provide opportunities for students to develop personal independence and initiative.

In a longitudinal study of development, Vaillant and Vaillant (1990) found that of intelligence, family background, and industry, a healthy sense of industry was the most significant factor in later personal adjustment, economic success, and interpersonal relationships. This finding is very encouraging, because it suggests that if teachers can help students acquire a sense of industry in responding to challenges, they can overcome many obstacles later in life.

As you study Erikson's work, keep in mind that children don't necessarily recognize the need to develop a sense of industry, competence, and success at the time they are going through the stage. It might appear, for example, that peer relationships are most important to them at this point in their lives. Erikson asserts, however, that during this period their main challenge is to develop a sense of competence and purpose which comes from accepting and meeting challenges.

Identity versus Confusion (Ages 12 to 18)

During adolescence, middle and junior-high school youngsters experience major physical, intellectual, and emotional changes. Many go through growth spurts, and their coordination doesn't keep up with their bodies. The magnitude of physical change in early adolescence is surpassed only during infancy. Adolescents experience new sexual feelings and, not quite knowing how to respond, they're frequently confused. They are concerned with what others think of them and are preoccupied with their looks. They are caught in the awkward position of wanting to assert their independence, yet longing for the stability of structure and discipline. They want to rebel, but they want something solid to rebel against. They write "Ms. Smith is a b_____" on the bathroom wall on Wednesday, but on Thursday they decide they really like her. Further, they would feel terrible if they thought she didn't like them.

3.5

What happens when students are consistently given schoolwork that is so easy they can complete it with little effort? Will this have a positive or a negative effect on their resolution of the industry/inferiority crisis? Explain. How would schoolwork that is too difficult influence development at this stage? Again explain.

3.6

Describe some specific items that you would expect to see on a report card designed to promote industry. What elements would be missing?

3.7

Which of the following is likely to contribute most to an adolescent's growing sense of identity: the formal school curriculum (e.g., math, English), extracurricular activities, friends, or family? Which contributes least? Explain.

3.8

Where would identity resolution likely be easier—in a rural community or in a large urban setting? Explain your choice.

During this period, youngsters are wrestling with the question *Who am I?* or **identity.** This, of course, doesn't mean that all teenagers are doomed to a period of distress and uncertainty. Most negotiate adolescence successfully, and most maintain positive relationships with their parents and other adults. Erikson, who coined the term **identity crisis**—*the feeling of uncertainty about who one is*—suggests that youngsters who have a basic sense of trust, can function on their own, aren't afraid to take initiative, and feel competent to overcome the uncertainty of adolescence and develop a firm notion of who they are and what their role in society should be.

Some contemporary theorists reject the term *crisis,* arguing that it suggests a sudden, intense upheaval of the self. They prefer the term *exploration,* because in their view it better reflects day-to-day experimentation with different roles and people (Berk, 1996).

Failure to form a viable identity results in role confusion, which prolongs adolescent characteristics and inhibits successful functioning as adults. We've all heard remarks such as, "He never grew up," or, "She still behaves like an adolescent." These descriptions typify people who have failed to resolve the identity–confusion crisis. Teachers can help in the process by providing structured but supportive classroom environments that encourage students to define themselves as developing young adults.

States of Identity Development.   Four seniors were talking about their after-high-school plans.

"I'm not sure what I want to do," Sandy commented. "I've thought about veterinary medicine, and I've also thought about teaching. I've been working at the vet clinic, and I really like it, but I'm not sure about doing it forever. I guess I should take some kind of interest inventory or something. I don't know."

"I wish I could do that," Ramon replied. "But I'm off to the university full-time in the fall. I'm going to be a lawyer. At least that's what my parents think. It's not a bad job, and they make good money."

Conversations with caring adults provide opportunities for adolescents to think about and refine their developing personal identities.

"How can you just do that, Ramon?" Nancy wondered aloud. "You don't really want to be a lawyer; you've said that before. Me, I'm not going to decide for a while. I'm only 18. I'm good in biology. I've thought about trying pre-med, and I'm going to take some more courses in biology-oriented stuff, but I'm not sure I'm ready for that many years of school. I'm going to think hard about it for a while. How about you, Taylor?"

"I'm going into nursing," Taylor answered. "I've been working part-time at the hospital, and it feels really good. I thought I wanted to be a doctor at one time, but I don't think I can handle all the pressures. I've talked with the counselors, and I think I can do the chem and other science. I guess we'll see."

The process of identity formation isn't smooth and uniform; it takes different paths, like a railroad train (Marcia, 1980). Sometimes it's sitting on a holding spur beside the main track; at others it's chugging full speed ahead.

Researchers have studied identity resolution by interviewing adolescents and asking them about commitments they've made to occupational, religious, and political choices (Marcia, 1980). The researchers found that adolescents tended to cluster around one of four positions (Marcia, 1987) and move from foreclosure to moratorium to achievement (Kroger, 1993). These are outlined in Table 3.2.

From the descriptions in Table 3.2, you can see that identity moratorium and identity achievement are healthy positions on the path to identity formation. With identity diffusion and identity foreclosure—less healthy positions—adolescents fail to wrestle with choices that will have important consequences for them throughout life.

Research helps in understanding this process. In a synthesis of eight studies, Waterman (1985) found that identity achievement more often occurs in the post-high-school years than during high school, in contrast with what Erikson's theory suggests. This finding was especially true for college students, who had more time to consider what they wanted to do with their lives. These results suggest that the uncertainty of adolescence is more related to increasing independence than it is to career or gender identity resolution.

3.9

Research indicates that, for American youngsters, identity resolution and formation are postponed until the post-high-school years. Why do these processes occur later for American youth than for youth in other countries?

Table 3.2 Positions in identity development

Position	Description and Example
Identity diffusion	Occurs when individuals fail to make clear choices. Confusion is common. Choices may be difficult, or individuals aren't developmentally ready to make choices. This state is illustrated by Sandy's comments.
Identity foreclosure	Occurs when individuals prematurely adopt ready-made positions of others, such as parents. This is an undesirable position, because decisions are based on the identities of others. Ramon's comments suggest this state.
Identity moratorium	Occurs when individuals pause and remain in a holding pattern. Long-range commitment is delayed. Nancy appears to be in this state.
Identity achievement	Occurs after individuals experience a period of crises and decision making. Identity achievement reflects a commitment to a goal or direction. Taylor's comments indicate that he has made this commitment.

Conflict with parents, teachers, and other adults peaks in early adolescence and then declines as teenagers accept responsibility and adults learn how to deal with the new relationship (Offer, Ostrov, & Howard, 1989; Steinberg, 1987). This helps explain why teaching junior-high or middle school students can be particularly challenging.

Helping Adolescents Grow.   Understanding emotionally developing adolescents helps a teacher better respond to their capricious behavior. Fads and bizarre clothing and hairstyles, for example, reflect teenagers' urges to identify with groups while simultaneously searching for their individuality. If their behaviors don't interfere with learning or the rights and comfort of others, they shouldn't be major issues. A teacher can help by spending time discussing students' concerns and simply talking with them openly and honestly. This is the best advice we can give teachers struggling to reach students like Sean.

Perhaps more significant is the sensitivity both Anne and Beth demonstrated in their efforts to reach Sean. Students, particularly at the middle and junior-high levels, need firm, caring teachers—teachers who the students think understand them yet who provide the security of setting limits for acceptable behavior. They don't need a teacher who is a buddy. They need a solid adult who can guide their intellectual and emotional growth (Emmer, Evertson, Clements, & Worsham, 1997).

3.10

Erikson's work suggests three major tasks during the school years: the development of initiative, industry, and identity. With which of the three are schools most successful? As a classroom teacher, what can you do to help students resolve the crisis in each area?

Intimacy versus Isolation (Young Adulthood)

During Erikson's sixth stage, individuals wrestle with their relationships with other people. A person with a firm sense of identity is prepared for **intimacy,** or *giving the self over to another,* based on something other than a basic need. Giving for the sake of giving without expecting something in return characterizes a positive resolution of the crisis at this stage. In contrast, people who fail to resolve the crisis remain emotionally isolated, unable to give and receive love freely.

Generativity versus Stagnation (Middle Adulthood)

The key characteristics of **generativity** are *creativity, productivity, and the concern for and commitment to guiding the next generation* (Erikson, 1980). Generative adults try to contribute to the betterment of society by working for principles such as a clean physical environment, a safe and drug-free social world, and adherence to the principles of freedom and dignity for individuals. Teachers who genuinely care about students and their learning exemplify people who have positively resolved the crisis at this stage. An unhealthy resolution leads to apathy, pseudointimacy, and self-absorption.

Integrity versus Despair (Old Age)

Erikson describes people who *accept themselves, conclude that they have only one life to live, live it about as well as possible, and have few regrets* as having **integrity.** They accept responsibility for the way they've lived and accept the finality of death. A person filled with regret for things done or left undone, worried that there is no turning back and that time is running out, is filled with despair.

Putting Erikson's Work into Perspective

Having read the descriptions of Erikson's eight stages, you probably have some questions about his theory. A frequent one is "When a crisis at a particular stage isn't

Teachers, in their commitment to helping young people, symbolize a positive resolution of the generativity versus stagnation stage of psychosocial development.

resolved, what happens later? Does the person not go on to the next stage?" Let's look at Sean and his development to begin answering these questions.

The evidence in our case study suggests that Sean didn't fully resolve the trust–mistrust crisis. However, this doesn't mean that it prevented him from wrestling with autonomy or initiative (although there is also some evidence that he lacked initiative). Rather, it has left him with a personality "glitch" that keeps him from functioning as fully as he might.

Sean's behavior also suggests that he is having problems resolving the identity–confusion crisis. His father's absence leaves him without an important male role model to help him in this process. This confusion, Erikson notes, can result in a negative identity, which rejects productive roles and substitutes negative ones. Sean may well grow up to be a successful adult, however, and the same is true for all of us.

No one knows for sure what the long-range ramifications of any personality imperfections might be. People who don't resolve the autonomy–doubt crisis, for example, may be less successful than their ability would indicate, because they are afraid to move forward on their own. On the other hand, they may find satisfying careers in a support role.

Rather than being absolute causes of behavior, "glitches" are simply that—personality imperfections that we all have in some form. Erikson's theory doesn't give specific answers, such as precisely when a problem leaves a person dysfunctional, but neither do other theories.

Because of its descriptive nature, Erikson's theory is difficult to document with empirical research. This is typical of personality theories; few have an extensive body of experimental data supporting them (Hall & Lindzey, 1978). Erikson's work, however, is intuitively sensible, and it helps us understand learners' developing personalities. We've all met people we admire because of their openness, drive, and enthusiasm. They seem to be comfortable around other people, have a good understanding of their own strengths and weaknesses, enjoy their work, and feel committed to contributing to society. However, we've also seen those who believe that others are trying to take advantage of them or are somehow inherently evil. We see good minds sliding into lethargy

3.11

You are teaching ninth-graders and you have a student whom you can't "get going." He will do what is required of him and no more. He does a good job on his required work, however, and he seems to be quite happy. Explain his behavior on the basis of Erikson's work.

as the result of apathy or even substance abuse. We are frustrated by people who are apathetic or lack a zest for living. Erikson's work helps us understand these problems.

As teachers, we can use Erikson's theory to gain insight into the personalities of our students and how they can be nurtured and strengthened. Further, we can see implications for ourselves in working with students at all school levels. It reminds us that we are there to do much more than help students learn to make subjects and verbs agree or to solve algebraic equations. We are also there to help them develop as individuals and relate productively to others.

Classroom Connections

Applying Erikson's Work in Your Classroom

1. Help students achieve a high degree of success, especially in the elementary school.
   - A sixth-grade teacher develops a grading system based partially on improvement so that each student can succeed by improving performance.
   - A second-grade teacher carefully covers each topic and provides precise directions before making seatwork assignments. He conducts "monitored practice" with the first few items to be sure all students get started correctly.

2. Be tolerant of honest mistakes when dealing with students at all levels.
   - A pre-algebra teacher, working with a student on simplifying expressions involving signed numbers, sees a student repeat a mistake explained only moments before. The teacher patiently reminds the student of the rule and then models the solution to the problem.
   - A kindergarten student responsible for watering the classroom plants knocks one over and spills the water. The teacher says evenly, "It looks like we have a problem. What needs to be done?" She pauses and continues, "Sweep up the dirt and use the paper towels to wipe up the water."

3. In a middle and junior-high school, provide the security of structure while allowing freedom of expression.
   - An eighth-grade history teacher consistently enforces her classroom rules and procedures. She also uses a few minutes of homeroom each day to discuss issues with students. They may say anything they wish other than criticizing people in the school by name.
   - A life-science teacher jokes with her students as they enter the classroom. When the bell rings, however, the students are settled and ready to begin working.

4. Know the emotional needs of young people and use that knowledge as an umbrella under which you conduct your instruction.
   - A junior-high earth-science teacher pays little attention to the attire and slang of his students as long as offensive language isn't used, the rights of others are recognized, and learning occurs.
   - After school, a seventh-grade geography teacher listens sympathetically as a girl talks about an incident in which her feelings were hurt as a result of an encounter with some of her friends.

5. Be a role model for students, both professionally and personally. With elementary students, model industry; with older students, also model the professionalism and individual dignity helpful in identity formation.
   - A middle-school teacher frequently comments on her own study in a master's program: how hard she has to work, how much she has learned during the previous year, and how good she feels about her new insights.
   - A fourth-grade teacher arranges his classroom procedures so that everyone—including

himself—is given responsibilities, including homework. He discusses the work that he takes home at night, stressing its importance for teaching and learning in the classroom.

- A tenth-grade English teacher stresses that discourtesy and mistreatment of others are mortal sins in her class. She pledges her own courtesy and preservation of everyone's individual dignity.

Self-Concept: Integrative Personal Development

One child announced at the dinner table that she was an honest person. When asked how she knew she was honest, she replied, "Because my teacher asked me to help her grade papers!" (Purkey & Novak, 1984, p. 27)

"I'll never forget my seventh-grade teacher. At that time I was overweight and wore braces on my teeth. Our teacher asked us to turn in a paper of different types of sentences. To demonstrate an exaggeration, I wrote, 'I am the most beautiful girl in the world.' The teacher wrote back: 'This is an exaggeration?' He'll never know how good he made me feel." (Purkey & Novak, 1984, p. 28)

As children develop, they grow not only in size, knowledge, and skills but also in their awareness and views of themselves as learners and as people. These views are positive when students enter school, but unfortunately often become less positive over time (Stipek, 1998). This is especially true for students who experience learning problems (Heward, 1996).

Self-Concept and Self-Esteem

The terms *self-concept* and *self-esteem* are commonly used to describe learners' views of themselves. They are often used interchangeably but in fact are quite distinct. **Self-concept** is *a cognitive appraisal of our physical, social, and academic competence*. In comparison, **self-esteem** or **self-worth** is *an affective or emotional reaction to the self* (Pintrich & Schunk, 1996). Self-esteem is significant, because researchers have found that learners with high self-esteem are confident, curious, independent, and motivated and do well in school. In contrast, low self-esteem has been linked to substance abuse, antisocial acts, adolescent pregnancy, suicide, and other self-destructive behaviors (Beane, 1991; Harter, 1990). We examine self-esteem in more detail later in the chapter.

3.12

Think about your own self-concept. For you, which is the most positive—physical, social, or academic self-concept? Why is that the case?

Sources of Self-Concept

As children develop, several factors influence their self-concepts. Young children's (three- to five-year-olds) self-concepts are concrete, focusing on tangible things like appearance, possessions, and everyday behaviors (Berk, 1996). This is consistent with Piaget's observation that young children's developing schemes depend heavily on direct experience with their environment.

As children grow older, interactions with others become increasingly influential. Initially, the most significant interactions are with parents, and during early school years teachers are important as well. Even young children sense whether adults have low or high expectations for them, and these expectations influence achievement (Phillips, 1990). As students progress through school, the influence of peers and friends increases, but adults remain important (Berk, 1994).

Self-Concept and Achievement

The relationship between general self-concept and achievement is positive but weak (Walberg, 1984). In attempting to understand why, researchers found that self-concept has at least three subcomponents—academic, social, and physical (Marsh, 1989)—with social and physical self-concepts being essentially unrelated to academic achievement (Byrne & Gavin, 1996; Marsh & Shavelson, 1985). This makes sense; we've all known socially withdrawn students who are happy as academic isolates, and we've also known popular students who are only average in schoolwork.

Academic Self-Concept

3.13

What is the primary way that social and physical self-concepts are developed in schools? What does this suggest about total school programs?

For teachers, the most important component of general self-concept is **academic self-concept,** *the aspect that deals with students' perception of their competence as learners.* Self-concept and school performance strongly interact. Children enter school expecting to learn and do well (Stipek, 1998), but as they progress, this expectation is altered by their accomplishments (Harter & Connell, 1984). When learning experiences are positive, self-concept is enhanced; when they're negative, it suffers.

Subject Matter Specificity. Although researchers find a moderate relationship between academic self-concept and achievement, the strongest correlations exist between specific academic self-concepts and their corresponding subject matter areas. For example, people with positive self-concepts of ability in math perform better on mathematical tests (and vice versa). Researchers have also found that concepts of ability in different subjects, such as math and English, become more distinct over time and that students become better able to differentiate between their performances in different areas (Marsh, 1992). Unfortunately, we've all heard people make statements such as, "I'm okay in English, but I'm no good in math." Some evidence suggests that comments such as these are based more on perceived ability resulting from lowered societal expectations of others than from actual ability (American Association of University Women, 1992).

3.14

What, specifically, provides students with information on which their academic self-concepts are based? Describe what you as a teacher can do to help low achievers form positive self-concepts.

The relationships between the components of self-concept and achievement are illustrated in Figure 3.1.

Improving Learner Self-Concept

The connections among self-concept, academic performance, and students' attitudes toward school have prompted efforts to improve the way students view themselves. These efforts have used two distinct approaches:

3.15

Does positive self-concept increase achievement, or does achievement improve self-concept? Explain your position.

- Attempts to improve self-concept directly
- Attempts to improve self-concept as a by-product of increased academic success

The first involves a variety of strategies, such as using multicultural learning materials with minority students, establishing residential summer camps, and implementing sensitivity training and support groups (Beane, 1991; Scheirer & Kraut, 1979). The other

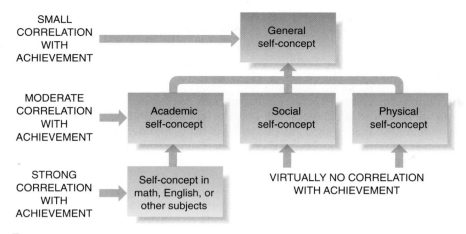

SMALL CORRELATION WITH ACHIEVEMENT

MODERATE CORRELATION WITH ACHIEVEMENT

STRONG CORRELATION WITH ACHIEVEMENT

General self-concept

Academic self-concept

Social self-concept

Physical self-concept

Self-concept in math, English, or other subjects

VIRTUALLY NO CORRELATION WITH ACHIEVEMENT

Figure 3.1 The relationships among the dimensions of self-concept and achievement

approach focuses on accomplishment and achievement (Stipek, 1998). As students experience success, their confidence grows and self-concepts improve.

These positions were tested in a federally funded, primary-grade program (Scheirer & Kraut, 1979). The education program that tried to improve self-concept directly stressed a learning environment of support and trust, with students selecting from a variety of stimulating materials. Program components were designed specifically to enhance participants' self-concepts. The program that attempted to increase self-concept as a by-product of academic success featured structured learning activities with immediate positive reinforcement. If increases in self-concept occurred, they would be outcomes of academic success.

Comparisons of the two approaches indicated that students in the second group not only learned more but also had more positive self-concepts. This study, as well as others reviewed by researchers, indicates that efforts to improve academic achievement through self-concept intervention alone are misguided (Scheirer & Kraut, 1979). This conclusion is further supported by more recent research on the formation of academic self-concept (Marsh, 1992). In forming self-concepts in academic areas, students use both external (e.g., "How do my knowledge and skills in this area compare with those of other students?") and internal (e.g., "How do my knowledge and skills in this subject compare with those in other subjects?") comparisons. Attempting to change students' self-concepts without improving their performance ignores the critical role that information plays in forming and changing self-concepts.

Self-Concept: Instructional Implications

The implications for teachers in the development of students' self-concepts are clear. They must design learning activities so that students are successful; if they do, self-concepts are likely to improve. The need for success and its impact on the developing self-concept are substantiated by classroom research. Berliner (1987) summarizes the research on success in this way:

It is now thought likely that a high level of success in a learning environment causes students to develop an enhanced self-concept as a learner. Thus, to build a positive self-concept, a teacher needs to design environments and make assignments so that students can have experience in attaining high levels of success. (p. 100)

The process is more complex, however, than just ensuring success. For self-concepts to improve, students must perceive learning activities as substantive and worthwhile (Ames, 1990; Clifford, 1990). Teachers who challenge students with worthwhile tasks and help them meet these challenges enhance both achievement and self-concept.

Classroom climate also influences self-concept (Beane, 1991). Positive teacher expectations communicate that all students can and will learn, and democratic classrooms in which students participate in decision-making foster initiative and self-direction. The combination of these elements creates an environment in which students both succeed and feel valued as developing people.

Grading practices also influence self-concept. Teachers who emphasize competition and encourage students to make social comparisons create win–lose environments (Cohen, 1991). In contrast, teachers who emphasize effort and individual improvement enhance self-concept by recognizing genuine progress.

3.16

How powerful are grades in influencing self-concept? How can teachers use grades as a positive influence on self-concept?

3.17

This section has focused on the relationship between self-concept and achievement. Does a similar relationship exist between self-esteem and achievement? Explain your position.

Ethnic Pride: Promoting Positive Self-Esteem and Ethnic Identity

Maria Robles squeezed her mother's hand tightly as they entered the busy doors of her new school. Her mother could tell she was nervous as she anxiously eyed the bigger boys and girls walking down the hallway.

As they stopped in front of the doorway marked Kindergarten, Room 3, Mrs. Avilla, a woman with a smiling face, came out to greet them.

"Hola. ¿Cómo te llamas, niña?" (Hello. What is your name, little one?)

Maria was still uneasy but, as she looked at her mother's face, she felt relieved.

"Dile tu nombre," (Tell her your name.) her mother prompted, squeezing her hand and smiling.

". . . Maria," she offered hesitantly.

Her mother added quickly, "Maria Robles. Yo soy su madre." (I am her mother.)

Mrs. Avilla looked on her list, found Maria's name, and checked it off. Then she invited them, in Spanish, to come into the room and meet the other boys and girls. Music could be heard in the background. Maria recognized some of her friends who were playing with toys in one corner of the room.

"Maria, ven aquí y juega con nosotros." (Maria, come here and play with us.)

Maria hesitated for a moment and looked up at her mother to see whether it was all right. When her mother smiled and nodded, Maria ran over to join her friends.

Self-Esteem and Ethnicity

We all wonder about our self-worth. Will others like us? Are we worthy of their love? Are we perceived by others as smart? beautiful? handsome? As you saw earlier, our interactions with others help shape our beliefs, and schools play an important role in this process. This applies to both self-concept and self-esteem.

Research suggests that culture plays an important role in the development of self-esteem in minority youth, and researchers have found that the self-esteem of minorities comprises two major components: personal and collective (Wright & Taylor, 1995).

Collective self-esteem refers to *children's perceptions of the relative worth of the groups to which they belong.* For all of us, our membership in families, peer groups, and ethnic groups contribute to our sense of self-worth. When we (and others) perceive these groups as valued and possessing status, our self-esteem is enhanced. The opposite is also true.

Children as young as Maria Robles know they are part of an ethnic minority, and research dating back to the 1930s indicates that ethnic minority children such as African Americans (Clark & Clark, 1939), Mexican Americans (Weiland & Coughlin, 1979), and Chinese Americans (Aboud & Skerry, 1984) evaluate their own ethnic reference groups lower than the White majority. These results suggest that simply being part of a minority group can make students feel less confident and good about themselves; this is a disturbing problem for all teachers who want their students to develop healthy self-esteem.

What can teachers do to combat this problem? They can make every effort to communicate to students that their ethnic heritage and language are not only recognized but also valued. In a test of this idea, researchers taught elementary native Canadian children in either their native (heritage) language or in a second language, such as French (Wright & Taylor, 1995). Children educated in their heritage language showed a sub-

3.18

What data do ethnic minority children use in forming these lower ethnic evaluations? How does this process compare with the process that occurs in forming personal self-esteem?

Teachers can help students develop ethnic pride and positive self-esteem by actively acknowledging and valuing the ethnic and cultural strengths different students bring to school.

stantial increase in their personal self-esteem, whereas children educated in the non-heritage second language did not. The researchers concluded that "early heritage language education can have a positive impact on the personal and collective self-esteem of minority language students" (p. 251).

Students who hear their home language used in the classroom learn that the language and the culture in which it is embedded is valued. Stories such as Maria Robles's are typical. Many students come to school wondering whether they will be welcomed and questioning whether the knowledge they bring with them will be valued. The way a teacher reacts to these students influences their views of their own self-worth.

Ethnic Pride and Identity Formation

Membership in an ethnic group also affects the process of identity formation. It affects who a person is and what he or she will become. For many minority youth, neighborhoods, family, and friends are important influences that shape their identities.

Sometimes the messages teenagers receive about their ethnic identities are mixed or even negative. An African American journalist reported, "If you were black, you didn't quite measure up. . . . You didn't see any black people doing certain things. . . . Well, it must mean that white people are better than we are" (Monroe, Goldman, & Smith, 1988, pp. 88–99). Similar problems with ethnic identity formation have also been documented with Mexican American (Matute-Bianchi, 1986) and Asian American (Wong-Fillmore, 1992) teenagers.

On a more positive note, research indicates that students who are encouraged and helped to explore their ethnic identities and who have adopted values from both the dominant culture and their own tend to have a clearer sense of their identity. They also have higher self-esteem and a more positive view of their ability to cope with their environment (Phinney, 1989; Phinney & Alipuria, 1990).

The research on both identity formation and influences on the self-esteem of minority children is clear. Minority students need to know that their cultures are valued and that the languages they bring to school are assets rather than obstacles or liabilities. Teachers play a crucial role in making every student feel wanted and loved by the overt and implicit messages they send through their teaching.

3.19

How might positive ethnic role models assist in the following identity resolution tasks: independence, career decision, sexual adjustment, and peer group relations?

Classroom Connections

Capitalizing on Diversity in Your Classroom

1. Build on students' cultures and ethnic backgrounds to develop positive self-esteem.

   - A first-grade teacher discovered that three different native languages were spoken in the homes of her students. With the help of other teachers and parent volunteers, she constructed a chart of common nouns and phrases (e.g., *chair, table, mother, hello*) in the different languages. She used the chart to explain to her students differences in the languages and to establish commonalities between them.

   - A social-studies teacher teaching in an ethnically diverse school encourages her students to do reports on the country from which their ancestors came. Students place the information they discover on a poster and bring in things from home, such as clothes and food, to illustrate the culture of the ancestral country.

- An elementary teacher emphasizes diversity in a unit on community. As the class discusses the community they live in, the teacher uses overlapping circles to show how different members of the community belonging to different groups contribute to the total community.

2. Use ethnic role models as a foundation for the development of students' personal identities.
   - A middle-school teacher in a career exploration unit makes a special effort to bring in minorities in different occupations and professions. He encourages them to talk openly about the challenges and satisfactions they encountered in pursuing their careers.
   - A social-studies teacher makes a special effort to emphasize the contributions of ethnic minorities and women to American society. As contemporary newspapers and magazines report the accomplishments of different ethnic groups, she brings these in to share with her students.

Development of Morality, Social Responsibility, and Self-Control

"Listen, everyone. . . . I need to go to the office for a moment," Mrs. Kellinger said as her students were completing a seatwork assignment. "You all have work to do, so work quietly on it until I get back."

The quiet shuffling of pencils and papers could be heard for a few moments, and then Gary whispered, "Psst, what math problems are we supposed to do?"

"Shh! No talking," Talitha said, pointing to the rules posted on the chalkboard.

"But he needs to know so he can do his homework," Krystal put in. "It's the evens on page 79."

"Who cares?" Dwain growled. "She's not here. She won't catch us."

What do students think about classroom rules? Perhaps more important, how do they think about the laws and conventions that make up the rules of society? What influences their interpretations of rules, and how do they learn to follow and modify them? In this section, we continue our discussion of student development to examine how children's thinking about issues of right, wrong, fairness, and justice change over time.

Increased Interest in Moral Education and Development

Over the last few years, interest in moral education and how it should be used to promote moral development has increased markedly (Wynne, 1997). In the general media, both *Time* and *Newsweek* devoted cover articles to the topic; within education, periodicals such as *Educational Leadership* and *Clearinghouse* did the same. During the second Clinton administration, two White House conferences on character education were held, and President Clinton referred to character education in both his 1996 and 1997 State-of-the-Union addresses.

Part of the reason for this growing interest in moral development is the perception that adolescents are being bombarded by a number of risk factors with moral undertones. Alcohol and drug abuse remain persistent problems among youth (Kuther & Higgins-D'Alessandra, 1997). Out-of-wedlock births to white adolescent females are at historical highs, as are homicide and suicide rates for white adolescent males (U.S.

Department of Health and Human Services, 1914–1993). The U.S. public is increasingly looking to moral education for solutions to problems such as these.

The need for moral education has also been voiced within the teaching profession (Tom, 1984; Goodlad, Soder, & Sirotnik, 1990). Some argue that teaching is an inherently moral activity, with value decisions around every instructional corner. This view separates the morality of teaching (e.g., who gets called on and who receives extra help) from the teaching of morality (e.g., how should we treat each other and why do we have classroom rules) (Buzzelli & Johnston, 1997). On a broader level, some argue that value conflicts and the decisions that follow are an integral part of applying knowledge within any profession (Stern, 1997).

Moral issues are also embedded in the curriculum. Social studies isn't a mere chronology of events; it is humans' responses to situation-specific moral dilemmas, such as war and peace and justice and equality (Sunai & Haas, 1993). Ethical issues have also been commonly used in literature designed for young people. For instance, Charlotte in *Charlotte's Web* was faced with the dilemma of saving Wilbur the pig at the loss of her own life. Old Yeller's master was faced with losing his dog or allowing the potential health menace of rabies. Students commonly study books such as *The Yearling* and *A Tale of Two Cities* not only because they are good literature but also because they introduce moral problems with no clear answers.

Most importantly, moral education is an essential and integral part of learner development. To develop as healthy individuals, learners need to acquire both the moral compass that values can provide and the thinking capacities to apply these values in intelligent ways. In addition, research indicates that the moral atmosphere of a school (e.g., democratic and prosocial versus authoritarian) can influence motivation and the value students place on school (Binfet, Schonert-Reicht, & McDougal, 1997). Moral development theory can help in understanding these issues.

Piaget's Description of Moral Development

Although most people think of Piaget primarily in the context of cognitive development, he examined the development of ethics and morals as well (1932/1965). He studied cognitive and moral development in much the same way: He presented children with problems or tasks, listened to their reactions, and asked questions to gain insight into their thinking.

He found that children's responses to moral problems could be divided into two broad stages of development on the basis of a principle he labeled "internalization" (Piaget, 1932/1965). **Internalization** refers to *the source of control for children's thoughts and actions*. In the first stage, which Piaget called *external morality,* children view rules as fixed and permanent and externally enforced by authority figures. External morality lasts to about age 10. In our introductory episode, Talitha, with her reference to the rules, demonstrated thinking at this stage. It didn't matter that Gary was only asking about the homework assignment; rules are rules. Dwain, who responded, "Who cares? She's not here. She won't catch us," was also responding at this level; he was focusing on the fact that no authority figure was there to enforce the rule. Piaget believed that parents and teachers who stress unquestioning adherence to adult authority retard moral development and encourage students to remain at this level (DeVries & Zan, 1995).

At the second stage, called **autonomous morality,** *children develop rational ideas of fairness and see justice as a reciprocal process of treating others as they would want to be treated.* Children at this stage begin to rely on themselves instead of others to regulate moral behavior. Krystal's comment, "But he needs to know so he can do his home-

3.20

Some people argue that schools should be value-free and avoid ethical and moral issues. Others advocate the active teaching of ethical and moral values. Which position is more valid? Explain your choice.

3.21

Use the concept of *egocentrism* (see Chapter 2) to explain the difference between external and autonomous morality. Describe what you as a teacher can do to help students progress from one stage to the next.

work," is characteristic of thinking at this stage: she views Gary's whispering as an honest request for assistance, rather than as a rule infraction.

Kohlberg's Theory of Moral Development

Steve, a high-school senior, is working at a night job to help support his mother, a single parent of three. Steve is a conscientious student who works hard in his classes, but he doesn't have enough time to study.

History isn't Steve's favorite course and, because of his night work, he has a marginal D average. If he fails the final exam, he will fail the course and won't graduate. He arranged to be off work the night before the exam so that he could study extra hard, but early in the evening his boss called, desperate to have Steve come in and replace another employee who called in sick at the last moment. His boss pressured him heavily, so Steve went to work reluctantly at 8:00 P.M. and came home exhausted at 2:00 A.M. He tried to study but fell asleep on the couch, with his book in his lap. His mother woke him for school at 6:30 A.M.

Steve went to his history class, looked at the test, and went blank. Everything seemed like a jumble. Clarice, one of the best students in the class, happened to have her answer sheet positioned so that he could clearly see every answer by barely moving his eyes.

From what you've read here, is Steve justified in cheating on the test?

What you've just encountered is a **moral dilemma,** which is *an ambiguous situation that requires a person to make a moral decision*. Steve was caught in a position that had no clear course of action; any decision had both positive and negative consequences. Students' responses to moral dilemmas provide some insight into their moral development (Rest, Thoma, Narvaez, & Bebeau, 1997).

Describe two personal examples of moral dilemmas that you've faced. Describe a moral dilemma that schools face.

Cheating is a persistent problem in classrooms. How students think about this problem and how teachers should respond to it depend on students' levels of moral development.

Influenced by the work of Piaget and John Dewey, Lawrence Kohlberg (1929–1987), a Harvard educator and psychologist, used dilemmas to study moral reasoning. While working with teenagers, he found that moral reasoning was developmental and, on the basis of research conducted in cities and villages in Great Britain, Malaysia, Mexico, Taiwan, and Turkey, concluded that the development of moral reasoning is similar across cultures. Using responses to hypothetical moral dilemmas such as the one you just read, Kohlberg (1963, 1969, 1981, 1984) developed a theory of moral development that extended Piaget's earlier work. Like Piaget, he concluded that morality develops in stages, and all people pass through all the stages in the same order but at different rates.

Kohlberg originally described moral development as existing in three levels consisting of two stages each. These levels represent different perspectives that people take as they wrestle with moral dilemmas or problems. The levels and stages are outlined in Table 3.3.

Table 3.3   Kohlberg's stages of moral reasoning

Level I Preconventional Ethics	The ethics of egocentrism. Typical of children up to about age 10. Called preconventional because children typically don't fully understand rules set down by others.
Stage 1: Punishment–Obedience	Consequences of acts determine whether they're good or bad. Individuals make moral decisions without considering the needs or feelings of others.
Stage 2: Market Exchange	The ethics of "What's in it for me?" Obeying rules and exchanging favors are judged in terms of the benefit to the individual.
Level II Conventional Ethics	The ethics of others. Typical of 10- to 20-year-olds. The name comes from conformity to the rules and conventions of society.
Stage 3: Interpersonal Harmony	Ethical decisions are based on concern for or the opinions of others. What pleases, helps, or is approved of by others characterizes this stage.
Stage 4: Law and Order	The ethics of laws, rules, and societal order. Rules and laws are inflexible and are obeyed for their own sake.
Level III Postconventional Ethics	The ethics of principle. Rarely reached before age 20 and only by a small portion of the population. The focus is on the principles underlying society's rules.
Stage 5: Social Contract	Rules and laws represent agreements among people about behavior that benefits society. Rules can be changed when they no longer meet society's needs.
Stage 6: Universal Principles	Rarely encountered in life. Ethics are determined by abstract and general principles that transcend societal rules.

As you read the following descriptions, remember that the specific response to a moral dilemma isn't the critical issue; the stage and level are determined by the *reasons* a person gives for making the decision. Let's see how this works.

Level I: Preconventional Ethics

The preconventional level is an egocentric orientation focusing on moral consequences for the self. As you would predict on the basis of their egocentrism, young children reason at this level.

The level consists of two stages: punishment–obedience and market exchange. Some research indicates that 15% to 20% of the U.S. teenage population still reason at this level (Turiel, 1973).

Stage 1: Punishment–Obedience. People reasoning at the **punishment–obedience stage** *make moral decisions based on their chances of getting caught and being punished.* Right or wrong is determined by the consequences of an action: If the child is punished, the act was wrong; if not, the act was right. A person encountering an unguarded wallet or purse and not taking it because of fear of getting caught is operating at this stage. The same principle applies in a classroom. A person who argues that Steve is justified in cheating because he could see every answer on Clarice's paper by barely moving his eyes and so he probably won't get caught is reasoning at Stage 1.

Stage 2: Market Exchange. At the **market exchange stage,** *people focus on the consequences of an action for themselves, but reciprocity is involved.* "An eye for an eye and a tooth for a tooth" or "Don't bite the hand that feeds you" reflect morality at this stage, and "You do something for me and I'll do something for you" is a key characteristic. A naive hedonism is used to judge the rightness or wrongness of an action.

Aspects of the political system exist at this stage. Political patronage, the tendency of successful office seekers to give their supporters "cushy" jobs regardless of qualifications, is an example of Stage 2 ethics.

Cheating is a common problem in classrooms. A person reasoning at Stage 2 might argue that Steve should go ahead and cheat because if he doesn't, he'll have to repeat the course and quit his job. From this perspective, "The right thing to do is what makes me the happiest." This reasoning again focuses on the self.

3.23

What teacher behaviors contribute to students continuing to reason at the preconventional level? What can teachers do to help students move to higher levels?

Level II: Conventional Ethics

As development progresses and egocentrism declines, students acquire the ability to see the world from others' points of view. Morality is no longer constrained by the immediate effects of punishment or reward, but is instead becoming linked to the perspectives and concerns of others. Values such as loyalty, others' approval, family expectations, obeying the law, and social order become prominent. Stages 3 and 4 reflect this orientation, and it is how the bulk of the population reasons.

Stage 3: Interpersonal Harmony. Individuals reasoning at Stage 3 do not manipulate people to reach their goals, as they might at Stage 2. Rather, the **interpersonal harmony stage** is characterized by *conventions, loyalty, and living up to the expectations of others.* The Stage 3 person is oriented toward maintaining the affection and approval of friends and relatives by being a "good" person. This is sometimes called the "nice girl/good boy" stage. A teenager on a date who meets a curfew because she doesn't want to worry her parents is reasoning at this stage.

A person reasoning at Stage 3 might offer at least two different perspectives on Steve's dilemma. One could argue that he needed to work to help his family, and therefore he was justified in cheating. A contrasting view, still at Stage 3, would suggest that he should not cheat, because people would think badly of him if they knew about it.

Reasoning at Stage 3 includes the danger of being caught up in the majority opinion. Accepting that cheating on one's income taxes is okay because "everybody cheats" is an example. We might call Stage 3 the "ethics of adolescence" because of the influence peers have on young people's thinking at this age.

Stage 4: Law and Order. A person reasoning at Stage 4 would argue that Steve should not cheat, because "It's against the rules to cheat." The focus at this stage is on adherence to laws and rules for their own sake, rather than on pleasing particular people, as in Stage 3. According to the ethics of the **law and order stage,** *laws and rules exist to guide behavior and should be followed uniformly.*

3.24

Suppose heavy traffic is moving on an interstate highway at a speed limit of 65. A sign appears that says, *Speed Limit 55.* The flow of traffic continues as before. How might a driver reasoning at Stage 3 behave, compared with a driver reasoning at Stage 4?

Concern for the orderliness of society is also characteristic of this stage, such as a person arguing that Steve should not cheat, because "What would our country be like if everybody cheated under those same conditions?" Concern for others is still the focus, but rules and order are key criteria at this stage. People reasoning at Stage 4 don't take the tag off the pillow because it says not to, and if checkout time is noon, they check out at noon. They don't care whether the rest of the world cheats on their income taxes; they pay theirs because the law says they must.

Level III: Postconventional Ethics

A person reasoning at Level III has transcended both the individual and societal levels and makes moral decisions based on principles. People operating at this level, also called *principled morality,* follow rules but also see that, at times, rules need to be changed or ignored. Only a small portion of the population attains this level, and most don't reach it until their mid- to late 20s.

Some of the great figures in history have sacrificed their lives in the name of principle. Sir Thomas More, who knew that he was, in effect, ending his own life by refusing to acknowledge King Henry VIII as the head of the Church of England, nevertheless stood on a principle. Mohandas Gandhi chose jail rather than adhere to England's laws as he applied the principle of nonviolent noncooperation; his work, as well, ultimately led to his death.

Stage 5: Social Contract. The person reasoning according to **social contract** understands that *a society of rational people needs socially agreed-on laws in order to function.* The laws are not accepted blindly or for their own sake; rather, they are based on the principle of utility, or "the greatest good for the greatest number," and are followed because they adhere to rights such as life, liberty, and the dignity of the individual.

3.25

How would a person at Stage 5 respond to the problem of people cheating on their income tax?

Stage 5 is the official ethic of the United States. The constitutional Bill of Rights is an example of a cultural social contract; for example, Americans agree in principle that people have the right to free speech, and the legal profession is conceptually committed to interpreting the laws in this light. In addition, the American system has provisions for changing or amending laws in the light of new values or conditions. A person reasoning at Stage 5 would say that Steve's cheating is wrong, because teachers and learners agree that the grades should reflect achievement. Cheating violates the agreement.

Stage 6: Universal Principles. **Universal principles** is the stage at which *moral reasoning is based on abstract and general principles above society's rules.* People at this stage define rightness in terms of internalized universal standards that go beyond concrete laws. "The Golden Rule" is a commonly cited example. Because very few people operate at this stage, and questions have been raised about the existence of "universal" principles, Kohlberg de-emphasized this stage in his later writings (Kohlberg, 1984).

Putting Kohlberg's Theory into Perspective

Research on Kohlberg's Work.   Kohlberg's work has been widely researched, and this research has led to the following conclusions (Berk, 1994; Taylor, 1987):

- Every person's moral reasoning develops through the same stages in the same order.
- People pass through the stages at different rates.
- Development is gradual and continuous, rather than sudden and discrete.
- Once a stage is attained, a person continues to reason at that stage and rarely regresses to a lower stage.
- Intervention usually results in moving only to the next higher stage of moral reasoning.

Despite this support for Kohlberg's theory, there have also been questions and criticisms.

> **3.26**
>
> Identify elements of Kohlberg's work that are similar to Piaget's.

Criticisms of Kohlberg's Work.   Kohlberg's original work has been criticized because of a lack of cross-cultural validations, the small number of people who reason at the postconventional level, and the uncertain connection between moral thought and moral behavior. Kohlberg contended that the moral dilemmas faced by individuals in all societies are similar, therefore the stages are the same across cultures. Cross-cultural research indicates that the stages do exist for people in other cultures and that children pass through these stages in the same sequence as they do in Western cultures. The rate and end point of moral development may vary, however, with the extent to which different societies encourage moral problem solving (Berk, 1994). Moral development may also vary with the extent to which different cultures encourage dialogue and debate about moral issues. Research grounded in social constructivist perspectives identifies social interaction as a critical component of moral development (Tappan, 1997).

Though Kohlberg attempted to make his levels content free, research suggests that thinking about moral dilemmas, like problem solving in general, is influenced by domain-specific knowledge (Bech, 1996). For example, a medical doctor asked to deliberate about an educational dilemma or a teacher asked to resolve a medical dilemma may be hampered by their lack of knowledge of the issues involved.

The problem of content also surfaces in cross-cultural studies; postconventional reasoning appears to be biased in favor of Western cultures. In describing Stage 5, for example, we used the phrase "rights such as life, liberty, and the dignity of the individual." The dignity of the individual certainly reflects Western values. Other cultures, such as the Amish and Native Americans, de-emphasize individuality, placing greater value on cooperation and collaboration. A person from a more group-oriented culture, for example, might respond to the cheating dilemma by saying, "He shouldn't have been placed in a situation like that. Other people—his mother, his teacher, and other students—should be helping him so that he wouldn't be forced into such a dilemma." Teachers should be sensitive to interpretations of morality that people from different cultures may carry with them.

Kohlberg's focus on moral reasoning rather than moral behavior has also been criticized. People may reason at one stage but behave at another. Reasoning and behavior are correlated, however. Kohlberg (1975) found that only 15% of students reasoning at the postconventional level cheated when given the opportunity to do so, that 55% of those reasoning at the conventional level cheated, and that 70% of those reasoning at the preconventional level cheated. In addition, adolescents reasoning at the lower stages are likely to be generally less honest and to engage in more antisocial behavior, such as delinquency and drug use (Gregg, Gibbs, & Basinger, 1994). In contrast, reasoning at the higher levels is associated with altruistic behaviors, such as defending free speech, victims of injustice, and the rights of minorities (Kuther & Higgins-D'Alessandra, 1997; Berk, 1994).

Gender Differences: The Morality of Caring.   Early research examining Kohlberg's theory identified differences in the ways men and women responded to moral dilemmas (Gilligan, 1982; Gilligan & Attanucci, 1988). Men were more likely to base their judgments on abstract concepts, such as justice, rules, individual rights, and obligations. Women, in contrast, were more likely to base their moral decisions on personal relationships, interpersonal connections, and attending to human needs.

These findings resulted in females' responses being scored lower, thus suggesting a lower stage of moral development (Haan, Smith, & Block, 1968; Holstein, 1976). Gilligan (1982) argued that the findings, instead, indicate an "ethic of care" in women which is not inferior; rather, Kohlberg's stage descriptions don't adequately represent female thinking. Caring appears to be more central to females' sense of identity and, when asked to identify moral dilemmas, they are more likely than males to choose interpersonal problems of real life rather than abstract and impersonal problems (Skoe & Dressner, 1994).

More recent research on gender differences is mixed, with some studies finding differences and others not (Leon, Lynn, McLean, & Perri, 1997). Like cross-cultural studies, Gilligan's research reminds us of the complexity of the issues involved in moral development.

3.27

On the basis of Gilligan's work, how might a woman respond to the problem of the student not knowing his assignment, presented in the case study at the beginning of this section? How might her response be different from that of a man?

The Moral Education versus Character Education Debate

Over the years, debate over the proper place of values and moral education in the curriculum has continued. At present, people generally agree that moral education is needed, but they disagree about the form it should take. This disagreement has polarized at two positions called *character education* and *moral education* (Wynne, 1997).

These two perspectives differ with respect to goals as well as methods of instruction. Character education emphasizes the transmission of moral values such as honesty and citizenship and the translation of these values into character traits or behaviors. Instruction in character education emphasizes the study of values, practicing these values both in school and out, and rewarding displays of these values.

Moral education, by contrast, is more value free, emphasizing instead the development of students' moral reasoning. Moral education uses moral dilemmas and classroom discussions to teach problem solving and to bring about changes in the way learners think with respect to moral issues.

These positions also differ in their views of learners' and teachers' roles. Learners are viewed by character educators as unsocialized at best, potentially evil at worst, and continually in need of moral guidance. A character education teacher serves as a lecturer/advocate, explaining and modeling appropriate values and reinforcing learners for displaying appropriate behaviors.

Moral educators view learners as undeveloped, needing cognitive stimulation to construct better and more comprehensive moral perspectives. A teacher using a moral education approach acts as a problem poser and facilitator, helping students grapple with complex moral problems. These differences are summarized in Table 3.4.

Critics of character education argue that it emphasizes indoctrination instead of education, it lacks attention to transfer, and its theoretical underpinnings focus on behavior instead of learner cognition (Kohn, 1997). Critics of moral education assert that it has a relativistic view of morals, with no right or wrong answers, and they further criticize the use of hypothetical and decontextualized dilemmas that are removed from real classroom life (Wynne, 1997).

Perhaps the greatest strength of the character education perspective is its willingness to identify and promote core values. For instance, values such as honesty, caring, and respect for others should undergird the way we structure our classrooms, interact with students, and expect them to treat each other. On the other hand, emphasizing student thinking and decision making is important as well, and this is the focus of the moral education perspective.

Let's pursue this topic a bit further.

Moral Development and Classroom Structure

Studying moral development is valuable for us as teachers, because it helps us understand that the way we structure our classrooms and interact with students influences their moral growth. If our goal is self-regulation, with students who understand and appreciate the need for orderly classrooms, we must explain the reasons for rules and involve them in the rule-setting process (McCaslin & Good, 1992). This emphasis on explanation and involvement changes the classroom culture from one in which there is an adherence to rules because punishment is threatened—an external form of regulation—to one in which rules are followed because students realize they're necessary—self-regulation.

Table 3.4 A comparison of character and moral education

	Character Education	Moral Education
Goals	Transmission of moral values	Development of moral reasoning capacities
	Translation of values into behavior	Decision making about moral issues
Instruction	Reading about and analyzing values	Moral dilemmas serve as the focus for problem-solving
	Practicing and rewarding good values	Discussions provide opportunities to share moral perspectives and analyze others
Role of a Teacher	Lecturer/advocate Role model	Problem poser Facilitator
View of Learner	Unsocialized citizen of the community needing moral direction and guidance	Undeveloped Uses information to construct increasingly complex moral structures

3.28

Explain why teachers reasoning at higher levels would likely be more democratic and involve students more in classroom discussions than teachers reasoning at lower levels.

Research indicates that moral development is enhanced in an atmosphere where a spirit of cooperation exists and adults are verbal, rational, and supportive (Berk, 1994; Boyes & Allen, 1993). Teachers who reason at higher stages of development promote this spirit to a greater extent than do those reasoning at lower levels (Strom, 1989). The opposite is also true. Students working in an environment where punishment or the threat of punishment is emphasized will obey rules, but growth in self-control and regulation suffers. (We discuss these ideas further in Chapter 11 when we study classroom management.)

Promoting Moral Development Through Peer Interaction

Teachers can also promote moral development by consciously creating opportunities for students to share and analyze their views. Let's look at an example.

> "We've been reading an interesting story, and now I'd like to focus on a particular incident in it. Let's talk a bit about the boy in the story who found the wallet. Would it be wrong for him to keep the money? . . . Okay, I see a lot of heads nodding. . . . Why? . . . Jolene?"
>
> "Because it didn't belong to him."
>
> "Helena?"
>
> "Because it was a lot of money, and his parents would probably make him give it back anyway."
>
> "Todd?"
>
> "Why not keep it? It wasn't his fault that the person lost it."
>
> "Juan?"
>
> "But what if the person who lost the money really needed it?"
>
> "Okay. Those are all good reasons. We'll return to them in a moment, but there are a lot of other interesting questions to consider. First, put yourself in his shoes. Would you keep the money? What else might the boy have done, rather than keep the money? If he gives the wallet back, does he have the right to expect a reward? What do you think?"

3.29

Predict, on the basis of Piaget's theory, what stage of cognitive development would be necessary in order for a learner to reason at the conventional level. What stage of cognitive development would be required for postconventional reasoning?

Research on Kohlberg's work indicates that moral development can be enhanced through classroom discussions that allow students to examine their own moral thinking and to compare it with that of others (Kuther & Higgins-D'Alessandra, 1997; Thoma & Rest, 1996). Interaction among peers is particularly effective because it encourages active listening and analysis of different moral positions (Kruger, 1992). Exposure to more complex ways of reasoning about moral dilemmas helps students reevaluate their own thinking by examining it in relation to others. These comparisons can disrupt a person's equilibrium and promote development.

Guidelines for effective discussions about moral dilemmas include:

- Focus on concrete moral conflicts and different ways of resolving them.
- Encourage students to consider the perspectives of others.
- Ask students to make personal choices in responding to dilemmas and to justify the choices.
- Analyze different courses of action by discussing the advantages and disadvantages of each.

In addition to systematically comparing different moral positions, the range of those positions also influences whether or not development will occur (Berk, 1996; Thoma & Rest, 1996). An optimal mix is one stage beyond learners' present reasoning; if learners are exposed to moral positions too far beyond their present level they have trouble relating the positions to their existing background knowledge and experience.

Discussing moral dilemmas provides students opportunities to analyze and evaluate their own moral views.

Moral Framework of Schools

Kohlberg's work also reminds us that much of what teachers do in schools is grounded in moral decisions. When teachers emphasize student responsibility, make rules that prevent students from ridiculing each other, emphasize industry, and advocate honesty, they are teaching ethics. Laws that apply to schools also promote these values. For example, Public Law 94–142, which requires that students with learning exceptionalities be placed in the least restrictive environment possible, is based on an ethical issue. It says that it is not fair to deny a student with an exceptionality access to the mainstream learning environment. (We examine PL 94–142 in detail in Chapter 5.)

Arguments that schools shouldn't teach morals are naive. Values are involved every time a teacher emphasizes one topic instead of another, and morals reflect the values of individuals as well as cultural groups. A more realistic approach is to become as well informed as possible. This allows you as a teacher to make sensitive and considered decisions based on your understanding.

3.30

Write a specific statement describing how you would respond to parents who strongly express the opinion that the teaching of morals should exist in the home and that teachers should not deal with the subject.

Classroom Connections

Developing Positive Self-Concepts in Your Classroom

1. Make students feel wanted and valued in your class.
   - A fourth-grade teacher starts the school year by having students write autobiographical sketches and bring in pictures of themselves taken when they were preschoolers. They list their strengths and weaknesses and describe what they want to be when they grow up.
   - A high-school teacher begins each school year by announcing that everyone is important in her classes and that she expects everyone to

learn. She structures her classrooms around success, minimizing competition. She also stays in her room every day after school and invites any students who are having problems to come by for help.

2. Provide learning experiences that promote success.
   - A fifth-grade teacher allows students to drop their lowest quiz grade, and he gives bonus points if students show consistent improvement.
   - A sixth-grade teacher has students keep portfolios of products they create in art, music, science, and social studies. She shares the portfolios with parents and encourages parents to take the portfolios home and discuss them with their children.

Applying Moral Principles in Your Classroom

3. Openly discuss ethical dilemmas when they arise.
   - A high-school teacher's students view cheating as a game, seeing what they can get away with. The teacher addresses the issue by saying, "Because you feel this way about cheating, I'm going to decide who gets what grade without a test. I'll grade you on how smart I think you are." This statement forms the basis for a discussion on fairness and cheating.
   - The day before a new student joins the class, a first-grade teacher discusses with the class how they would feel if they were new, how new students should be treated, and how they should treat each other in general.

4. Make and enforce rules requiring ethical treatment of each other.
   - A seventh-grade teacher has a classroom rule that students may not laugh, snicker, or make remarks of any kind when one of their classmates is trying to answer a question. In introducing the rule, she has the students discuss the reasons for it.
   - A second-grade teacher is explaining classroom rules at the beginning of the school year. One of them is "Respect other students' property." In the discussion, the teacher encourages students to think about the importance of the rule from other students' perspectives.

5. Model ethical behavior for students.
   - A science teacher makes a commitment to students to have all their tests and quizzes graded by the following day. One day, he is asked, "Do you have our tests ready?" "Of course," he responds. "I made an agreement, and people can't go back on their agreements."
   - A group of tenth-graders finishes a field trip sooner than expected. "If we just hang around a little longer, we don't have to go back to school," someone comments. "Yes, but that would be a lie, wouldn't it?" the teacher counters. "We said we'd be back as soon as we finished."

Windows on Classrooms

As you've studied this chapter, you've seen how the characteristics of preschool and primary-age learners, elementary students, and adolescents affect the ways they feel about themselves and the way they learn. You've seen how an environment that combines structure with opportunities for autonomy and decision making and teachers who are sensitive to their students promote personal, social, and emotional development.

Let's look now at another teacher working with a group of middle-school students. As you read the case study, compare the teacher's approach to the suggestions you've studied in the chapter.

"Gee, this is frustrating," Helen Sharman, a seventh-grade teacher, mumbled as she was scoring a set of quizzes in the teachers' workroom after school.

"What's up?" her friend Natasha asked.

"Look," Helen directed, pointing to Item 6 on the quiz that read:

Theirs were the first items to be loaded.

"These students just won't think at all," Helen continued. "Three quarters of them put an apostrophe between the *r* and the *s* in *theirs*. The quiz was on using apostrophes in possessives. I warned them I was going to put some questions on the quiz that would make them think and that some of them would have trouble if they weren't on their toes. I should have saved my breath. . . . Not only that, but I had given them practice problems to work that were just like those on the quiz. We had one almost exactly like Number 6, and they still missed it. . . . And I explained it so carefully," she mumbled, shaking her head.

Helen returned to scoring her papers.

Hearing Helen mumble some more, Natasha asked, "Not getting any better?"

"No," Helen said firmly. "Maybe worse."

"What are you going to do?"

"What's really discouraging is that some of the students won't even try. Look at this one. Half of the quiz is blank. This isn't the first time Kim has done this either. When I confronted him about it last time, he said, 'But I'm no good at English.' I replied, "But you're doing fine in science and math." He thought about that for a while and said, 'But, that's different.' I wish I knew how to motivate him. You should see him on the basketball floor—poetry in motion—but when he gets in here, nothing."

"That can be discouraging. I've got a few like that myself," Natasha replied empathically.

"What's worse, I'm almost sure some of the students cheated. I left the room to go to the office, and when I returned, several of them were talking and had guilt written all over their faces."

"Why do you suppose they did it?" Natasha returned.

"I'm not sure; part of it might be grade pressure. I grade on the curve, and they complain like crazy, but how else am I going to motivate them? Some just don't see any problem with cheating. If they don't get caught, fine. I really am discouraged."

"Well," Natasha shrugged, "hang in there."

The next morning, Helen returned the quizzes.

"We need to review the rules again," she commented as she finished. "You did so poorly on the quiz, and I explained everything so carefully. You must not have studied very hard."

"Let's take another look," she went on. "What's the rule for singular possessives?"

". . . Apostrophe *s*," Felice volunteered.

"That's right, Felice. Good. Now, how about plurals?"

"*S* apostrophe," Scott answered.

"All right. But what if the noun doesn't end in *s*? . . . Russell?"

"Then it's like singular. . . . It's apostrophe *s*."

"Good. And how about pronouns?"

"You don't do anything," Connie put in.

"Yes, that's all correct," Helen nodded. "Why didn't you do that on the quiz?"

". . ."

"Okay, look at Number 3 on the quiz."

It appeared as follows:

The books belonging to the lady were lost.

"It should be written like this," Helen explained, and she wrote "The lady's books were lost" on the chalkboard.

"Ms. Sharman," Nathan called from the back of the room. "Why is it apostrophe *s*?"

"Nathan," Helen said evenly. "Remember my first rule?"

"Yes, Ma'am," Nathan said quietly.

"Good. That's the second time today. If you speak without permission again, it's a half hour after school.

"Now, to answer your question, it's singular. So that's why it's apostrophe s.

"Now look at Number 6." Helen waited a few seconds and then continued, "You were supposed to correctly punctuate it. But it's correct already because *theirs* is already possessive. Now, that one was a little tricky, but you know I'm going to put a few on each quiz to make you think. You'd have gotten it if you were on your toes."

Helen identified three more items that were commonly missed. She then gave the students a re-view sheet for some additional practice.

"Now, these are just like the quiz," she said. "Practice hard on them now, and we'll have another quiz on Thursday. Let's all do better. Please don't let me down again.

"And one more thing. I believe there was some cheating on this test. If I catch anyone cheating on Thursday, I'll tear up your quiz and give you a failing grade. Now, go to work."

The students then worked on the practice exercises as Helen walked among them, offering periodic suggestions.

Questions for Discussion and Analysis

Analyze Helen's lesson in the context of the information in this chapter. In doing your analysis, you may want to consider the following questions. In each case, be specific and take information directly from the case study in answering these questions.

1. How might Erikson explain Kim's behavior in Helen's class?
2. Using findings from the research on self-concept, explain Kim's behavior.
3. Using concepts from Kohlberg's theory, analyze Helen's cheating problem. From Kohlberg's perspective, how well did she handle this problem?
4. If you think Helen's teaching could have been improved on the basis of the information in Chapter 3, what suggestions would you make? Again, be specific.

Summary

Erikson's Theory of Personal and Social Development

Erikson's psychosocial theory, an effort to integrate personal and social development, is based on the assumption that development of self is a response to needs and this development occurs in stages, each marked by a psychosocial challenge called a *crisis*. As people develop, their motivations change.

According to Erikson, positive resolution of the crisis in each stage results in an inclination to be trusting, feelings of autonomy, willingness to take initiative, and a sense of industry, from the period of birth through approximately the elementary school years. Continued resolution of crises leaves people with a firm identity, the ability to achieve intimacy, desire for generativity, and finally a sense of integrity as life's end nears. As teachers work with students, they should keep these developmental challenges in mind and structure their classrooms and interactions with students to facilitate growth in these areas.

Self-Concept: Integrative Personal Development

Self-concept, based largely on experience, describes people's cognitive assessments of their physical, social, and academic competence. In comparison, self-esteem is an affective evaluation of ourselves. Academic self-concept, particularly in specific content areas, is correlated with achievement, but achievement and physical and social self-concepts are essentially unrelated.

Attempts to improve students' self-concepts by direct intervention have been largely unsuccessful. In contrast, attempts to improve self-concept as an outcome of increased success and achievement have been quite successful. This finding suggests that teachers should direct their efforts toward improving students' effort and achievement, then self-concept will improve as well.

Development of Morality, Social Responsibility, and Self-Control

Piaget is identified with cognitive development, but he studied moral development as well. He suggests that individuals progress from external morality, in which rules are enforced by authority figures, to autonomous morality, in which they see morality as rational and reciprocal.

Lawrence Kohlberg's theory of moral development was influenced by Piaget's work. Kohlberg presented people with moral dilemmas—problems requiring moral decisions—and, on the basis of their responses to the dilemmas, developed a classification system for moral reasoning. At the first level, called *preconventional ethics,* people make egocentric moral decisions focused on consequences for themselves. At the *conventional ethics* level, people's moral reasoning focuses on the consequences for others, and at the *postconventional ethics* level, moral reasoning is based on principle. Kohlberg suggested that conventional reasoning required concrete operational thinking, and that postconventional reasoning required formal operational thinking.

Character education advocates emphasize the study, practice, and reinforcement of moral values. In contrast, moral education proponents emphasize the development of moral reasoning and students' thinking about moral issues.

Teachers can promote moral development in their classrooms by emphasizing personal responsibility and the functional nature of rules designed to protect the rights of others. Students should be encouraged to think about topics such as honesty and respect for others in terms of consequences for others and basic principles of human respect. As teachers interact with students, they should recognize the powerful influence they have in encouraging the moral development of their students.

Important Concepts _____

academic self-concept (p. 80)
autonomous morality (p. 86)
autonomy (p. 72)
collective self-esteem (p. 82)
crisis (p. 71)
generativity (p. 76)
identity (p. 74)
identity crisis (p. 74)
industry (p. 73)

initiative (p. 72)
integrity (p. 76)
internalization (p. 86)
interpersonal harmony stage (p. 89)
intimacy (p. 76)
law and order stage (p. 90)
market exchange stage (p. 89)
moral dilemma (p. 87)
psychosocial theory (p. 70)

punishment–obedience stage (p. 89)
self-concept (p. 79)
self-esteem (p. 79)
self-worth (p. 79)
social contract stage (p. 90)
trust (p. 71)
universal principles stage (p. 90)

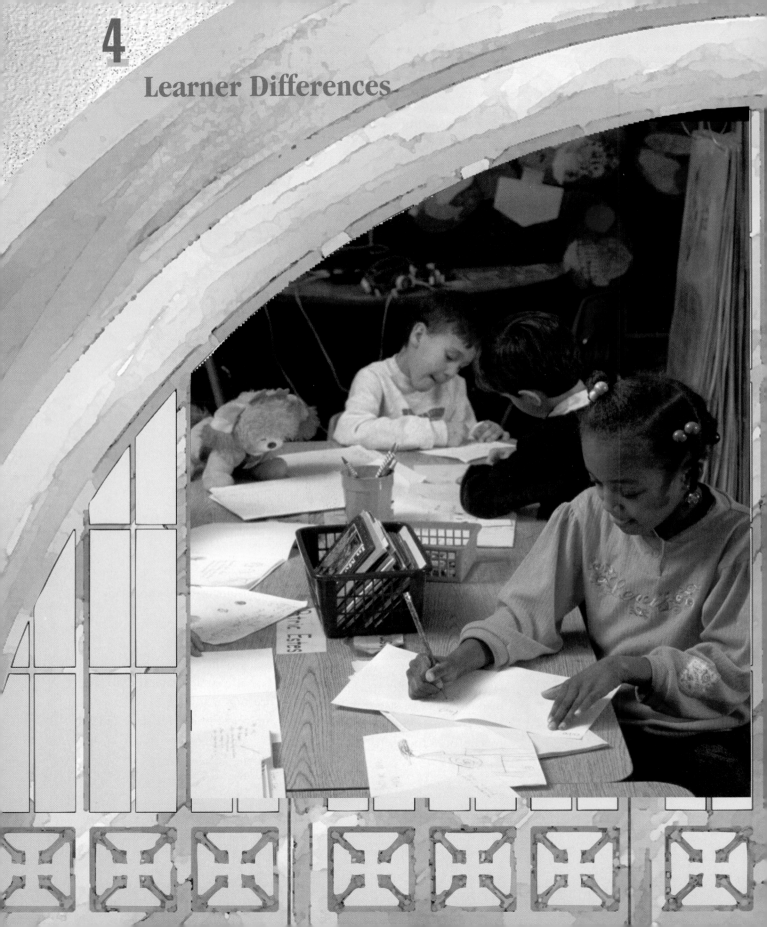

4

Learner Differences

CHAPTER OUTLINE

Tim Wilkinson is a fifth-grade teacher in a large urban elementary school. He has 29 students—16 girls and 13 boys. His group includes ten African Americans, three students of Hispanic descent, and two Asian Americans. Most of his students come from low-income families.

He smiled slightly as he watched the students, bent over their desks, busy with seatwork. He enjoyed working with the students, and was fascinated by the differences in their backgrounds. As Tim walked among his students, he glanced at Selena's work. As usual, it was nearly perfect. Everything was easy for her, and she seemed to be a happy, well-adjusted child.

He smiled slightly as he walked by Helen's desk. She was his "special project," and she had begun to blossom in response to his attention and effort. The quality of her work had improved dramatically since the beginning of the year.

As he stepped past Juan, Tim's warm glow turned to concern. Juan had been quiet from the first day of school, and he was easily offended by perceived slights from his classmates. Because his parents were migrant workers, the family moved constantly, and he had repeated the fourth grade. Now his parents were separated, and his mother had settled in this area so that the children could stay in the same school.

Juan had to struggle to keep up with the rest of the class. Spanish was his first language, and Tim wasn't sure how much of his instruction Juan understood. What seemed certain, however, was that Juan was falling farther and farther behind, and Tim didn't know what to do. Not knowing where else to turn, he consulted the school psychologist.

When we enter our classrooms for the first time, a sea of faces appears before us. In some ways these students seem very much alike; for example, they are nearly the same age, they have similar interests, and they study common subjects and topics. A closer look, however, reveals many differences. Almost certainly, we have both males and females in our classes. We know from our study of Chapters 2 and 3 that students develop at different rates. Learning is nearly effortless for some; others struggle with even basic ideas. A few have affluent parents; others' parents barely eke out a living. Depending on location, we have students with different ethnic and cultural backgrounds—African American, Hispanic, Asian, European, Native American, and others—in our classes.

Suddenly, our sea of faces turns into 30 individuals! Unfortunately, some demographic combinations may put our students at risk of not being able to fully benefit from the educational system. In this chapter, we examine these differences among students and the implications they have for teachers.

After completing your study of this chapter, you should be able to meet the following objectives:

- Explain how different views of intelligence influence your teaching.
- Define socioeconomic status and explain how it may affect school performance.
- Explain the role that culture and language play in learning.
- Describe the influence of gender on different aspects of school success.
- Describe ways that schools and classrooms can be adapted to meet the needs of at-risk students.

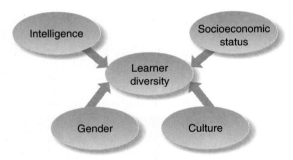

Figure 4.1   Sources of learner individuality

As we saw in the opening case, Tim's concerns for Juan are important. In a perfect world, all learning would be as easy as it is for Selena, and teaching would be a nearly effortless pleasure. Teachers know, however, that students vary in ability and in many other ways. They truly are individuals, and teachers must keep this in mind when they make professional decisions. Figure 4.1 illustrates some of these sources of individuality.

At the top of Figure 4.1 is *intelligence,* or aptitude. It determines how quickly and easily a person might learn, and in some instances, whether the learning is even possible.

Socioeconomic status (SES) refers to parents' income, occupation, and level of education, all of which influence student learning. Children of high-SES parents are likely to have a wealth of school-related experiences, and they are usually well nurtured physically. In contrast, children of low-SES parents often come from homes where parents spend much of their time and energy trying to meet essential needs. Some children even lack nutrition and a permanent place to live, and they may come to school emotionally ill-prepared for its demands.

Culture and *ethnicity* also influence school success. Cultural background and values can be strong foundations on which learning is based, or they can be obstacles to both achievement and motivation. Teachers who value students' cultural backgrounds and build on them help make all students feel accepted and capable of learning.

4.1

How does the practice of building on students' cultural backgrounds illustrate Piaget's concepts of *schemes, assimilation,* and *accommodation?*

Gender is also a source of individuality. In the United States, males and females are perceived and treated differently. Unfortunately, these perceptions and treatments can result in different expectations and achievement for boys and girls.

This chapter focuses on individual differences among students and how these differences affect their learning. Let's begin with a discussion of intelligence.

Intelligence

Intelligence: What Does It Mean?

Everyone has a commonsense notion of what intelligence is; it's how "sharp" people are, or how much they know, how quickly they learn, and how perceptive and sensitive they are. Teachers have an intuitive sense of intelligence and use quizzes, assignments, and students' comments to gauge their abilities. Used properly, this intuition can help teachers design learning activities that best match students' abilities; misused, it can lead to lowered expectations and false stereotypes (Good & Brophy, 1997). Tim's sensitivity and concern guided him as he considered seeking additional help for Juan. A teacher less alert than Tim might miss the fact that Juan is struggling, or worse yet, write him off on the grounds that he is too far behind the others.

Experts define **intelligence** as three dimensional: (a) *the capacity to acquire knowledge,* (b) *the ability to think and reason in the abstract,* and (c) *the capability for solving problems* (Snyderman & Rothman, 1987; Sternberg, 1986). The capacity to acquire knowledge has also been called *aptitude,* and some learning theorists have equated it with the time and quality of instruction needed to master a subject (Bloom, 1981; Carrol, 1963). According to this model, learners with high aptitude need less time and instruction than those whose aptitude is lower. In seeing Juan falling farther and farther behind, Tim was intuitively reacting to this dimension.

From another perspective, intelligence is simply defined as the attributes that intelligence tests measure. Let's examine some of them.

> **4.2**
>
> Which of the three dimensions of intelligence is most important? least important? How is your answer influenced by the culture you live in, twentieth-century America, as compared with a primitive, nomadic culture?

Measuring Intelligence

Following are some items commonly found on intelligence tests:

1. Cave : Hole :: Bag : ____ (Cave is to hole as bag is to ____ ?)
   a. paper   b. container   c. box   d. brown
2. Sharon had X amount of money, and this could buy eight apples. How much money would it take to buy four apples?
   a. 8X   b. 2X   c. X/2   d. 4X
3. Inspect the following list of numbers for five seconds.

   9   7   4   6   2   1   8   3   9

   Now cover them and name the digits in order from memory.

Items like each of these have been used on standardized intelligence tests, and an individual's intelligence is inferred from her or his performance on such a test.

Examination of these items makes one aspect of the tests strikingly clear: Experience is an important factor in test performance (Perkins, 1995). For instance, the first item requires both vocabulary and an understanding of analogies, and experience with

> **4.3**
>
> How does experience influence a person's "capacity to acquire knowledge"? Explain your answer with a specific example.

analogies would certainly improve performance. The second item is based on background in math. Even the third item, a seemingly simple memory task, can be improved with experience and training (Brown, Bransford, Ferrara, & Campione, 1983).

The impact of experience on intelligence test performance corroborates Piaget's work. In Chapter 2, you saw that experience is one factor affecting cognitive development and that children who have the advantage of rich experiences consistently perform better than their less-experienced peers. Clearly, intelligence tests measure something more than raw, or innate, ability.

Intelligence: One Trait or Many?

Because scores on different measures of intelligence, such as verbal and numerical ability and abstract reasoning, were all highly correlated, early researchers believed intelligence to be a single trait. Spearman (1927), one of the major early figures, described it as "g" or general intelligence. Raymond Cattell (1963, 1971), one of Spearman's students, later expanded the description to include *fluid intelligence* (which reflects general ability and adaptability to novel tasks measured by tests such as matrices and block designs) and *crystallized intelligence* (which reflects people's experience as measured by school tasks, such as vocabulary and math problems). As the field developed, other kinds of intelligence, such as verbal, mathematical, spatial, and perceptual, were proposed (Jensen, 1987). Contemporary researchers have further extended the idea that intelligence is composed of several abilities, as we'll see in the next section (Woodcock, 1995).

Guilford's Structure of Intellect (SOI)

4.4

Consider Guilford's view of intelligence again. Did he believe intelligence was a single trait or composed of multiple traits? Explain.

J. P. Guilford (1967) believed that intelligence depends on *what* people are thinking about (content), their mental *operations,* and the *products* of these operations. He developed a *structure of intellect (SOI)* model that describes intelligence as the intersection of four content areas, five cognitive operations, and six products. For example, remembering a telephone number requires a memory operation in a symbolic content area to produce a single product—the number (Perkins, 1995).

When analyzed with the Guilford model, school curricula focus a disproportionate amount of time and resources addressing limited aspects of intelligence, such as memorizing facts and definitions, while virtually ignoring others, such as evaluation and the search for relationships (Gall, 1984; Goodlad, 1984). Proposed changes in curricula, particularly in math and science, are attempting to address this imbalance by increasing the emphasis on problem solving and processes such as hypothesizing, analyzing, and evaluating (American Association for the Advancement of Science [AAAS], 1993; National Council of Teachers of Mathematics [NCTM], 1991). We discuss these changes in Chapter 9, which examines learning in different content areas.

4.5

What implications would Guilford's model have for intelligence testing? for reporting test scores?

Guilford's pioneering work is valuable because it encouraged researchers and educators to broaden their concept of ability, but the complexity of the model makes it difficult to apply in classrooms.

Gardner's Theory of Multiple Intelligences

Influenced by Guilford's original work, Howard Gardner (1983) concluded that most conceptions of intelligence were too narrow and should be broadened beyond the confines of traditional academic subjects. He describes eight major and relatively independent dimensions of intelligence and makes a persuasive argument for the idea of multiple talents.

Gardner originally described seven intelligences, but he has now expanded his theory to include an eighth. He calls it "naturalist intelligence" and describes it as "the ability to recognize and classify plants, minerals, and animals, including rocks and grass and all varieties of flora and fauna. The ability to recognize cultural artifacts like cars or sneakers may also depend on the naturalist intelligence" (Chekley, 1997, p. 9). Table 4.1 outlines these dimensions.

Gardner's argument for multiple intelligences derives from two sources. One is research on people with brain damage indicating neural functioning is localized and specific to a single domain, such as speech or aesthetic ability. The second is the variety of skills found in modern society. Many people are not high in verbal or logical dimensions but excel in others, such as spatial ability (artists and architects) and interpersonal skills (effective counselors and empathic teachers).

Gardner's ideas make intuitive sense. For example, we all know people who don't seem very "sharp" analytically but who have excellent instincts for getting along with others. This ability serves them well, and in some instances they're more successful than their "brighter" counterparts. Others seem very self-aware and have the ability to capi-

Table 4.1 Gardner's theory of multiple intelligences

Dimension	Example
Linguistic intelligence: Sensitivity to the meaning and order of words and the varied uses of language	Poet, journalist
Logical-mathematical intelligence: The ability to handle long chains of reasoning and to recognize patterns and order in the world	Scientist, mathematician
Musical intelligence: Sensitivity to pitch, melody, and tone	Composer, violinist
Spatial intelligence: The ability to perceive the visual world accurately, and to re-create, transform, or modify aspects of the world on the basis of one's perceptions	Sculptor, navigator
Bodily-kinesthetic intelligence: A fine-tuned ability to use the body and to handle objects	Dancer, athlete
Interpersonal intelligence: The ability to notice and make distinctions among others	Therapist, salesperson
Intrapersonal intelligence: Access to one's own "feeling life"	Self-aware individual
Naturalist Intelligence: The ability to recognize similarities and differences in the physical world	Naturalist, biologist, anthropologist

Source: Adapted from H. Gardner and Hatch (1989) and Chekley, 1997.

Spatial intelligence includes the ability to perceive and re-create physical relations in the world.

Bodily-kinesthetic intelligence allows dancers and athletes to use their bodies in effective and creative ways.

talize on their strengths and minimize their weaknesses. Gardner would explain these examples as interpersonal and intrapersonal intelligence, respectively.

Gardner's Theory: Educational Applications. Attempts to apply Gardner's ideas to school settings have focused on both curriculum and instruction. Curriculum developers have attempted to prepare materials in underrepresented areas of the curriculum; modules to develop skills in areas such as imaginative writing, visual arts, and music notation are being pilot-tested in both elementary and secondary schools (Gardner & Hatch, 1989).

In planning instruction, teachers are encouraged to introduce and foster the knowledge and skills emphasized in the different intelligences (Armstrong, 1994). Table 4.2 presents some classroom applications of Gardner's theory. He cautions, however, that not all ideas or subjects can be approached with each intelligence: "There is no point in assuming that every topic can be effectively approached in at least seven ways, and it is a waste of effort and time to attempt to do this" (Gardner, 1995, p. 206).

Sternberg's Triarchic Theory of Intelligence

Robert Sternberg (1988, 1990), like Gardner, approaches intelligence from a multi-ability perspective. Sternberg proposes a triarchic theory of intelligence composed of three parts: (a) processing components—skills used in problem solving, (b) contextual components—links between intelligence and the environment, and (c) experiential components—mechanisms for modifying intelligence through experience.

Sternberg's theory is based on the idea that intelligence can be separated into processes that influence the way people think about the world and solve problems. These processes and their features are illustrated in Figure 4.2.

4.6

On which of Gardner's eight intelligences does the typical school curriculum focus most strongly? On which report card—an elementary or a secondary—are more of the intelligences evaluated? Why is this the case?

Table 4.2   Instructional applications of Gardner's multiple intelligences

Dimension	Application
Linguistic	How can I get students to talk or write about the idea?
Logical/Mathematical	How can I bring in number, logic, and classification to encourage students to quantify or clarify the idea?
Spatial	What can I do to help students visualize, draw, or conceptualize the idea spatially?
Musical	How can I help students use environmental sounds, or set ideas into rhythm or melody?
Bodily/Kinesthetic	What can I do to help students involve the whole body or to use hands-on experience?
Interpersonal	How can peer, cross-age, or cooperative learning be used to help students develop their interactive skills?
Intrapersonal	How can I get students to think about their capacities and feelings to make them more aware of themselves as persons and learners?
Naturalist	How can I provide experiences that require students to classify different types of objects and analyze their classification schemes?

Figure 4.2   Sternberg's triarchic model of intelligence

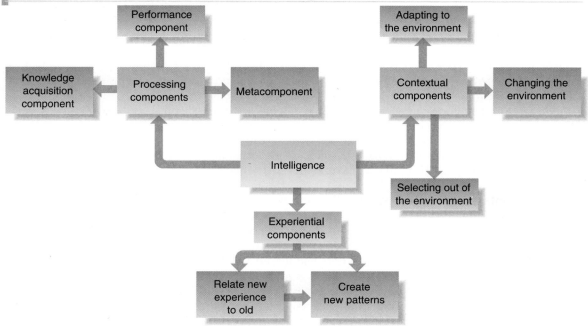

Intelligence can be enhanced by learning activities that emphasize abstract reasoning and problem solving.

Processing Components. The most basic parts of Sternberg's model are the processing components learners use to solve problems: *a knowledge acquisition component,* a *performance component,* and a *metacomponent.* Sternberg describes these components as analogous to trainees, labor, and management in a corporation. Knowledge acquisition components (trainees) allow people to learn new information, performance components (labor) actually work with problems, and metacomponents (management) manage the other aspects of intelligence. Intelligent behavior includes selecting effective problem-solving strategies, monitoring progress, and changing the approach if it doesn't work.

The components interact when people apply intelligence to a complex task such as writing a term paper (Sternberg, 1988). Metacomponents decide on a topic, plan the paper, and monitor progress as it's written. Knowledge acquisition components research the topic and combine facts into integrated ideas, and performance components do the actual writing. The three work together to produce a final product.

4.7

Illustrate the three processing components with an example such as buying a car.

4.8

Consider Sternberg's strategies for dealing with the environment—adapting to it, changing it, and selecting out of it. Which do schools emphasize the most? Which *should* they emphasize most? least?

Contextual Components: Intelligence and the Environment. The contextual components attempt to explain how intelligence relates to operating in the everyday environment. To reach goals, intelligent people adapt to the environment, change it, or select out of it when necessary. For example, in an attempt to get a good grade in a college course, a student adjusts her note-taking and studying in response to a professor's testing procedures (adapts to the environment). She can't clearly hear the presentation, so she moves up front (changes the environment). Despite these efforts, she just isn't learning enough, so she drops the class (selects out of the environment). In each case, the student is sensitive to the effect that environment is having on performance. Sternberg considers this an important part of intelligence.

Experiential Components: Modifying Intelligence Through Experience. The third aspect of Sternberg's theory explains how intelligence is modified by experience. In Sternberg's view, intelligent behavior has two important characteristics: (a) the ability to cope effectively with novel experiences and (b) the ability to solve problems efficiently and automatically. An intelligent person learns from experience by relating new experiences to old and converting this information into patterns that can be used automatically and efficiently. For example:

> A beginning reader encounters the word *she*. The teacher says, "Shheee."
> Then the reader encounters the word *show*. The teacher says, "This word sounds like `Shho.'"
> Next, the student sees the word *ship*. He tries pronouncing it himself: "Shhip." He now has a rule to decode future words. When *s* and *h* are together, they go "shh."

According to Sternberg, an intelligent child recognizes patterns quickly and is able to use rules automatically. The ability to analyze data and find patterns increases with age and makes older children more efficient problem solvers. This ability to process information efficiently is one cornerstone of increased intellectual functioning (Sternberg, 1988).

Educational Implications of Sternberg's Work. Sternberg's view of intelligence suggests that learners should be given experiences that require them to relate new to existing ideas, rather than focus on the drill and practice of basic skills.

Sternberg views intelligence as alterable, capable of being improved; this view obviously has implications for teaching. According to Sternberg, intelligence is a complex process that can be divided into subcomponents to be trained and improved upon in school. For example, if solving analogies is an important part of intelligence (and intelligence tests), then it should be possible to improve intelligence and intelligence test performance by giving students experience with analogies. This issue—the extent to which intelligence can be altered—is the topic of the next section.

Intelligence: Nature versus Nurture

No aspect of intelligence has been debated more hotly than the issue of heredity versus environment. The extreme **nature view of intelligence** asserts that *intelligence is solely determined by genetics;* the **nurture view of intelligence** emphasizes the *influence of the environment.* Differences between these positions become very controversial when race or ethnicity are considered. For example, research indicates that cultural minorities, as a group, consistently score lower on intelligence tests than American white children (Brody, 1992). People who emphasize the nurture view explain this finding by arguing that minority children have fewer stimulating activities while they are developing.

On the other hand, people adhering to the nature view argue that heredity is the more important factor. In the highly controversial book *The Bell Curve,* Hernstein and Murray (1994) concluded that the contribution of heredity outweighed environmental factors in minority populations, especially African Americans.

Most experts take a position somewhere in the middle, believing that a person's intelligence is influenced by both nature and nurture (Yee, 1995; Weinberg, 1989). In this view, a person's genes provide the potential or upper boundaries for intelligence, and stimulating environments make the most of the raw material. Unfortunately, the

4.9

Identify at least two ways in which Sternberg's and Piaget's theories are similar. What implications do these similarities have for schools?

4.10

Of the three legs of Sternberg's triarchic theory, which is most clearly related to Spearman's notion of "g" or general intelligence? What do the other two legs attempt to explain about intelligence?

opposite is also true; most learning environments do not provide maximum stimulation to reach full potential (Ceci, 1990; Loehlin, 1989). For example, in one study researchers tracked children born of low-income parents but adopted as infants into high-income families. The experiences the children were provided produced an average IQ 14 points higher than that of comparable siblings (Schiff, Duyme, Dumaret, & Tomkiewicz, 1982).

Intelligence also changes over time. One review found IQ changes of 28 points from early childhood to adolescence; one seventh of the students had changes of more than 40 points (McCall, Appelbaum, & Hogarty, 1973)! Although some testing error is likely, intelligence itself was probably altered in many cases because of changes in an individual's social setting, level of intellectual challenge, or others' expectations (Perkins, 1995).

Efforts to improve intelligence have also been fruitful. Attempts to directly teach the cognitive skills tapped by intelligence tests have been successful with preschool and elementary students (Consortium for Longitudinal Studies, 1983; Sprigle & Schoefer, 1985), adults (Whimbey, 1980), and students with learning disabilities (Brown & Campione, 1986). A longitudinal study of disadvantaged, inner-city children also indicated that early stimulation can have lasting effects on IQ (Garber, 1988).

4.11

If environments to promote an increase in intelligence were designed, what aspects of typical American environments would need to be changed?

Ability Grouping

Although other adaptations exist (we discuss them in detail in Chapter 5), the most common way schools have responded to differences in learner ability is by **ability grouping,** *which places students together on the basis of ability and attempts to match instruction to the needs of different groups*. Because ability grouping is so common, yet controversial and politically charged, we examine it in this section.

4.12

If forced to choose between between-class ability grouping and within-class ability grouping, which would Guilford and Gardner prefer? Why?

Types of Ability Grouping

Ability grouping in elementary schools is popular (Clements & Evertson, 1982), and it typically exists in three forms. They are described and illustrated in Table 4.3. Many teachers of elementary students endorse ability grouping, particularly in reading and math.

In middle, junior high, and high schools, ability grouping goes further, with high-ability students studying advanced and college preparatory courses and their low-ability

4.13

Why is within-class grouping so uncommon in secondary schools?

Table 4.3 Types of ability grouping in elementary schools

Type	Description	Example
Between-class grouping	Divides students at a certain grade into levels, such as high, average, and low	A school with 75 third graders divides them into one class of high achievers, one of average, and one of low.
Within-class grouping	Divides students in a class into subgroups based on reading or math scores	A fourth-grade teacher has three reading groups based on reading ability.
Joplin plan	Regroups across grade levels	Teachers from different grade levels place students in the same reading class.

counterparts receiving vocational or work-related instruction. In some cases, students are grouped only in certain areas, such as English or math; in other cases, it exists across all content areas—a practice called *tracking*. **Tracking** is *the practice of placing students in different classes or curricula on the basis of ability*. Some form of tracking exists in most middle, junior high, and high schools (Braddock, 1990).

Ability Grouping: Research Results

Why is ability grouping so pervasive? Advocates argue that it enhances instruction by allowing teachers to adjust the rate, methods, and materials to better meet students' needs. Because pace and assessment are similar for a particular group, instruction is easier for the teacher (Cotton & Savard, 1981).

Critics, on the other hand, identify a number of problems with all forms of ability grouping:

- Within-class grouping creates logistical problems, because different lessons and assignments are required and monitoring students in different tasks is difficult (Good & Brophy, 1997; Oakes, 1992).

- Improper placements occur, and placement tends to become permanent. Cultural minorities are underrepresented in high-ability classes (Good & Marshall, 1984; Grant & Rothenberg, 1986; Oakes, 1992).

- Low groups are stigmatized. The self-esteem and motivation of low groups suffer (Good & Marshall, 1984; Hallinan, 1984).

- Homogeneously grouped low-ability students achieve less than heterogeneously grouped students of similar ability (Good & Brophy, 1997).

> **4.14**
>
> Explain how ability grouping could affect students' self-esteem and motivation.

Negative Effects of Grouping: Possible Explanations

Negative effects of grouping are related, in part, to the quality of instruction. Presentations to low groups are more fragmented and vague than those to high groups; they focus more on memorizing than understanding, problem solving, and "active learning". Also, students in low-ability classes are often taught by teachers who lack enthusiasm and stress conformity versus autonomy and the development of self-regulation (Good & Brophy, 1997; Oakes, 1992; Ross, Smith, Loks, & McNelie, 1994).

Grouping also affects the students themselves. In addition to lowered self-esteem and motivation to learn, absentee rates tend to increase. One study found that absenteeism increased from 8% to 26% after transition to a tracked junior high (Slavin & Karweit, 1982), with most of the truants being students in the low-level classes. Tracking can also result in the racial or cultural segregation of students making social development and the ability to form friendships across cultural groups difficult (Oakes, 1992).

Grouping: Implications for Teachers

Suggestions for dealing with the problems of grouping vary. At one extreme, critics argue that the negative effects of grouping are so pernicious that the practice should be abolished completely. Grant and Rothenberg (1986) summarize this position:

> We suggest . . . that there is a fundamental conflict between the practice of ability grouping and public schools' avowed goal of providing equal opportunity to

Figure 4.3 Suggestions for reducing the negative effects of grouping

1. Keep group composition flexible and reassign students to other groups when their rate of learning warrants it.
2. Make every effort to ensure that the quality of instruction is as high for low-ability students as it is for high-ability students.
3. Treat student characteristics as dynamic rather than static; teach low-ability students appropriate learning strategies and behaviors.
4. Avoid assigning negative labels to lower groups.
5. Constantly be aware of the possible negative consequences of ability grouping.

all students. More equitable alternatives must be sought, even if they involve major changes in classroom organization. (p. 47)

An enthusiastic second-grade teacher will be teaching science to all three classes at her grade level and is considering ability grouping. What advice would you give her? Provide a specific rationale for your advice. Would your advice change if the grade level were sixth instead of second?

A more moderate position suggests that grouping may be appropriate in some areas, such as reading and math (Good & Brophy, 1997), but that every effort should be made to de-emphasize groups in other content areas. Researchers have found that use of the Joplin plan in reading, combined with heterogeneous grouping in other areas, can have positive effects on reading achievement without negative side effects (Slavin, 1987). At the junior and senior high levels, between-class grouping should be limited to the basic academic areas, with heterogeneous grouping in others.

When grouping is necessary, specific measures to reduce the negative effects should be taken. Summaries of some suggestions are presented in Figure 4.3.

The suggestions in Figure 4.3 are demanding. Teachers must constantly monitor both the cognitive and affective progress of their students and make careful decisions about group placements. The need to maintain high expectations and instructional flexibility in this process cannot be overemphasized (Bixby, 1997).

Classroom Connections

Applying an Understanding of Ability Differences in Your Classroom

1. Remember that intelligence test scores are just one indicator of school ability.
   - In deciding whether to place a student in a special education class, a team of teachers and the guidance counselor consider grades,

work samples, and teacher observations, in addition to intelligence test scores.

2. Be cautious when using intelligence test scores to make educational decisions about cultural minorities.
   - A first-grade teacher working in an inner-city school consults with the school psychologist in

interpreting intelligence test scores. She reminds herself of the effect that language and experience can have on test performance.

3. Use instructional strategies that minimize narrow definitions of aptitude and maximize student interest and effort.
   • A math teacher allows students two opportunities to pass his quizzes. When they need extra help, he uses peer tutoring and special small-group work as additional aids.
   • An English teacher makes two types of assignments: required and optional. Seventy percent of the assignments are required for everyone; the other 30% provide students with choices, and they negotiate with the teacher on the specific assignments.

4. Consider the implications of multiple intelligences for teaching and learning.
   • In a unit on the Revolutionary War, a teacher has all students take a test on basic information, but bases 25% of the unit grade on special projects. Groups of students research topics such as the music and art of the times and present their information to the class on poster boards, in video and audio tape recordings, or in replicas of battle sites.

Using Grouping Appropriately in Classrooms

5. View group composition as flexible, and reassign students to other groups when warranted by their learning progress.
   • A team of four first-grade teachers meets at the end of each grading period to reexamine groups and to move students when appropriate.

6. Use heterogeneous grouping whenever possible.
   • A second-grade teacher uses different ability groups in his reading instruction but uses whole-class instruction when he does units on poetry and American folktales.

7. When using ability groups, make every effort to ensure that the quality of instruction is the same for each ability level.
   • A teacher has a colleague observe and monitor her questioning strategies during a series of language arts lessons. She asks the colleague to record her questions and to whom they're addressed to ensure that each ability group receives the same amount of active teaching and appropriate mix of high- and low-level questions.

Socioeconomic Status (SES)

One of the most powerful factors influencing school performance is **socioeconomic status (SES),** *the combination of parents' incomes, occupations, and levels of education.* SES consistently predicts intelligence and achievement test scores, grades, truancy, and dropout and suspension rates (Ballantine, 1989; Macionis, 1994). In a recent review of the topic Konstantopoulas (1997) concluded, ". . . the relationship between test scores and SES is one of the most widely replicated findings in the social sciences" (p. 5). School dropout rates for students from poor families are twice those of the general population; for students from the poorest families, they exceed 50% (Catterall & Cota-Robles, 1988). Figure 4.4 identifies SES as an important source of learner individuality.

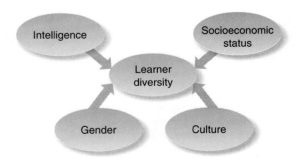

Figure 4.4 Sources of learner individuality: Socioeconomic status (SES)

Influence of SES on Learning

Never before have schools attempted to teach so many students who are physically and mentally ill-prepared to learn. A combination of economic and social forces threatens the ability of many students to profit from their educational opportunities. Consider these statistics:

- One fourth of U.S. children currently live below the poverty level, the highest percentage in 20 years. Fifteen million children are being raised by single mothers whose family income averaged $11,400 in 1988 dollars.

- Forty-four percent of African American children and 36% of Latino children live in poverty.

- Between one fourth and one third of today's children have no adult at home when they return home from school.

- Twenty percent of America's preschoolers have not been vaccinated against polio (Hodgkinson, 1991; Kellog, 1988; U.S. Department of Education, 1993).

Socioeconomic Status, Physical Needs, and Experience

4.16

Look ahead in your text to page 406, where Maslow's hierarchy of needs is described. Read this section and then explain, on the basis of Maslow's work, why children of poverty might be ill-equipped for learning.

How does SES influence learning? One way is through basic needs. Many families lack adequate medical care, and an increasing number of children are coming to school without proper nourishment. In addition, homelessness is becoming a major problem; experts estimate that families now account for one third of the homeless, that more than 500,000 children were homeless in 1989, and that 43% of school-age homeless children do not attend school at all (Lawler-Prince & Holloway, 1992).

Poverty also influences the quality of home life. Unstable work conditions increase economic problems that lead to parental frustration, anger, and depression. These pressures can lead to family problems and marital conflicts and result in less stable and nurturant homes (Conger et al., 1992). Children of poverty often come to school without a sense of safety and security, so they are less well equipped to tackle school-related tasks.

SES also influences children's background experiences. High-SES parents are more likely than low-SES parents to provide their children with:

- Educational activities outside school (e.g., visits to art, science, and history museums; attendance at concerts; books borrowed from the library)

- Learning materials at home (e.g., computers, pocket calculators, newspapers, encyclopedias, dictionaries)

- Lessons outside school (e.g., art, music, religion, dance, computer)

4.17

The term *cultural capital* uses an analogy to compare cultural experiences to money in the bank. How are early experiences like money in the bank? How are they different?

These activities complement and reinforce classroom learning by providing an experiential base for school activities (Peng & Lee, 1992). Some researchers call these experiences "cultural capital" that forms a foundation for the concepts young children bring to school (Ballantine, 1989). In studying Piaget's work in Chapter 2, you found that these early experiences are crucial to intellectual development. Bloom (1981) estimated that 80% of human potential intelligence is developed by age 8; this point underscores the importance of early, family-based experiences.

Recent work with minority populations documents the untapped potential of family and home resources (Halle, Kurtze-Costes, & Mahoney, 1997). Researchers found

Parents promote both cognitive and language development by discussing ideas and experiences with their children.

"funds of knowledge," informal networks of information that minority families use to deal with lack of money and access to services (Moll, Amanti, Neff, & Gonzolez, 1992). Teachers can use these funds of knowledge to make connections with students' homes and help students develop pride in the resources available to them.

Interaction Patterns in the Home

SES also influences learning through the interaction patterns of parents and their children (Hess & McDevitt, 1984). Low-SES parents are more likely to "tell," rather than explain. Their language is less elaborate, their directions are less clear, and they are less likely to encourage problem solving. High-SES parents, in contrast, talk more with their children, explain ideas and the causes of events, and encourage independent thinking. In addition, high-SES parents are more likely to ask "wh" questions *(who, when, where, and why)*, promoting language development and preparing their children for the kind of verbal interaction found in the schools. Sometimes called "the curriculum of the home," these rich interaction patterns, together with the experiences described in the previous section, provide a strong foundation for reading and vocabulary development (Walberg, 1991).

Attitudes and Values

The impact of SES is also transmitted through parental attitudes and values. Reading is a classic example. Adults who have books, newspapers, and magazines around the home and read themselves have children who are more likely to read, and students who read at home show larger gains in reading achievement than those who don't (Anderson,

Hiebert, Scott, & Wilkenson, 1985). When involved in school activities, these children are familiar with the power of the printed word and are eager to read.

The educational aspirations parents have for their children are probably the most powerful variables affecting achievement; parents who expect their children to graduate from high school and attend college have children who achieve more than the children of parents with lower aspirations. These expectations are communicated through dialogues between parents and children. High-achieving students talk frequently with their parents about school activities, topics they're studying, and their high school programs (Peng & Lee, 1992).

Extracurricular activities provide a rich opportunity for parents to become involved in their children's education. One mother commented, "When she sees me at her games, when she sees me going to open house, when I attend her Interscholastic League contests, she knows I am interested in her activities. Plus, we have more to talk about" (Young & Scribner, 1997, p. 12). Student participation in extracurricular activities has two significant benefits: it involves students in the life of the school, and it provides an arena in which parents and their children can interact.

Compared with low-SES parents, middle-class parents also play the "schooling game" better, being much more likely to monitor their children's learning progress and to contact schools for information (Rothman, 1990). In one study of eighth-graders, researchers documented how middle-class parents "managed" the system, "steering" their sons and daughters into college-prep high school courses (Baker & Stevenson, 1986). Low-SES parents, in contrast, allowed their children to "drift" into classes, relying on the decisions of others. The low-SES students often got lost in the shuffle, ending up in inappropriate or less challenging classes and tracks.

Differences between low- and high-SES families also reflect the emphasis placed on student autonomy and responsibility. High-SES parents emphasize self-direction, self-control, and individual responsibility; low-SES parents, in contrast, place greater emphasis on conformity and obedience (Ballantine, 1989).

To succeed in schools, low-SES students need more structure and motivational support than their high-SES peers. In addition, they need help in seeing connections between learning tasks and the outside world, as well as in understanding that effort leads to accomplishment.

4.18

Of the three major factors influencing SES—occupation, income, and level of education—researchers have found that the last is most influential in school performance. Explain why this is the case.

SES: Some Cautions

As with all sources of diversity, teachers should exercise caution in applying information about SES to individual students or families. These are general patterns that may not apply to each individual. Keeping this fact in mind can help prevent inappropriately lowered expectations for students from low-income families. Many low-income families provide not only a rich learning environment but also a strong system of parental support. Tapping into and using this system is one way of promoting learning for these children.

Culture

Think about the way you dress, the music you like, the kinds of things you eat, how you spend time with your friends, and the kinds of recreation you enjoy. These and other factors, such as religion, family structure, and values, are all part of your culture.

Culture refers to *the attitudes, values, customs, and behavior patterns that characterize a social group* (Banks, 1997). Its enormous impact on even the most basic aspects of our lives is illustrated in the following quote:

> Culture not only helps to determine what foods we eat, but it also influences when we eat (for example, one, three, or five meals and at what time of the day); with whom we eat (that is, only with the same sex, with children or with the extended family); how we eat (for example, at a table or on the floor; with chopsticks, silverware, or the fingers); and the ritual of eating (for example, in which hand the fork is held, asking for or being offered seconds, and belching to show appreciation of a good meal). These eating patterns are habits of the culture. (Gollnick & Chinn, 1986, pp. 6–7)

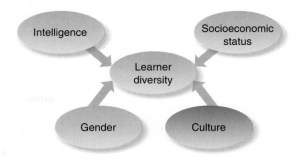

Figure 4.5 Sources of learner individuality: Culture

Like SES, culture influences school success through the attitudes, values, and ways of viewing the world that are held and transmitted by it (see Figure 4.5).

Ethnicity

An important part of culture is a person's ethnic background. **Ethnicity** refers to *a person's ancestry; the way individuals identify themselves with the nation from which they or their ancestors came* (Gollnick & Chinn, 1994). Members of an ethnic group have a common:

- history
- set of customs and traditions
- language (although sometimes not spoken)
- value system

More than 170 Native American and 100 non-Native American ethnic groups live in the United States. The largest in the school-age population is African American, comprising about 15% of the total. Hispanic groups—Mexican, Puerto Rican, Cuban, Central, and South Americans—make up 10% of the school-age population, and Asian American students—Chinese, Japanese, Filipino, Korean, and Vietnamese—total about 3% (U.S. Department of Education, 1994).

More than 7 million people immigrated to the United States during the 1970s, and another 7 million came during the 1980s. Between 1980 and 1994 the number of Asian American students increased by almost 100%, Hispanic students increased by 46%, African American students increased by 25%, and Caucasian students increased by only 10% (U.S. Bureau of Census, 1996). Experts estimate that the number of ethnic minorities in the school-age population will increase to 40% by the year 2000 (Villegas, 1991). Each of these groups brings a distinct set of values and traditions that influences student learning.

Culture and Schooling

A second-grade class in Albuquerque, New Mexico, was reading *The Boxcar Children* and was about to start a new chapter. The teacher said, "Look at the illustration at the beginning of the chapter and tell me what you think is going to happen." A few students raised their hands. The teacher called on a boy in the back row.

4.19

Explain the influence of culture on learning from a constructivist perspective. Which theorist—Piaget or Vygotsky—places more emphasis on culture? Explain.

4.20

How do the foods Americans commonly eat in their day-to-day living suggest increasing ethnic diversity in the U.S. culture? Is this diversity greater or less than in the past?

He said, "I think the boy is going to meet his grandfather."

The teacher asked, "Based on what you know, how does the boy feel about meeting his grandfather?"

Trying to involve the whole class, the teacher called on another student—one of four Native Americans in the group—even though she had not raised her hand. When she didn't answer, the teacher tried rephrasing the question, but again the student sat in silence.

Feeling exasperated, the teacher wondered if there was something in the way the lesson was being conducted that made it difficult for the student to respond. She sensed that the student she had called on understood the story and was enjoying it. Why, then, wouldn't she answer what appeared to be a simple question?

The teacher recalled that this was not the first time this had happened, and that, in fact, the other Native American students in the class rarely answered questions in class discussions. She wanted to involve them, wanted them to participate in class, but could not think of ways to get them to talk. (Villegas, 1991, p. 3)

Why do students respond differently to instruction? How does culture influence school-related attitudes and values? How do communication patterns vary from culture to culture? Is classroom structure a factor? What can teachers do to build on the culturally influenced behavior patterns their students bring to school? In this section, we examine these questions, together with the relationships between culture and (a) attitudes and values, (b) adult–child interactions, (c) classroom organization, and (d) school communication.

Attitudes and Values

Our students come to us with a long learning history. In their homes they have learned to talk, dress, care for themselves, and function as family members. On their streets and playgrounds they have learned to interact with their peers, make friends, and solve interpersonal problems. When they enter our classrooms, they bring attitudes and values with them that can either complement or work against school learning. Research on different minority populations provides insights into how these attitudes and values influence learning.

Ogbu (1992) divides minority cultures in the United States into two broad categories: voluntary and involuntary. Members of *voluntary minorities,* such as recent Chinese, Vietnamese, and Indian immigrants, came to the United States seeking a better life; schooling, hard work, and integration are seen as vehicles to accomplishing it. In contrast, some *involuntary minorities,* such as African Americans, were brought into the United States against their will, and others, such as Native Americans, were conquered.

4.21

Identify another example of a voluntary and an involuntary minority. Identify an example that is not clearly one or the other.

Ogbu (1992) suggests that the two groups approach assimilation and integration into U.S. culture (and schooling) in different ways. Voluntary minorities see school as an opportunity for quick assimilation and integration into the economic and social mainstream. Involuntary minorities, because of a long history of separatism and low status, defend themselves through isolation, or cultural inversion. **Cultural inversion** is *"the tendency for involuntary minorities to regard certain forms of behavior, events, symbols, and meanings as inappropriate for them because these are characteristic of white Americans"* (Ogbu, 1992, p. 8). To adopt these attitudes, values, and ways of behaving is to reject their own culture, to become different from their peers and family.

Language is an example. Students are hesitant to drop the use of non-Standard English dialects in favor of "school English" because it would alienate their peers and distance their families. The same problem occurs in second-language learning. Research indicates that immersion programs that encourage students to drop their native language in favor of English cause distancing problems with parents, many of whom cannot speak English (Wong-Fillmore, 1992).

School success is often interpreted as rejecting a native culture; to become a good student is to become "White"—adopting White cultural values and rejecting their own. Students who study and become actively involved in school risk losing the friendship and respect of their peers. Ogbu believes that in many schools peer values either don't support school learning or actually oppose it; students form what he calls "resistance cultures" (Ogbu, 1987). Low grades, management and motivation problems, truancy, and high dropout rates are symptoms of this cultural conflict.

Ogbu (1987) encourages teachers to help minority students adapt to the dominant culture (including schools) without losing their cultural identity, a process he calls "accommodation without assimilation." Others use the term "alternation"—the ability to comfortably function in both cultures (Hamm & Coleman, 1997). The challenge for teachers is to help students learn about the "culture of schooling"—the norms, procedures, and expectations necessary for success in school—while honoring the value and integrity of the students' home cultures.

Minority role models are especially powerful in helping minority youth understand how they can succeed without losing their ethnic or cultural heritage. One commented,

It all started in the second grade. One faithful (sic) Career day at Jensen Scholastic Academy in my teacher Mrs. F.'s room a M.D. came to speak to the class about his career as a doctor. Reluctantly I can't remember his name but from that day forward I knew I was destined to be a doctor. From that point on I began to take my work seriously, because I knew to become a doctor grades were very important. Throughout my elementary career I received honors. In the seventh grade I really became fascinated with science, which I owe all to my teacher Mr. H. He made learning fun and interesting. I started to read science books even when it wasn't necessary, or I found myself watching the different specials on Channel 11 about operations they showed doctors performing. When I entered Kenwood Academy I decided to take Honors Biology which was very helpful. I wanted to be in a medical program at U.I.C. but I received a B second semester so I did not get chosen. That incident did not discourage me one bit. Through high school I continued my science classes. (Smokowski, 1997, p. 13)

Role models provide minority learners with evidence that they can succeed, and success can be accomplished without sacrificing their cultural identity.

Cultural Differences in Adult–Child Interactions

Children from different cultures also learn to interact with adults in different ways; sometimes it complements communication in schools, and sometimes it doesn't. This phenomenon can be illustrated with one of your author's personal experiences.

I was a Chicago-raised person living in the South for the first time. I soon developed a warm relationship with a family having three children, ages 3, 7, and 10. I reacted when the children would always call me "Dr. Kauchak" and my fiancee "Miss Lake," rather than "Don" and "Kathy," as we preferred. We thought these addresses were formal, but quaint. The parents also referred to us in this way, so we didn't press the issue. As we worked in schools, we noticed that middle-class children said, "Yes, ma'am," and, "No, ma'am," when talking with teachers. We came to realize that these formal (to us) ways of addressing adults were expected by both middle-class families and the teachers who came from these families. To

4.22

Why are positive minority role models important for the concept of *accommodation without assimilation?* Is the concept consistent or inconsistent with the idea of America as a "melting pot"?

Minority role models help minority youth understand how they can succeed without losing their ethnic or cultural heritage.

encourage these children to call us by our first names would have been inappropriate in social situations and in conflict with accepted behavior in the schools.

Although the previous case reflects a minor (and positive) cultural difference, others can result in misunderstanding or even conflict. An experience described by a principal working with Pacific Island students is an example. The principal had been invited to a community awards ceremony at a local church that was to honor students from her school. She gladly accepted, arrived a few minutes early, and was ushered to a seat of honor on the stage. After an uncomfortable (to her) wait of over an hour, the ceremony began, and the students proudly filed to the stage to receive their awards. Each was acknowledged, given an award, and applauded. After this part of the ceremony, she had an eye-opening experience.

> The children all went back and sat down in the audience again, and the meeting continued on to several more items on the agenda. Well, the kids were fine for a while, but as you might imagine, they got bored fast and started to fidget. Fidgeting and whispering turned into poking, prodding, and open chatting. I became a little anxious at the disruption, but none of the other adults appeared to even notice, so I ignored it, too. Pretty soon several of the children were up and out of their seats, strolling about the back and sides of the auditorium. All adult faces continued looking serenely up at the speaker on the stage. Then the kids started playing tag, running circles around the seating area and yelling gleefully. No adult response—I was amazed, and struggled to resist the urge to quiet the children. Then some of the kids got up onto the stage, running around the speaker, flicking the lights on and off, and opening and closing the curtain! Still nothing from the Islander parents! It was not my place, and I shouldn't have done it, but I was so beyond my comfort zone that with eye contact and a pantomimed shush, I got the kids to settle down.

I suddenly realized then that when these children. . . come to school late, it doesn't mean that they or their parents don't care about learning . . . that's just how all the adults in their world operate. When they squirm under desks and run around the classroom, they aren't trying to be disrespectful or defiant, they're just doing what they do everywhere else. (Winitzky, 1991, pp. 137–138)

This experience gave the principal insights into the ways (and reasons) her students often acted as they did. Students bring with them ways of acting and interacting with adults that may differ from the traditional teacher-as-authority-figure role. (We discuss the difficult question of what to do about these differences later in the chapter.)

Classroom Organization: Working with and Against Students' Cultures

In most classrooms, emphasis is placed on individual responsibility, which is often reinforced by grades and competition. Competition demands successes and failures, and the success of one student is often tied to the failure of another (Cushner, McClelland, & Safford, 1992).

Contrast this orientation with the learning styles of the Hmong, a mountain tribe from Laos that immigrated to the United States after the Vietnam War. The Hmong culture emphasizes cooperation, and Hmong students constantly monitor the learning progress of their peers, offering help and assistance. Individual achievement is de-emphasized in favor of group success. A researcher working with the Hmong described her classroom in this way:

> When Mee Hang has difficulty with an alphabetization lesson, Pang Lor explains, in Hmong, how to proceed. Chia Ying listens in to Pang's explanation and nods her head. Pang goes back to work on her own paper, keeping an eye on Mee Hang. When she sees Mee looking confused, Pang leaves her seat and leans over Mee's shoulder. She writes the first letter of each word on the line, indicating to Mee that these letters are in alphabetical order and that Mee should fill in the rest of each word. This gives Mee the help she needs and she is able to finish on her own. Mee, in turn, writes the first letter of each word on the line for Chia Ying, passing on Pang Lor's explanation.
>
> Classroom achievement is never personal but always considered to be the result of cooperative effort. Not only is there no competition in the classroom, there is constant denial of individual ability. When individuals are praised by the teacher, they generally shake their heads and appear hesitant to be singled out as being more able than their peers. (Hvitfeldt, 1986, p. 70)

Consider how well these students would learn if instruction were competitive and teacher centered, with few opportunities for student help and collaboration.

Native Americans experience similar difficulties with competitive classrooms. They are also taught that cooperation is important; they view competition as silly, if not distasteful. When these children enter school and are asked to compete in the classroom, they experience cultural conflict (Phillips, 1983). Getting good grades at the expense of their fellow students is both strange and offensive. Raising hands and jousting for the right to give the correct answer isn't congruent with the ways they interact at home. The result is that Native American students are often forced to choose between two cultures, and too often they conclude that schools are not for them. (We examine competitive classroom structures and their impact on motivation in Chapter 10.)

4.23

Ogbu's concept of *accommodation without assimilation* requires considerable teacher judgment and tact to implement. Explain specifically how you, if you were a teacher working with the Pacific Island children in this anecdote, would deal with their conception of time and their spirited behavior in your classroom.

4.24

How do Native Americans' views of competition and cooperation illustrate Ogbu's concept of *cultural inversion*?

School Communication Patterns: Cultural Matches and Mismatches

Cultural conflict can occur in communication. A study of differences in language patterns between White and African American students illustrates this possibility (Heath, 1982). For example, teachers would say, "Let's put the scissors away now." White students, accustomed to this indirect way of speaking, interpreted this as a command; African Americans did not. Failure to obey was then viewed as either a management or motivation problem—a result of the mismatch between home and school cultures.

Similar disparities caused problems during instruction. From their home experience, White children were accustomed to using language to explore abstract relationships and were asked questions requiring specific answers, such as, "Where's the puppy?" and "What's this story about?" African American children were accustomed to questions that were more "open-ended, story-starter" types that did not have a single answer. African American children "were not viewed as information-givers in their interactions with adults, nor were they considered appropriate conversation partners and thus they did not learn to act as such" (Heath, 1982, p. 119). When these children went to school, they were unprepared for the verbal give-and-take of fast-paced, convergent questioning.

Made aware of these differences, teachers incorporated more open-ended questions in their lessons, and they worded commands more directly, such as "Put your scissors away now." They also helped African American students become more comfortable with answering factual questions. In this way, effective bridges were built between African American students' natural learning styles and the schools.

Cultural Matches with School Learning

Culture can also complement school learning. In a cross-cultural study comparing Chinese, Japanese, and American child-raising practices, researchers found significant differences in parental support for schooling (Stevenson, Lee, & Stigler, 1986). Over 95% of native Chinese and Japanese fifth-graders had desks at home on which to do their homework; only 63% of the American sample did. Also, 57% of the Chinese and Japanese parents supplemented their fifth-graders' schoolwork with additional math workbooks, as compared with only 28% of the American parents. Finally, 51% of the Chinese parents and 29% of the Japanese parents supplemented their children's science curriculum with additional work, compared with only 1% of the American parents.

A study attempting to understand the phenomenal successes of Indo–Chinese children in U.S. classrooms further documents the effects of home values on learning (Caplan, Choy, & Whitmore, 1992). In examining the school experiences of Vietnamese and Laotian refugees who had been in the United States for a relatively short time (an average of 3½ years), the researchers found amazing progress. The Indo–Chinese children received better than a B average in school, and scores on standardized achievement tests corroborated the grades as reflecting true achievement, not grade inflation.

In attempting to explain this encouraging pattern of school acculturation and progress, the researchers looked to the families. They found heavy emphasis on the importance of education, hard work, autonomy, perseverance, and pride. These values were reinforced with a nightly ritual of family homework in which both parents and older siblings helped younger members of the family. Indo–Chinese high schoolers spent an average of 3 hours a day on homework; junior high and elementary students spent an average of 2½ hours and 2 hours, respectively, compared with the 1½ hours a day U.S. junior and senior high students spend on homework.

4.25

On the basis of the 1986 study by Stevenson et al., what would you infer about the attitudes, beliefs, and values of Japanese, Chinese, and American parents? Does this inference apply to all members of these groups? What does this tell you about the process of inferring cultural attributes?

Culture and Learning: Deficit or Difference?

In the previous sections, you've seen how cultural differences can affect school success. Efforts have been made to synthesize this information into theories that can be used to further explain the relationship between school learning and culture.

Cultural deficit theories *suggest that "the linguistic, social or cultural backgrounds of minority children prevent them from doing well academically"* (Villegas, 1991, p. 5). These theories have at least three weaknesses. First, they don't account for the many successes of different cultural groups. Second, because of their negative orientation, they result in lowered expectations for minority students. Third, they can't explain why the longer some minorities are in school, the farther behind they fall. If deficit theories were valid, the gap should be greatest when students first enter school and should gradually narrow over time (Villegas, 1991).

Cultural difference theories *emphasize the strengths of different cultures and look for ways that instructional practice can recognize and build on those strengths* (Tharp, 1989; Villegas, 1991). They begin with the premise that different cultural groups have unique ways of learning and that no single way of teaching is most effective for all. They then attempt to understand different cultural groups and to adapt instruction to best meet these groups' learning needs. Evidence supports their premise, and we discuss implications for teaching cultural minorities on the basis of this concept.

Using Ogbu's concept of *cultural inversion,* explain why some minorities might fall farther and farther behind.

Culturally Responsive Teaching

Culturally responsive teaching *acknowledges cultural diversity in classrooms and accommodates this diversity in instruction* (Gay, 1997). It does this in three important ways, which are illustrated in Figure 4.6.

Accepting and Valuing Differences

By recognizing and accepting student diversity, teachers communicate that all students are welcome and valued. This notion is important for every learner, but particularly so for cultural minorities, who may feel alienated from school. Teachers need to develop healthy communication channels with minority students and help them understand that school success and belonging to their minority culture are not antagonistic.

Genuine *caring* is the critical element in the process; students quickly see through artificial attempts to communicate caring, and lip service to minorities will be seen as superficial. This dilemma can be difficult, of course, because teachers can never be certain that their intentions are being accurately perceived. Teachers can, however, take the following actions, which are rarely misperceived:

- Time: Giving your time is one of the most effective ways to communicate caring.

- Personal Interest: All people react positively to someone taking an interest in their personal lives.

- Involvement: Teachers who try to involve all students equally in classroom activities communicate that everyone is important and that each student's contributions to learning activities are valued.

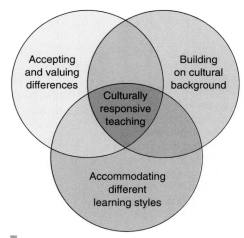

Figure 4.6 Characteristics of culturally responsive teaching

Accommodating Different Learning Styles

Teachers who are sensitive to possible differences between home and school patterns are in a position to adapt their instruction to best meet their students' needs. For example, you saw earlier that the values of Native Americans often clash with typical classroom practice. Recognizing that these students learn more effectively when cooperation rather than competition is emphasized, teachers can incorporate peer tutoring and cooperative learning to complement teacher-centered approaches (we describe cooperative learning in Chapter 13). These adaptations can result in increased learning for all students (Slavin, 1995).

Another example illustrates how sensitive and creative teachers can accommodate different cultural learning styles. When one teacher learned that Asian American students are often overwhelmed by the hustle and bustle of American schools (Park, 1997), she tried to keep her classroom quiet and orderly. She also found that Asian Americans are often shy and sometimes reluctant to speak in class, so she made a special effort to promote their participation by using open-ended questioning and by encouraging them to speak loudly and clearly (Shields & Shaver, 1990)

Building on Students' Cultural Backgrounds

Effective teachers also learn about their students' cultures and use these to develop personal pride and motivation in their students, as the following illustration demonstrates:

> In one third-grade classroom with a predominately Central American student population, youngsters are greeted most mornings with the sound of salsa music in the background, instruction takes place in both English and Spanish, magazines and games in both languages are available throughout the classroom, maps of both the United States and Latin America line one wall with pins noting each student's origin, and every afternoon there is a Spanish reading lesson to ensure that students learn to read and write in Spanish as well as English. . . . The teacher argues very clearly that a positive instructional environment for these students must be tailored to the home cultures. (Shields & Shaver, 1990, p. 9)

The benefits of this approach are felt in both the classroom and the home. In addition to increases in student achievement, parents are more positive about school, which in turn enhances student motivation, and a positive learning cycle is created. Students bring with them a wealth of experiences embedded in their home culture. Sensitive teachers build on these experiences to help all students reach their full potential.

Culture and Language: English Dialects

Language is a powerful and important aspect of culture and ethnicity, both here and in other countries. For instance, because of political pressure, both English and French are official languages in Canada, and labels, signs, and other information are printed in both languages. Language plays a central role in what Delpit (1995) calls "codes of power," the cultural and linguistic conventions that control access to doors of opportunity in our society. Because language is so important, we devote the next two sections to a discussion of its influence on learning.

English Dialects: Research Findings

Anyone who has traveled can confirm the fact that the United States has many regional and ethnic dialects. A **dialect** is *a variation of Standard English that is distinct in vocab-*

4.27

To work effectively with students from different cultures, teachers must understand those cultures. Explain the advantages of learning about students' cultures from both a cognitive and an affective perspective.

4.28

How would behaviorism explain the development of dialects? How would social cognitive theory explain them?

ulary, grammar, or pronunciation. Everyone in the United States speaks a dialect; people merely react to those different from their own (Wolfram, 1991). An important question is, How should teachers deal with dialects in classrooms?

Research indicates that use of non-Standard English results in lowered teacher expectations for student performance (Bowie & Bond, 1994) and lowered assessments of students' work and the students themselves (Taylor, 1983). Teachers often confuse non-Standard English with mistakes during oral reading (Washington & Miller-Jones, 1989) and some critics argue that dialects, such as Black English, are substandard, lacking in structure and complexity. Linguists, however, argue that these variations are just as rich and semantically complex as Standard English (Labov, 1972; Rickford, 1997).

A controversy over *ebonics*—a term created by combining *ebony* and *phonics* used to describe an African American dialect—erupted in California when the Oakland school board wanted to use ebonics to help children learn Standard English (McMillen, 1997). Proponents claimed that ebonics would help African American students form a bridge between home and school cultures and better understand instruction. Critics contended that the move was political, would isolate African American children, and would "dumb-down" the curriculum.

Dialects in the Classroom: Implications for Teachers

You saw earlier that culturally responsive teaching begins with accepting and valuing differences, and this is particularly important when responding to learners with non-standard dialects. Keep in mind that dialects are both functional and valued in the culture of students' neighborhoods. Requiring that they be eliminated communicates that differences are neither accepted nor valued.

A primary reason for teaching Standard English is that it allows access to other educational and economic opportunities. Students realize this when they interview for their first job or when they plan for post-high-school education. So, what should a teacher do when a student says, "I ain't got no pencil," bringing a nonstandard dialect into the classroom? Opinions vary from "rejection and correction" to complete acceptance. The approach most consistent with culturally responsive teaching is to accept the dialect and build on it (Speidel, 1987). For example, when the student says, "I ain't got no pencil," the teacher (or adult) might say, "Oh, you don't have a pencil. What should you do, then?" Although results won't be apparent immediately, long-range benefits are promising.

Language differences don't have to form barriers between home and school. **Bidialecticism,** *the ability to switch back and forth between a dialect and Standard English,* provides the best of both worlds, allowing access to both (Gollnick & Chinn, 1994). As another example of culturally responsive teaching, a teacher explicitly taught differences between Standard and Black English, analyzing the strengths of each and respective places for their use (Shields & Shaver, 1990). The teacher read a series of poems by Langston Hughes, the African American poet, focusing on the ability of Black English to create vivid images. The class discussed the contrast with Standard English and ways in which differences between the two languages could be used to accomplish different communication goals.

4.29
State one disadvantage and one advantage of the "rejection and correction" approach. Identify an advantage and a disadvantage of the complete acceptance approach.

Culture and Language: English as a Second Language

In an urban fourth-grade class composed of 11 Asian and 17 Black children, Sokhom, age 10, has recently been promoted to the on-grade-level reading group and is doing well. Instead of being "pulled out" of her regular classroom for special instruction in English, she now spends her whole day in the mainstream classroom. At home, she pulls out a well-worn English–Khmer dictionary that she says her father bought at great expense in the refugee camp in the Philippines. She recounts that when she first came to the United States and was in second grade, she used to look up English words there and ask her father or her brother to read the Cambodian word to her; then she would know what the English word was. Today, in addition to her intense motivation to know English ("I like to talk in English. I like to read in English, and I like to write in English."), Sokhom wants to learn to read and write in Khmer and, in fact, has taught herself a little via English.

In another urban public school across the city, Maria, a fifth-grader who has been in a two-way maintenance bilingual education program since prekindergarten, has both Spanish and English reading every morning for 1¼ hours each, with Ms. Torres and Mrs. Dittmar, respectively. Today, Mrs. Dittmar is reviewing the vocabulary for the story the students are reading about Charles Drew, a Black American doctor. She explains that "influenza" is what Charles's little sister died of. Maria comments that "you say it [influenza] in Spanish the same way you write it [in English]."

In the same Puerto Rican community, in a new bilingual middle school a few blocks away, Elizabeth, a graduate of the two-way maintenance bilingual program mentioned above, hears a Career Day speaker from the community tell her that of two people applying for a job, one bilingual and one not, the bilingual has an advantage. Yet Elizabeth's daily program of classes provides little opportunity for her to continue to develop literacy in Spanish; the bilingual program at this school is primarily transitional. (Hornberger, 1989, pp. 271–272)

As a result of rapidly increasing immigration (more than 7 million people a decade during the 1970s and 1980s), increasing numbers of students with limited backgrounds in English are entering American classrooms. Coming with their families from places such as Southeast Asia, the Middle East, Haiti, and Mexico, the number of non-English-speaking and limited-English-proficient (LEP) students is growing at about 4% a year—about twice the population growth rate for the nation (Catterall & Cota-Robles, 1988). The number of language minority students increased by more than 50% between 1985 and 1991, and between 1991 and 1993 the language minority population increased 12.6% versus an increase of only 1.02% for the general population (Weaver & Padrón, 1997).

The diversity is staggering. Currently, 2.3 million LEP students in U.S. schools (U.S. Department of Education, 1993) and about 50% of all California students speak a language other than English as their primary or only language (Fitzgerald, 1995). In the Los Angeles School District, more than 81 languages are represented, with as many as 20 found in some classrooms. Nationwide, the number of students whose primary language is not English is expected to triple during the next 30 years (Pallas, Natriello, & McDill, 1989).

This diversity presents challenges to both the students and the schools. A study in California found that 45% of Hispanic students do not complete high school, and 40% leave school before tenth grade (Cortes, 1986). In response to these trends, in 1988 the U.S. Department of Education listed as its first research priority "the teaching and learning of reading, writing, and language skills, particularly by non- or limited-English speaking students" (U.S. Department of Education, 1988, p. 192). This language diversity poses a challenge to teachers because most instruction is verbal. How should schools respond to this linguistic challenge? Bilingual programs offer one solution.

Types of Bilingual Programs

True bilingual programs offer instruction to non-native English speakers in two languages: English and their primary language. They attempt to maintain and enhance the native language while building on it to teach English. The term *bilingual,* however, has been expanded to refer to a range of second-language programs (Allen, 1992; Stowe, 1992). We look at three of them: maintenance programs, transitional programs, and English as a second language (ESL) programs.

Maintenance Bilingual Programs. **Maintenance bilingual programs** *teach in both the native language and English, maintaining and building on the students' native language* (Gollnick & Chinn, 1994). Also called "two-way" bilingual programs because of the interaction between the two languages (Ovando, 1997), maintenance programs are found primarily at the elementary level, with the goal of developing students who are truly bilingual. Maria, the fifth-grader in the episode above, had both a Spanish- and an English-speaking teacher to help her develop proficiency in both languages. Maintenance programs have the advantage of maintaining students' heritage, language, and culture. They are difficult to implement, however, because they require groups of students with the same native language and bilingual teachers or teacher teams in which one member speaks the heritage language.

Transitional Bilingual Programs. **Transitional bilingual programs** *use the native language as an instructional aid until English is proficient.* Transitional programs begin with the first language and gradually develop learners' English proficiency. The transition period is often too short, however, leaving the students inadequately prepared for learning in English (Gersten & Woodward, 1995). In addition, loss of the first language and lack of emphasis on the home culture can result in communication gaps between children who no longer speak the first language and parents who don't speak English.

English as a Second Language (ESL) Programs. Although, technically, all bilingual programs fit this category because mastery of English is a goal, **English as a second language (ESL) programs** *focus explicitly on the mastery of English.* Unlike the other

4.30

Using Piaget's concepts of *equilibrium, assimilation,* and *accommodation,* describe the process of second-language learning in maintenance programs.

4.31

Identify at least one similarity and one difference between maintenance and transitional programs. From an economic perspective, with the current emphasis on a move to a global economy, which approach would be preferable?

Effective bilingual programs teach English while building on and enriching student's native language.

programs, they emphasize learning English and mainstreaming students into regular classrooms. Sokhom, the Cambodian student in the episode above, was initially in a pull-out ESL program until she could function in an English-only environment. Pulling students out of the regular classroom, however, disrupts the continuity of their instruction, and cultural discontinuities similar to those associated with transitional programs can result. ESL programs are common when classes contain students who speak a variety of languages, making maintenance or transitional programs difficult to implement.

4.32

Describe an ESL program based on behaviorist principles. Describe one based on social cognitive theory.

Teachers should be cautious when they work with students from ESL programs not to overestimate their English proficiency. After about two years in a language-rich environment, students develop **basic interpersonal communication skills,** *a level that allows students to interact conversationally with their peers* (Cummins, 1991). However, it may take an additional five to seven years to develop **cognitive academic language proficiency,** *a level that allows students to handle demanding learning tasks in an abstract curriculum.*

Evaluating Bilingual Programs

In comparing bilingual with English-only programs, researchers have found that students in bilingual programs achieve higher in math and reading and have more positive attitudes toward school and themselves (Arias & Casanova, 1993; Díaz, 1983). Also, because of their exposure to two languages, they better understand the role of language in communication (Díaz, 1990).

These findings make sense. Programs that use a student's native language not only build on an existing foundation but also say to the student, "To do well in school, you don't have to forget the culture of your home and neighborhood."

Teaching Bilingual Students

Teachers are crucial to the success of bilingual programs. Let's see why.

> Tina Wharton had read about diversity in her education classes, but she wasn't expecting what she encountered when she took a job in a suburb of Los Angeles. Her first-grade class of 29 students had 9 who spoke Spanish as their first language. In working with them, she knew that building communication skills would need to be a top priority in her class.
>
> At the suggestion of other teachers, she wrote to each of the parents—in Spanish—and asked for their help. With the aid of Spanish-speaking teachers, she labeled all the objects in the room with both Spanish and English names and encouraged students to learn to read both. Her class made frequent field trips to local parks, a nearby food-processing plant, and the airport. After they returned, they talked about their trips, and students drew pictures and wrote about their visits. She enlisted the aid of several parents and had these stories transcribed into both Spanish and English.
>
> Six blocks down the street, Jim Harrison taught the brothers and sisters of Tina's students in his middle-school science class. He had attended a workshop on the problems that LEP (limited-English-proficient) students might encounter in different content areas and adjusted his classes accordingly. He used hands-on activities, de-emphasized reading, and paired LEP students with other students to discuss and write about the experiments. At the beginning of each unit, he used demonstrations, concrete examples, pictures, and diagrams to introduce new vocabulary and abstract ideas.

It is likely that you will teach students whose first language is not English, and you can use a number of strategies to help LEP students learn both English and academic content. These begin with awareness and move to language and concept-development strategies.

Awareness. Research indicates that a surprising number of teachers are unaware of the home languages that students bring to school; one study found that teachers recognized only 27% of the non-native English speakers in one sample of Asian students (Schmidt, 1992). Teachers can't adjust their teaching to meet the needs of LEP students if they aren't aware that these students exist. A related problem is that many teachers believe that learning a second language depends on losing the first (Weaver & Padrón, 1997). Instead, research suggests that effective ESL teachers build on both the language and background experiences of their ESL students (Gersten, 1996). Talking with counselors, administrators, other teachers, the students and their parents can help teachers learn about their learners' backgrounds. Then teachers can communicate with actions and words that they respect and value this diversity.

Facilitating Language and Concept Development. Students learn English by using it in their day-to-day lives. In large part, language is a skill, and students in general—LEP students in particular—need to spend as much time as possible literally "practicing the language" (Fitzgerald, 1995; Ravetta & Brunn, 1995). Teacher-centered instruction, in which the teacher talks most of the time and students listen passively, should be avoided (Adamson, 1993). Instead, students should be provided with concrete experiences and opportunities to talk, write, and read about them. Also, open-ended questions that allow students to respond without the pressure of giving specific answers are valuable tools for eliciting student responses (Langer, Bartolome, Vasquez, & Lucas, 1990). Let's see what this looks like in the classroom.

> Felyce Marquez has a group of eight non-native English speakers in her second-grade class of 24 students. She has been reading a story to her class from a book liberally illustrated with pictures depicting the events in the story. As she read, she showed the pictures and had the students identify the object or event being illustrated, such as a cave in the woods that the boy and girl in the story decided to explore.
> After she finished reading the story, she continued by discussing the events in it.
> "Please tell us something you remember about the story. . . . Carmela?" she began.
> ". . . A boy and a girl," Carmela responded hesitantly.
> "Yes, good, Carmela," Felyce smiled. "The story is about a boy and a girl," and she pointed again to the picture of the boy and girl.
> "Tell us something about the boy and girl. . . . Segundo."
> ". . . Lost . . . cave."
> "Yes," Felyce nodded encouragingly. "The boy and girl were exploring a cave and they got lost," again pointing to the pictures in the book. "What do you think exploring means? . . . Anyone?"

Felyce employed at least three simple, but effective, strategies to promote language and concept development in her students (Ovando, 1997). First, she used pictures to provide concrete reference points for the vocabulary she was developing. Second, she used open-ended questions to allow Carmela and Segundo to "practice" using English without the pressure of providing a specific answer. Third, she modeled elaborated descriptions such as, "The boy and girl were exploring a cave and they got lost," in response to Segundo's ". . . Lost . . . cave." The strategies took little preparation; all she needed was the book with pictures. These same strategies can be used in the content areas as well. When consistently used, they can do much to help students develop their language while simultaneously learning concepts.

Other strategies proven effective with ESL students include:

- Modifying speech by slowing down and simplifying vocabulary and supplementing words with gestures and pictures
- Using small-group activities to provide opportunities for interaction
- Supplementing verbal instruction with visuals such as charts and diagrams
- Relating new vocabulary to native terms
- Encouraging writing and reading through creative and interactive tasks (Ovando, 1997; Weaver & Padrón, 1997)

These strategies not only help ESL learners but also enrich instruction for all students.

4.33

Use the concept of *zone of proximal development* to explain the difference between successful and unsuccessful bilingual programs.

Classroom Connections

Using Socioeconomic Status and Culture as Tools to Understand Your Students

1. Communicate with students about who they are and who you are.
   - On the first day of class, a sixth-grade teacher has students write essays about themselves. He has them include a description of their favorite activities, the kind of music they like, and any information they want to include about parents, caregivers, or other close relatives. He asks them to include, if they would like, anything about school that scares them or makes them worry. He writes an essay of his own and shares it with his students.
   - A math teacher makes an effort to get to know each of his students. He tries to learn something personal about each and refers to it in one-on-one conversations.

2. Make an attempt to learn about the cultures of the students you are teaching.
   - A third-grade teacher asks her students about their after-school activities and their holiday customs. She designs classroom "festivals" that focus on different cultures and invites parents and other caregivers to help celebrate and contribute to enriching them.

- A high-school teacher in an inner-city school makes himself available before and after school. Although the focus in these sessions is on academics, the conversation often turns to students' lives and the problems they encounter in school.

3. Accept and value the language diversity in your classroom.
   - As they use variations of Standard English in his classroom, a fifth-grade teacher asks his students to describe the meanings of vocabulary and phrases and where they originated. He describes the explanations as interesting and paraphrases them in different ways in Standard English.

4. Use instructional strategies that accommodate diversity.
   - A physical-education teacher uses the "buddy system" to help students with limited English skills participate in class. She asks bilingual students with well-developed English skills to pair with less-proficient students to explain rules and concepts during instruction and games.
   - A second-grade teacher strategically uses seating patterns to foster class cohesion and inter-group friendships. She puts the desks in

groups of four and places students from different ethnic groups and ability levels in the same group.

5. Use concrete examples and open-ended questions to help learners acquire experiences and reference points for language.

   • A first-grade teacher working in a low-SES classroom begins her lesson with a demonstration, concrete example, or hands-on experience. She begins discussions by asking individual students to describe what they see in the examples. On the basis of their observations, she guides them to an understanding of the topic.

6. Make students aware of the values and accomplishments of ethnic minorities.

   • A second-grade teacher emphasizes values, such as courtesy and respect, that cross all

cultures. He has students discuss the ways values, such as respect for others, are displayed differently in various cultures.

• An art teacher decorates the room with pictures of Native American art and discusses its quality and contributions to the general field of art.

• An inner-city American history teacher displays pictures of prominent African Americans and discusses the contributions they made to the American way of life. She emphasizes that many history books often under-represent the contributions of minorities and females.

• A teacher with many Hispanic students in her classroom points out the accomplishments of Americans of Latin heritage, such as the Cuban population in Miami and the prominent Hispanic politicians around the country.

Gender

What Marti Banes saw on her first day of teaching advanced-placement chemistry was both surprising and disturbing. Of the 26 students watching her, only two were female, and they were sitting quietly in the back of the room. One reason that Marti had gone into teaching was to share her interest in science with other females, but this situation gave her little chance to do so.

The fact that some of our students are boys and others are girls is so obvious that we sometimes miss this important difference. When we're reminded, we of course notice that boys and girls look different and often act and think differently from each other. In this section, we examine gender-related student differences and explore their implications for teaching (Figure 4.7).

Differences exist in boys' and girls' developmental rates; girls develop faster, with differences in verbal and motor skills appearing at an early age. Boys and girls are different in other areas as well, and these differences appear as early as the preschool years. Girls tend to play with dolls and other girls and gravitate toward activities such as make-believe and dress-up. Boys play with blocks, cars, dinosaurs, and other boys. Why? Like the nature–nurture argument regarding intelligence, this question is controversial, but much of the evidence points to an interaction between genetics and environment (Berk, 1996). Genetics result in physical differences such as size and growth rate, and may also influence other differences such as temperament, aggression, and early verbal and exploratory behaviors (Berk, 1996). Girls and boys are also treated differently by their par-

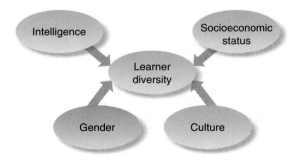

Figure 4.7 Sources of learner individuality: Gender

ents, peers, and teachers, and they grow up looking and acting different. Unfortunately, differences in societal support can result in differences in achievement between males and females.

What should teachers do? Opinions vary from accepting them as a natural part of the differences between the sexes to minimizing them at every opportunity. Consider these findings:

- In the early grades, girls are ahead of or equal to boys on almost every standardized measure of achievement and psychological well-being. By the time they graduate from high school or college, they have fallen back. Girls enter school even or ahead, but leave behind.

- In high school, girls score lower on the SAT and ACT, which are critical for college admission. The greatest gender gaps are in science and math.

- Boys are much more likely to be awarded state and national college scholarships.

- Women score lower on all sections of the Graduate Record Exam, the Medical College Admissions Test, and admission tests for law, dental, and optometry schools (Sadker, Sadker, & Long, 1997).

Let's examine some proposed explanations for these findings.

Different Treatment of Boys and Girls

Societal and Family Influences

In 1993, Mattel attempted to market a new "Teen Talk Barbie," which said the following things when you pressed her tummy:

"I like shopping."
"I like boys."
"Math class is tough."

Mattel withdrew this recording under a storm of protest, yet this is an example of how our society perpetuates differences between males and females.

From the day they are born, male and female babies are treated differently. Girls are given pink blankets, are called cute and pretty, and are handled delicately. Boys are dressed in blue, are regarded as handsome, and are seen as tougher, better coordinated, and hardier. Fathers are rougher with their sons and engage them in more physical stimulation and gross motor play; they tend to be gentler with their daughters and offer more sex-stereotyped toys, such as dolls and stuffed animals (Ruble, 1988). Differences in treatment continue in later years. In high school, girls become cheerleaders for the boys, who become football or basketball players.

Unfortunately, these differences include expectations for school success. Parents—probably unconsciously—often communicate different expectations for their sons and daughters. Researchers have found that parents' gender-stereotyped attitudes toward girls' ability in math adversely influenced their daughters' achievement in math and their attitudes toward it. A longitudinal study indicated that girls who thought they were good at math declined from 64% in third grade to 57% in seventh grade and 48% in eleventh grade; boys' attitudes only dropped from 66% in third grade to 60% in eleventh grade (Nagy-Jacklin, 1989). Unfortunately, girls grow up perceiving math as a

4.34

Mattel presumably thought the phrases uttered by the Teen Talk Barbie were inoffensive, or they wouldn't have included them. What does this view suggest about the values of different groups in the United States? What implications do these values have for you as a teacher?

male domain, severely limiting many of their career options (Eccles, Jacobs & Harold, 1990).

Given this differential treatment, it's not surprising that early research on gender effects found differences between boys and girls in different academic areas. Boys did better in math and on visual and spatial tasks (e.g., those required in geometry); girls did better on verbal skills (Maccoby & Jacklin, 1974). In addition, researchers found small differences favoring boys in science, both in achievement and participation (Fennema, 1987). These differences were small, and within any population, we expect to find boys and girls who don't follow this pattern.

Other research offers more encouraging results. One review concluded that current gender differences in verbal ability are "negligible," that differences in quantitative ability and science are "declining," and that small differences in visual and spatial tasks are probably due to uneven opportunities to practice these skills (Linn & Hyde, 1989). These researchers further concluded that gender "differences were always small, that they have declined in the last two decades . . . and that educational programs can influence when differences arise" (p. 17). However, despite small and declining differences in *average* science and math achievement, significant differences exist at the extremes (Nowell, 1997). These differences at the upper end are especially troubling because this is the pool for future scientists and mathematicians (Fan, Chen, & Matsumata, 1997). How do school programs contribute to differences that do exist, and what can teachers do to ensure that boys and girls are provided equal opportunities for success in their classroom?

Different Treatment in Schools

Unfortunately, societal influences sometimes carry over into schools and result in different treatment for boys and girls. According to persistent gender stereotypes, teachers view boys as more independent thinkers and more likely to do better in math and science because these are "male" subjects. Girls, in contrast, are viewed as more submissive and conforming (Fennema & Peterson 1987; Grant, 1984).

Both male and female teachers treat boys and girls differently. They interact with boys more often (Sadker & Sadker, 1985) and ask them more questions—questions that are more conceptual and abstract (Sadker, Sadker, & Klein, 1991). Boys receive more approval, are taught more directly and listened to more, and are rewarded more for creativity (Torrance, 1983).

Researchers also found that boys are more likely to ask questions and make comments about ideas being discussed in class (Sadker et al., 1991). The differences increase as students move through school, with an especially noticeable drop at the middle-school level. In the seventh grade, girls initiated 41% of the student–teacher interactions (compared with 59% for boys); by eighth grade, this number had dropped to 30%. This drop appears at the time when adolescent girls are often wrestling with their sex-role identities. In a society that often views female roles as submissive and conforming, middle-school girls may feel uncomfortable asserting themselves as independent learners. One solution to this problem is to call on volunteers and nonvolunteers as equally as possible, providing equal opportunities for boys and girls to participate (Allermatt, Jovanovic, & Perry, 1997). This is especially important in math and science, where girls are more hesitant to participate.

This decline of female-initiated contacts might also be a result of different treatment. Boys were eight times more likely than girls to call out in class, and the teacher's most frequent response was to accept the call-out and continue. When girls did the same, the teachers were more likely to reprimand or correct the student, reinforcing

4.35

How would an extreme "nature" position describe gender differences? How about an extreme "nurture" position? How would an interactionist position describe these differences?

4.36

Explain the decline in gender-related differences in achievement. Predict what will happen in the future in this area.

4.37

Explain why an increase in male-initiated contacts during middle school years might occur.

boys for aggressive intellectual behaviors and punishing girls for those same behaviors (Sadker & Sadker, 1985).

Interestingly, when teachers were asked to analyze videotapes of classroom interactions containing differential treatment of boys and girls, they failed to see these patterns. In fact, despite the fact that boys participated more than girls by a ratio of three to one, teachers concluded that girls received more teacher attention than boys (Sadker & Sadker, 1985).

Experiences in Science and Math. Girls also have different experiences in science and math classes. When teachers organized science demonstrations, 79% were carried out by boys (Sadker et al., 1991). At the third-grade level, 51% of boys reported experience with microscopes compared to 37% of girls. In an eleventh-grade sample, 49% of males, but only 17% of females, reported experience with electrical equipment. Coincidentally, girls' attitudes toward science, science courses, and science careers all declined as they grew older (American Association of University Women, 1992).

The slight advantage for males in math can also be explained by differential teacher treatment and expectations. In Sweden, where sex role differences are less emphasized, differences in math achievement tend to be smaller (Svenson, 1971). In the United States, girls attending all-female schools take more math and science and have higher achievement in these areas (Finn, Dulberg, & Reis, 1979). In regular public schools, girls are much less likely to take nonrequired math and science courses (Pallas & Alexander, 1983). When they do take math, they are less confident than boys and more likely to attribute success to luck than ability (Stipek & Gralinski, 1991). Achievement differences in math between boys and girls decrease when girls take more math courses (American Association of University Women, 1992). Instruction also appears to make a difference; girls do better in math when it is taught in noncompetitive, cooperative small groups (Fennema & Peterson, 1987), and in classrooms that emphasize labs and relate content to students' background experiences (Lee, Burkam, & Smerdon, 1997).

Gender Stereotyping Influences Career Decisions. Differences in students' views of gender-appropriate careers appear as early as kindergarten (Kochenberger-Stroeher, 1994). Significantly, when the children chose nontraditional roles for males or females, their choice was based on personal experience (e.g., "One of my friends' dad is a nurse").

These gender-stereotypic views influence career decisions. In 1980, 30% of college-bound high school women, compared with 50% of comparable men, planned to study science and engineering in college. At the doctoral level, the differences were even greater: Only 25% of the doctoral degrees in science and engineering were awarded to women (National Research Council, 1980). More recent research shows that this trend continues: girls were less than half as likely as boys to pursue careers in engineering and physical and computer sciences (American Association of University Women, 1992). The percentage of female doctors (20%), lawyers (21%), and engineers (8%) remains disturbingly low (U.S. Bureau of the Census, 1996).

Gender Differences: Implications for Teachers

Significantly, girls who go into science-related fields reported that the encouragement received from teachers was a critical factor in their career decisions (American Association of University Women, 1992). Further, intervention studies designed to increase female participation in math and science resulted in girls having more positive attitudes

---

4.38

Explain why teachers might have difficulty recognizing different treatment of boys and girls.

4.39

Explain female achievement in math and science, using Erikson's stage of identity versus confusion as the basis for your explanation.

4.40

How do you think gender-related differences in math and science are influenced by SES? What implications does this have for teachers of low-SES students?

Science activities that actively involve female students in designing and carrying out science experiments help combat gender stereotypes that the sciences are a male domain.

about math and taking more courses in these central areas (Fennema & Koehler, 1983; Mason & Kahle, 1989).

Teachers can help reverse the negative impact of gender stereotyping in education. As with many aspects of individual differences, the first step is awareness. Teachers who know they may unconsciously treat boys and girls differently are more sensitive to their own behavior. The next step is to make every effort to treat boys and girls as equally as possible and to encourage the same academic behaviors in both.

"Academic" behavior is a key idea. You're not saying that boys and girls are the same in every way, and you're not asking them to be. You are, however, suggesting that, academically, they will be given the same opportunities and encouragement.

Open communication is critical. Simply telling the students that teachers often treat boys and girls differently and that you're going to try to treat them equally is a positive step. Then make your best effort to be true to your commitment.

At-Risk Students

I was told that "the class was all right, but some children were pretty hopeless." I was also told that the children were used to working through their arithmetic book and were tested at the end of each week. After receiving the first test papers in long division, most of which were disastrous, I did not know what to do. Nothing in my training had prepared me for a class where some children failed because they did not understand the meaning of zero, some because they had not learned how to carry over numbers from one stage to another; others seemed to have very little understanding of division and would try to divide the smaller number by the larger one, while some children seemed confused and unable to make any sense of the set number work.

I subsequently divided the papers into small groups according to the main errors they revealed, and spent my next lunch breaks working with the children on their own specific difficulties. I soon realized that some of the "hopeless" children were pretty bright, but for different reasons had lost confidence in their ability to cope with their schoolwork. However, I found out that when each child was helped to understand the specific problem in arithmetic that had been holding him back, his progress was not only remarkable, but also quite out of proportion to the effort I invested. (Butler-Por, 1987, p. 3)

The school population is changing. For example, an increasing percentage of students don't come from two-parent households where the father works and the mother stays home. Instead, both parents probably work, and the likelihood of a single-parent family is much higher than it's been in the past (Maciones, 1994).

Who are the students of tomorrow? The class of 2001, which started kindergarten in 1988, has this profile:

- Minority enrollment levels now range from 70% to 96% in the nation's 15 largest school systems.
- Twenty-five percent of U.S. children currently live below the poverty level, the highest proportion in more than 20 years.
- Fifteen percent of U.S. schoolchildren today have a physical or mental disability.
- Fourteen percent are children of teenage mothers.
- Fourteen percent are children of unmarried parents.
- Ten percent have poorly educated, sometimes functionally illiterate, parents.
- Between one fourth and one third of today's schoolchildren have no adult at home when they return from school.
- Twenty-five percent (or more) will not finish high school (Kellogg, 1988).

These figures have critical implications for schools and teachers. Educating these children will be more difficult: the students of tomorrow will be more academically and linguistically diverse, less cared for, and less ready to profit from schools. To meet the challenge, teachers will have to adapt their instruction to meet the needs of these students.

At-Risk Students: A Definition

Let's look again at Juan in our case study at the beginning of the chapter. He is a cultural minority from a low-SES background, he missed a great deal of school, and he was retained in the fourth grade. His tendency to be easily offended suggests low self-esteem. Juan exhibits several characteristics of an at-risk student (see Table 4.4).

At-risk students *are those in danger of failing to complete their education with the skills necessary to survive in a modern technological society* (Slavin, Karweit, & Madden, 1989). The term came into wide use after the National Commission on Excellence in Education proclaimed the United States a "nation at risk" (National Commission on Excellence in Education, 1983). The report emphasized the critical link between education and economic well-being in the modern technological society. Since that time, much attention has been given to problems and issues relating to at-risk students (Vito

4.41

Using our discussion of the influences of SES and home culture on learning, explain why at-risk students are more difficult to teach. What instructional adjustments need to be made?

4.42

Why are at-risk students increasingly seen as both educational and economic problems? Will this trend increase or decrease? Why?

Table 4.4 Characteristics of at-risk students

Background Factors	
Low SES	Minority
Inner city	Non-native English speaker
Male	Divorced families
Transient	

Educational Problems	
High dropout rate	Management problems
Low grades	Low self-esteem
Retention in grade	High criminal activity rates
Low achievement	Low test scores
Low involvement in extracurricular activities	Dissatisfaction with and lack of interest in school
Low motivation	
Poor attendance	High suspension rates
High rates of drug use	

& Connell, 1988). It is a virtual certainty that you will have some of these students in your classes.

At-risk students have learning problems and adjustment difficulties, and they often fail even though they are capable of succeeding (Scott, 1988; Vito & Connell, 1988). These students used to be called *underachievers,* but the term *at-risk* more clearly signals the long-term consequences of school failure. A male high-school dropout, for example, will earn a quarter of a million dollars less over a lifetime than a high-school graduate. Families whose primary breadwinners lack high-school diplomas earned 30% less in 1987 than they did in 1973 (adjusted for inflation) (Mishel & Frankel, 1991). Many blue collar and nonskilled jobs that existed earlier no longer exist today and are becoming even rarer in our technologically oriented society.

We see from Table 4.4 that at-risk students suffer from myriad academic, social, and emotional problems. The presence of "male" as a background factor needs clarification. Though research shows that males are more likely to experience difficulties in school and to drop out, many low-SES female students who either leave school before graduation or graduate with inadequate survival skills will live in poverty. Girls who drop out commonly do so for school-related reasons and are more likely to end up in poverty than male dropouts (American Association of University Women, 1992). In addition, many girls who drop out are pregnant and are left with the burden of single parenting on a below-the-poverty-level income. Being at risk is a problem facing both male and female students.

Before continuing, let's consider a note of caution. Some educators worry that use of the term *at-risk* is ill-advised because it blames students for the problem and doesn't hold schools accountable for their education (Franklin, 1997; Benard, 1994). Critics contend that the term results in low expectations for success and concomitant low achievement. Teachers need to guard against negative stereotyping as they work with these students and continually ask themselves, "Am I providing every opportunity for success for all students?" The following sections describe some practices to help ensure that this occurs.

At-Risk Students: Promoting Resilience

Continuing research on at-risk students has resulted in the concept of *resilience*. **Resilience** *results in a heightened likelihood of success in school and in other aspects of life despite environmental adversities* (Wang, Haertel, & Walberg, 1995). Researchers have become interested in resilience for both theoretical and practical reasons. Theoretically, the study of resilience helps us understand the larger process of development, especially as it occurs in at-risk youth. Practically, the study of resilient youth offers the possibility of practices that result in healthy, academically successful learners.

The study of resilience focuses on youth who have survived and even prospered despite obstacles such as poverty, poor health care, and fragmented services. Resilient children have well-developed "self systems," including high self-esteem and feelings that they are in control of their destinies. They are good at setting personal goals, possess good interpersonal skills, and have positive expectations for success (Benard, 1993; Wang et al., 1995). These strengths pay off in higher academic achievement, motivation, and satisfaction with school (Waxman & Huang, 1996).

How do these adaptive skills develop? Resilient children come from families that are nurturant and caring. Their families provide structure and hold high moral and academic expectations for their children (Masten, Morison, Pelligrini, & Tellegen, 1990). Resilient youth also come from schools that are both demanding and supportive; in many instances, schools served as a home away from home (Haynes & Comer, 1995). Let's look more closely at these connections between school experiences and the development of resiliency.

4.43

Identify two of Gardner's multiple intelligences that are particularly important for resilient children.

Resilient children come from homes and classrooms that are supportive but demanding and where caring adults provide nuturant challenge.

Effective Schools for At-Risk Students

Important research has been conducted on schools that are effective in developing student resilience (Good & Brophy, 1986; Wang et al., 1995). In these schools, students and teachers treat each other with respect, and personal responsibility and cooperation are stressed (Kim, Solomon, & Roberts, 1995; Roberts, Horn, & Battistich, 1995). The meaning and purpose of rules are emphasized, and mastery of content rather than passive attendance is required. Interestingly, these same characteristics seem to apply to other countries and cultures; a study done with at-risk students in Israel arrived at essentially the same conclusions (Gaziel, 1997). The characteristics of these schools are summarized in Figure 4.8.

4.44

Why are these characteristics of effective schools especially important for at-risk students?

Effective Teachers for At-Risk Students

While well organized and academically focused schools are important, they are not sufficient. Teachers are the critical factors in at-risk learners' success and development (Waxman, Huang, Anderson, & Weinstein, 1997). What makes an effective teacher for at-risk students? How do teachers help students develop resilience and make connections between their lives and the classroom? Let's have students from two different studies tell us. First, a ninth-grader offers this view:

> Well it's like you're family, you know. Like regular days like at home, we argue sometimes, and then it's like we're all brothers and sisters and the teachers are like our guardians or something.
> And the teachers really get on you until they try to make you think of what's in the future and all that. It's good. I mean it makes you think, you know, if every school was like that I don't think there would be a lot of people that would drop out. (Greenleaf, 1995, p. 2)

Now, an interview offers an additional perspective:

> *Melinda:* I act differently in his [Appleby's] class—I guess because of the type of teacher he is. He cuts up and stuff. . . . He is hisself—he acts natural—not tryin' to be what somebody wants him to be . . . he makes sure that nobody makes fun of anybody if they mess up when they read out loud.
> *Bernard:* [I like him] just by the way he talk, he were good to you . . . he don't be afraid to tell you how he feels—he don't talk mean to you, he just

Figure 4.8 Characteristics of effective schools

- Safe, orderly school climate
- Concentration on academic objectives
- Positive teacher attitudes and high expectations for all students
- Continuous monitoring of student performance
- Emphasis on the development of cooperation, a sense of community, and prosocial values
- Emphasis on student responsibility and self-regulation; decreased emphasis on external controls
- Strong parental involvement

speak right to you . . . some teachers only likes the smart people—and Coach Appleby don't do that.

LaVonne: Appleby's fun, he helps you when you feel bad, he'll talk to you. Appleby's got his own style, he makes his own self . . . he's not a brag . . . he get(s) into it—what they [the students] like. Appleby always has this funny grin. . . . He's funny, he tells jokes, laughs with the class. He makes me want to work, he makes me want to give and do something. . . . He show me that I can do it. (Dillon, 1989, pp. 241–242)

Alienation from school is a pattern that emerges from the research on at-risk students (Dillon, 1989; Goodenow, 1992a). Boredom, lack of involvement, and feelings of not belonging keep them on the fringe, prevent them from participating in school experiences, and inhibit motivation. When bright spots appear, they are often the result of teachers who care about these students as people and who communicate this caring through their actions.

A study of at-risk students at an urban junior-high found that teachers differed in their ability to help these students; the terms *high impact* and *low impact* were used to describe these differences (Kramer-Schlosser, 1992). High-impact teachers attempted to create caring, personal, learning environments and assumed responsibility for their students' progress. They talked with students, found out about their families, and shared their own lives. They maintained high expectations, used a variety of teaching strategies, and emphasized success and mastery of content. They motivated students through personal contacts, instructional support, and attempts to link school to students' lives.

Low-impact teachers, in contrast, were more authoritarian. They distanced themselves from students and placed primary responsibility for learning on them. They viewed instructional help as "babying the student" or "holding the student's hand." Instruction was teacher-directed and lecture-oriented, and primary responsibility for motivation was the student's.

In light of these differences, the effects are not surprising. At-risk students thought of low-impact teachers as adversaries, to be avoided if possible, tolerated if not. In contrast, they sought out the high-impact teachers, both in class and out. Researchers highlighted the human elements of caring and communication in concluding that "relationships with teachers were related to marginal students' behaviors and attitudes. Marginal students reported losing interest in learning when teachers distanced themselves" (Kramer-Schlosser, 1992, p. 138). Another study found effective teachers for at-risk students to be approachable, pleasant, easy to relate to, accepting, concerned, caring, and sensitive to the needs of students (Sanders & Jordan, 1997).

Personalized, caring, learning environments are important for all students; for at-risk students, they may be essential. But beyond the human element, what else can teachers do?

4.45

How are the characteristics of high-impact teachers similar to those of effective schools for at-risk students? What additional characteristics are added?

Effective Instruction for At-Risk Students: Structure and Support

When students entered the classroom, they saw a review assignment written on the chalkboard. As Mrs. Higby took roll and prepared for the lesson, they routinely started on the assignment.

At exactly 9:05, Mrs. Higby began with a brief review of the previous day's lesson. Both the pace and accuracy of the answers convinced her that the class knew the content and was ready to move on.

As she introduced two-column subtraction, she explained the new idea, guided the students through the steps by using manipulatives, and used questioning to link the manipulatives to the written numerals. Then she had students solve problems on their own mini-chalkboards and hold them up to allow her to check their solutions. Whenever mistakes occurred, she stopped, analyzed the errors, and helped students correct them.

When 90% of the class was correctly solving the problems, the teacher started the students on seatwork, which they checked in pairs when they were done. As they worked, she gave some extra help to those still having difficulty, periodically getting up to respond to pairs who disagreed with each other or had questions.

How should regular classroom teachers adapt their instruction to meet the needs of at-risk students? The overall suggestion is to offer more structure and support, while still emphasizing the learning strategies that will help these students become independent learners. In a review of the research in this area, Brophy (1986) concluded that "research has turned up very little evidence suggesting the need for qualitatively different forms of instruction for students who differ in aptitude, achievement level, socioeconomic status, ethnicity or learning style" (vol. IV, p. 122).

In short, teachers of at-risk students don't need to teach in fundamentally different ways; they need to provide enough instructional support to ensure student success while at the same time teaching students strategies that allow them to take control of their own learning. Effective strategies for at-risk students are outlined in Table 4.5 (Brophy, 1986; Gladney & Green, 1997; Wang et al., 1995). These are characteristic of good instruction in general; their importance with at-risk students is even more crucial.

4.46

Earlier, at-risk students were described as having poorer motivation than their not-at-risk peers. How do *greater structure and support, more frequent feedback, higher success rates,* and *high expectations* address this problem?

Table 4.5 Effective instruction for at-risk students

Characteristic	Description
Greater structure and support	Course expectations need to be clearly laid out, and assignments and grades need to be designed to encourage achievement.
Active teaching	The teacher needs to carry the content to students personally through interactive teaching rather than depend on curricular materials, such as the text or workbooks.
Instruction emphasizing student engagement	Interactive teaching with high questioning levels invites students to participate in lessons. Open-ended questions allow successful responses and give students a chance to explain their thinking.
More frequent feedback	Student progress should be monitored frequently through classroom questions, quizzes, and assignments.
Higher success rates	Classroom questions, assignments, and quizzes should be designed to maximize opportunities for success.
High expectations	Teachers should assume that all students can learn and emphasize higher order thinking in all classes.
Emphasis on learning strategies	Teachers teach and model learning strategies, emphasizing how they contribute to effective learning.
Emphasis on student motivation and self-regulation	Teachers stress the importance of student control over their own learning; teachers demonstrate and model how learning tasks can be accomplished through proactive planning, monitoring, and self-assessment.

Effective Instruction for At-Risk Students: The Need for Challenge

Increased structure and support may not be enough, however. One study of at-risk high school students found that many effective instructional practices were being implemented (Miller, Leinhardt, & Zigmond, 1988). The schools were adapting at every level, from school policies to classroom instruction, and this adaptation kept students in school. However, researchers also found

- Lowered expectations for students,
- Lack of emphasis on higher level thinking and problem solving, with a concomitant increase in low-level worksheets, and
- Student apathy and boredom.

In essence, the increased structure and support had resulted in a remedial program that lacked intellectual rigor and excitement.

Several programs have been developed to provide challenge for at-risk students. The *Accelerated Schools Program* builds on student strengths by combining high expectations with an enriched curriculum, focusing on a language-based approach in all academic areas (Levin, 1988; Rothman, 1991). The *Higher Order Thinking Skills Program (HOTS)* focuses on teaching students skills such as inferencing and generalizing to help at-risk students understand the process of understanding and how it contributes to learning (Pogrow, 1990).

Results from both programs have been encouraging. One Accelerated Schools site in San Francisco registered the highest achievement gains on standardized test scores in the city, and spring-to-spring comparisons of achievement gains in one HOTS program showed students were 67% above the national average in reading and 123% higher in math (Rothman, 1991).

Common to both programs are high expectations, emphasis on enrichment versus remediation, and the teaching of higher order thinking skills and cognitive strategies. Research in this area indicates that these strategies should be integrated into the regular curriculum, so that students can see their usefulness in practice (Means & Knapp, 1991).

The dilemma in working with at-risk students is how to be structured and responsive while still presenting a challenging intellectual menu. It isn't an easy task, but it can be done. It requires caring teachers, effective instruction, and administrative support. Admittedly, it requires enormous effort from teachers. However, seeing students who were previously unsuccessful and apathetic succeed and meet challenges can also be enormously rewarding.

4.47

Think about classes you've attended in which the content is trivial or the standards are low. How satisfied were you after you finished the classes? Why did you feel this way? What implications does this have for your teaching?

Classroom Connections

Eliminating Gender Bias in Your Classroom

1. Be sensitive to the possibilities of unconscious gender bias.
   - A junior-high teacher checks her interaction with her students by periodically videotaping one of her classes. She checks the tape to ensure that boys and girls are called on equally, are asked the same number of high-level questions, and receive the same quality of feedback.

- A first-grade teacher consciously deemphasizes sex roles and differences in her classroom. She has boys and girls share equally in chores and she eliminates gender-related activities, such as competition between boys and girls and forming lines by gender.

2. Actively attack gender bias in your teaching.
   - At the beginning of the school year, a social-studies teacher explains how gender bias hurts both sexes, and he forbids sexist comments in his classes. As classes study historical topics, he emphasizes the contributions of women and how they have been ignored by historians, and he points out the changes in views of gender over time.
   - A second-grade teacher selects stories and clippings from newspapers and magazines that portray women in nontraditional roles. She matter-of-factly talks about nontraditional careers with the students in reference to "when you grow up."

Using Effective Teaching Practices for At-Risk Students in Your Classroom

3. Communicate positive expectations by carefully specifying the procedures and requirements for your class.
   - A fourth-grade teacher spends the first two weeks of school teaching her students her classroom procedures. She makes short assignments, carefully monitors students to be certain the assignments are turned in, and immediately calls parents if an assignment is missing. This positive beginning lays the foundation for the rest of the year.
   - A junior-high math teacher takes extra time explaining his course procedures to his basic math classes. He explains how homework and quizzes contribute to the overall grade. He emphasizes the importance of attendance and effort and expects all to pass his course. He makes himself available before and after school for help sessions.

4. Make active attempts to involve parents or guardians in your classroom.
   - An English teacher sends home a description of his class expectations at the beginning of the school year. He makes this letter upbeat and positive and carefully explains student work requirements and grading practices. He also invites questions and comments from parents or other caregivers.
   - An inner-city elementary teacher makes a special effort to make parents welcome at parent–teacher conferences. She mails a letter of invitation a week before the conference and sends home an additional reminder with students. So that parents feel comfortable, she puts a welcome sign on the door and provides light refreshments in the waiting area.

5. Maintain high levels of student involvement in your teaching.
   - A sixth-grade teacher arranges the seating in her classroom so that minority and nonminority students are mixed. She combines small-group and whole-class instruction and, when she uses groupwork, she arranges the groups so they comprise high and low achievers, minorities and nonminorities, and boys and girls.
   - In language-arts activities, a teacher builds her teaching around questioning and examples. She comments, "My goal is to call on each student in the class at least twice during the course of a lesson. I also use a lot of repetition and reinforcement as we cover the examples."

6. Give frequent quizzes and return them the following day to provide feedback.
   - An earth-science teacher gives students a short quiz of one or two questions every day. It is discussed at the beginning of the following day, and students calculate their own averages each day during the grading period.

7. Use grading practices that promote success and encourage effort and achievement.
   - An eighth-grade math teacher computes students' averages after the third week of the grading period, shares them with students, and, from that point on, awards bonus points for improvement on tests and quizzes. She writes a brief note on the paper every time students improve, praising them for their effort and achievement.

Windows on Classrooms

Throughout this chapter, you've seen how sources of individuality—intelligence, socioeconomic status, culture, language, and gender—can influence learning. You also saw how some unfortunate combinations of these factors can place students at risk. Further, you've examined the implications these factors have for teachers: sensitivity to differences, building on students' backgrounds, structure and support, active teaching, frequent feedback, and high success rates with appropriate challenge.

Now read the following case study and assess the teacher's effectiveness in the context of the information you've studied.

Diane Smith is a fifth-grade teacher at Oneida Elementary, a school in a lower-middle-class section of the city. The school is crowded, and Diane has 33 students, 14 of whom are ethnic minorities, in a classroom built for 25. The students sit facing each other across an aisle as shown in the outline of her classroom on the next page. Her desk, with a filing cabinet behind it, is on one side of the screen—the chalkboard is behind the screen—with an area for the students to file papers on the opposite side of the screen, next to the door. A worktable is at the back of the room, and the pencil sharpener (ps) is near the door.

Diane has her day scheduled as follows:

8:55–9:00	Roll; announcements
9:00–10:00	Reading
10:00-11:00	Math
11:00–11:30	Science
11:30–11:45	Silent reading
11:45–11:55	Prepare for lunch
11:55–12:30	Lunch
12:30-12:35	Bathroom break
12:35–1:45	Language Arts
1:45–2:15	Social Studies
2:15–2:45	P.E.
2:45–3:00	Evaluate day; give homework; prepare for dismissal
3:00–3:15	Dismissal

In language arts, Diane has already covered adjectives with her students and now wants to cover the comparative and superlative forms of adjectives.

We join her class at 12:33 as the students are filing into the room from their lunch break. As they come into the room, they look at the screen and see a series of ten sentences on the overhead with directions stating, "Number your paper from 1 to 10, write down the adjective in each of the sentences, and also identify the noun that it modifies."

Her students move to their desks, take out paper, and begin working on the exercises.

At 12:35, all students are seated and busy. As the students are working, Diane surveys the room, identifying students who have pencils of different lengths and students whose hair colors vary. Deciding that she will use these as examples for her lesson, rather than the pencils and colored pieces of paper she brought with her, she puts the pencils and paper back into her filing cabinet.

"I can't see," Rick, the shortest boy in the class, announces as he bobs up and down in his desk next to the table at the back of the room.

"Rick and David (the student next to Rick in the last row near the table), move your desks into the aisle so that you will be able to see the screen," Diane directs.

Diane then walks among the students to see how they are doing. As she surveys their work, she sees that Eric and Amado have missed Item 3 but that the rest of the students have gotten all the exercises correct.

The students finish at 12:45, and Diane begins, "It looks like we're in good shape on these exercises, but let's go over them just to be sure."

Diane goes over each exercise, identifying both the adjective and the noun in each case.

At 1:05 they finish, and Diane announces, "Okay, very good, everyone. Now put your materials away, and we'll move on to today's lesson."

At 1:06, the students have their papers in their desks and

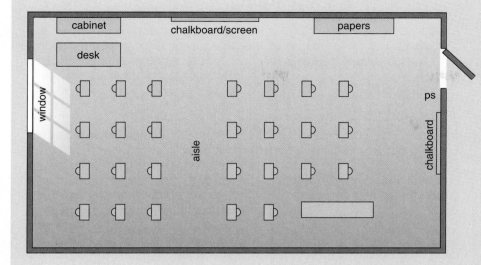

Diane begins, "Calesha and Daniel, hold your pencils up high so that everyone can see. What do you notice about the pencils? . . . Naitia?"

". . . Calesha's is red and Daniel's is blue."

"Okay. What else?" Diane smiles. . . . "Sheila?"

"You write with them."

"Indeed you do!" Diane nods and smiles again. "What else, Kelvin?" she asks quickly.

"Calesha's is longer."

"That's true," Diane confirms. "Does everyone see that? Hold them up again," she directs energetically.

Calesha and Daniel hold their pencils up again, and Diane moves to the chalkboard and writes:

> Calesha has a long pencil.
> Calesha has a longer pencil
> than does Daniel.

"Now, let's look at Matt and Leroy. What do you notice about their hair? . . . Judy?" Diane asks as she walks down the aisle.

As she walks back to the front of the room, Diane takes a note Elaine has been writing to Hanna, folds it so that Elaine sees she doesn't read it, and says quietly, "Please pay attention. You can have this back after school."

"Leroy's is black, and Matt's is brown," Randy responds.

"Okay. Good, Randy. So who has darker hair?"

"LEROY!" several in the class blurt out.

"Okay, everyone. I understand your eagerness, and I think it's good," Diane waves at the class. "Just as a reminder, what is one of our most important rules in here? . . . Todd?"

"We wait until you call on us before we answer."

"Okay. Excellent, everyone. You've all done very well with this. We just need a little reminder now and then.

"Now, let's see where we are. What did we say about Leroy's and Matt's hair? . . . Vicki?"

"Leroy's was darker."

"Good!" and Diane then writes three more sentences on the chalkboard, and they appeared as follows:

> Calesha has a long pencil.
> Calesha has a longer pencil
> than does Daniel.
> Leroy has black hair.
> Matt has brown hair.
> Leroy has darker hair than
> does Matt.

"Now, let's look at the adjectives in the sentences and compare them with each other. How do they compare? . . . Heather?"

". . . The adjectives in the bottom sentences have an -er on the end of them," Heather responds hesitantly.

"Yes, good," Diane smiles reassuringly.

"So, what are we doing in each of the sentences? . . . Jason?" Diane continues.

"We're comparing two things to each other."

"Very good, Jason! And what are we comparing in the first sentence? . . . Lawsikia?"

"The length of the pencils."

"And how about the second sentence? . . . Jana?"

"The color of Leroy's and Matt's hair."

"Good! Now, Calesha and Daniel, hold your pencils up again, and Kerri and David, you hold yours up too. Now, what do you notice? . . . Tom?"

"Kerri's pencil is longer than any of the others."

"Good, Tom. We can see that it is. Now, look at Teresa's hair. What do you notice about it? . . . Angie?"

"It's blonde."

"Yes, it is," Diane nods, and she then writes the following three more sentences on the chalkboard:

Calesha has a long pencil.
Calesha has a longer pencil than does Daniel.
Kerri has the longest pencil.
Leroy has black hair.
Matt has brown hair.
Teresa has blonde hair.
Leroy has darker hair than does Matt.
Leroy has the darkest hair.

"Now, what do you notice about the adjectives in the third set of sentences? . . . Sean?"

Sean suddenly looks up at the sound of his name. ". . . Could you repeat the question?"

"What do you notice about the adjectives in the third set of sentences?" Diane repeats.

". . . They have -est on the end of them," Sean says hesitantly.

"Okay. Good, Sean. And what did we do in each of those cases? . . . Spence?"

"We compared the pencils and the hair."

"How many pencils? . . . Steve?"

"Four."

"And how many people's hair? . . . Debbie?"

"Three."

"So, how do we write adjectives if we compare two things? . . . Todd?"

"We put an -er on the end of them."

"And suppose we have three or more things. Then what? . . . Sara?"

"We put an -est on them."

"Very good, everyone. In describing nouns, if we're comparing two, we use the comparative form of the adjective, which has an -er on the end, and if we have three or more, we have an -est on the end of the adjective.

"Now, look," Diane continues, and she reaches back and takes a tennis ball and a golf ball from her desk. "Write a sentence that tells us about the size of the two balls."

The students then take out paper and begin writing their sentences. As they work, Diane walks up and down the rows, looking at each student's work.

"Now let's look at some sentences," Diane begins after a few

minutes. "Someone volunteer a sentence, and I'll write it on the chalkboard. . . . Okay, Rashad?"

"The tennis ball is bigger than the golf ball," Rashad volunteers.

"Very good, Rashad. And why did you write bigger with an 'er' in your sentence?"

"We're comparing the size of two balls."

"That's excellent. Now, I want you to write a paragraph that has in it at least two examples that use the comparative form of adjectives and at least two other examples that use the superlative form of the adjectives. Underline the adjectives in each case."

The students then begin writing their paragraphs. As they work, Diane circulates among them, periodically stopping for a few seconds to comment on a student's work and to offer suggestions.

At 1:40, Diane announces, "All right, everyone. Please turn in your paragraphs; we're going to get ready for social studies."

The students then pass their papers forward. By 1:45, the students have turned in their papers and have their social studies books out and waiting.

Questions for Discussion and Analysis

Analyze Diane's teaching. In conducting your analysis, consider the following questions. In each case, be specific and take information directly from the case study to defend your assessment.

1. Describe how Diane provided structure and support in her teaching. How effective was this structure and support?

2. Did Diane demonstrate active teaching? Cite specific examples to support your answer.

3. To what extent was Diane's teaching designed to emphasize active engagement of the students? Again, cite specific examples.
4. How did Diane attempt to ensure success in her teaching?
5. Most of Diane's students are from relatively low SES backgrounds. Overall, how effective was her teaching for these students?
6. To what extent did Diane display culturally responsive teaching in her lesson?
7. To what extent did Diane's teaching reflect sensitivity to gender issues?
8. How effective was Diane's teaching for at-risk students?

Summary

Students differ in intelligence, socioeconomic status (SES), culture, and gender, each of which influences learning. Certain combinations of these factors place students at risk of not being able to take full advantage of their educational experience.

Intelligence

Intelligence is the ability to think and reason abstractly, to solve problems, and to acquire new knowledge. Some theories suggest that intelligence is a single entity; others describe intelligence as existing in several forms.

Experts disagree about the contributions of heredity and environment on the development of intelligence. *Nature* advocates argue that intelligence is genetically determined; *nurture* proponents contend that it is influenced primarily by a child's cumulative experiences. Most theorists believe that intelligence is determined by a combination of the two.

The most common response to differences in ability has been to group students according to those differences. Within- and between-class ability grouping is common in elementary schools; tracking is prevalent in middle and secondary schools. Ability grouping can lower performance and stigmatize students in low-ability classes.

Socioeconomic Status

Socioeconomic status (SES) includes parents' income, occupation, and level of education. SES can strongly influence student attitudes, values, background experiences, and school success.

Culture

Culture helps determine the attitudes, values, customs, and behavior patterns a child brings to school. The match between a child's culture and the school has a powerful influence on school success. Culturally responsive teaching creates links between a student's culture and classroom instruction.

Language

Language is a crucial aspect of culture and ethnicity. An increasing number of students are coming to U.S. classrooms with limited expertise in English. Bilingual programs are designed to teach English while maintaining the first language. ESL programs attempt to teach English as quickly as possible.

Gender

Gender differences in aptitude or intelligence are minor and are caused primarily by different treatment of boys and girls. Teachers can minimize the negative effects of gender differences by treating boys and girls equally and by actively combating negative stereotypes in their teaching.

At-Risk Students

At-risk students are more likely to exit school with subminimal learning skills. Effective schools for at-risk students stress high expectations, an academic focus, continuous monitoring of progress, and strong parent involvement. Effective programs for at-risk students prevent rather than remediate learning problems by being flexible and adaptive to student needs. Effective teachers for at-risk students hold high expectations for academic success, use a variety of instructional and motivational strategies, and demonstrate caring through sincere interest in students' lives. Effective instruction for at-risk students provides greater structure and support, more active teaching, greater student engagement, and more feedback with higher success rates. Research also documents the need for challenge in classes for at-risk students; effective teachers balance support with challenge to create lessons that are both stimulating and successful. The study of resilient youth provides teachers with an overall goal for their work with at-risk students, as well as concrete suggestions for developing healthy students.

Important Concepts

ability grouping (p. 110)

at-risk students (p. 136)

basic interpersonal communication skills (p. 128)

bidialecticism (p. 125)

cognitive academic language proficiency (p. 128)

cultural deficit theories (p. 123)

cultural difference theories (p.123)

cultural inversion (p. 118)

culturally responsive teaching (p. 123)

culture (p. 117)

dialect (p. 124)

English as a second language (ESL) programs (p. 127)

ethnicity (p. 117)

intelligence (p. 103)

maintenance bilingual programs (p. 127)

nature view of intelligence (p. 109)

nurture view of intelligence (p. 109)

resilience (p. 138)

socioeconomic status (SES) (p. 113)

tracking (p. 111)

transitional bilingual programs (p. 128)

5

Learners with Exceptionalities

CHAPTER OUTLINE

Sabrina Curtis is a beginning first-grade teacher in a large inner-city school district. She survived the hectic first weeks of school and was beginning to feel comfortable as she worked her way into the routines of teaching. At the same time, something bothered her.

"It's kind of frustrating," she admitted, sandwich in hand as she shared her half-hour lunch break with Clarisse, a "veteran" of three years who had become her friend and confidant. "I'm teaching the students, but some of them just don't seem to 'get it.'"

"Maybe you're being too hard on yourself," Clarisse responded. "Students are different. Remember some of the stuff you studied in college? One thing they emphasized was that it just takes some students a little longer to mature."

"Well, . . . yes, . . . I understand that, but that seems almost too easy. I still have this feeling. For instance, there's Rodney. You've seen him on the playground. He's a cute boy, but his engine is stuck on fast," she smiled wryly, rolling her eyes up. "I can barely get him to sit in his seat, much less work.

"When he sits down to do an assignment, he's all over his desk, squirming and wiggling. It takes just the smallest distraction to set him off. He can usually do the work when he sticks to it, but that's a major challenge for him. I've spoken with his mother, and he's the same way at home. I wonder if he has some type of learning disability.

"Then there's Amelia; she's so sweet, but she simply doesn't get it. I've tried everything under the sun with her. I explain it, and the next time, it's as if it's all brand new again. I feel sorry for her, because I know she gets frustrated because she can't keep up with the other students. What she seems to lack are basic learning strategies such as paying attention and keeping track of her assignments. When I work with her individually, it seems to help, but I wish I had more time to spend with her. I just see her falling farther and farther behind."

"Maybe it's not your fault. You're supposed to be bright and energetic and do your best, but you're going to burn yourself out if you keep this up," Clarisse encouraged. "Check with the Teacher Assistance Team. Maybe these students need some extra help."

As you saw in Chapter 4, students differ in several ways, and effective teachers consider these differences when they plan and teach. In some cases, the *differences are such that special help and resources are needed to help students reach their full potential.* In these cases, the students are said to have **exceptionalities.** These exceptionalities range from mild learning disabilities and physical impairments to gifted and talented. Help and resources include special schools, self-contained classrooms, resource rooms, and inclusion in regular classrooms with the support of specially trained professionals.

Special education refers to *instruction designed to meet the unique needs of students with exceptionalities.* In the past, special education often meant separate classrooms for these students; today the practice of inclusion attempts to integrate students with exceptionalities into the regular flow of school and classroom life. Inclusion requires teachers in regular classrooms to play an ever-increasing role in identifying and teaching students who need special help. This chapter is designed to help you prepare for that role.

After you have completed your study of this chapter, you should be able to meet the following objectives:

- Explain the role of classroom teachers in working with students with exceptionalities.
- Explain how different exceptionalities—mental retardation, learning disabilities, behavior disorders, communication disorders, and visual and hearing impairments—affect student learning.
- Describe different methods of identifying and teaching students who are gifted and talented.
- Explain how instructional strategies can be adapted to meet the needs of students with exceptionalities.

Incidents like the ones in the opening case study are not uncommon. Although we can't be certain from the brief descriptions, Rodney and Amelia may have problems that prevent them from taking full advantage of their educational opportunities. As teachers, we all work with students who, despite our best efforts, fail to learn as their classmates do.

Students with Learning Problems

The terms *children with exceptionalities, special education students, children with handicaps, students with special needs,* and *individuals with disabilities* have all been used to describe students needing additional help to reach their full potential. Currently, the term *students with disabilities* is often preferred, because it emphasizes that disabilities can be altered and that they don't necessarily result in handicapped performance (Hallahan & Kauffman, 1994). On any given day, about 5 million students are enrolled in special programs, two-thirds of them for relatively minor problems (Heward, 1996). Approximately 1 of 10 students in a typical school receives special education services and the kinds of disabilities range from mild learning problems to physical impairments such as deafness and blindness (U.S. Department of Education, 1994). Federal legislation has created categories to identify specific learning problems, and educators use these categories in developing programs to meet the needs of each type of student.

Use of categories and the labeling that results is controversial (King-Sears, 1997). Advocates argue that categories provide a common language for professionals and encourage specialized instruction that meets the specific needs of all students (Heward, 1996). Opponents claim that categories are arbitrary, many differences exist within the categories, and categorizing encourages educators to treat students as labels rather than as people (Podell & Soodak, 1997). Despite the controversy, however, these categories are widely used, so teachers need to be familiar with the terms and the implications they have for working with students.

Figure 5.1 represents the percentage of students in each of the categories commonly used in education (U.S. Department of Education, 1994). The figure shows that three categories—mental retardation, learning disabilities, and behavior disorders—make up a large majority of the total population (about 70%) of students with disabilities, and they are ones you will most likely encounter in your classroom.

Mental Retardation

Gail Toomey watched her first-grade class as they worked on their reading assignment. Most of the class was working quietly, with occasional whispers and giggles. Stacy, in contrast, was out of her seat for the third time, supposedly sharpening her pencil. Gail had reminded her once to sit down and this time went over to see what the problem was.

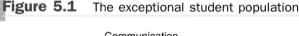

Figure 5.1   The exceptional student population

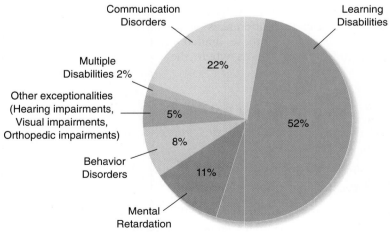

Source: U.S. Department of Education (1994).

"I can't do this! I don't get it!" Stacy responded in frustration when Gail asked her why she hadn't started her work.

After helping her calm down, Gail worked with Stacy for a few moments, but she could tell by Stacy's responses and her facial expression that she truly didn't "get" the assignment. Gail made a note to herself to talk to a special educator about Stacy.

5.1

Why might some educators prefer the term *intellectually handicapped*?

All first-grade teachers have had experiences similar to Gail's. Stacy, like Amelia in our opening case study, seems to be slower than others and may be frustrated because she can't keep up with her peers. Unfortunately, this problem is often not identified until students are well into their school experience—sometimes several years. Many of these students have mild mental retardation. (You may also encounter the terms *educationally* or *intellectually handicapped,* which some educators prefer.)

The American Association on Mental Retardation (AAMR) defines **mental retardation** as follows:

Mental retardation refers to substantial limitations in present functioning. It is characterized by significantly subaverage intellectual functioning, existing concurrently with related limitations in two or more of the following applicable adaptive skill areas: communication, self-care, home living, social skills, community use, self-direction, health and safety, functional academics, leisure, and work. Mental retardation manifests before age 18. (AAMR Ad Hoc Committee on Terminology and Classification, 1992, p. 5)

This definition emphasizes two important characteristics (Turnbull, Turnbull, Shank, & Leal, 1995). The first identifies limitations in intellectual functioning, as indicated by difficulties in learning; the second focuses on adaptive skills, such as communication, self-care, and social ability. The characteristics suggest the need for support that shifts the focus from the person's limitations to an array of services designed to meet the person's needs.

5.2

In Chapter 4, *intelligence* was defined as "the capacity to acquire knowledge, the ability to think and reason in the abstract, and the capability for solving problems." To which of these is adaptive behavior most closely related? least related?

Prior to the 1960s, definitions of mental retardation were based primarily on below-average scores on intelligence tests, but this approach had at least three problems. First, any test has built-in error, and this imprecision means that decisions about people should be made with caution. Second, disproportionate numbers of minorities and non-English-speaking students were identified as mentally retarded and placed in inappropriate educational settings (Hallahan & Kauffman, 1994; Hardman, Drew, & Egan, 1996). Third, individuals with the same IQ scores varied widely in their ability to cope with the real world, and the differences were unpredictable based on the tests alone (Heward, 1996). Because of these limitations, the definition was broadened to include adaptive functioning. This is where the classroom teacher's input is essential.

Levels of Mental Retardation

There are four levels of mental retardation, and each relates to the amount of support needed (Luckasson et al., 1992):

- Intermittent: Support on an as-needed basis
- Limited: Support consistently needed over time
- Extensive: Regular (e.g., daily) support required
- Pervasive: High-intensity, potentially life-sustaining support required

This classification system replaces the one based on IQ scores. That system categorized people as having either mild (50 to 70 IQ), moderate (35 to 50 IQ), or severe and profound (IQ below 35) mental retardation. The transition from the older, IQ-anchored system to the new one is not complete, so you might encounter both in your work.

Programs for Students With Mental Retardation

Programs for students who have intermittent (mild) mental retardation focus on creating support systems to augment existing instructional programs. These students are often placed in regular classrooms and instruction is adapted to meet their special needs. Attempts are made to help students fit in both socially and academically.

Research indicates that these students often fail to acquire basic learning strategies (such as maintaining attention, organizing and memorizing new material, and studying for tests) that regular students pick up naturally (Choate, 1997; Heward, 1996). Amelia, in our opening case study, was an example of a student who needed additional instructional support to help her function in the classroom. Sabrina recognized this need and attempted to provide additional support by working with her one-on-one.

5.3

Again consider the definition of intelligence from Chapter 4 referred to in Note 5.2. To which of these dimensions is strategy training most directly targeted? Explain.

Learning Disabilities

Tammy Fuller, a middle-school social-studies teacher, was surprised as she scored Adam's test. He seemed to be doing so well. He was rarely absent, paid attention, and participated willingly and intelligently. Why was his test score so low? Tammy made a mental note to watch him more closely, because his classroom behavior and his test performance were inconsistent.

In her second unit, Tammy emphasized both independent and collaborative work, so she prepared study guide questions and had students work in groups to study the material. As she circulated around the room, she noticed that Adam's sheet was empty; when she asked him about it, he mumbled something about not having time the night before. Because the success of the unit depended on students coming to class prepared, Tammy asked Adam to come in after school to complete his work.

Adam arrived promptly at 3:10 and opened his book to the chapter. When Tammy stopped to check on his progress 15 minutes later, his page was blank; in another 15 minutes, it was still virtually empty.

As she sat down to talk with him, he appeared embarrassed and evasive. When they started to work on the questions together, she discovered that he couldn't read the text.

Some students, such as Adam, have *average* or *above average intelligence* but, despite teachers' best efforts, have a difficult time learning. These are students with **learning disabilities (LDs),** *difficulties in acquiring and using listening, speaking, reading, writing, reasoning, or mathematical abilities* (The National Joint Committee on Learning Disabilities, 1994). Problems with reading, writing, and listening are most common.

Learning disabilities are presumed to be due to central nervous system dysfunction, and they may exist along with, but are not caused by, other handicapping conditions such as sensory impairment or cultural differences. Experts also agree that many differences exist among students with learning disabilities (Podell & Soodak, 1997).

Although it is probable that every classroom will have students with learning disabilities they are often overlooked because learning disabilities are difficult to identify.

5.4

Identify at least one similarity and one difference between learning disabilities and intellectual disabilities or mental retardation.

Students with learning disabilities comprise the largest group of students with exceptionalities—approximately 4% of the total school-age population. The category first became widely used in the early 1960s, and the number of school-age children diagnosed as LD has continually increased, so that they comprise over half of all children with disabilities (U.S. Department of Education, 1994).

Characteristics of Students with Learning Disabilities

Students with learning disabilities have problems such as those outlined in Table 5.1. However, each student with a learning disability is unique, and educational adaptations should be individualized.

Some of these characteristics are typical of general learning problems or immaturity. Unlike developmental lags, however, problems associated with learning disabilities often increase over time instead of disappear. Students fall farther behind in achievement, management problems increase, and self-esteem decreases (Hardman et al., 1996; Heward, 1996). Lowered achievement and reduced self-esteem exacerbate each other and result in major learning problems.

Rodney, in the case study at the beginning of this chapter, may have a learning disability. He's hyperactive, easily distracted, and has difficulties focusing his attention. Sabrina is wise in seeking additional help for him. The characteristics he displays suggest either a learning disability or attention deficit/hyperactivity disorder.

Table 5.1   Characteristics of students with learning disabilities

General Patterns
Hyperactivity and fidgeting
Lack of coordination and balance
Attention deficits
Disorganization and tendency toward distraction
Lack of follow-through and completion of assignments
Uneven performance (e.g., capable in one area, extremely weak in others)

Academic Performance	
Reading	Lacks reading fluency
	Reverses words (e.g., *saw* for *was*)
	Frequently loses place
Writing	Makes jerky and poorly formed letters
	Has difficulty staying on line
	Is slow in completing work
	Has difficulty in copying from chalkboard
Math	Has difficulty remembering math facts
	Mixes columns (e.g., 10s and 1s) in computing
	Has trouble with story problems

Attention Deficit/Hyperactivity Disorder

Attention deficit/hyperactivity disorder (AD/HD) is *a learning problem characterized by students' inability to focus their attention on the learning task at hand*. Attention problems and hyperactivity are often connected with a learning disability; estimates indicate that at least a third of students with learning disabilities also have attention problems (Hallahan & Kauffman, 1994).

The American Psychiatric Association (1994) has identified three categories of AD/HD: (a) *inattentive*—students who are forgetful, easily distracted, and have problems focusing their attention; (b) *hyperactive-impulsive*—students who fidget and talk excessively; or (c) *combined*—a category that includes characteristics of the other two. Characteristics of AD/HD include:

- Difficulty in concentrating and failure to finish tasks
- Failure to listen and easy distractibility
- Inordinate need for supervision
- Impulsiveness (e.g., acting before thinking, shifting from one activity to another)
- Frequent calling out in class and difficulty awaiting turns

Collectively, these characteristics suggest an impaired ability to delay responding to stimuli (Barkley, 1994). It's easy to see why students with AD/HD have difficulties adjusting to the "sit-down" pace of school life, where many activities are done quietly at a desk (Nahmias, 1995).

AD/HD usually appears early (at age 2 or 3), and up to three to nine times as many boys as girls are identified (American Psychiatric Association, 1994). Treatments range from medication (e.g., the highly controversial drug Ritalin) to reinforcement programs and structured teaching environments (described later in this chapter). Diagnosis and treatment of AD/HD are usually done in consultation with medical experts.

5.5

Explain the high ratio of boys to girls with AD/HD from a genetic or nature position, from an environmental or nurture position, and from an interactionist position.

Identifying and Working with Students Who Have Learning Disabilities

As with all exceptionalities, identification is the first step, and it must be done early to prevent damaging effects from accumulating. Although early identification is essential, at least two factors complicate the process. First, uneven rates of development can easily be mistaken for learning disabilities, and second, classroom management issues can complicate identification. Students with learning disabilities frequently display inappropriate classroom behavior, and misbehaving students are referred as LD at a much higher rate than those who behave. On the other hand, LD students who comply with rules and complete assignments on time are often passed over for referral. These patterns can be gender related; more boys than girls are identified because boys tend to act out, whereas girls tend to be quiet.

Using Classroom-Based Information for Identification.   The teacher plays an important role in identifying and working with a learning disability. Information taken from teachers' assessments of behavior, anecdotal records, direct observation, and curriculum-based measurements are combined with test scores. Often, a discrepancy model, which looks for differences in three areas, will be used to diagnose the problem (Salvia & Ysseldyke, 1988):

5.6

Why wouldn't the discrepancy model be useful in identifying students who have an intellectual disability or mental retardation?

1. Differences between intelligence and achievement test performance
2. Differences between intelligence test scores and school achievement
3. Large differences between subtests on either intelligence or achievement tests

The rationale is that performance in one area, such as an intelligence test, should predict performance in others; when the two are not comparable, a learning disability may be the cause.

Earlier we mentioned the problem of labeling. Critics contend that LD is a catch-all term for students who have learning problems (Kavale & Forness, 1995; Podell & Soodak, 1997). Part of this criticism results from the rapid growth of the category—nonexistent in the early 1960s to the largest at present. Before using the learning disability label, teachers should examine their own instruction to ensure it meets the needs of different students.

Adaptive Instruction.   Students with learning disabilities require modified instruction and teacher support. Because learning disabilities have different causes, the most effective strategies are tailored to meet each student's needs. One study of 25 learning disabled college students illustrates the range of modifications that increase success (Cowan, 1988). These students budgeted their time carefully, attended class regularly, and completed all work on time. To compensate for reading deficits, they always read in a quiet environment, subvocalized (read aloud to themselves), and even purchased previously highlighted books. In writing, they used a dictionary, frequently substituted an easier word if they had trouble spelling one, and asked other people to proofread their papers. Other strategies included using taped textbooks, tape-recording lectures to compensate for poor note taking, and asking for extra time on tests or for someone to help them read through the test questions.

5.7

Which of these adaptations could be most easily taught and incorporated into the regular classroom? What role might the teacher play?

Behavior Disorders

> Kyle came in from recess sweaty and disheveled, crossed his arms, and looked at the teacher defiantly. The playground monitor had reported another scuffle. Kyle had a history of these disturbances and was a difficult student. He struggled at his studies but could handle them if provided with enough structure. When he became frustrated, he would sometimes act out, often ignoring the feelings and rights of others.
>
> Ben, who sat next to Kyle, was so quiet that the teacher almost forgot he was there. He never caused problems. In fact, he seldom participated in class. He had few friends and walked around at recess by himself, appearing to consciously avoid other children.

Although their behaviors were very different, these two students both have a *behavior disorder.* This term is often used interchangeably with *emotional disturbance, emotional disability,* or *emotional handicap,* and you may encounter any of these terms in your work. *Behaviorally disordered* is sometimes preferred because it focuses on overt behavior instead of internal causes.

Students with **behavior disorders (BD)** *display serious and persistent age-inappropriate behaviors that result in social conflict, personal unhappiness, and school failure* (Kirk & Gallagher, 1989). In this definition, the terms *serious* and *persistent* are important. Many children occasionally fight with their peers, and all children go through periods when they want to be alone. When these patterns are chronic and interfere with normal development and school performance, however, a behavior disorder may exist.

Prevalence of Behavior Disorders

Estimates of the frequency of behavior disorders vary (Hardman et al., 1996). Some suggest that about 1% of the total school population and about 8% of the special education population have the problem (U.S. Department of Education, 1994), whereas others suggest that it's closer to 6% to 10% of the total population (Hallahan & Kauffman, 1994). Identification is a problem because the characteristics are elusive. In a study of teachers' assessments of 1,586 kindergarten through sixth-grade students, 60% of the students were classified as having a behavior problem at least once, but only 7% were identified as having problems serious enough to require special help (Rubin & Balow, 1978).

5.8

Offer another explanation for the disproportionate number of boys who are referred for special help because of behavior disorders (think about our discussion of gender and cultural differences in Chapter 4).

Kinds of Behavior Disorders

There are two types of behavior disorders, *externalizing* and *internalizing* (Hallahan & Kauffman, 1994). Students like Kyle fall into the externalizing category, with characteristics such as hyperactivity, uncooperativeness, defiance, hostility, and even cruelty. Externalizing children often don't respond to typical rules and consequences. Males are

Students with behavior disorders fall into two major categories; externalizing, characterized by acting out, and internalizing, characterized by social withdrawal and anxiety.

three times more likely to be labeled as having an externalizing behavior disorder than females, and a higher incidence of this category exists in low-SES and minority students. Evidence suggests that some aggressive behaviors are learned from aggressive parents and peers (Hallahan & Kauffman, 1994).

Internalized behavior disorders are characterized by social withdrawal, guilt, depression, and anxiety. Like Ben, these children lack self-confidence and are often shy, timid, and depressed—sometimes suicidal. They have few friends and are isolated and withdrawn (Walker & Bullis, 1991). Because they don't have the high profile of the acting-out student, they may go unnoticed, so a teacher's sensitivity and awareness is crucial in identifying these students.

Students with behavior disorders often have academic problems, some of which are connected with learning disabilities (Gelfand, Jenson, & Drew, 1988). The combination of these problems results in a dropout rate of 40%, the highest of any group of students with special needs (U.S. Department of Education, 1994).

Teaching Students with Behavior Disorders

Behavior Management Strategies. Students with behavior disorders often have problems monitoring and controlling their behaviors. Regular classroom teachers can help by providing an environment that invites participation and success while providing structure through clearly stated and uniformly enforced rules and expectations.

Behavioral management strategies can also be used. Some of them include:

- Positive reinforcement—Identifying and rewarding positive behaviors (e.g., negotiating for a wanted toy)

- Replacement—Teaching appropriate behaviors that substitute for inappropriate ones (e.g., expressing personal feelings versus verbal aggression toward another student)

- Extinction—Ignoring disruptive behaviors

5.9

Identify at least two similarities and two differences between students with learning disabilities and those with behavior disorders.

- Time out—Removing the child from opportunities for reward for brief periods of time
- Overcorrection—Requiring restitution beyond the damaging effects of the immediate behavior (e.g., requiring a child to return one of his own cookies in addition to the one he took from another student)

Self-Management Skills. Teaching self-management skills can also be effective in working with students with behavior disorders (Heward, 1996). For instance, students might be helped to identify behaviors they want to increase (such as making eye contact with the teacher) or decrease (such as finger-snapping or playing with a pencil). They are then taught to evaluate their behaviors when a timer goes off at their desks. By counting and graphing the results, students monitor their own behavior over the course of the day. The teacher also meets with them—frequently at first—to reinforce progress and to set new goals. This strategy has been successful in increasing behaviors, such as paying attention and responding in class, as well as decreasing others, like talking out and leaving seats without permission (Alberto & Troutman, 1995).

Teacher Flexibility and Sensitivity.   Students with behavior disorders can be difficult to teach, and frustrated teachers sometimes forget that they have unique needs. A school psychologist describes an encounter that illustrates this point.

> The psychologist was testing a four-year-old who had been referred to her for aggressive behaviors and acting "out of control in the classroom." The psychologist found the young boy to be friendly, polite, and cooperative, and the session went smoothly until the child announced he was done. When the psychologist tried to get him to continue, a behavioral outburst followed with screaming, kicking, and shoving and the boy running out of the room.
>
> I assumed the testing phase of the evaluation was over and started writing a few notes. . . . A few minutes later, however, the little boy returned . . . and said that he was ready to continue. After another 10 minutes or so . . . the child again said, "I'm done now," to which I replied, "That's fine." The child calmly got out of his chair, walked around the room for a minute, and then sat down to resume testing. This pattern was repeated. . . .
>
> It was easy to see in a one-to-one testing situation that this child recognized the limits of his concentration and coped with increasing frustration by briefly removing himself. . . . It is equally easy to see, however, how this behavior created problems in the classroom. By wandering around, he would be disrupting the learning of other children. When the teacher tried to make him sit back down, she was increasing his frustration by removing from him the one method he had developed for coping. (Griffith, 1992, p. 34)

But how do teachers deal with this behavior in the regular classroom? The psychologist suggested marking an area in the back of the room where the child could go when he became frustrated. With this safety valve in place, the teacher could return to her teaching and work with the boy on other, long-term coping strategies. By attempting to understand the acting-out child as an individual, the teacher was able to continue with her instructional agenda while meeting the needs of the student.

5.10

Which behavioral management strategy would be most effective in working with Kyle, the student at the beginning of this section? least effective? Explain.

Classroom Connections

Teaching Students with Exceptionalities in Your Classroom

1. Identify resources that are available for working with students with exceptionalities.
   - A beginning teacher talked with other teachers about their past experiences in working with students with exceptionalities: What approaches worked for them? Who was especially helpful in working with these students? Who would they turn to when they needed help?
   - A first-year teacher talked with the principal about programs and personnel available in the building and the school district. She made an effort to introduce herself to the special education team in the building and found out how the referral process works.

2. Use a variety of data sources for help in identifying and understanding the students with exceptionalities in your classroom.
   - A third-grade teacher started the school year by giving her students diagnostic work sheets in all the subject-matter areas. The work within each assignment was arranged in order of difficulty. After the teacher had a complete battery from each student, she spent a weekend reviewing the worksheets and identifying each student's strengths and weaknesses.
   - A junior-high teacher was having trouble with one student. After talking with the student's other teachers, he looked over her previous record and discussed the problem with the guidance counselor. Then he called the student in and talked with her about the problem directly.

3. Work to create a positive classroom learning environment for students who are mainstreamed in your classroom.
   - At the beginning of the school year, a first-grade teacher explains to the class where resource students go and why. He explains that all people are different and that some people learn in different ways.
   - A sixth-grade teacher sits with his pull-out students in one-to-one sessions to voice his support for the program and to explain that any assignments they miss will be written on assignment sheets for them. He also sends a letter home to parents, explaining these procedures and inviting their questions or comments.

Communication, Visual, and Hearing Disablities

In the previous section, we discussed mental retardation, learning disabilities, and behavior disorders, each of which interferes with learning in the regular classroom. In this section, we examine communication, visual, and hearing impairments, which can also influence learning.

Communication Disorders

Communication disorders interfere with students' abilities to receive and understand information from others and express their own ideas and questions. They exist in two forms. **Speech or expressive disorders** *involve problems in forming and sequencing* *sounds*. Examples are stuttering and mispronouncing words, such as saying, "I taw it" for "I saw it." **Language or receptive disorders** *include problems with understanding language or in using language to express ideas*. Language disorders are often connected to other problems, such as a hearing impairment, learning disability, or mental retardation.

As Table 5.2 indicates, there are three kinds of speech, or expressive, disorders. If they are chronic, a therapist is usually required, but sensitive teachers can help students cope with the emotional and social problems that are often associated with them.

Language Disorders

Language disorders are more serious than speech disorders and go beyond the production of sounds. The vast majority of students learn to communicate quite well by the time they start school, but a small percentage (less than 1%) experience problems expressing themselves verbally.

Symptoms of a language disorder include

- Seldom speaking, even during play,
- Using few words or very short sentences, and
- Overrelying on gestures to communicate.

The causes of language disorders include hearing loss, brain damage, learning disabilities, mental retardation, severe emotional problems, and inadequate experiences in a child's early developmental years. If they suspect a communication disorder, teachers should keep cultural diversity in mind. As you saw in Chapter 4, English is not the primary language for many students. The difficulties involved in learning both content and a second language should not be confused with communication disorders. These students will respond to an enriched language environment and teacher patience and understanding. Students with language disorders require the help of a language specialist.

Helping Students with Communication Disorders

Primary tasks for the teacher working with students who have communication disorders are identification, acceptance, and follow-through on classroom instruction. As with other exceptionalities, teachers play an important role in identification because they are in the best position to assess students' performances in classroom settings. Modeling and

5.11

Should teachers' interaction patterns, such as calling on students and waiting for them to answer, be different for students with speech disorders? Why or why not?

Table 5.2 Kinds of speech disorders

Disorder	Description	Example
Articulation disorders	Difficulty in producing certain sounds, including substituting, distorting, and omitting	'Wabbit' for rabbit 'Thit' for sit 'Only' for lonely
Fluency disorders	Repetition of the first sound of a word (stuttering)	'Y, Y, Y, Yes'
Voice disorders	Problems with the larynx or air passageways in the nose or throat	High-pitched or nasal voice

encouraging acceptance are crucial because teasing and social rejection can cause lasting emotional damage. It is not easy being a student who talks differently. In communicating with these students, a teacher should be patient and refrain from finishing sentences and correcting speech problems in class; this calls attention to the problem. In addition, cooperative and small-group activities provide opportunities for students to practice their language skills in informal and less threatening settings.

Visual Disabilities

One in ten students enters school with some type of visual impairment (Kirk & Gallagher, 1989). Fortunately, most can be corrected with glasses, surgery, or therapy. In some situations, though—approximately 1 child in 1,000—the impairment cannot be corrected. People with this condition have a **visual disability,** *an uncorrectable impairment that interferes with learning in the regular classroom.*

About 64% of visual impairments exist at birth, and most children are screened for visual problems when they enter elementary school. Some, however, do appear during the school years as a result of growth spurts, and teachers should remain alert to the possibility of an unscreened visual impairment in students. Some symptoms of vision problems are outlined in Figure 5.2.

Research on people with visual disabilities reveals little or no lag in intellectual development (Kirk & Gallagher, 1989), but word meanings in language development may not be as rich or elaborated because of the students' lack of visual experience with the world. As a result, hands-on experiences are even more important for students with visual disabilities than they are for other learners.

5.12

How would Piaget and Vygotsky each react to instructional modifications emphasizing hands-on experience for visually disabled students?

Working with Students Who Have Visual Disabilities

Suggestions for working with visually disabled students include seating them near chalkboards and overheads, verbalizing while writing on the board, and ensuring that duplicated handouts are dark and clear (Heward, 1996). Large-print books and magnifying aids also help adapt instructional materials. Peer tutors can provide assistance in explaining and clarifying assignments and procedures.

Figure 5.2 Symptoms of potential visual problems

1. Holding the head in an awkward position when reading, or holding the book too close or too far away.
2. Squinting and frequently rubbing the eyes.
3. Tuning out when information is presented on the chalkboard.
4. Constantly asking about classroom procedures, especially when information is on the board
5. Complaining of headaches, dizziness, or nausea.
6. Having redness, crusting, or swelling of the eyes.
7. Losing place on the line or page and confusing letters.
8. Using poor spacing in writing or having difficulty in staying on the line.

Source: Hallahan and Kaufman (1994).

Adaptive instructional devices, such as machines and books with large print, and braille printers and books, allow students with visual disabilities to integrate into the regular classroom.

Two possible side effects of a visual disability are lowered self-esteem and *learned helplessness.* Learned helplessness results from teachers and other students overreacting to the disability and doing for the student what the student, with training, can do alone. This can result in an unhealthy dependence on others and can compound self-esteem problems (Hallahan & Kauffman, 1994).

Hearing Impairments

Hearing impairments can be divided into two categories. A student who has a **partial hearing impairment** *uses a hearing aid and hears well enough to be taught through auditory channels.* A student who is **deaf** *has hearing that is impaired enough so that other senses, usually sight, are used to communicate.* Only about 1 student in 1,000 is deaf; 3 to 4 in 1,000 are severely hard of hearing (Kirk & Gallagher, 1989).

Hearing impairments result from rubella, or German measles, during pregnancy, heredity, complications during birth or pregnancy, meningitis, and other childhood diseases (Kirk & Gallagher, 1989). Unfortunately, in almost 40% of cases involving hearing loss, the cause is unknown; this makes prevention and remediation more difficult.

A trained audiologist working in a school screening program is the best method of identifying students with hearing problems, but these programs don't exist everywhere, and students can be overlooked because of transfers or absences. When such an omis-

Figure 5.3   Indicators of hearing impairment

1. Favoring one ear by cocking the head toward the speaker or cupping a hand behind the ear.
2. Misunderstanding or not following directions, and exhibiting nonverbal cues (e.g., frowns or puzzled looks) when directions are given.
3. Being distracted or seeming disoriented at times.
4. Asking people to repeat what they have just said.
5. Poorly articulating words, especially consonants.
6. Turning the volume up loud when listening to cassette recorders, radio, or television.
7. Showing reluctance to participate in oral activities.
8. Having frequent earaches or complaining of discomfort or buzzing in the ears.

Source: Adapted from Kirk and Gallagher (1989).

sion happens, the classroom teacher's awareness of the signs of hearing difficulties is essential. These are outlined in Figure 5.3.

Working with Students Who Have Hearing Impairments

Lack of proficiency in speech and language are the learning problems that result from hearing impairments. These problems affect content areas that rely on reading, writing, and listening. Teachers should remember that these language deficits don't mean the learners are unintelligent; students with hearing impairment can learn if appropriately helped.

Programs for students with hearing impairment combine mainstreaming with supplementary special education classes; 92% of students who are deaf are in full- or part-time special education classes, and about half of these are mainstreamed in regular classes (Kirk & Gallagher, 1989). Supplementary programs for students who are deaf include using whatever hearing there is together with lipreading, sign language, and finger spelling. Total communication, which uses the simultaneous presentation of manual approaches (signing and finger spelling) and speech (through speech reading and residual hearing), is becoming more popular (Heward, 1996).

> **5.13**
>
> What can teachers do to make their classrooms instructionally friendly for students who have hearing impairment?

Students Who Are Gifted and Talented

What is it like to be gifted in a regular classroom? Listen to one nine-year-old:

> Oh what a bore to sit and listen,
> To stuff we already know.
> Do everything we've done and done again,
> But we still must sit and listen.
> Over and over read one more page
> Oh bore, oh bore, oh bore.
> Sometimes I feel if we do one more page
> My head will explode with boreness rage
> I wish I could get up right there and march right out the door. (Delisle, 1984, p. 72)

While we don't think of gifted and talented students as having an exceptionality, they also are often unable to reach their full potential in the regular classroom. **Gifted and talented students** are *those at the upper end of the ability continuum who need supplemental help to realize their full potential*. At one time, the term *gifted* was used to identify these students, but the category has been enlarged to include both students who do well on IQ tests (typically 130 and above) and those who demonstrate above-average talents in such diverse areas as math, creative writing, and music (Davis & Rimm, 1993; Subotnik, 1997).

The history of gifted and talented education in the United States began with a longitudinal study of gifted students by Louis Terman (Terman, Baldwin, & Bronson, 1925; Terman & Oden, 1947, 1959). He used teacher recommendations and IQ test scores to identify 1,500 gifted individuals to track over a lifetime of development (the study is projected to run until 2010). In addition to finding that these students did better academically, Terman also found that they:

Enrichment activities provide opportunities for gifted students to explore alternative areas of the curriculum.

- Were better adjusted as children and adults
- Were better achievers and learned more easily
- Had more hobbies
- Read more books
- Were healthier

This and more current research has done much to dispel the stereotype of gifted students as maladjusted and narrow "brains" (Moon, Zentall, Grskovic, Hall, & Stormont-Sprugin, 1997).

Present views of gifted and talented students see them as possessing diverse abilities and needs. The current definition used by the federal government identifies them as possessing demonstrated or potential abilities that give evidence of high performance capability in areas such as intellectual, creative, specific academic or leadership ability, or in the performing and visual arts, and who by reason thereof require services or activities not ordinarily provided by the school. (U.S. Congress, Educational Amendment of 1978 [PL 95–561, IX(A)])

Another popular definition uses three criteria (Renzulli, 1986):

1. Above-average ability
2. High levels of motivation and task commitment
3. High levels of creativity

According to this definition, not only are gifted people "smart," but they also use this ability in focused and creative ways.

Creativity: What Is It?

Creativity is *the ability to identify or prepare original and divergent solutions to problems*. Creativity and IQ are related but not identical (Sternberg, 1989; Torrance, 1995); intellectual ability that is at least average can be thought of as a necessary, but not suf-

5.14

The definition of gifted and talented has changed over time. What similarities exist between this trend and trends with respect to other types of exceptionalities?

ficient, component of creativity. People who score low on IQ tests typically don't score high on measures of creativity; people who score high on IQ tests may or may not score high on measures of creativity.

Research indicates that creativity can be taught but that some people are more creative than others (Torrance, 1986). Like intelligence, it is probably influenced by both genetics and the environment.

Research suggests that creativity utilizes three kinds of intelligence (Sternberg & Lubart, 1995): *Synthetic intelligence* allows a creative person to see a problem in a new way. *Analytic intelligence* allows a person to recognize which new ideas are productive and allocate resources to solve the problem. In using *practical intelligence,* a creative person promotes an idea by using feedback from others. In all three, the emphasis is on problem solving in real-world settings.

J. P. Guilford (1967, 1988), whose work we examined in Chapter 4, was an influential researcher in the area of creativity. He emphasized divergent thinking, or the ability to generate a variety of original answers to questions. Divergent thinking has three dimensions:

- fluency—the ability to produce many ideas relevant to a problem
- flexibility—being able to break from an established set to generate new perspectives
- originality—the facility for generating new and different ideas.

To illustrate each, let's look at a social studies class discussing the problem of world hunger. Fluency would result in many solutions to the problem, such as growing food in domes in deserts, altering humans' genetic makeup so that they require less food, and growing food on the moon; flexibility would cast the problem in a new light (e.g., from economic or political rather than traditional perspectives); and originality would produce new and creative solutions to the problem (e.g., superpower cooperation).

More recently, Howard Gardner (1993), who we also studied in Chapter 4, defined the creative person as "a person who regularly solves problems, fashions products, or defines new questions in a domain in a way that is initially considered novel but that ultimately becomes accepted" (p. 35). Notice here that creativity is viewed as a recurring trait, rather than as a one-time event. Also, creativity typically occurs within, rather than across, domains, such as within art or music but not both. As with most aspects of learning, creativity requires background knowledge (Sternberg & Lubart, 1995). Knowledge makes a person aware of what has gone before—prevents "reinventing the wheel"—and allows a person to concentrate on new ideas instead of existing ones.

Teachers play an important role in developing students' creativity (Esquival, 1995). Their attitudes, the learning environments they create, and the way they interact with students all communicate whether or not they value creativity.

Measuring Creativity

Creativity is usually measured by giving students a verbal or pictorial stimulus and asking them to generate as many responses as they can, such as listing as many uses as possible for a brick (e.g., doorstop, bookshelf, paperweight, weapon, building block) or suggesting ways to improve a common object such as a chair (Davis, 1989). Pictorial tasks involve turning an ambiguous partial sketch into an interesting picture. Responses are then evaluated in terms of fluency, flexibility, and originality. Current ways of mea-

5.15

A science class is discussing the problem of pollution and the environment. Explain how the creative elements of fluency, flexibility, and originality might be evident in a class discussion.

5.16

Think about the research findings on creativity. Problem solving includes an important component that also exists in creativity. What do you suppose this component is?

suring creativity are controversial, with critics charging that existing tests are too narrow and fail to capture its different aspects (Sternberg, 1989; Ward, Ward, Landrum, & Patton, 1992).

Identifying Students Who Are Gifted and Talented

Meeting the needs of gifted and talented students requires early identification. Failure to do so can result in gifted underachievers with social and emotional problems linked to boredom and unmotivating school experiences (Clinkenbeard, 1992). A study of 1,172 school districts across the United States found that they use the following identification methods (Wilkie, 1985):

Identification Method	Percentage of Districts Using
Teacher nomination	91%
Achievement test	90%
Intelligence test	89%
Grades	50%
Peer and self-nomination	6%

Experts question relying so heavily on achievement and intelligence tests and recommend more flexible and less culturally dependent measures. These include creativity measures, peer and parent nomination, and classroom-based efforts by teachers to identify gifted minorities (Davis & Rimm, 1993).

As with all exceptionalities, teachers play a critical role in identifying gifted and talented students, because they constantly work with these students and can identify strengths that tests often miss. Unfortunately, some research indicates that teachers often confuse conformity, neatness, and good behavior with being gifted and talented (Davis & Rimm, 1993).

Minorities are underrepresented in gifted programs, and the reasons include limited definitions of giftedness, lack of culturally sensitive means of assessing potential, and over-reliance on standardized tests (Strom, 1990; Tomlinson, Callahan, & Lelli, 1997). For example, standardized tests are usually verbal and in English. Students for whom English is a second language have two challenges—the test itself and understanding and responding in English. Minority students also may not understand the "classroom game" as well as other students, which teachers interpret as lack of ability or potential (Subotnik, 1997). In addition, minority youth may lack gifted role models, or mentors, who have succeeded in school or in work (Pleiss & Feldhusen, 1995; Tomlinson et al., 1997).

What should teachers look for? Experts have identified the following characteristics of the gifted and talented (Davis & Rimm, 1993):

- Likes to work alone
- Is imaginative, enjoys pretending
- Is highly verbal and flexible in thinking
- Is persistent, stays with a task
- Goes beyond assignments
- Is often bored with routine tasks
- Is sometimes impulsive, with little interest in details

5.17

On the basis of the criteria *above-average ability, high levels of motivation and task commitment,* and *creativity,* which method of identifying gifted students is probably most effective? least effective?

5.18

Why is curriculum compacting most easily adopted in areas such as math and reading?

Working with these students can be challenging; their giftedness places unique demands on teachers, and the flexibility of teachers' responses can make school a happy or an unhappy experience for these students.

Programs for the Gifted: More and Faster or Deeper and Different?

Programs for the gifted and talented are based on one of two ideas: acceleration and enrichment. **Acceleration** *keeps the curriculum the same but allows students to move through it more quickly.* **Enrichment** *provides richer and varied content through strategies that supplement usual grade-level work.* Table 5.3 offers examples of each.

Time for acceleration or enrichment can be generated with a process called **curriculum compacting,** which is *an approach to individualization that identifies mastered content, concentrates on content not yet mastered, and uses the time saved for acceleration or enrichment* (Reis, 1992). For example, a primary teacher might pretest math skills at the beginning of a new unit and then focus on unmet objectives, freeing students to pursue additional math topics or content in other areas. The practice evolved from research indicating that gifted students were often asked to spend time on content they already understood (Renzulli, Smith, & Reis, 1982). One study of curriculum compacting found that gifted students had already mastered from 25% to 75% of the math and language arts curriculum before it was taught (Reis & Purcell, 1992).

Which is better: acceleration or enrichment? Critics of enrichment call it busywork and irrelevant, contending that students should be provided a healthy menu of regular academic fare. Critics of acceleration point to the narrowness of the regular curriculum, the dangers of pushing students too fast, and possible social mismatches in relating to older students. Research found that accelerated students surpassed by nearly one grade level the achievement of nonaccelerated students of equal age and intelligence (Kulik & Kulik, 1984). These students were also equivalent in achievement to older, talented, but nonaccelerated students. No affective differences, such as attitudes toward school or

Table 5.3 Options in enrichment and acceleration programs

Enrichment Options	Acceleration Options
1. Independent study and independent projects	1. Early admission to kindergarten and first grade
2. Learning centers	2. Grade skipping
3. Field trips	3. Subject skipping
4. Saturday programs	4. Credit by exam
5. Summer programs	5. College courses in high school
6. Mentors and mentorships	6. Correspondence courses
7. Simulations and games	7. Early admission to college
8. Small-group investigations	
9. Academic competitions	

self-concept, were found. A ten-year longitudinal study also found no negative effects resulting from acceleration (Swialth & Benbow, 1991).

Supporters point to these studies as evidence for the superiority of acceleration (Feldhusen, 1989). Critics counter that the comparison is unfair because the outcomes of enrichment, such as creativity and problem solving, are not easily measured on standardized achievement tests. Which is better? There is obviously no easy answer, and the debate is likely to continue.

5.19

Which strategy—enrichment or acceleration—would be easiest to implement in the regular classroom? Why?

Classroom Connections

Teaching Students with Disabilities in Your Classroom

1. Work closely with parents and other professionals to understand the special needs of students with physical disabilities in your classroom.

   • A second-grade teacher, knowing a student with hearing impairment would be in her class, talked with the student's previous teacher and discussed strategies that had worked for him. She also met with the special education teacher, who gave her materials on working with those who have hearing impairment. She also made a special effort to communicate with the student's parents about the student's strengths and needs.

   • A high-school math teacher works with parents and the special education specialist in his school to adapt his instruction for a student with partial vision. He seats her at the front of the room, consciously uses the front chalkboard, and makes a special effort to write clearly, using large numbers and letters. He also repeats written information aloud. If the print on quizzes and assignments is too small, he enlists the aid of other students in recopying problems.

2. Help other students understand the disability and enlist their aid in helping the student.

   • Before a blind student was transferred into a sixth-grade teacher's class, the teacher held a class meeting at which she discussed the new student's disability and asked the other students to think of ways to make the classroom a positive learning environment.

   • A junior-high teacher noticed nervous shuffling and muffled laughter when a quiet boy stuttered during the first week of class. The next day, the teacher sent the student to the office on an assignment and discussed the problem with the rest of the class. She explained how everyone stutters when nervous and how important it is to give each student a chance to participate. In the next few days, she made a special effort to call on the student, especially when she thought he knew the answer. When the student responded, she was careful to make eye contact and not interrupt or complete sentences for the boy.

Teaching Gifted and Talented Students in Your Classroom

3. Prevent boredom in the classroom by providing supplementary activities.

   • A sixth-grade teacher confers with her students who are gifted and talented at the beginning of each grading period to identify areas of interest and to outline projects. After students have finished their regular work, they are free to read books and work on their projects.

   • A junior-high math teacher pretests students at the beginning of each unit. Whenever a student has mastered the concepts and objectives of the unit, he or she receives an honor pass to work on an alternative activity in the school media center. The activities may be extensions or applications of the concepts taught in the unit, or they may involve learning about mathematical principles or math history not usually taught in the regular classroom.

4. Integrate activities that require creativity and critical thinking in the classroom.
   - A high-school social studies teacher caps off every unit with a hypothetical problem (e.g., What would the United States be like today if Great Britain had won the Revolutionary War?). Students work in groups to address the question.
   - A junior-high science teacher begins every unit with a problem or question (e.g., How are birds and airplanes similar?). She leaves the question unanswered and returns to it for discussion at the end of the unit.

Changes in the Way Teachers Help Students with Exceptionalities

In the past, students with exceptionalities were separated from their peers and placed in segregated classrooms or schools. Instruction in these classrooms, however, was often inferior, achievement was no better than in regular classrooms, and students didn't learn the life skills needed to live in the real world (Bradley & Switlick, 1997). Educators looked for other ways to help these students.

Federal Laws Redefine Special Education

In 1975, the U.S. Congress passed Public Law 94–142, the *Individuals with Disabilities Education Act (IDEA),* which is intended to ensure a free and public education for all students with exceptionalities. IDEA, combined with more recent amendments, provides the following guidelines for working with students having exceptionalities:

- Identify the needs of students with exceptionalities by nondiscriminatory assessment.
- Involve parents in developing each child's educational program.
- Create an environment that is minimally restrictive.
- Develop an individualized education program (IEP) of study for each student.

IDEA has affected every school in the United States and has changed the roles of regular and special educators.

The Evolution Toward Inclusion

As educators realized that segregated classes and services were not meeting the needs of students with exceptionalities, they wrestled with alternatives. One of the first was **mainstreaming,** *the practice of moving students with exceptionalities from segregated settings into regular classrooms.* Popular in the 1970s, mainstreaming had advantages and disadvantages (Hardman et. al, 1996). It began the move away from segregated services and allowed students with exceptionalities and other students to interact. Unfortunately, however, students with exceptionalities were often placed into classrooms without the necessary support and services.

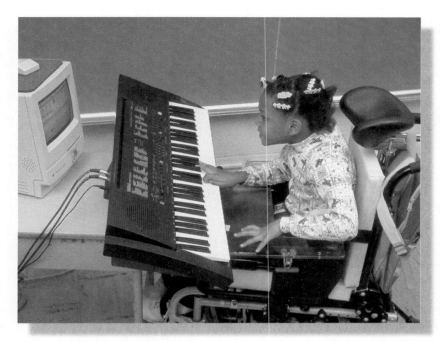

The least restrictive environment provides students with opportunities to develop to their fullest potential.

As educators grappled with these problems, they developed the concept of the **least restrictive environment (LRE),** *one that places students in as normal an educational setting as possible while still meeting their special academic, social, and physical needs.* Broader than the concept of *mainstreaming,* the LRE can consist of a continuum of services, ranging from mainstreaming to placement in separate facilities. Mainstreaming occurs only if parents and educators decide it best meets the child's needs.

Central to the LRE is the concept of **adaptive fit,** *the degree to which a student is able to cope with the requirements of a school setting and the extent to which the school accommodates the student's special needs* (Hardman et al., 1996). Adaptive fit requires an individualized approach to dealing with students having exceptionalities; it can only be determined after an analysis of a student's specific learning needs. As educators considered mainstreaming, LRE, and adaptive fit, they gradually developed the concept of *inclusion.*

Inclusion is *a comprehensive approach to educating students with exceptionalities that advocates a total, systematic, and coordinated web of services.* Inclusion has three components:

1. Placing students with special needs in a regular school campus
2. Creating appropriate support and services to guarantee an adaptive fit
3. Coordinating general and special education services

Inclusion is both proactive and comprehensive; it makes all educators responsible for creating supportive learning environments and leaves open the possibility of services being delivered in places other than the regular classroom (Larrivee, Semmel, & Gerber, 1997). Its thrust is to include students with exceptionalities in regular classrooms whenever possible, but it also allows for delivering services in other places (Bradley & Switlick, 1997).

5.20

Imagine drawing two circles, one inside the other. Which would represent an LRE, and which would be mainstreaming?

5.21

Identify at least two advantages of inclusion. Identify at least one potential problem with inclusion.

Inclusion creates a web of services to integrate students with exceptionalities into the educational system.

A Legal Framework for Working with Students Who Have Exceptionalities

Kevin had mild retardation and had been going to a resource program for an hour a day during his elementary school years. The resource teacher worked closely with the regular teacher to ensure that Kevin's work in each classroom was consistent. Through their combined efforts, they were able to help him learn in the regular classroom, even though his achievement test scores were well below his grade level.

The move to junior high posed new challenges for Kevin. He would have five teachers instead of one, and the prospect of moving from one class to the next was frightening. Before school started, Mr. Endo, Kevin's resource teacher in the junior high, called a meeting of Kevin's parents and teachers. They discussed Kevin's strengths and weaknesses and what kinds of teaching strategies had worked at his old school. He liked science and art, and a special effort was made to provide him with some additional science materials. Out of this meeting came an *individualized education program* (IEP) that provided short- and long-term goals and additional teaching strategies to use with him. The IEP would take effect with the start of his next semester and would guide teachers during the next year, after which it would be reviewed and revised. The group shared the IEP with Kevin, who was more at ease knowing that he was being looked after.

As you saw in the previous section, IDEA fundamentally changed the way schools educate students with exceptionalities. This change occurred through specific provisions that require:

- due process through parental involvement
- protection against discrimination in testing
- least restrictive environment (LRE)
- an individualized education program (IEP)

Let's look at these provisions.

Due Process Through Parental Involvement

Due process guarantees parents' involvement in identifying and placing their children in special programs, access to school records, and the opportunity for an independent evaluation if they're not satisfied with the initial one. Legal safeguards are also in place if parents don't speak English; they have the right to an interpreter, and their rights must be read to them in their native language. Involving Kevin's parents in developing his IEP is one facet of due process.

Protection Against Discrimination in Testing

The law requires that any testing used in the placement process will be conducted in a student's native language by qualified personnel, and that no single instrument, such as an intelligence test, can be used as the sole basis for placement. In response to a court

5.22

Kevin's parents were involved in the development of his IEP. What educational advantages might come from this involvement?

5.23

You suspect that a Hispanic student in your class, who speaks halting but understandable English, has a learning disability in math. Because he speaks understandable English, can he be given a placement test written in English? Explain.

Teachers and other professionals meet with parents to design an IEP that meets a student's individual learning needs.

decision (Larry P. v. Riles, 1979), California severely restricted the use of standardized intelligence tests in identifying minority children with disabilities. In recent years, increased emphasis has also been placed on a student's classroom performance and general adaptive behavior (Heward, 1996).

Least Restrictive Environment (LRE)

The intent of an LRE is that all students have the right to learn in an environment that best promotes their academic and social growth. They are taken out of the regular classroom only when an exceptionality is such that regular classes with the use of supplementary help cannot meet their needs.

The LRE provision means that *you will have students with exceptionalities in your classroom,* and you will be asked to work with special educators to design and implement programs for these students. The thrust of the LRE is that students with exceptionalities should participate as much as possible in the regular school agenda, including academics, recess, lunch in the cafeteria, regular school assemblies, and extracurricular activities. The form of these programs varies with the nature of the problem and the capabilities of the students. Figure 5.4 presents a continuum or cascade of services for implementing the LRE, starting with the least confining at the top and moving to the most confining at the bottom. The word *cascade* is used by special educators to label the connectedness of levels; if students can't succeed at one level they are moved to the next.

5.24

How could integration into the regular classroom help a student with special needs improve academic performance? self-concept? peer acceptance?

Figure 5.4 Educational service options for implementing the LRE

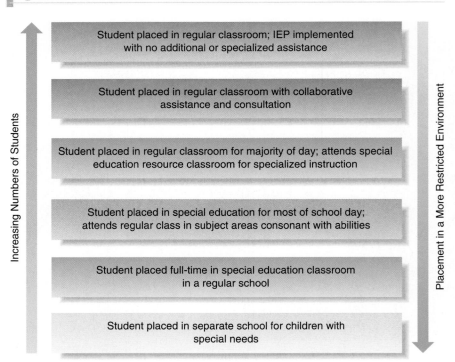

Increasing Numbers of Students

Placement in a More Restricted Environment

Student placed in regular classroom; IEP implemented with no additional or specialized assistance

Student placed in regular classroom with collaborative assistance and consultation

Student placed in regular classroom for majority of day; attends special education resource classroom for specialized instruction

Student placed in special education for most of school day; attends regular class in subject areas consonant with abilities

Student placed full-time in special education classroom in a regular school

Student placed in separate school for children with special needs

These placement options represent a continuum from greater to lesser involvement in the regular classroom. The goal of inclusion is to identify the point on the continuum that best meets the student's needs.

Individualized Education Program (IEP)

To ensure that inclusion works and learners with exceptionalities don't get lost in the regular classroom, an **individualized education program (IEP)**—*an individually prescribed instructional plan devised by special education and classroom teachers, other resource professionals, and parents*—is prepared. It specifies the following:

- An assessment of the student's current level of performance
- Long- and short-term objectives
- Services or strategies to be used
- Schedules for implementing the plan
- Criteria to be used in evaluating the plan's success

Teachers and other professionals meet with parents to design an IEP that meets a student's individual learning needs. When completed, the IEP must be approved and signed by the student's parents or legal guardians; this signals their involvement in the process and their approval of the product.

Figure 5.5 presents a sample IEP. It has three important features. First, the initials of all participants indicate that its development was a cooperative effort. Second, the specific information in Columns 3, 4, 5, and 6 and in Section 7 guides the classroom teacher and special education personnel when they implement it. Third, the parent's signature indicates that they were involved in developing the plan and agree with its details.

5.25

Which of the options in Figure 5.4 will serve the greatest number of students with exceptionalities? the smallest number? What implications does this have for you as a regular classroom teacher?

Functions of the IEP

The IEP performs at least four functions. First, it provides support for the classroom teacher, who may be uncertain about dealing with students with special needs. Second, it creates a link between the regular classroom and the resource team. Third, it helps parents monitor their child's educational progress. Fourth, and most important, it provides a program to meet the individual needs of the student.

IEPs often provide for work in settings outside the regular classroom, such as a resource room; at other times, they focus exclusively on adaptations in the regular classroom. They are most effective when the two are coordinated, such as when a classroom teacher working on word problems in math asks the resource teacher to focus on the same type of problems (Choate, 1997).

5.26

Explain specifically how an IEP addresses the previously discussed concepts of *due process, parental involvement,* and *least restrictive environment.*

Curriculum-Based Measurement

To assist both the classroom teacher and the special education teacher in designing IEPs, educators are placing increased emphasis on **curriculum-based measurement,** *which assesses learners' performance in specific areas of the curriculum* (Shinn & Hubbard, 1992). As opposed to broader measures, such as standardized achievement tests, curriculum-based measurement identifies specific areas in which students need help, such as finding the main idea in reading or knowing multiplication facts. Identifying these areas helps the team to be specific in designing IEPs.

5.27

Describe a curriculum-based measurement designed to measure a student's ability to find "main ideas." Be specific in your description.

Figure 5.5 Individualized education program (IEP)

INDIVIDUAL EDUCATION PROGRAM

Date _____3-1-98_____

(1) Student

Name: Joe S.
School: Adams
Grade: 5
Current Placement: Regular Class/Resource Room

Date of Birth: 10-1-86   Age: 11-5

(2) Committee

		Initial
Mrs. Wrens	Principal	*D.A.W.*
Mrs. Snow	Regular Teacher	*AS*
Mr. LaJoie	Counselor	*JLJ*
Mr. Thomas	Resource Teacher	*M.T.*
Mr. Ryan	School Psychologist	*H.R.R.*
Mrs. S.	Parent	*J.S.*
Joe S.	Student	*Joe S.*

EP from _3-15-98_ to _3-15-99_

(3) Present Level of Educational Functioning	(4) Annual Goal Statements	(5) Instructional Objectives	(6) Objective Criteria and Evaluation
MATH Strengths 1. Can successfully compute addition and subtraction problems to two places with regrouping and zeros. 2. Knows 100 basic multiplication facts. Weaknesses 1. Frequently makes computational errors on problems with which he has had experience. 2. Does not complete seatwork. Key Math total score of 2.1 Grade Equivalent.	Joe will apply knowledge of regrouping in addition and renaming in subtraction to four-digit numbers.	1. When presented with 20 addition problems of 3-digits numbers requiring two renamings, the student will compute answers at a rate of one problem per minute and an accuracy of 90%. 2. When presented with 20 subtraction problems of 3-digit numbers requiring two renamings, the student will compute answers at the rate of one problem per minute with 90% accuracy. 3. When presented with 20 addition problems of 4-digit numbers requiring three renamings, the student will compute answers at a rate of one problem per minute and an accuracy of 90%. 4. When presented with 20 subtraction problems of 4-digit numbers requiring three renamings, the student will compute answers at a rate of one problem per minute with 90% accuracy.	Teacher-made tests (weekly) Teacher-made tests (weekly) Teacher-made tests (weekly)

(7) Educational Services to be provided

Services Required	Date initiated	Duration of Service	Individual Responsible for the Service
Regular Reading-Adapted	3-15-98	3-15-99	Reading Improvement Specialist and Special Education Teacher
Resource Room	3-15-98	3-15-99	Special Education Teacher
Counselor Consultant	3-15-98	3-15-99	Counselor
Monitoring diet and general health	3-15-98	3-15-99	School Health Nurse

Extent of time in the regular education program: 60% increasing to 80%
Justification of the educational placement:

It is felt that the structure of the resource room can best meet the goals stated for Joe; especially when coordinated with the regular classroom.

It is also felt that Joe could profit enormously from talking with a counselor. He needs someone with whom to talk and with whom he can share his feelings.

(8) I have had the opportunity to participate in the development of the Individual Education Program.
   I agree with Individual Education Program   (✓)
   I disagree with the Individual Education Program (   )

Parent's Signature ___*Mrs S.*___

Source: Adapted From *Developing and Implementing Individualized Education Programs* (3rd ed.) (pp. 308, 316) by B. B. Strickland and A. P. Turnbull, 1990, New York: Macmillan. Reprinted by permission.

The Teacher's Role in Inclusive Classrooms

In earlier sections, you learned about different kinds of disabilities, how they affect the students you teach, and how views of special education have changed over time. In this section, we shift our focus to strategies regular classroom teachers use to help these students reach their potential. In this process, they have three roles:

- helping identify students with exceptionalities
- teaching students with exceptionalities in the regular classroom
- fostering other students' acceptance of students with exceptionalities

Let's look at them.

Identifying Students with Exceptionalities

Because regular classroom teachers work with these students every day, they are in the best position to help identify students with exceptionalities. Identification often begins by simply monitoring a student's learning progress on typical classroom tasks. In doing so, teachers should remember that a disproportionate number of males and cultural minorities tend to be identified (Hardman et al., 1996). This imbalance suggests that you should ask yourself, for example, whether a difficulty truly indicates a learning problem or if some other factor might be operating. This is the dilemma that Sabrina Curtis faced in our opening case study as she worked with Rodney and Amelia.

Prereferral Strategies: Gathering Data for Instructional Problem Solving

Current approaches to identification encourage the use of a team-based problem-solving model with the teacher as the key member. The process begins when a learning problem is suspected; the teacher's first step is to diagnose the problem and try different instructional strategies.

If this fails, other educators are called in and additional data are gathered, including standardized test scores, classroom performance, and interviews with parents and other teachers.

If the data warrant additional help, a "prereferral team" is formed, often consisting of the school psychologist, a special educator, and the classroom teacher. The team further evaluates the problem, suggests ways that classroom procedures could be modified to create a better adaptive fit, and assists the classroom teacher in modifying instruction. The teacher will be expected to document the strategies attempted in solving the problem (Hallahan & Kauffman, 1994). Specifically, the teacher should describe:

| 5.28 |
| Why are tests, quizzes, papers, and other work samples important in the referral process? How is using them similar to the concept of *curriculum-based measurement,* discussed earlier? |

- The nature of the problem
- How it affects classroom performance
- Dates, places, and time the problem has occurred
- Strategies the teacher has tried
- Evidence of the strategies' successes

Before a referral is made, the classroom teacher should also check the student's records to see if the student has had a previous evaluation, has any physical problems, has been included in other special programs, or is qualified for special services (Hallahan & Kauffman, 1994).

Teachers should also communicate with parents *prior* to initiating a process. Parents need to be informed and involved for at least three reasons:

1. Due process legally requires their involvement.
2. They can provide valuable information about the student's history.
3. Involving parents is a professional courtesy.

When considering a referral, the teacher should check with school administrators or the school psychologist to learn about the school's policy. If the referral results in a recommendation for special services, an IEP is then prepared.

Teaching Students with Exceptionalities

Almost certainly, some of your students will have exceptionalities, and you will be expected to teach them as effectively as possible. Fortunately, changes are more in *how* than in *what* you teach (Choate, 1997). One teacher working in an inclusive classroom commented,

> I wasn't sure that I knew what to do for special ed kids. And now I think I do
> know what to do for special ed kids and it's not a whole lot different than . . .
> what I've always done for regular ed kids (Oka, Kolar, Rau, & Stahl, 1997, p. 10).

Also, special educators should be available to you—*resource teachers* who can help you modify instruction for your students with exceptionalities; the *prereferral teacher assistance teams* we discussed earlier; and *site-based* or *collaborative consultation* teams—as resources.

Effective Teaching for Inclusive Classrooms

Most modifications that work with students having exceptionalities are based on principles of effective teaching that work with all students, such as managing a classroom effectively, matching learning tasks to student abilities, and providing frequent and specific practice and feedback (Mercer & Mercer, 1993). This is encouraging because it means the knowledge and effective strategies that teachers use with regular students need only to be adapted, not fundamentally changed. Table 5.4 outlines these teaching practices.

As described in Table 5.4, teachers need to structure their time so that students have meaningful learning tasks and the opportunity to learn. The classroom should be emotionally warm and supportive, and students must believe that they can and will learn. Management reinforces instruction, and disruptions should be minimized. Tasks should be designed so that students have high rates of success on classwork and homework. Finally, effective feedback reinforces instruction and provides learning correctives. These teaching strategies are effective for students in general and are particularly important for students with exceptionalities.

Of the five areas, the most challenging is adapting instruction to ensure high success rates. This often means spending more time with individual learners and providing more opportunities for practice and feedback. For example, teachers may need to shorten assignments, giving 10 instead of 20 problems, or a teacher might break an assignment of 20 problems into four groups of 5, with opportunities for teacher, peer, or self-checking after each group.

Adapting Instruction. To help students overcome a history of failure and frustration and to convince them that renewed effort will work, teachers often have to adapt their methods. Peer tutoring has been used effectively, and much of the benefit comes from

5.29

Examine the teaching strategies in Table 5.4. Which of these focus on achievement-oriented goals? Which focus on affective or motivational goals? What do your answers suggest about working effectively with students having exceptionalities?

Table 5.4   Effective teaching practices for inclusion

Practice	Description
Effective instruction	• Meaningful learning tasks
	• High rates of on-task behavior
	• Minimal losses of instructional time to transitions and disruptions
Warm academic climate	• Supportive responses to *all* students—particularly those mainstreamed
	• Supportive responses when problems occur (e.g., "I know we can learn this if we try.")
Effective classroom management	• Structured and orderly classroom
	• Minimal use of punishment
	• Minimal loss of instructional time to manage misbehavior
High success rates	• Correct answers to most teacher questions
	• Success rate of 80%–90% on seatwork and homework assignments
Effective feedback	• Feedback that is immediate
	• Feedback that provides information (e.g., "Good, Sarah. You remembered to borrow from the tens column.")
	• Feedback that includes no criticism

doing the actual tutoring (Miller, Barbetta, & Heron, 1994). Home-based tutoring programs that involve parents can also be effective (Barbetta & Heron, 1991). You can set up a home-based tutoring program by contacting parents and explaining specifically what they can do in working with their youngster. Additional adaptations are outlined in Table 5.5.

A Successful Homework Program.   Increased structure and support is an essential characteristic of successful adaptive instruction. Students with learning problems need to be taught in small steps, with an effort to promote as much success as possible. Inappropriate assignments, or homework that is too difficult, can be frustrating for the regular student; for students with learning problems, it can be devastating.

One successful homework program made a concerted effort to ensure student success (Rosenberg, 1989). Homework was an extension of seatwork successfully completed in class. Parents' assistance was solicited; they orally administered a quiz each night on material being studied and confirmed the completion of the homework and quiz with their signatures.

The signature was both concrete and symbolic; it was a concrete indicator that parents were participating in their child's homework and, symbolically, it provided a link between home and school. To reinforce students, points were used; students received some points for doing homework and additional ones for doing both homework and the quiz. The program was demanding, but results indicated the time and energy were well spent.

> **5.30**
>
> Earlier, we said that most modifications for mainstreamed students were more of degree than of kind. Explain this statement using Rosenberg's (1989) homework study as a focus.

Technology can be used to provide students with exceptionalities opportunities for practice with frequent and specific feedback.

Adapting Reading Materials.   Reading poses particular problems, because the special texts students need are usually unavailable. However, teachers can supplement the materials they have by

- Setting goals at the beginning of an assignment,
- Using advance organizers that structure or summarize passages,
- Introducing key concepts and terms before students read the text,
- Creating study guides with questions that focus attention on important information, and
- Asking students to summarize information in the text. (Graham & Johnson, 1989)

These strategies increase reading comprehension with regular learners (Dole, Duffy, Roehler, & Pearson, 1991), and using them with mainstreamed students provides an additional level of support.

Strategy Training: Learning How to Learn

Strategy training is one of the most promising approaches to helping students with learning problems. A strategy is a plan for accomplishing a learning goal. Let's see how a strategy might be applied when encountering a task such as learning a list of ten spelling words. For example, a student might say to himself,

"Okay, . . . ten words for the quiz on Friday. That shouldn't be too hard. I have two days to learn them.

Table 5.5 Instructional adaptations for students with exceptionalities

Skill Area	Adaptations
Math	• Model correct solutions on the chalkboard. • Use peer tutors to explain problems. • Break long assignments into several shorter ones. • Encourage the use of calculators and other manipulative aids.
Reading	• Use old textbooks and other alternative reading materials at the appropriate level. • Use study guides that identify key concepts. • Preteach difficult concept before presenting a reading passage. • Encourage group assignments in which students assist each other.
Spelling	• Avoid spelling as a grading criterion. • Focus on spelling words used in science, social studies, and other areas. • Stress mastery of several short spelling lists, rather than one long list. • Encourage students to proofread papers, circling words of which they're uncertain.
Writing	• Increase time allotted for writing assignments. • Allow assignments to be typed, rather than handwritten. • Allow reports to be taped or dictated to others. • Encourage daily writing through the use of short, creative assignments.

Source: Dolgins, Myers, Flynn, and Moore (1984).

"Let's see. These are all about airports. Which of these do I already know—*airplane, taxi, apron,* and *jet?* No problem. Hmmm. . . . Some of these aren't so easy, like *causeway* and *tarmac.* I don't even know what a 'tarmac' is. I'll look it up. . . . Oh, that makes sense. It's the runway. I'd better spend more time on these words. I'll cover them up and try to write them down and then check 'em. Tonight, I can get Mom to give me a quiz, and then I'll know which ones to study extra tomorrow."

This student was strategic in at least two ways. Separating the words he already knew from those he didn't, spending extra time on the difficult ones, and looking up *tarmac* in the dictionary indicate the presence of clear learning goals. He also took a deliberate approach to the task, matching his effort to the difficulty of the problem. He allocated more time to the words he didn't know and skipped the ones he did. In addition, he monitored his progress through quiz-like exercises (Palincsar & Brown, 1987).

In contrast, students with learning difficulties often approach learning tasks in a "strategically inactive" manner, either approaching a learning task passively or using the same strategy for all learning goals (Montague, 1990). For example, they might approach a spelling task, such as the one above, by merely reading the words, rather than by trying to actually spell them—a passive approach. They also spend an equal amount of time on the words they already know and make little effort to test themselves to receive feedback.

5.31

How, specifically, might a teacher instruct students to more strategically attack the spelling list in the example?

In contrast with most students, who learn strategies naturally as they progress through school, students with learning problems often have to be explicitly taught them. Teacher modeling and explanation are essential, together with opportunities for practice and feedback (Miller, 1990).

Collaborative Consultation: Help for the Classroom Teacher

Collaboration between regular and special educators is essential if inclusion is to work. In the *consulting teacher model,* a special education expert assists the classroom teacher in meeting the classroom needs of students requiring special help (Hardman et al., 1996). In working with the classroom teacher, the consulting teacher can perform a number of valuable functions, such as:

- Assist in collecting assessment information
- Maintain students' records
- Develop special curriculum materials
- Coordinate the efforts of team members in implementing the IEP
- Work with parents
- Assist the regular teacher in adapting instruction

Perhaps most important is helping the regular teacher adapt instruction. One way to do so is through collaborative team teaching, which allows more efficient use of special education resources and a reduction of the stigma of pull-out programs. Research on collaborative team teaching is encouraging, indicating that learning environments improve and resources and instructional variety increase (Pugach & Wesson, 1995).

Strategies for Social Integration and Growth

Among the most difficult obstacles that students with exceptionalities face are the negative attitudes of others and the impact of these attitudes on their confidence and self-esteem (Chapman, 1988; Moon et al. 1997). Often, a student who has a disability and is labeled as different is neither well understood nor accepted by other students.

In addition, these students are often behind in their academic work, frequently act out in class, and sometimes lack social skills. Further, being pulled out for extra help calls attention to their differences (Hallahan & Kauffman, 1994). Special efforts are needed to promote their acceptance in regular classrooms.

Attempts to foster acceptance have focused on three approaches:

- helping regular students understand and accept students with exceptionalities
- helping students with exceptionalities behave acceptably
- using strategies that encourage social interaction and cooperation

Helping Regular Students Understand and Accept Students with Exceptionalities

Regular students often have negative attitudes toward students with exceptionalities, because they don't understand the disabilities. The first approach attempts to change that. Providing information about disabilities and promoting interaction between regular and mainstreamed students can help (Heward, 1996). Successful strategies include:

Creative teachers design learning activities that allow students of differing abilities to interact and learn about each other.

- films and discussions of disabilities
- teaching students the manual alphabet
- having students perform routine activities when blindfolded
- using wheelchairs and crutches

In addition, teachers can promote acceptance by calling on all students—including those with exceptionalities—regularly, using cooperative learning that puts learners with exceptionalities into direct contact with other students, and identifying areas of interest or strength (e.g., art or science). Above all, teachers communicate through their language and actions that they value these students as individuals, expect them to learn, and want to have them in their classrooms.

5.32

How does mainstreaming help foster acceptance of students with exceptionalities? In addition to mainstreaming, what else is necessary?

Helping Students with Exceptionalities Behave Acceptably

A second approach to social integration attempts to improve the social skills of students with exceptionalities, who often misbehave, acting out because of frustration or learned inappropriate behaviors (Zens, Curtis, Graden, & Ponti, 1988). Ways of changing these behaviors include contracts that specify appropriate behavior in advance, and individual

5.33

Describe two similarities between teaching students with exceptionalities social skills and teaching them cognitive strategies.

or group reward systems where individuals or the whole class receives tokens or points for desired behavior.

Students with disabilities often avoid contact with regular students because they lack the social skills to make friends. Teachers can help by modeling and coaching. For example, a teacher says, "Barnell's over there on the playground. I think I'll say, 'Hi, Barnell! Want to play ball with me?' Now you try it, and I'll watch." Another strategy is to teach social problem solving; for instance, a teacher comments, "Hmm. Mary has a toy that I want to play with. What could I do to make her want to share that toy?" Direct approaches have proved successful in teaching social skills such as empathy, perspective taking, negotiation, and assertiveness (Anderson, Nelson, Fox, & Gruber, 1988; Vaughn, McIntosh, Spencer, & Rowe, 1990).

Using Strategies that Encourage Social Interaction and Cooperation

One obstacle to social integration is the classroom itself. Students often work alone and grades are based on competition rather than cooperation. Peer tutoring and cooperative learning can help break down these barriers (Bradley & Switlick, 1997).

Peer Tutoring. Peer tutoring places students in groups of two or three and provides them with structured learning activities, including practice and feedback. For example, after introducing a new concept in math, the teacher assigns students in pairs to work on practice exercises. Students take turns tutoring and being tutored, one doing the sample problems and the other checking the answers and providing feedback. Various combinations have been used: high and low ability, students with and without exceptionalities, and students with exceptionalities tutoring each other. All have proved successful in teaching content (Fuchs, Fuchs, Mathes, & Simmons, 1997) while also pro-

Cooperative learning activities encourage students to interact as they learn content and depend on each other for mutual help and support.

moting social interaction and improved attitudes toward those with exceptionalities (Miller et al., 1994). For both cognitive and affective gains to be maximized, it is important that students with exceptionalities have opportunities to tutor and be tutored.

Training for the tutors is essential, however; research indicates that the quality of the instruction during peer tutoring can be improved markedly by teaching students to be more interactive and task oriented in their feedback (Fuchs, Fuchs, Bentz, Phillips, & Hamlett, 1994).

Cross-age tutoring, in which older students tutor younger ones, appears to be an especially promising practice for students with disabilities. In one study, upper elementary students categorized as having either a learning disability or behavior disorder served as tutors for first-graders (Top & Osgthorpe, 1987). After 12 weeks of tutoring, both the tutors and those tutored showed significant learning gains. In addition, tutors increased in their perceptions of their general academic ability and their reading/spelling ability. Anyone who has taught something successfully knows how personally fulfilling it can be. Successful tutoring appears to provide feelings of competence and satisfaction that can improve self-concept.

Cooperative Learning. Cooperative learning strategies place students in teams and encourage them to work toward common goals. Students are rewarded for helping and encouraging other students to learn. Cooperative learning strategies have been used effectively at all grade levels and in all content areas. They have been found to increase achievement, improve attitudes toward minorities and those with disabilities, and increase inclusion in mainstream classroom activities (Slavin, 1995). We discuss cooperative learning in more detail in Chapter 13.

Classroom Connections

Teaching Students With Exceptionalities in the Regular Classroom

1. Adapt regular instruction to meet the unique needs of students with exceptionalities.
   - A third-grade teacher circulates around the room after an assignment is given, making sure his mainstreamed students understand the directions. If necessary, he gathers them together in a small group or works with them one-on-one to go over the directions again.
   - A junior-high math teacher has organized a buddy system in which his abler students are paired with mainstreamed students. A short training program teaches students how to assist with homework assignments and helps them understand the difference between academic and nonacademic help.

2. Teach students with exceptionalities learning strategies they can use in the classroom.
   - An English teacher teaches and models strategies step-by-step. A unit on writing one-paragraph essays taught students to use four steps:
     a. Write a topic sentence.
     b. Add two reasons they believe it is the topic sentence.
     c. Add a summary sentence.
     d. Reread and edit it.
   - An elementary math teacher teaches problem-solving strategies by thinking aloud at the

chalkboard while she's working through a problem. She breaks word problems into the following steps:

a. Read: What is the question?

b. Reread: What information do I need?

c. Stop and think: What do I need to do—add, subtract, multiply, or divide?

d. Compute: Put the correct numbers in and solve.

e. Label and check: What answer did I get? Does it make sense?

Fostering Acceptance of All Students in Your Classroom

3. Emphasize the value of diversity in the classroom.

   • A first-grade teacher began a unit on diversity with a discussion of how all students in the class were similar. The next day, he focused on diversity, both physical and cultural. Students drew pictures of themselves, and the teacher helped each student point out on the pictures, "I'm me because . . ."

   • A junior-high homeroom teacher begins the school year by asking students to fill out an autobiographical fact sheet that asks them to think about their favorites (e.g., food, hobby, movie), as well as their strengths and weaknesses. The teacher, too, fills out a fact sheet and puts them all up on the bulletin board. The teacher discusses these in the first few weeks to get to know students and to introduce the idea "Different is great."

4. Deal with the subject of exceptionalities in an open and straightforward manner.

   • An elementary teacher uses role playing and modeling to discuss problems such as teasing and laughing at others, and she specifically emphasizes treating students who look or act different with the same respect that other students receive.

   • A junior-high-school English teacher uses literature, such as *Summer of the Swans* by Betsy Byars, as a springboard for talking about individual differences. Students are encouraged to reflect on their own individuality and how important this is to them.

Windows on Classrooms

As you've studied this chapter, you've examined characteristics of students with exceptionalities, and you've learned that they all can learn if you adapt your instruction to meet their needs. Efficient use of time, a supportive academic climate, effective classroom management, high success rates, and frequent and informative feedback are important in helping students with exceptionalities achieve their maximum potential.

Read the following case study and assess the teacher's effectiveness in the context of the information you've been studying.

Mike Sheppard is a math teacher at Landrom Junior High School. He teaches three sections of seventh-grade pre-algebra and two sections of eighth-grade algebra.

We join him in his second-period pre-algebra class on Thursday morning. The day before, Mike introduced his class to a procedure for solving word problems, and he modeled the solution of some examples by using the procedure. He then assigned five problems for homework.

Mike has 28 students in his second-period class, which includes five students with exceptionalities: Herchel, Marcus, and Gwenn, who have learning disabilities, and Todd and Horace, who have behavior disorders. Herchel, Marcus, and Gwenn each have problems with decoding words, reading comprehension, and writing. Todd has been described by other teachers as verbally abusive, aggressive, and lacking in self-discipline. He is extremely active and has a difficult time sitting through a class period. Horace is just the opposite: a very shy, timid, and withdrawn boy.

It is 10:07, and Herchel, Marcus, and Gwenn are among the first of Mike's students to file into class. As the students come in, they look in anticipation at the screen in the front of the room. Mike typically displays one or more problems on the overhead for the students as "warm-up" exercises, which they are directed to complete while he takes roll and completes other beginning-of-class routines.

Mike watches and, as soon as Herchel, Marcus, and Gwenn are in their seats, he slowly reads the displayed problem: "On Saturday, the Trebek family drove 17 miles from Henderson to Newton, stopped for 10 minutes to get gas, and then drove 22.5 miles from Newton through Council Rock to Gildford. The trip took 1 hour and 5 minutes, including the stop. On the way back, they took the same route but stopped in Council Rock for lunch. Council Rock is 9.5 miles from Gildford. How much farther will they have to drive to get back to Henderson?"

As Mike reads, he points to each displayed word. "Okay," he smiles after he finishes reading.

"Do you know what the problem is asking you?"

"Could you read the last part again, Mr. Sheppard?" Gwenn asks.

"Sure," Mike nods, and repeats the part of the problem that describes the return trip, again pointing to the words as he reads.

"All right, jump on it. Be ready because I'm calling on one of you first today," he again smiles and touches each of them on the shoulder.

The students are in their seats, and most are studying the screen as the bell rings at 10:10. Mike quickly takes roll and then moves back to Todd's desk.

"Let's take a look at your chart," he says. "You've improved a lot, haven't you?"

"Yeah, look," Todd responds, proudly displaying the following chart.

	2/9–2/13	2/16–2/20	2/23–2/27
Talking out	|||| |||| |||| ||||	|||| ||||	|||| ||
Swearing	|||| ||||	|||| ||	||||
Hitting/ touching	|||| |||	|||| ||||	|||
Out of seat	|||| |||| |||| |||	|||| |||| |||| ||||	|||| |||| |||| |||
Being friendly	||	||||	|||| ||

"That's terrific," Mike whispers to Todd as he leans over the boy's desk. "You're doing much better. We need some more work on 'out-of-seat,' don't we? I don't like getting after you about it, and I know you don't like it either," he went on. "Stop by after class. I have an idea for you. I think it will help. Don't forget to stop. I'll give you a pass to your next class if you're

late. . . . Okay. Get to work on the problem." Mike then gives Todd a light thump on the back and returns to the front of the room.

Mike monitors the students and, seeing that most of them have either finished the problem or have stopped working, he begins at 10:15, "Okay, everyone. How did you do on the problem?"

Amid a mix of "Okay," "Terrible," "Fine," "Too hard," some nods, and a few nonresponses, Mike begins, "Let's review for a minute. . . . What's the first thing we do whenever we have a word problem like this?"

He then looks knowingly at Marcus, remembering his pledge to call on one of them first. . . . "Marcus?"

"Read it over at least twice."

"Good. . . . That's what our problem-solving plan says," Mike continues, pointing to a chart hanging from the top of the chalkboard that has the following information on it.

PLAN FOR SOLVING WORD PROBLEMS

1. Read the problem at least twice.
2. Ask the following questions:
   What is asked for?
   What facts are given?
   What information is needed that we don't have?
   Are unnecessary facts given? What are they?
3. Make a drawing.
4. Solve the problem.
5. Check to see whether the answer makes sense.

"Then what do we do? . . . Melissa?"

"See what the problem asks for."

"Very good. What is the problem asking for? . . . Rachel?"

". . . How much farther they will have to drive?"

"Excellent. Now, think about this. Suppose I solved the problem and decided that they had 39½ miles left to drive. Would that make sense? Why or why not? Everybody think about it for a moment."

Mike hesitates for several seconds and then says, "Okay. What do you think? . . . Herchel?"

". . . I . . . I . . . don't know."

"Oh, yes you do," Mike encourages. "Let's look. . . . How far from Henderson to Gildford altogether?"

"Thir . . ." Rico begins until Mike puts his hand up, stopping him in mid-word. He then waits a few seconds as Herchel studies the sketch on his paper that appears as follows:

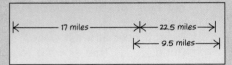

". . . 39 and ½ miles," Herchel says uncertainly. "Oh! . . . The whole trip was only that far, so they couldn't still have that far to go."

"Excellent thinking, Herchel. See, I told you that you knew. That's very good.

"Now go ahead, Rico. How far do they still have to go?"

"Thirty miles," Rico, one of the higher achievers in the class, responds quickly.

"Good," Mike nods. "Someone explain carefully how Rico might have gotten that. . . . Go ahead, Brenda."

". . . The total distance is 39½ miles over, . . . and they came back 9½, . . . so, 39½ minus 9½ is 30."

"Good, Brenda, that's a good, clear description.

"Now," Mike goes on, "is there any unnecessary information in the problem?"

"Yes!" several students respond at once.

"Okay. Like what? . . . Horace?" Mike asks, lowering his tone of voice slightly and moving toward Horace's desk.

". . ."

"Look at the problem," Mike encourages softly.

". . ."

"How long did the trip take?"

". . . An hour and 5 minutes."

"And again, what does the problem ask us for?" Mike continues, nodding to Horace.

". . . How much farther they had to drive."

"Excellent, so the amount of time they took is irrelevant," Mike shrugs, raising his tone of voice and turning back to the front of the room.

"What does *irrelevant* mean?" he asks, suddenly turning back to the class.

"Not necessary," Sherry volunteers quickly.

"Heck," Mike snaps his fingers. "I thought I had you on that one. You're on your toes today," he grinned at the class.

Mike guides the class toward identifying other items of unnecessary information in the problem, and then he asks students to raise their hands, holding up three fingers if they had solved it correctly, two fingers if they had solved it but got an incorrect answer, and one finger if they had gotten no solution. Seeing about a third of the class holding up three fingers, he thinks wryly, "We're going to need some work on this material."

"Okay. Not too bad for the first time through," he continues cheerfully. "Let's take a look at your homework."

Mike then goes through each homework problem just as he did the first one, asking students to relate the problems' parts to each of the steps in the problem-solving plan, drawing a sketch on the chalkboard, and calling on a variety of students to supply specific answers and describe their thinking as they worked their way to the solutions.

With 20 minutes left in the period, he assigns ten more problems for seatwork/homework, and the students begin working.

Once the class is working quietly, Mike nods to Herchel, Marcus, and Gwenn, and the three of them quietly get up from their desks and move to a table at the back of the room. The four of them sit at the table, with Gwenn and Marcus on one side of Mike and Herchel on the other.

"How'd you do on the homework when we went over it?" Mike asks. "Do you think you get it?"

"Sort of," Gwenn responds, and the other two nod.

"Good," Mike smiles. "Now, let's see what we've got, but before we start," he continues, "I noticed your drawing on our practice problem," he says to Herchel. "Let's take another look at it. . . . Go ahead and get it out."

Herchel then gets out his sketch.

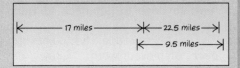

"Take a good look at it," Mike directs. "What looks funny? . . . Gwenn, you and Marcus look too."

"The 9½ miles is longer than the 22½ miles," Gwenn answers after looking at the sketch for a few seconds.

"Exactly," Mike nods. "Now remember, this has to make sense. We know that 22½ is longer than 9½, and also we know that 22½ is longer than 17. So, when you make your sketches, be sure they make sense. Now, you all can do this work. So, I want to see good work from each of you. Okay? Good," he finishes, nodding encouragingly.

"Okay. Go ahead and read the first problem, Gwenn."

"Ramon b . . . b . . . "

"Bought," Mike interjects.

"Bought," Gwenn continues, ". . . bought a CD for $13.95." She finishes reading the problem, haltingly, and with Mike's help.

"Okay. What are we trying to find in this problem?"

"How much more the first CD cost than the cassette?" Marcus answers.

"Good. You all understand the problem?"

The three nod.

"Okay. Let's look at the next one. . . . Go ahead and read it, Marcus."

Mike goes through each of the problems with the three students to be sure they are able to read the problems and comprehend the information in each. As they work, in-dividual students periodically come back to the table and briefly ask questions. Mike then momentarily stops his work with Marcus, Herchel, and Gwenn to answer the question and then returns to working with them. He also stops briefly to go over and speak to Connie and Pamela, who are whispering.

After he returns, he says, "There are about five minutes left in the period. Run back to your desks now and see whether you can get one or two of them done before the bell rings."

Mike then watches as the students work until the bell rings.

As the students file out of the room, Mike catches Todd's eye,

Todd stops, and Mike then leads him to a small area in the back of the room, partially enclosed but facing the front of the class.

"Look here," Mike directs. "Here's what we'll do. When you have the urge to get out of your seat, you quietly get up and move back here for a few minutes. Stay as long as you want, but be sure you pay attention to what we're doing. When you think you're ready to move back to your seat, go ahead. All I'm asking is that you move back and forth quietly. . . . Okay? . . . What do you think?"

Todd nods, and Mike then puts his arm around him and says, "You're doing so well on everything else; this will help, I think. You're a good student. You hang in there. . . . Now, get out of here," Mike smiles, giving Todd a little push. "Here's a pass into Mrs. Miller's class."

Questions for Discussion and Analysis

Now analyze Mike's teaching. In conducting your analysis, you may want to consider the following questions. In each case, be specific and take information directly from the case study to defend your assessment.

1. Describe Mike's use of time. How efficiently did he use his time?
2. Did he create a warm academic climate for his students? Cite specific evidence from the case study.
3. How effective was Mike's classroom management? Again cite specific evidence.
4. How did Mike attempt to ensure success in his teaching?
5. What did Mike do to alter instruction for his students with learning disabilities? How effective were these modifications?

6. What did Mike do to meet the needs of his students with behavior disorders? How effective were these interventions?

7. Give Mike's teaching an overall assessment; use the information in this chapter as a basis for your conclusions. You may also want to consider your answers to Items 1 through 6 in making your analysis.

Summary

Students with Learning Problems

Many students with exceptionalities have mild learning problems that interfere with classroom performance but do not require separate instructional settings. Students who have mental retardation have below average intellectual functioning and impairment in adaptive behavior. Students with learning disabilities have normal levels of intellectual capability but below-average academic performance. Students with AD/HD have difficulties focusing their attention on the learning task at hand. Classroom teachers play an integral part in identifying these students and helping to adapt instruction to meet their needs.

Behavior disorders involve serious, persistent, and age-inappropriate behaviors that interfere with learning and social development. Externalizing behavior disorders are characterized by behaviors such as hyperactivity, uncooperativeness, and defiance. Students with internalizing disorders are withdrawn, depressed, or anxious. Both types of behavior disorders respond to teaching strategies that provide structured support and teach prosocial behaviors.

Communication, Visual, and Hearing Disorders

Communication disorders include speech or expressive disorders, which involve problems in forming and sequencing sounds. Language or receptive disorders are more global and involve problems with the ability to understand or use language to express ideas. Care should be taken to differentiate language disorders from culturally influenced difficulties encountered in learning English as a second language.

Other disabilities include visual and hearing disorders. Although less common than other disabilities, these disorders can be serious because of their potentially adverse influence on communication channels that affect learning. In both instances, teachers can take adaptive steps to modify instruction to meet the special needs of these students.

Students Who Are Gifted and Talented

Gifted and talented students are at the upper end of the ability continuum and display unique talents in specific domains. Acceleration moves these students through the regular curriculum faster; enrichment provides alternative instruction to encourage student exploration.

Changes in the Way Teachers Help Students with Exceptionalities

In the past, students with exceptionalities were often segregated from the regular classroom. Mainstreaming placed them in the regular classroom. Inclusion attempts to take the process a step further by creating a web of services that ensures student success and learning.

A Legal Framework for Working with Students Who Have Exceptionalities

A series of federal laws has changed the way teachers work with students who have exceptionalities. These laws require that students with exceptionalities be taught in the LRE, guaranteed due process through parental involvement, protected against discrimination in testing, and provided with IEPs.

The Teacher's Role in Inclusive Classrooms

Teachers perform three essential roles in effective inclusive classrooms: identification, instruction, and social integration and growth.

Effective instruction for students with exceptionalities uses basic principles of effective teaching, such as effective management and high success rates as a foundation. In addition, strategy instruction teaches students to approach learning tasks by setting and monitoring progress toward goals.

Social acceptance for students with exceptionalities can be promoted through modeling, practice, and feedback. Attitudes of other students can be improved through instructional approaches focusing on increased understanding and through strategies such as peer tutoring and cooperative learning, which provide students with opportunities to interact in productive ways.

Important Concepts _____

acceleration (p. 170)

adaptive fit (p. 173)

attention deficit/hyperactivity disorder (AD/HD) (p. 157)

behavior disorders (BD) (p. 159)

creativity (p. 167)

curriculum-based measurement (p. 177)

curriculum compacting (p. 170)

deaf (p. 165)

enrichment (p. 170)

exceptionalities (p. 152)

gifted and talented students (p. 167)

inclusion (p. 173)

individualized education program (IEP) (p. 177)

language or receptive disorders (p. 163)

learning disabilities (LDs) (p. 155)

least restrictive environment (LRE) (p. 173)

mainstreaming (p. 172)

mental retardation (p. 154)

partial hearing impairment (p. 165)

special education (p. 152)

speech or expressive disorders (p. 162)

visual disability (p. 164)

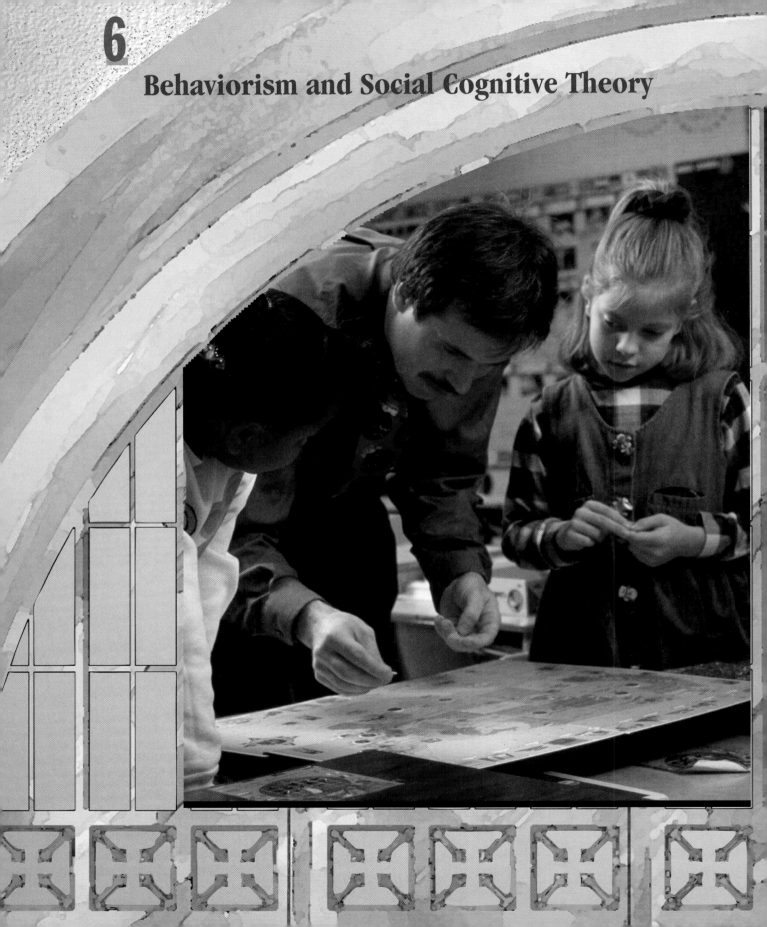

6

Behaviorism and Social Cognitive Theory

Tim, a tenth-grader, was taking Algebra II and had been doing fairly well—getting a few C's but mostly B's on the weekly tests. In fact, he had become fairly confident about his ability to do algebra until the last test, when something inexplicably went wrong. For some reason, he became confused, got solutions mixed up, seemed to "blank out," panicked, and badly failed the test. Even with his parents' sympathy and support, he was devastated. On the next test, he was so anxious and nervous that when he started, the first few answers he circled on his problems had wiggly lines around them from his shaking hand.

"What if I flunk again? . . . I still don't get this stuff. . . . What am I doing in here?" he thought as he struggled with the problems. Although he did better than he had on the previous test, he still barely passed it.

"I'm not sure I can do this," he concluded.

After making only a halfhearted effort on the next test and again barely passing it, he thought, "Maybe I should drop algebra."

He was also more nervous when he took chemistry tests than he had been previously, even though he hadn't done poorly on any chemistry exam. Fortunately, he still did fine in his English and world history classes.

Mrs. Lovisolo, his Algebra II teacher, talked with him, exhorting him to remember that he had only failed one test and hadn't been making his usual effort as he studied.

"Thanks, Mrs. Lovisolo," Tim said, on the brink of tears, "but math . . . is so hard for me. I don't know. Maybe geometry is as far as I can go."

"I don't want to hear those words," she said with a supportive smile. "Now, I want you to relax. You

can do this work. I'm going to keep an eye on you in class, and if you're having trouble, just let me know and we'll work together after school. Okay?"

". . . Okay," Tim said and, although he remained unconvinced, he vowed to redouble his efforts.

Tim's friend Susan sat directly in front of him in Algebra II; another friend, Karen, sat behind him, and he talked with them about his uneasiness. They always did so well on the tests.

Karen was sympathetic, but shrugged. "I pay close attention in class and always do the problems," she commented, "and the tests aren't all that bad."

"I think they're tough," Susan retorted, "so I really study for them. How about if we get together and study?" Susan added. "Maybe it would help, and it could be kinda fun. . . . You want to?"

"Sure," Tim responded uncertainly. Then after thinking about it some more, it sounded like a really good idea. "Yeah, . . . yeah, that would be great!"

Anticipating working with Susan, he thought to himself determinedly, "She has to study hard, and she can do it. I oughta be able to do better."

On Thursday, the night before the next test, Tim went to Susan's home to study with her. In the process, he saw how she selected problems from the book and solved them completely in writing, rather than just reading over the sample problems and explanations. As she began working on her third problem, he asked her why she was doing another one.

"I try to do as many different kinds as I can, to be sure I don't get fooled on the test," she explained. "That way, I'm more confident when I go into the test.

". . . See, this one is different," she continued. "The first thing I look for is how it's different. Then I try it. . . . See, on this one I think we need to find c with . . . you know . . . like b, and then we . . . like get two equations . . . Now it's simpler."

"I sometimes make even . . . a little chart. I try to do at least three problems of each one, . . . of each type we study, and then I check 'em off as I do them. It's sort of fun; . . . I can see I'm making some progress. If I get 'em all, . . . I treat myself with a bowl of ice cream."

". . . Good idea," Tim nodded. "I usually do one, maybe two and if I'm okay on them, I quit," he shrugged.

Tim now has a goal to do three problems of each type, selecting the odd problems so that he can check the correct answers in the back of the book. Also, when Mrs. Lovisolo uses a term in class that he doesn't understand, he writes it down, together with the definition, and then studies it so that he immediately understands what she means when she uses it in her explanations.

Tim did much better on the next test. "Whew, what a relief," he said to himself.

He was still somewhat nervous for the following week's test, but his effort had paid off, and he did very well; in fact, his score was the highest for the year. ". . . Maybe I can do this after all," he concluded with an inward smile.

His new strategy seems to be working; he's less nervous, and his test scores are steadily improving. With each success, he's more comfortable, and he has brought his average back up to nearly a B since his bad experience.

L earning is at the core of any study of educational psychology, and this text focuses on what teachers can do to promote learning in all students. This chapter is the first of three devoted to theoretical descriptions of the topic. We begin by describing learning from a behaviorist perspective. This is followed by a discussion of social cognitive theory, a view of learning that includes elements of behaviorism but that goes beyond it to examine processes, such as learners' beliefs and expectations, that behaviorists don't consider. In Chapters 7, 8 and 9, we extend this discussion to examine cognitive learning in greater detail.

After you've completed your study of this chapter, you should be able to meet the following objectives:

- Explain how classical conditioning can influence student learning.
- Explain student behavior by using concepts such as *reinforcement, punishment, generalization, discrimination, satiation,* and *extinction*.
- Describe the influence of different reinforcement schedules on student behavior.
- Identify examples of modeling and vicarious learning in classroom situations.
- Describe how self-regulation influences student learning.

Behaviorist Views of Learning

Tim's experience in the opening case illustrates the theme of this section. The incident involved *learning,* and in this section of the chapter we examine learning from a behaviorist point of view. According to this view, **learning** is *a relatively enduring change in observable behavior that occurs as a result of experience* (Skinner, 1953; Walker, 1996). Notice that this definition focuses on observable behaviors. Behaviorism doesn't consider any ideas, insights, goals, or needs that are "in learners' heads."

Consider our definition again. It says that the change in behavior is relatively enduring. We all have seen or experienced temporary changes in behavior resulting from illness, injury, or emotional distress. These changes would not be classified as learning.

In addition, changes in behavior resulting from maturation are not considered learning. For example, a 15-year-old can carry a large bag of groceries that his 6-year-old brother cannot even lift. He is bigger and stronger as a result of maturation. Parents say with excitement that their small child has "learned" to walk but, although some experience with crawling is certainly a factor, walking depends more on maturation than on learning.

Let's look again at Tim's situation. He makes wiggly lines around his problems. This behavior is observable and, based on the example, it was relatively enduring. His making wiggly lines was a result of his experience on the earlier test. We would say that these wiggly lines are "learned" behaviors. Other learned behaviors are illustrated in the case study as well, and we discuss them later in the chapter.

In this section we examine three types of learning according to behaviorism. They are outlined in Figure 6.1.

> **6.1**
>
> Identify two other types of enduring behaviors that would not be called learning. Give an example of each type.

Contiguity

Suppose someone asks you, "What is 7 times 8?" and you immediately respond, "56." Your response is the result of learning that occurs through **contiguity,** or *the simple pairing of stimuli (S) and responses (R).* Contiguity is based on the principle that if two sensations occur together often enough, they become associated (Guthrie, 1952; Walker, 1996). **Stimuli** are *all the sights, sounds, smells, and other influences the senses receive from the environment.* **Responses** are *the behaviors that result from the association.* If you pair 7×8 with 56 often enough, you respond "56" when you see 7×8 or hear

> **6.2**
>
> A teacher asks students, "When was the Magna Carta signed?" They are unable to answer. Explain their inability to answer; use the principle of contiguity as the basis for your explanation.

Figure 6.1 Types of learning in behaviorism

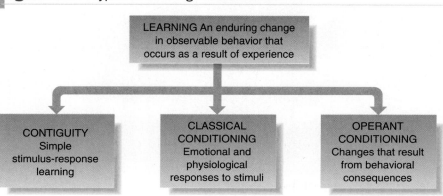

LEARNING An enduring change in observable behavior that occurs as a result of experience

CONTIGUITY
Simple
stimulus-response
learning

CLASSICAL
CONDITIONING
Emotional and
physiological
responses to stimuli

OPERANT
CONDITIONING
Changes that result
from behavioral
consequences

"What is 7 times 8?" Seeing or hearing the 7 × 8 is the stimulus, and 56 is the response. Contiguity occurs in classrooms when stimuli and responses are paired and repeated, such as drill-and-practice activities with flash cards. Tim was applying the principle of contiguity when he wrote new terms and definitions and practiced them.

Classical Conditioning

Although stimulus–response pairings can be used to explain fact learning and other simple behaviors, most learning is more complex. This complexity was originally described by Ivan Pavlov, a Russian physiologist who won a Nobel Prize in 1904 for his work on digestion. As a part of his research, he had his assistants feed dogs meat powder, so that their rates of salivation could be measured. As the research progressed, however, the dogs began to salivate at the sight of the assistants, even when they weren't carrying meat with them (Pavlov, 1928). This startling phenomenon resulted in a turn in Pavlov's work and opened a new field of study called **classical conditioning,** or *respondent learning,* because *the learner is responding to the environment.*

Flash cards and drill and practice help students learn facts through contiguity.

In Pavlov's experiments a dog's initial salivation was an **unconditioned response;** *a reflexive, involuntary response* induced by the meat powder, which was an **unconditioned stimulus,** *the original stimulus that produces an unconditioned response.*

Now the process becomes a bit more complex. Initially, Pavlov's dogs didn't react one way or another to the lab assistants; they were **neutral stimuli,** *stimuli that don't produce any response.* In time, however, the lab assistants became *associated* with the meat, and they elicited salivation all by themselves. The lab assistants became **conditioned stimuli,** which are *stimuli that become associated with unconditioned stimuli* and produce **conditioned responses,** *responses identical or similar to the unconditioned responses.*

Let's see how Tim *learned* to fear tests, based on these ideas. Initially, he didn't react to tests one way or another; they were neutral stimuli. Then he failed the test and was devastated by his failure. Subsequent tests became *associated* with his initial failure, resulting in his nervousness, as evidenced by the wiggly lines around his answers.

Our examples illustrate the essential characteristics of classical conditioning. They are outlined below.

6.3

Identify the unconditioned and conditioned stimuli and the unconditioned and conditioned responses in Tim's case.

- Classical conditioning is a form of learning. Tim's behavior underwent an enduring change as a result of his experience—he *learned* to be nervous in tests, just as Pavlov's dogs *learned* to salivate at the sight of the lab assistants.

- Classically conditioned responses are *emotional or physiological* and *involuntary* (Walker, 1996). Tim's nervousness was an emotional response, and it was out of his control; he didn't choose to be nervous when he took Algebra II tests.

- Conditioned and unconditioned stimuli, which are *unrelated,* became *associated.* Pavlov's assistants and the meat powder, which weren't related in any way, became associated, and Tim's tests became associated with failure.

- Conditioned and unconditioned responses are *identical or similar.* In Pavlov's experiments, they were identical. In Tim's case, devastation and anxiety are related emotions.

Classical Conditioning in the Classroom

Classroom examples of classical conditioning are actually quite common. For example, many students experience test anxiety (Pintrich & Schunk, 1996). It's not uncommon for some young children to become physically ill in anticipation of school, and some parents are reluctant to attend school functions or respond to teacher requests because of past unpleasant experiences at school. Classical conditioning helps us explain these problems.

6.4

Using concepts from classical conditioning, explain a child becoming ill in anticipation of school, and explain why a parent might be reluctant to attend school functions.

It can also help us explain positive feelings toward school and can help sensitize teachers to the importance of a positive emotional climate in their classrooms. Some researchers, in fact, suggest that the emotional reactions associated with the topics they study are the most meaningful experiences learners have (Gentile, 1996). For example, suppose students—often uneasy about a new school, class, or topic, such as a difficult idea in math—are treated with warmth, caring, and encouragement by their teachers. Learners respond positively to these displays of genuine warmth and encouragement. If teachers are consistently caring and encouraging, students will begin to associate school

Classical conditioning helps teachers understand how supportive classroom environments and warm and caring teachers result in positive feelings toward schools and learning.

and studying with the teacher's encouragement, and the school will elicit comfortable and safe feelings in the students. These relationships are outlined in Table 6.1.

Generalization and Discrimination

6.5

One of this text's authors gets a funny feeling when he enters a dentist's office. This doesn't happen when he goes to see a medical doctor. Using the concepts of *generalization* and *discrimination,* explain the feeling.

Let's look once more at our opening case study. In addition to his nervousness when he took his Algebra II tests, Tim became nervous when he took chemistry tests, even though he hadn't done poorly on any of them. His fears had generalized to chemistry. **Generalization** *occurs when a stimulus related to the conditioned stimulus elicits the conditioned response all by itself.* The physical sciences are somewhat related to algebra, so chemistry tests are stimuli related to the algebra tests, and they elicited the conditioned response—nervousness.

The process can also work in a positive way. Students who have come to associate school with the caring of one teacher may, through generalization, have similar reactions to other classes, club activities, and school-related functions.

The opposite of generalization is discrimination. **Discrimination** is *the ability to give different responses to related but not identical stimuli.* For example, Tim is nervous

Table 6.1   Promoting positive classroom climate

Unconditioned Stimuli	Unconditioned Responses
Teacher displays warm, caring, and encouraging behaviors	Learners' feelings of comfort

Conditioned Stimuli	Conditioned responses
Classrooms and topics (which have become associated with the teacher's manner)	Learners' feelings of comfort

during chemistry tests, but not during those in English and history. He discriminates between English and algebra, as well as between history and algebra.

Extinction

In our case study, we saw that Tim has been doing better since he started working with Susan and changed his study habits. In time, if he continues to succeed, his nervousness will disappear, or the conditioned response will become extinct. **Extinction** _occurs when the conditioned stimulus occurs repeatedly in the absence of the unconditioned stimulus._ Eventually, the conditioned stimulus no longer elicits the conditioned response. In Tim's case, repeated test taking (the conditioned stimulus) occurring without failure (the unconditioned stimulus) will, in time, no longer result in nervousness (the conditioned response).

Classroom Connections

Applying Contiguity in Your Classroom

1. Carefully consider the forms of fact learning for which students will be responsible. Provide frequent review and drill to cement the contiguous links in the facts.
   - An elementary teacher takes a few minutes each morning to review difficult multiplication facts in a simple drill-and-practice activity.
   - A history teacher wants students to remember several crucial dates. She identifies the dates and their significance on a handout and tells students they're responsible for knowing the information. She reviews the material with them periodically before they are tested.

Applying Classical Conditioning in Your Classroom

2. Provide a safe and warm environment so that the classroom will be associated with positive emotions.
   - A first-grade teacher greets each of her students with a smile when they come into the room in the morning. She makes an attempt to periodically ask each of them about their family, a pet, or some other personal part of their lives.
   - A junior-high teacher makes a point of establishing and enforcing rules that forbid students to ridicule each other in any way, particularly when they're involved in class discussions or responding to teacher questions. He makes respect for each other a high priority in his classroom.

3. When questioning students, put them in safe situations and arrange the results to ensure a positive outcome.
   - A fourth-grade inner-city teacher tries to get all his students to participate by doing the following:
     a. When calling on reluctant responders or low-achieving students, he begins with questions such as, "What do you notice about the problem?" and "How would you compare the two examples?" These are questions for which virtually any answer is appropriate.
     b. When students are unable or unwilling to respond, he prompts them until they give an acceptable answer. (Effective prompting techniques are discussed in Chapter 11.)
     c. He calls on all students in his class, so that being in his class becomes associated with responding and making an effort.

4. Provide students with practice in anxiety-inducing situations.
   - A senior-high math teacher deals with test anxiety by specifying precisely what information students are accountable for on tests. He gives them sample items to practice on and provides ample opportunity to go over problem areas before the test.

- When a middle-school social-studies teacher encounters students who are anxious about making a presentation to the whole class, she has them come in and make their presentations to her alone so that they can practice and she can provide reassurance and support.

Operant Conditioning

So far, we've progressed from simple S–R pairings, which apply to fact learning (contiguity), to more complex S–R relationships (classical conditioning), and we've used these relationships to help explain emotional and physiological reactions to classroom activities and other events. These explanations are inadequate, however, because people often initiate behaviors, rather than merely respond to stimuli. In other words, people "operate" on their environments, which is the source of the term *operant conditioning*.

This leads us to the work of B. F. Skinner (1904–1990), a behavioral psychologist whose influence in the mid-1960s was so great that heads of psychology departments late in the 1960s identified him as the most influential psychologist of the twentieth century (Myers, 1970). Skinner argued that, instead of merely responding to stimuli, learners' actions are more controlled by the consequences of the behavior than by events preceding the behavior. A **consequence** is *an outcome (stimulus) occurring after the behavior that influences future behaviors*. For example, a teacher's praise after a student answers is a consequence. Being stopped by the highway patrol and fined for speeding is also a consequence. Test results and grades are consequences, as are recognition for outstanding work and reprimands for inappropriate behavior.

Operant and classical conditioning are often confused. To help clarify the differences, a comparison of the two is presented in Table 6.2. We see that learning occurs as a result of experience for both classical and operant conditioning, but the type of behavior is different and the behavior and stimulus occur in the opposite order for the two.

Let's turn to a detailed discussion of operant conditioning and the different consequences of behavior as they are presented in Figure 6.2.

Reinforcement

Imagine that during a class discussion you make a comment and your instructor responds, "That was a very insightful idea. Good thinking." The likelihood that you'll try to make another comment in the future increases. The instructor's comment is a **reinforcer,** *a consequence that increases the frequency or duration of a behavior*. The *process of applying reinforcers to increase behavior* is called **reinforcement,** and it exists in two forms: positive and negative.

★**Positive Reinforcement.** **Positive reinforcement (PR)** is *the process of increasing the frequency or duration of a behavior as the result of presenting a reinforcer*. In class-

6.6

A child approaches a dog and is bitten. From that point on, the child is filled with fear whenever a dog approaches, and the child runs away. Describe the classically conditioned aspect of this example, and also describe the operantly conditioned aspect of this example.

Table 6.2 A comparison of classical and operant conditioning

	Classical Conditioning	**Operant Conditioning**
Behavior	Involuntary (Person does not have control of behavior) Emotional Physiological	Voluntary (Person has control of behavior)
Order	Behavior follows stimulus	Behavior precedes stimulus (consequence)
How learning occurs	Neutral stimuli become associated with unconditioned stimuli	Consequences of behaviors influence subsequent behaviors
Example	Learners associate classrooms (initially neutral) with the warmth of teachers, so classrooms elicit positive emotions.	Learners attempt to answer questions and are praised, so their attempts to answer increase.
Key researcher	Pavlov	Skinner

Figure 6.2 Consequences of behavior

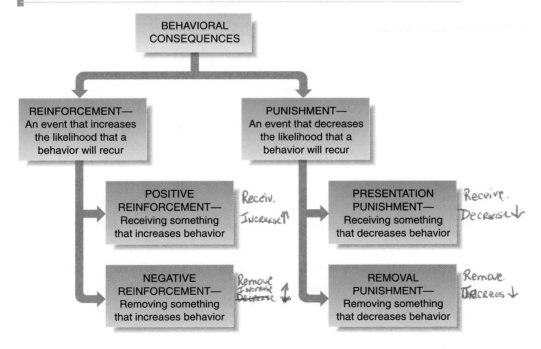

Positive reinforcers, such as grades, can be powerful motivators for students.

6.7

Praise, though well intended, isn't always a positive reinforcer. How do we know when it isn't?

rooms we typically think of a positive reinforcer as something desired or valued, such as your instructor's comment, but an *increase* in student horseplay following a reprimand, for example, can also indicate that positive reinforcement is occurring.

Teacher praise in all its forms is perhaps the most common positive reinforcer in classrooms. High test scores, "happy faces" for young children, tokens that can be cashed in for privileges, and stars on the bulletin board all can act as positive reinforcers for students. Likewise, attentive looks from students, student questions, high student test scores, and compliments from students or their parents serve as positive reinforcers for teachers.

The Premack Principle.

Don Zentz's jazz band students love playing modern, upbeat jazz-rock compositions, but are less enthusiastic about some of the standards.

"No, not 'Mood Indigo' again," they protest when he holds up the sheet music for the Duke Ellington classic.

"A good job one time through it, and we'll do 'Watermelon Man,'" he counters.

"All right! Let's do it!" they shout.

In this example, Mr. Zentz employed the Premack Principle, named after David Premack (1965). Also called "Grandma's rule" ("First eat your vegetables, and then you can have dessert"), the **Premack Principle** says that *a more frequent or more preferred activity can be used as a positive reinforcer for a less frequent or less preferred activity*. Mr. Zentz's students preferred playing "Watermelon Man" to "Mood Indigo," so he used it as a reinforcer for playing the less preferred piece.

A geography teacher who has students wanting to do their map projects says, "All right, as soon as you've finished identifying the longitude and latitude of the five cities

I've given you, you may begin your map projects," is also using the Premack Principle. It affords both teachers and students a variety of instructionally related reinforcers that are easy to administer.

Negative Reinforcement. You've just completed a strenuous workout, and your body is "achy," so you decide to take aspirin to get some relief and help you sleep better. It works, and the next time you work out you take the aspirin again. In fact, some times you take the aspirin before you work out to avoid the aches and pains.

These examples illustrate the concept of **negative reinforcement (NR)** which is *the process of removing or avoiding a stimulus to increase behavior* (Skinner, 1953). Notice that although the term *negative* appears in the label, negative reinforcement results in an *increase* instead of a decrease in behavior. In our example, the "achy" muscles were the stimuli that were removed when you took the aspirin, so your behavior increased; you took the aspirin more readily the next time. You also *avoided* the achy muscles on another occasion by taking the aspirin before you worked out.

Notice that when negative reinforcement is applied, one of two situations exists:

1. Learners *are in* the situation before they demonstrate the behavior. Your muscles ached before you took the aspirin.
2. Learners can avoid a consequence (you took the aspirin to avoid the achy muscles).

Punishment

Positive and negative reinforcers are consequences that strengthen behavior. *Some consequences, however, weaken behaviors or decrease their frequency. They are called* **punishers** *and the process of using these consequences to decrease behavior is called* **punishment.**

Presentation Punishment. From Figure 6.2, you can see that **presentation punishment (PP),** *occurs when a learner's behavior decreases as a result of being presented with a punisher.* Presentation punishment is intended when students have to pick up lunchroom trash because they were rowdy or when teachers verbally reprimand students for misbehavior. Picking up the trash and the reprimands are intended as punishers designed to decrease the unwanted behaviors.

Removal Punishment. There are two kinds of punishment illustrated in Figure 6.2. Whereas presentation punishment is the process of weakening a behavior by presenting a punisher, *decreasing behavior by removing a stimulus or the inability to get positive reinforcement (PR) is* **removal punishment (RP).** As with negative reinforcement, the learner is in the situation prior to the consequence; but unlike negative reinforcement, removal punishment reduces rather than increases behavior.

A fairly common and somewhat controversial application of removal punishment is called *time-out.* A misbehaving student is removed from the class and physically isolated behind filing cabinets or some other barrier. The rationale is that removal from the class eliminates the student's chances to get positive reinforcement, so isolation acts as a form of removal punishment. In other cases, students are sent to another teacher's classroom or kept in detention after school. In the case of detention, the student's opportunity to play and interact with classmates is taken away. When not used excessively, time-out can be an effective management technique (Skiba & Raison, 1990; White & Bailey, 1990).

6.8

Judy is off-task in your class, and you admonish her for her misbehavior. However, in a few moments she's off-task again. What concept from operant conditioning does this situation illustrate? Explain.

6.9

Darren's behavior is disruptive to the point that his teacher finally writes a referral and Darren is sent to the school dean. Unfortunately, Darren's behavior is even worse the next day, so he is again sent out of class. What concept from behaviorism is best illustrated by Darren's behavior? Explain.

6.10

Picking up the trash and reprimands are *intended* as punishers. How would we know if they *actually are* punishers? What would indicate to us that they are reinforcers instead?

6.11

Corporal (physical) punishment is presentation punishment that is still used in some schools. Using classical conditioning as a basis, describe an important undesirable outcome that might result from using corporal punishment.

6.12

Explain how allowing students to talk with each other during detention or even allowing them to finish their homework might defeat its purpose.

Let's consider another teacher's application of removal punishment.

Bette Ponce has been having management problems with her second-grade class. To try to solve these problems, she hands each of her second-graders a small packet containing three slips of paper every morning when they come into the room. Each time a student breaks one of her classroom rules, a slip of paper is taken from that student's packet. Bette then calls the parents of any students who lose all three slips during the course of the day. Losing all three slips for a second day results in half an hour of detention.

Bette also combines positive reinforcement with the program. Any student who has ten or more slips left in his or her packet by the end of the week can trade the slips for free time and other rewards.

Bette's system is sometimes called **response cost,** *the application of removal punishment by taking away reinforcers already given.* Bette's students are given the slips of paper, which they lose for infractions of the rules. Traffic fines, revoked drivers' licenses, backing up ten yards for holding in football games, and loss of free classroom time previously earned are all additional examples of response cost.

Using Punishers: Research Results.   What long-range impact does the use of punishment have on learners? Is it effective? Does it work? Should it ever be used?

6.13

You want to teach a desired behavior, and you want to use behaviorism as the basis for doing so. Describe specifically how you would accomplish this.

Work done in the 1950s indicated that punishers only temporarily weakened undesirable behaviors (Sears, Maccoby, & Levin, 1957), but these findings were later refuted (Johnson, 1972). If the punisher is severe enough, behavior can be suppressed, and using punishers may be justified in extreme cases. Chronically and severely disruptive students do not have the right to destroy the classroom environment for students who want to learn, and if the only alternative is removing the disrupters, this action may be appropriate. Remember, however, that a punisher doesn't teach desired behaviors; it only suppresses undesirable ones. Students must still be taught appropriate behaviors.

Sensitivity and good judgment are required in using punishers. For instance, if punishers are routinely used, students may become desensitized to punishment, the teacher may become aversive, and punished students may generalize their aversion to the class, other teachers, and the school (Jenson, Sloan, & Young, 1988). A classroom management system based primarily on punishers is flawed and should be reexamined.

As an alternative, many educational leaders emphasize positive reinforcement. For example, everyone's heard the maxim "Catch 'em being good." Research indicates that systems focusing on positive behaviors are vastly superior to those emphasizing a decrease in inappropriate behaviors (Williams, 1987).

Focusing exclusively on positive behaviors isn't a panacea, however. After all aversive consequences are eliminated, some students may actually become more disruptive (Pfiffer, Rosen, & O'Leary, 1985; Rosen, O'Leary, Joyce, Conway, & Pfiffer, 1984). A probable solution is a combination of classroom rules with clear consequences. We discuss these issues in detail in Chapter 11.

Operant Conditioning: Applications

In the previous section, we introduced operant conditioning concepts and began to examine their classroom applications. We turn now to a more systematic look at those applications.

Generalization and Discrimination.   We examined generalization and discrimination when we discussed classical conditioning, and now we consider them from an operant

Figure 6.3　Squares and a rectangle

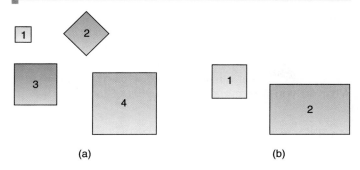

(a)　　　　　　　　　　　(b)

perspective. As an example, suppose kindergarten students see shapes such as those in Figure 6.3a, and respond with "square." Similarly, after dissecting a shark or frog, biology students recognize the heart in each case. Both the squares and the hearts are similar but not identical. The squares differ in size and orientation, and a shark's heart is two-chambered, whereas a frog's is three-chambered. Nevertheless, students learn that they are all squares or hearts despite these differences. They have generalized.

Like classical conditioning, **generalization** *is giving the same response to similar but not identical stimuli.* The responses are voluntary, however, rather than involuntary—as they are in the case of classical conditioning—and result from reinforcers. For example, children are reinforced for saying the first shape in Figure 6.3b is a square but are told, "No, it's a rectangle," when they say the second shape is a square. This feedback helps them learn to *discriminate* between the two shapes. Likewise, the biology student who recognizes the difference between the frog's heart and its liver is also discriminating.

Discrimination *is the ability to give different responses to similar but not identical stimuli.* The importance of discrimination is illustrated in reading readiness tasks in which young children learn to respond differently to *p* and *q* or *b* and *d* and other related letters. They learn these discriminations through feedback.

Generalization and Discrimination: The Role of Feedback.　The need to generalize and discriminate is obvious. It would be impossible, for example, for children to learn each individual shape they encounter; to help them, shapes are categorized into concepts such as *square, circle,* and *rectangle.* On the other hand, if they couldn't discriminate between concepts, the world would be incredibly confusing. The role of teachers in this process is to provide feedback. **Feedback** *is information about the accuracy or appropriateness of a response,* and it has been consistently linked to student learning (Weinert & Helmke, 1995).

Effective feedback has four essential characteristics:

1. It is immediate.
2. It is specific.
3. It provides corrective information for the learner.
4. It has a positive emotional tone (Brophy & Good, 1986; Murphy, Weil, & McGreal, 1986).

To illustrate these ideas, let's examine three examples.

Mr. Dennis:	What kind of figure is shown on the overhead, Jo?
Jo:	A square.
Mr. Dennis:	Not quite. Help her out, . . . Steve?

> **6.14**
>
> Identify two differences between generalization and discrimination in the context of operant conditioning, compared with generalization and discrimination in the context of classical conditioning.

Ms. West:	What kind of figure is shown on the overhead, Jo?
Jo:	A square.
Ms. West:	No, it's a rectangle. What is the next figure, . . . Albert?

Ms. Baker:	What kind of figure is shown on the overhead, Jo?
Jo:	A square.
Ms. Baker:	No, remember we said that all sides have the same length in a square. What do you notice about the lengths of the sides in this figure?

6.15

You're teaching students about adjectives and you display the sentence, "The damaged car sped quickly away from the scene of the accident," on the overhead and then ask, "What is the adjective in this sentence?" Bryan answers, "accident." Based on the characteristics of effective feedback, state specifically what you would say to Bryan.

In comparing the three examples, you can see that the feedback is *immediate* in each case, but that Mr. Dennis's feedback gave Jo no information about her answer other than it was incorrect; it was not *specific* and provided no *corrective information*. Ms. West's feedback was specific, but it gave Jo no corrective information. Ms. Baker, in contrast, provided specific, corrective information in her feedback.

The examples provide no information about the emotional tone of the feedback. Positive emotional tone means that teachers are supportive in their responses to student answers. Harsh, critical, or sarcastic feedback detracts from both learning and student motivation (Pintrich & Schunk, 1996).

Praise.   Because it is probably the most well known and adaptable form of teacher feedback, we examine praise in this section. Research reveals some interesting patterns:

6.16

Using classical conditioning as a basis, explain why harsh, critical, or sarcastic feedback might detract from learning and motivation.

- Praise is used less often than most teachers believe—less than five times per class.

- Praise for good behavior is quite rare, occurring once every two or more hours in the elementary grades and even less as students get older.

- Praise tends to depend as much on the type of student—high achieving, well behaved, and attentive—as on the quality of the student's response.

- Teachers praise students based on the answers they expect to receive as much as on those they actually hear (Brophy, 1981).

Effective praise includes the characteristics of effective feedback but goes beyond them (Figure 6.4). Using praise effectively is complex and requires sound teacher judgment (Brophy, 1981). For example, praise must be perceived as sincere to be credible. However, effusive praise after every answer loses its credibility even if the teacher is sincere. This is particularly true with older students. They tend to discount praise they per-

Figure 6.4   Characteristics of effective praise

Praise genuinely

Praise immediately

Praise specifically

Praise incidental answers

Praise effort

Praise judiciously

ceive as invalid and interpret praise given for easy tasks as indicating that the teacher thinks they're not intelligent (Emmer, 1988; Good, 1987a).

Young children, on the other hand, tend to take praise at face value and bask in praise given openly in front of a class, whereas junior-high students may react better if it's given quietly and individually (Stipek, 1984). High-anxiety students and those from low-SES backgrounds tend to react more positively to praise than their more confident and advantaged counterparts.

Finally, although research indicates that specific praise is more effective than general praise, if every desired answer is praised specifically, it begins to sound stilted and artificial, and the flow of a lesson can be disrupted. You must judge the appropriate mix of specific and general praise.

Rosenshine (1987) offers a solution to this dilemma. He suggests that praise for student answers that are delivered with confidence should be simple and general. In contrast, praise for student answers that are correct but tentative should be specific and provide additional or affirming information.

Praise that comes from a respected teacher can be a powerful reinforcer for students of all ages.

Shaping. Let's turn now to another application of positive reinforcement.

"I start out praising every answer even if it's only partially right," Ms. Brugera commented. "I also praise them for trying even if they can't give me an answer. Then as they improve, I praise them only for better, more complete answers, until finally they have to give well thought-out explanations before I'll say anything."

"I don't," Mr. Jordan responded. "I like to give a lot of praise, but I think praising every answer takes too much time. I also think if you do too much, you lose your credibility, so I start right off praising them only when they give me a really good answer."

According to Ms. Brugera, her students aren't always able to give her the answers she is after, so she praises partial answers and even effort. Gradually, they have to give more complete responses to earn her praise. She is applying the concept of **shaping,** *the process of reinforcing successive approximations of a desired behavior.* Although Ms. Brugera was obviously after the correct answer, student effort was a beginning step, and a partially correct response was a close approximation of the desired behavior. By reinforcing each step, she hoped to eventually get complete and thoughtful answers from her students.

Reinforcement Schedules. Even though you may not have played them, you likely understand how slot machines work. You insert a coin, pull the handle, and hope for some coins in return. Sometimes a few coins drop into the tray; many times they don't. The coins you receive are reinforcers, and if you continue to receive them, you're likely to continue playing. Since you only periodically receive the coins, you're on an **intermittent reinforcement schedule,** which is *the process of reinforcing a behavior only periodically.* If you received coins every time you pulled the handle, you would be on a **continuous reinforcement schedule,** which occurs when *every response is reinforced.* These two basic types illustrate **reinforcement schedules,** which describe *pat-*

6.17

Based on Piaget's work in Chapter 2 and Erikson's work in Chapter 3, explain why younger and older students might respond differently to praise. Why might older students interpret praise for easy tasks negatively?

6.18

Felicia, one of your students, puts her pencil down and says, "I can't do these!" when given a math assignment. Describe specifically how you could use shaping to help Felicia.

terns in the frequency and predictability of reinforcers. By praising every student answer, Ms. Brugera initially used a continuous schedule in her shaping process, whereas Mr. Jordan used an intermittent schedule.

There are two types of intermittent reinforcement schedules. **Interval schedules** *distribute reinforcers based on time;* **ratio schedules** *base reinforcers on the number of responses.* Teachers use a **fixed-interval schedule** *when they reinforce learners on a predictable time interval,* such as every three minutes or every day. A **variable-interval schedule** *changes the amount of time between reinforcers in an unpredictable way.*

Mr. Jordan praised students on the basis of responses, rather than time, and he praised on the basis of his judgment of the answer's quality, rather than every fifth answer, for example. He was using a **variable-ratio schedule,** which is *a schedule that reinforces students in an unpredictable way based on the number of responses.* If he had chosen to praise every third or fifth or some other numbered answer, he would have been using a **fixed-ratio schedule,** which is *a schedule that reinforces students in a predictable way based on the number of responses.*

Some of the ways that continuous and intermittent reinforcement schedules are used in classrooms is outlined in Table 6.3.

These different schedules are important to you as a teacher because each has advantages and disadvantages. A continuous schedule yields the fastest rates of initial learning, so, for example, it can be effective when students are initially learning to solve equations. On the other hand, the behaviors are less persistent; i.e., learners quickly stop displaying the behaviors when the reinforcers are removed

Fixed schedules also have disadvantages: behavior increases rapidly just before the reinforcer is given and then decreases rapidly and remains low until just before the next reinforcer is given. For instance, if you give a quiz every Friday—a fixed-interval schedule—students may study diligently on Thursday and then not study again until the following Thursday.

This might suggest using a variable-interval schedule, such as giving "pop" quizzes. This strategy, however, has its own disadvantages. It can cause high anxiety in students and detract from their motivation to learn. The best compromise is probably brief, frequent, announced quizzes once a week or even more often (Eggen, 1997; Kika, McLaughlin, & Dixon, 1992).

6.19

What specific type of reinforcement schedule are people on when they play a slot machine?

6.20

To encourage on-task behaviors, a teacher has a classroom beeper that periodically makes a noise. If students are on-task when the beeper goes off, the class gets points toward a party. What reinforcement schedule is the teacher using? Explain.

6.21

Explain how pop quizzes might increase test anxiety; use classical conditioning as a basis for your explanation.

Table 6.3 Reinforcement schedules and examples

Schedule	Example
Continuous	A teacher "walks students through" the steps for solving simultaneous equations. They are liberally praised at each step as they first learn the solution.
Fixed-ratio	The algebra teacher announces, "As soon as you've done two problems in a row correctly, you may start on your homework assignment so that you'll be able to finish by the end of class."
Variable-ratio	Students volunteer to answer questions by raising their hands and are called on at random.
Fixed-interval	Students are given a quiz every Friday.
Variable-interval	Students are given unannounced quizzes.

Potency and Satiation. As you would expect, reinforcers vary in their effectiveness. Behaviorists use the term **potency** to refer to *a reinforcer's ability to strengthen behaviors*. Reinforcement potency depends on at least three factors:

- The learners themselves. High test scores and recognition, for example, are effective reinforcers for some students but not for others.

- The source of reinforcers. For instance, compliments are more potent reinforcers when they come from respected teachers than from those less respected.

- The frequency of reinforcers. A simple "Excellent!" written beside a response on a test paper can be a potent reinforcer, but if it appears too often or is written on every student's paper, it can lose its potency.

When *a reinforcer occurs so frequently that it loses its potency,* **satiation** is the result. Mr. Jordan demonstrated that he was aware of the possibility of satiation when he chose to be judicious in his use of praise.

Satiation can be used to eliminate the power of a reinforcer. For example, we've all heard the tale of the father who catches his son smoking behind the barn and then forces the boy to smoke the rest of the pack of cigarettes. Although we wouldn't recommend the father's technique, classroom applications of satiation have been used successfully. Let's look at an example.

> Ms. Ortega was having a problem with chronic note-passing in her seventh-grade English class, so she developed the following plan. After identifying the culprits, she required them to write a long personal note to a friend near the end of class while the other students began their homework. The note could not be related to classwork, nor could it be copied, and she required it to be a full handwritten page. She didn't read any of the notes but did inspect them to be certain they were of proper length. If they weren't, she demanded that the students continue writing until the page was full or until the period ended.
>
> By the end of the second day, several of the students asked whether they could stop writing notes and work on their homework, and by the end of the third day, Ms. Ortega stopped the process. She has not had problems with note-writing in her class since that time.

This example again illustrates the importance of teacher sensitivity and professional judgment. For instance, Ms. Ortega made a point of not reading any of the notes, so she didn't embarrass the students or violate their privacy. She required that the topic be some form of personal note so that note-writing became the aversive behavior. Had she allowed them to write about a class topic, the topic or writing itself could have become aversive instead.

Ms. Ortega was also respected by the students as a teacher who was strict but fair. She cared about her students and communicated that she expected them to learn. Had these factors not existed, her application of satiation might not have succeeded.

Extinction. You saw in our opening case study that Tim's nervousness was reduced with each test and that, in time, it could be eliminated. This was an example of extinction with classical conditioning.

Operantly conditioned behaviors can also become extinct, as illustrated in the following example.

> Renita, a tenth-grader, enjoyed school and liked to respond in her classes. She was attentive and raised her hand, eager to answer most teachers' questions. She said she could "stay awake better when the teacher asks questions."

6.22

With what kind of a reinforcement schedule—continuous or intermittent—would satiation occur first? What implication does this have for your teaching?

6.23

Using concepts from classical conditioning, explain how writing might become aversive if used as a form of punishment.

Mr. Frank, her world-history teacher, asked a few questions but usually lectured. Renita raised her hand when he did ask a question, but someone would usually blurt out the answer before she could respond.

Renita rarely raises her hand now and often catches herself daydreaming in world history.

6.24

Explain specifically the difference between extinction in the context of operant conditioning and extinction in the context of classical conditioning. What key feature is similar in both?

This situation demonstrates how operantly conditioned behaviors can become extinct and, further, how important the way we teach is in promoting student attention and learning. For Renita, being called on by the teacher reinforced both her attempts to respond and her attention. Because she wasn't called on or allowed to respond, she wasn't reinforced, and her behaviors were becoming extinct. **Extinction,** *from an operant perspective, is the elimination of a response as a result of nonreinforcement.*

Often, teachers don't interact enough with their students; this is unfortunate because classroom interaction and learning are closely related (Good & Brophy, 1997; Nystrand & Gamoran, 1989). Renita's experience illustrates one aspect of this relationship, and our study of behaviorism helps us understand why classroom interaction and learning are so closely related. (We discuss the role of interaction in detail—both teacher to student and student to student—in Chapters 11, 12, and 13.)

6.25

Identify one characteristic that satiation, extinction, and punishment have in common. Describe the specific differences in each.

Cues: Antecedents to Behavior. In our discussion so far, we have emphasized the consequences of behavior. What do we do, however, when we identify behaviors that we want to reinforce, but we can't because students don't demonstrate the behaviors? For instance, we ask questions, and we want to reinforce students' answers, but often they don't answer or they answer incorrectly. Unfortunately, this situation often occurs with the very kind of student—low achieving or poorly motivated—we're trying to involve in the first place.

We can provide **cues,** *antecedent stimuli that prompt the learner to display the desired behavior.* For example:

Mrs. Wendt was working with her fourth-graders on adverbs. She wrote this sentence on the chalkboard:

"John quickly jerked his head when he heard his name called."

Then she asked, "What is the adverb in the sentence? . . . Wendy?"
". . ."
"Look at the sentence. What did John do?"
". . . He . . . er . . . jerked . . . his head."
"How did he jerk it?"
". . . Ahh . . . quickly."
"So what is the adverb?"
". . . Is . . . it . . . quickly?"
Mrs. Wendt smiled, "Yes! Well done, Wendy."

6.26

Look again at the example with Mrs. Wendt. Identify the specific cues she used to help Wendy respond.

Mrs. Wendt provided cues that allowed Wendy to produce the desired behavior, which Mrs. Wendt then reinforced.

Cues come in other forms as well. When a teacher moves to the front of the class, turns off the light switch, or walks among the students as they do seatwork, she is cuing them to turn their attention toward her, become quiet, or remain on-task. In each case, the desired behavior can then be reinforced. Expert teachers use both verbal and nonverbal cues to develop routines that result in smoothly running classrooms (Cazden, 1986; Doyle, 1986).

Teacher questions act as effective cues to elicit responses from a number of students.

Implications of Behaviorism for Instruction.   What do the applications you've studied in this section suggest for the way students learn and the way we should teach? Think about how you learned many of the grammar rules you use in your writing. Most of us have completed many exercises similar to "Juanita and (I, me) went to the football game." The assumption is that being able to complete exercises such as these will ultimately result in us becoming skilled writers. This type of exercise is so common that we may not realize it is based on principles of behaviorism.

According to behaviorism, information must be broken down into small, specific items. This allows learners to display and teachers to focus on observable behaviors; teachers can *see* whether the learner identifies the "I" or the "me" in the sentence above, for example. If learners demonstrate the behaviors, they're reinforced; if not, they receive corrective feedback until they do. This tactic promotes generalization and discrimination.

The teacher's role is to present information in highly organized and tightly sequenced segments that help learners demonstrate the desired behaviors. Learners are viewed as passive recipients of the information, and learning is described as hierarchical, with prerequisite skills mastered before more advanced ones are tackled.

Historically, programmed learning, teaching machines, and many of the early instructional computer programs were based on behaviorist principles. Criticisms of this approach have increased in recent years, and we discuss these criticisms in the next section.

Putting Behaviorism into Perspective

Like virtually any theory, behaviorism has both its proponents and its critics. In this section we examine some of the arguments related to behaviorism.

6.27

Using the behaviorist concepts of generalization and discrimination, describe the teachers' goal in the (I, me) exercise.

Criticisms of behaviorism include:

- Assuming learners are passive, as behaviorists do, isn't valid. Teachers can attest to the misconceptions and sometimes "off-the-wall" ideas students bring to the classroom. They don't acquire these ideas through reinforcement; instead, they are actively trying to make sense of the world and, to them, these idiosyncratic and sometimes bizarre notions make sense.

- Behaviorism is unable to adequately explain higher-order functions, such as language. For instance, Chomsky and Miller (1958) demonstrated that even people with small vocabularies would have to learn sentences at a rate faster then one per second throughout their lifetimes if their learning were based on responses and reinforcers.

- Much of what we learn is not effectively acquired through reinforcement of small, specific, decontextualized items of information. For example, we learn to write effectively by practicing writing in meaningful contexts, not by responding to exercises such as "Juanita and (I, me) went to the football game."

- Offering reinforcers for engaging in intrinsically motivating activities appears to decrease interest in the tasks (Deci & Ryan, 1987; Kohn, 1993; Schwartz, 1990). The use of rewards may detract from intrinsic interest in learning.

Finally, some criticisms of behaviorism are philosophical, with critics arguing that schools should attempt to promote learning for its own sake rather than learning to receive rewards (Anderman & Maehr, 1994). Other critics argue that behaviorism is essentially a means for controlling people, rather than helping students learn to control their own behavior (Kohn, 1993).

On the other hand, we all know that our experiences undeniably influence the ways we behave, and the influence of experience on behavior is at the core of behaviorism. For example, virtually all teachers understand that a timely, genuine compliment can exert a powerful influence on students' motivations as well as how they feel about themselves. Also, how many of us would continue working if we stopped receiving pay checks, and do we lose interest in our work merely because we get paid for it?

Further, research indicates that reinforcing appropriate classroom behaviors, such as paying attention and treating classmates well, decreases misbehavior (Elliot & Busse, 1991), and behaviorist classroom management techniques are sometimes effective when others are not (Emmer & Evertson, 1981).

Finally, proponents argue, if reinforcers enhance learning, such as learning a mathematical operation, they have still acquired the ability, and the ability won't disappear merely because praise or some other reinforcer has been removed (Chance, 1993).

Behaviorism isn't a complete explanation for learning and behavior, and it is neither a panacea nor a totally ineffective view of learning. As with most of what we know about teaching and learning, effective application of behaviorism requires the careful judgment of an intelligent teacher.

Classroom Connections

Applying Operant Conditioning in Your Classroom

1. When using behavioral methods, use reinforcement rather than punishment if possible. When punishment is necessary, use removal punishment rather than presentation punishment.
   - After giving an assignment, a first-grade teacher circulates around the room and gives tickets to students who are working quietly. The tickets may be exchanged for opportunities to play games and work at learning centers.
   - A fifth-grade teacher gives students "behavior points" at the beginning of the week. If they break a rule, they lose a point. At the end of the week, a specified number of remaining points may be traded for free time.

2. Carefully select reinforcers for their potency.
   - A seventh-grade teacher asks students what they would like as rewards. (They typically suggest watching videos or being given free time to visit.) Then she tries to use their suggestions, so they feel as though they have influence over their environment.
   - A math teacher increases the potency of grades as reinforcers by awarding bonus points for improvement. After an average for each student is determined, she offers them incentive points for scoring higher than their average.

3. Promote generalization and discrimination by encouraging students to make comparisons among examples and other information.
   - A life-science teacher, in a unit on deciduous and coniferous trees, asks students to compare a pine and an oak tree. He helps them identify the essential differences between the trees by asking specific questions.
   - A teacher praises a third-grader who, on her own, notices that frogs and toads are not the same and that frogs climb trees but toads don't.

4. Use appropriate schedules of reinforcement.
   - At the beginning of the school year, a first-grade teacher plans activities that all students can do. She praises liberally and rewards frequently. As students get used to first-grade work, she requires more effort.
   - A second-grade teacher is careful to provide compliments on an intermittent basis for consistent work and effort. She knows that students who do steady, average to above-average work and are not disruptive tend to be taken for granted and are often "lost in the shuffle."
   - An algebra teacher gives frequent announced quizzes to prevent the decline in effort that can occur after reinforcement with a fixed-interval schedule.

5. Provide clear, informative feedback on student work.
   - A sixth-grade teacher has students do sample math problems that are similar to their homework, the class goes over the problems, and the teacher answers any questions they have before having them work independently.
   - A high-school history teacher uses essay items to teach, not just to assess. With each essay question, she provides written feedback to each student, giving a concrete explanation for the grade. If this is too time-consuming, she prepares an "ideal" response to the item and shares it with the class, specifically explaining grading criteria.

6. Shape desired behaviors.
   - A language-arts teacher begins a unit on paragraph writing by assigning a written paragraph from each student. As she scores them, she is initially generous with positive comments, but she becomes more critical as time goes on and the students' work improves.
   - A second-grade teacher openly praises a student whose behavior is improving. With continued improvement, she requires longer

periods of acceptable behavior to earn the praise.

7. Provide cues for appropriate behavior.
   • After completing a lesson and assigning seatwork, a seventh-grade English teacher circulates around the room, reminding students both verbally and nonverbally to begin working.

• Before students line up for lunch, a first-grade teacher reminds them to stand quietly while waiting to be dismissed. When they're standing quietly, she compliments them on their good behavior and lets them go to lunch.

Comparing Behaviorism and Cognitive Learning Theory

6.28

Using your own experiences with learning as a basis, identify at least two other mental processes that occur within people.

In the first section of the chapter we discussed learning with a focus on observable behaviors and the factors that influence them; hence the name *behaviorism.* We are now making a transition to *cognitive learning theories,* or theories that focus on learners' internal thought processes. This doesn't mean that cognitive theories pay no attention to observable behavior, but the emphasis has shifted to processes that occur within the learner, such as beliefs and expectations.

Behaviorists' and cognitive theorists' views of learners and learning differ in several ways, as outlined in Table 6.4. For example, while behaviorists view learners as passive, cognitive psychologists view learners as actively attempting to make sense of the world. Behaviorists focus on changes in observable behavior; cognitive theorists believe that learners' internal processes are more interesting. Consequently, cognitive approaches to instruction emphasize helping learners organize and make sense of information. When cognitively-oriented teachers focus on behaviors, it's to help them understand what's going on in learners' minds.

Table 6.4 A comparison of behaviorist and cognitive theories

	Behaviorism	Cognitive Theories
View of learners	Passive—respond to experience	Active—form meaningful ideas
Theoretical focus	Observable behavior	Mental processes
Definition of learning	Change in observable behavior, resulting from experience	Changes in mental "structures" that provide the capacity to demonstrate behaviors
Source of information about learners	Observation of learner behaviors	Inferences about internal processes (based on observable behaviors)
Goal of learning experiences	Demonstrate desired behavior	Form meaningful ideas
Teacher's role	Organize information, administer reinforcers and punishers	Organize information, guide developing understanding

To illustrate differences in the ways behaviorists and cognitive theorists view learning, try the following exercise (Murdock, 1992). Study the items on the following list for three seconds each, cover the list with a piece of paper, and then count backward from 20 by twos. (Counting backward is intended to keep you from repeating the words over and over to yourself.)

After you've finished counting, try to write down as many of the words as possible in any order.

Apple	Hammer	Banana	Goat
Cat	Pear	Hamster	Broom
Shovel	Parrot	Vice	Horse
Dog	Saw	Orange	Peach

If you're like most people, you didn't write the word in the order they appeared; instead you organized them into groups, such as tools, fruits, and animals, that were more meaningful to you. Organizing the information is a mental process that we *inferred* took place, based on the appearance of the list. The study of this and other mental processes is the focus of cognitive learning theory.

While behaviorists and cognitive learning theorists differ in several ways, they agree on two important points.

- Learning depends on experience.
- Learning is strongly influenced by feedback.

Experience is at the core of behaviorism, but in Chapter 2 we saw that Piaget and Vygotsky, both cognitive theorists, viewed experience as critical for development as well. They disagree, however, on how experience influences learning. We will examine the disagreements as we continue our study of learning.

Feedback is also critical to both theories. Behaviorists tend to interpret feedback in terms of reinforcers and punishers, whereas cognitive theorists think of it as information learners use to see if their understanding of the world is valid.

6.29

Explain a person's tendency to organize the information in the list on the basis of behaviorism.

Social Cognitive Theory

"What are you doing?" Jason asked Kelly as he came around the corner and caught her in the act of swinging her arms back and forth.

"I was sort of practicing my batting swing," Kelly responded with a red face. "I was watching a game on TV last night, and noticed the way those guys swing. It always looks so easy, but they hit it so hard. It just seems like I should be able to do that. It was running through my head, so I just had to try it."

Three-year-old Jimmy crawled up on his dad's lap with a book. "I read too, Dad," he said as his father put down his own book to help Jimmy up on his lap.

"Wait a minute," Mrs. Edwards said as she saw Joanne struggling with the microscope. "Let me show you once more. . . . Now, watch closely as I adjust the microscope. This is important because these slides crack easily and are expensive. The first thing I think about is getting the slide in place. Otherwise, I might not be able to find what I'm looking for in the microscope. Then I want to be sure I don't crack the slide while I lower the objective lens, so I watch from the side. Finally, I slowly raise the objective lens until I have the object in focus. You were trying to focus as you lowered it. It's easier and safer if you try to focus as you raise it. Now go ahead. You try it."

Students are able to learn a wide range of complex behaviors through modeling.

6.30

Using the examples above, explain why the term *social* appears in *social cognitive theory.* Also explain why *cognitive* appears in *social cognitive theory.*

What do these events have in common? Although they involve three distinct situations—a girl practicing her softball swing, a child wanting to be like his father, and a girl learning a laboratory technique—they all involve learning by observing the behavior of others.

Researchers have become interested in what happens as people learn by watching others and have found that the process is more complex than the simple imitation of others' behaviors. This line of inquiry, pioneered by Albert Bandura (1925–   ) and originally called *observational learning,* has evolved into what is now known as *social cognitive theory* (Bandura, 1986).

Social cognitive theory *examines the processes involved as people learn from observing others and gradually acquire control over their own behavior.* Social cognitive theory has its historical roots in behaviorism but goes well beyond it. Let's look at some differences between the two.

Differences Between Behaviorism and Social Cognitive Theory

Social cognitive theory differs from behaviorism in at least three ways: (a) the way learning is viewed, (b) the way interactions among behavior, the environment, and personal factors are described, and (c) the way reinforcement and punishment are interpreted. Let's examine these differences more closely.

Views of Learning

From our discussion in the last section, we can see why the word *cognitive* is in *social cognitive theory.* Kelly, for example, didn't try to imitate the baseball swing until the next day, which means her observations of the players on television had to be stored in her memory. Also, her comment, "It just seems like I should be able to do that," suggests a belief about her ability that influenced her behavior. Beliefs are internal processes that behaviorists don't consider.

Interactions Among Behavior, the Environment, and Personal Factors

Whereas behaviorism only examines the influence of the environment on behavior, social cognitive theory suggests that behavior, the environment, and personal factors all influence each other. For instance, Tim's low score on his algebra test (an environmental factor) influenced his belief (a personal factor) about his ability to do algebra. His belief, in turn, influenced his behavior (he adapted his study habits) and his behavior influenced the environment (he went to Susan's home to study). Social cognitive theorists call these mutual influences *reciprocal causation.*

Interpretations of Reinforcement and Punishment

Behaviorists and social cognitive theorists interpret the influence of reinforcement and punishment differently. For behaviorists, reinforcers and punishers are direct causes of behavior; for social cognitive theorists, reinforcers and punishers cause people to form *expectations* about consequences that are likely to result from various behaviors. For example, if you study hard and do well on a test, you expect to do well on a second test by studying the same way. If you see someone being reinforced for a certain behavior, you expect to be reinforced for a similar behavior. Like beliefs, expectations are mental processes, occurring within learners, that influence their behavior.

The fact that people form expectations about consequences means they're aware of the behaviors that will be reinforced. This is important because, according to social cognitive theory, reinforcement only changes behavior when learners know what behaviors are being reinforced (Bandura, 1986). Tim believed that his changed study habits were the cause of his improved scores, so he maintained those habits. If he had believed that some other strategy was more effective, he would have used that strategy. Tim wasn't passively responding to reinforcers; he was actively assessing the effectiveness of his strategy.

These factors have two implications for teachers. First, teachers should explain what behaviors will be reinforced so students can adapt their behavior accordingly; second, learners need feedback so they know what behaviors have resulted in desired consequences. (As we said in the last section, all views of learning view feedback as essential; here we see its role in social cognitive theory.) For instance, if a student gets full credit for an essay item on a test but doesn't know why the credit was given, she may not know how to respond correctly the next time.

Non-Occurrence of Expected Consequences. Social cognitive theory also helps us explain behavior when expectations aren't met. For example, suppose your instructor gives you a homework assignment, you work hard on it, and then she doesn't collect it. The non-occurrence of the expected reinforcer (credit for the assignment) can act as a punisher. You will probably be less inclined to work hard for the next assignment. Just as the non-occurrence of an expected reinforcer can act as a punisher, the non-occurrence of an expected punisher can act as a reinforcer (Bandura, 1986).

6.31

Greg concludes, "I seem to have a feel for French," as he begins his homework. His teacher often compliments him on the high quality of his written work, and his effort has continually increased. Explain these incidents using reciprocal causation as a basis for your explanation,

6.32

In thinking back to our study of behaviorism, we see that no discussion of *expectations* took place. Explain why that would have been the case.

6.33

Look again at the incident with Greg in Note 6.31. Behaviorists would describe Greg's increased effort as the result of being positively reinforced by the teacher's compliments. How would social cognitive theorists explain Greg's increased effort?

6.34

A student knowingly breaks a classroom rule, but the teacher doesn't notice. Regarding the rule, what is the student likely to do in the future? Explain on the basis of the information in this section.

Modeling

6.35

Consider the statement "Modeling doesn't work unless the observer sees the model being reinforced." Is that statement true or false? Explain.

Central to social cognitive theory is the idea that people learn through interacting with and observing each other. The primary mechanism in this process is **modeling,** *which refers to changes in people that result from observing the actions of others.* Tim, for example, observed that Susan was successful in her approach to studying for exams. As a result, he imitated her behavior; imitation is one form of modeling.

The importance of modeling in our everyday lives is difficult to overstate. Modeling helps explain the powerful influence of culture on student learning described in Chapter 4. Parents are urged to use correct grammar and pronunciation in talking to their infants in hopes of promoting language development. Studies of disadvantaged youth indicate that a lack of appropriate adult role models is one reason they have difficulty handling the problems they encounter (Ogbu, 1987).

6.36

A teacher shows her students Dr. Martin Luther King Jr.'s famous "I Have a Dream" speech. What form of modeling is illustrated in the speech?

In addition to direct modeling (as illustrated by Tim's imitation of Susan's behavior or children imitating their parents), at least two other forms of modeling exist—symbolic and synthesized (Bandura, 1986). They are described in Table 6.5. Common to each is the fact that people learn by observing the actions of others.

Cognitive Modeling

6.37

Identify an example of cognitive modeling in the opening case study in which Tim and Susan were working together.

An application of modeling that is increasingly emphasized in instruction is called cognitive modeling. **Cognitive modeling** *involves modeled demonstrations, together with verbal descriptions of the model's thoughts and actions* (Pintrich & Schunk, 1996). As Mrs. Edwards demonstrated how to use the microscope, for example, she also described her thinking, ". . . The first thing I think about is getting the slide in place. Otherwise, I might not be able to find what I'm looking for in the microscope. Then I want to be sure I don't crack the slide while I lower the objective lens, so I watch from the side."

Cognitive modeling allows learners to benefit from the thinking of experts. When teachers think aloud about the information their students are studying, or when they encourage other students to explain their thinking, they provide students with specific, concrete examples of how to think about and solve problems.

6.38

Using the concept of *expectations* as a basis, explain how vicarious reinforcement and punishment can change a person's behavior.

Vicarious Learning

Although merely observing the actions of other people can affect a learner, the effects are amplified if the learner also observes the consequences of those actions. This is

Table 6.5 Different forms of modeling

Type	Description	Example
Direct modeling	Simply attempting to imitate the model's behavior	Tim imitates Susan in studying for exams. A first grader forms letters in the same way a teacher forms them.
Symbolic modeling	Imitating behaviors displayed by characters in books, plays, movies, or television	Teenagers begin to dress like characters on a popular television show oriented toward teens.
Synthesized modeling	Developing behaviors by combining portions of observed acts	A child uses a chair to get up and open the cupboard door after seeing her brother use a chair to get a book from a shelf and seeing her mother open the cupboard door.

called **vicarious learning,** and it *occurs when people observe the conse-quences of another person's behavior and adjust their own behavior accordingly.* For example, Tim saw how well Susan did on tests with her approach to studying, so he was *vicariously reinforced* through her success. When students hear a teacher say, "I really like the way Jimmy is working so quietly," they are being vicariously reinforced, and when a student receives a verbal reprimand for leaving his seat without per-mission, other students in the class are *vicariously punished.* Modeling and vicarious learning work together to affect behavior in several ways. Let's look at them.

Effects of Modeling on Behavior

Modeling can affect behavior in at least four ways: (a) learning new behaviors, (b) facilitating existing behaviors, (c) changing inhibitions, and (d) arousing emotions.

Both teachers and other students can act as effective motivators and role models for other students.

Learning New Behaviors

Through modeling, people can acquire behaviors they weren't able to display prior to observing the model. Examples include being able to properly swing a forehand after seeing a tennis instructor demonstrate it, or being able to factor a trinomial after watching a teacher execute the procedure.

Facilitating Existing Behaviors

You're attending a concert, and at the end of one of the numbers, someone stands and begins to applaud. Others notice and, after hesitating briefly, join in to create a stand-ing ovation. Obviously, people already know how to stand and clap. The person "facil-itated" yours and others' behaviors through modeling.

We also saw this demonstrated in Tim's behavior. He practiced solving problems prior to tests, but by his own admission, "I usually do one, maybe two, and if I'm okay on them, I quit." After observing Susan, he modified his behavior and increased his efforts.

Changing Inhibitions

An **inhibition** is a *self-imposed restriction on one's behavior,* and modeling can either strengthen or weaken the inhibition. Unlike facilitating existing behaviors, inhibitions involve socially unacceptable behaviors, such as breaking classroom rules (Pintrich & Schunk, 1996).

Pedestrians stopped at a red light are more likely to obey or disregard that red light if they see others doing the same, for example. If a teacher has a classroom rule requiring students to raise their hands before speaking, students are less likely to break the rule if they see one of their peers reprimanded for doing so. The inhibition against speaking without permission is strengthened. On the other hand, if a student speaks without permission and isn't reprimanded, other students are more likely to do the same. The inhibition is weakened.

6.39

A second-grade teacher and several members of the class see Shelley throw a pencil at Kim. The teacher can't decide whether to reprimand Shelley publicly or private-ly. What would social cog-nitive theory suggest? Identify at least two other factors the teacher should consider in making the de-cision.

Arousing Emotions

Finally, a person's emotional reaction can be changed by observing a model's display of emotions. For example, observing the uneasiness of a diver on a high board may cause an observer to become more fearful of the board as well. If you see a couple having a heated argument at a party, you find yourself feeling awkward and embarrassed. Notice here that the emotions modeled aren't necessarily the same ones aroused in others. You see anger modeled, but your emotions are more likely to be embarrassment or uneasiness.

On the positive side, the emotional arousal effect of modeling is a strong endorsement for teacher enthusiasm. Observing teachers genuinely enjoying themselves as they discuss a topic can help generate similar excitement in students.

From these examples, you can see that modeling can result in behavioral, cognitive, and even affective outcomes. Behavioral outcomes occur when behaviors are learned or facilitated; cognitive outcomes result from observing the consequences of others' actions, such as the example in which a student broke a classroom rule, and affective outcomes are the result of modeling emotions.

Learning from Models: The Processes Involved

In the previous section, we described some effects of modeling: learning and facilitating behaviors, changing inhibitions, and arousing emotions. How do these effects occur, and what mechanisms are involved?

Learning from models involves four processes: attention, retention, reproduction, and motivation (Bandura, 1986). They're illustrated in Figure 6.5.

Attention

Learning begins when the observer attends to the behavior of the model. Merely attracting the learner's attention isn't enough to make learning effective, however. The learner's attention must be drawn to the critical aspects of the modeled behavior (Bandura, 1986). For example, when Tim worked with Susan, he was able to directly observe her study strategies, and he identified the important aspects of her behavior that he intended to imitate. As another example, if an English teacher is trying to teach students to write clear expository essays, merely sharing well-written paragraphs probably won't be enough; the teacher will have to direct students' attention to specific elements that made the paragraphs well written.

Retention

Once students are attending to the important aspects of the modeled behavior, it must be transferred to memory before it can be reproduced. This transfer involves mentally verbalizing the steps or visually representing the processes in some way. (We discuss the processes involved in transferring information to memory in Chapter 7.)

Reproduction

Having attended to and retained the modeled behaviors, learners are now ready to reproduce the behaviors on their own. The information in memory can now be used to guide the learners' performance. In classrooms, however, this often doesn't happen. Although teachers have modeled the desired behaviors, students often can't reproduce

6.40

Research indicates that teachers who model persistence in problem-solving tasks have students who persist longer than teachers who don't (Zimmerman & Blotner, 1979). Which modeling effect is best illustrated in this research finding? Explain.

6.41

Earlier we discussed the effectiveness of teacher think-alouds. Based on the processes of attention and retention, explain why think-alouds are effective.

Figure 6.5 Processes involved in learning from models

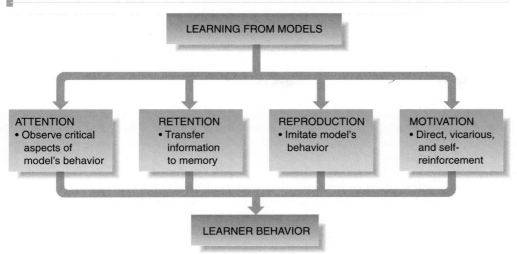

them. To help, teachers often walk them through the process, providing feedback along the way. To illustrate, let's look at a teacher who has modeled the procedure for solving simultaneous algebraic equations but whose students are having difficulty solving them on their own.

> "Let's look up here," Sally Hernandez commented after seeing that her students were struggling with the assigned problems. "I see you're still having a little difficulty, so let's look at another example.
> "Try this one," she said, writing on the chalkboard:
>
> $$4a + 6b = 24$$
> $$5a - 6b = 3$$
>
> "What's one way of solving this problem? . . . Alfino?"
> ". . . By addition."
> Sally nodded. "How do we know that will work?"
> "There's a 6b in the first equation and a negative 6b in the second equation," Kim volunteered.
> "Yes. Good, Kim. That's the key that determines whether you can use addition. Let's go on. What do we do first? . . . Lakesha?"
> ". . . We add the two equations together."
> "And we get? . . . Hue?"
> ". . . Nine a plus zero b equals 27."
> "Okay," Sally smiled. "And what is the value of a? . . . Chris?"
> ". . . Three."
> "Good! That's right. Now let's find the value of b. What should we do first? . . . Mitchell?"

Through questions and feedback, Sally helped her students reproduce the behaviors she had modeled. The importance of her guidance has been confirmed by research (Rosenshine, 1983). Not all students pay close attention when teachers teach, and the connections between the modeled behaviors and the way learners represent them in memory often aren't ideal. As a result, the retention phase is often a shaky foundation for reproducing the modeled behavior. Sally helped overcome those difficulties by

6.42

As Sally questions, she first asks the question, pauses briefly, and then calls on a student. By pausing in this way, Sally is implementing what concept from behaviorism that was discussed earlier in the chapter?

guiding students' initial reproductions as a group process. This tactic allowed her to provide immediate feedback in the case of incorrect answers, and cues when students were unable to answer. Sally's strategy is sometimes described as *controlled practice* (Murphy, Weil, & McGreal, 1986).

Motivation

The motivation component of learning from models illustrates an important difference in the way social cognitive theorists and behaviorists view reinforcement. As we saw earlier, behaviorists suggest that reinforcers are direct causes of behavior; in contrast, social cognitive theorists interpret direct and vicarious reinforcers as sources of motivation by causing learners to form expectations.

According to social cognitive theorists, people imitate others' behaviors if they expect to be reinforced for doing so. Sally's students reproduce the behaviors she modeled, for example, because they expected to be reinforced with high test scores and good grades for doing so. Tim imitated Susan's behavior for the same reason.

Vicarious learning operates as well. When a teacher praises Tommy, one of her first graders, for working quietly, other students are likely to imitate Tommy's diligent behavior because they are vicariously reinforced; they expect to be reinforced for similar behaviors. Likewise, when an English teacher recognizes a student for bringing in a review of a new biography of Ernest Hemingway, the class is vicariously reinforced, and similar behaviors are more likely to occur in the future.

Finally, as learners see themselves making genuine progress as a result of imitating a model's behavior, they may experience self-reinforcement. In many ways, this feeling of accomplishment is the most motivating reinforcer of all.

Effectiveness of Models

As you might expect, not all models are equally effective, and learners are more affected by some models than others. A model's effectiveness depends on at least three factors: (a) perceived similarity, (b) perceived competence, and (c) perceived status.

Perceived Similarity

When we observe a model's behavior, we are more likely to imitate it if we perceive the model as similar to us (Schunk, 1987). In addition, several models are more effective than a single model or even a few. One reason for this is that the likelihood of finding a model perceived to be similar to the observer increases as the number of models increases. Although students can learn academic skills from models of either gender, they are more likely to imitate behaviors from same-sex models, for example, probably because of perceived similarity. This is one reason it is important to present a balanced curriculum that accurately portrays the contributions of women and minorities, and it highlights the importance of nontraditional career models (e.g., female engineers) in helping students develop nonsexist views of possible occupations.

Perceived Competence

Perception of a model's competence interacts with perceptions of similarity to influence a model's effectiveness. Students are more likely to imitate those perceived as competent models than those perceived as less competent, regardless of similarity. In Tim's

6.43

One group of students watched teachers successfully solve math problems, a second group watched peers do the same, and a third group saw no models. Which group successfully solved the most math problems, and which group solved the fewest? Explain the results on the basis of the information in this section.

case, although Susan was his classmate, it is unlikely he would have imitated her behaviors had she not been a successful student.

Perceived Status

Individuals acquire social status by distinguishing themselves from others in their fields, and people tend to imitate these individuals more often than others. Professional athletes, popular rock stars, and world leaders are all high-status models. At the school level, high-school athletes, cheerleaders, and in some cases even gang leaders may have high status for other students.

Teachers are also influential models. Despite concerns expressed by educational reformers and teachers themselves, they remain and will continue as powerful influences on students.

Status has an additional spill-over effect. High-status models often get tacit credit for competence outside their own areas of expertise. This is the reason you see professional basketball players (instead of nutritionists) endorsing breakfast cereal, and actors (instead of engineers) endorsing automobiles and motor oil.

Self-Regulation

Earlier, you saw that learners' beliefs and expectations can influence both behavior and the environment. This is accomplished through the process of **self-regulation,** *students using their own thoughts and actions to reach academic learning goals*. Self-regulated learners identify goals and adopt and maintain strategies for reaching these goals.

To illustrate the process of self-regulation, let's look at Tim's case once more. He *chose* to go to Susan's home to study. He didn't go because he had been reinforced for doing so in the past, and he wasn't immediately reinforced when he did go. Not until after he had developed a pattern of changed study strategies, which he monitored himself, was he reinforced with higher test scores.

Self-regulation is critical to understanding social cognitive theory because much of human behavior occurs without immediate reinforcement; the consequences exist too far in the future to affect behavior in the present (Bandura, 1986). Without self-regulation, people wouldn't maintain the behavior until it could be reinforced.

Self-regulation has four aspects: goal setting, self-observation, self-assessment, and self-reinforcement. Let's see how each can influence classroom learning.

Goal Setting

Goal setting is a critical component of self-regulation. Goals not only establish purposes for a student's actions but also provide ways of measuring progress. Susan, in our opening case study, set the goal of working at least three of each type of problem, and Tim imitated her behavior by setting goals of his own.

Challenging but realistic goals and goals set by students themselves are often more effective than those imposed by the teacher (Schunk, 1994; Spaulding, 1992). An important role for teachers is to help students learn how to set effective goals. (We examine goal setting again in Chapter 10 when we consider the relationship between goals and learner motivation.)

Self-Observation

Once goals have been set, self-regulated learners monitor themselves to determine the progress they're making. Susan, for example, pointed out, "I sometimes even make a lit-

6.44

Consider the effect of a model's status on the behavior of observers. Does this effect illustrate the concept of *reinforcement potency?* Explain why or why not.

6.45

Think about your work in this class. Identify at least two goals that you could use to increase your learning. Based on information from the text, explain why you believe the goals are effective.

A teacher can help students develop self-regulation by providing them with complex learning activities that require goal setting, and monitoring of learning progress.

tle chart. I try to do at least three problems of each type we study, and then I check them off as I do them." Self-observation allowed Susan to monitor her own progress.

Students can be taught to monitor a variety of behaviors. For example, they can keep a chart and make a check every time they catch themselves "drifting off" during an hour of study, the number of times they go off-task during seatwork, the number of times they blurt out answers in class, or, on the positive side, the number of times they use a desired social skill (Jenson et al., 1988).

Self-observation combined with appropriate goals can change student behavior, sometimes dramatically (Mace, Belfiore, & Shea, 1989; Mace & Kratochwill, 1988). With effort and teacher monitoring and support, study habits and concentration can be improved and social interactions can be made more positive and productive.

6.46

Think about one of the goals you identified in Note 6.45. Now describe a simple form of self-observation that you could use to monitor your progress toward the goal.

6.47

Again consider one of the goals you identified in Note 6.45. Describe a form of self-assessment that you could use to measure your success in reaching the goal.

Self-Assessment

Schools historically have been places where a person's performance is judged by someone else. Although teachers can provide valuable feedback in assessing student performance, they don't have to be the sole judges; students can learn to assess their own work (Stiggins, 1997). For example, students can assess the quality of their solutions to word problems by learning to ask themselves whether their answers make sense and to compare their answers with estimates. Tim was involved in a form of self-assessment when he checked his answers against those given at the back of the book.

Developing self-assessment skills takes time, and students won't automatically be good at it. The best way to help students develop these skills is to be sure their goals are specific and quantitative, as Susan's and Tim's were. Helping students make valid self-assessments based on accurate self-observations is one of the most important instructional tasks teachers face.

Self-Reinforcement

We all feel good when we accomplish a goal, and we often feel regretful or even guilty when we don't, vowing to do better in the future (Bandura, 1989). As learners become self-regulated, they learn to reinforce or punish themselves for meeting or failing to meet their goals.

Self-reinforcers and self-punishers can be an internal pat on the back, or they can be something more tangible, such as Susan's, "If I get all of them right, I treat myself with a bowl of ice cream." A powerful form of self-reinforcement is the feeling of accomplishment that can result from setting and meeting challenging goals.

Self-reinforcement is somewhat controversial. Some researchers argue that it is unnecessary, that goals, self-observation, and self-assessment are sufficient in themselves (Hayes et al., 1985). Others argue that self-reinforcement can be a powerful strategy, particularly for low achievers. In one study, low achievers were taught to award themselves points, which they could use to buy privileges, when they did well on their assignments. Within a few weeks, the low achievers were achieving as well as their classmates (Stevenson & Fantuzzo, 1986). Bandura (1986) argues that rewarding oneself for good work can lead to higher performance than goals and self-monitoring alone.

Putting Social Cognitive Theory into Perspective

Like all descriptions of learning and behavior, social cognitive theory has its strengths. For example, the influence of modeling as both a tool for learning and an influence on behavior is difficult to overstate, and social cognitive theory overcomes some of the limitations of behaviorism by helping us understand the importance of learner beliefs and expectation on their actions.

However, like any theory, social cognitive theory has limitations. Some of them are:

- Although not to the extent behaviorism does, it treats learners as somewhat passive (e.g., learners merely imitate behaviors they observe in others).

- It is unable to explain why learners attend to and imitate some modeled behaviors but not others.

- It doesn't account for the learning of complex tasks, such as learning to write (beyond mere mechanics).

- It isn't able to explain the role of context and social interaction in complex learning environments. For example, research indicates that student interaction in small groups facilitates learning (Greeno, Collins, & Resnick, 1996; Shuell, 1996). The processes involved extend well beyond modeling and imitation.

We identify these limitations as a reminder that every theory of learning is incomplete, able to explain some aspects of learning but not others. This is why it's important for teachers to understand different views of learning together with their strengths and limitations.

Classroom Connections

Applying Social Cognitive Theory in Your Classroom

1. Act as a role model for your students.
   - A school committee charged with improving the quality of instruction developed the following guidelines to encourage teachers to be good role models.
     a. Treat students with respect and courtesy. Avoid criticism and any form of sarcasm.
     b. Require that students respect you and each other. Enforce this rule consistently.
     c. Communicate your interest in reading and studying.
     d. Approach the topics you teach with enthusiasm, energy, and effort.

2. As you model the skills you teach, use think-alouds to verbally illustrate your thinking.
   - A kindergarten teacher helping students form letters says, "I start with my pencil here and make a straight line down," as she begins to form a *b*.
   - A physics teacher solving acceleration problems involving friction writes $F = ma$ on the chalkboard and says, "First, I think about finding the net force on the object. Let's see what the problem tells me."

3. As students are learning to reproduce skills, provide group practice by walking them through examples before having them practice on their own.
   - A sixth-grade teacher has his class adding fractions with unlike denominators. He displays the problem $1/4 + 2/3 = ?$ and then begins, "What do we need to do first? . . . Karen?" He

continues until the class works through the problem and then does a second example the same way.

4. Use vicarious reinforcement to increase the effectiveness of modeling.
   - As one reading group moves back to their desks, a first-grade teacher comments loud enough for the class to hear, "I like the way this group is returning to their desks. Karen, Vicki, Ali, and David each get a star because they have gone so quickly and quietly."
   - An art teacher hands back students' pottery projects. She then displays several excellent pieces and comments, "Look at these, everyone. These are excellent. Let's see why. . . ." This art teacher accomplished three things. First, the students whose pottery was displayed were directly reinforced, but they weren't put on the spot because the teacher didn't identify them. Second, the class was vicariously reinforced. Third, the teacher gave the class feedback and provided a model for future imitation.

5. Promote self-regulation in your students.
   - A geography teacher helps her students set individual goals by asking each to write a study plan. She returns to the plan at the end of the unit and has each student assess his or her progress.
   - A fifth-grade teacher works with students to design a checklist for monitoring desired social skills in cooperative learning groups. They use the checklist to assess their interaction skills at the end of each cooperative learning session.

Dealing with Diversity: Behaviorism and Social Cognitive Theory

As Carlos entered his second-grade classroom early Tuesday morning, he heard salsa music in the background. Donna Evans sometimes played it as she prepared her classroom for the day. The walls were decorated with colorful prints from Mexico and Central America, and vocabulary cards in both Spanish and English were hung near the blinds, chalkboard, clock, file cabinet, and other areas in the room.

"Buenos días, Carlos. How are you today?" Donna asked. "You're here very early."

". . . Buenos días. . . . I'm fine," Carlos responded, smiling as he went to his desk to take out his homework from the night before.

Donna watched Carlos for a few moments as he worked in the empty room. Then she walked over to him, put her hand on his shoulder, and asked, "What are we working on today, Carlos? . . . Math?"

"I cannot do it! I do not understand," Carlos replied in his halting English, frustration in his voice.

As Donna looked over his shoulder at the 12 problems she had assigned for homework, she noticed that he had done the first two correctly, but then had forgotten to borrow on the next three, and had left the last seven undone.

"Carlos, look," she said, kneeling down so that she was at eye level with him. "You did the first two just fine. Then you forgot an important step. Look here. . . . How is this problem different from this one?" she asked, pointing to the two following problems.

$$
\begin{array}{cc}
36 & 45 \\
-14 & -19 \\
\end{array}
$$

". . . The numbers . . . are different."

"Okay," she smiled. "What else?"

". . . This one . . . is bigger," he said, pointing to the 45 and then to the 36.

"How about the 9 and the 5? . . . Which is bigger?"

". . . This," pointing at the 9.

"Good, and how about the 6 and the 4?"

". . . Here," referring to the 6.

"And where is the bigger one in each case?"

". . . There," Carlos said, pointing to the 6 in the first problem, ". . . and there," pointing to the 9 in the second.

"Very good, Carlos. This is very important," she continued. "Now, let's work this one together. . . . Watch what I do."

Donna worked with Carlos as they solved the next two problems, carefully discussing her thinking and what they were doing as they went along, comparing problems that require regrouping to those that don't.

"Now try the next three on your own," she said, "and I'll be back in a few minutes to see how you're doing. Remember what Juanita's father said about becoming a scientist when he came and visited our class. You have to study very hard and do your math. I know you can do it, especially because you already did it on the first two. . . . Now go ahead."

Carlos nodded and then bent over his work and was finishing the last of the three problems as the other students were coming into the classroom. Donna went to him, checked his work, and commented, "Very good, Carlos. You got two of them right. Now check this one. You have just enough time before we start."

In another elementary school in the same city, Roberto shuffled into class and hid behind the big girl in front of him. If he was lucky, his teacher wouldn't discover that he hadn't done his homework—12 problems! How could he ever do that many? Besides, he wasn't good at math.

Roberto hated school. He was very uncomfortable. It seemed so strange and foreign. His teacher would sometimes frown when he spoke, because his English wasn't as good as most of the other students'. Sometimes when the teacher talked, he couldn't understand what she was saying.

Even lunch wasn't much fun. If his friend Raul wasn't there, he would eat alone. One time when he sat with some other students, they started laughing at the way he talked, and they asked what he was eating when he had tortillas for lunch. He couldn't wait to go home.

As you saw in Chapter 4, students from different cultures sometimes feel that they aren't welcome and don't belong in their classes. Schools seem strange and cold, and classrooms are threatening. School tasks are difficult, and failure is all too common. Behaviorism and social cognitive theory can help teachers understand why schools aren't friendlier places for these students and what can be done about this problem.

Classical Conditioning: Learning to Like and Dislike School

You learned earlier in the chapter that classical conditioning occurs when neutral stimuli become associated with unconditioned stimuli. Although you may have heard about schools from your parents or siblings, schools are essentially neutral stimuli when you first enter them, and initial experiences influence your emotional reactions to them (Gentile, 1996).

We respond instinctively to warmth and support, as Carlos did to Donna's manner. In time, school becomes associated with a teacher like Donna, and the school and class elicit positive emotions similar to those Donna caused with her behavior. Had Donna been of Hispanic background, Carlos's experience might have been still more positive, but we can all create warm and supportive environments for our students, regardless of their or our ethnic origins.

Unfortunately, the opposite can also be true, as it was in Roberto's case. School was not associated with positive feelings for him, and he didn't feel wanted, safe, or comfortable.

Motivating Hesitant Learners

When students are struggling, how can modeling and appropriate use of reinforcers enhance their efforts? The answer to this question both influences initial learning and affects lifelong views of competence.

Let's look again at Donna's work with Carlos.

- She reinforced him for the problems he had done correctly.

- She provided corrective feedback to help him understand where he had made mistakes.

- She reduced the task to three problems to ensure that the reinforcement schedule would be motivating.

- She used both direct and cognitive modeling to show him the correct procedures for solving the problems.

- She helped Carlos increase his sense of accomplishment by encouraging him and by providing only enough assistance so that he could do the problems on his own.

In her work with Carlos, Donna supported his efforts by applying concepts from both behaviorism and social cognitive theory. This support can increase learner motivation as well as increase opportunities for success.

6.48

Using the terms *unconditioned stimulus, unconditioned response, conditioned stimulus,* and *conditioned response,* explain how Donna Evans's room made Carlos feel good about being there.

6.49

If Donna Evans checked and reinforced Carlos for every three problems that he completed, what schedule of reinforcement would she be using?

Learning theories help teachers understand how their classrooms influence learners from diverse backgrounds differently.

Roberto: A Study in Contrasts

Let's compare Roberto's experience to Carlos's. To Roberto, the classroom was a strange and unfriendly place. His teacher didn't greet him, and nothing in the classroom made him feel welcome. When the problems seemed impossible, no one came to help. He had already "learned" that he wasn't "good" at math.

In Chapter 4, we examined the ways students from different backgrounds and cultures respond to schooling. In this chapter, behaviorism and social cognitive theory help us understand how factors such as caring, reinforcement, modeling, and feedback can be used to help all students learn successfully.

Classroom Connections

Capitalizing on Diversity in Your Classroom

1. Make your classroom a place that welcomes all students.
   - An elementary teacher invites students to bring in posters and pictures to decorate their room. On Friday afternoons during earned free time, she allows them to bring in and play music.
   - An inner-city social-studies teacher displays pictures of historical minority figures around

her room. Throughout the year, she refers to these people and emphasizes that American history is the story of all people.

2. Provide instructional support to ensure as much success as possible.
   - An English teacher assigns a research paper at the beginning of the term. He breaks the assignment into parts, such as doing a literature search, making an outline, and writing a first draft before the final paper is finished. He meets with students each week to check their progress and give them feedback.
   - A fifth-grade teacher uses student graders to provide immediate feedback on math assignments. Two students are chosen each week and are provided with answers for each day's assignment. After students have completed their work, they have it checked immediately; if their scores are below 80%, they see the teacher for help.

Windows on Classrooms

From reading the chapter's opening case study and the content of each section, you've seen how contiguity, classical and operant conditioning, modeling, vicarious learning, and self-regulation can be used to explain the behavior of students.

Let's look now at a case study describing a teacher working with his students. As you read the case study, analyze the teacher's effectiveness in applying the behavioral and social cognitive principles described in the chapter.

Warren Rose is a seventh-grade math teacher working on a unit on decimals and percents. He's beginning class on Thursday of the third week of the grading period.

"Here are your tests from last Thursday," Warren said as he handed the students their papers. "The ones you missed have a check by them. Your grades are at the top of your paper."

Warren paused briefly and then said, "Be sure you write your grade in your notebook."

He paused for a few minutes as the students looked over their tests. He then said, "Okay. Pass the tests back in. . . . Remember now, the next test is at the end of next week, so you need to work hard to be ready for it."

The students passed their test papers forward, and as he picked up the last one, he redirected their attention by saying, "All right, everyone, let's look up here at the problems on the chalkboard. . . . I realize that percents and decimals aren't your favorite topic, and I'm not wild about them either, but we have no choice, so we might as well buckle down and learn them.

"Let me show you a few more examples," he continued, and he then displayed the following problem on the overhead:

You have gone to the mall, shopping for a jacket. You see one that looks great, originally priced at $84, marked 25% off. You recently got a check for $65 from the fast-food restaurant where you work. Can you afford the jacket?

"Now," he continued. "The first thing I think about when I see a problem like this one is, 'What does the jacket cost now?' I have to figure out the price, and to do that I will take 25% of the $84. . . . That means I first convert the 25% to a decimal. I know when I see 25% that the decimal is understood to be just to the right of the 5, so I move it two places to the left. Then I can take .25 times 84."

Warren demonstrated the process as he spoke, working the problem through to completion. He then had the students work one at their desks and discussed their solutions. He then said, "Okay, do you all understand?"

Hearing no response, Warren then said, "Okay, for homework, do the odd problems on page 113. The answers are at the back of the book."

"Do we have to do all six of them, . . . the word problems?" Robbie asked.

"Why not?" Warren answered after looking at the problems he had assigned.

"Aww, . . . gee, Mr. Rose," Will put in, "they're so terrible hard."

"Uh hunh," Ginny added. "I can't ever do 'em."

". . . Yeah, and they take so long," Mark added. "All I ever do is math . . . I get so sick of it."

Several other students chimed in, arguing that six word problems were too many.

"Wait, . . . people, please," Warren held up his hands. "All right. You only have to do the first four word problems . . . but! . . . you have to promise not to complain if I give you homework over the weekend."

"Yeah!" the class shouted.

"All right, Mr. Rose," Matt nodded. "You've got a deal."

"Yikes, Friday," Helen commented to Jenny as they walked into Warren's room Friday morning. "I . . . like . . . blanked out last week. I get so nervous when he makes us go up to the board, and everybody's . . . like staring at us. If he calls me up today, I'll die."

Warren had the students exchange their papers, score the homework, and pass their papers forward. He then turned to the day's work by saying, "Let's look at this problem on the chalkboard,"

A bicycle selling for $145 was marked down 15%. What is the new selling price?

"First, let's estimate so that we can see whether our answer makes sense. About what should the new selling price be? . . . Helen?"

". . . I . . . You . . . I'm not sure," Helen stammered.

"Callie, what do you think?"

". . . I . . . think it would be about $120."

"Good thinking. Describe for everyone how you arrived at that."

". . . I . . . Well, 10% . . . would be $14.50, . . . so 15% would be about another $7, . . . well, about another $7, . . . so that would be about $21, and $21 off would be a little over $120."

"Good," Warren nodded. "Now, let's go ahead and solve it. What do we do first? . . . David?"

". . . We . . . er . . . we make the 15% into a decimal."

"Good, David. Now, what next? . . . Leslie?"

"Take the .15 times the 145."

"Okay. Do that everybody. . . . What did you get? . . . Someone?"

". . . $200.17," Cris volunteered. ". . . Whoops, . . . that . . . can't be right. . . . That's more than the bicycle cost to start with. . . . Wait, . . . $21.75."

"Good," Warren smiled. "That's what we're trying to do. We are all going to make mistakes, but if we catch ourselves, we're making progress. Keep it up. You can do these problems. Now what do we do?" he continued.

". . . Subtract," Matt volunteered.

"All right, go ahead," Warren directed.

". . . $142.83," Molly answered.

"Now, think about that for a second. What was our estimate?"

"What? . . . Oh, yeah, . . . No, . . . wait, . . . $123.25."

"What did you do the first time?" Warren queried.

". . . Wrong decimal point."

"Okay, good work. Now, let's look at another one," Warren responded, and then he displayed the following problem:

Christy has a job working at a novelty store, making $5.25 an hour. After 4 months on the job, her boss gave her an 8% raise. What does she make now?

"Let's see who can solve this one. . . . Go ahead, Helen."

". . . I . . . I don't know," Helen said after looking at the problem briefly.

"Shannon?"

". . . Make . . . a decimal out of the 8% and . . . times it by $5.25," Shannon responded.

"Good, Shannon. Let's do it, everybody." Warren then watched as the students solved the problem, and the class worked two more examples together. Then he said, "For homework, do the problems on page 116, and look, only four word problems."

The class began the problems, and Warren circulated around the room as they worked. Seeing Kevin had the wrong answer on the second word problem, he commented, "Look at this one again, Kevin. I know you can figure it out. Try it again. I'll be around to check on you in a few minutes."

As he continued his monitoring, he saw that Helen was just staring at her paper. "How are you doing?" he smiled.

". . . I'm lost. . . . I don't know what I'm doing," she shrugged in frustration, pointing at the second word problem.

"Here, let me show you," Warren said encouragingly. "I know that math is a little tough for you. Watch what I do."

Warren then solved the problem while Helen watched.

"There, you see. Not so bad. Now, you try the next one."

Warren again circulated among the students, making occasional comments and suggestions. "How're you coming?" he said as he walked by Kevin. "Very good, I see you figured it out. That's super."

"Let's look at the next one," he said to Helen, seeing that she had gotten the third one wrong. "First, remember that you have to change the percent to a decimal, and then the problem says that the value *increased* by 30%. You subtracted, and you didn't change the percent to a decimal. Here, let me show you." He then carefully solved the problem and left the solution with Helen.

Warren continued monitoring the students until there were two minutes left in the period. "All right, everyone, the bell is going to ring in two minutes. Get everything cleaned up around your desks and get ready to go."

Questions for Discussion and Analysis

Analyze Warren's teaching in the context of the information in this chapter. In conducting your analysis, you may want to consider the following questions. In each case, be specific and take information directly from the case study in conducting your analysis.

1. How well did Warren apply an understanding of classical conditioning in working with his students? Provide a specific example that illustrates classical conditioning.

2. Describe specifically how operant conditioning affected the behavior of both Warren and the students. What might Warren have done to change the effect?

3. Identify at least two examples in the case study where Warren (perhaps inadvertently) negatively reinforced student behaviors that detracted from student's learning.

4. How well did Warren apply an understanding of reinforcement schedules in his teaching (and particularly in his testing)? Provide a specific explanation based on your understanding of reinforcement schedules and information taken from the case study.

5. Assess Warren's use of feedback and praise in the lesson. Describe specifically what he might have done to improve it. Be sure to refer directly to the case study in making your assessment.

6. How effectively did Warren provide cues to elicit behaviors that he could then reinforce?

7. Assess Warren's modeling in his lesson. Identify at least one positive and one negative example.

8. What could Warren have done to increase his students' self-regulation? Be specific in your response.

Summary

Contiguity and Classical Conditioning

Contiguity helps explain the learning of simple memorized information through the pairing of stimuli and responses. Classical conditioning occurs when a formerly neutral stimulus becomes associated with a naturally occurring (unconditioned) stimulus to produce a response similar to an instinctive or reflexive response. Classical conditioning helps teachers understand emotional reactions such as test anxiety and how students learn to be comfortable in school environments.

Operant Conditioning

Operant conditioning focuses on overt, voluntary responses that are influenced by consequences. Praise, high test scores, and good grades are consequences that increase behavior and are called reinforcers, whereas reprimands are consequences that decrease behavior and are called punishers. The schedule of reinforcers influences both the rate of initial learning and the persistence of the behavior.

Comparing Behaviorism and Cognitive Learning Theory

In making the transition from behaviorism to cognitive learning theories, we see several differences. Whereas behaviorists view learners as passively responding to their experience, cognitive theorists view them as actively attempting to make sense of those experiences. Behaviorists focus on observable behavior; cognitive theorists emphasize the mental processes that cause behaviors. Cognitive theorists make inferences about mental processes based on their observations of behavior, whereas behaviorists focus exclusively on the behaviors they observe. For behaviorists, the goal of learning is to demonstrate desired behaviors, and the teacher's role is to reinforce them appropriately. For cognitive theorists, the goal is to form meaningful ideas, and the teacher's role is to help guide the process.

Social Cognitive Theory

Social cognitive theory extends behaviorism and focuses on the influence that observing others has on behavior. It considers, in addition to behavior and the environment, learners' beliefs and expectations. Social cognitive theory suggests that reinforcement and punishment affect learners' motivation, rather than directly cause behavior.

Modeling lies at the core of social cognitive theory. Modeling can be direct (from live models), symbolic (from books, movies, and television), or synthesized (combining the acts of different models). It can cause new behaviors, facilitate existing behaviors, change inhibitions, and arouse emotions. In learning from models, observers go through the processes of attention (observation), retention in memory, reproduction of the observed behavior, and motivation to produce the behavior in the future.

Learners become self-regulated when they set learning goals on their own, monitor their progress toward the goals, and assess the effectiveness of their efforts.

Important Concepts

classical conditioning (p. 198)

cognitive modeling (p. 220)

conditioned responses (p. 199)

conditioned stimuli (p. 199)

consequence (p. 202)

contiguity (p. 197)

continuous reinforcement schedule (p.209)

cues (p. 212)

discrimination (pp. 200, 207)

extinction (pp. 201, 212)

feedback (p. 207)

fixed-interval schedule (p. 210)

fixed-ratio schedule (p. 210)

generalization (pp. 200, 207)

inhibition (p. 221)

intermittent reinforcement schedule (p. 210)

interval schedules (p. 209)

learning (p. 197)

modeling (p. 220)

negative reinforcement (NR) (p. 205)

neutral stimuli (p. 199)

positive reinforcement (PR) (p. 202)

potency (p. 211)

Premack Principle (p. 204)

presentation punishment (PP) (p. 205)

punishers (p. 205)

punishment (p. 205)

ratio schedules (p. 210)

reinforcement (p. 203)

reinforcement schedules (p. 209)

reinforcer (p. 203)

removal punishment (RP) (p. 205)

response cost (p. 206)

responses (p. 197)

satiation (p. 211)

self-regulation (p. 225)

shaping (p. 209)

social cognitive theory (p. 218)

stimuli (p. 197)

unconditioned response (p. 199)

unconditioned stimulus (p. 199)

variable-interval schedule (p. 210)

variable-ratio schedule (p. 210)

vicarious learning (p. 220)

7

Cognitive Views of Learning

David Shelton has been preparing a unit on the solar system for his ninth-grade earth science class. From his filing cabinet, he retrieved a color transparency showing the sun throwing off globs of gases into space. He assembled a large model of the solar system to illustrate the planets in their orbital planes and their relative distances from the sun. Finally, he prepared a large matrix, made from a roll of chart paper, and taped it to the back wall of the room.

David began his unit on Monday by saying, "We're getting ready to study the solar system for the next several days, so I've prepared some things to help us get started. Take a look at the chart I made," he said, pointing to the back of the room.

"This chart is going to help us learn about the solar system. . . . But first, we need information to fill in the chart. . . . So, I want you to work in your groups to gather the information. Think about it for a moment and decide which planet you want. If more than one group wants a

planet, you'll have to negotiate to see which one gets its first choice."

The students turned to their groups, talked briefly, and quickly made their choices, compromising in a few cases.

David listed the groups' choices on the chalkboard and then directed the students to books, videos, computer software, and other resources in the room. The students spent the rest of Monday's class gathering their information and putting it on the chart with marking pens.

At the beginning of Tuesday's class, David displayed and briefly discussed the color transparency showing the sun throwing off globs of gases into space. He also referred to the model of the solar system he had assembled and suspended from the ceiling after school on Monday. He reminded the class that it might serve as a frame of reference for their study. The students then spent the rest of Tuesday's class continuing to put information into the chart.

On Wednesday, David began, "Let's review what we've found out so far. Then I'm going to do a little demonstration, and I want you to think about how it relates to what you've been doing."

After completing his review, David tied a pair of athletic socks to a three-foot piece of string, another pair to a five-foot piece of string, and whirled the two around his head simultaneously to demonstrate that the planets revolve around the sun on the same plane and in the same direction.

After the students made a number of observations about what they saw, he continued, "Now our job gets a bit more challenging. Each group should identify a piece of information from the chart that might explain or provide evidence about how the solar system was formed. . . . Let me give you an example. . . . For instance, when we look at Pluto, we see that the plane of its orbit is different from the plane of all the other planets. What Tanya, Juan, and Randy, who

	Mercury	Venus	Earth	Mars	Jupiter	Saturn	Uranus	Neptune	Pluto
Orbital plane									
Diameter									
Distance from sun									
Length of year									
Length of day									
Average surface temperature									
Gravity (compared to earth)									

are studying Pluto, must do is figure out why it's different," he said pointing to the orbital plane cell for Pluto on the chart, "and be able to explain to the rest of the class why you think that's the case. Use any of the information you have—the demonstration I just did, the transparency, the model we have hanging from the ceiling—and anything else."

"Let me give you one more example," he went on. "Here," referring to the diameter and gravity cells for Saturn. "Saturn is much bigger than Earth, but its gravity is about the same as Earth's. Now why might that be the case? . . . Karen, Jack, and Karl will have to explain that to the rest of us. . . . Okay, see what I mean? . . . If you get totally stuck, let me know, and I'll come around and help you. Any questions? . . . Go ahead."

The room was again quickly filled with the buzz of voices as the students prepared for the discussion to follow. As they worked, David moved from group to group, offering periodic comments, suggestions, and compliments to groups that were working hard.

"Pluto wasn't part of the solar system to begin with," Juan commented to Randy and Tanya as they started their work.

"What do you mean?" Randy responded.

"I was watching *Nova* with my mom, and the narrator said that scientists think Pluto was an asteroid floating around and the sun kinda grabbed it. . . . See, when Mr. Shelton did that thing with the socks, the socks stayed sorta level," he continued, moving his hand back and forth to demonstrate a flat plane.

"What's that got to do with it?" Randy asked, still confused.

"Oh, I get it! Pluto isn't level with the rest of them," Tanya interrupted.

"Gee, I didn't even notice that," Randy lamented.

"Yeah, and look there," Tanya added, pointing to the chart. "See how little Pluto is? It's the littlest one, so it would be sorta easy to capture."

"And it's the last one," Randy added, beginning to warm to the task. "I better write some of this stuff down, or I'll never remember it."

David listened as the students talked, and then he suggested, "I think you're doing a super job, but you might be forgetting something. Take another look at the transparency and see how it relates to what you're talking about. . . .Look at how the globs are coming off the sun, and look at the title of the transparency."

The students studied the transparency for a moment, and Juan finally said, "Look, all those globs are even too, you know, level, like the socks. . . . And it says, 'One Theory of the Formation of the Solar System.' So, that's how the planets were made."

"Now, what was that again about Pluto being the littlest?" Randy wondered. "What's that got to do with anything?"

"If it was really big and floating around out there, the sun's gravity might not be strong enough to grab it," Juan offered.

"But it's easier to grab if it's little," Tanya added.

The students continued their work for a few more minutes, and then David called the class together. "Now, let's see what we've got. Are you all ready? . . . Which group wants to go first? . . ."

"We will," Tanya offered after several seconds.

"Go ahead."

"We can explain why Pluto isn't on the same plane with the other planets," she continued, pleased with her group's accomplishments. "It wasn't part of the solar system when it was first made."

"Now, the rest of you should be asking for what . . . what else do you need to know?" David probed.

" . . . "

"You should be asking for evidence," David continued after hearing no response. "Each group needs to provide evidence that makes sense to the rest of us. . . . Go ahead, Tanya, or Juan, or Randy."

Juan and Randy motioned for Tanya to continue. "It's the littlest one, and it's way out there," motioning to the end of the model.

"Does that support or contradict what the group said?" David queried.

"Supports," Lori volunteered.

"How?" David nodded, gesturing for her to continue.

"If it were captured from somewhere else, it makes sense that it would be the last one."

"Wait, Mr. Shelton, you're going too fast. I'm getting lost. What is this about supporting the theory?" Alfredo asked.

"That's a good question, Alfredo. Let's think about that one, everyone. What do you think?"

". . . If the rest of the solar system were already in place, and if Pluto came by and was snagged by the sun's gravity, then it would be the farthest one out," Dena offered.

"I see that, but what if Pluto was snagged first? Then how could it be the farthest out?" Alfredo continued.

". . . Yes, but we found out that the planets weren't snagged; they spun off as molten stuff . . . globs. So Pluto, if it was caught by the sun, would be the last one," Dena replied.

"What do you think, Alfredo?" David gestured.

". . .Yeah, I see what she means . . . .I guess it makes sense."

"And, also, it isn't in line with the others," Juan added, motioning with his hand to indicate that its orbital plane was different from the others, "And its path is funny too. Sometimes it's actually inside Neptune's."

"And what did we call the paths?" David probed.

"Orbits," several of the students responded in unison.

"Excellent, everyone. See how this relates to what Dena said a minute ago? When I think of location and orbit, the first thing that pops in my mind is 'origin.' I relate the location and orbit to their origins," David continued, thinking aloud for the students.

The groups continued to present their information and explanations until David saw the period was nearing an end. "Okay, everyone. We'll continue tomorrow. You've done an excellent job of gathering and relating items of information about the solar system. Now, to check on us, I have a short assignment. For tonight's homework, I want you to write a paragraph summarizing how Earth became a member of the solar system and compare that with how Pluto became a member. Use all the information we have and today's discussion to help you. This should take less than a page."

"Just a reminder in passing," he added as he pointed to the overhead. "This is just one theory of how the solar system was formed. There are others, but we're focusing on this one for now. Also remember," David emphasized, "the information must be in a paragraph. Don't just write down isolated sentences."

As the students began their summaries, David circulated around the room, answering questions and offering suggestions.

We began Chapter 6 by examining behaviorism and its emphasis on experience and observable behavior. We then turned to social cognitive theory and saw that although it has behavioral roots, it marked a transition from behaviorism to more cognitively oriented learning theories. We continue our discussion of cognitive learning theories in this chapter and in Chapter 8, expanding our discussion to include cognitive processes such as attention, perception, imagery, encoding, elaboration, and organization that help make information meaningful.

We begin this chapter with a discussion of information processing, one of the most thoroughly studied cognitive learning theories. We then examine constructivism, a view of learning receiving increasing emphasis in both psychology and education.

After you've completed your study of this chapter, you should be able to meet the following objectives:

- Describe the components of information processing, including sensory memory, working memory, and long-term memory.
- Explain the role of cognitive processes in learning.
- Explain how teachers can help students develop metacognitive abilities.
- Identify the essential elements of constructivist views of learning.
- Describe the implications that constructivism has for teaching.

Cognitive Views of Learning

As you saw in Chapter 6, behaviorists explain learning as a change in observable behavior that occurs as a result of experience. In contrast, **cognitive learning theories** *explain learning by focusing on changes in mental processes that people use in their efforts to make sense of the world.* These processes are used for tasks as simple as remembering a phone number and as complex as solving detailed math problems. The influence of cognitive learning theories on education has increased steadily during the last 40 years (Bruer, 1993; Mayer, 1996; Greeno, Collins, & Resnick, 1996).

From a cognitive perspective, **learning** is *a change in a person's mental structures that provides the capacity to demonstrate different behaviors.* These "mental structures" include knowledge, beliefs, goals, expectations, and other components "in the learner's head." In David Shelton's lesson, for example, Randy consciously thought about his need to take notes, and Tanya, Randy, and Juan all used *higher-order reasoning* to help them relate information from the chart, transparency, model, and demonstration. Cognitive learning theories stress the importance of mental processes, such as reasoning, and focus on what is happening in the learner. These processes allow learners to actively interpret and organize information, an underlying principle of all cognitive theories.

7.1

In our study of behaviorism, we didn't discuss any of these internal mental processes. Why not?

Information Processing

Cognitive psychology is an eclectic theoretical orientation. There isn't *one* cognitive theory of learning, but rather a cluster of cognitive theories. We begin by examining information processing, one of the first and most influential of the cognitive views of learning. **Information processing** *is a cognitive theory that examines the way knowledge* *enters and is stored in and retrieved from memory*. It has been the most prominent cognitive theory during the twentieth century, and has important implications for teaching (Mayer, 1996).

Models: Aids to Understanding

Think back for a moment to courses you've taken during your schooling. You probably studied geography, perhaps chemistry, and now you're taking educational psychology. In geography, you examined the face and makeup of the earth, and in chemistry, you studied the structure of the atom. Because you can only directly experience a small portion of the earth, you doubtless made frequent use of maps and globes. The globe is a miniature representation of the earth, faithful in shape and proportion—a *model*. Likewise, in chemistry you cannot directly observe the atom with all its individual parts, so scientists created a model, such as the one in Figure 7.1, to help people visualize it. In this case the **model** is *a representation that allows learners to visualize what they can't observe directly.*

People encounter a similar situation when they try to visualize what occurs during information processing. They can't directly observe the structures and mechanisms that operate when they process information, so they use a model to help represent this process. The model in Figure 7.2 represents a current view of how cognitive psychologists think the mind processes information (Atkinson & Shiffrin, 1968; Leahey & Harris, 1997).

The information-processing model of learning is based on a computer analogy.

> The human–computer analogy is based on the observation that both computers and humans engage in cognitive processes such as learning (or acquiring knowledge), remembering (or retrieving knowledge), making decisions, answering questions, and so on. Computers perform cognitive tasks by processing information—taking symbols as input, applying operators to the input, and producing output—so it follows that perhaps humans are also information processors (Mayer, 1996, p. 153).

The model has three major components:

1. Information stores
2. Cognitive processes
3. Metacognition

Figure 7.1   Model of an oxygen atom

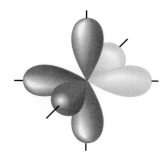

7.2

There is an important difference between the model of the atom and the model of Earth. What is this difference? The information-processing model is more like which of the two? Explain.

Models allow students to visualize abstract relationships that are often difficult to understand.

Figure 7.2 An information-processing model

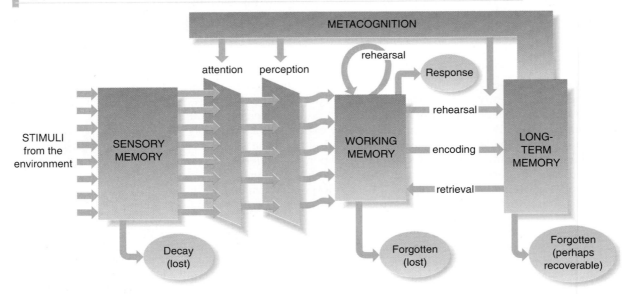

7.3

In the model in Figure 7.2, fewer lines connect "attention" and "perception" than connect "sensory memory" and "attention." Why is this the case?

Information stores are *repositories used to hold information.* They are analogous to computer files, filing cabinets, or address books where people store information. The information stores in the information-processing model are *sensory memory, working memory,* and *long-term memory.*

The second component consists of **cognitive processes,** *intellectual actions that transform information and move it from one store to another.* These processes include *attention, perception, rehearsal, encoding,* and *retrieval.* Cognitive processes are analogous to the programs that direct and transform information in computers.

The third component of the information processing model is **metacognition,** which is *knowing about and having control over cognitive processes* (Hiebert & Raphael, 1996; Paris, Wasik, & Turner, 1991). When Randy decided to take notes because he realized that note taking would help him pay attention better, he was demonstrating knowledge of and control over his attention. Metacognition is a form of self-regulation. It controls and directs the processes that move information from one store to another.

First, we focus on the information stores. Then, we discuss the processes that move information from one store to another. We complete the discussion with an analysis of the metacognitive abilities that regulate those processes.

Sensory Memory

People are constantly bombarded with stimuli from their environment. The sound of a lawn mower, the acrid smell of car exhaust, a teacher's voice, words on a book page, and other students shuffling in their seats are all stimuli. These stimuli are what people "process" when they learn and remember, and this processing begins with the senses.

Hold your finger in front of you and rapidly wiggle it. Do you notice a faint "shadow" that trails behind your finger as it moves? Or, suppose someone says, "That's an oxymoron," and you respond, "Ox see what?" as you repeat part of the word without understanding it. The "shadow" and the fact that you're able to repeat the word even though it's meaningless are both representations of stimuli that are retained in your sensory memory.

Sensory memory is *the information store that briefly holds stimuli from the environment until they can be attended to and further processed* (Neisser, 1967). The material in sensory memory is ". . . thought to be completely unorganized, basically a perceptual copy of objects and events in the world" (Leahey & Harris, 1997, p. 106). Sensory memory is nearly unlimited in capacity, but if processing doesn't begin almost immediately, the memory trace quickly fades away (in about .5 to 1 second for vision and 3 to 4 seconds for hearing (Leahey & Harris, 1997).

Sensory memory is critical to further processing. In trying to read, for example, if the words at the beginning of a sentence were lost from your sensory memory before you got to the end, it would be impossible to get any meaning from the sentence. The same is true for spoken language. Sensory memory allows you to hold information long enough to transfer it to working memory, the next store.

Working Memory

Working memory is *the information store that retains information as the person consciously works with it*. It is where deliberate thinking takes place. It is a "workbench" of memory that temporarily holds information as it is being used or worked on (Gagne, Yekovich, & Yekovich, 1993; Leahey & Harris, 1997). For example, consider students working on comparison shopping problems who are to determine whether 32 ounces of rice for $1.97 is a better buy than 48 ounces of rice at $2.79. These figures, the mental arithmetic, and the answers are all temporarily stored in working memory. After the computations are completed, a decision is made and some information is moved to long-term memory. The remaining details are swept off the workbench and forgotten. Retaining details like these would clog people's memories with useless information.

Working memory has two important characteristics: (a) It screens information that comes into it, and (b) it is limited in capacity and duration (without rehearsal, it can hold about five to nine items for about 10 to 20 seconds for adults) (Miller, 1956).

Working Memory as a Screen

As people are constantly bombarded by stimuli, working memory screens these stimuli and decides what to do with them. There are three choices:

1. Disregard the information (purge from memory).
2. Retain the information in working memory by repeating it over and over (rehearsal).
3. Transfer the information into long-term memory through rehearsal or by connecting it with information already there (encoding).

To illustrate these choices, let's look again at Randy's experience. Tanya said that Pluto was the smallest planet, so it was easy to capture. This information entered Randy's working memory. Later, however, he had to ask Tanya and Juan what Pluto being small had to do with anything. Because he had not connected it to information already in long-term memory, it was lost. In contrast, Juan connected the information by linking Pluto's size to the sun's gravity and the orbit of the other planets, successfully encoding it into long-term memory.

7.4 In this section, we said that information in sensory memory is completely unorganized. What does *unorganized* mean? In which memory store does organization take place?

7.5 Research indicates that multiple questioning—asking a second question before a student has a chance to respond to the first one—detracts from learning. On the basis of what you know about sensory memory, explain why multiple questioning is ineffective.

7.6 The next day you remember some of the information from the comparison shopping problem, such as $1.97 for the rice. Was this information retained in your working memory, or had it been moved to long-term memory? How do you know? As you think about these questions, where is your thinking taking place?

Figure 7.3   Characteristics of working memory

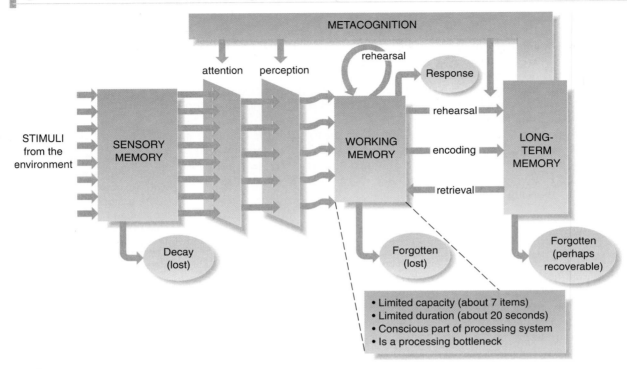

7.7

In Figure 7.3 there is a rehearsal "loop" above "working memory" and a response arrow coming out of "working memory." What is each intended to help you understand?

Why was the information lost from Randy's working memory? Why don't people retain all of the information they hear or read? The characteristics of working memory, which are summarized in Figure 7.3, help answer these questions.

Limitations of Working Memory

Working memory's most important characteristic is the fact that it is limited in capacity (Miller, 1956); it can hold only small amounts of information for limited periods of time. As a result, it is often a "processing bottleneck" (Gagne et al., 1993). Randy probably

Working memory is the "workbench" where students think about and solve problems.

lost the relationship between size and origin because his working memory was "overloaded"; it never made it through the bottleneck. These limitations of working memory can be partially overcome, however, with *chunking* and *automaticity*.

Increasing Processing Efficiency: Chunking.   **Chunking** is *the process of combining separate items into large, meaningful units* (Miller, 1956). To illustrate, try this simple exercise. Look at the following row of letters for 5 seconds.

A E E E G G I I I I L N N N N R R S S T T

Now cover them up and try to write down all 21 letters in any order. How did you do? Most people are unable to remember the list even though the letters are presented in alphabetical order, all but two are repeated and grouped together, and you're told that there are 21 letters in all. The capacities of their working memories have been exceeded.

Now look at the same letters presented as follows:

LEARNING IS INTERESTING

Now you have no trouble remembering the letters because they have been "chunked" into three meaningful words (three units) and into a meaningful sentence (one unit).

Table 7.1 presents other examples of chunking. In each case, you can see that remembering the chunk requires less working memory space than the individual items of information, because you remember the chunked information as a single unit.

Increasing Processing Efficiency: Automaticity.   A second way of increasing the efficiency of working memory is to make the mental processes involved in a task virtually automatic. **Automaticity** *refers to mental operations that can be performed with little awareness or conscious effort* (Schneider & Shiffrin, 1977). Driving a car is a simple example. Once learned to automaticity, people can drive and do other things, such as talk and listen, at the same time.

7.8

Why would a health club prefer to advertise its telephone number as 2HEALTH rather than 243–2584?

Table 7.1   Saving working memory space through chunking

Information "Unchunked"	Information "Chunked"
u, n, r	run
2492520	24 9 25 20
jump jumping hit hitting fight fighting run running	When adding a suffix, double the final consonant when the consonant is preceded by a vowel.
Cooking oil / Water	Less dense materials float on more dense materials (if they don't mix).

As teachers interact with students, processes developed to the point of automaticity allow them to think on their feet while still maintaining the flow of the lesson and monitoring the classroom.

7.9

Two students are about equal in general ability, but one is a better algebra student than the other. Using the information in this section, explain why the better algebra student would likely be more successful in physics than the other student.

7.10

Working memory has been described as a "processing bottleneck." What does this phrase mean? What can teachers do about this bottleneck?

As automaticity develops, the time and effort to perform tasks is dramatically reduced (LaBerge & Samuels, 1974). For example, decoding words in reading and using grammar and punctuation in writing must be largely automatic, so that working memory space is left for comprehension and composition (Samuels, 1988). The same applies in math, where basic operations such as addition and multiplication must be automatic, to allow working memory to be used for problem solving. When learners must consciously focus on basic operations, not enough working memory space remains to perform complex operations such as thinking about the problem, selecting a strategy, computing an answer, or evaluating the validity of the answer.

Limitations of Working Memory: Implications for Instruction. One solution to the problem of working memory limitations is to practice basic skills to the point of automaticity. A second is to use teaching aids that present information in both oral and printed form (Mousavi, Low, & Sweller, 1995) together with high levels of interaction in learning activities. In combining the model and chart with his verbal presentation, David Shelton helped both visual and verbal learners overcome the limitations of working memory. Also, his questioning gave him immediate feedback about whether his students' working memories were overloaded. Had they been, he would have known immediately, because students would have been unable to answer his questions correctly.

The opposite is true in a lecture, in which the pace and amount of information can easily exceed learners' working memory capacities. When this happens, students grasp what they can, take notes so that they can rehearse the information later, or, out of frustration, tune out altogether.

Long-Term Memory

Long-term memory is *our permanent information store.* In a sense, it's like a library with millions of entries and a network that allows them to be retrieved for reference and use. It differs from working memory in both capacity and duration. Whereas working memory is limited to approximately seven chunks of information for a matter of seconds, long-term memory's capacity is vast (some argue nearly unlimited) and durable. Some experts suggest that information in it remains virtually forever (Ashcraft, 1989). These traits are evidenced, for example, when environmental cues trigger a person's recall of events he or she hasn't remembered in years (Schab, 1991). Although the information hasn't been recalled in a very long time, it has been stored in long-term memory.

Representing Knowledge in Long-Term Memory

Let's examine this vast information repository. What is it like? Does it have different compartments? In what form is information stored?

Declarative and Procedural Knowledge

One of the most widely accepted descriptions of the way knowledge is stored in long-term memory is based on the concepts of *declarative* and *procedural knowledge* (Anderson, 1990). **Declarative knowledge** is *knowledge of facts, definitions, procedures, and rules,* whereas **procedural knowledge** is *knowledge of how to perform activities.* For example, a learner who says, "To add fractions, you must first have like denominators," knows the rule for adding fractions but might not be able to actually perform the operation. Being able to state the rule is a form of declarative knowledge, whereas being able to actually add the fractions involves procedural knowledge. Declarative knowledge can be determined directly from a person's comments, whereas procedural knowledge is inferred from the person's performance. Information about the planets in our opening case study is declarative knowledge; procedural knowledge was required to write the summary David assigned.

7.11

In a class, you state, "When using adjectives in writing, the adjective always precedes the noun it describes." Does your statement represent declarative or procedural knowledge? Explain.

Representing Declarative Knowledge.   Declarative knowledge is represented in a variety of forms, which are outlined below and described in Table 7.2 (Gagne et al., 1993).

- Propositional networks
- Linear orderings
- Images
- Schemas

Propositional networks combine **propositions,** *the smallest bits of information a person can judge to be true or false* (such as "Pluto is a planet") into interrelated knowledge structures. Propositions are the heart of declarative knowledge; they are the kernels of information learners store in long-term memory. Linear orderings organize information such as the alphabet or days of the month into stable and coherent patterns. In contrast with both propositional networks and linear orderings, images store physical characteristics of information in memory in the form of mental pictures or snapshots. Imagery can also be useful in executing procedures. For example, athletes often visualize a smooth performance before doing it.

Table 7.2 Representing declarative knowledge in memory

Type of Representation	Description	Example
Prepositional Networks	Sets of interconnected items of declarative knowledge	Combining propositions such as "Pluto is a planet" and "It is the smallest," into a network
Linear Orderings	Ranking or ordering items of declarative knowledge according to some dimension	Representing the days of the week in order in memory
Images	Mental pictures	An image of a map of Canada and the United States representing the land area of each
Schemas	Combinations of propositions, images, and linear orderings	Randy's and Juan's schemas for parts of the solar system

7.12

You have a thorough understanding of cognitive development, whereas one of your friends' understanding is much less thorough. In what two ways do your schemas differ? Explain.

7.13

How would Juan's schema look if he simply memorized the information about the planets' names, their order from the sun, and their orbital planes?

Schemas: Combinations of Propositions, Images, and Linear Orderings. Propositions, images, and linear orderings "represent information at the level of a single idea, image, or relation" (Gagne et al., 1993, p. 81). We know, however, that combining single bits of information into more general patterns is a more efficient way of processing information, and this leads us to the concept of *schemas*.

Theorists don't agree on a single definition, but **schemas** (also called *schemata*) are commonly described as *organized networks of connected information* (Anderson, 1990; Hiebert & Raphael, 1996; Voss & Wiley, 1995). Schemas are individually constructed, dynamic, and contextual (Wigfield, Eccles, & Pintrich, 1996). As a way of understanding schemas, look at Figure 7.4, which illustrates Randy's schema for the solar system.

This illustration, though it doesn't capture any imagery that Randy may have used, shows how his ideas were organized. It suggests that he has linked Pluto and the solar system to the sun, and that globs and the orbital plane are loosely linked to the sun as well. His understanding of the relationship between the sun, the globs, and the orbital plane is uncertain, however, as indicated by the dotted lines, and none of the information is linked to the origins of the solar system, as illustrated by the "origins" label sitting alone.

In contrast, Figure 7.5 illustrates the way Juan organized the ideas in the lesson. Juan understood how the origins of the solar system, the orbital plane, the location of Earth, and Pluto's size and distance from the sun were all related, as indicated by the links in Figure 7.5. These links have important implications for both learning and retention, as we'll see shortly.

Schemas as Scripts. Schemas can also guide a person's actions. For example, when you first go into a university class, you may ask the following:

What are the instructor's expectations?

What are the course requirements?

How should I prepare for quizzes and other assessments?

How will I interact with my peers?

Initial answers come from your schema for the proper way to operate in university classes. One kind of schema is a **script,** which is *"an organized plan of action in a* *particular situation"* (Walker, 1996, p. 231). The script guides your behavior as you prepare for and attend class. In this regard, scripts contain some procedural knowledge, as well as propositions about ways to interact with other students, images of past classes, and linear orderings about what tasks to complete first.

Schemas: Implications for Teaching. Schema theory is important because it helps teachers understand why background knowledge is so important in learning. Learners' schemas interact with new information and influence the way they interpret it. To illustrate, let's look again at a portion of David Shelton's lesson.

Juan:	Pluto wasn't part of the solar system to begin with.
Randy:	What do you mean?
Juan:	I was watching *Nova* with my mom, and the narrator said that scientists think Pluto was floating around and the sun kinda grabbed it. . . . See, when Mr. Shelton did that thing with the socks, the socks stayed sorta level.
Randy:	What's that got to do with it?
Juan:	Well, look. (pointing to the model)
Tanya:	Oh, I get it! Pluto isn't level with the rest of them.
Randy:	Gee, I didn't even notice that.

Because his schema was more complex and interrelated, Juan was able to relate David's demonstration to both a television documentary and information in the unit. In contrast, Randy initially didn't even notice one of the relationships. The concept of *schemas* and how they affect learning helps us understand why Juan's and Randy's experiences were different.

Well-developed and integrated schemas, such as Juan's, represent **generative knowledge,** *knowledge that can be used to interpret new situations* (Mayer & Wittrock, 1996), as opposed to **inert knowledge** which *exists in isolated pieces.* Inert knowledge can't be used to make connections, and it's a pervasive problem in classrooms.

The way topics are presented is critical for developing generative knowledge. To learn effectively, students must experience information represented in different ways and connect it to other ideas through discussion and interpretation. The matrix and the information the students gathered; David's transparency, model, and demonstration; and the discussion that followed were all attempts to help students develop generative knowledge. The role of schemas and generative knowledge again demonstrates an underlying principle in all cognitive learning theories: *Learners are not passive recipients of information but, rather, active organizers of their own understanding.*

Figure 7.4 Schema illustrating Randy's understanding

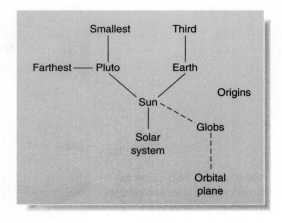

Figure 7.5 Schema for Juan's understanding

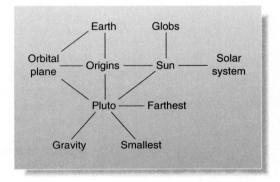

7.14

Research indicates that high-SES students are generally more successful in school than low-SES students. Using the information in this section, explain this research result.

A teacher can help students develop generative knowledge by encouraging them to connect ideas and share these connections with others.

Representing Procedural Knowledge in Memory: Conditions and Actions. As you saw earlier, procedural knowledge is knowledge of "how to do things." In implementing procedural knowledge, learners need to *adapt* to changing *conditions* and then *act* according to these conditions. For example, in adding fractions, if the denominators are the same, you merely add the numerators. If they are different, you must find a common denominator and then add the numerators. The conditions for adding fractions are different depending on the denominators, and the ability to add them correctly depends on recognizing these conditions and responding appropriately. Procedural knowledge also depends on declarative knowledge; you must first *know the rule* to adapt to the different conditions and correctly perform the addition.

Acquiring Procedural Knowledge. Procedural knowledge is typically acquired in three stages (Anderson, 1995; Gagne et al., 1993). In the *declarative stage,* learners acquire declarative knowledge about the procedure, such as being able to describe how to shift gears when driving or state rules for adding fractions. Performing the action is painstaking at this stage, and occupies most of learners' working memory space.

During the *associative stage* learners are able to combine steps and perform the procedure, but must still think about what they are doing (Anderson, 1990). With additional practice, learners finally move to the *automatic stage,* during which they're able to perform the process with little conscious thought or effort. A person's ability to shift gears smoothly, maneuver through traffic, and simultaneously carry on a conversation illustrates this stage.

Importance of Context in Acquiring Procedural Knowledge. Applying procedural knowledge first requires that learners identify conditions in a problem situation before they can appropriately apply procedures. To become proficient, students should use procedural knowledge in a variety of **contexts**, which *involves embedding problems and exercises in realistic settings*. This will help them learn to identify conditions for

7.15

You are given a problem that asks, "How much pizza have you eaten if you eat a piece from a pizza cut into six pieces and another piece from an identical pizza cut into eight pieces?" What are the conditions and what are the actions required in this problem? What declarative knowledge is required in solving the problem?

individual problems, yet appropriately generalize on the procedures. This means, for example, that students should be learning mathematical operations by solving realistic word problems as soon as possible, and should be practicing grammar and punctuation rules in the context of their own writing, not in isolated sentences. Having students complete decontextualized exercises, such as finding common denominators in abstract problems, doesn't provide them with opportunities to identify conditions and apply the appropriate actions. (We examine the role of context again later in this chapter and in Chapter 8.)

As a review, take a moment now to examine Figure 7.6, which presents a summary of the characteristics of long-term memory.

7.16

You're a math teacher. Describe specifically what you might do to give your students practice in identifying appropriate conditions for adding fractions.

Classroom Connections

Applying an Understanding of Sensory Memory in Your Classroom

1. As information is presented, give students time to process it before changing the stimulus.
   - A third-grade teacher displays problems on the overhead projector and waits until the students have copied the problems before she starts talking.
   - In a social studies lesson, a teacher puts a map on the overhead and says, "Look at the map of the neighborhood where our school is located. I'll stop for a second to give you an opportunity to examine it. Then we'll go on."

2. Ask only one question at a time. Otherwise, the memory trace for succeeding questions may be lost before students can attend to them.
   - A first-grade teacher gives students directions for seatwork by presenting them slowly and one at a time. She asks different students to repeat the directions before she has them begin.

Applying an Understanding of Working Memory in Your Classroom

3. Keep descriptions short to prevent overloading students' working memories. Use questions to encourage transfer to long term memory.
   - A teacher in a woodworking class begins by saying, "The hardness and density of wood from the same tree varies, depending on the amount of rainfall the tree has received." He waits a moment, holds up two pieces of wood, and says, "Look at these wood pieces. What do you notice about the rings on them?"

4. To develop automaticity, provide frequent practice and review in basic skills.
   - A first-grade teacher begins language arts each morning by having students write one or two sentences about some event of the night before. She selects samples to review the basic structure of sentences.

5. Encourage organization by identifying and highlighting key points in your presentation and writing them on the chalkboard or overhead.
   - A history teacher prepares an outline of the events that led up to the Revolutionary War. As he presents the information, he refers to the outline for each important point and encourages students to use the outline to organize their note taking.

Applying an Understanding of Long-Term Memory in Your Classroom

6. Encourage students to explore relationships among ideas to help in developing complex networks and schemas.
   - During story time, a first-grade teacher asks the students to explain how the events in a story contribute to the conclusion.

Figure 7.6 Characteristics of long-term memory

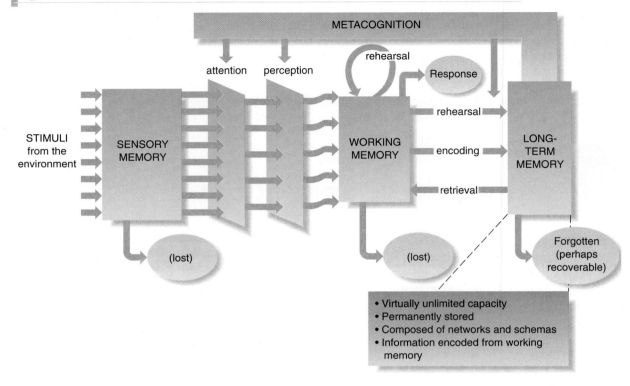

- A third-grade teacher presents examples of writing in which facts, inference, and opinions are embedded and asks students to explain how fact, inference, and opinion are each similar to and different from each other.
7. Connect new ideas to previous learning.
  - In developing the rules for multiplying fractions, a math teacher asks the class, "How does this process compare to what we did when we added fractions? What do we do differently? Why?"

8. Encourage meaningful learning by presenting topics in context.
  - An English teacher presents the rules for singular and plural possessives in the context of a passage about the school. She guides students into an understanding of the rules by using the passage.
  - A sixth-grade math teacher reviews percentages by bringing in newspaper ads and having students compute the percentages saved on CD's and tapes on sale.

Cognitive Processes

Let's return to our model. We've just described the information stores: sensory memory, working memory, and long-term memory. You've seen the characteristics of each, and understand how information is represented in long-term memory. Let's shift our attention to the processes that move information from one store to another: *attention, perception, rehearsal, encoding,* and *retrieval.* These are highlighted in Figure 7.7.

Attention: The Beginning of Information Processing

Consider the room you're in right now. A myriad of stimuli exist—pictures, furniture, other people moving and talking, the whisper of an air conditioner—even though you're not aware of some of them. Others, however, attract your **attention,** which is *the process of consciously focusing on a stimulus or stimuli.*

Reexamine the model in Figure 7.7. "Attention" appears next to "sensory memory," and is where processing begins. All additional processing depends on whether and how well learners attend to appropriate stimuli in the learning environment.

Attracting and Maintaining Student Attention.   Attracting and maintaining student attention is a critical first step in teaching. Teachers should plan their lessons so students attend to what is being taught and ignore outside noises and other stimuli irrelevant to the learning experience (Brophy & Good, 1986; Rosenshine & Stevens, 1986). If a teacher pulls a live, dripping, wriggling crab out of a cooler to begin a lesson on crustaceans, for example, even the most uninterested student is likely to pay attention.

Attention-getters exist in a variety of forms. Demonstrations, displays on transparencies, pictures, maps, graphs, thought-provoking questions, even the chalkboard can attract students' attention. Enthusiastic teachers move around the classroom, change their rate, pitch, and intensity of speech, and use gestures and other energetic movements to maintain attention. Additional examples of attention-getting events are presented in Table 7.3.

Figure 7.7   Cognitive processes in the information-processing model

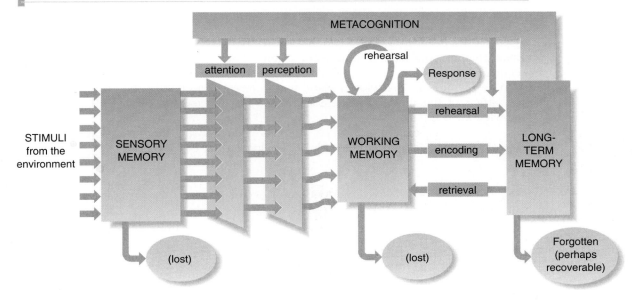

Table 7.3 Instructional strategies to attract attention

Type	Example
Demonstrations	A physical science teacher pulls a student in a chair across the room to demonstrate force and work in a physical science class.
Discrepant events	A world history teacher who usually dresses conservatively comes to class in a sheet, makeshift sandals, and a crown to begin a discussion of ancient Greece.
Visual displays	A health teacher displays a chart showing the high fat content of some popular foods.
Thought-provoking questions	A history teacher begins a discussion of World War II with the question, "Suppose Germany had won the war. How might the world be different now?"
Emphasis	A teacher says, "Pay careful attention now. The next two items are very important."
Student names	In her question and answer session, a teacher always asks her question, pauses briefly, and then calls on a student *by name* to answer.

7.19

One teacher asks, "John, why do you think people are fascinated by the legends of King Arthur?" Another asks, "Why do you think people are fascinated by the legends of King Arthur? . . . John?" How will these two questioning patterns influence John's attention and that of the rest of the class?

David Shelton attracted learners' attention in several ways. Perhaps most significant was his demonstration with the strings and socks, but his model, transparency, and matrix were effective as well. The use of students' names is also a powerful attention-getter. Effective teachers direct their questions to individual students, and when this becomes a pattern, attention and achievement increase (Kauchak & Eggen, 1998; Kerman, 1979).

Perception: Finding Meaning in Stimuli

Perception is *the process by which people attach meaning to their experiences*. After attending to certain stimuli in their sensory memories, processing continues with perception. Perception is critical because it influences the information that enters working memory. Information in working memory is in the form of "perceived reality," not "true reality." If students misinterpret or misperceive the teacher's examples, the information that enters working memory will be invalid, as will the information they transfer to long-term memory.

Background Knowledge Affects Perception. Background knowledge in the form of schemas affects both perception and subsequent learning. This explains why Randy didn't even "notice" that Pluto's plane was different from that of the other planets. His *perception* of the model and demonstration was affected by his lack of background knowledge.

As another example, science students are studying the formation of calcium deposits from hard water and see the following on the chalkboard:

$$CaCO_3 + CO_2 + H_2O \rightarrow Ca + 2HCO_3$$

For learning to be effective, students must accurately perceive several aspects of this equation:

- A symbol without a subscript implies one atom of the element in the compound.
- Some elements have two letters in their symbols; others have only one.
- The subscript indicates the number of atoms of the element.

Accurate perceptions of these features depend on students' background knowledge with respect to chemical equations.

An effective way of checking students' perceptions is to review by asking open-ended questions (Kauchak & Eggen, 1998). For example, after writing the equation on the chalkboard, the science teacher might ask, "Look at the equation. What do you notice about it?" If students can't identify essential information, such as the elements involved, the numbers of each in the compounds, and what the arrow means, the teacher would know that their perceptions are inaccurate or incomplete, and she could then adjust her review to cover these features.

Rehearsal: Retaining Information Through Practice

You have your students' attention; you've checked to make sure their perceptions are accurate; and the information is now in working memory. Knowing that it will remain there for only a short time, what can you do to move important parts into long-term memory? Rehearsal is one of the most commonly used strategies, and occurs in two forms: maintenance rehearsal and elaborative rehearsal (Craik & Lockhart, 1972).

Maintenance rehearsal is *the process of repeating information over and over, either aloud or mentally, without altering its form*. It is analogous to rehearsing a piece of music. When people do so, they play the music as written; they don't alter it or change its form.

As an example, suppose you're adding a series of numbers on a calculator. Rather than read a number and punch it in, to speed up the process you might read four numbers, repeat them once or twice, and punch in all four in the same action. This is a form of maintenance rehearsal used to retain information in working memory until you choose to do something with it.

If information is rehearsed enough, it can sometimes be transferred to long-term memory (Atkinson & Shiffrin, 1968). This is an inefficient method of transferring information, however and, not surprisingly, it's one of the first memory strategies that develops in young children (Berk, 1997).

Rehearsal can be made more effective by capitalizing on the fact that memory tends to be associative. **Elaborative rehearsal** is *the process of associating information the person wants to remember with information already stored in long-term memory*. For instance, if you know that the Civil War was fought during the years 1861 to 1865, you can remember approximately when Lincoln was elected president, because you associate it with the Civil War. Let's see how this happens in the classroom.

7.20

We said that perception depends on background knowledge. How is background knowledge organized in learners' memories?

7.21

You've just looked up a telephone number and want to remember it long enough to call the person. What strategy would you most likely use? What if you wanted to remember it for a longer period of time?

7.22

Look again at the information-processing model in Figure 7.7. What in the model is intended to help you understand that some information can be transferred to long-term memory through rehearsal?

Effective teachers use a variety of visual aids to attract and maintain students' attention.

> T: What year did we say Lincoln was elected? . . . Jane?
> S: . . . 1865?
> T: Let's back up a minute. What year did we say the Civil War began?
> S: 1861.
> T: Good, and how were his election and the start of the Civil War connected?
> S: The South thought Lincoln as president would be . . . like an abolitionist, . . . sort of, so they thought they had to secede, . . . like it was their only choice.
> T: So would Lincoln's presidency start before or after the Civil War started?
> S: . . . Must be before. . . . Oh, yeah. It was 1860.

The information that rehearsal—both maintenance and elaborative—moves to long-term memory is primarily factual (Bruning, Schraw, & Ronning, 1995), as we see in the example with the Civil War and Lincoln presidency. More complex information requires more complex processing, which leads us to the concept of encoding.

Meaningful Encoding: Making Connections in Long-Term Memory

7.23

What is the difference between elaborative rehearsal and encoding? Why is understanding the difference important?

Encoding is perhaps the most critical cognitive process in the information-processing model. **Encoding** *occurs when a person forms mental representations of complex information and stores them in memory* (Siegler, 1991). Meaningful encoding involves organizing and connecting information to information that already exists in long-term memory. **Meaningfulness** *describes the number of connections or associations between an idea and other ideas in long-term memory* (Gagne et al., 1993). For example, Juan formed a mental representation of the solar system's formation by connecting the globs thrown off from the sun—stored in long-term memory—to the formation of the planets. He also encoded the information about Pluto's different origin by associating it with the fact that its orbital plane was different from that of the other planets.

Organizing and attaching new information to old is a critical element of learning, and this is the reason that background knowledge and an understanding of schemas is important. The more "old" information that exists, the more locations a learner has to connect the new information and the more likely it is to be meaningfully encoded.

Making Information Meaningful

How effectively learners represent information in their memories—i.e., how well information is encoded—depends on how meaningful it is to them, and cognitive views of learning emphasize learners' active role in this process. Teachers can support learners, however, by applying three principles in their instruction:

7.24

We've said that complex and interrelated schemas organize information more meaningfully than less complex schemas. Why don't these complex schemas overload learners' working memories?

1. Organization increases meaningfulness by imposing order and connections in new information.
2. Elaboration increases meaningfulness by linking new, complex information to existing schemas.
3. The more cognitively active learners are, the more they learn.

These principles are illustrated in Figure 7.8 and discussed in the sections that follow.

Organization.   In our discussion of long-term memory, you saw that learners store knowledge in the form of schemas that combine propositions, images, and linear orderings. Schemas are important because they organize information. **Organization** is *the process of clustering related items of content into categories or patterns.* David Shelton's model of the solar system displayed the sun, the relative distances of the planets, and the orbital plane and helped students see the relationships among the different parts. Research in reading (Eggen, Kauchak, & Kirk, 1978), memory (Bower, Clark, Lesgold, & Winzenz, 1969), and classroom instruction (Cruickshank, 1985; Mayer, 1997) confirms the value of organization in promoting learning.

Information can be organized in several ways. Among them are:

- Charts and matrices—useful for organizing large amounts of information into meaningful patterns. David Shelton used a matrix in his lesson to help his students organize their thoughts about the planets. Table 7.4 contains an additional example from American history.

- Hierarchies—effective when new information can be subsumed under existing ideas. We made frequent use of hierarchies in our discussion of behaviorism in Chapter 6. Figure 7.9 contains an additional example from English.

- Models—helpful for representing relationships that cannot be observed directly. David Shelton's model of the solar system and the models in this chapter that illustrate the different aspects of information processing are examples.

- Outlines—useful for representing the organizational structure in a body of written material. The outlines at the beginning of each chapter in this book are examples.

Other types of organization include graphs, tables, flowcharts, and maps. Each is intended to make information meaningful by illustrating relationships among different parts (Mayer, 1997). Learners should be encouraged to adapt these forms of organization as personal study strategies to help them in their efforts to encode information.

Organizers, such as charts, hierarchies, and models, can also be used to capitalize on **imagery**—*the process of forming mental pictures.* For instance, as you study information processing, you can picture the model in your mind, "seeing" that working memory is smaller than sensory and long-term memory, and noticing that the lines emerging from perception are curved, which reminds you that individuals perceive information differently. The organization of the model, together with your use of imagery, further enhance the meaningfulness of the information (Clark & Paivio, 1991).

7.25

Look again at the chart organizing information about immigrants (Table 7.4 on the next page). Identify at least three patterns in the chart that would help make the information meaningful to learners.

7.26

You're an English teacher and you use the hierarchy displayed in Figure 7.9 on the next page. What, in addition to displaying the hierarchy, would you have to do to ensure that your students find the information about verbals meaningful? Describe specifically what you would do.

7.27

Think about the use of charts, matrices, and outlines from the perspective of information processing. What function would they serve for beginning lessons? What function would they serve later in lessons?

Figure 7.8 Making information meaningful

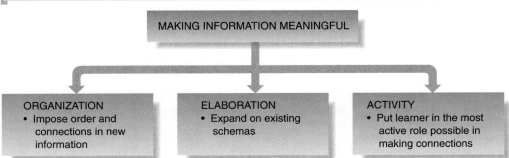

Table 7.4 Chart used to organize information in American history

	Italians	Chinese
Reasons for coming	Small farms that couldn't support families	Overpopulation
	Population increase	Fixed status
	Poor land, poor equipment	Inefficient warlords
	Few factories and plants in which to work	High taxes
	Heavy taxes	Crop failures and famine
	Stories of wealth in America	Active recruitment—promise of high wages
Characteristics	Lower socioeconomic class	Originally coolie laborers
	Large families	Tight family structure
	Tight family structure	Low literacy rate in English
	Low literacy rate in English	Laborers' jobs
	Quick to learn English	Slow to learn English
Assimilation	First generation: very religious, little outside contact	Settlement in Western U.S.
	Second generation: increased intermarriage	Togetherness
		Establishment of "Chinatowns"
	Third generation: "Americanized"	Preservation of Chinese customs

Source: Strategies for Teachers: Teaching Content and Thinking Skills, 3rd ed., by P. Eggen and D. Kauchak, 1996, Needham Heights, MA: Allyn & Bacon. Copyright 1996 by Allyn & Bacon. Adapted with permission.

7.28

Research indicates that students commonly think green plants get their food from the environment, as animals do, rather than make their own. Does this research finding imply that the information is *not* organized for these students? Explain.

As we close this section, a word of caution: *While it's important, organizing content—by itself—doesn't ensure learning.* If the organizational structure doesn't make sense to learners, they will (mentally) reorganize the information in a way that does make sense to them, they will memorize snippets of it, or they will reject or ignore it. For organization to be effective, students must understand the relationships in the information.

Interaction is crucial to this process. David Shelton, for example, not only used his model, demonstration, and matrix but also guided his students' developing understand-

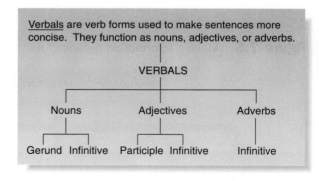

Figure 7.9 Organizational hierarchy in English

Teachers help students encode information in effective ways by organizing content and sharing this organization with students.

ing with questioning and class discussion. It is critical that organization be combined with high levels of interaction if information is to be meaningful to students.

Elaboration.   To begin this section, let's look again at David Shelton's lesson. He began his Wednesday class by saying, "Let's review what we've found out so far. Then I'm going to do a little demonstration, and I want you to think about how it relates to what you've been doing."

By having students review their current understanding and expanding on it with his demonstration, David capitalized on **elaboration** which is *the process of making complex information meaningful by forming additional links in existing knowledge or adding new knowledge* (Willoughby, Wood, & Khan, 1994). It occurs in a noisy party, for example, when you miss some of a conversation; you fill in details, trying to make sense of the message. You do the same as you read or listen to a lecture. You expand on and sometimes distort information to make it fit your expectations and current understanding.

Elaboration can enhance meaningfulness in one or both of two ways. For example, when Tanya said, "Oh, I get it! Pluto isn't level with the rest of them," she formed an additional link in her schema without adding any new information. This is one type of elaboration.

David's review capitalized on a second type. It reactivated his students' schemas (organized background knowledge), to which the information from Wednesday's lesson would be attached. Teacher questioning, such as David's, can be a powerful tool to encourage student elaboration (Seifert, 1993; Simpson, Olejnik, Tam, & Suprattathum, 1994).

In addition to questioning, teachers can promote elaboration by using two additional strategies:

- **Analogies,** which are *comparisons in which similarities are created between otherwise dissimilar ideas* (Mayer & Wittrock, 1996; Zook, 1991).

- **Mnemonic devices,** which are *strategies that promote meaningfulness by forming associations between items or ideas that don't exist naturally in the content* (Leahey & Harris, 1997).

7.29

Look again at Figures 7.4 and 7.5. How do these figures illustrate the information in this section?

7.30

Identify at least one similarity between elaboration and elaborative rehearsal. Identify at least one difference.

7.31

You're a language arts teacher and have discussed direct objects. Describe specifically how you would begin a lesson on indirect objects to capitalize on elaboration.

Meaningfulness is enhanced when students are encouraged to find connections in the new material they are learning.

For example, in an attempt to make information processing more meaningful to you, we presented an analogy between it and a computer. Another analogy from science is:

> Our circulatory system is like a pumping system that carries the blood around our bodies. The veins and vessels are the pipes, and the heart is the pump.

In this case, the circulatory system (the new information) is linked to pipes and a pump (familiar ideas). As a result, links between the new information and information in long-term memory are created.

Mnemonic devices use acronyms, such as HOMES (Huron, Ontario, Michigan, Erie, and Superior), NASA (National Aeronautics and Space Administration) and SCUBA (self-contained underwater breathing apparatus), or place information to be remembered into statements or phrases that are meaningful to learners, such as "Every good boy does fine," for E, G, B, D, and F—the names of the notes on the treble clef staff. Mnemonics are successfully used in classrooms to help students remember vocabulary, names, rules, and other kinds of factual knowledge. As these devices are used to recall information, learners remember the mnemonic and then link it to the items it represents. Figure 7.10 includes some additional examples.

7.32

What is an important limitation in the classroom use of mnemonics?

Activity. Students actively participating in learning is at the heart of cognitive learning theories. You first saw activity emphasized in our study of Piaget and Vygotsky in Chapter 2, and you're seeing in our discussion of information processing that learners are viewed as cognitively active. Active learning encourages meaningful encoding.

"Activity" isn't as simple as it appears on the surface, however (Robins & Mayer, 1993). For instance, since "hands-on" activities are strongly encouraged in science

Figure 7.10 Examples of mnemonic devices

Biology
Kingdom, Phylum, Class, Order, Family, Genus, Species

King Phillip came over from Greece singing.

Astronomy
Mercury, Venus, Earth, Mars, Jupiter, Saturn, Uranus, Neptune, Pluto

My very educated mother just served us nine pizzas.

Grammar
Spelling rules

"I" before "e" except after "c."

The Calendar
Days of the months

Thirty days hath September, April, June, and November . . .

instruction, if learners are working with materials, such as magnets and objects, teachers often assume that active learning is taking place. This isn't necessarily the case. If the goal isn't clear, or if students aren't encouraged to articulate their understanding and describe the connections between new information and information already in long-term memory, learning isn't meaningful. "Hands-on" activities don't necessarily mean "minds-on" activities.

The same is true with manipulatives in math (Ball, 1992), cooperative learning, or any other strategy that is intended to promote active learner participation. Because learners are physically active, or are talking, we assume that learning is taking place. This may not be the case.

Activity can also be deceiving at an individual level. For example, consider two chemistry students who use the worked examples in their text to help them understand the material in the chapter.

> Selena reads the sample problem and then carefully reads through the solution provided by the text's authors. Gretchen covers up the solution, first trying to work the problem on her own and then comparing the solution in the book to hers.

At a casual glance, both girls appear to be actively studying. However, Gretchen is in a more mentally "active" mode than Selena. By preparing a solution that she can compare to the one provided, she is actively processing information, forming links between the problems and information in long-term memory.

As another example, how do you use the margin notes in each chapter? Do you read them and then read the feedback provided in the supplement, or do you read them, write an answer, and then compare your answer with the feedback? The latter more "actively" involves you in creating links and making the content meaningful.

A number of teaching and learning strategies encourage active learning:

- Putting content in the form of problems to solve, rather than information to be memorized.
- Employing questions that require students to analyze, rather than recall, information.

7.33

One student highlights entire paragraphs of her text, whereas another highlights only sentences and small sections. Which of the two is likely to be the more "active" in her study? Explain.

Active learning encourages students to encode information in meaningful ways.

- Requiring students to provide evidence for conclusions, rather than merely form conclusions.
- Developing lessons with examples and applications, instead of definitions.
- Using tests and quizzes that require application, rather than rote memory.

In each of these strategies, students are cognitively active, the activity is purposeful, and connections and deep processing are required.

Levels of Processing: An Alternate View of Meaningful Encoding

Think again about David Shelton and the matrix he used to organize information about the solar system. To guide his students as they processed the information, he could have asked:

"Which planet is the fourth one from the sun?"

"What patterns can you find in the information in the chart?"

"Why do you suppose Mercury is so hot on one side and so cold on the other?"

Which of these would result in the most learning?

Levels of processing is *a view of learning that suggests that the more deeply information is processed, the more meaningful it becomes.* Although originally proposed as an alternative to the three-store information-processing model (Craik & Lockhart, 1972), more recent views describe it as a way of processing information into long-term memory (Cermak & Craik, 1979). The more deeply information is processed, the more connections are made and the more meaningful the information becomes. For instance, merely asking students to identify the fourth planet from the sun is a "shallow" form of processing, whereas asking students to find patterns in the chart or to explain why the temperature on Mercury varies so much requires much deeper processing.

To find patterns, students must identify relationships in items of information, such as visualizing the four inner planets as small and relatively close to the sun, compared with the outer planets, which (except for Pluto) are much larger and more distant. Explaining temperature differences on Mercury also requires a deeper level of processing because it requires identifying cause-and-effect relationships among temperatures, Mercury's period of rotation, its gravity, and atmosphere. Teachers should be continually looking for ways to encourage students to process information in as deep a way as possible by looking for relationships in the information they're learning.

7.34

Identify three kinds of questions that would promote deep levels of processing. Identify one kind of question that would promote shallow processing.

Classroom Connections

Applying an Understanding of Attention in Your Classroom

1. Use examples in your teaching that attract students' attention.
   - A teacher introducing the concept of *pressure* to her science students has them stand by their desks, first on both feet and then on one foot. They then discuss the force and pressure on the floor in both cases.
   - An economics teacher introduces the concept of *opportunity cost* by saying, "You could spend your after-school time at a job, or you could socialize with your friends. If you work, what happens?" She then guides them to the idea that the opportunity cost for the job is the amount of time they don't get to spend with their friends.

2. Call on all students equally and by name to capitalize on the attention-arousing element.
   - A first-grade teacher calls on all students, including those who don't have their hands up. He tells them in advance what he is going to do and explains why it is important.
   - A third-grade teacher mentally keeps track of who she has called on. She periodically asks, "Who have I not called on lately?" to be sure students are treated as equally as possible.

3. Use emphasis to ensure that students attend to important information in the lesson.
   - An earth-science teacher emphasizes, "Class, listen carefully now, because the idea of volcanism is important to the way landforms are created."

Applying an Understanding of Perception in Your Classroom

4. Check to be certain that students are perceiving your examples accurately.
   - A geography teacher, when teaching about landforms, shows her class a series of colored slides. After displaying each one, she asks the students to describe the slide before she moves on to the next.

Using Organization in Your Classroom

5. Carefully organize the information you present to your students.
   - A biology teacher displays an outline of the topics covered to that point in the unit and then highlights the topics to be covered in the current day's lesson.
   - A math teacher presents a flowchart with a series of questions students are encouraged to ask themselves as they solve word problems. She then models the process, using the flowchart as a guide.

Using Imagery in Your Classroom

6. Whenever possible, encourage students to form images of the topics they study.
   - A geography teacher encourages her students to visualize flat parallel lines on the globe as they think about latitude, and vertical lines coming together at the North and South Poles as they think about longitude.
   - A language-arts teacher asks students to imagine how the characters would look in the books they read. She asks them to describe the characters in detail, including their facial features, the way they wear their hair, how they're dressed, and how they act.

Applying Elaboration in Your Classroom

7. Relate new information to previously learned material.
   - A fourth-grade teacher states, "We've been studying the digestive system. We're turning now to the circulatory system. As we study the circulatory system, think about aspects of it that are similar to or different from the digestive system."

- An art teacher begins, "Color is one way to give pictures depth. Perspective is another. As we study perspective, keep in mind how both it and color interact to give the perception of depth."

8. Ask questions requiring students to make comparisons, find relationships, and search for patterns.
   - A science teacher states, "We've just examined physical changes. How does this compare with chemical changes? Can you give me an example of each?"
   - A class studying Shakespeare is asked, "How are the plot and the setting related in *Macbeth?*"
   - A math teacher asks, "Why are the units for volume *cubic* centimeters, whereas the units for area are *square* centimeters?"

9. Review at the beginning and end of each class period.
   - A class studying American literature is asked, "We started our discussion of Hemingway's *The Sun Also Rises* yesterday. What were the key ideas we discussed?"
   - A math teacher states, "Our class period is nearly over, so let's review what we've learned today. We know some new formulas. Who can tell me how we would find the volume of this box?"

10. Ask for and use examples to illustrate abstract ideas.
    - A third-grade teacher demonstrates that heat causes expansion by placing a balloon-covered soft drink bottle in a pot of hot water. He supplements the demonstration with a drawing simulating the spacing and motion of the air molecules.
    - An English teacher dealing with the concept of *internal conflict* in literature displays the following on the overhead: "Joanne didn't know what to do. She was looking forward to the class trip, but if she went, she wouldn't be able to take the scholarship qualifying test."

Applying an Understanding of Activity in Your Classroom

11. Actively involve students in the learning process.
    - In discussing word problems, a math teacher asks individual students to explain how they arrived at their solutions and why they chose a particular process.
    - A history teacher begins new topics with a description of a historical event and asks students why they think the event occurred. The unit is then developed around the students' search for an explanation.

Forgetting

No discussion of memory would be complete without considering **forgetting,** which is *the loss of, or inability to retrieve, information from memory.* Forgetting is both a very real part of people's everyday lives ("Now, where did I put those car keys?") and an important factor in school learning.

Let's look again at the information-processing model first presented in Figure 7.2. There you see that information can be lost from the memory stores in different ways. If a person doesn't quickly attend to the information in sensory memory, it is lost and cannot be retrieved. Information can be retained in working memory if it is rehearsed; otherwise, it is disregarded or purged and cannot be recovered. In the case of long-term memory, information has been rehearsed enough to be transferred to long-term memory or has been encoded in some way. Why can't the learner find it or use it?

Forgetting as Interference.   One view of forgetting uses the concept of **interference,** which is *the loss of information because something else learned either before or after detracts from the learning* (Postman & Underwood, 1973; Schunk, 1996). We've all had the experience of understanding an idea, even being quite confident and comfortable with it, but later, after learning a related idea, being uncertain about the original one. The idea of interference helps in explaining this experience.

When we examine topics commonly taught in schools, we can see how interference occurs. For example, students learn that possessives are formed by adding an apostrophe *s* to singular nouns. They also study plurals and contractions, and they find that the apostrophe is used differently: It comes after the *s* in some cases, it appears before the *s* in the case of plural nouns such as *women* and *children,* and it comes between letters in the case of contractions. Students' understanding of plural possessives and contractions can interfere with their understanding of singular possessives and vice versa.

One solution to the problem of interference is review and comparison. After a new topic is discussed, teachers should compare it with closely related information already studied and identify easily confused similarities. Doing so elaborates on the original schema, reducing interference.

A second solution to the problem of interference is to teach closely related ideas together—for example, adjective and adverb phrases, longitude and latitude, and adding and subtracting fractions with similar and different denominators (Hamilton, 1997). As teachers present related ideas together, they need to highlight the relationships for students, emphasize differences, and identify areas that are easily confused.

Forgetting as Retrieval Failure

Phew, this test is a bear. Maybe I should have studied more last night. Oh, well, almost done.

   Now for the fill-in-the-blanks section. First question: Landing site for the Allied invasion of France? I know that. I remember reading it in the text and seeing it in my notes.

   Paris? No, that's inland. We talked about Calais. No, that was a diversion to trick Germany. Darn! I know that I know it. . . . Why can't I think of the name?

Encoding is important because, without it, information won't be meaningfully stored in long-term memory. However, unless the learner can **retrieve** the information—*pull it into working memory again for further processing*—it's useless. It's like putting information into a file folder and then trying to figure out where the folder is stored; the information is there but can't be found. Many researchers believe that learners don't literally "lose" information when they forget, but rather they can't retrieve it (Ashcraft, 1989).

In attempting to retrieve information, people are often aware they've stored something in long-term memory, but they can't put their mental "finger" on it. Researchers call this the "tip-of-the-tongue" phenomenon (Brown & McNeill, 1966), and it occurs when, for example, you see a face and say, "I know that person, but I can't place her," or in classrooms when students think, "I saw that in the book. Now, what did it say?" The student trying to remember Normandy knew the information was there; the problem was finding it. This brings us to the role of context.

The Role of Context In Retrieval.   You saw earlier that context is important in acquiring procedural knowledge, and it is also important for encoding and retrieval. For

7.35

In which case would interference be most likely to occur: when studying similes and metaphors, or when studying figures of speech and parts of speech? Explain.

7.36

How would meaningfulness affect the tip-of-the-tongue phenomenon?

7.37

Explain why encoding specificity might be harmful in classroom learning. What can teachers do to help learners cope with its effects?

7.38

Consider David Shelton's lesson again. Prepare an introduction to his lesson that would put the lesson in the context of a problem as suggested in this section.

instance, you know a person at work or school but you can't remember her name when you see her at a party. The party is a different context from the one in which the information was encoded. This contextual influence on retrieval is sometimes called the *encoding specificity hypothesis* (Tulving, 1979).

David Shelton capitalized on the impact of context when he presented his information about Pluto in different ways. He didn't merely *say* that the first eight planets had one origin and that Pluto had another. Instead, he presented the information in the context of the planets' orbital planes, their direction of revolution, and the origin of the solar system. He also asked questions such as, "Does that support or contradict what the group said?" By encouraging his students to learn new information in a variety of ways, he increased the likelihood of later retrieval (Martin, 1993).

Metacognition: Knowledge and Control of Cognitive Processes

We have now examined the first two parts of the information-processing model. We've studied the memory stores—sensory memory, working memory, and long-term memory—and the cognitive processes—attention, perception, rehearsal, encoding, and retrieval—that move information from one store to the next.

These cognitive processes are not simple mechanisms that merely turn on or off, however. To be useful, they must be integrated so they can be used strategically. Metacognition serves this function. (We examine the relationships between learner motivation, metacognition, and self-regulation in depth in Chapter 10.)

Earlier in the chapter we said **metacognition** is *knowing about and having control over cognitive processes*. The metacognitive components of the information-processing model are illustrated in Figure 7.11.

Metacognition operates from the beginning of the learning process, starting with attention. If you choose to sit near the front of the class so you don't drift off, for example, you are demonstrating meta-attention.

Figure 7.11 Metacognition in the information-processing model

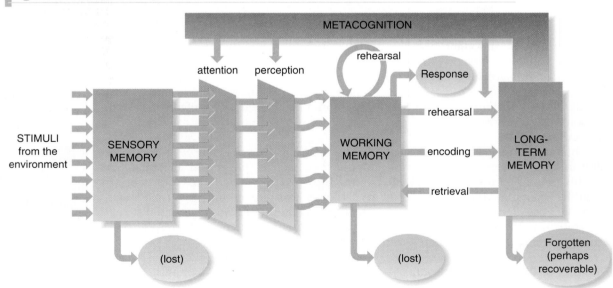

Metacognition can play a role in perception as well. Being aware of the possibility of misperceiving something and consciously reserving judgment until you have additional information demonstrates awareness of and control over your perception.

Metacognition also helps regulate the flow of information through working memory. For example, we've all been in situations where we've had to remember a phone number. If we're going to dial the number immediately, we simply rehearse; if we're going to call later, we'll probably write the number down. Each decision is strategic, influenced by our goal and the awareness and control over our memories—metamemory. Alfredo, in David's lesson, demonstrated metamemory when he said, "Wait, Mr. Shelton, you're going too fast. I'm getting lost. What is this about supporting the theory?" He was aware that he was missing some of the information, and he demonstrated control over his memory by asking David to slow down and explain the information about Pluto. The ability to monitor the processing of information in working memory is critical because of its limited capacity.

Finally, metacognition involves awareness and control of long-term memory and encoding. For example, knowing that you tend to associate items of information in long-term memory rather than store them in isolation can help you consciously look for relationships in the topics you study. *Being aware* of the way you store information and *making a conscious effort* to look for relationships is a form of metacognition.

7.39

As you are reading you encounter an unfamiliar word. You reread the sentence to try to figure out the meaning of the word. Is your behavior strategic? Explain.

7.40

Identify two common strategies that you (and most other university students) use to help you learn.

The Development of Metacognition

As students develop their metacognitive abilities, they learn to use **strategies**—*plans for accomplishing learning goals*—effectively (Berk, 1997). For instance, summarizing would be a strategy for increasing comprehension of a written passage, or a mnemonic could be a strategy to remember something such as the names of the Great Lakes.

Young learners are often passive; they don't realize that they can influence the learning process. As they develop, however, they acquire an increasing number of strategies, the strategies become more efficient, and the strategies are used more selectively (Berk, 1997).

Meta-Attention: Development of Attention Strategies. **Meta-attention** is *awareness and control of attention*. Research on meta-attention indicates that older children are more aware of the role of attention in learning than their younger counterparts, are better at directing their attention toward important information in a learning task, and are also better at ignoring distracting or irrelevant stimuli (Berk, 1997; Scholnick, 1995).

Although meta-attention develops naturally during the school years, efforts by teachers can enhance it. Let's look at an example.

Mrs. Mahera began working with her first-graders by saying, "We know how important it is to pay attention." She then modeled attention by focusing on a sample seatwork assignment, working carefully, and keeping her eyes on the paper.

Then she had Mrs. Morton, her parent volunteer, talk, and she listened intently to Mrs. Morton, maintaining eye contact and keeping her hands and body still. She next modeled inattention in both an interactive and a seatwork situation.

She then asked, "Now, am I paying attention?" as she modeled inattention to seatwork by gazing out the window and playing with objects on her desk. She demonstrated several more examples, had the students classify them as attention or inattention, and then told the students, "I am going to click the 'cricket,' and if you're paying attention each time I click it, make an X in a box." She showed the students a sheet of paper with several boxes drawn on it and passed each student a sheet. She went on, "Each time you hear a click, put an *X* in the next box if you're paying attention."

The next morning and for several consecutive mornings, Mrs. Mahera demonstrated and had students demonstrate attentive and inattentive behaviors as part of the class routine. As time went on, students' attention improved markedly. (based on Hallahan et al., 1983)

7.41

On which aspect of meta-attention was Mrs. Mahera primarily focusing?

Young children often don't realize that they're inattentive, and this awareness needs to be developed. With time and teacher assistance, meta-attention increases, and students can begin the process of becoming self-regulated learners.

Metamemory: Development of Memory Strategies. An eight-year-old is describing her strategy for remembering a telephone number:

> Say the number is 663–8854. Then what I'd do is say that my number is 663, so I won't have to remember that really. And then I would think now I've got to remember 88. Now I'm eight years old, so I can remember, say my age two times. Then I say how old my brother is, and how old he was last year. And that's how I'd usually remember that phone number. [Interviewer: Is that how you would most often remember a phone number?] Well, usually I write it down. (Kreutzer, Leonard, & Flavell, 1975, p. 11)

7.42

What are some indicators that teachers can use to gauge whether metamemory is operating in students? What can teachers do to encourage metacognitive growth in this area?

Information-processing researchers have also found developmental differences in **metamemory,** *which is knowing about and regulation of memory strategies.* The eight-year-old used a sophisticated strategy, linking the numbers to information that was already encoded in her memory.

Older children and adults are much better than young children at using strategies for remembering information (Short, Schatschneider, & Friebert, 1993). For example, nursery school students given a list of objects to memorize in order didn't use rehearsal as a strategy. Fourth graders, in contrast, both rehearsed aloud and anticipated succeeding items by naming them before they were shown by the experimenter (Flavell, Friedrichs, & Hoyt, 1970). Similar patterns have been found with categorizing and imagery as strategies; kindergartners don't use them, whereas fourth graders can and do (Berk, 1997).

7.43

Most college and university students take notes as a strategy. Does note taking better illustrate meta-attention or metamemory? Explain.

Besides using different strategies, older learners are more aware of their memory limitations. For example, when asked to predict how many objects, such as a shoe or ball, they could remember from a list, nursery school students predicted 7; when tested, they remembered fewer than 4 (Flavell et al., 1970). Adults given the same task predicted an average of 5.9 and actually remembered 5.5 (Yussen & Levy, 1975). These examples illustrate not only differences in memory capacities but also differences in students' awareness of them.

Instruction can help students become aware of their memory capacities and the importance of matching strategies to task demands (Huet & Mariné, 1997). For simple tasks, such as remembering a class assignment, a simple strategy like writing it down is enough. For more complex tasks, like understanding written material, more sophisticated strategies such as summarizing or self-questioning are required. The goal for teachers at all levels should be the development of students who take responsibility for their own learning.

Classroom Connections

Applying an Understanding of Interference in Your Classroom

1. Teach closely related ideas together, stressing similarities and differences.
   - A life-science teacher combines the topics of reptiles and amphibians in the same unit, stressing the features that make them different.
2. Carefully review and compare closely related topics after they're covered.
   - A teacher presenting a unit on verbals states, "We've finished our discussion of participles now. Yesterday, we covered gerunds. Tell me the key difference between the two and give us an example of each."

Applying an Understanding of Retrieval in Your Classroom

3. Present information in enriched contexts.
   - A life-science teacher begins a unit on arteries and veins by saying, "We've all heard of hardening of the arteries, but we haven't heard of 'hardening of the veins.' Why not? Are we using the term *artery* to mean both, or is there a difference? Why is hardening of the arteries bad for people? I'm going to write these questions down so that we keep them in mind as we study arteries, veins, and capillaries."

Applying an Understanding of Metacognition in Your Classroom

4. Consciously teach students about the role of attention in learning.
   - A fourth-grade teacher plays an attention game with his students. During a lesson, he'll hold up a card with the sentence "If you're paying attention, raise your hand." He'll then acknowledge those who are and encourage them to share their strategies for maintaining attention during class.
   - A social-studies teacher tries to teach attention-monitoring skills by saying, "Suppose you're reading and the book states that there are three important differences between capitalism and socialism. What should you do?"
5. Teach students the importance of listening carefully.
   - To encourage students to listen to each other, a middle-school teacher periodically has the class write down what a student has just said in answering a question. She has them monitor their listening and try to continually improve.
6. Model metacognitive abilities for your students.
   - A ninth-grade economics teacher says, "Whenever I read something new, I always ask myself, 'How does this relate to what I've been studying? For example, how is the liberal economic agenda different from the conservative economic agenda?'"
   - In a health lesson, a third-grade teacher says, "If I understand what Dana meant by her comment, she is suggesting that we should stay away from smoky places because of the danger of secondhand smoke." The teacher then asks the students why they think Dana would make such a statement, and leads them to conclude that she was aware of the possibility of misperceiving Dana's comment.
   - A chemistry teacher, in trying to help his students remember the symbols for elements in the periodic table, asks students to volunteer any mnemonic devices and images they use.

As a warm-up activity for his world geography class, Mike Havland asked his students to turn to page 267 of their text, on which was a "modern" map of Europe.

As Carl looked at the map, he thought it looked familiar. "Yeah," he thought, "there's England, France, Germany, and Russia. Hey, there's Yugoslavia. That's where Goran's grandparents came from."

Next to him, Celeena, whose father was a career military man with whom she had traveled all over Europe, was also looking at the map, but with a look of disbelief. "How old *is* this book?" she thought. "Look at Yugoslavia. It doesn't exist anymore. It's been torn apart. Hmm, where's Barcelona? . . . Oh yeah. Down there on the coast of Spain. We saw it when we went to the Olympics several years ago."

After a few minutes, Mike began. "Okay, everyone. It's important to have some idea of the geography of Europe, because the geography reflects an important idea that we'll return to again and again." With that, he wrote on the chalkboard: "The history of Europe reflects the tension between nationalism and intercountry cooperation."

He continued by saying, "As you've already noticed, the face of Europe is continually changing, reflecting the ebbs and flows of nationalistic fervor and efforts to reduce cultural and trade barriers."

As he was talking, he noticed a few nods but more blank looks. Celeena sat knowingly, while Carl thought, "What's he talking about? nationalism? cultural and trade barriers? What is this?"

Not knowing what to do about the blank looks, Mike continued with his planned lecture.

7.44

Consider the following two statements: "Many students have less well developed schemas than other students" and "Many students have different schemas than other students." On the basis of the information in this section, which is the more accurate statement?

Teachers know that background knowledge is a powerful influence on perception and encoding. Students come to class with widely varying experiences, and dealing with this diversity is one of the biggest challenges facing all teachers (Veenman, 1984).

Diversity and Perception

Background knowledge resulting from experience powerfully influences perception. As you saw in Mike's lesson, what students perceive from something complex, such as a map, largely depends on what they already know. This notion has been verified in areas as varied as chess, reading, math, and physics (Glover, Ronning, & Bruning, 1990).

Experience affects both *what* and *how much* students learn. For example, one student seeing a movie on the Vietnam conflict interprets the war as an effort to stop the spread of communism, whereas another perceives it as the imposition of American values on a distant country. When Carl viewed the map of Europe, he perceived an accurate representation; when Celeena viewed it, she perceived it as an antiquated document. Learners' schemas influence the way they perceive information.

Diversity, Encoding, and Retrieval

Just as learners' background knowledge influences their perceptions, it also influences how effectively they encode new information. Celeena, for example, has a richer geography background than Carl. As a result, the statement "The history of Europe reflects the tension between nationalism and intercountry cooperation," was meaningful to her, whereas it meant little to Carl; he had little in his background to which ideas such as "nationalism" and "intercountry cooperation" could be linked.

We've all been in situations when a presentation or passage in a book doesn't make sense, and we've all been in conversations in which we're not connecting with

The diverse experiential backgrounds of students can be used to enrich the learning experiences of all students.

the other person. In each case, we may lack the background to which new information can be linked, so meaningful encoding doesn't occur.

Instructional Adaptations for Background Diversity

What can teachers do when this lack of encoding happens in the classroom? Research suggests several strategies (Brenner et al. 1997; Glover et al., 1990):

- Begin lessons by asking students what they know about the topic you're planning to teach.
- Provide background experiences with rich examples and representations of the content you're teaching.
- Use open-ended questions to assess student perceptions of your examples and representations.
- Use the experiences of students in the class to augment the backgrounds of those lacking the experiences.

For example, it would have been easy for Mike to say, "Celeena, you lived in Europe. What do people in Europe say about the conflict in the former Yugoslavia?" Also, because *nationalism* was an organizing idea for much of what followed, Mike could have asked, "What does *nationalism* mean? Give an example of strong and weak nationalism." If students are unable to respond, he must alter his plans to focus on the concept, laying the groundwork for subsequent learning. For example, he could have used the school as context for his discussion of nationalism by describing school spirit, pride in the school, and the school's traditions as analogies for the feelings of nationalism in European countries. The analogies would make the notion of nationalism more meaningful for students, and subsequent encoding and retrieval would be improved (Zook, 1991). The ability to adapt lessons in this way is one characteristic of teaching expertise.

7.45

We recommended in this section, "provide background experiences with rich examples and representations of the content you're teaching." Describe specifically what is meant by "rich examples and representations."

Classroom Connections

Capitalizing on Diversity in Your Classroom

1. Assess students' backgrounds prior to lessons.
   - A second-grade teacher begins a unit on communities by requesting, "Tell us what you know about the community we live in." He encourages a number of students to respond so that he can get an accurate idea of what students know.
   - An art teacher begins a unit on perspective by asking students to sketch a three-dimensional scene. He has students put their names on the back of the sketches and then discusses the sketches during the following class period.

2. Use open-ended questioning to assess students' perceptions.
   - A fourth-grade teacher begins a unit on the North and South prior to the Civil War by preparing a matrix comparing the economy, geography, and climate of the North and South. He displays the matrix and says, "Now, tell us what you see in the first column on the chart. . . . Anything you notice or observe there?"
   - An English teacher puts a sonnet on the overhead and says, "Someone describe what's on the overhead." In the discussion that follows, he tries to relate characteristics of sonnets to the students' observations.

3. Have students with different backgrounds share their experiences and ideas.
   - A sixth-grade teacher beginning a study of plants says to a student whose parents own a greenhouse, "Melinda, you've had some interesting experiences working with plants and crops. Tell us about the kinds of plants your parents grow, what they're used for, and anything else about plants you think might be interesting."

4. Provide concrete experiences to develop learners' background knowledge.
   - As an introduction to the study of refraction, a science teacher has students put coins in opaque dishes and then back up until they can't see the coins. She then has a partner pour water into the dish until the coin becomes visible. Finally, she shows a model illustrating how the light rays are bent when they enter and leave the water.
   - Before beginning a unit on geometric shapes, a kindergarten teacher has his students draw, color, and cut out squares, triangles, rectangles, and circles. He then has students identify examples of the shapes around the classroom.

Putting Information Processing into Perspective

Information processing has been the most influential cognitive theory of learning in the twentieth century (Mayer, 1996). It offered a workable alternative to behaviorism, and provided both teachers and researchers with useful concepts that helped them better understand learning.

Like virtually all theories, however, information processing has its critics (Derry, 1992; Mayer, 1996). Some of these criticisms are outlined in the following paragraphs.

First, the computer as a metaphor for the mind has both strengths and weaknesses. Concepts such as working and long-term memory help us understand and explain how information is acquired and stored. But learners aren't computers. They enter our classrooms with a variety of emotions, beliefs, expectations, and personal goals, all of which influence learning. Information processing has been criticized for ignoring these factors.

In addition, critics argue that information processing fails to take into account the context in which learning occurs, tacitly assuming that learning is learning, no matter where it occurs. Research indicates, however, that the social environment strongly effects what is learned and how it transfers to other settings (Greeno et al. 1996).

Finally, critics contend that information processing doesn't adequately emphasize the extent to which learners actively construct their own understanding (Derry, 1992). In the next section we examine constructivism, a cognitive learning theory that addresses this criticism.

Constructivism

To begin this section, let's look in on a classroom of 29 fourth-graders working in a math lesson.

Jenny Newhall, a fourth-grade teacher, wants her students to develop their problem-solving skills, learn to work collaboratively in groups, and learn that a balance beam balances when the weight times the distance on one side equals the weight times the distance on the other. She begins the lesson by giving each group of students a balance beam and directing them to place weights on it as shown in the following drawing:

Video Case

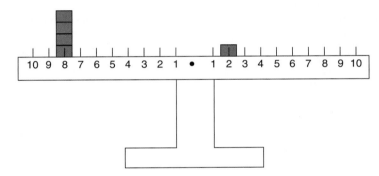

The students' task is to make the beam balance by adding more weights, without moving any of the existing weights. To encourage individual problem solving, she first asks each student to write down a possible solution. Then the individuals share their solutions with their teammates and the groups discuss the validity of each solution, deciding which solution to try first.

Let's join one of the groups—Molly, Suzie, Tad, and Drexel—as they explain their strategies.

"I think we should put 3 on 10, because 4 and 8 is the same as 32—like 32 on one side. And since we only have 2 on the other side, we need to make them equal. So 3 on 10 would equal 30 and so we'd have 32 on both sides," Molly offers first.

"I did a short one," Drexel adds. "4 times 8 is 32 and 1 times 2 is 2. 6 times 5 is 30 and 30 plus 2 is 32."

Suzie then offers hers. "There are 4 on the 8 and 1 on the 2. I want to put 3 on the 10 so there will be 4 on each side."

As Jenny joins the group she listens to the different solutions and asks Tad if he has one to add. When he hesitates, she asks if he wants to think about the ones already offered.

Tad replies, "These three, I guess."

Jenny then encourages each of them to explain and defend their solutions and decide which they want to try first on the balance beam.

Suzie begins by asserting, "See, if 4 is on each side, that'll make 8, which is even and it'll even out."

"Drexel's will work, too," Molly interjects. "Let's try it second [after the 3 on the 10], 'cause we may not be able to fit five weights on the balance . . . Do you agree? . . . Yes or no? . . . Okay? . . . Tad, what's your prediction?"

"I never had time to write it," Tad replies, shrugging.

Suzie suggests an alternate solution. "Put 2 weights on the 10 and 1 on the 6."

The group considers this suggestion until Jenny returns to the group and asks, "Why did you decide to try the 3 on 10 as your first choice?"

"'Cause it would make 4 here and 4 there," Suzie offers.

"Also, if you times that, it'll be 32, and it'll also equal 32 on this side. So it'll make it equal. 4 times 8 is 32 and 3 times 10 is 30 plus two is 32," Molly adds.

"Your second choice was 5 on 6?" Jenny interjects.

"I think we should make it third 'cause it may not work [physically] and mine may."

"Suzie, why do you think yours should be second?" Jenny asks.

"'Cause 5 tiles won't fit on there."

"Molly, why do you think 5 on 6 should still be second?" Jenny asks.

"Because I think it's the second best that will work."

"Why?" Jenny probes.

"What was yours again, Suzie?" Jenny asks.

"Put 2 on 10 and 1 on 6."

"See, 2 on 10 is 20, and 1 on 6 will only make it 26," Molly counters.

Jenny asks, "When you do the multiplying they need to be the same on both sides? Is that what you're telling me? And you think that what you have down for the third one is not going to be heavy enough, and so that's why you want Drexel's idea to be second? Well, you guys need to decide that. Talk it over and decide."

As Jenny circulates around the room the group discusses the different options.

When Jenny returns, Suzie volunteers, "We've decided to keep the same order" (to try the 6 × 5 solution second).

"What made you decide to keep it as it is?" Jenny asks.

"Because mine. . . . It kind of sunk in what she said when we add them up—it won't be even. It kind of sunk in."

"And that was a good compromise. She gave her point of view and you could see the rationality of it," Jenny offers.

They then add 3 to the 10 spot and wait for the balance to stop jiggling.

"That one has more weight," Tad asserts as the beam tips to the side where they added weights.

After a few moments it balances and Suzie cries out, "It's perfect! It works!"

Next they try adding 5 weights on 6, but because of a balance malfunction, it doesn't balance. Molly and Drexel are convinced of the validity of their answer. Suzie and Tad, unsure of this solution, want to physically experiment with other options, which they do unsuccessfully.

Jenny then calls the whole class together to discuss the solutions different groups formed. Allison suggests the 3 on 10 strategy. Jenny asks for a volunteer to draw and explain this solution and Danielle goes up to the board and draws the following diagram:

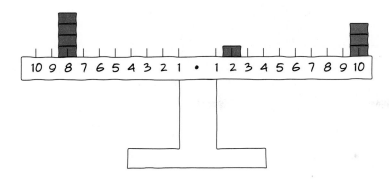

"Danielle, can you explain why that works?" Jenny asks.

"Because there are 4 tiles on each side and so that makes it equal."

Paraphrasing, Jenny adds, "So there are 4 tiles on this side and 4 on the other and that made it work. Does anyone else have another explanation why that worked? Can someone tell us why that works in a different way? Mavrin? Can you go up to the board and explain it a different way? Can you write something to show us why it works?"

Mavrin then writes the following under the balance beam on the board:

$$8 \times 4 = 32 \quad = \quad (10 \times 3) + 2 = 32$$

"Do you see what he's done?" Jenny asks. "He has a number sentence on both sides. Over on this side he came up with 8 times 4, which is 32. When he started out with just a 2 over here, what do you think Mavrin thought to himself to figure this problem out? Blair?"

"He needed something to add to 2 to make it 32."

"And since we already have 2, now he needs something to add up to . . . Blair?"

"30."

"And that's why he had to put the 3 on the 10," Jenny adds. "Now, Becky, you had a different solution. Would you go up and do the one you had?"

Becky erases Mavrin's answer and puts the following on the board:

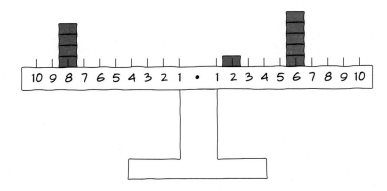

"Now, can you write a number sentence underneath to show us how that works?" Jenny encourages. After Becky writes a number equation on the board, Jenny explains Becky's solution, referring to both the balance beam on the board and the number sentence underneath it. She then gives the groups the following problem to solve:

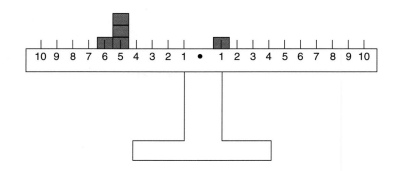

Again, students in each group are encouraged to come up with their own individual solutions. When Jenny calls the class back together she asks Suzie to share her answer. She goes to the front of the room and draws the following on the board:

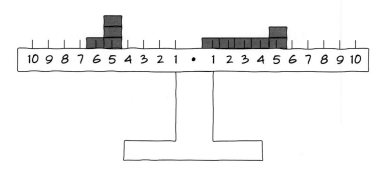

With Jenny's help, Suzie writes the following number sentence on the board:

$$(3 \times 5) + 6 = 21 \quad = \quad 1 + 2 + 3 + 4 + 5 + 5$$

"Add that up and see what you get," Jenny directs Suzie. "You boys and girls at your seats could be adding this up to see if it comes up to 21."

Suzie concludes that the numbers add up to 22, and Jenny responds, "Does anyone else have a different answer?" The lesson continues with other students offering and explaining additional possible solutions.

After the lesson, an interview was conducted with Molly, Suzie, Tad, and Drexel to determine their understanding of balance beam problems. Molly and Drexel thoroughly understood the principle, but Tad and Suzie initially did not. As the interview progressed, both Suzie and Tad learned to solve balance beam problems, but this occurred only after additional discussion and experimentation with the balance beam.

Emerging Role of Constructivism in Education

You first encountered the idea of knowledge construction in Chapter 2, when we saw that, instead of recording understanding delivered from others, learners "construct" their understanding of the topics they study. We now want to consider this view of learning in more detail.

The influence of constructivism in teaching and learning has increased over the last several years. The shift toward literature-based approaches to reading, for example, and process approaches to writing are both grounded in constructivism (McCarthy,

1994). The *Curriculum and Evaluation Standards for School Mathematics* (National Council of Teachers of Mathematics, 1989) and the *Benchmarks for Science Literacy* (American Association for the Advancement of Science, 1993) both have a constructivist foundation, and modern school textbooks are also being influenced by constructivist views of learning (e.g., Thompson, McLaughlin, & Smith, 1995). The increasing influence of constructivism can be seen across the school curriculum.

Different Views of Constructivism

We said at the beginning of this chapter that there isn't *a single* cognitive theory of learning, and the same is true of constructivism (Driscoll, 1994; Greeno et al., 1996). Constructivists disagree on the nature of knowledge and the importance of different elements in the knowledge construction process. We describe two positions in this section.

The first position, based largely on Piaget's work, is called *cognitive constructivism* (Cobb, 1994; Greeno et al., 1996). It focuses on internal, individual constructions of knowledge (Fowler, 1994; Moshman, 1982). In this view, knowledge does not exist, as such, in the social environment; rather, social interaction is important primarily as a stimulus or catalyst for individual, internal cognitive conflict. When one child suggests an idea that causes disequilibrium in another, for example, the second child might resolve the disequilibrium by individually constructing, or reconstructing, his or her understanding. As an example, let's look at some brief dialogue between two children on a playground.

Devon:	"Look at the bugs." (holding a beetle between his fingers and pointing at a spider)
Gino:	"Yech . . . Put that thing down. Besides, that's not a bug. It's a spider." (gesturing to the spider)
Devon:	"What do you mean? A bug is a bug. They look the same."
Gino:	"Nope. Bugs have six legs. See. (touching the legs of the beetle). He has eight legs. . . . Look." (pointing to the spider).
Devon:	"So, . . . bugs . . . have . . . six legs, and spiders have eight."

Cognitive constructivists' interpretation of the episode would suggest that Devon's equilibrium was disrupted by the discussion, since he saw evidence that the beetle and spider were different, and—individually—he resolved the problem by reconstructing his thinking to accommodate the evidence.

Cognitive constructivism emphasizes learning activities that are child-determined and discovery-oriented. For instance, cognitive constructivists in math argue that children learn math facts more effectively if they discover these facts based on what they already know, rather than have them presented by a teacher or other expert (Pressley, Harris, & Marks, 1992).

Cognitive constructivism poses a dilemma for educators. One interpretation of Piaget's work is that it ". . . fundamentally distrusted all attempts to instruct directly" (Resnick & Klopfer, 1989, p. 3). A different interpretation suggests that interaction is important for learner growth, but that teachers need to guard against imposing their thoughts and values on developing learners (DeVries, 1997). Both interpretations minimize the role of the teacher in directly instructing students in basic knowledge and skills. So, other than providing materials and a supportive learning environment, what is the teacher's role in this process? This question has never been satisfactorily answered for classroom teachers (Airasian & Walsh, 1997; Greeno et al., 1996).

Social interaction in small-group work provides opportunities for students to refine their own ideas as they shape the ideas of others.

A second position, strongly influenced by Vygotsky's (1978) work, is called *social constructivism* (Bruning et al., 1995; Turner, 1995). Although social constructivists vary in what they emphasize (e.g., Greeno et al., 1996; Rogoff, 1990), they agree that knowledge exists in a social context and is, at least initially, shared with others rather than represented solely in the mind of an individual (Cole, 1991). Social constructivists acknowledge the contributions of others in learning. As people interact, the process of sharing results in learners refining their own ideas and helping shape the ideas of others. For example, social constructivists, instead of concluding that Devon individually reconstructed his understanding of insects and spiders in an effort to re-establish equilibrium, would argue that Devon's understanding was increased *as a direct result* of the exchange with Gino. Further, they would assert that the dialogue between the two played an important role in helping Devon arrive at a clearer understanding of insects and spiders.

This interpretation has important implications for instruction and helps resolve the Piagetian constructivists' dilemma. It "does not suggest that educators get out of the way so children can do their natural work, as Piagetian theory often seemed to imply" (Resnick & Klopfer, 1989, p. 4). Unlike the Piagetian-based downplaying of the role of the social environment, social constructivism highlights that role and suggests that teachers consider all the traditional questions of teaching: how to organize and implement learning activities, how to motivate students, and how to assess learning. It answers these questions, however, with a focus on learners' own constructions of understanding within a community of learners (Greeno et al., 1996; Shuell, 1996).

Characteristics of Constructivism

Despite their differences, most constructivists agree that four characteristics influence all learning, as outlined in Figure 7.12 (Bruning et al., 1995; Mayer, 1996).

7.46

Both cognitive and social constructivism emphasize the importance of social interaction. They differ, however, in defining the function it performs. Describe this difference.

Figure 7.12   Characteristics of constructivism

- Learners construct their own understanding.
- New learning depends on current understanding.
- Learning is facilitated by social interaction.
- Meaningful learning occurs within authentic learning tasks.

Learners Construct Understanding

The core idea of constructivism—knowledge construction—emphasizes the central role learners play in developing their own understanding. Brophy observes,

> Current research, while building on the findings indicating the vital role teachers play in stimulating student learning, also focuses on the role of the student. It recognizes that students do not passively receive or copy input from teachers, but instead actively mediate it by trying to make sense of it and to relate it to what they already know (or think they know) about the topic. Thus, students develop new knowledge through the process of *active construction*. (1992, p. 5)

We saw the process of "knowledge construction" in Jenny Newhall's students. Suzie and Tad struggled with the idea that length times weight on one side equals length times weight on the other. Suzie, especially, characterized this struggle. At first she believed that four weights on each side were all that were needed to balance the beam. Then she reconsidered, commenting, ". . . It kind of sunk in what she [Molly] said when we add them up. . . . it won't be even." But this understanding was fragile, and she rejected it when the balance didn't work with the "6 on 5" solution.

You can see from the students' comments that they didn't "receive understanding" from Jenny. Rather, they were faced with the problem of understanding an abstract idea and, in their efforts to understand, they discussed it, conducted experiments, and constructed their own meaning. This process of constructing understanding is the core of constructivism.

Jenny played an important role in the process. She could have simply explained the idea that length times weight on one side equals length times weight on the other side; this is what teachers commonly do. But abstract explanations don't do much to help ideas "make sense." In contrast, Jenny demonstrated skill and expertise in guiding students to a more mature understanding of the principle (length times weight on one side equals length times weight on the other). Most important, the ideas began to make sense to them.

We also saw elements of constructivism in David Shelton's lesson. Both Jenny's and David's work illustrate an important implication for instruction based on constructivism: *The way information is presented is critical.* Instead of lecturing, Jenny and David *guided* their students to an understanding of the content in the lessons. In the extreme, lecturing and explaining are based on behaviorist views of learning; treating learners as passive recipients of understanding.

7.47

What concept from Piaget's theory best illustrates Suzie's thinking when she concluded that to balance the beam the number of weights on each side of the balance needed to be equal?

7.48

Identify two similarities between information processing and constructivism. Identify one important difference.

New Learning Depends on Current Understanding

7.49

Identify at least four ways in which background knowledge can be organized. What implications do they have for instruction?

7.50

Using Piaget's work as a basis, explain why people are reluctant to modify their existing understanding of the way the world works.

We emphasized the role of background knowledge and current understanding when we discussed the importance of making information meaningful in information processing. Constructivists also emphasize the importance of students' current understanding; they see new learning interpreted in the immediate *context* of current understanding, not first as isolated information that is later related to existing knowledge.

This principle was explicitly illustrated in Jenny's lesson. For example, Molly and Drexel had fairly sophisticated understandings of how balance beams worked, even at the beginning of the lesson; Suzie thought that the principle simply involved keeping the number of weights on each side the same, and Tad wouldn't venture a guess. As they dialogued, these differences became evident and influenced their ability to benefit from the lesson.

Jenny's students were reluctant to give up their ideas about the balance beam. This became clear in the interview with the four students. In spite of the instruction, dialogue, and correctly modeled solutions, Suzie retained the view that the beam would balance if the number of weights on each side was the same. It wasn't until this understanding was directly confronted (in the interview) that she changed her view, finally concluding that the weight times the distance on each side had to be equal. This reluctance to give up current understandings helps us understand why merely telling or explaining to students—such as Jenny explaining the principle behind balance beams—aren't effective. Students must be provided with experiences that make sense to them, or current understandings are unlikely to mature or change.

Teaching strategies based on constructivism require teachers who are responsive to the learning needs of students.

Learning Is Facilitated by Social Interaction

Jenny's lesson also underscores the importance of social interaction in learning. Dialogue in the group allowed Molly and Drexel to share their correct solution, and provided opportunities for Suzie to share her solution. This resulted in continued dialogue that helped both Suzie and Tad move in the direction of a clearer understanding.

The importance of social interaction was also illustrated in the whole-group discussion. For example, Danielle's initial understanding, like Suzie's, was that keeping the number of weights equal on both sides of the balance was all that mattered. Without social interaction, it is unlikely that her understanding would have changed.

Jenny's guidance was critical in this process. She provided enough support with her questions and cues to help students make progress, but not so much that she reduced their active role in the learning activity. Giving the appropriate amount of support is a very sophisticated process requiring a great deal of teacher expertise (Brown, 1994).

To emphasize the importance of social interaction, researchers have called for the creation of "communities of learners" within classrooms (Brown & Campione, 1994). Learning communities encourage students to take responsibility for their own learning through cooperative ventures. Both Jenny and David Shelton attempted to create learning communities by forming groups that were responsible for problem solving. As students worked on problems, both teachers facilitated the process by offering only enough guidance to ensure they were making progress and by encouraging students to listen to the solutions of their peers.

Importance of Dialogue in Learning. You've seen how important social interaction is in the learning process. The way more knowledgeable members of the culture—the teachers, in these cases—assist in learning is through dialogue, both teacher–student and student–student. As an example, let's look again at some of the dialogue from Jenny's lesson.

> *Jenny:* Your second choice was 5 on 6?
> *Suzie:* I think we should make it third 'cause it may not work [physically] and mine may.
> *Jenny:* Suzie, why do you think yours should be second?
> *Suzie:* 'Cause 5 tiles won't fit on there.
> *Jenny:* Molly, why do you think (5 on 6) should still be second?
> *Molly:* Because I think it's the second best that will work.
> *Jenny:* Why? . . . What was yours again, Suzie?
> *Suzie:* Put 2 on 10 and 1 on 6.
> *Molly:* See, 2 on 10 is 20 and 1 on 6 will only make it 26.
> *Jenny:* When you do the multiplying they need to be the same on both sides? Is that what you're telling me? And you think that what you have down for the third one is not going to be heavy enough and so that's why you want Drexel's idea to be second? Well, you guys need to decide that. Talk it over and decide.

Jenny circulates around the room then returns to the group.

> *Suzie:* We've decided to keep the same order. (To try the 6 × 5 solution second)
> *Jenny:* What made you decide to keep it as it is?
> *Suzie:* Because mine. . . . It kind of sunk in what she said when we add them up—it won't be even. It kind of sunk in.

7.51

Constructivists might have one criticism of the social interaction illustrated in David Shelton's teaching. What might this criticism be?

7.52

On the basis of the information in this section, does constructivism have more implications for curriculum development or for instruction? Explain.

> *Jenny:*   And that was a good compromise. She gave her point of view and you could see the rationality of it.

This dialogue was primarily teacher-facilitated. Let's look at an example of student–student dialogue from David's lesson.

> *Juan:*   Pluto wasn't part of the solar system to begin with.
> *Randy:*   What do you mean?
> *Juan:*   I was watching *Nova* with my mom, and the narrator said that scientists think Pluto was floating around and the sun kinda grabbed it. . . . See, when Mr. Shelton did that thing with the socks, the socks stayed sorta level.
> *Randy:*   What's that got to do with it?
> *Juan:*   Well, look. (pointing to the model)
> *Tanya:*   Oh, I get it! Pluto isn't level with the rest of them.
> *Randy:*   Gee, I didn't even notice that.
> *Tanya:*   Yeah, and look there. (pointing to the chart) See how little Pluto is. It's the littlest one, so it would be sorta easy to capture.
> *Randy:*   And it's the last one.

Both forms of dialogue allow learning to move from the external, socially shared level, to the individual, internalized level (McCarthy, 1994). Socially shared ideas provide opportunities for students to rethink and reconstruct their internal ideas about the world.

Meaningful Learning Occurs Within Authentic Learning Tasks

Think about Jenny's lesson once more. In it, she used concrete materials to help students advance their current understanding of balance beams. The lesson used an **authentic task,** which is *a classroom learning activity that requires understanding similar to understanding that would be used in the world outside the classroom.* Her students were able to experiment on their own to investigate how their ideas would work in the real world.

Authentic tasks simulate real-world problem situations and provide students with practice in thinking in realistic, lifelike situations (Needels & Knapp, 1994). Teachers provide this practice by posing problems that are embedded in realistic situations. Authentic situations also increase students' motivation to learn, which in turn further increases learning.

Jenny could have enhanced the applicability of her task by asking the students to think about their prior experiences with teeter-totters and levers. This would have allowed them to use their background knowledge to attack their problem. Other examples of authentic tasks include actually going to a supermarket to do comparison shopping problems, writing a persuasive essay for a school or class newspaper, and conducting an ecological study of a stream or tract of land near a school.

> **7.53**
>
> Identify at least two types of authentic learning tasks that we have included in this text.

Putting Constructivism into Perspective

Like behaviorism and other cognitive theories, constructivism is controversial and has its critics. In this section we outline some of the controversies surrounding this view and consider some cautions that researchers are suggesting.

Constructivist Controversies

In addition to differences between cognitive and social constructivist views of learning, constructivists also disagree about the kind of learning that occurs and the context in which it takes place. *Situated learning* is one of these controversies.

Situated Learning.   Most educational psychologists think of learning as something that occurs within the individual, and this learning is transferred to other settings (Driscoll, 1994; Schunk, 1996). Proponents of **situated learning,** in contrast, *emphasize that much of what we learn is social in nature, context-bound, and tied to the specific situation in which it is learned* (Lave, 1988; Greeno, 1997). For example, research indicates that people can perform sophisticated mathematical operations in jobs such as selling merchandise or delivering milk but are unable to use the same operations to solve similar, classroom-based problems (Brown, Collins, & Duguid, 1989). Situated learning is viewed as a form of apprenticeship in which new members become enculturated into the language, customs, and beliefs of a learning community (Greeno, 1997).

At the extreme, however, situated learning suggests that learning is bound to the specific concrete situation in which it occurs, and transfer is difficult, if not impossible (Anderson, Reder, & Simon, 1996). Transfer, however—while admittedly difficult—can and does occur, and expert teachers design learning experiences that encourage this process.

The Nature of Knowledge.   A second constructivist controversy centers on the nature of knowledge itself. Does knowledge correspond to some external reality, or is it personally and idiosyncratically constructed? This latter view, called "radical constructivism," emphasizes that all knowledge is relative, individual, and different for each person (Derry, 1992; Phillips, 1995, 1996). In its extreme, it questions the existence of objective reality, suggesting that the only reality that exists is what an individual perceives and constructs.

This view is interesting at a philosophical level, but it both minimizes and confuses the central role teachers and schools play in helping learners acquire the knowledge, or powerful cognitive tools, that exists in cultures (Osborne, 1996). For example, understanding math helps us quantify the world and gives us tools that support the other disciplines; knowing science helps us understand how the world operates; art and literature provide us with insights into the human condition. The concepts and principles in these disciplines are important, not as dogma, but as powerful ways of looking at and thinking about the world, and teachers play a crucial role in helping students acquire them.

Constructivist Cautions

Constructivism provides us with powerful ideas about how children learn. However, like any other theory of learning and human behavior, it doesn't give us a complete picture of teaching and learning. Experts warn against the rejection of other theories of learning in favor of a full-scale adoption of constructivist ideas (Airasian & Walsh, 1997; Anderson et al., 1995, 1996).

For instance, discovery—commonly interpreted as the instructional approach most consistent with constructivism—has both advantages and disadvantages. While valuable for promoting learner involvement and motivation, it probably isn't the most effective way to learn complex strategies or develop automaticity (Anderson et al., 1995; Weinert & Helmke, 1995). Discovery also requires a great deal of teacher time, effort and expertise (Airasian & Walsh, 1997). Teachers need to use a variety of approaches, both learner-centered and teacher-centered to help students learn as much as possible. Chapters 12 and 13, which focus on teacher- and learner-centered instruction, analyze the strengths and weaknesses of different strategies.

Classroom Connections

Applying Constructivism in Your Classroom

1. Develop learning activities around realistic problems.

   • In a unit on percent increase and decrease, a math teacher has students go to malls and find examples of clothes that have been marked down. He also brings in newspaper ads. The class discusses the examples and calculates the amount saved in each case.

   • An elementary social studies teacher has students describe their favorite forms of recreation and the way they're dressed while they participate in these. She also asks students who have moved to this area from other parts of the country to do the same for their previous locations. She then asks them to explain differences and guides a discussion of how climate and geography relate to lifestyle.

2. Teach new ideas in the context of current understandings.

   • A third-grade teacher beginning a unit on crustaceans, insects, and arachnids asks students to tell her as many things as they can think of about crabs, lobsters, and "bugs." She then presents examples of each and has the students compare the characteristics.

   • An English teacher has students describe what they know about writing persuasively. She then has them describe what they might want to know about this form of writing. She follows this discussion with examples of effective and ineffective persuasive essays.

3. Create a "learning community" environment in your classroom.

   • An English teacher discussing *The Scarlet Letter* has the students share their individual perceptions of the characters, the events, and how those impressions were formed.

   • A science teacher discussing heat and expansion has the students articulate their understanding of a series of demonstrations that illustrate the relationship. Where there are disagreements in understanding, she encourages her students to explain and defend their understanding to each other.

Windows on Classrooms

At the beginning of the chapter, you saw how David Shelton planned and conducted his lesson in an effort to make the information meaningful for his students and help them construct their own understanding of the topic he was teaching. Then you saw how Jenny Newhall attempted to apply the characteristics of constructivism with her fourth graders.

Let's look now at another teacher as she conducts a lesson with a group of high school students studying the novel *The Scarlet Letter.* As you read the case study, consider the extent to which the teacher applied the information you have studied in this chapter in her lesson.

Video Case

Sue Southam, an English teacher at Highland High School, is discussing Nathaniel Hawthorne's *The Scarlet Letter.* This novel, set in Boston in the 1600s, describes a tragic and illicit love affair between the heroine (Hester Prynne) and a minister (Arthur Dimmesdale). The novel gets its title from the letter *A* meaning "adulterer," that the Puritan community makes Hester wear as punishment for her adultery. The class has been discussing the book for several days; the focus for this lesson is Reverend Dimmesdale's character.

After the class enters the room and quickly settles down, Sue begins by briefly reviewing the novel's plot to date.

She then asks about Hester's illicit lover. After the class identifies Dimmesdale as the baby's father, Sue challenges them by asking, "How do you know the baby is Dimmesdale's? What are the clues in the text in Chapter 3? . . . Nicole?"

"He acts very withdrawn. He doesn't want to look her in the face and doesn't want to be involved in the situation."

"Okay, anything else, any other clues?"

"The baby . . . it points at Reverend Dimmesdale."

"Good observation. That is a good clue and one of my favorite scenes from the novel," Sue adds.

After several more comments, Sue pauses and says, "Class, I'd like to read a passage to you from the text describing Dimmesdale. Listen carefully, and then I'd like you to do something with it."

After reading the paragraph, Sue continues, "In your logs, jot down some of the important characteristics in that description. If you were going to draw a portrait of him, what would he look like? Try to be as specific as possible. Try that now."

Sue gives the students a few minutes to write in their logs and then, with a questioning look, continues by asking, "If you were directing a film of *The Scarlet Letter,* what would Dimmesdale look like? . . . Mike?"

". . . Thin, 5 feet 10, nervous, trembling lips," Mike offers.

"Yeah, and he's always mopping his brow with a handkerchief," Todd adds, gesturing with his hands as if he's mopping his brow.

"What else?" Sue encourages.

"Wire-framed glasses," Tamara contributes.

"With brown, melancholy eyes," Jeremy adds.

After the class discusses additional characteristics, Sue shifts gears by asking, "What do these characteristics tell us about Dimmesdale as a person? . . . Anyone? . . . Sonya?"

"I think he's worried about getting caught."

". . . Kasha?"

"I think he feels bad about what has happened to Hester. He feels guilty," Kasha adds.

After a few additional comments, Sue says, "Let's see whether we can find out more about the Dimmesdale character through his actions. I'd like you to listen carefully while I read the speech by Reverend Dimmesdale in which he confronts Hester Prynne in front of the congregation and exhorts her to identify her secret lover and partner in sin. Think about both Dimmesdale's and Hester's thoughts while I'm reading."

She reads Dimmesdale's speech, and after she's finished, she divides the class into Dimmesdales and Hesters by counting "One, two" in front of different rows around the room.

Then she says, "Now I'd like you to role-play; pretend you're either Hester or Dimmesdale during the speech. All the 'ones' are Dimmesdales, and all the 'twos' are Hesters. Dimmesdales, in your logs I want you to tell me what Dimmesdale is really thinking during this speech. Hesters, I want you to tell me what Hester is thinking while she listens to Dimmesdale's speech. Write in your logs in your own words what the private thoughts of your character are. Do that right now, and then we'll come back together in a few minutes."

As students write in their logs, Sue circulates around the room, clarifying the task and encouraging students to be creative in their perspectives.

After giving them a few minutes to write in their logs, she sorts them into groups of four, with each group comprising two Hesters and two Dimmesdales. Once students are settled, she says, "In each group, I want you to start off by having Dimmesdale tell what he is thinking during the first line of the speech. Then I'd like a Hester to respond. Then continue with Dimmesdale's next line, and then Hester's reaction. Go ahead and share your thoughts in your groups."

After giving students about 5 minutes to share their perspectives, she reconvenes the class with, "Okay, let's hear it. A Dimmesdale first. Just what was he thinking during his speech? . . . Mike?"

"The only thing I could think of was, 'Oh God, help me. I hope she doesn't say anything. If they find out it's me, I'll be ruined. . . . And then here comes Hester with her powerful speech," Mike concludes, turning to his partner in the group, Nicole.

With a nod, Sue acknowledges Mike's reply and gestures to Nicole. "Nicole, what do you think Hester is thinking during this speech?"

"I wrote, 'Good man, huh. So why don't you confess then? You know you're guilty. I've admitted my love, but you haven't. Why don't you just come out and say it?'"

"Interesting. . . . What else? How about another Hester? . . . Sarah?"

"I just put, 'No, I'll never tell. I still love you, and I'll keep your secret forever,'" Sarah offers.

Sue pauses for a moment, looks around the room, and comments, "Notice how different the two views of Hester are. Nicole paints her as very angry, whereas Sarah views her as still loving him." Sue again pauses to look for reactions. Karen raises her hand, and Sue nods to her.

"I think the reason Hester doesn't say anything is that people won't believe her because he's a minister," Karen suggests. "She's getting her revenge just by being there reminding him of his guilt."

"But if she accuses him, won't people expect him to deny it?" Brad adds, responding to Karen.

"Maybe he knows she won't accuse him because she still loves him," Julie offers.

"Wait a minute," Jeff interrupts, gesturing with his hands. "I don't think he's such a bad guy. I think he feels guilty about it all, but he just doesn't have the courage to admit it in front of all of those people."

"I think he's really admitting it in his speech but is asking her secretly not to tell," Caroline puts in. "Maybe he's really talking to Hester and doesn't want the rest of the people to know."

The class continues, with students debating the hidden meaning in the speech and trying to decide whether Reverend Dimmesdale is really a villain or a tragic figure.

As the end of class nears, Sue says, "Interesting ideas . . . And who haven't we talked about yet? . . . Sherry?"

"Hester Prynne's husband . . . ?"

". . . Who's been missing for several years," Sue adds.

"Tomorrow, I'd like you to read Chapter 4, in which we meet Hester's husband. That's all for today. Please put the desks back . . . . Thank you."

Summary

Cognitive Views of Learning

Behaviorism and cognitive learning theories differ fundamentally in that behaviorism treats learners as passively responding to the environment, whereas cognitive theories assume that learners are mentally active and construct their own understanding of the topics they study.

Cognitive theories acknowledge the role of environmental influence but emphasize internal, mental processes in attempting to understand learning. Behavioral theories contend that mental processes are not necessary to explain learning; rather, one looks to stimuli and reinforcers in the environment. Cognitive theories were developed, in part, because behaviorism was unable to adequately explain both research results and everyday events, especially complex phenomena such as language learning and problem solving.

Information Processing

Information processing is a cognitive view of learning that compares human thinking to the way computers process information. Information stores—sensory memory, working memory, and long-term memory—hold information; cognitive processes, such as attention, perception, rehearsal, and encoding, move the information from one store to another.

Information received by sensory memory is moved to working memory through the processes of attention and perception. Working memory, with its limited capacity, can easily be overloaded and become a bottleneck to subsequent processing. The capacity of working memory can, in effect, be increased through chunking and making aspects of processing automatic.

Information-processing theory assumes that knowledge is encoded in long-term memory in complex interrelationships (schemas) of declarative knowledge (which includes knowledge of facts, concepts, and other ideas) and procedural knowledge (which is knowledge of how to perform operations, such as writing an essay). Information processing is governed by metacognition—an awareness of and control over the processes that move information from one store to another. As metacognitive knowledge and skills improve, learners develop the capacity for self-regulation.

Information that is meaningful is interconnected with other information in memory, and an important goal in teaching is to help learners increase the number of connections between individual items of information. A teacher can make information meaningful by putting learners in the most active role possible, encouraging visual imagery, organizing content in various ways, and encouraging learners to elaborate on their own understanding. Mnemonic devices help create connections in information where no natural connection exists.

Constructivism

Although all cognitive views of learning focus on learners being active, constructivism places more emphasis than other cognitive theories on learners constructing their own understanding. Constructivists disagree on the nature of knowledge, but they generally agree that learners construct their own understanding, that new learning exists in the context of prior understanding, that learning is enhanced by social activity, and that authentic tasks promote learning. Many constructivists suggest that teachers should create a learning community where teachers and students work together to solve problems.

Important Concepts _____

analogies (p. 261)

attention (p. 255)

authentic task (p. 284)

automaticity (p. 247)

chunking (p. 247)

cognitive learning theories (p. 242)

cognitive processes (p. 244)

contexts (p. 252)

declarative knowledge (p. 249)

elaboration (p. 261)

elaborative rehearsal (p. 257)

encoding (p. 258)

forgetting (p. 266)

generative knowledge (p. 251)

imagery (p. 259)

inert knowledge (p. 251)

information processing (p. 242)

information stores (p. 244)

interference (p. 267)

learning (p. 242)

levels of processing (p. 264)

long-term memory (p. 249)

maintenance rehearsal (p. 257)

meaningfulness (p. 258)

meta-attention (p. 269)

metacognition (pp. 244, 268)

metamemory (p. 270)

mnemonic devices (p. 261)

model (p. 243)

organization (p. 259)

perception (p. 256)

procedural knowledge (p. 249)

propositions (p. 249)

retrieve (p. 267)

schemas (p. 250)

script (p. 250)

sensory memory (p. 245)

situated learning (p. 285)

strategies (p. 269)

working memory (p. 245)

Complex Cognitive Processes

CHAPTER OUTLINE

Laura Hunter, a fifth-grade teacher at Bennion Elementary School, was reading her notes as she planned for the following week's instruction. She keeps a journal in which she writes comments about units and lessons and refers to them as she plans to teach the topics the next time.

She reacted with a nod when she read a note from the previous year—"Seem to understand perimeter, but can't find area; don't know how to begin. Memorize"—referring to a section on finding the area of irregularly shaped plane figures. Reflecting on her experience, Laura decided, "I'm going to try to make it

more real for them this year. I need a real problem instead of that stuff in the book, something they can relate to."

After considering a series of possibilities, she thought, "Why not use the classroom? The carpeted area has an irregular shape." She thought about it some more and then decided, "What the heck, I'll give it a try. It can't be any worse than last year. All we need to do is measure the classroom and take it from there. I bet they'll like it."

After her beginning-of-class routines were completed the following Monday, she began by reviewing the concepts of area and perimeter.

"Okay," she began, "What kinds of things have we been talking about?"

"Area," the class responded in unison.

Video Case

"Before that we talked about perimeter," Laura continued. "Can someone tell us what perimeter is? . . . Sam?"

"It's the length of the line going around the outside," Sam answered.

"Right, right, and what's the example we used? Like if we were building a playground, it would be the . . ."

"Perimeter," several students mumbled.

"Fence," others said simultaneously.

"Right," Laura acknowledged. "It would be like the fence around it. . . . And then we talked about area. What's the area? . . . If you were going to build that same playground and you were going to cover it, with green stuff, . . . Elise what would that be?"

"The inside of the shape," Elise answered.

"The inside of the shape, . . . like how many squares of grass you would need, or sand, like how many squares of sand you would need to cover it.

"And here's the problem," Laura continued. "We're going to use this as a guide," displaying the following on the overhead.

"First, identify the problem," she said, referring to the overhead. . . . "Now here's the problem. . . . You know how the first floor has blue carpeting. . . . The second floor is going to get carpeting too. But Mr. Garcia needs some help in determining what kind of carpeting to get for this room. We know that it's going to be blue, but he doesn't know how much it's going to be. . . . And we've made some changes. When the computers came in, they decided with kids sitting there so many times, moving their feet around, they want to put linoleum underneath where all the computers are. . . . So, your job is going to be to figure out how much carpeting we need."

Laura paused for a moment to let the students think about what she had said, and then she broke the students into groups and had each decide what their problem was and how they would represent it.

The students worked together for several minutes, then Laura had each of the groups report their results to the class.

"Fred, what did your team decide you were supposed to do?" Laura began.

"Measure the area."

"Okay; Grant, can you give me some more details?"

"We decided we should measure the perimeter around and about two feet from the computers and the linoleum and measure all around."

"Okay, anything you want to add, Sam?"

"If we like . . . like with that post, if we have an area that has part of a linoleum there we could, we would figure out the area including the linoleum, . . . figure out just the linoleum and then subtract the linoleum from the total area."

"I'm going to put 'remember the linoleum' so you remember to go through that process," Laura noted, writing on the overhead.

"Okay, have we identified all the parts of the problem? . . . Paige, do you want to add anything?"

"Ahh . . . we could make a drawing of the outside of the room."

"You guys, are you listening?" Laura admonished two of the boys who were whispering.

"Like on the graph paper like we did yesterday. Write the measurements on the side," Paige continued.

"Okay, outside measurements," Laura repeated as she wrote down what Paige said.

"Okay, who else? . . . Jamison?"

"We decided we had to get the perimeter before we could get the area. Everything else is the same."

"Okay, do I need to add anything else here to identify what the problem is? . . . Okay, so now we know what the problem is."

Laura then had students measure different parts of the room in their groups.

As the students worked, a dispute arose in one of the groups over the best way to measure the linoleum. Some just wanted to count the squares, while others advocated measuring the perimeter. Laura encouraged them to resolve the dispute "mathematically".

"Let's talk about how that went," Laura smiled as she reconvened the class. . . . "On a scale of one to five, one it went totally great, and five means you were totally frustrated; . . . one, . . . two, . . . three, . . . four, . . . five," she counted to a sprinkling of hands, with the most appearing when she counted three.

"Uh-oh," she smiled, seeing that some students had raised their hands when she counted 5. "Jamison, why were you so frustrated?"

"Because nobody would listen to me. . . . I couldn't tell my points," he answered.

"Okay. Sam, was that why you were frustrated?" she asked, turning to Sam.

"I was frustrated because I was almost a hundred percent sure that I got it right but my team was like, 'We're not going to listen to you'," he replied.

Laura chuckled and then said, "So, it's hard to know something that you think you know about math but having to prove it to somebody else. . . . That's the hardest part about math, proving what you know to somebody else.

"So, who thought it was a good experience? Nephi, you had a one. What did you like about it; what went well?"

"That our side was easy. We knew that each tile square was one foot, one square foot, and so all we had to do was count the tiles this way and that way, and measure the little pieces of tile."

"Yeah, it's kind of like the area assignment that we did, that already had the grid marked on it, so you just had to count, but one of your teammates had trouble, because it wasn't an exact square tile, it was part of a tile," Laura elaborated.

". . . Grant?" she continued.

"Ours was pretty easy too, but when we were measuring we were wondering how far from what was going to be the triangle we should measure. We just measured from a certain point. And also we had stuff that was in the way."

"Yeah, it would be a lot easier if it were a completely empty room," Laura acknowledged.

Using the information gathered from each group, Laura constructed a diagram of the room and distributed it. "I'm going to put one of these on each table," Laura said, changing the direction of the lesson.

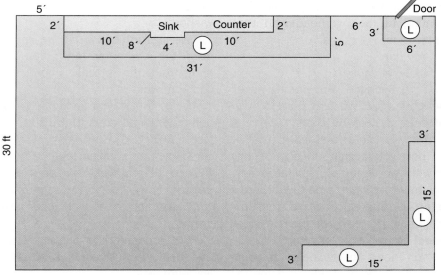

"Now, on the side where the sink is, the L with a circle. Can you tell us what that means, the L word? . . . Kelly?" Laura began.

"Linoleum."

"Linoleum, right. It's kind of an abbreviation for linoleum or tile."

She then continued, "Everybody sees that the distance across the front of the chalkboard is 30 feet," pointing to the diagram "Okay, let's talk about the sink side. How many feet are there between the edge and the start of the counters?"

"Five feet," several students answered in unison.

"Five feet; that little symbol means feet. . . . and how many feet for the length of that counter?"

"31," several students again said in unison.

"Okay, everybody see that? . . . Let's look back up here at our overhead. . . . Another way we can look at this map is to say it's representing the problem . . . I've heard it called a diagram. What you're looking at is a representation of the problem. . . . Okay, everybody look up here again. What's your job going to be to do? . . ."

"The problem" and "Solve the problem" could be heard.

"Do we want to add any more steps to this part?" Laura asked. ". . . We did these things. We measured the area, we measured the perimeter. . . . Did we do all these things?"

"Yeah," most of the students replied in unison.

"Are we through?" Laura wondered.

"No," the students again answered in unison.

"We didn't measure the area. We still have the whole inside of the classroom. We just measured the perimeter," Nephi volunteered.

"Okay, you guys understand what Nephi's saying?" Laura queried.

"Yeah," several students respond.

"So, . . . Nephi, what do I need to add up here?" Laura continued, pointing to the overhead with the problem-solving steps.

"You don't."

"Okay, because. . . . ?"

". . . Because you already have the perimeter. We just have to do the area . . . of the class."

"Okay," Laura nodded. "That's the part you're going to be working on with your team. . . . What I want you to do is this step right here. Select a strategy," Laura replied, again pointing to the problem-solving model on the overhead projector.

"You need to decide with your team what the best way is going to be to measure the area of this shape," she directed. "I only want to know right now the area of the carpet. I only want to know how much carpet I need to buy.

"You can go ahead and get started."

The students then turned back to their groups to try to decide how best to calculate the area.

As students attempted to solve the problem, they came up with two basic strategies. One was to find the area of the whole room and subtract the linoleum; the other was to find the area of an interior rectangle in the room and then add extra, irregularly shaped carpeted areas.

"One more minute." Laura called to the groups.

"Okay, let's look back up here at our diagram," Laura directed after the class had again re-assembled. "In the select-your-strategies part, there were a lot of different strategies that I saw as I was walking around. Raise your hand and tell me what one of the strategies was. . . . Yashoda."

"We figured out, . . . we multiplied the perimeter. And then we subtracted the places where the linoleum was."

"Okay, when you multiplied the perimeter, what does it give you?"

"1440."

"Okay, that's called the . . . ?"

"Area," several students responded.

"Okay, and what was your next step?"

"We measured everything first, and then we subtracted where the linoleum was."

"Okay, raise your hand if your team tried that strategy," Laura directed.

Students from several groups raised their hands.

"Raise your hand if you tried a different strategy."

Several more students raised their hands.

"Matt, explain what your team did," Laura directed.

"We had two strategies. I'll do the first one that we tried. We took . . . , we squared it off, like covering up this," Matt responded, pointing to the diagram, "and then we multiplied the, the we got the middle, and then we were going to put the other pieces together . . . on it."

"Okay, I'm going to put 'found measurements and add area' Is that okay?" Laura asked.

"Uh-hunh," Matt answered.

After each team offered their strategies, Laura again changed the direction of the lesson, saying, "I have a green marker and a blue paper at each table. Raise your hand if you don't have one.

"Here's your job. . . . The person with the green marker, your job is to draw lines on your diagram that illustrate, to show us how you solved the problem. . . . The person with the blue paper, your job is to write down three conclusions your team decided on about the problem. . . . When you're finished, what do you need to do?"

"Put our markers down," the students answered.

After discussing the strategies they used to solve the problem, each group reported on their progress.

"One of our conclusions was, 'Put all the pieces together,'" Matt explained for his team. "We took all the extra pieces that we had and we added them together. . . . Our team had a little difficulty working together," Matt continued shyly.

"So you guys said you had a problem with conclusions because you had trouble working together. . . . Could you make a conclusion about working together?" Laura smiled.

". . ."

"Any ideas?"

"Uhmm, we could have . . . ideas about working together? Yeah, we had trouble with that," Matt stumbled.

"What could you have done to solve that problem?" Laura asked.

"We could have listened to each other better," Matt concluded.

"Yes, that's a good conclusion too."

After each group described their strategy, Laura put the diagrams and conclusions on a bulletin board to share with others.

She then continued, "Most of you said you took the 30, which is the width of the room, and the 48, which is the length of the room, and Sam already said the formula for that was 30 feet times 48 feet. . . . Would you say, as a strategy for solving a problem like this, that that would be a good place to start?

"Yeah," several students responded.

"Okay, and what was another step that most of you used to carry out the strategy? . . . Justin?"

"Subtract."

"Okay, and before you do that you had to find the area of the linoleum, and then subtract it. . . . Were there other ways to solve this problem?

"Yeah," several students again responded.

"Did we get different answers? . . . Okay, tell me what the answer was that you got. How many square feet of carpet?" Laura asked one of the groups.

"1,173."

"Okay," and she nodded to another group.

"1,378."

"1,347," a third group reported.

"1,169," a fourth group added.

"1,600," the last group put in.

"Well, are you guys comfortable with that?"

Several students said "No," while a few said, "Yes."

"If you were the person purchasing the carpet, would you be comfortable with that? . . ." Waiting for an answer Laura paused.

"If you were the person *estimating* would you be comfortable with that?" Laura continued.

Most of the class said they wouldn't be comfortable if they were the person purchasing the carpet, but offered that they would be if they were merely estimating.

"If you were going to redo this tomorrow, what could we do to be more accurate? . . . Talk to your team for 30 seconds," Laura then directed.

The students talked to their teammates and offered some suggestions, such as remeasuring the room, rechecking to see if the strategy made sense, and even asking the janitor about the dimensions of the room.

Chuckling at the last suggestion, Laura said, "That's a strategy called 'Ask an expert,'" and she then had the students get ready for recess.

In this chapter, we extend our study of cognitive theory by examining the content students learn and the strategies they use to increase that learning. We begin by examining concepts, one of the most common forms of classroom content. We continue with an analysis of problem solving, which is being increasingly emphasized in schools. We then move to a discussion of the strategic learner and how students can use self-regulation to take responsibility for their own learning. We complete the chapter with a discussion of transfer—how understanding in one setting can be applied in others.

After you've completed your study of this chapter, you should be able to meet the following objectives:

- Explain the application of concept learning to classroom activities.
- Apply problem-solving strategies to well-defined and ill-defined problems.
- Explain how thinking skills can be used in classroom learning activities.

- Describe how study strategies can be used to increase student learning.
- Discuss ways of increasing transfer of learning

Teachers often encounter challenges similar to those Laura Hunter faced in the opening case study. Students struggle with certain topics, and teachers are often frustrated in their efforts to help. As a result, they approach a topic reluctantly the next time they teach it, or even skip it completely. Laura took a positive approach instead. Knowing that her students had tried to "memorize their way through" the unit the year before, she increased her efforts to make the information meaningful to them. She also recognized that the unit involved different types of learning, and she consciously directed her teaching to each. We examine these aspects of learning in this chapter, beginning with concepts.

Concept Learning

Concepts: Categories that Simplify the World

8.1

Think about this book and the class that's using it. Identify at least five concepts that you've learned in your study to this point.

Concepts, or *mental abstractions that categorize sets of objects, events, or ideas,* represent a major portion of the school curriculum, and much of teachers' efforts are directed at teaching them (Klausmeier, 1992). The categories, based on rules or prototypes, help simplify the world for learners. For example, if learners saw the polygons in Figure 8.1, they would describe them all as triangles, even though the shapes vary in size and orientation. "Triangle" represents a mental category into which all examples of triangles can be placed.

People use concepts because they simplify the world. The concept of *triangle* allows people to think and talk about the examples in Figure 8.1 as a group, instead of as specific objects. Having to remember each separately would make learning impossibly complex and unwieldy.

Although not the central focus, concepts were important in Laura's lesson. She began, for example, by reviewing the concept of *perimeter;* the students' ability to solve the problem depended on their having a clear concept of *area.* Significantly, both concepts were elaborated in the context of the lesson, rather than in isolation, and each time the students used them, their understanding evolved as the concepts were developed in new and richer contexts (Brown, Collins, & Duguid, 1989).

8.2

Identify at least two concepts each in music, art, and physical education.

Examples of concepts in language arts, social studies, math, and science are presented in Table 8.1. This is only a brief list, and you can probably think of many more for each area. Concepts are also taught in other areas, such as music, art, and physical education. In addition, students learn abstract concepts such as *honesty* and *justice* as they go through school and life.

Figure 8.1 Triangles

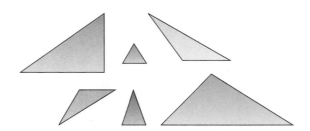

Table 8.1 Concepts in different content areas

Language Arts	Social Studies	Science	Math
Adjective	Culture	Acid	Prime number
Verb	Longitude	Conifer	Equivalent fraction
Plot	Federalist	Element	Set
Simile	Democracy	Force	Addition
Infinitive	Immigrant	Inertia	Parabola

Characteristics: The Defining Features of Concepts

Some concepts, such as those Laura taught, have clear and precise **characteristics** (sometimes called *attributes* or *features*), which are *a concept's defining elements.* Perimeter, for example, has one essential characteristic—the distance around a closed, plane figure. Other characteristics, such as the size or shape of the figure, are not essential, so learners can classify the circumference of a circle, the distance around a rectangle, and the amount of fence around an irregularly shaped playground all in the category, *perimeter.* These nonessential characteristics don't alter the concept.

Factors Influencing the Ease of Learning Concepts

The ease of learning a concept is directly related to the *number* of characteristics and how tangible and *concrete* they are (Tennyson & Cocchiarella, 1986). When a concept's characteristics are concrete and observable, concept learning is simplified. You saw this with *triangle;* the same is true for other concrete concepts, such as *adjective, latitude,* and *mammal.*

Others are much more difficult. Could you, for example, precisely describe what makes a democracy a democracy? Most people can't, because its characteristics are abstract and not precisely defined; it has "fuzzy boundaries" (Schwartz & Reisberg, 1991). Concepts such as *democracy* are often effectively learned with a **prototype,** which is *the best representative of its category* (Busmeyer & Myung, 1988; Nosofsky, 1988; Schwartz & Reisberg, 1991). When we teach concepts, we try to present a prototype as one of our first illustrations to provide a clear example for students.

Examples: The Key to Learning and Teaching Concepts

Regardless of the complexity of a concept, the key to effective concept teaching is a carefully selected set of **examples,** or *prototypes that tell the learner what the concept is,* and nonexamples, which illustrate what the concept is not (Tennyson & Cocchiarella, 1986). As you prepare to teach concepts ask yourself, "What can I show the students, or what can I have them do that will clearly illustrate the concept?" The best examples are ones in which characteristics are observable or the example is the best prototype available. To illustrate this idea, look at the following examples of the concept *snurf.* Can you identify its characteristics?

8.3

Think about the concepts of *adjective* and *conifer* in Table 8.1. What are the characteristics of these concepts?

8.4

Consider the concepts of *noun* and *culture.* On the basis of the information in this section, which of the two should be easier to learn? Explain your answer.

8.5

Identify two additional concepts that have fuzzy boundaries and are therefore better described with a prototype than with characteristics.

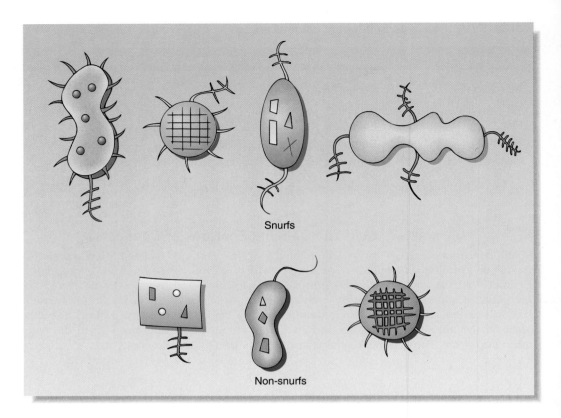

Snurfs

Non-snurfs

8.6

In teaching a concept, should you first present an example, or should you first present a nonexample? Why? Would there ever be exceptions to this order?

You can see that snurfs are curved shapes with cross-hatched tails. All other characteristics are irrelevant. You can also see nonexamples—cases that are not snurfs. In situations where a concept can easily be confused with a closely related concept, nonexamples are particularly important (Tennyson & Cocchiarella, 1986). For example, if a teacher wants her students to understand the concept *reptile*, she would include a frog—an amphibian—as a nonexample, to be certain that students don't confuse reptiles and amphibians. The strategies discussed in the next sections capitalize on these ideas.

Strategies for Teaching Concepts

Concept learning involves two goals: (a) acquiring the concept itself and (b) relating the concept to other concepts in a complex schema. Let's look at three strategies that attempt to reach these goals.

Rule–Example: An Expository Concept-Teaching Strategy

The *rule–example strategy* is a method of teaching concepts that includes four steps (Tennyson & Cocchiarella, 1986):

1. Define the concept, link it to a superordinate concept, and identify its essential characteristics.
2. Clarify terms in the definition.
3. Provide positive and negative examples.

Effective teachers use concrete examples to help students learn concepts and relate them to the real world.

4. Provide additional unlabeled examples, asking students to identify those that are examples and explain the basis for their selection, or have students provide their own examples.

In the rule–example strategy, a **definition,** which is *a statement that includes the concept name, a superordinate concept, and the concept's characteristics,* is presented first. For instance, a definition of the concept *metaphor* might be, "A metaphor is a figure of speech in which two objects are compared in a nonliteral way and the words *like* or *as* are avoided." A **superordinate concept** is *a larger class into which the concept fits. Figure of speech* is the superordinate concept for the concept *metaphor.* In this definition, ". . . in which two objects are compared in a nonliteral way and the words *like* or *as* are avoided," describes the characteristics of the concept. The definition and superordinate concept help embed the concept into a meaningful schema (Murphy & Allopena, 1994).

In the second step, the teacher helps students clarify terms and ideas in the definition, such as knowing what ". . . compared in a nonliteral way . . ." means.

The third step is critical. Here, students use *examples,* such as, "John's Camaro is a lemon," "My grandmother's hat was a garden of daisies," and "Autumn leaves are hands wrinkled with age," together with *nonexamples,* such as "Hurricane Andrew hit the Florida coast like a truck" "I'm as hungry as a bear," and "I had a million pages of homework last night," to identify essential characteristics of the concept. Students analyze the examples and nonexamples as they're presented, identifying similarities and differences in them and explaining why the examples are metaphors and the others are not.

Finally, the teacher presents additional examples and nonexamples and has students classify them or produce their own. When the examples illustrate the concept's

8.7

What is a superordinate concept to the concept *adjective?* What is the difference between the *concept* adjective and the *name* adjective?

8.8

Think again about teaching the concept *adjective.* Would a noun, a verb, or an adverb be the best nonexample? Why? To which cognitive process in the information-processing model in Chapter 7 does the use of examples and nonexamples most closely relate?

characteristics and students are actively involved in accurately analyzing them, the strategy is effective.

Example–Rule: An Inductive Concept-Teaching Strategy

Example–rule is an alternative strategy that begins with examples and guides learners to the definition of the concept; it reverses the sequence of the rule–example process. As a comparison, let's look again at the concept *metaphor* and the same examples.

The teacher would present two or three examples, such as:

John's Camaro is a lemon.
My grandmother's hat was a garden of daisies.

and

Autumn leaves are hands wrinkled with age.

She would then ask students what patterns they see in the examples and would guide them to conclude that a comparison exists in each, and the comparison isn't literal, i.e., John's Camaro isn't literally a lemon. Next, the teacher would present *nonexamples,* such as

Hurricane Andrew hit the Florida coast like a truck.
I'm as hungry as a bear.

and

I had a million pages of homework last night.

She would then ask the students how the second set of sentences was different from the first, guiding them to conclude that no comparison existed (as in "I had a million pages of homework last night.") or the comparisons in the second set used the terms *like* or *as*. She would then guide them to form a definition based on the patterns they observed.

The rule–example strategy has the advantage of being time efficient, whereas the example–rule strategy can be more motivating and promote more student involvement and higher-order thinking than the rule–example strategy.

Concept Mapping: Embedding Concepts in Complex Schemas

Concept mapping, *a teaching strategy in which the relationships among concepts are represented visually,* focuses explicitly on the goal of helping learners relate a concept to other concepts in complex schemas (Novak & Gowin, 1984; Novak & Musonda, 1991). Concept mapping is a form of organization—one way information can be made meaningful. The visual aspects of concept mapping also allow learners to use imagery as a way of representing information. Concept maps can be presented first by teachers as they model the strategy; later, students can then develop their own. Figure 8.2 illustrates a concept map for closed plane figures.

The concepts in Figure 8.2 are organized hierarchically. Not all concepts are hierarchical, however, so other types of maps may be more appropriate. Figure 8.3 illustrates a network, which is similar to a hierarchy, except the arrows illustrate different types of relationships among the concepts.

The point in concept mapping is that students use the map to construct relationships that embed the concept into an organized framework, which increases its meaningfulness. The form students use should be one that best illustrates the associations. Hierarchies often work best in math and science; in other areas, such as reading, social studies, and literature, a network may be better.

8.9

Create a network for the concept *operant conditioning.*

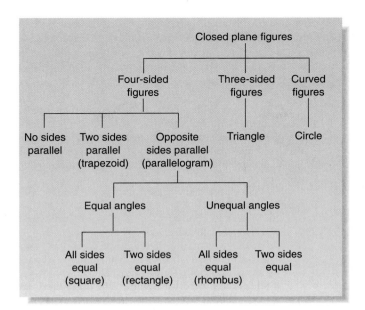

Figure 8.2 Concept map for closed plane figures

Concept Learning: Misconceptions and Conceptual Change

The importance of background knowledge was a theme emphasized in Chapter 7, and it is important in concept learning as well. Although we have emphasized the importance of examples and nonexamples, remember that students process these examples in the context of their background knowledge, and if misconceptions exist, they can be hard to eliminate (Brandes, 1995).

An example from educational psychology is the concept of *negative reinforcement*. We repeatedly emphasized that negative reinforcers *increase* behavior by removing a consequence. We carefully illustrated the concept with several examples because

8.10

You find that your social-studies students tend to view communism and fascism as synonymous. Describe specifically what you would do to eliminate this misconception.

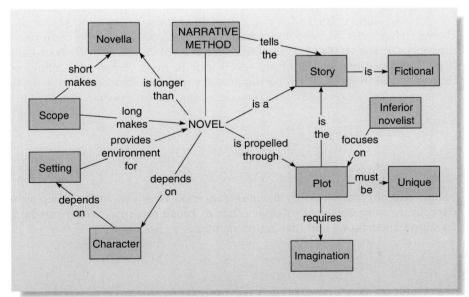

Figure 8.3 Network for parts of a novel

learners commonly confuse negative reinforcers with punishers, believing that negative reinforcers decrease behavior. Similar examples can be found in many areas. For instance, in science, students often confuse *reptiles* and *amphibians* and *spiders* and *insects*. Students give up misconceptions reluctantly and only when they are directly confronted (Chinn & Brewer, 1993). Let's look at an example.

> Elaine Madison has been working with her middle-school students on basic science concepts and has defined *force* as any push or pull and *work* as the combination of force and movement. She knows that students often incorrectly think that work is done if effort is expended, regardless of whether movement occurs.
>
> To try to eliminate these misconceptions, she suggested, "Kari, stand up and hold up the chair."
>
> Kari stood, lifted the chair that was at the side of the room, and remained standing motionless.
>
> "Now," Elaine continued. "Is Kari doing any work?"
>
> "Yes," Jared volunteered.
>
> "What did we say the definition of work is?" Elaine probed.
>
> "The combination of force and movement," Natalie offered.
>
> "Okay, is Kari doing any work?" Elaine went on.
>
> "If she stands there for a while, she'll get tired, and you get tired when you work," Jared persisted.
>
> "But she's not moving," Kathy added. "For work to be done, there has to be movement."
>
> "That doesn't make sense," Jared continued. "That means you can get tired without doing any work."
>
> "What actually makes you tired?" Elaine queried.
>
> "Holding up the chair."
>
> "Sure. So, the effort of holding up the chair would make any of us tired. Effort is the force we're exerting, and exerting a force can make us tired."
>
> The class continued to discuss the example, noting that Kari actually did do work when she first lifted the chair. They then discussed additional examples, noting that because of their day-to-day experience, they tend to equate effort, work, and being tired. Finally, Jared reluctantly accepted the idea that work requires movement.

8.11

Which of the concepts from Piaget's work discussed in Chapter 2 best helps you understand why students are reluctant to give up their misconceptions?

As we said earlier and we see from this example, misconceptions are difficult to change. They exist because they make sense to us, and changing them requires restructuring our schemas. It's also possible that a student like Jared will revert back to his earlier thinking—work equals effort—even though he accepted the definition; additional examples and discussion will be required for him to restructure his ideas. Alert teachers are aware of this possibility and provide additional experiences.

Relating Concepts to Each Other: Principles, Generalizations, and Academic Rules

People simplify the world by forming concepts. They can further simplify their experience by relating concepts to each other in broad patterns, which can be powerful in forming explanations and making predictions.

Principles are *relationships between concepts that are accepted as valid for all known cases.* The terms *principles* and *laws* are often used interchangeably. The following are examples:

- Like magnetic poles repel and unlike poles attract.
- The greater the force on an object, the greater its acceleration.
- Moving objects tend to keep moving in a straight line unless a force acts on them.

Principles are an important part of the school curriculum, particularly in the sciences. They are valuable because they connect concepts and help in summarizing large amounts of information. Principles also play a vital role in problem solving, as you'll see later in the chapter.

Generalizations are *relationships between concepts that have known exceptions.* For instance:

- People immigrate for economic reasons.
- Thunderstorms occur during the afternoon hours.
- People who consume large quantities of fat have a higher incidence of heart disease than those who don't.

Although each statement describes a relationship, they have obvious exceptions. For example, some people immigrate for religious or political reasons, some thunderstorms occur during other parts of the day, and some people who consume large quantities of fat (e.g., Eskimos) have little evidence of heart disease.

Much of the health-related information we get from the medical profession is in the form of generalizations, and most of the patterns described in this text are also generalizations. "Teachers who use their time effectively have students who learn more than those who don't" is an example. If, for instance, examples aren't clear, or discussions aren't focused and meaningful, learning is reduced regardless of how well teachers use their time.

Academic rules, a third type of statement linking concepts, *describe relationships between concepts that have been arbitrarily derived by people.* For example:

- A pronoun must agree with its antecedent in number and gender.
- When making nouns ending in *-y* plural, drop the *-y* and add *-ies* if the *-y* is preceded by a consonant, but add *-s* if the *-y* is preceded by a vowel.
- To round off a number, if the last digit is 5 or above, round up, and if the last digit is 4 or below, round down.

Whereas principles and generalizations describe patterns observed in the natural world, rules are arbitrary conventions. For instance, adjectives precede the nouns they modify in English, whereas in French and Spanish they follow nouns. Academic rules are important, however, because they provide consistency. If there were no rules for forming plurals, for example, writing would be chaotic and communication would suffer. One part of Laura's lesson involved rules. When Yashoda found the area of a rectangular portion of the classroom, for instance, she was following a rule for calculating area.

8.12

Would the statement "When students are praised for desirable behavior, the behavior increases" be more accurately called a principle or a generalization? Explain your answer with a specific example.

8.13

Principles, generalizations, and academic rules have an important feature in common. What is this feature? What is the primary difference between a generalization and an academic rule?

Classroom Connections

Applying Concept Learning in Your Classroom

1. Use examples that include all the information learners need to understand the concept.
   - A physical education teacher was helping her students learn to serve a tennis ball. She videotaped several people, some with good serves and others with poor ones. During the next class period, she showed the class the videotapes and discussed the differences before having them practice their own serves.
   - A fourth-grade teacher's students were having difficulty understanding the concept of *ecosystem*. She went into her stack of *National Geographics* and cut out several pictures of different ecosystems—a jungle, a desert, and northern tundra. As she presented the pictures, she discussed them with her students and helped them identify the characteristics of ecosystems in each.

2. Link essential characteristics to examples.
   - A kindergarten teacher wanted her class to understand the concept of *living thing*. She displayed and discussed examples, such as themselves, their pets, grass near the school grounds, and plants in their classroom. They identified "the ability to grow and change," and "the need for food and water" as two characteristics that the examples had in common.
   - A language-arts teacher, working with her class on summary sentences, displayed paragraphs on the overhead. With her guidance, the class analyzed the summary sentences in each paragraph, determining which were good and poor and explaining why in each case.

3. Link new concepts to related concepts.
   - The term *cultural revolution* came up in a social-studies lesson. The teacher asked the students to compare cultural revolutions to other revolutions they had studied, such as the Industrial Revolution and the American Revolution, pointing out similarities and differences in each case.
   - An earth-science class was learning about "old" and "new" geologic formations. The teacher showed slides of the two kinds of formations, with examples of young mountains and young rivers serving as the nonexamples for the old mountains and old rivers. The class then related "old" and "new" mountains and rivers to climate, weathering, and erosion, which had been discussed in earlier lessons.

Teaching Principles, Generalizations, and Academic Rules in Your Classroom

4. Provide examples that illustrate the relationship you're teaching.
   - A science teacher, wanting his students to understand the principle "The longer the vibrating column, the lower the pitch," had students lay rulers on their desks, extend different lengths of the rulers over the edge, and snap the rulers to hear differences in pitch.
   - A first-grade teacher wants her students to understand the rules for basic punctuation. She has students write several sentences, and she writes some, too. As students share theirs, and as she shares hers, she helps the class recognize that each sentence begins with a capital letter and ends with a punctuation mark.

5. Have students apply relationships to new situations.
   - The science teacher working with length and pitch put different amounts of water into three identical soft-drink bottles and asked students to predict how the amount of water would affect pitch. He then had students blow across the bottle openings to make sounds and asked them to relate the different pitches to the differing amounts of space and water in each bottle.

Jody Curtis is a third-grade teacher in an ethnically diverse school. Of her 27 students, more than a third are non-native English speakers. They come from a variety of backgrounds and have widely varying experiences.

Jody is beginning a unit on reptiles. She prepared by gathering colored pictures from magazines and other sources. She knew that her class had studied amphibians in the second grade, and she planned to build on their knowledge by comparing reptiles to amphibians.

As she showed each picture, she called on different students to describe and discuss what they observed. Disagreements began to emerge almost immediately.

"They're sort of worms, except they have eyes," Sarina suggested. "They wiggle when they move."

"No, they got bones," Miguel countered.

"Yeah, I saw a skeleton once," Bryan added. "It looked funny, but it had bones."

When the discussion turned to reproduction, there was more disagreement.

"They lay eggs in a nest like birds," Monica said.

"Uh huh," Jamille agreed. "In the water."

"No, they have babies like dogs and cats," Manuel retorted, arguing that the young were born alive.

They even disagreed about basic features.

"They're yucky and slimy," Sanra asserted.

"Gross," Lucia added. "All slippery and gross."

"What makes you say that?" Jody wondered aloud.

". . . Uhh."

"No," Muhammed interjected. "My brother has a snake, and I felt it. It was dry, not slimy. It was smooth and clean," he added, reacting to the skeptical looks on his classmates' faces.

"What's your reaction to what Muhammed said?" Jody turned to Lucia, trying to reinvolve her in the discussion.

"I . . . I . . . What do you mean, reaction?"

"I mean, how does Muhammed's experience compare to what you said?"

". . . I . . . don't know."

"Tell us about your experience with snakes," Jody encouraged.

". . . My brother caught one in a pond, and he was holding it up by its head, . . . and I was so scared, and finally I touched it, . . . and it was all wet and slimy."

Jody and her students continued the discussion for the remainder of the science period.

As she reflected on it, Jody was struck by two aspects of the lesson. First, students' experiences with reptiles varied widely and, as a result, they had very different preconceptions about reptiles.

Second, the way the students responded to the interaction in the lesson also varied. Some were confident, whereas others were less comfortable, perhaps even confused. For example, when Jody asked Lucia, a non-native English speaker of Hispanic background, "What makes you say that?" Lucia was uncertain about how to respond. Jody was asking her to provide evidence for her conclusion that snakes are slippery and gross, but Lucia didn't realize that this is what the question called for. A similar thing happened when Jody asked her, "What's your reaction to what Muhammed said?" and her effort to clarify the question by asking, "I mean, how does Muhammed's experience compare to what you said?" still didn't help. Until she simply asked Lucia to describe her experience with snakes, Jody had little insight into Lucia's understanding.

8.14

What factor in Piaget's descriptions of development best explains why the students came to the lesson with strong preconceptions about reptiles? What other factor from Piaget's work is critical in helping a student change preconceptions if they're invalid? Explain.

Differences in background experiences and patterns of interaction require two kinds of instructional adaptations. Let's look at them.

Accommodating Differences in Background Experiences

To begin this section, let's look at what Jody did to follow up with her students:

> To deal with the differences in the students' experiences, Jody arranged to have several reptiles brought to class. She had Muhammed bring his brother's snake, and she went to a pet store and talked the owners into letting her borrow a turtle and a lizard.
>
> The next day, as students observed and handled the animals, they realized that snakes do have bones and that reptiles have dry, clean skin. Using additional photos, Jody showed how some reptiles laid their eggs in the ground, whereas others are born alive. On the basis of their new experiences, even Sanra and Lucia reluctantly agreed that reptiles are usually dry and clean.

Because Jody was able to provide concrete experiences for the students, their concept of *reptile* was clarified and enriched. Providing these experiences can be demanding—Jody had to go to a pet store to get a live turtle and lizard, for example—but the results are worth the effort. Merely explaining that snakes are usually dry and clean would have been unconvincing for students such as Sanra and Lucia.

Although Jody's was a science lesson, similar approaches can be used in other content areas. If students are consistently misspelling the same types of words, for example, teaching rules that directly address the errors allows students to restructure their understanding (Hall, Gerber, & Stricker, 1989). When adapting their instruction, teachers design their lessons to build on students' current understandings. This is congruent with both information-processing and constructivist approaches to instruction.

Accommodating Differences in Patterns of Interaction

Although accommodating differences in background is challenging, dealing with differences in patterns of interaction can be even more difficult, because these differences are easy to miss. A teacher less sensitive than Jody, for example, might not have persisted with Lucia, concluding instead that the girl didn't understand the topic or was a generally weak student.

In Chapter 4, we addressed the issue of discontinuities between the home and the school, and this might explain Lucia's reluctance to answer. As it turns out, her reasoning wasn't faulty, and her misconception about snakes was sensible. On the basis of her experience, snakes *are* slippery and gross. It's also likely that her home experience didn't prepare her for questions such as "What makes you say that?" "What's your reaction to what Muhammed said?" and ". . . how does Muhammed's experience compare to what you said?" When Jody persisted and asked her about her experience with snakes, the basis for Lucia's comment was revealed. Had Lucia been familiar with the questioning patterns in the class, she would have responded to Jody's first question by simply saying something such as, "I felt a snake once and it was slippery and gross."

Helping students learn to interact effectively in school is an important teacher task. "The key challenge for schools is to introduce and enculturate students into these school-based discourses without denigrating their culturally specific values and ways of using language" (Michaels & O'Connor, 1990, p. 18).

Teachers can help students acquire these "school effective" ways of interacting in at least three ways (Michaels & O'Connor, 1990). First, they can provide and lead discussions that build on common experiences, such as having the students observe, describe, and discuss the reptiles Jody brought to class.

8.15

What concept from Chapter 7 best helps you understand why the way students respond to your questioning and other aspects of instruction vary so much?

By designing activities that encourage student involvement and group problem solving, teachers help students acquire and understand classroom-effective ways of interacting.

Second, during the discussions, they can introduce "new kinds of talk," such as Jody's questions that asked for evidence. Because the "new talk" was related to concrete and familiar experiences—snakes and Muhammed's comments in Jody's lesson—the questions gradually become meaningful.

Third, teachers can discuss the "new talk" explicitly. For instance, Jody could discuss the intent of questions such as "What makes you say that?" with the students and model responses to them. As students become familiar with patterns of classroom questioning and discussion, and they see that teachers are explicitly trying to involve them, they learn that their contributions are valued.

As teachers work with their students, they should monitor their own communication and realize that students' inability to respond may indicate miscommunication rather than lack of understanding, as was illustrated in the example with Lucia. Asking open-ended questions, as Jody did when she asked Lucia to describe her experience with snakes, is an excellent way to informally assess learners' current understanding.

Classroom Connections

Capitalizing on Diversity in Your Classroom

1. Assess students' background knowledge related to the topics you plan to teach.

• A health teacher beginning a study of nutrition and eating habits asks her students to describe what they believe to be a good meal.

- A math teacher beginning a unit on percentage increase and percentage decrease preassesses students by giving them several problems that require changing fractions to decimals and decimals to percentages.

2. Adapt instruction to students' different backgrounds.
   - A middle-school English teacher finds that several of his students don't use Standard English in speaking and writing. He regularly assigns them short essays and encourages them to express themselves in whatever way they're comfortable. He then builds on the students' thinking and helps them learn to rephrase their writing to conform to standard practice by providing examples of correctly written passages and pairing students who act as peer editors for each other's work.
   - A sixth-grade teacher beginning a unit on Central America asks his students to describe their lives in their neighborhoods. He reminds them that this is their local "culture" and to use it as a comparison when they study the different cultures in Central America.

3. Provide examples that are meaningful for all the students in the class.
   - To illustrate the concept of *adverb,* a fifth-grade teacher has a student walk quickly across the front of the room, asks students to describe how the student walked, and writes on the chalkboard: "Brenda walked quickly across the front of the room." As students discuss the sentence, the teacher leads them to conclude that *quickly* tells how Brenda walked, so it describes the verb in the sentence.
   - A third-grade teacher demonstrates the process of multiplication by having students make four groups of seven interlocking cubes, then three groups of eight interlocking cubes, and six groups of eight interlocking cubes. She then writes on the chalkboard

$$4 \times 7 = 28$$
$$3 \times 8 = 24$$
$$6 \times 8 = 48$$

and leads the class in a discussion of what the numeral means in each case, carefully linking each numeral to the sets of cubes.

Problem Solving

As an introduction to this section, think about the following.

- You want to write a greeting card to a friend who has moved to New York, but you don't know her address.

- You're planning to paint your living room. To determine how much paint you should buy, you need to know the area of the ceiling and walls.

- You're a teacher, and your seventh-graders resist thinking on their own. They expect to find the answer to every question laid bare by the textbook.

What do the three incidents have in common? Although they look different, each can be described as a *problem*. A **problem** *exists when you're in a state that differs from a desired goal or end state and there is some uncertainty about reaching the goal state* (Bransford & Stein, 1984). "In short, a problem occurs when a problem solver has a goal but lacks an obvious way of achieving the goal" (Mayer & Wittrock, 1996, p. 47). In the cases above, for example, our goals are finding the address, knowing the area of the ceiling and walls, and having students think on their own. The desired states are knowing the address, knowing the area, and the students thinking for themselves.

You can see from our examples that we're thinking of problems quite broadly. Needing to determine how much paint to buy is commonly viewed as a problem, for example, but we might not think of wanting to know an address as a problem.

Thinking of problems more broadly is beneficial in at least two ways. First, it recognizes the pervasiveness of problem solving in our everyday lives; and second, it allows people to apply general strategies to solve virtually all problems (Bruning et al., 1995).

Problem Solving: Theoretical Perspectives

Problem solving is grounded in both information-processing and constructivist views of learning. For example, both views see background knowledge as a foundation on which additional learning is based, and expert problem solvers have a great deal of well-organized background knowledge. In addition, expert problem solvers are strategic in their approaches to solving problems, they have well-developed metacognitive abilities, they organize their understanding in ways that overcome the limitations of working memory, and they develop their expertise through practice and experience. Each characteristic is grounded in information processing.

In addition, we will see that problem solving is facilitated by social interaction, and authentic problems are more effective than less meaningful problems. These are constructivist notions. Keep both of these views in mind as you study the following sections.

Well-Defined and Ill-Defined Problems

Problem-solving theorists find it useful to distinguish between well-defined and ill-defined problems (Eysenck & Keane, 1990; Simon, 1978). A **well-defined problem** is *one in which the goal is clear and the potential solutions are known or can be easily accessed,* whereas an **ill-defined problem** *has an ambiguous goal and no generally agreed-on strategy for solving it* (Dunkle, Schraw, & Bendixon, 1995; Mayer & Wittrock, 1996). Our first two examples are well defined: wanting to know the address and the area of the ceiling and walls are unambiguous, and straightforward strategies for finding each exist. Many problems in math, physics, and chemistry are well defined, such as this example:

> *Roger and Diana are selling lemonade. The lemonade mix was $.40 for a package that made two quarts. They sold the lemonade at $.10 for an eight-ounce glass and sold a total of 15 quarts. How much money did they make on each glass they sold?*

Although students often have difficulty solving this type of problem, its goal is clear and specific strategies exist for solving it. Most of students' experiences in school focus on well-defined problems.

In contrast, students not wanting to think for themselves is an ill-defined problem. The goal state isn't clear: teachers are often not even sure what "thinking" means and a readily agreed-on strategy for getting students to "think" doesn't exist. The problem can be solved with several strategies, and several "right" answers can be found.

Routine and Nonroutine Problems

Problems can also be classified as routine or nonroutine (Mayer & Wittrock, 1996). A routine problem is one for which a ready-made procedure for finding the solution exists. For instance, if a student has been practicing problems, such as 492 × 55, then

8.16
You don't know the meaning of a word, so you look it up in a dictionary. Under these conditions, is not knowing the meaning of the word a problem? Explain.

8.17
Was the problem Laura Hunter's students attempted to solve well defined or ill defined? Explain.

8.18
You're involved in a relationship with a member of the opposite sex but the relationship isn't as satisfying as you would hope. Is this a well-defined or an ill-defined problem? Explain.

631×87 is a routine problem. If a new procedure for finding the solution is required, the problem is nonroutine. Since Laura Hunter's students had to devise their own procedure for finding the area that needed carpeting—because it was an irregular shape—they were working on a nonroutine problem. Most problems learners face in school are routine, but real-world problems generally are not (Mayer & Wittrock, 1996).

The distinction between problems and "non-problems" isn't clear or distinct. For instance, most experts would contend that not knowing the definition of a word isn't a problem if a dictionary is available. If one isn't available, however, not knowing the word might be a problem. Also, some experts might suggest that routine problems aren't really "problems," arguing that the goal is clear and no uncertainty exists about reaching the goal. Others describe them as problems, however (e.g., Mayer & Wittrock, 1996), and we have chosen this conception.

A General Problem-Solving Model

Since the 1950s, computer scientists and cognitive psychologists have worked to develop approaches to problem solving that can be applied across a variety of domains. This work has led to the development of the five-step problem-solving model illustrated in Figure 8.4 and discussed below (based on work by Bransford & Stein, 1984).

Identifying the Problem

Question: There are 26 sheep and 10 goats on a ship. How old is the captain?

Amazingly, in one study, 75% of the second-graders who were asked this question answered 36 (cited in Prawat, 1989)! Obviously, these students had difficulty understanding what the problem was asking.

It appears that identifying a problem is simple and straightforward but, in fact, it is one of the most difficult aspects of problem solving. It requires patience and a willingness to avoid committing to a solution too soon (Hayes, 1988).

Four obstacles to effective problem finding are:

- lack of experience in defining problems
- the tendency to rush toward a solution before the problem has been clearly identified
- the tendency to think convergently
- lack of domain-specific knowledge (Bruning, Schraw, & Ronning, 1995).

Figure 8.4 A general problem-solving strategy

Lack of Experience in Defining Problems. If you think about your own experience, how much formal training have you had in searching for and defining problems? Most problem-solving experiences in schools are in math at the lower grades and in math, chemistry, and physics in the upper grades. These problems are usually well defined and presented by the teacher or textbook. Students often go through 13 or more years of formal schooling and have virtually no experience in framing and defining problems.

Tendency to Rush Toward a Solution. Novice problem solvers tend to "jump" into a solution before they've clearly identified the problem (Shoenfeld, 1989; Van Leuvan, Wang, & Hildebrandt, 1990). The second-graders who added sheep and goats to get the age of the captain illustrate this tendency. Even university students will quickly select and persist with a strategy despite the fact that it isn't working or making sense (Schoenfeld, 1989).

Tendency to Think Convergently. In contrast with **convergent thinking,** which is *thinking that tends to focus on one solution to a problem,* **divergent thinking** *occurs when problem solvers consider solutions that are novel or even seemingly inconsistent* with what appears to be the original problem.

For example:

> Paula Waites, a second-year teacher, is having classroom management problems. Her students are inattentive and disruptive, and despite clearly stated rules and an effort to enforce them consistently, the behaviors persist.
>
> "I'm not sure what to do," Paula confided to her friend, Linda, an eight-year veteran. "I know I'm supposed to be consistent, and I'm trying. I told them I mean business, and I've written several referrals during the past week, but it isn't helping that much. I guess I'll just have to get tougher, but I hate coming down on them all the time. I've thought and thought about it, and that's all I can come up with."
>
> "I'm not sure," Linda responded, "but maybe you ought to try something a little different."
>
> "I don't know what you mean."
>
> "Maybe try working up a few really nifty activities, even if it takes some extra work. If the students like them, maybe they'll behave better. . . . Whenever my students are acting up, the first thing I ask myself is whether I'm doing a good job of motivating and involving them in my lessons. I mean, that isn't always the case, but it's often a factor in their behavior."
>
> "Gee, I guess I never actually thought about approaching it that way. I admit that most of what I do is lead discussions about what they've read or were supposed to read in the book."
>
> A week later, Paula reported that she had been experimenting with different motivational strategies and that her students were behaving much better.

In this case, Linda prompted Paula to look at her problem in a different way. What on the surface appeared to be a management problem was actually a problem with student motivation caused by unimaginative instruction. Paula was so focused on

8.19

How effective was Laura Hunter in helping her students acquire experience in defining problems? Describe specifically what she might have done to be more effective.

8.20

What is the most effective thing a teacher can do to prevent students from rushing toward a solution before they fully understand the problem?

A teacher can help students learn general problem-solving strategies by focusing their attention on specific strategies, such as identifying and representing the problem during their problem-solving efforts.

management that she was unable to see the problem in another way until Linda prompted her.

Learning to think divergently results from having a variety of experiences requiring divergent thinking. This suggests a critical role for teachers. As they guide students' discussions of problems, they can ask questions that encourage thinking about the problems in different ways. As students acquire experience, they gradually develop their abilities to think divergently.

Lack of Domain-Specific Knowledge. In Chapter 7, we emphasized the importance of schemas in organizing learners' background knowledge, and background knowledge is no less important in problem solving. Teachers can help students access background knowledge by encouraging them to analyze and discuss problems before attempting to identify solutions (Bernardo, 1994; Lawson & Chinnappan, 1994).

This isn't as easy as it appears, however. As we saw in our opening case study, Laura had students review *area* and *perimeter,* and they spent a considerable amount of time analyzing the problem. However, in spite of this discussion, her students didn't know how to find areas of nonroutine problems, nor did they fully understand the concept *area.* This lack of background knowledge might explain why students got different answers to the problem.

Representing the Problem

The second step of the general problem-solving model involves representing the problem. Using some form of visual or written representation of the problem is often useful because it helps frame the problem in a larger context and connect it to learners' existing background (Lovett & Anderson, 1994). As an example, look again at the diagram that Laura Hunter's students used to represent their problem.

One advantage in putting problems on paper is that the load on working memory is reduced. You know from Chapter 7 that working memory's capacity is limited, and many problems are so complex that working memory can easily be overloaded. A picture or diagram, such as Laura's students used, helps to identify important aspects of the problem. Without it, their working memories could be overloaded.

Selecting a Strategy: Algorithms and Heuristics

After the problem has been identified and represented, a strategy for solving it must be selected. This is the third step in the model.

Suppose you're given the following problem:

A coat costing $90 is marked 25% off. What is the sale price of the coat?

In responding to a well-defined, routine problem, a person often can apply an **algorithm** or *specified set of steps for solving problems.* Algorithms are academic rules. For instance, the algorithm for finding the cost of the coat could be summarized as follows:

Convert the 25% to a decimal.

Multiply 90 by .25.

Subtract the result from 90.

When you subtract whole numbers with regrouping, add fractions with unlike denominators, and solve algebraic equations, you are using algorithms.

Many problems can't be solved with algorithms, however. Algorithms don't exist for ill-defined problems, and many well-defined problems also lack algorithms. In those cases, problem solvers use **heuristics,** which are *general, widely applicable problem-solving strategies* (Mayer, 1992). Some common heuristics include (a) trial and error, (b) means–ends analysis, (c) working backward, and (d) drawing analogies.

Trial and Error. Trial and error is obviously an inefficient strategy, but it is one that problem solvers often try first when faced with unfamiliar problems. Trial and error can be valuable pedagogically, however, because it allows learners to explore the specifics of new problems, and experience is one of the most important factors in acquiring expertise (Hayes, 1988; Wagner & Sternberg, 1985). As learners gain experience, they switch to more efficient strategies.

Means–Ends Analysis. **Means–ends analysis** is *a heuristic in which the problem solver attempts to break the problem into subgoals and works successively on each.* Laura Hunter's students used means–ends analysis in solving their problem. One of the strategies they used was: (a) Find the area of the whole room then (b) subtract the areas of the noncarpeted portions. In this way they used their knowledge of routine problems (finding the area of a rectangle) to help then solve a nonroutine problem (finding the area of an irregular shape).

Means–ends analyses is one of the most effective strategies for solving ill-defined problems. Because ill-defined problems have ambiguous goals, identifying subgoals that may need to be operationally defined helps problem solvers "get a handle" on the problem. In the case of the seventh-graders who don't want to "think," for example, we might operationally define "thinking" as an inclination to search for relationships in the topics they study, to make conclusions on the basis of evidence, and to remain open-minded. We can then design learning activities that provide experiences for them in these areas.

8.21

Think back to the problem of painting your living room presented at the beginning of our discussion of problem solving. Suppose paint costs $21.99 per gallon. Describe an algorithm you could use to find the cost of painting your living room.

8.22

Think again about the ill-defined problem of a personal relationship that is less satisfying than you would like it to be. Describe a means–ends analysis that might be used to "solve" the problem.

Small groups provide an effective means of teaching problem-solving heuristics.

Working Backward. Suppose you're faced with the problem of running late for appointments and then feeling uneasy and stressed in the process. One person dealt with this problem by starting with the time of the appointment and backing up 45 minutes because, "It takes less than 45 minutes from where I work to anyplace else in town. Then if I get caught in traffic, I know I'll have a few extra minutes." This is a simple example of "working backward."

Drawing Analogies. **Drawing analogies** is *an attempt to solve unfamiliar problems by comparing them with familiar ones that have already been solved* (Mayer, 1992). The more background knowledge learners have with the analogy, the more effective it will be for helping learners solve the unfamiliar problem. This is true for both teacher-generated and learner-generated analogies (Pittman & Beth-Halachmy, 1997). Once Laura's students, for example, were able to accurately solve the carpeting problem, they would probably be able to solve area problems with other irregular plane figures by drawing analogies between the two.

8.23

Students often have difficulty using the drawing analogies strategy. What is the most likely reason they have this difficulty? Explain.

Implementing the Strategy

The key to successfully implementing the strategy is clearly defining and representing the problem and selecting an appropriate algorithm or heuristic. If these processes have been effective, implementing the strategy is essentially routine. If learners are unable to implement a strategy, they should rethink the original problem or the strategy they've selected.

Evaluating the Results

Evaluating results is the final step in problem solving. Although this step seems basic, it is often difficult for learners. Let's look at an example.

> One boy, quite a good student, was working on the problem "If you have six jugs, and you want to put two thirds of a pint of lemonade into each jug, how much lemonade will you need?" His answer was 18 pints. I (Holt) said, "How much in each jug?" "Two thirds of a pint." I said, "Is that more or less than a pint?" "Less." I said, "How many jugs are there?" "Six." I said, "But that doesn't make any sense." He shrugged his shoulders and said, "Well, that's the way the system worked out." (Holt, 1964, p. 18)

This case illustrates a common problem. Getting an answer, regardless of whether or not it makes sense, is typically the students' goal. Young children in particular have trouble at this stage, wanting to rush through, get on to the next problem, and finish the assignment (Schunk, 1994). This occurred in Laura's class, where several of the students were satisfied with widely discrepant answers.

Much of the improvement in problem-solving ability results from effective evaluation (L. Baker, 1989; Zimmerman, 1990). Teachers can help in this process, particularly in math, by having students estimate answers before they begin. Estimates require thought, and when answers and estimates are far apart, questions are raised. The habit of estimating is an important disposition that teachers should try to help students develop.

8.24

Think about the boy's comment, "That's the way the system worked out." Describe specifically what you might do to help him arrive at a valid solution to the problem.

Expert–Novice Differences in Problem-Solving Ability

To this point, we have identified well-defined, ill-defined, routine, and nonroutine problems, and discussed a general problem-solving model. As educators, however, we still have a "problem" of our own: research indicates that many of our students are not very good at solving problems (Applebee, Langer, Mullis, & Jenkins, 1990; Bruer, 1993; Mayer & Wittrock, 1996). This is our "initial state." Our goal state is for them to be better problem solvers.

One way to approach this problem is to examine expert problem solvers, compare them with novices and, keeping these differences in mind, guide learners as they try to develop expertise. An **expert** is an *"individual who is highly skilled or knowledgeable in a given domain"* (Bruer, 1993, p. 12). A **novice** *isn't knowledgeable or skilled*. Research has identified four important differences between experts and novices in problem-solving ability (Bruning et al., 1995; Glaser & Chi, 1988). They're outlined in Table 8.2 and discussed in the paragraphs that follow.

Differences between experts and novices can be largely traced to experience and background knowledge, which allow experts to overcome the limitations of working memory. For example, experts represent problems effectively because their complex schemas allow them to recognize patterns and "chunk" large amounts of information into smaller units that don't exceed working memory's capacity.

Also, because experts have a great deal of experience, having solved many similar problems in the past, "specific experiences are represented in memory as 'cases' that are indexed and searched so that they can be applied analogically to new problems that occur" (Bransford, 1993, p. 4). Because of experts' experience and practice, much of their knowledge is automatic, allowing them to focus on the overall problem instead of

8.25

How could a teacher increase students' expertise about a topic without teaching any new information about it?

Table 8.2 Expert–novice differences in problem-solving ability

Area	Experts	Novices
Representing problems	Search for context and relationships in problems.	See problems in isolated pieces.
Problem-solving efficiency	Solve problems rapidly and possess much knowledge that is automatic.	Solve problems slowly and focus on mechanics.
Planning for problem solving	Plan carefully before attempting solutions to unfamiliar problems.	Plan briefly when attempting solutions to unfamiliar problems; they quickly adopt and try solutions.
Monitoring problem solving	Demonstrate well developed metacognitive abilities; they abandon inefficient strategies.	Demonstrate limited metacognition; they persevere with unproductive strategies.

8.26

How do students develop automaticity? What might be an obstacle to the development of automaticity?

8.27

Could two people have the same "amount" of knowledge, yet one be an expert and the other a novice? Explain.

8.28

Taking existing knowledge into account is identified as a characteristic of deliberate practice. Explain why this characteristic is important.

specific mechanics (Bruer, 1993). Automaticity, together with seeing patterns, frees working memory, leaving space available for metacognition—monitoring their progress and assessing the validity of their solutions.

In summary, experts are, "faster, more efficient, and more reflective *because of the depth and breadth of their knowledge*" (Bruning et al., 1995, p. 195). The need for thorough background knowledge is difficult to overstate. Effective problem solving involves access to substantial well-organized, domain-specific knowledge (Bransford, 1993; Mayer, 1992).

Developing Expertise: Role of Deliberate Practice

As we began this section, we said that one way to improve the problem-solving abilities of students is to examine expert problem solvers. But how did these experts get that way? Research indicates that much of what characterizes expertise is teachable (Gagne, Yekovich, & Yekovich, 1993). Researchers emphasize the importance of *deliberate practice,* which has four characteristics:

1. Learner motivation to attend to the task and exert effort
2. Instruction that takes learners' preexisting knowledge into account
3. Knowledge of results and feedback
4. Opportunities for learners to repeatedly perform similar tasks (Ericsson, Krampe, & Tesch-Romer, 1993).

You've already seen how important background knowledge is in acquiring expertise, and providing students with the opportunity to repeat tasks and receive feedback makes sense. One additional essential element is learner motivation.

Acquiring Expertise: The Importance of Motivation

Research clearly indicates that if learners are to develop problem-solving expertise, they must acquire a great deal of experience in solving problems (Bransford, 1993; Bruning et al., 1995). To acquire this experience requires motivated students. This isn't easy; students often complain about and try to avoid word problems in math, for example, because they are difficult and require thinking. Unless teachers consciously plan for learner motivation in their efforts to improve problem solving, they are likely to have little success with all but the most successful and highly motivated students (Pintrich, Marx, & Boyle, 1993). With these ideas in mind, we turn to suggestions for helping learners become better problem solvers.

Cognitive Approaches to Problem Solving: Helping Learners Become Better Problem Solvers

From our study of information processing in Chapter 7, we learned that background knowledge in the form of learners' schemas is critical to learning. We also understand the importance of monitoring our own learning (metacognition) and the importance of practice in developing automaticity.

As we continued our discussion of cognitive learning, we identified four characteristics of constructivism (Figure 7.12):

1. Learners construct their own understanding.
2. New knowledge depends on current understanding.

3. Learning is facilitated by social interaction.
4. Meaningful learning occurs within authentic learning tasks.

We now want to apply elements of both of these theories to problem solving. As you read the following sections, keep two questions in mind:

1. How are the elements incorporated into the suggestions for improving learner problem solving?
2. How effectively did Laura Hunter apply these elements in her lesson?

With these questions in mind, let's look at several specific strategies for teaching problem solving, as outlined in Figure 8.5.

Capitalize on Social Interaction

Research indicates that encouraging students to discuss and analyze problems increases understanding and promotes transfer (Perry, Vanderstoep, & Yu, 1993; Stern, 1993), and the importance of social interaction is supported by constructivist views of learning. Teachers can apply this research in classrooms by arranging learning activities that encourage students to think about their problem-solving strategies and to share their thoughts with others. Laura, for example, had her students work cooperatively to both gather information and attempt solutions to problems, and she also involved the whole class in discussion when they explained their strategies and evaluated results.

Present Problems in Meaningful Contexts

In looking at Laura's lesson again, you can see she attempted to reach her goal of finding the areas of irregular plane figures by embedding her learning activity in a problem involving carpeting her classroom, which was an "authentic task." Embedding problems in concrete contexts can significantly improve problem-solving ability (Mayer, 1992).

Information processing supports the importance of practice and experience in developing expertise. One way of acquiring experience is to solve a wide variety of examples embedded in different contexts. For example, to extend their learning, Laura's students need to solve other area problems, such as the surface areas of objects in the room or in their homes. A variety of contextualized problem-solving experiences provides opportunities for students to embed specific solutions in larger conceptual frameworks, which increases the chances for transfer (Reed, Willis, & Guarino, 1994). In addition, presenting problems in meaningful contexts can increase learner motivation, which is critical if learners are to persist long enough to develop problem-solving expertise.

8.29

Research indicates that discussing math problems qualitatively (without numbers) before attempting the actual solutions facilitates problem solving. Explain why this would happen.

8.30

You saw in Chapter 7 that context is important in helping students develop procedural knowledge. Explain why this is the case. Describe the declarative and procedural knowledge that Laura Hunter's students needed in order to solve the "carpeting the room" problem.

Figure 8.5 Improving learner problem solving

- Capitalize on social interaction
- Present problems in meaningful contexts
- Provide practice in problem finding
- Provide scaffolding for novice problem solvers
- Teach general problem-solving strategies

Provide Practice in Problem Finding

Laura had clear goals for the lesson, but she didn't give her students as much practice in identifying and defining the problem for themselves as she might have. Earlier, we said that learners get little practice in finding and identifying problems and this was largely true in Laura's case.

She could have given the students some experience in problem finding in a variety of ways. One possibility might be to begin by saying something such as, "Our room is really noisy, particularly when we leave or come in. . . . What might we do about this?" The discussion could then be guided to the possibility of carpeting, which would lead to how much carpeting was necessary, which was the problem the students examined. The discussion could have been completed in a matter of minutes and would have given the students some valuable experience in problem finding.

As teachers acquire experience in guiding learners' problem solving, they will learn to recognize opportunities to help learners identify problems. The first step is to be aware of the need to move back, to involve students in *identifying* problems instead of handling students problems.

8.31

Why do students in formal school settings get so little practice in finding and defining problems?

Provide Scaffolding for Novice Problem Solvers

Social constructivism, grounded in Vygotsky's views, emphasizes the importance of *scaffolding* in assisting learning. As learners attempt to solve problems, teachers provide enough scaffolding to ensure that learners make progress *on their own,* but not so much guidance that the learners' active role in the process is reduced. A painter's scaffold supports the painter, but the painter does the painting; the teacher provides support, but the students solve the problems.

Three forms of scaffolding can be particularly helpful: analyzing worked examples, visually representing problems, and cognitive apprenticeships.

8.32

What kinds of scaffolding did Laura Hunter provide in her lesson?

Analyzing Worked Examples.   In traditional problem-solving instruction, teachers typically display one or more problems and present and model the solutions. Students then try to imitate the teacher's behavior, often with little understanding. In contrast, analyzing problems, discussing them in detail, and then relating the solutions to them makes the entire process much more meaningful.

The value of analyzing worked examples is confirmed by research (Carroll, 1994). Students using worked examples made fewer errors, completed the work more rapidly, and required less assistance from the teacher than students who received traditional explanations, even outperforming students who received individualized instruction. In addition to helping students solve the immediate problems, analyzing worked examples increases their understanding of the broader principles involved (Reed et al., 1994).

The combination of the worked examples *with discussion* makes the learning experience especially meaningful for students. Worked examples alone are insufficient; without discussion, learners often miss important aspects of the process, and are likely to try to memorize the steps in it instead of developing a meaningful understanding (Chi, Bassok, Lewis, Reiman, & Glaser, 1989).

8.33

Using constructivism as a basis, explain why discussion is so important to learning problem solving.

Visually Representing Problems.   We know from our study of information processing that the limitations of working memory are obstacles we all face when trying to solve problems. This obstacle is particularly important for novices because they represent problems less efficiently than experts. Putting as much information as possible on paper helps reduce this load and improves problem-solving efficiency. Drawings and diagrams are particularly helpful because they often result in reconceptualizing the problem and encourage the use of analogies as a strategy. As Laura's students worked, they used the diagram they had prepared, and this diagram guided their problem-solving efforts.

Cognitive Apprenticeship. One form of scaffolding is **cognitive apprenticeship,** *which occurs when a less skilled learner works at the side of an expert* (Collins, Brown, & Holum, 1991; Collins, Brown, & Newman, 1989). Cognitive apprenticeship involves modeling, teacher think-alouds, teacher questions to promote active student involvement, coaching, and gradually removing support as the apprentice becomes proficient. (We discuss think-alouds and coaching in more detail in the next section.) In an apprenticeship model, teachers attempt to make tasks authentic to build on the motivation and meaningfulness that are characteristic of tasks situated in the workplace, outside of school (Good & Brophy, 1997).

8.34

What elements of cognitive apprenticeship did Laura Hunter incorporate in her lesson?

Teach General Problem-Solving Strategies

Research indicates that although general strategies in the absence of domain-specific knowledge are of limited value, within specific domains, such as mathematics, they can increase problem-solving abilities (Mayer, 1992; Resnick, 1987).

Teachers can help learners think in terms of general strategies by modeling the thinking involved. Thinking aloud provides a model for students and also allows those less confident to see that it's alright to take risks and make mistakes. As with all forms of teaching, an accepting teacher attitude is essential. By inviting alternative solutions, emphasis is placed on the general problem-solving process, rather than on getting the right answer to a specific problem.

Teachers can also help students acquire general problem-solving skills through explicit instruction in the form of "coaching" (Collins et al., 1989). For example, as students work in small groups to solve problems, the teacher can ask questions to help the students develop an awareness of the problem-solving process:

8.35

Explain why general problem-solving strategies would be more effective within a particular domain than across domains.

What (exactly) are you doing? (Can you describe it precisely?)

Why are you doing it? (How does it fit into the solution?)

How does it help you? (What will you do with the outcome when you obtain it?)

(Shoenfeld, 1989, p. 98)

In time and with practice, students begin to think in terms of general problem-solving strategies, and their problem-solving skills improve.

This completes our discussion of problem solving. You can see how cognitive views of learning provide a conceptual foundation for helping students improve their problem-solving abilities, and you saw how Laura Hunter implemented these principles in her teaching. In the next section, we continue our discussion of cognitive applications by looking at learners as strategy users. As learners become more strategic in their thinking, they become more successful in all forms of learning, including concept learning and problem solving.

Classroom Connections

Teaching Problem Solving in Your Classroom

1. Teach students general problem-solving strategies.
   - A third-grade math teacher spends time at the beginning of the school year teaching her students to break down problems into subgoals; she uses categories such as "We know" and "We need to know." She provides practice and spends considerable class time discussing general approaches to problem solving.

2. Make problems as concrete as possible and discuss them qualitatively before attempting to solve them.
   - A middle-school math teacher teaches the first stage of problem solving by having his students practice putting problems into their own words. He asks them to replace the variables in an equation by using a concrete description, such as a person's age or a number.

3. Put problems into meaningful contexts.
   - A second-grade teacher has a "problem of the week" activity. Each student in the class is required to bring in at least one "real world" problem each week. She selects from among them, and the class works on them in groups. She is careful to ensure that each student has a problem selected during the year.

4. Provide students with practice in problem finding.
   - A second-grade teacher begins a lesson on graphing by asking students how they might determine what people's favorite jelly beans are. She helps them identify a problem and guides their discussion of how to represent and solve it.

5. Teach students to evaluate the products of their problem solving.
   - A middle-school math teacher requires his students to write down an estimate of the answer before actually solving the problem. After the problem is solved, he requires students to compare the two answers.
   - A science teacher requires her students to underline the part of the word problem that suggests or requests units, such as *square centimeters* and *meters per second*. After students solve the problem, they have to draw a line from their answer to the underlined part.

The Strategic Learner

8.36

Think about "the effort to become self-regulated" as a problem. Is it well defined or ill defined? Explain. What is the initial state assumed to be in this problem?

As we studied information processing, we saw that metacognition is important for understanding and regulating our cognitive processes. We employ metacognition, for example, when we take notes on what we've read to help remember the content of the passage—an example of metamemory. The more effectively we employ metacognition, the more self-regulated we become.

Taking notes can also be described as a **cognitive strategy,** which we defined in Chapter 7 as *a plan for accomplishing a learning goal,* that includes cognitive operations above and beyond the processes directly entailed in carrying out a task (Pressley et al., 1990). Taking notes involves operations beyond simply reading the passage, for example. Do you write notes in the margins as you read, highlight parts of the text, or reorganize your notes after class? These, too, are strategies designed to increase your understanding of the content.

As we saw above, cognitive strategies are grounded in information-processing theory, and an enormous amount of research documents their effectiveness (Rosenshine, 1997). In this section we examine cognitive strategies and ways teachers can help learners become "strategic."

Cognitive Strategies, Concept Learning, and Problem Solving: How Are They Different?

Although cognitive strategies, concept learning, and problem solving are similar in several ways, they have several important differences. First, concepts, problems, and the relationships among them are declarative knowledge and tend to be domain-specific. Triangles, rectangles, and the formulas for finding their areas, for example, fall into the domain of mathematics or, more specifically, the geometry of plane figures. In contrast, strategies are a form of procedural knowledge that can be used in a variety of situations. Once students learn to monitor their comprehension, they can use the skill as a strategy in history, biology, or English classes, for example. The fact that cognitive strategies can be used in a variety of situations makes them one of the most powerful forms of school learning.

Another important difference is that whereas learning concepts and other forms of content are goals in themselves, strategies are tools, means to ends. When students learn to summarize, for instance, the goal is to make other information meaningful, and summarizing is a tool used to reach the goal.

Although the majority of cognitive strategy research has focused on reading (Duffy, 1992; Pressley, Johnson, Symons, McGoldrick, & Kurita, 1989), other studies have examined strategy use in a variety of areas, including problem solving in math and science, writing, and study skills (Rosenshine, 1997). From this research, at least three characteristics of effective strategy users have been identified: (a) a broad background of knowledge, (b) a repertoire of strategies, and (c) well-developed metacognitive abilities. Let's examine them.

> **8.37**
> Concepts were described as declarative knowledge, while strategies were a form of procedural knowledge. What implications do these differences have for instruction?

Characteristics of Effective Strategy Users

Broad Background Knowledge

The importance of a broad knowledge base has been emphasized repeatedly in both Chapter 7 and this chapter. It is no less important with effective strategy use. Trying to encode information and represent it in memory without a strong knowledge base as an anchor makes strategy use difficult if not impossible (Pressley, Borkowski, & Schneider, 1987). Research underscores this point in a study in which reciprocal teaching—a strategy we discuss in Chapter 9—was used with science students. Researchers found that without sufficient background knowledge students used the strategy to "predict trivia, to summarize details, and to clarify big words" (Anderson & Roth, 1989, p. 300). Additional research in science indicates that students using deep processing strategies were able to generate questions, create images, and use analogical thinking (Chinn, 1997), all of which require extensive background knowledge. Implementing strategies across the curriculum requires adequate background knowledge within students and instructional scaffolding that activates this knowledge.

A Repertoire of Strategies

Just as effective problem solvers have wide experience in solving problems, effective strategy users have a variety of strategies from which to choose. For instance, they are able to take notes, skim, use outlines, take advantage of bold and italicized print, and capitalize on examples. They are able to use heuristics, such as means–ends analysis to break ill-defined problems into manageable parts. Without a repertoire of strategies, learners are unable to match strategies to different contexts and goals. This leads us to the importance of metacognition.

Well-Developed Metacognitive Abilities

Have you ever commented, "I studied all the wrong stuff for that test," or "I worked so hard, and I don't understand why I didn't do better"? Most people have. Unfortunately, people often fail to match their efforts to goals and monitor whether their strategies are working.

Effective strategy users constantly monitor their progress to see whether the strategy they're using is as effective as it should be (Weinstein, 1994). Monitoring the effectiveness of a strategy involves *awareness of* and *control over* strategy use. These are metacognitive abilities.

8.38

Well-developed metacognitive abilities and background knowledge are described as characteristic of what other concept discussed in this chapter?

In addition, effective strategy users possess *conditional knowledge*—knowing where and when to use a strategy (Anderson, 1990; Pressley, et al. 1987). If the goal is to get an overview of a passage, for example, good readers skim it, looking at headings and searching for major ideas. They match the strategy (skimming) to the goal (getting an overview of the content). On the other hand, if the goal is to acquire a deep understanding of the content, good readers select a different strategy, such as summarizing, note taking, or self-questioning. They realize that goals and conditions are different and adapt their strategies accordingly.

Research on good and poor readers corroborates these characteristics. Compared to poor readers, good readers possess more strategies, use them spontaneously, match strategies to tasks (conditional knowledge), and continually evaluate whether their study skills are working; their metacognitive abilities are well developed (Pressley et al., 1989; Wade, Trathen, & Schraw, 1990). Teachers help learners improve their metacognitive use of strategies by encouraging them to think about and discuss when and why a specific strategy is effective (Carpenter, Levi, Fennema, Ansell, & Franke, 1995).

Having examined the characteristics of effective strategy users, let's turn now to some specific strategies.

Study Strategies

When students attempt to *increase their understanding of written materials and teacher presentations,* they commonly use **study strategies.** In this section, we examine different study strategies, beginning with basic study skills.

Basic Study Skills

Basic study skills are simple, commonly used ones, such as *highlighting* and *taking notes.* Highlighting is a popular strategy, and its value lies in the thought that goes into making the decision about what is important enough to highlight (Anderson & Armbruster, 1984; Moreland, Dansereau, & Chmielewiski, 1997). This, of course, is the most difficult part. Some students avoid the decision by highlighting entire sections, believing they're studying when, in fact, the process is little more than the combined acts of reading and physically marking the text.

Students often have difficulty making decisions about what information is most important. They tend to focus on the first sentence of paragraphs; items that stand out, such as those in **boldface** or *italics* (Mayer, 1984); or those that are intrinsically interesting, often missing important ideas embedded in the body of a passage (Garner, Alexander, Gillingham, Kulikowich, & Brown, 1991).

As with highlighting, effective note taking depends on the learner's decision about what is important. Some students attempt to write down as much of what the teacher says as possible, thus avoiding analyzing the message and deciding what is important—the crux of note taking. Teachers can help learners develop note-taking skills by signally important points and transitions, modeling the process, and having students practice with specific topics (Deshler & Shumaker, 1993; Rickards, Fajen, Sullivan, & Gillespie, 1997).

8.39

How is the ability to identify important ideas related to background knowledge?

8.40

The difference between effective and ineffective highlighting and note taking most closely relates to what concept in Chapter 7?

Study strategies such as note-taking and outlining are effectively learned through teacher modeling, think-alouds, and discussion.

Research indicates that *effective* note taking significantly improves classroom learning and that it can be taught (Kiewra, 1989). Teachers can help students improve their note-taking skills and ability to make decisions about what is important by providing them an outline or matrix to fill in and by modeling thinking while identifying important information. For example, a teacher discussing the characteristics of Eastern and Western Europe prior to the collapse of communism might present a skeleton matrix like the one shown in Table 8.3. As information is discussed, students process and record it in the matrix. This instructional scaffold helps them learn to make comparisons, identify important information, and organize their note taking (Kiewra, 1989).

Other special representations, such as hierarchies, outlines, concept maps, networks, and even pictures, can help students organize information as they take notes and study written materials (Dansereau, 1985; Novak & Gowin, 1984). Again, teachers help students learn to do this by modeling and by making their own thinking public through think-alouds.

8.41

On the basis of your study of Chapter 7, explain why organized note taking is important.

Comprehension Monitoring

Comprehension monitoring (Palincsar & Brown, 1984) is *the process of periodically checking to see whether you understand the material you're reading or hearing.* It is an advanced study strategy, and it requires well-developed metacognitive abilities. Low achievers and those lacking self-regulation seldom check themselves and fail to take action when they don't comprehend (Baker & Brown, 1984). Failure to monitor comprehension is a common problem, even with college students. You may have heard friends say something like, "I knew the stuff. The test was just so tricky." In fact, they probably didn't know the material because of ineffective comprehension monitoring (L. Baker, 1989; Mayer, 1992).

Let's look at two important comprehension monitoring strategies—summarizing and self-questioning.

Summarizing. Learning to **summarize,** or *prepare a concise statement of the essential meaning of a verbal or written passage,* is a powerful comprehension-monitoring strategy. Teaching students to summarize takes time and requires training, but upper elementary students and higher can become skilled with it (Pressley et al., 1989). Training usually consists of walking students through a passage and helping them: (a) identify and delete unimportant information, (b) construct general descriptions for lists of items, and (c) construct a topic sentence for each paragraph. Although time-consuming, training results in increased comprehension (Anderson & Armbruster, 1984; Brown & Palincsar, 1987). We examine summarizing in more depth in Chapter 9 when we focus on cognition in reading.

Self-Questioning. A second effective way of learning to monitor comprehension is through self-questioning (Dole, Duffy, Roehler, & Pearson, 1991). It occurs when stu-

Table 8.3   Matrix used to guide note taking

	Economic Philosophy	Economic State	Political System	Other Factors
Western Europe				
Eastern Europe				

dents stop periodically as they read and ask themselves questions about the material. **Elaborative questioning,** which is *the process of drawing inferences, identifying relationships, citing examples, or identifying implications of the material being studied,* is a particularly effective form of self-questioning. You saw in Chapter 7 that elaboration was one way to promote meaningfulness, and students can also use the process as an effective comprehension-monitoring strategy. Three elaborative questions are especially effective:

1. What is an additional example of this idea?
2. How is this topic similar to/different from the one in the previous section?
3. What is this a part of?

To illustrate these strategies, consider your own study of this chapter. As you were studying the section on the relationships among concepts, you could have asked yourself questions, such as:

What is another example of a generalization or academic rule?

How are generalizations and academic rules similar? How are they different?

Into what category do generalizations and academic rules fit?

Elaborative self-questioning creates links between new information and knowledge in long-term memory, improving both comprehension and learning.

8.42

To what concept does "creates links between new information and knowledge in long-term memory" refer?

Strategies for Improving Comprehension Monitoring

In an effort to help learners improve comprehension-monitoring abilities, researchers have developed comprehensive study systems specifically focusing on those abilities. Because the strategies are complex, they require extensive training. We describe two of these strategies in this section.

8.43

In one situation, you're reading an article in a news magazine to prepare for a discussion in a world history class. In another, you're reading a unit on DNA in a biology text. For which of the two will SQ4R probably be more helpful? Explain.

SQ4R. One of the oldest study systems, SQ4R (Survey, Question, Read, Reflect, Recite, Review) teaches students to attack a text and monitor comprehension in a series of sequential steps (Thomas & Robinson, 1972). A hybrid of an earlier system called SQ3R (the additional R is for *reflect*), SQ4R has proven effective for both learning and retention (Adams, Carnine, & Gersten, 1982). The steps in SQ4R are outlined in Figure 8.6.

Figure 8.6 The steps in SQ4R

S	Survey	Skim material. Use headings as guides.
Q	Question	Construct questions about material.
R	Read	Read, using questions as guides.
R	Reflect	Think about what has been read. Relate ideas to what is already known.
R	Recite	Answer questions. Relate information to headings.
R	Review	Organize information. Restudy difficult material.

Source: Improving Reading in Every Class: A Source Book for Teachers by E. Thomas and H. Robinson, 1972, Boston: Allyn & Bacon. Copyright 1972 by Allyn & Bacon. Adapted by permission of the publisher and the author.

MURDER. A more recent comprehension-monitoring system uses a mnemonic aid to help students remember the steps (Dansereau, 1985). The MURDER (Mood, Understanding, Recall, Digest, Expand, Review) system is more complex and specific than the SQ4R system. The steps are outlined in Figure 8.7.

Research done with college students supports the effectiveness of the MURDER system. Trained students scored more than 30% higher than those in a control group on post-tests and also reported favorable attitudes toward the system. Three-month follow-up questionnaires revealed continued use and favorable attitudes (Dansereau, 1985).

8.44

Think again about reading a topic in biology, such as genetics or DNA. Which of the strategies—SQ4R or MURDER—is probably better for helping you understand the content? Explain your answer, making specific reference to the characteristics of each strategy.

Helping Students Become Effective Strategy Users

To help students become effective strategy users, researchers advocate explicitly teaching the strategy by using modeling and think-alouds (Rosenshine, 1997). The teacher then provides instructional scaffolding as learners practice applying it, gradually withdrawing support as students become more competent (Rosenshine, 1997; Rosenshine & Meister, 1994). Let's look at a teacher applying these processes.

> Donna Evans, a middle-school geography teacher, began her lesson by saying, "We need to read the section of our text that describes the low-latitude climates, middle-latitude climates, and high-latitude climates. Let's talk for a few minutes about how we can help ourselves remember and understand what we've read.
>
> "One way to help us be more effective readers is to summarize the information we read into a few short statements. This is a very useful reading skill. First, it makes the information easier to remember, and second, it helps us compare one climate region with another. We can use this skill whenever we're studying a specific topic, such as climates, and later when we study culture and economics. You can do the same thing when you study different classes of animals in biology or parts of the court system in your government class.
>
> "Now go ahead and read the passage and see if you can decide what makes a low-latitude climate a low-latitude climate," she said.
>
> After giving the class a few minutes to read the section, Donna continued, "As I was reading, I kept asking myself what makes the low-latitude climates what they are. Here's how I thought about it. I read the section, and at first it looked as if the low-latitudes were hot and wet. Then I saw that some of them are hot and dry. So it looks like there are two major types: one humid and the other dry. Close to the equator, the humid tropical climate is hot and wet all year. A little farther away, it

Figure 8.7   Sequential steps in MURDER

M Mood	Plan for study. Schedule time. Monitor concentration.
U Understanding	Identify important and difficult ideas.
R Recall	Paraphrase content. Map key concepts.
D Digest	Reflect. Identify key points and trouble spots.
E Expand	Ask how information is applied.
R Review	Analyze errors on quizzes. Modify study methods.

Source: Learning Strategy Research by D. Dansereau. In J. Segal, S. Chipman, and R. Glaser (Eds.), *Thinking and Learning Skills* (Vol. I), 1985. Hillsdale, NJ: Erlbaum. Copyright 1985 by Lawrence Erlbaum. Reprinted by permission.

has wet summers and dry winters. For the dry tropical climate, high-pressure zones cause deserts, like the Sahara.

"Now, let's all give it a try with the section on the middle-latitude climates. Go ahead and read the section and see whether you can summarize it the way I did."

The class read the passage, and after they were finished, Donna began, "Okay. Give me a summary, someone. . . . Go ahead, Dana."

Dana offered her summary, and Donna and other class members responded, adding information and comments to what Dana said. They then practiced again with the section on the high-latitude climates.

In this episode Donna demonstrated at least four characteristics of effective strategy instruction:

- She explicitly taught the skill, explaining how it worked and why it was important. (She modified the skill slightly, focusing on the characteristics of the climate region, rather than merely identifying a topic sentence and supporting details. In this way, it better fit her content area.)

- She attempted to increase students' metacognitive awareness of the skill by identifying where it is useful, both in geography and in other parts of the curriculum.

- She modeled the skill with students.

- She had students practice the skill, providing feedback in the process.

Notice also that although Donna focused explicitly on summarizing, she also modeled self-questioning when she said, "I kept asking myself, 'What makes the low-latitude climates what they are?'" Helping students see the larger picture by combining strategies in this way makes strategy instruction even more effective (Duffy, 1992).

8.45

Explain how Donna's approach is related to information processing. Also explain how it is related to social cognitive theory.

Thinking Skills

The terms *thinking skills* and *critical thinking* are often used interchangeably. Regardless of the terms, the development of critical and analytical learners is at the core of cognitive approaches to teaching. If learners are to be self-regulated, they must be able to use information to analyze and evaluate ideas and to construct solutions to problems. One approach to this challenge is through the development of students' critical thinking skills.

Definitions vary. Some describe **thinking skills** as the *behaviors and thoughts problem solvers engage in that enhance the problem solving process* (Mayer & Wittrock, 1996). Others describe them as *the ability to accurately and efficiently gather, interpret, and evaluate information* (Perkins, 1987). Interest in thinking skills/critical thinking has grown in recent years because of several factors, outlined in Table 8.4 (based on work by Bransford, Goldman, & Vye, 1991).

Although thinking skills are closely related to study skills, the two differ in scope. Study skills focus on learning from teacher presentations and written materials. Thinking skills are broader; they're used to process information in a general sense, and from multiple sources (Jones, 1995). For example, reading a column in the editorial section of a newspaper, you might ask a question or summarize the passage to increase your comprehension of it. When you go beyond comprehension of the passage, however, to look for evidence for the author's position or to question whether the author is justified in taking the position he or she does, you are thinking critically.

Table 8.4 Factors contributing to the interest in teaching thinking

Factor	Description
Poor test scores	American students score poorly on tests that require thinking (e.g., writing persuasive essays, solving word problems in math, using formal and informal reasoning).
Concerns of business leaders	Business leaders believe that high school and college graduates cannot speak and write effectively, learn on the job, and use quantitative skills.
Increased need for thinking in the future	Many future jobs will require complex learning skills and the ability to adapt to rapid change. Thinking will no longer be in the domain of a select few.
National needs and personal rights	The primary weapon against being exploited by selfish leaders is the ability to think (Machado, 1980). A major impediment to peace in the world is irrational behavior (Nickerson, 1986).

Teaching Thinking: Within or Outside the Regular Curriculum?

8.46

Explain why efforts to teach thinking outside the context of the regular curriculum have been generally unsuccessful. (Hint: Think about one of the themes of Chapters 7 and 8.)

Over the years, many programs have been developed to teach different aspects of thinking outside traditional content courses. Among them are the CoRT Thinking Program (de Bono, 1976), Philosophy for Children (Lipman, Sharp, & Oscanyan, 1980), and Project Intelligence/Odyssey (Hernstein, Nickerson, Sanchez, & Swets, 1986). The problem with these programs has been that the skills rarely transfer to the regular curriculum (Bransford et al., 1991).

A trend that began in the 1980s and continues today is the *explicit teaching of thinking* within the context of the *regular curriculum*. Emphasis on either without the other is likely to be less effective than combining the two. Nickerson (1988) summarizes this position:

> On the one hand, it is important to treat the skills, strategies, attitudes, and other targeted aspects of thinking in such a way that students come to understand their independence from specific domains and their applicability to many; on the other, it seems equally important to demonstrate their application in meaningful contexts, so students witness their genuine usefulness. (p. 34)

Current approaches to teaching thinking skills vary but are generally organized around four basic elements, illustrated in Figure 8.8 (adapted from Nickerson, 1988).

Basic Processes

Basic processes *are the fundamental components or "tools" of thinking.* With some variation from one source to another (Beyer, 1988; Kneedler, 1985; Presseisen, 1986), most experts include the processes summarized in Table 8.5.

You can think of these processes as the basic building blocks of thinking. By focusing on these processes and subprocesses, we attempt to break the complex phenomenon of thinking into teachable and learnable parts.

Laura Hunter emphasized these processes when she had her students compare the strategies they used to solve their problem. The comparisons helped her students see patterns in their thinking. David Shelton, in his astronomy lesson in the opening case study of Chapter 7, also emphasized these processes when he encouraged his students

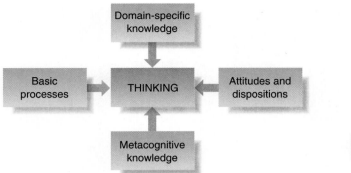

Figure 8.8 Elements of thinking

to explain different characteristics related to planets on the basis of the information students had available to them.

Research on the teaching of thinking skills supports the idea of focusing on basic processes, which are specifically described, modeled, and practiced with feedback (Beyer, 1984). By integrating thinking skills into the regular school curriculum, teachers not only teach thinking but also help their students process information in a deeper, more meaningful way (Bransford et al., 1991; Van Leuvan et al., 1990).

Domain-Specific Knowledge

Like the other aspects of cognitive learning discussed in Chapter 7 and in this chapter, domain-specific knowledge is critical to the teaching of thinking. To think, a person must think *about* something; domain-specific knowledge is the content in a given area on which a person focuses thinking skills. "The importance of domain-specific knowledge to thinking is not really debatable. To think effectively in any domain one must

8.47

Which of the basic processes in thinking could a preoperational learner use? What processes would require concrete operational thinking? formal operational thinking? Explain in each case.

Table 8.5 Basic processes in thinking

Process	Subprocesses
Observing	Recalling Recognizing
Finding patterns and generalizing	Comparing and contrasting Classifying Identifying relevant and irrelevant information
Forming conclusions based on patterns	Inferring Predicting Hypothesizing Applying
Assessing conclusions based on observation	Checking consistency Identifying bias, stereotypes, clichés, and propaganda Identifying unstated assumptions Recognizing overgeneralizations or undergeneralizations Confirming conclusions with facts

Asking students to compare and contrast, analyze, and make predictions encourages them to use and develop higher level cognitive processes.

know something about the domain and, in general, the more one knows the better" (Nickerson, 1988, p. 13).

Metacognitive Knowledge

We emphasize metacognition throughout this text. In the context of thinking skills, metacognition means that the learner knows when to use the different basic processes, how they relate to domain-specific knowledge, and why they're used. Effective thinkers not only find patterns and form conclusions based on evidence, for example, but also are keenly aware of what they're doing. Talking about thinking as it occurs in the classroom is an effective way to develop students' metacognitive knowledge (Adams, 1989). Explicitly focusing on and discussing metacognitive skills increases both reading comprehension and mathematical problem solving (Mayer & Wittrock, 1996).

Motivational Factors

Experts are becoming increasingly aware of the role motivation plays in thinking (Pintrich & Schunk, 1996; Resnick, 1987). Learner motivation determines the attitudes and dispositions students bring to their learning experiences, and attitudes are an essential component of thinking, influencing how and when thinking skills will be used. Examples include the inclination to rely on evidence in making conclusions; the ability to respect opinions that differ from your own; a sense of curiosity, inquisitiveness, and a desire to be informed; and a tendency to reflect before acting (Nickerson, 1988; Tishman, Perkins, & Jay, 1995). Each of these influences students' inclinations to use thinking strategies.

Much of a teacher's effort in teaching thinking is directed toward helping learners develop these inclinations. For example, we want our students to ask themselves,

"Where is the author coming from?" when they read a political commentary, knowing that political orientation will slant the author's opinion. In school, we want learners to be skeptical about the truth of rumors, and in classroom settings, we want them to constantly wonder, "What does this relate to?" and, "How do we know?"

Attitudes and dispositions often can't be taught directly. They're learned primarily by modeling; students disposed to think critically and accurately usually have teachers who demonstrate and set this tone for them.

This completes our discussion of critical thinking, the second major category of cognitive strategies emphasized in U.S. schools. We now turn our attention to *transfer,* a variable that influences how successfully concept learning, problem solving, and strategy use are applied in future learning situations.

8.48

How do you know when students have a positive attitude toward something such as math? How about a positive attitude toward a specific thinking skill?

Classroom Connections

Teaching Cognitive Strategies in Your Classroom

1. Teach study strategies across the curriculum.
   - A sixth-grade teacher introduces note taking as a listening skill and then provides note-taking practice in science and social studies by using a skeletal outline to organize his presentations and by requiring students to take notes from his presentations.
   - A home economics teacher introduces outlining at the beginning of the school year. Later, she collects students' outline notes of her lectures and gives them feedback on the quality of the notes.

2. Teach students to analyze their study strategies and to match them to learning tasks.
   - A biology teacher reviews for a unit test by surveying the important concepts and then describing the types of items on the test, such as essay and multiple choice. Then he asks for volunteers to share ways of studying that they have found effective.

Teaching Critical Thinking in Your Classroom

3. Plan and conduct lessons to promote thinking.
   - A first-grade teacher recaps every field trip by asking students to list things they saw on the trip. Then the class categorizes items and thinks of names for the categories.
   - A social-studies teacher develops much of the content in her units with charts, graphs, and tables. She begins the units by asking her students to first make observations, then comparisons, then conclusions based on the comparisons. Finally, they generalize whenever possible and analyze their thinking to see whether they have over- or under-generalized.

4. Use questioning to promote thinking.
   - A fifth-grade teacher makes an effort to ask questions that promote thinking in his students. He has a list he calls "The Big Five," and looks for opportunities to ask them whenever he can:
     What do you see? notice? observe?
     How are these alike? How are they different? Why?
     What would happen if . . .?
     How do you know?
   - An English teacher attempts to help his students analyze literature. As they talk about a work, he constantly asks, "Why do you say that?" and, "What in the story supports your idea?"

Transfer of Learning

Consider the following situation:

> You get into your car, insert the key into the ignition, and the seat belt buzzer goes off. You quickly buckle the belt. Or anticipating the buzzer, you buckle the belt before you insert the key.

Think now for a moment before reading further. What concept from behaviorism does your behavior—buckling the seat belt—best illustrate? Behaviorists would describe this as an example of *negative reinforcement*. If you identified it as such, you have demonstrated **transfer,** *which ". . . occurs when a person's prior experience and knowledge affect learning or problem solving in a new situation"* (Mayer & Wittrock, 1996, p. 48). You have applied your understanding of the concept of *negative reinforcement* to the situation with the seat belt.

> Transfer makes survival possible by allowing humans to adapt to new situations. Schools are not able to teach students everything they will need to know, but rather must equip students with the ability to transfer—to use what they have learned to solve new problems successfully or to learn quickly in new situations. (Mayer & Wittrock, 1996, p. 49)

Merely recalling information, however, doesn't involve transfer. If, for example, your instructor has previously discussed buckling the seat belt as an example of negative reinforcement and if you later identify it as such, there is no transfer. You merely remembered the information.

With respect to problem solving, transfer occurs when students are able to solve problems they haven't previously encountered and, in the case of study skills, transfer occurs when students use self-questioning, for example, in areas other than reading.

8.49

One learner transfers understanding of a topic to a new situation, whereas another learner does not. Describe the difference in the two learners' schemas.

Positive and Negative Transfer

Positive transfer occurs when learning in one situation *facilitates* performance in another, whereas negative transfer occurs when one situation *hinders* performance in another (Mayer & Wittrock, 1996). As a simple example, if students know that a mammal nurses its young and breathes through lungs and then, using these characteristics, conclude that a whale is a mammal, they demonstrate positive transfer. On the other hand, if they believe that a fish is an animal that lives in the sea and then conclude that a whale is a fish, negative transfer occurs.

General and Specific Transfer

At one time, educators believed that taking courses such as Latin, Greek, and mathematics were valuable not only for learning Latin, Greek, and math, per se, but also to "discipline" the mind. The hope was these courses would strengthen learners' general thinking ability. If these beliefs had been confirmed, they would involve **general transfer,** *which is the ability to take knowledge or skills learned in one situation and apply them in a broad range of different situations.* For example, if becoming an expert chess player would help a person learn math more easily because both require logic, general transfer would occur. **Specific transfer** *is the ability to use information in a setting similar to the one in which the information is originally learned.* If having learned that *photos* means "light" in Greek results in a learner better understanding words such as *photography* and *photosynthesis,* specific transfer occurs.

Students learn to transfer when teachers provide varied learning experiences and invite students to make connections between classroom content and the real world.

Unfortunately, as researchers found more than 80 years ago and have since confirmed repeatedly, transfer is quite specific (Driscoll, 1994; Perkins & Salomon, 1989; Thorndike, 1924). Studying Latin, for example, results in learners acquiring expertise in Latin and perhaps specific transfer to the Latin roots of English words; it does little to improve thinking in general. Teachers can, however, significantly increase their students' ability to transfer.

8.50

One of the themes of Chapters 7 and 8 can help in explaining why transfer tends to be more specific than general. Identify it, and offer an explanation.

Factors Affecting the Transfer of Learning

At least five factors affect students' ability to transfer: (a) the similarity between the two learning situations, (b) the variety of learners' experiences, (c) the quality of learners' experiences, (d) the context of learners' experiences, and (e) the depth of understanding and practice. Let's examine them.

Similarity Between the Two Learning Situations

As our discussion of general and specific transfer implies, the more closely the two learning situations are related, the more likely transfer is to occur. For instance, if students have encountered examples of mammals such as dogs, cats, horses, and deer, they are likely to identify a cow as a mammal because cows are similar to the other examples. By comparison, learners are less likely to transfer the concept of *mammal* to bats because bats aren't as closely related to the original examples.

With respect to problem solving, when first-graders are given the following problem, *Angi has two pieces of candy. Kim gives her three more pieces of candy. How many pieces does Angi have now?*

they do well on this one:

> *Bruce had three pencils. His friend Orlando gave him two more. How many pencils does Bruce have now?*

When they're given the problem about Angi and Kim followed by this problem:

> *Sophie has three cookies. Flavio has four cookies. How many do they have together?*

they perform less well (Riley, Greeno, & Heller, 1982). The first set of problems are more closely related than the second set. These results demonstrate how specific transfer can be.

Variety of Learning Experiences

8.51

Think back to David Shelton's lesson at the beginning of Chapter 7. Describe the different knowledge representations he used. How do they represent adequate variety? Explain.

The variety of learning experiences is perhaps the most important factor affecting transfer. *Variety* means that a topic has been covered in several ways from a number of perspectives and is sometimes called "multiple knowledge representations" (Brenner, et al., 1997; Spiro, Feltovich, Jacobson, & Coulson, 1992). As learners construct understanding and prepare for transfer, each case or example adds different and useful connections that others miss. One way of visualizing this variety of examples is to think of "crisscrossing" a conceptual landscape, providing multiple paths for retrieval and connections to other ideas (Spiro et al., 1992). For instance, if the topic is reptiles, adequate variety means that examples of snakes, alligators, turtles, and lizards are included to help students understand the breadth and depth of the concept. Conversely, inadequate variety results in students undergeneralizing and forming an incomplete concept that fails to transfer. The same applies when teaching relationships among concepts, problem solving, and cognitive strategies: The greater the variety of applications, the greater the likelihood that students' understanding will transfer (Stein, 1989; Sternberg & Frensch, 1993).

Quality of Learning Experiences

Quality refers to the extent that experiences are meaningful for learners (Brooks & Dansereau, 1987; Mayer, 1987). In the case of concept learning, this means *the essential characteristics of the concept are observable in the examples and are understood by learners.* In the case of the concept of *adverb,* for example, students should understand that the meaning of each verb, adjective, or adverb used as an example is being altered by the adverb modifying it. When Karen Johnson (in Chapter 2) compressed the cotton in the drinking cup to illustrate the concept *density,* she created a high quality example; the students could see that the same amount of cotton was occupying less space.

In the case of principles, generalizations, or academic rules, *quality* refers to how clearly the *relationship* between the concepts is illustrated. Seeing a balloon actually expand over a heated bottle is a higher quality example than a picture or verbal statement when trying to teach the principle "Heat makes materials expand."

With respect to problem solving, high-quality problems have real-world applications and are meaningful to students' lives. Problems that students identify or generate themselves are particularly powerful. Laura Hunter capitalized on the value of real-world applications in guiding her students as they found the area of the classroom carpet.

Context of Learning Experiences

8.52

One teacher displays "Karen quickly jumped to her feet," whereas another displays "quickly," "very," "openly," and "rapidly" as examples of adverbs. Which display is of higher quality? Explain.

In Chapter 7, we noted that learners don't merely encode information; they encode it together with the context in which it exists (Brown et al., 1989). The role of context has important implications for teaching in general and transfer in particular. For transfer to occur, knowledge and skills learned in one context must be applied in others. This is unlikely to happen unless learning experiences are embedded in varied contexts. Laura Hunter, for example, embedded her entire problem-solving experience in the context of a practical problem that her students could directly relate to.

Applications of principles and generalizations should, like problem solving, be made in real-world contexts. For instance, when teaching "Heat makes materials expand," students should have opportunities to examine applications, such as why an unopened can of pork and beans explodes when placed over a campfire and why bridges have expansion joints.

Similar situations exist for grammar and punctuation rules in language arts. Rather than isolated sentences, rules should be presented in the context of written passages, such as the following description designed to teach rules for forming plural nouns:

8.53

Assess the variety and quality of the examples in the passage you've just read. Support your assessment with information taken directly from the passage.

> Jefferson, one rural **county** among several **counties,** has six **schools**—one high **school,** two elementary **schools,** and one middle **school.** Five of the **schools** are in Brookesville, the largest **city** in Jefferson **county. Schools** in the three **cities** nearest Brookesville are Brookesville's biggest rivals. The **schools** in all the **cities** hold an annual athletic and scholastic competition.
>
> The two **women** advisors of the debate team and the **woman** who coached the softball team were proud of both the performance of the **students** from Big Tree High School and their appearance. (The school is named after a 600-year-old **tree** that stands prominently in a grove of oak **trees** near the school grounds.) One **student** took all-around honors, and four other **students** won medals. One **girl** and one **boy** were honored for their work in math, and two **boys** and two **girls** wrote exemplary **essays.** One **essay** was voted top of the competition. It described a **child** and how she helped several other **children** learn to cope with difficulty.
>
> The students all looked the part of **ladies** and **gentlemen.** Each young **gentleman** wore a shirt and tie, and each young **lady** wore a dress or pant suit.

If explicit teaching of rules is a goal, embedding them in context makes sense. The goal in understanding rules is to help learners write correctly, and rules in context are more similar to writing than those presented in the abstract. Increasing the similarity of the learning situations increases the likelihood of transfer.

Depth of Understanding and Practice

The more time learners spend studying a topic, the more likely transfer is to occur (Glick & Holyoak, 1987; Voss, 1987). The key here is *depth* of understanding versus breadth (Brophy, 1992). "Schools should pick the most important concepts and skills to emphasize so that they can concentrate on the quality of understanding rather than on the quantity of information presented" (Rutherford & Algren, 1990, p. 185).

Practice also influences depth of understanding. The more opportunities learners have to practice, the greater their depth of understanding and, again, the greater the likelihood of transfer (Cormier, 1987; Perkins & Salomon, 1987).

Student discussion also facilitates transfer; as students share ideas and analyze their interconnections, they gain insights into the ways ideas apply in different settings (Vanderstoep & Siefert, 1994).

Dispositions, Metacognition, and General Transfer

Although transfer of learning tends to be specific, *dispositions,* or the attitudinal element of learning, can transfer in a general sense (Prawat, 1989). A disposition to be open-minded, to reserve judgment, and to search for facts to support conclusions is a general disposition. Domain-specific knowledge is required for understanding the conclusion and the relevant facts, but the disposition is a general orientation. In addition, self-regulation can be a general disposition that transfers to a number of situations. Schoenfeld (1989), after acknowledging that much learning and problem solving is domain-specific, concludes:

> At the level of self-regulation, however, the issues appear to be the same across subject-matter boundaries. Are things going well as you perform a complex task? If yes, then leave well enough alone. If not, then there might be things you can do—and here, the details might be domain-specific. (p. 95)

Teachers encourage transfer of these dispositions through modeling across disciplines and by the day-in and day-out message that learning is a meaningful activity facilitated by cognitive monitoring.

8.54

Students most commonly learn dispositions in either or both of two ways. What are they?

Classroom Connections

Promoting Transfer in Your Classroom

1. Provide a wide range of examples and applications for the content you teach.

   - A fifth-grade teacher provides practice in writing paragraphs by requiring students to report their science experiments in paragraph form. She also requires appropriate paragraph structure in social studies reports and letters to foreign pen pals. Before each assignment, she reminds students of key points in paragraph structure before they begin their writing.

   - A geometry teacher illustrates applications of course content with examples from architecture. He also uses photographs from magazines and slides to illustrate how math concepts relate to the real world.

2. Plan representations that provide the information students need for understanding the topics they study.

   - A history teacher writes short cases to illustrate concepts, such as *mercantilism,* that are hard to understand from text alone. He guides students' analyses of the cases, helping them identify the essential characteristics of the concepts.

   - An English teacher prepares a matrix illustrating the characters, setting, and themes for several of Shakespeare's plays. Students use the information in summarizing and drawing conclusions about Shakespeare's works.

3. Embed information in meaningful contexts.

   - A fifth-grade teacher selects samples of student writing to teach grammar and punctuation rules. She copies samples onto overheads and uses the samples as the basis for her instruction.

   - A science teacher begins a discussion of light refraction by asking students why they can see better with their glasses on than they can without them. He tries to begin each new topic with a problem presented in a personalized way.

4. Use regular reviews to strengthen ideas and to provide practice with broad applications.

   - A chemistry teacher includes at least one problem from the previous topic on every new problem sheet. During the week before the grading period ends, she gives an assignment sheet containing problems from each topic covered during the grading period.

   - A fourth-grade social studies teacher caps each unit with the following questions:
     What have we learned in this unit?
     Why is it important?
     What does it have to do with our world today?

Windows on Classrooms

At the beginning of this chapter, you saw how Laura Hunter planned and conducted her lesson in an effort to promote thinking and problem solving in her students. Let's look now at a teacher with a group of second-graders involved in a lesson on graphing. As you read the case study, consider the extent to which the teacher applied the information in this chapter in her lesson.

Suzanne Brush, a second-grade teacher at Webster Elementary School, has her students involved in a unit on graphing.

After students settled down for math, she began, "I'm planning a party for us, and when I was doing that, a question came to my mind. I thought maybe you could help me solve it today. I need to know how I can figure out the class's favorite kind of jelly bean. If you can help me out with that, raise your hand."

Several students offered suggestions and, after considerable discussion, they finally settled on giving each student a variety of jelly beans and having them indicate which one was their favorite.

"It just so happens," Suzanne smiled as they decided on the idea, "that I did bring in some jelly beans today, and you'll be able to taste the jelly beans and vote for your favorite flavor."

She then handed out a baggy with seven different-flavored jelly beans in it to each student. After Suzanne directed the students to taste all the jelly beans before they chose their favorite, the students opened the bags and began tasting them as Suzanne monitored the process.

"Okay," she started when everyone was done tasting. "Right now I need your help. . . . Raise your hand, please, if you can tell me what we can do now that we have this information. . . . How can we organize it so that we can look at it as a whole group? We want the favorite flavor jelly bean. . . . Jacinta?"

"See how much people like the same one, and see how much people like other ones," Jacinta responded.

"Okay. . . . Can you add to that? . . . Josh?"

"You can like write their names down and see how many . . . like black, . . . how many ones are black," Josh answered uncertainly.

"That was right in line with what Jacinta said," Suzanne smiled and nodded. "Here's what we're going to do. Stacey and someone else, when we first started off, mentioned that we could graph the information, and so we have set up here . . . We have an empty graph up in the front of the room," she continued, moving to the front of the room and displaying the outline of a graph that appeared as follows:

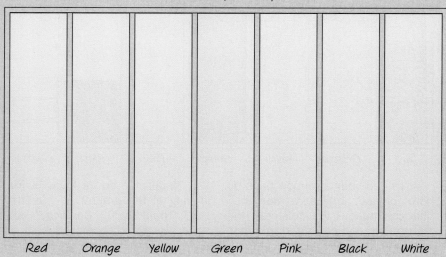

Most Popular Jelly Bean

| Red | Orange | Yellow | Green | Pink | Black | White |

"Yes, Justin," she nodded in response to his raised hand.

"See like which ones like, like red, get the people that like red and write it down; get all the colors and like red and like yellow, green, orange, black, yellow, white," he suggested haltingly, as Suzanne carefully monitored the attention of the rest of the students while Justin made his suggestion.

"That's a great idea," she smiled. "We're going to do that," explaining that she had a series of cut out cardboard squares that matched the colors for the graph. She directed individual students to come to the front of the room and paste the color of square that represented their favorite color on the graph. After all the groups were done, the graph appeared as follows:

Most Popular Jelly Bean

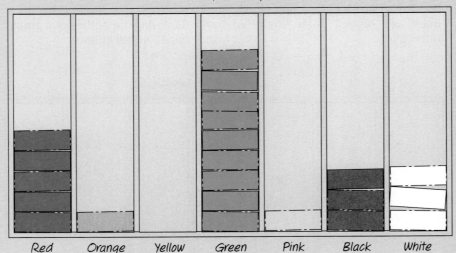

Red   Orange   Yellow   Green   Pink   Black   White

"I need your attention back up here, please, for just a moment," she continued. "We collected the information and organized the information up here on the graph. Now we need to look at and analyze the information. I need you to tell me what we know by looking at the graph up here. . . . What do we know? Please look at the graph up front. . . . Candice, what do we know?" she asked as she walked toward the middle of the room.

"People like green," Candice answered.

"Candice said most people like the green jelly beans. . . . Candice, how many people like green?"

". . . Nine."

"Nine people like green. . . . And how did you find that out? Can you go up there and show us how you read the graph?"

Candice went up to the graph and moved her hand up from the bottom, counting the green squares as she went.

"What else do we know by just looking at the graph? . . . Justin? . . . Thank you, Candice," she added as Candice moved back to her desk.

"There's three people that like black and three people that like white."

"Three people like black and three people like white," Suzanne repeated, pointing to the black and white columns on the graph. "Let's let Stacey add some more to that."

"No one liked yellow," Stacey answered.

"Nobody picked yellow," Suzanne repeated.

"Okay, what else do we know from looking at the bar graph? . . . Andrew?"

"One took orange."

"Only one person picked orange," Suzanne repeated.

"And one person picked pink. . . . Okay, here we go. . . . How many more people liked green than red?" she asked, changing the direction of the questioning. "How many more people liked the green jelly beans than the red? Look up at the graph. Try to find out the information, set up the problem, and then we'll see what you come out with. You have to have a problem set up on your paper."

Suzanne watched as the students looked at the graph and began setting up the problem. She commented, "Quite a few hands, and a few people are still thinking," as she moved across the room. She stopped briefly to offer Carlos some help, continued watching the students as they finished, and then said, "I'm looking for a volunteer to share an answer with us. . . . Dominique?"

"Nine plus 5 is 14," Dominique answered.

"Dominique says 9 plus 5 is 14. Let's test it out," Suzanne

said, asking Dominique to go up to the graph and show the class how she arrived at her answer.

Dominique went to the front of the room as Suzanne said, "We want to know the difference. . . . How many more people liked green than red, and you say 14 people, . . . 14 more people liked green. Does that work?" Suzanne said, pointing at the graph.

Dominique looked at the graph for a moment and then said, "I mean 9 take away 5."

"She got up here and she changed her mind," Suzanne said with a smile to the rest of the class after Dominique made her comment. "Tell them."

"Nine take away 5 is 4," Dominique said.

"Nine take away 5 is 4," Suzanne continued, "so how many more people liked green than red? . . . Carlos?"

"Four," Carlos responded.

"Four, good, four," she smiled at him warmly. "The key was you had to find the difference between the two numbers.

"Raise your hand," she then continued, "if you can make up a problem like that, as I just set up and asked the whole class. . . . Okay, Jacinta."

"We could take pieces of paper and get all the students different colors . . . ," Jacinta began.

"Oh, I see. . . . You're giving me a different example of something that we could collect information on and graph. . . . Let's look at the one we have up there though. Could you just think of another problem that we could ask everyone to figure out?"

"How many more reds there are? . . . How many more people like red than black?" Jacinta responded haltingly.

"How many more people liked red than black?" Suzanne repeated. "Go ahead and do it," she said to the class.

She watched as students solved the problem, and responding to Timmy energetically waving his hand, she nodded for him to answer.

"Two," he said.

"And how did you get your answer? What problem did you set up?"

"Five take away 3," Timmy explained.

Suzanne then continued, "I have one more question, and then we'll switch gears a little bit. How many people participated in this voting? How many people took part or participated in this voting?"

Suzanne watched as students turned to the problem and then said, "Matt? . . . How many people?" she said as she saw that students were finished and several had their hands raised.

"Twenty-four," Matt answered.

"Twenty-four," Suzanne repeated. "How many people in the room right now?"

"Uhmm, 25," he answered.

"Is that where you got your answer?" she asked, leaning over him and touching his shoulders. What was the problem you set up?"

"How many people voted," he answered.

"Matt said 24. Did anyone get a different answer? So we'll compare. . . . I can't call on you if you're jumping up and ooing," she said as she walked among the students with their hands waving energetically.

"Robert?"

"Twenty-two."

"How many people got 22 for their answer?"

A number of hands went up, and Suzanne asked, "How many people got a different number?" which was followed by a few hands.

"How did you solve the problem?" she asked, walking past the table and motioning to Robert. "That's the most important thing."

"Nine plus 5 plus 3 plus 3 plus 1 plus 1 equals 22," he answered quickly.

"Where'd you get all those numbers?"

"There," he said, pointing to the graph.

"He went from the highest to the lowest, and the answer was 22. . . . Matt, why isn't it 24?" Suzanne asked walking back toward him, smiling.

". . ."

"Raise your hand if you didn't put a square up there," she directed to the class, and she explained why the answer wasn't 24.

". . . Okay, I need your attention," she said changing the direction of the discussion, "so that I can explain to you six fun and exciting centers that you're going to be working at this morning. You have in front of you your brown center folder. You'll start with your first center number. I'm going to explain the centers very quickly, and then you're going to break up into those groups and begin working."

The students then moved to the centers. In one, students attempted to flip a penny into a cup and fill in a bar graph comparing their attempts to their successful tries. In another, they tallied the number of students who had birthdays each month and entered the information on a bar graph. In a third, they used pictures to make a graph of the type of transportation each student used to get to school. In a fourth, they looked at a videotape of children at play, and measured and graphed their times in different activities. A fifth group went out of the classroom, interviewing people about their favorite soft drinks, tallying the results in a graph. A sixth group called four pizza delivery places, priced the cost of comparable pizzas, entered the information on a graph, and explained why they would choose a particular pizza place.

As time for lunch neared, Suzanne called the groups back together. After the students were settled, she said, "Raise your hand if you can tell me what you learned this morning in math."

"How to bar graph," Jenny responded.

"How to bar graph," Suzanne repeated. "More important, when we set up a problem, what do we have to do to solve the problem. . . . Timmy?"

"Add or subtract."

"Okay, but we have to decide *what*, before we add or subtract?"

"The numbers."

"So, we have to collect the information, then we have to organize it, and we organized it by setting up a bar graph, something that we can look at and talk about and decide what we need to do with the information. And we set up some problems, and we solved them. It's a nice way to look at information and make decisions about certain things, and at your centers too. . . . Do you have any questions about your centers?" she asked as she ended the lesson.

Questions for Discussion and Analysis

Analyze Suzanne's lesson now in the context of the information in this chapter. In doing your analysis, you may want to consider the following questions. In each case, be specific and take information directly from the case study.

1. How effectively did Suzanne teach problem solving in her lesson? To what extent did she apply the suggestions for helping students become better problem solvers in her lesson? Explain, using information taken directly from the case study.

2. To what extent did Suzanne encourage critical thinking in her lesson? What could she have done to give students more practice in developing critical thinking abilities? Explain.

3. How effective would Suzanne's lesson have been for promoting transfer? Explain, using information taken directly from the case.

4. Offer an overall assessment of Suzanne's lesson, based on the content of this chapter. What could she have done to improve the lesson? Be specific in any suggestions you make.

Summary

Concept Learning

Concepts help people make sense of the world by grouping stimuli with similar characteristics into categories. Concepts with few concrete characteristics are easier to learn than those with many characteristics or characteristics that are more abstract. Learners construct an understanding of concepts by analyzing a wide variety of examples in which the characteristics are observable.

Principles, generalizations, and academic rules further simplify the world by describing relationships among concepts. Principles and generalizations describe observed relationships, principles being accepted as true and generalizations having known exceptions. Academic rules are relationships arbitrarily derived by people. Each relationship is learned through a variety of examples followed by applications, just as a concept is.

Problem Solving

Problems describe situations in which individuals have goals but lack obvious ways of achieving them. Well-defined problems have clear goals and clear paths for achieving them; ill-defined problems have ambiguous goals and no clear means of achieving them.

Experts in any domain have thorough knowledge backgrounds organized into complex schemas that allow them to represent problems as relationships in context, to process problems quickly and in some cases automatically, and to monitor their problem-solving efforts effectively. Novices have schemas that are less well developed, often represent problems in isolated pieces, and don't monitor their efforts effectively. Experts spend more time thinking about and planning for problem solving than novices. Teachers can help students become better problem solvers by helping them understand and acquire the problem-solving strategies of experts.

The Strategic Learner

A strategy is a plan for achieving a specific learning goal. Self-regulated learners, in addition to setting and monitoring goals, assume responsibility for their learning and are effective strategy users. Effective strategy users have broad background knowledge, a repertoire of strategies to choose from in reaching their goals, and well-developed metacognitive skills.

Study skills are strategies used to increase comprehension of information in teacher presentations and written text. Comprehensive strategies (like SQ4R and MURDER) as well as specific strategies (like summarizing and self-questioning) are effective in monitoring and improving comprehension.

Thinking skills or critical thinking include reflective strategies designed to improve understanding and decision making. Critical thinking requires thorough domain-specific knowledge, the ability to use basic cognitive processes, well-developed metacognitive ability, and dispositions for open-mindedness and a respect for evidence. Research indicates that critical thinking is most effectively developed in the context of specific topics.

Transfer of Learning

Transfer occurs when learners are able to apply previously learned information to a new setting. Specific transfer involves an application in a situation closely related to the original; general transfer occurs when two learning situations are quite different. Transfer also depends on the amount of time and practice that learners spend on a topic, the quality and variety of the representations they study, and the context in which learning experiences are embedded. Research indicates that transfer tends to be specific. Metacognitive and self-regulatory skills, however, may transfer across domains.

Important Concepts

academic rules (p. 305)

algorithm (p. 314)

basic processes (p. 330)

characteristics (p. 299)

cognitive apprenticeship (p. 321)

cognitive strategy (p. 322)

comprehension monitoring (p. 326)

concepts (p. 298)

concept mapping (p. 302)

convergent thinking (p. 313)

definition (p. 301)

divergent thinking (p. 313)

drawing analogies (p. 316)

elaborative questioning (p. 327)

examples (p. 299)

expert (p. 317)

generalizations (p. 305)

general transfer (p. 334)

heuristics (p. 315)

ill-defined problem (p. 311)

means–ends analysis (p. 315)

novice (p. 317)

principles (p. 305)

problem (p. 310)

prototype (p. 299)

specific transfer (p. 334)

study strategies (p. 324)

summarize (p. 326)

superordinate concept (p. 301)

thinking skills (p. 329)

transfer (p. 334)

well-defined problem (p. 311)

9
Cognition in the Content Areas

CHAPTER OUTLINE

Carla Thompson, a fifth-grader in Hannah Brown's class, sat looking out the window.

She thought to herself, "Man, this is hard. . . . I'm s'posed to make a report on Michigan, . . . and I have to write about 'agricultural products,' and I'm not even . . . really sure what that means. . . . Now what? . . . I'll look in the book. Where was this stuff? Yeah, here it is. Yikes! Three pages. How am I gonna get this down to three paragraphs? I better write some stuff down. . . . Let's see. . . . I'll list everything, like cherries, dairy products, and stuff, and then see if any things go together. . . . At least that's a start," she shrugged.

Suddenly, Carla's work was interrupted by Hannah's voice. "Okay, everyone, you need to put away your social-studies writing assignment and get ready for math," she said.

When the shuffling subsided, Hannah continued, "Class, you'll remember we've been working on how to spend the money the class earned for winning the city's environmental education poster contest. We've got $50, and lots of ideas about how to spend it," Hannah went on, pointing to the board where items like pizza party, trip to the zoo, and software games for the room were listed.

"You remember yesterday we asked everyone to rank these in terms of their first, second, and third choices. Now we need to figure out what to do with the information we collected, which I've put on this sheet that I'm handing out. I'd like you to get into your groups and discuss what to do next."

As Carla slid her desk next to Carlos, Shelly, and Tran, she whispered, "What are we supposed to do?"

"Easy, just tell Mrs. Brown what's our favorite way to spend the money," Carlos replied. "We just need to see which things got the most ones."

"But what about the second and third choices?" Shelly asked. "If you don't get your first choice, shouldn't your second and third ones count?"

"But how do we do that?" Tran wondered as he studied the sheet in front of them.

As different groups discussed the problem, Hannah circulated around the room asking questions and encouraging students to represent their ideas in some form of graph.

After lunch, Carla returned from the playground and fanned herself while Mrs. Brown got out the supplies she needed for her science lesson. These included a basketball, tennis and golf balls, and a flashlight.

She began by asking, "Who remembers what we've been talking about? . . . Sarina?"

"The solar system?"

"And what have we found out about our solar system? Nikita?"

"Well, the sun's in the middle of it."

After reviewing additional information about the sun and the planets, Hannah continued, "Anybody notice what the moon looked like last night? . . . Dewayne?"

"Umm, . . . it was only a piece . . . kind of like almost a half."

"Good, Dewayne. Yes, it was almost a half moon. What makes the moon look like that? . . . Anyone? . . . Look at these pictures [holding up several pictures of the moon in different phases]. Why is the moon completely round sometimes, a half moon at others, and almost nothing or a crescent at other times? Any ideas? . . . Kira?"

". . . Clouds?"

"Tyrone?"

". . . The atmosphere?"

"Kevin?"

". . . It might . . . have something . . . to do with the sun, . . . like solar flare-ups, . . . or whatever."

"Those are all interesting ideas. Let's see if we can figure this question out. First I need some volunteers up here to hold the sun, the moon, and the earth. Let me see. . . ."

Students learn a great deal in schools. They study math, science, reading, social studies, art, music, and other disciplines. How they learn the content in these areas is similar in many ways, and as we discussed theories of learning in Chapters 6 and particularly 7 and 8, we illustrated them with examples from each. Our goal was to demonstrate that learning theories are valuable because they help us understand learning in different contexts.

However, a growing body of research suggests that different forms of content present unique learning challenges (Bruning, Schraw, & Ronning, 1995; Mansilla & Gardner, 1997). In this chapter, we examine learning in four areas: reading, writing, math, and science. Our goal is two-fold. First, we want to see how cognitive learning theories can help us understand the unique aspects of learning in each of these areas. Second, we want to describe instructional strategies that support cognition in each.

After you've completed your study of this chapter, you should be able to meet the following objectives:

- Explain the developmental process of learning to read and how teachers can implement strategies to help students learn to read.

- Analyze cognitive factors influencing the process of learning to write and explain how teachers can facilitate students in this process.

- Describe current views of learning in mathematics and explain implications for instruction in math.

- Explain how students' conceptions of science content influence learning in that area and describe instructional strategies to confront those conceptions.

Learning to Read and Teaching Reading

What is reading? What does it mean to learn to read, and how can teachers help learners in the process? These questions guide us in this first section of the chapter.

We've organized this section into two parts: *learning to read,* which is emphasized in the lower elementary grades, and *reading to learn,* which occurs when students develop enough expertise to use reading as a learning tool—arguably the most powerful tool they'll acquire in school (Adams, 1990). The importance of learning to read can't be overestimated; it opens educational and occupational doors that no other form of learning can. Let's try to understand this process.

Learning to Read

Try reading the following passage.

> We see that two high-energy phosphate groups, one from ATP and one from GRP, each yielding −7.3 kcal/mole under standard conditions, must be expended to phosphorylate one molecule of pyruvate from phosphoenolpyruvate, which requires input of 14.8 kcal/mol under standard conditions. In contrast, when phosphoenolpyruvate is converted in pyruvate during glycolysis, only one ATP is generated from ADP. Although the standard free-energy change G of the net reaction learning to phosphoenolpyruvate synthesis is +0.2 kcal/mol, the actual free-energy change G under intracellular conditions is very strongly negative, about −6.0 kcal; it is thus essentially irreversible.

Did you understand what you "read"? Were you able to pronounce most of the words? If you experienced difficulties, you can understand how students who are not good readers struggle with textbooks. You can also begin to appreciate the developmental process young students go through to figure out how written language works.

Reading is *the translation from symbols or letters to thoughts or speech* (Bruning et al., 1995). The purpose in reading is to get meaning from what we read. Learning to read is a developmental process that builds on **background knowledge**—*general declarative knowledge about the world*—and **linguistic knowledge**—*a person's understanding of the different dimensions of language.* These two kinds of knowledge are acquired by children as they interact with the world and other people.

Reading as a Developmental Process

The process of learning to read begins at birth. Stimuli in the home, walks around the neighborhood, trips to the supermarket, and many other experiences provide background for forming concepts about the world. The richer these experiences, the greater the wealth of *background knowledge* beginning readers bring to the classroom.

Rich experiences with language also influence *linguistic knowledge.* Conversations with adults and peers provide opportunities to learn both vocabulary and the way language works. Exposure to books and other print media, such as cereal boxes and stop signs, helps the learner understand that symbols correspond to both sounds and meaning. Opportunities to sit on someone's lap and talk and think about books help children understand what words and books are about and motivate them to learn to read.

This view of language learning, called **emergent literacy,** *emphasizes that learning to read and write is a gradual process that develops over time* (Clay, 1975). It parallels and depends upon learning to communicate orally (Peregoy & Boyle, 1997). If children are immersed in a world of words, they begin to understand and appreciate the powerful role that printed and spoken words play in communication (Hiebert & Raphael, 1996). Background and linguistic knowledge interact to influence the process of learning to read, as we'll see in the following sections.

9.1

Explain how a trip to the zoo could help develop both background and linguistic knowledge.

Background Knowledge

When learners enter first grade they bring with them an impressive store of background knowledge and a vocabulary of between 5,000 and 6,000 words with which to talk about their experiences (Chall, Jacobs, & Baldwin, 1990). As we saw in Chapter 7, this background knowledge is stored as *schemas*—organized networks of connected information—in long-term memory. These schemas influence both perception and encoding. Let's see how background knowledge lays a foundation for reading.

What is happening in the following passage?

> Toby wanted to get a birthday present for Chris. He went to his piggy bank. He shook it. There was nothing in it. (Adapted from Bruning et al., 1995)

9.2

Chapter 7 described two forms of knowledge in long-term memory: declarative and procedural. What kind of knowledge did you use to make sense of the passage about the piggy bank? In what form is this knowledge stored?

Why did Toby go to the piggy bank? What did he think was in it? How did he know it was empty? Answering these questions (and making sense of the passage) requires background knowledge, as did the passage about energy at the beginning of this section. The information that students extract from text can be categorized as either text explicit (Toby wanted to get Chris a birthday present) or text implicit (Toby expected money in his piggy bank) (Raphael & Pearson, 1985). The background knowledge learners bring to a reading passage allows them to make text-implicit inferences and strongly influences the meaning they take away from what they read.

Linguistic Knowledge

The importance of linguistic knowledge is illustrated by the following passage.

> *Once upon a time a wimmy Wuggen zonked into the grabbet. Zhe was grolling for poft because zhe was very blongby.*

What kind of wuggen was it? What was the wuggen doing and why? Successful answers to these questions require linguistic knowledge, an understanding of the different dimensions of language. The dimension of linguistic knowledge that you used to make sense of the wuggen passage was syntax, the way words in larger units make sense. For example, we know what kind of wuggen it was (a wimmy one) because, in English, adjectives precede nouns.

Other dimensions of linguistic knowledge that contribute to learning to read include:

9.3

How is linguistic knowledge similar to background knowledge? How is it different? Explain.

- Print awareness—understanding that letters and symbols, such as McDonald's golden arches and a child's name on his door, mean something.
- Graphic awareness—recognizing that letters have different shapes or configurations (e.g., *d* and *p*) and that words include letters.
- Phonemic awareness—understanding that speech incorporates a series of individual sounds.
- Syntactic awareness—understanding how sentence-level patterns influence both meaning (e.g., "He did go." versus "Did he go?") and pronunciation (e.g., "read" in "He read the book." versus "Let's read a book.") (Lomax & McGee, 1987)

Reading educators disagree about the relative importance of background and linguistic knowledge in learning to read, as we'll see in the next section (Hempenstall, 1997).

Conflicting Conceptions of Learning to Read

More disagreements probably exist in reading instruction than in any other area of education. Jeanne Chall, in her 1967 landmark book, *Learning to Read: The Great Debate,* divided reading methods into two categories: *meaning-emphasis* and *code-emphasis* approaches. Though understanding is the goal for both methods, they use different strategies to help learners reach that goal.

These camps are deeply divided (Hempenstall, 1997). In 1995, California adopted two statutes called the ABC laws, which require code-based approaches in the schools, because leaders there believed that low reading test scores resulted from meaning-emphasis approaches (Halford, 1997). Let's look at both approaches.

Meaning Emphasis Approaches. **Meaning-emphasis methods** *focus on general comprehension by stressing the functional nature of printed words.* Two prominent meaning-emphasis approaches include *language experience* and *whole language.*

Language experience *uses children's oral language, based on their everyday experiences, as the basis for dictated stories that become the text for learning to read.* Language experience advocates stress the importance of individual students' background experiences in making reading meaningful. From an information processing perspective, language experience should work because the stories are based on information stored in long-term memory. Constructivists explain the effectiveness of language experience by emphasizing that creating a story based on prior knowledge is an authentic task for each learner.

A more recent and comprehensive meaning-emphasis approach, called **whole language,** *integrates reading into the total literacy process (i.e., learning to speak, listen, write, and read).* Most whole-language classrooms use literature as the foundation of the reading process. Books, projects, tapes, and videos are used to discover connections between vocabulary and concepts related to a topic. Three important characteristics of whole language include the following:

1. It uses language to think about and describe experiences, and builds bridges between spoken and written language.
2. It emphasizes the use of language to communicate with others.
3. It applies language across the curriculum, connecting content areas.

Let's see how these characteristics are illustrated in a classroom example.

> Samantha Taylor's third-grade classroom was a beehive of activity. One corner was decorated with a giant paper spider web with drawings and students' written descriptions comparing spiders' eight legs with insects' six. These came from books and videotapes the students had been studying and from a field trip to a park near the school. Students were taking turns reading the descriptions, matching them to the drawings, and checking their answers with a key on the back.
>
> Several students were at their desks, writing about a visit from one of the parents, an entomologist, who had brought a mounted insect collection to class. The rest of the students would later read these descriptions. In a third corner, students were manipulating multiples of six and eight in math to find patterns, and discussing their thinking and answers with each other.
>
> Samantha had the rest of the class in a half circle in front of her. She was reading *The Very Quiet Cricket* by Eric Carle, about a cricket who could not find another cricket to talk to among the insects it encountered in a field. When she neared the end, she stopped and asked each student to create an ending for the story and to share it with the group. Later in the day, students compared their story endings to the book's.

Samantha capitalized on the first characteristic of whole-language instruction by having students write about things they had experienced—insects, the field trip, and the

9.4

Using the piggy bank passage as an example, explain how both code- and meaning-emphasis approaches are necessary for comprehension.

Whole language helps learners see connections between the natural communication processes of speaking, listening, writing, and reading.

visit from the parent. Second, by having the students write and have other students read what they wrote, her instruction complemented children's natural tendency to communicate with others. In time, learners see how reading, speaking, and writing are interrelated, and they learn to communicate clearly (Needels & Knapp, 1994).

Third, whole-language instruction emphasizes the use of language across the curriculum. Teachers will use science, for example, as an opportunity to practice language as well as to study science concepts. Samantha capitalized on this dimension by having her students discuss their thinking and answers in their math activity.

Because of its emphasis on concrete experiences, whole language is consistent with Piaget's view of cognitive development. Its emphasis on dialogue and communication also makes it compatible with social constructivist views of learning.

Code Emphasis Approaches. **Code-emphasis approaches** to reading *stress learning the correspondence between letters and sounds.* Advocates claim that once learned, decoding strategies can be used to identify new words as well as to recognize words learners already know. **Phonics,** probably the most prominent of these approaches, *stresses learning basic letter–sound patterns and rules for sounding out words.* Most code-oriented approaches begin with attention to phonemic awareness.

9.5

How is whole language similar to language experience? How is it different?

Phonemic Awareness. Whenwehearsomebodytalkthesoundscometousinacontinuous-stream. We are able to make sense of the stream by dividing it into separate words or phrases that have meaning. A prerequisite to learning to read is the ability to do the same with spoken and printed words (e.g., cat = k aa tuh). This can be difficult for young children, because they think of words as carrying meaning; focusing on the sounds of words requires a different and sometimes more abstract way of thinking (Tompkins, 1997).

Researchers measure phonemic awareness by asking learners to

- segment words (What are the two sounds in "go"?).
- identify first and last sounds in a word (What sound does "hat" begin with? end with?).
- delete first or last sounds (What would "ham" sound like without the "h"?).
- substitute first and last sounds (Say "ball." Now instead of "b" begin the word with a "t."). (Bradley & Bryant, 1991)

Why are these skills important and how do they contribute to learning to read?

Research supports the need for phonemic awareness (Hiebert & Raphael, 1996). For example, older poor readers scored lower on phonemic awareness than did younger good readers, in spite of the fact that the older readers had exposure to more words (Pennington, Groisser, & Welsh, 1993). Also, young children taught phonemic awareness were more skilled in reading individual words, scored higher on standardized reading tests, and spelled words more accurately than comparable students who did not receive the same training (Bradley & Bryant, 1991; Spector, 1995). Significantly, these differences on standardized reading test scores lasted up to five years.

Decoding. To illustrate the process of decoding, try to read these imaginary words:

figt

phrend

blud

nale

> **9.6**
>
> Is phonemic awareness declarative or procedural knowledge? Explain. What implications does this have for instruction?

Code emphasis approaches to reading stress letter–sound connections in language.

Most people come up with fight, friend, blood, and nail. How do we do this?

American English comprises about 40 sounds or phonemes (Adams, 1990; Tompkins, 1996). These include

- consonants (e.g., *d, b, t*).
- vowels—both long and short (e.g., *hat* and *hate*).
- blends (e.g., *bl, st, tr*).
- digraphs (e.g., *sh, ch, th*).
- diphthongs (e.g., *oi, oy, ou, ow, ar, er, ir, or, ur*).

9.7

What phonetic generalizations allowed you to decode the *ph* in *phrend* and the *ale* in *nale*?

Phonics emphasizes that these approximately 40 sounds are represented by a fixed number of letter and letter combinations, and that once these sounds are learned, we can sound out any new word. Unfortunately, there isn't one-to-one correspondence between letters and sounds (e.g., the *c* in *cent* and the *c* in *cat*) or between letter combinations and sounds (e.g., *change, chaos,* and *chiffon*). However, a number of generalizations such as, "when c is followed by an a, o, or u, it makes a 'k' sound and when followed by an i, e, or y it makes an 's' sound," work often enough to allow learners to use them quite effectively (Tompkins, 1997).

Advocates of decoding argue that, once learned, these strategies allow readers to decipher words automatically and that ". . . as less attention is required for decoding, more attention becomes available for comprehension (Samuels, 1979, p. 405). To test this hypothesis, researchers trained second- through fifth-grade poor readers to decode rapidly by using flashcards that had either single words or phrases on them (Tan & Nicholson, 1997). On a comprehension task in which the target words were embedded in longer passages, the trained group performed better than students who didn't receive such training. Researchers suggested that learning words to the point of automaticity helped bypass a bottleneck in working memory. They believed this strategy was especially effective because the students (a) had not received previous decoding instruction, and (b) the instruction during this experiment also focused on the meaning of words.

While most reading experts believe that decoding is an essential part of successful reading (Adams, 1990; Calfee, 1994; Pressley, 1994), they stress that additional strategies are necessary if students are to become skilled in reading to learn.

9.8

For which of the two approaches—meaning-emphasis or code-emphasis—would background knowledge be more important? For which of the two would linguistic knowledge be more important?

Reading to Learn

At about third grade, the emphasis changes from learning to read to reading to learn. The same controversies persist, however. In reading to learn, **data-driven models** *stress decoding and view reading as a sequential, letter-by-letter, word-by-word analysis of text* (Bruning, et al., 1995). **Conceptually driven views** *suggest that the meaning learners take from text is determined by individual expectations and prior knowledge.* Most experts advocate a combination of the two, in which automatized decoding is guided by background knowledge and strategies (Just & Carpenter, 1987; Kintsch, 1986). In this section we examine how learners use these processes to construct meaning from text.

Components of Comprehension

In Chapter 8, we found that "strategic learners" have broad background knowledge, a repertoire of strategies (particularly comprehension strategies), and well-developed metacognitive abilities. These characteristics are critical in comprehending written text (Mayer, 1999). They are illustrated in Figure 9.1 and discussed in the sections that follow.

Background Knowledge. As we saw earlier, the background knowledge that we bring to text influences both comprehension and attention. It tells us what to look for and how to make sense of ambiguities. Our ability to understand the energy and piggy bank passages, for instance, depended on our background knowledge in these areas.

As another example, read the following passage:

> The procedure is actually quite simple. First you arrange items into different groups. Of course one pile may be sufficient depending on how much there is to do. If you have to go somewhere else due to lack of facilities that is the next step; otherwise, you are pretty well set. It is important not to overdo things.
>
> That is, it is better to do too few things at once than too many. In the short run this may not seem important but first, the whole procedure will seem complicated. Soon, however, it will become just another facet of life. It is difficult to foresee any end to the necessity for this task in the immediate future, but then, one never can tell. After the procedure is completed, one arranges the materials into different groups again. Then they can be put into their appropriate places. Eventually they will be used once more and the whole cycle will then have to be repeated. However, that is part of life. (Bransford & Johnson, 1972, p. 722)

Did you realize that the passage was about washing clothes? If you didn't, don't worry. A group of college students was told beforehand that the paragraph was about washing clothes; a second group wasn't. The students who were told judged the passage twice as comprehensible and remembered twice as much information from it (Bransford & Johnson, 1972). Activating background knowledge increases comprehension.

Background knowledge also influences attention during reading. Students were asked to read the following passage from one of two perspectives—as a prospective home buyer or as a thief. Take one of these perspectives and see what you notice.

> The two boys ran until they came to the driveway.
> "See, I told you today was good for skipping school," Mark asserted. "Mom is never home on Thursday."
> Tall hedges hid the house from the road so the pair strolled across the finely landscaped yard.
> "I never knew your place was so big," Pete said.
> "Yeah, but it's nicer now since Dad had the new stone siding put on and added the fireplace."
> There were front and back doors and a side door which led to the two-car garage, empty now except for three 10-speed bikes.
> They went in the side door, Mark explaining that it was always open in case his younger sisters got home earlier than their mother.
> Pete wanted to see the house so Mark started with the living room. It, like the rest of the downstairs, was newly painted.
> Mark turned on the stereo, the noise of which worried Pete. "Don't worry, the nearest house is a quarter of a mile away," Mark shouted.
> Pete felt more comfortable observing that no houses could be seen in any direction beyond the huge yard. (Adapted from Pichert & Anderson, 1977)

If you read from a burglar's perspective, you probably noted that the house was unlocked, isolated, shielded from view, and full of expensive items like stereos and bikes. A home-buyer's perspective might focus on the size of the lot, stone siding and

Figure 9.1 Characteristics of effective strategy users

Have broad background knowledge

Have a repertoire of comprehension strategies

Have well-developed metacognitive abilities

9.9

The text makes the statement, "Activating background knowledge increases comprehension." Explain how this statement relates to information processing views of learning.

9.10

Your social studies students are reading a section on the agricultural products of your state. You want them to understand the connection between these products and geography and climate. What can you do to encourage this focus in their reading?

The background knowledge learners bring with them to the reading process facilities comprehension.

9.11

Prior to assigning a diffi- cult science passage on the influence of ecology on plant and animal growth, a sixth-grade teacher discussed the ecological environment that students lived in. How might this help students with their reading task?

fireplace, and two-car garage. This is exactly what the researchers found: the perspec- tive taken influenced what readers attended to and the kind of information gleaned from text (Pickert & Anderson, 1977).

In both the clothes-washing and house examples, *schema activation* guided both attention and comprehension. Schemas influence reading comprehension in at least three ways:

- They guide attention by helping us differentiate between important and unimportant information.
- They help us search our memories to provide "slots" for assimilating new information.
- They allow us to make predictions and inferences, filling in gaps and making connections that aren't always apparent in what we read. (Bruning et al., 1995)

Teachers can facilitate comprehension by helping learners access their background knowledge and providing background information prior to reading difficult passages.

Comprehension Strategies.   Comprehension strategies allow us to actively attack print, making sense of passages that aren't clear (Heibert & Raphael, 1996). In Chapter 8, we found that two strategies in particular are effective for promoting comprehension: sum- marizing and self-questioning. In reading to learn, they can be very powerful.

Summarizing may be most powerful. One review concluded that, ". . . the evi- dence to date in favor of this strategy as a facilitator of comprehension and memory is so striking that we recommend the procedure without hesitation" (Pressley, et al., 1989, p. 9). Summarizing is effective because it encourages learners to

- Read for meaning,
- Identify important information, and
- Describe content in their own words. (Hidi & Andersen, 1986)

Identifying important information in what we read is a critical skill. Without it, learners can't allocate their study efforts strategically.

This ability develops over time. Researchers found, for example, that third- and fifth-graders couldn't differentiate between more and less important ideas, seventh-graders were beginning to develop some proficiency, and high-school students were quite good at it (Brown & Smiley, 1977). Further, when given extra time to study a passage, fifth-graders showed no improvement in the amount of important information recalled, seventh-graders showed some, and high-schoolers showed a great deal (Brown & Smiley, 1978). The high-school students were allocating their study efforts more strategically than the younger students.

Learning to put summaries into words takes time and effort. Learners initially tend to select words and phrases from the original text rather than put ideas into their own words. Teachers can help learners develop summarizing strategies in a number of ways:

- Focus on a specific paragraph and help students identify the main idea in it.
- Encourage students to describe main ideas in their own words.
- Use modeling and think-alouds to demonstrate how strategies like outlining and concept mapping can be used to show the connections of ideas in a longer passage.
- Require students to apply these strategies across the curriculum.

Self-questioning can also be a powerful strategy, and one of its most critical components is the ability to draw inferences from the material being studied. For example, what is happening here?

The driver started the car and entered traffic.

Was a key involved in the process?

Was the car in neutral when the engine started?

Did the driver check the traffic flow before entering it?

Did this take place in the city or the country?

Your ability to answer these questions depends upon your ability to make text-implicit inferences. Research indicates that good readers are better than poor readers at making these inferences and that teaching readers to make inferences improves comprehension (Fielding & Pearson, 1994).

Metacognition. In Chapter 7 we found that metacognition involves students' *knowledge* and *regulation* of their cognitive processes during learning. As we read, metacognition allows us to *monitor* our comprehension; it tells us when text makes sense and when it doesn't. For example, read the following passage.

> Many fish live at the bottom of the ocean, where no light can reach. Fish need light to see and find their favorite food, which is a red fungus that grows at the bottom of the deepest parts of the ocean. Being able to find this fungus is very important because a closely related one, which is green, is poisonous. (Adapted from Markman, 1979)

9.12

What features of this text help you identify important information?

9.13

Middle-school students taught outlining strategies improved both their recall and comprehension scores (Taylor & Beach, 1984). Explain how outlining can improve comprehension.

Comprehension strategies allow learners to attack reading passages and construct meaning from text.

Something is wrong here. How can the fish differentiate red from green fungus if there is no light at the bottom of the ocean? When similar inconsistent or contradictory passages were either read to or by younger and older readers, researchers found that

- most sixth-graders can explain why they reread an unclear passage; second-graders can't (Myers & Paris, 1978).

- young readers have problems identifying inconsistencies in text (Markman, 1979).

- when students were told to look for inconsistencies, sixth-graders' performance increased but third-graders' didn't (Markman, 1979).

- children as young as third grade can learn to identify inconsistencies when provided with examples (Markman & Gorin, 1981).

- skilled readers allocate more of their processing time to inconsistent than to consistent parts of passages (Baker & Anderson, 1982).

9.14

Why is rereading a passage an example of metacognition? In your answer, explain the differences between the younger and older students.

Metacognition develops over time, but the process can be facilitated by effective instruction (Hiebert & Raphael, 1996). **Reciprocal teaching,** *is a teaching strategy specifically designed to help students learn to monitor their comprehension* (Palincsar & Brown, 1984; Palincsar, Brown, & Martin, 1987). When using this strategy, students take turns leading dialogues that combine clarifying, summarizing, and predicting into a coherent sequence. These steps, which students apply to each paragraph they read, are outlined in Figure 9.2. Through first seeing these comprehension strategies modeled by the teacher, and then having opportunities to practice, learners internalize the strategies to the point where they use them automatically when they read.

The designers of the strategy emphasize the importance of explicitly teaching it. In doing so, the teacher first describes and models each step. Then students practice the skill and receive feedback. As they gradually internalize the strategy, more responsibility is transferred to them as they assume the role of the teacher when new passages are read and discussed.

Figure 9.2 Comprehension-monitoring steps in reciprocal teaching

1. Summarize	the paragraph for the main idea.
2. Construct a text question	that captures the essence of the passage.
3. Clarify	any points in the passage that are not clear.
4. Predict	what the author is going to say in the next paragraph.

Source: Reciprocal Teaching of Comprehension Strategies: A Natural History of One Program for Enhancing Learning by A. Brown and A. Palincsar, 1985, The Center for the Study of Reading. Copyright 1985 by The Center for the Study of Reading. Reprinted by permission.

Let's look at the strategy in use with a group of students who have read a section of a story about aquanauts. The discussion begins with a student question:

Student 1:	(Question) My question is, what does the aquanaut need when he goes under water?
Student 2:	A watch.
Student 3:	Flippers.
Student 4:	A belt.
Student 1:	Those are all good answers.
Teacher:	(Question) Nice job! I have a question too. Why does the aquanaut wear a belt? What is so special about it?
Student 3:	It's a heavy belt and keeps him from floating to the top again.
Teacher:	Good for you. Now how about a summary for the paragraph?
Student 1:	(Summary) For my summary: This paragraph was about what aquanauts need to take when they go under the water.
Student 5:	(Summary) And also why they need that gear.
Student 3:	(Clarify) I think we need to clarify *gear*.
Student 6:	That's the special things they need.
Teacher:	What's another word for *gear*?
Student 5:	In this story it might be equipment, the equipment that makes it easier for the aquanauts to do their job.
Student 1:	I don't think I have a prediction to make.
Teacher:	(Prediction) Well, in the story they tell us that there are "many strange and wonderful creatures" that the aquanauts see as they do their work. My prediction is that they'll describe some of these creatures. What are some of the strange creatures you already know about that live in the ocean?
Student 6:	Octopuses.
Student 3:	Whales?
Student 5:	Sharks?

(Palincsar & Brown, 1986, pp. 771–772)

Reciprocal teaching is one of the most thoroughly developed and researched study strategies, and it has proven successful with both high and low achievers (Kelly, Moore, & Tuck, 1994; Rosenshine & Meister, 1994). However, it is designed to be used with six to eight students at a time, as opposed to class-size groups, and parts of the strategy are difficult to implement in different content areas. For example, Brady (1990) found that clarifying and predicting were difficult in studying social studies, because of the structure and density of the material. The benefits of question generating and summarizing, however, are well documented (Rosenshine & Meister, 1994).

9.15

How did the teacher provide instructional scaffolding during this reciprocal teaching lesson?

9.16

Explain how structure and density influence students' ability to clarify and predict in social studies texts?

Classroom Connections

Helping Students Learn to Read

1. Create a literacy-rich classroom learning environment.
   - A kindergarten teacher labels common objects around the room like clocks, doors, windows, and chairs. She also puts a sign on each student's desk and chair that says "Maria's desk" and "Antonio's chair."
   - A first-grade teacher creates a number of literacy-focused learning centers. In one, students can read along with big-print books while they listen on tape. Another contains games where learners match words to pictures. In a third, parent volunteers help students create their own stories.

2. Provide a balanced approach that includes both code- and meaning-emphasis components.
   - A first-grade teacher incorporates phonics as one important part of learning to read. During the first part of the year, he uses word families (e.g., *cat, bat, hat*) to illustrate letter–sound correspondence. Later, he encourages students to read predictable books (that repeat the same sentences over and over) to develop reading fluency. He uses students' own writing to forge links between spoken, written, and read words.
   - When second-graders encounter a word that they don't know, they are encouraged to use two strategies: (1) what does context tell you about the meaning of the word, and (2) sound it out and see if it makes sense.

Helping Students Read to Learn

3. Teach students to activate prior knowledge prior to reading.

   - A middle-school teacher uses the KWL strategy (What do I Know?; What do I Want to know?; What have I Learned?) to activate background knowledge (Ogle, 1986). Before reading a passage, she has them list and organize all the information they know about a topic and identify questions that need answering. After reading the passage, the class discusses what they learned from the passage and what additional information they want to know.
   - A fourth-grade teacher uses webbing and concept mapping to help students remember and organize background information before they read chapters in their science and social studies texts.

4. Actively teach comprehension strategies.
   - A middle-school teacher found that her students had problems identifying the main idea in paragraphs. She used think-alouds and modeling to teach finding or constructing the main idea, then gave her students practice and feedback using passages from different texts.
   - A teacher taught reciprocal teaching to her fifth-graders in stages. During whole group instruction, she modeled the strategy and then asked students to practice the steps while she provided feedback. Then she used one small group as the focus and asked the rest of the class to analyze and critique. Finally, she broke the whole class into small groups, monitoring them and providing feedback to the whole group at the end of the lesson.

Learning to Write and Teaching Writing

Learning to write is a complex cognitive task requiring thought and effort by learners and expertise by teachers. To better understand how we learn to write, we compare it to problem solving, and consider what teachers can do to facilitate the process. Let's begin by looking at two sixth-graders faced with a writing task.

Luis and Dave glanced at the blank page in front of them. Both appeared deep in thought. On the board their teacher had written:

> What is your favorite hobby or form of recreation? Why do you like to do this? What does it tell us about who you are?

The assignment was a beginning-of-the-year activity designed to build classroom community and help students get to know each other.

Luis looked at the blank page again and started thinking. He took out a second piece of paper and started jotting down some ideas. He circled some of these words and drew arrows connecting them. As he did, he would periodically glance at the board to remind himself of the task. As he drew on his paper he said to himself, "Now, . . . why is Mrs. Greenleaf asking us to do this? . . . Oh, . . . yeah, to share something about ourselves with the class. What about myself would they be interested in? Stamp collecting—nah, too nerdy. How about soccer? Wonder if they know anything about soccer? I like to play soccer, but I'm not sure how to explain why. Hmm . . . why don't I start out by listing some of the things I like about soccer and see if they make sense."

Dave, in contrast, sat slouched at his desk, tapping his pencil against the desk and looking out the window.

"Hobby? Recreation? What does she mean? Favorite . . . I like to do all kinds of things. Why do I like them? I don't know. How long does this have to be? Lunch is only half hour away—if I can just finish it by then, I won't have to take it home. . . . Well, here goes. 'My favorite sport is soccer. I like to play soccer. I play sweeper on my team.'"

Writing as Problem Solving

Some experts describe writing as a form of problem solving (Kellogg, 1994). When we face a writing task, we try to define and mentally represent it, just as we do when we have a problem to solve.

Two factors influence this process. The first is the **task environment,** *which includes the writing assignment itself and available resources.* The task environment determines how complex defining the problem will be (Hayes & Flower, 1986). For example, if you're required to write an essay describing the implications of cognitive learning theory for teaching, you're likely to first consider the assignment itself: what it's about, how long it needs to be, who you're writing for, and why you're writing the essay (e.g., for a grade, extra credit, learning exercise, or portfolio entry). Then you probably will want to know what resources you can use, such as collaborating with others, or referring to articles and papers. Accomplished writers consider elements of the task environment automatically; novices often need help in considering resources. The components of the task environment are illustrated in Figure 9.3.

Knowledge is a second factor influencing the writing process. As we saw in Chapter 8, background knowledge is critical for problem solving, and it is equally important for writing (Kellogg, 1994). Writers draw on at least two kinds of knowledge when they write, the first being conceptual or *domain-specific knowledge.* When faced with the

<aside>
9.17

The first three steps in the problem-solving model described in Chapter 8 were *identify the problem, represent the problem,* and *select a strategy.* Explain how these processes were different for Luis and Dave.
</aside>

<aside>
9.18

Using the implications of the cognitive learning theory writing assignment as an example, explain how resources influence the writing task.
</aside>

Figure 9.3 Elements of the writing task environment

educational psychology writing task, for example, you will first assess what you know about the topic and how this knowledge can be used to complete the assignment.

The second is **discourse knowledge,** or *an understanding of how language can be used to communicate.* Communication through writing is facilitated by conventions such as indenting the beginnings of paragraphs, capitalizing the first words of sentences and using appropriate punctuation. As opposed to domain-specific knowledge, which is a form of declarative knowledge, discourse knowledge is a form of procedural knowledge. Figure 9.4 shows knowledge added to the writing model.

The Writing Process

Armed with our understanding of the task environment, together with our conceptual and discourse knowledge, we're ready to begin. Or are we? Research examining learners' strategies as they grapple with a writing task suggests that strategies can be divided into three stages:

- Planning,
- Translating, and
- Revising. (Hayes & Flower, 1986; Hayes, 1996)

These stages are combined with the elements of the task environment and our knowledge to provide a comprehensive model of writing, as seen in Figure 9.5.

Planning

During the **planning stage** *we set goals and generate and organize ideas* (Mayer, 1999). *Goal setting* identifies the purpose for the product. It can be as vague and general as filling up a page with words or as complex as trying to inform or persuade another person.

Once goals are set, *generating ideas* provides the raw material for our efforts. Internal processes (like brainstorming) and outside sources (such as books and journals,

Figure 9.4 The influence of task environment and knowledge on the writing process

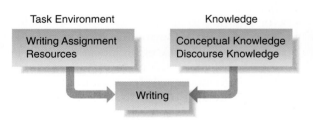

9.19

How are linguistic and discourse knowledge similar? different? What implications do these similarities and differences have for instruction?

9.20

In Figure 9.5, arrows that connect planning, translating, and revising go both ways. Why do they go both ways? Provide an example to explain your answer.

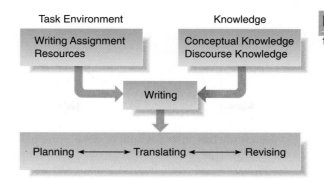

Figure 9.5 A model of the writing process

the Internet, notes, and other people) can both be used to generate ideas. Once generated, the ideas need to be *organized* in some coherent way.

These processes are consistent with cognitive learning theory. For instance, constructivists view the planning process as the creation of new ideas based on learners' existing understanding, and they emphasize the importance of authentic writing tasks and scaffolding. Information-processing theorists emphasize the existence of declarative and procedural knowledge (in the form of strategies) in long-term memory.

We saw these processes in Luis's efforts. His goal was to share something of himself with his classmates. He took a few moments to generate ideas and he organized his ideas by drawing arrows to connect them.

It was quite different with Dave. His goal was to get the job done by lunch. He started writing immediately, and any ideas he generated evolved as he wrote them. Because of this inattention to planning, it is unlikely that he will generate a high-quality product.

9.21

How was Luis's and Dave's writing assignment authentic? What might have made it more so?

Learning to write is a complex process that involves planning, translating, and revising.

Research confirms these differences. Good writers devote up to two thirds of their writing time to planning, focusing on large issues such as the audience and how the final product holds together (Matsushashi, 1987). Less effective writers jump into the task with little forethought, focusing their planning on specifics, such as how to begin, and adding sentences as they think of them. These differences parallel those between expert and novice problem solvers: when faced with unfamiliar problems, experts plan carefully before attempting solutions, whereas novices plan only briefly before jumping into a solution.

Research has also identified developmental trends in planning (Bereiter & Scardamalia, 1987). Five- and six-year-olds, for example, have difficulties generating ideas, likely as a result of their limited background knowledge (Caccamise, 1987).

Eight- to twelve-year-olds can generate ideas but have trouble evaluating and organizing them. We saw this in Dave's writing, which was primarily "knowledge telling"—spewing out ideas in much the same form as they were generated. This results in short and disorganized final products (Stotsky, 1990).

Teaching planning strategies improves writing. For example, teaching college students to list ideas and organize them in outlines improves written products. We should emphasize, however, that simply listing ideas without organizing them or considering their relevance—as in brainstorming—did little to improve writing (Kellogg, 1987). If college students need instruction in writing strategies, younger learners need it even more.

The importance of planning can be explained on the basis of information processing (Kellogg, 1994). If writers fail to plan, during translation their working memories are overloaded with two simultaneous tasks—planning and translating. Further, we would predict that planning strategies would be effective based on our understanding of metacognition.

Translating

In the **translation stage,** *we put our ideas on paper in an effort to communicate with others.* Though the products appear on paper, the major work in this stage is done in working memory, where ideas and words interact. This poses problems for young and inexperienced writers. Let's look again at the challenges Dave and Luis faced as they attempted to translate their ideas into words. Dave wrote:

> My favorite sport is soccer. I like to play soccer. I play sweeper on my team. Sweeper is import . . . ("Hmm, how do you spell *important?* . . . Oh well.") Playing sweeper is fun because we get to go after the ball a lot. Me and Luis are the best sweepers on the teem. Coach says we're import . . . because . . . Coach says he needs us to keep the other team from . . . scoring. That's why I like soccer. The end.

In the desk next to Dave, Luis is also translating his ideas into words.

> My favorite sport is soccer. I like playing on a team. There is lots of action, and when you work hard you can win. Teamwork is import . . . importund. Dave and I are both sweepers on the team. Our job is to stay in front of the goal. We make sure no clear shots are taken at the goal.
>
> When you are a sweeper there is lots of responsubility. People really depend on you when you're the sweeper. Sweepers help a team win.

In comparing the two essays we see that Dave and Luis both struggled with translating their ideas into meaningful sentences that follow spelling and grammar conventions. They used invented spellings, wrote around words they didn't know how to spell, and used simple sentence structure.

There are important differences, however. Dave's is essentially a string of unconnected sentences. Luis's, in contrast, suggests some organization, and it also indicates effort to write to an audience. For instance, when he introduced the term *sweeper* he didn't assume the reader knew what the term meant. Dave used the same term but didn't define it, and he also used the word *we* to refer to someone he hadn't yet discussed. Let's see how these problems correspond to patterns researchers have documented in developing writers.

Writers face several simultaneous challenges as they attempt to put their ideas on paper (Nystrand, 1986):

- Graphic challenges   writing legibly so that others can read what's written

- Syntactic challenges   using appropriate grammar and punctuation

- Semantic challenges   using ideas that make sense to readers

- Textual challenges   creating sentences and paragraphs that form a cohesive whole

9.24

Which of these translation challenges can be addressed during the planning phase?

Young writers often use so much working memory space on the first two levels that little is left for the other two tasks. Significantly, instruction designed to improve first-graders' handwriting skills improves general writing ability (Berninger, et al., 1997).

Attempts to consciously bypass these hurdles have proven successful. For example, to bypass the graphic challenge, researchers allowed fourth- and sixth-graders to dictate rather than write their own essays (Bereiter & Scardamalia, 1987). This resulted in essays that were twice as long and better quality. To bypass the syntactic challenge, young writers can be allowed to initially make grammatical errors and use invented spellings, saving the corrections for the revising stage (Atwell, 1987; Graves, 1994). In fact, overemphasis on grammar and punctuation, as evidenced by red ink corrections all over an assignment, can discourage developing writers from taking risks.

Even simple words of encouragement influence the amount young students write. For example, for both fourth- and sixth-graders, written cues to continue writing (e.g. "You're doing fine. Now what do you want to say next?") resulted in essays that were 50% longer than those for whom cues weren't given (Scardamalia, Bereiter, & Goel, 1982). Writing tasks, even short ones, can seem monumental to young writers, and teachers' support and encouragement are important emotional scaffolds for them.

Revising

In the **revising stage,** *we reflect on what we've written and edit and improve our initial attempts.* It involves at least three tasks:

- Improving the overall structure and organization of the piece.

- Ensuring that the meaning of sentences and paragraphs is clear.

- Detecting and correcting errors in spelling and grammar. (Hayes & Flower, 1986)

Let's look at Dave's essay again and see what he might do to improve it.

My favorite sport is soccer. I like to play soccer. I play sweeper on my team. Sweeper is import . . . ("Hmm, how do you spell *important* . . . Oh well."). Playing sweeper is fun because we get to go after the ball a lot. Me and Luis are the best sweepers on the teem. Coach says we're import . . . because . . . Coach says he needs us to keep the other team from . . . scoring. That's why I like soccer. The end.

The essay could be improved in at least three ways. First, it could be organized so there is a logical flow of ideas from the beginning to the end. For example, after saying that his favorite sport is soccer, he might write a sentence like, "I like it because I play sweeper, and sweepers get to go after the ball a lot." Second, he could define *sweeper* and help the reader understand that the first *we* in the passage refers to himself and the other sweeper. Third, spelling and punctuation could be cleaner. Each of these aspects, while demanding, can be taught.

Research on the revision process has produced the following generalizations:

- As writers improve, they spend more time on organization and less on superficial issues like spelling and grammar.

- Expert writers spend a greater proportion of their total writing time on revising than do novices.

- Even skilled (and older) writers have problems detecting errors—especially their own. (Fitzgerald, 1987; Hayes & Flower, 1986)

Research indicates that revising greatly improves writing quality and that experts are better at this process than novices (Hayes & Flower, 1986). Information-processing theory explains this in two ways. First, the information in experts' long-term memories is better organized and, second, their writing strategies are more developed.

Instruction can help learners improve their revising strategies. For example, sixth-graders who were taught to add, delete, substitute, and rearrange their written products did significantly more revising than comparable students who received no instruction. Also, their stories improved more than the stories by students who did not receive strategy instruction (Fitzgerald & Markman, 1987).

9.25

Using information processing as a basis, what could teachers do to improve the revision process?

Helping Students Learn to Write

Writing instruction is changing (Mayer, 1999; Kellogg, 1994). Historically, writing was viewed as the process of creating a product by applying specific procedures. Transmitting information succinctly and accurately was emphasized. Current views describe writing as a process of solving problems and transforming information in an attempt to communicate ideas. These differences are summarized in Table 9.1.

Let's look at the implications these differences have for the way we teach students to write.

Table 9.1 Changes in views of writing

	Previous View of Writing	Present View of Writing
Definition of writing	Writing as a product	Writing as a process
Goal of writing	Disseminate knowledge	Transform knowledge
View of the writing process	Composition	Communication
Learner task	Application of procedures	Solve problems

A Cognitively Oriented-Writing Classroom

Jennifer Stevens, Luis and Dave's sixth-grade teacher, read their essays before putting them on the bulletin board to share with others.

"Looks like we've got some work to do this year," she thought with a shake of her head as she finished stapling the last one on the board.

The next day she began her language arts class by saying,

"Class, this year we're going to practice our writing. I know all of you can write because I read the essays you wrote about yourselves. But I think you can become better writers by thinking about what you're doing while you're writing.

"Let me show you what I mean. Let's imagine that I need to write an essay about how to do something, like fix a bicycle tire. What's the first thing that I'd do?"

After listing suggestions from the class on the overhead, Jennifer continued, "These are all good ideas, and I think you'll see that many of them are included in a strategy sheet that I want to share with you.

"When we write something new, it's like thinking on paper, but before we put our ideas down, we need to think about what we're going to say. I have a planning sheet that will help each of you become better writers."

With that she shared this overhead (Figure 9.6) with the class.

"Now, the first thing I need to think about is, Who am I writing this paper for? Probably this person has ridden a bicycle and knows some names for the parts but maybe doesn't know how to fix a tire. That's why I'm writing this paper."

Figure 9.6   Cues to aid a writing assignment

Planning to Write

Name _____   Date _____

TOPIC _____

Who: Whom am I writing for?

_____
_____
_____

Why: Why am I writing this?

_____
_____

What: What do I know? (Brainstorm)

1. _____
2. _____
3. _____
4. _____

How: How can I group my ideas?

_____   _____
_____   _____
_____   _____

How will I organize my ideas?
_____ Comparison/Contrast   _____ Problem/Solution
_____ Explanation   _____ Other

Source: Adapted from Englert, Raphael, and Anderson (1989).

9.26

Identify an example of each of the characteristics of present views of writing listed in Table 9.1 in Jennifer's lesson.

Jennifer went through the rest of the planning sheet, then she gave the class a new topic—making a sandwich—and had each student go through the steps, first individually and then with a partner. Finally, the class as a whole discussed what they had learned.

As we saw earlier, learning to write is complex, but teachers can help with effective instruction that incorporates the following:

- Teach writing strategies through modeling and think-alouds.
- Embed strategies in a context of writing with a purpose.
- Provide students with opportunities to practice strategies and receive feedback from peers and the teacher.
- Create a community of writers where learners share their works, discuss their thinking, and dialogue with their peers (Bruning et al., 1995; Mayer, 1999).

9.27

What did Jennifer do to ensure that the strategies students were learning were flexible and could be applied to other situations?

Teach Specific Strategies. Writing instruction has moved away from a product-oriented, one-right-way approach toward an approach that emphasizes strategies that can be used with different topics and audiences. For example, since organization is a problem for developing writers, teaching students different ways to organize information—such as outlining or creating hierarchies—provides them with strategies that can be used with a variety of writing tasks.

How much structure should we provide in teaching these strategies? This question was answered convincingly by a review that compared

- teacher-centered expository approaches that focused on grammar, punctuation, and standard formats,
- "pure" discovery approaches that gave students ample opportunities to write but left them largely on their own, and
- guided discovery that was interactive, using structured rating sheets and teacher and peer feedback to assess student writing.

The guided discovery approaches proved to be three times more effective than pure discovery and four times more effective than traditional, teacher-centered, expository approaches (Hillocks, 1984). As we saw in Jennifer's lesson, modeling, think-alouds, and opportunities for teacher–student interaction can provide the structure that students need to learn writing strategies.

Embed Strategies in a Larger Context. While learners need structure and guidance to learn specific writing strategies, these strategies should be embedded in the context of writing for a purpose. For example, opinions written to the editor of a school newspaper, inquiries to audiotape and CD catalogues, and letters to pen pals in other cities all provide opportunities to see how writing relates to the real world.

9.28

What did Jennifer Stevens do to embed her writing instruction into a larger context?

Most importantly, the teaching–learning process must be contextualized and situated within the actual writing process, rather than talked about abstractly or removed from the process and reduced to a set of memorized writing principles, scripts, or rules. (Englert, Raphael, Anderson, Anthony, & Stevens, 1991, p. 364)

The researchers found consistent results favoring contextualized strategies for high and low ability students as well as those with learning disabilities (Englert et al., 1991).

Creating a community of writers provides opportunities for developing writers to share their works and receive feedback from their peers.

Provide Opportunities for Practice and Feedback.   As we saw in Chapter 8, an essential component of helping students become effective strategy users is the opportunity to practice strategies in a variety of settings and receive feedback. Learning to write is no different. Students need opportunities to learn strategies in one context and practice them in a variety of others to ensure transfer and retention (Bruning et al., 1995; Englert et al., 1991; Mayer, 1999).

Create a Community of Writers.   When we write, we share both our ideas and ourselves, and this sharing involves taking risks. In the past, writing was a solitary task and learning to write was viewed as something best done alone. As constructivist views of learning have become more prominent, this view has changed. Growth in the process requires a community of colearners that we can become a part of and learn from. Just as learning communities support learning in reading (Palincsar & Brown, 1984), math (Forman, 1996), and science (Linn, Songer, & Eylon, 1996), they provide developing writers with support, differing perspectives, and feedback. Social interaction, which has proven to be effective in promoting learning in general (Brown, 1994; Rogoff, 1990), also appears to be an essential ingredient in learning to write.

Classroom Connections

Helping Students Learn To Write

1. Teach specific strategies through modeling and think-alouds.
   - A third-grade teacher is trying to help students understand strategies to organize their writing. She begins by saying, "Let's brainstorm some ideas about pets for our writing assignment." After writing a number of ideas on the board she asks them to connect related ideas through webbing.
   - To teach revision strategies, a high-school teacher places an example of a short writing assignment with organization, clarity, grammar, and punctuation errors on an overhead. She asks, "Where should we start?" With input from the class she systematically revises the essay, starting with clarity issues and then moving to grammar and punctuation problems.

2. Embed specific strategies in a context of writing with a purpose.
   - To help his students understand how audience influences the way persuasive letters are written, a middle-school teacher allows his students to write letters to the school board and parents to try to convince these groups to oppose a proposed dress code. Before writing the letters, the teacher assigns students to groups, has them think of arguments that would persuade their audience, and discusses the ideas with the whole class before the class writes their letters.
   - A sixth-grade teacher reinforces her writing instruction by asking students to use planning and revision strategies in their social studies reports. She asks them to first turn in an outline, then a first draft to which other students respond, and, finally, a final revision.

3. Give students opportunities to practice strategies and receive feedback.
   - A fifth-grade teacher has students write in their journals the first 15 minutes of each day. She collects the journals each Friday and writes comments and questions in an effort to promote clarity.
   - A middle-school teacher breaks students into groups and gives students an editing checklist to provide feedback to each others' writing. The checklist asks students to evaluate organization, clarity, punctuation, and grammar. Students then revise their works based on this peer feedback.

4. Create a community of writers.
   - A high-school teacher uses response groups as a way to provide peer feedback to each others' works. Students read their works out loud and others in the group comment on what was clear, what wasn't, and what they liked about the essays.
   - A second-grade teacher works with her students to write simple stories that they convert into books. Each child's book is bound by parent volunteers in the school publishing room. Students then take turns sitting in the author's chair and reading their book to the class.

The Challenge of Diversity in Learning to Read and Write

As we've seen in the previous two sections, learning to read and learning to write are cognitively challenging tasks for all learners. This is especially true for non-native English speakers and cultural minorities. Obstacles for these learners include:

- Background knowledge that differs from topics they're asked to read and write about.
- Lack of linguistic knowledge in English, including vocabulary and structural knowledge.
- Problems with confidence in their ability to use English to read and write. (Hernandez, 1997; Peregoy & Boyle, 1997)

These learners have a working knowledge of their home languages and they want to learn to use English to communicate with others. In this section, we examine ways that teachers can help learners with diverse backgrounds in learning to read and write English.

Creating a Supportive and Language-Rich Learning Environment

Classrooms can be scary places for students, especially when they are unable to understand much of what occurs. Effective teachers of cultural minority and English-as-a-second-language learners make special efforts to explain the structure of the day and preview future learning activities. Let's look at an example:

> Ms. Reed meets with a group of seven English-language learners several times during the day for a variety of reasons (e.g., language arts instruction, one-on-one tutoring). One recurring theme in these meetings, which may last anywhere from 3 to 30 minutes, is to discuss and describe future events and activities. For example, Ms. Reed spent 15 minutes on activities and discussion that focused on an impending field trip to a nearby forest. During this meeting, she told the students about the forest, provided pictures of the terrain, and provided new vocabulary that they would be having to deal with in their interactions with the nature guides. During this interaction, she was able to address individual questions that students had about the forest and what they would be encountering there. (August & Pease-Alvarez, 1996, p. 39)

These discussions allowed the teacher to explain classroom procedures and assess and supplement learners' background knowledge, and gave the students a chance to ask questions and practice using English.

Perhaps most important is Ms. Reed's willingness to take the time to work with these students, which communicates caring and a commitment to their learning. If cultural minorities feel welcome, their motivation to learn English and immerse themselves in the mainstream of the classroom and school may increase dramatically.

9.29

Why might classroom procedures be confusing to minority or non-English speaking students?

Providing Scaffolding in Literacy Activities

Scaffolding in literacy activities can take a number of forms. Some of them are described in the following sections.

Background Knowledge

Gaps in background knowledge present barriers for both reading and writing. Comprehension depends on a range of cultural factors that may not be evident to the teacher. For example,

> A middle-school text about an adolescent testing the limits of her personal freedom with her parents . . . may be largely incomprehensible to students from cultures

that place more value on respecting parents and less on individuality—not because they fail to understand the words or even the sentences, but because they fail to grasp the cultural value Americans place on individuality. And it is this social factor that shapes the meaning of the text. (Williams & Snipper, 1990, p. 22)

As another example, when Ms. Reed was previewing the forest field trip, one of the students mistook the word *guide* for the word *guy* and asked, "How can the guys have names like Mary and Suzy?" As sensitive teachers talk with their students, they diagnose and build on gaps in background knowledge.

Linguistic Scaffolds

Effective instruction for cultural minority students also provides linguistic scaffolds. In working with non-native English speakers, "accept and build upon"—a strategy recommended for working with learners having non-standard dialects—can be effective. For example, Natalia, a native Russian speaker in this country for only four months says:

Natalia:	I putting the marker on the points.
Teacher:	Those are called dots. You're putting the marker on the dots.
Natalia:	The dots.

(Peregoy & Boyle, 1997, p. 52)

By focusing on the vocabulary term *dots* and ignoring grammatical errors such as *I putting,* the teacher helps Natalia build her word knowledge in a supportive manner.

The same supportive scaffolding is effective when evaluating students' writing products. For example, when evaluating the following writing sample produced by Jorge, a fairly fluent Hispanic third-grade reader who is just learning to read and write in English, a teacher would want to identify and build on his strengths.

Jorge Describes the Differences Between Two Kinds of Birds

Tey are the same becaes the bofe of them haves two eggs and there head and there foot and they are not the same becaes they don't eat the same thing and ther beak and one place is the mountain and one is the valley. the end. (Peregoy & Boyle, 1997, p. 201)

We see that Jorge's content knowledge is quite good (he is able to identify similarities and differences in the birds' eggs, heads, beaks, food, and location), and he is willing to use invented spelling to convey ideas. Building on these strengths, a teacher would help him develop spelling, grammar, and punctuation skills.

Meaningful Learning Activities

Perhaps the most important strategy in helping cultural minority and ESL students learn to read and write is to embed literacy tasks within a larger contextual framework. As opposed to abstract or fragmented literacy assignments, contextualized comprehensive tasks provide concrete experiences for students to read and write about.

The sea is a radiant water galaxy. It's a world of its own in a special way. Under its foam created surface, there exists a universe of plant and animal life. With the tiniest microscopic beings to the most humumgus creature that ever lived, the sea is alive! (Kids of Room 14, 1979, p. 1)

This is the opening passage of a 79-page book that Lynda Chittenden's fourth- and fifth-graders produced as a result of their study of the sea near their school. The class

9.30

How could the invented spellings that students use be interpreted as a strength rather than a weakness?

took several field trips to the sea, visited a seal rookery, observed gray whales migrating, observed dolphins in training, and had marine biologists visit their classrooms. They recorded their experiences in learning logs. One journal entry read like this,

> Today I learned how important it is to have blubber. Our class went swimming in a
> 40 degree pool. I did learn that I COULD swim in that temperature. But, I couldn't
> even breathe the first time I jumped in. Gradually I got better. I could swim two
> laps without flippers. But I still don't see how a whale could live in 33 degree
> water, even with layers and layers of blubber. (Kids of Room 14, 1979, p. 16)

First-hand experiences made abstract ideas—such as relationships between water temperature and blubber—meaningful to students.

Integrated units such as these are effective for English language learners because they provide rich opportunities to use language in purposeful activities (Peregoy & Boyle, 1997).

Learning and Teaching Mathematics

We began the chapter by looking in on a fifth-grade classroom. Let's look in on another now.

> Gena Evans, the teacher, walked casually to the front of the room holding a banana. As she began to peel it, she looked at it pensively and said, "I wonder how much banana I'm actually getting for my money. . . . Look at that (pointing to the peel). Sure is a lot of peel. . . . I wonder how much I'm paying for peel."
>
> "Same thing with oranges," Kevin interjected. "I had an orange this morning, and it was all peeling."
>
> "That's an interesting idea," Gena nodded. "I wonder if we get more for our money with bananas or with oranges. . . . Any idea how we might figure that out. . . . Thinking about my banana again, if I paid 49 cents a pound for it, how much was I paying for the peel?
>
> "Tell you what," she continued after a few seconds of silence. "I want you to work in your teams for a few minutes, and let's see if we can figure out how to determine which one, a banana or an orange, gives us more for our money."
>
> Used to doing groupwork, Gena's students quickly went to work, while Gena circulated among them, listening to their discussions and making brief comments.
>
> After a few moments she called for their attention and asked for their ideas.
>
> "We think . . . we should put a banana peel down and also an orange peel, and . . . see which is thicker," Andrea volunteered for her team.
>
> "What if some bananas are thicker, . . . I mean if their skin is thicker?" Devon wondered.
>
> "Good question," Gena nodded. "What do the rest of you think?"
>
> "Maybe we could have a bunch of bananas, . . . and oranges too," Shelly offered. "Then they might . . . sort of . . . even out."
>
> "What do you mean, 'even out'?" Gena wondered.
>
> "Well, like, . . . you know we could have . . . a thick one . . . and a thin one and . . . some others, and then we . . . like, . . . you know, like . . . we even them out, sorta."
>
> "You mean like find the average," Gena smiled.
>
> "Yeah," Shelly nodded.
>
> "How could we find the average?" Gena wondered.
>
> After a few more comments, Gena saw that her students were uncertain about the concept of averaging, so she did an example using several of the children's

heights. She then had them do some additional examples, where they first estimated the average weight of several students, calculated the average, and did the same with the lengths of their arms. This took up the remainder of their time, and Gena changed their homework assignment for the next day to problems that required them to find averages.

The next morning Gena had the children review what they had done, and then asked, "So, where are we with the banana peel problem?"

"We think we oughta weigh the banana and orange, . . . and then peel 'em, . . . and then weigh them without the peels," Candice began.

"How about weigh the peelings too?" Brad wondered.

"Well, yeah, I . . . guess so."

"We should do a bunch of them and find the average," Latasha suggested, remembering yesterday's work.

The class generally agreed that weighing the bananas and oranges and peels was a good strategy. Some suggested that they should weigh the unpeeled and peeled bananas and oranges and compare them. Others suggested that they should weigh the unpeeled bananas and oranges and the peels and compare them. Still others thought it would be better if they did both.

Gena encouraged each of the strategies, commenting that often there isn't necessarily one best way to attack a problem. Then, over the next three days, the students tried their strategies, got results, and discussed and evaluated what they had done.

Changing Views of Learning Mathematics

As cognitive views of learning have become more prominent, they have helped us better understand the complexities of learning, including the role that learner motivation, beliefs, expectations, and strategies play in determining how much students learn. To place this understanding in context, let's first look at the way learning and instruction in mathematics have historically been viewed.

Historical Views of Learning

Historically, math in this country has been taught in a highly proceduralized way (Woodward, Baxter, & Robinson, 1997). For example, students learned to convert fractions to percents by (a) dividing the numerator of the fraction by the denominator, and (b) moving the decimal point two places to the right. For instance, converting 3/8 to a percent involves: $8\overline{)3.0} = .375 = 37.5\%$. Emphasis was on mastery of the algorithm.

9.31

How does the learning of math as procedures parallel historical trends in the history of writing instruction?

This approach—though not always a conscious application—was consistent with behaviorism. The steps are specific and observable, and learners can be reinforced for demonstrating the steps or given corrective feedback if they don't.

There are at least two problems with this method. First, students learn to perform the operations but don't understand why, so they do poorly on more complex tasks requiring the operations; i.e., transfer is limited. We can see how this might happen. For instance, other than simply accepting it because we're told to do so, why do we place a decimal point after the 3 when we divide it by 8? Also, we're told that 3/8, .375, and 37.5% are equivalent. On the surface, 3/8 and .375 don't appear to be related; what allows us to simply move the decimal point two places and then add the percent symbol? Understanding math requires more than the manipulation of symbols.

Second, learners commit random and chronic errors and fail to question the validity of their answers. This is due to lack of conceptual understanding as well as confusion with the algorithms themselves; they forget or misapply some of the steps.

Culture of the Classroom

Classroom culture refers to *characteristics of the teaching/learning environment, including the values, expectations, language, learning experiences, and unspoken rules, and conventions that guide the day-to-day operation of the classroom* (Tishman, Perkins, & Jay, 1995). Classroom culture influences learning in a number of ways, including the beliefs learners acquire and the strategies they use.

Beliefs about Learning Mathematics.   Research indicates that many American students hold negative and unproductive beliefs about learning mathematics.

- Math learned in school has nothing to do with the real world (Davis, 1989; Greer, 1993; Verschaffel, De Corte, & Lasure, 1994).

- The ability to do mathematics is innate; i.e., some have it and some don't (Hess, Chih-Mei, & McDevitt, 1987; Stevenson, Lee, & Stigler, 1986).

- Solving a math problem shouldn't take more than a few minutes. Problems that take longer are impossible to solve (Schoenfeld, 1988).

- Math consists primarily of rules and procedures to be memorized, there is only one right way to solve a problem, and the goal in doing mathematics is to get the right answer (Lampert, 1990; Schoenfeld, 1992b).

The sources of these beliefs are complex. Society as a whole and teachers in particular hold similar beliefs about mathematics (De Corte, Greer, & Verschaffel, 1996). As teachers interact with students and structure their math lessons, these beliefs become part of the classroom culture.

Learner Strategies.   Classroom culture also results in students acquiring superficial coping strategies for solving problems. A common one is looking for key words, such as *altogether,* which suggests that addition is the operation required, or *how many more,* which implies subtraction. Others include performing the operation most recently taught, or looking at cues in chapter headings of the text.

Unfortunately, these strategies often bypass understanding completely, yet can be quite successful (Schoenfeld, 1991). When they don't work, learners are often at a total loss, resulting in accepting results that make no sense in the real world. For example, consider the following problem:

> *The fourth-graders at Washington Elementary School are going on a field trip, and the school is scheduling buses. If each bus has a capacity of 40 and 140 students are making the trip, how many buses are required?*

In a problem such as this, learners commonly react to specific words in the problem, such as, *If each . . . has a capacity,* and *how many . . . are required?* They may decide that division is the required operation, get an answer of three and a half, and conclude that three and a half buses are required, without reacting to the fact that half a bus is meaningless.

Learning Mathematics: Cognitive Perspectives

The increasing influence of cognitive views of learning has helped us understand why unproductive learner beliefs and superficial strategies can detract from a meaningful understanding of mathematics.

9.32

Look again at the list of beliefs about learning mathematics. Which of the beliefs is most strongly related to learners' tendency to be satisfied with "three and a half buses" as an answer to the problem?

Effective mathematics instruction emphasizes learning strategies aimed at deep understanding.

These theoretical views are corroborated by research. American students tend to fare poorly in international comparisons of achievement, particularly compared to students in China and Japan (National Center for Educational Statistics, 1992). These differences appear in overall achievement, measures of mathematical reasoning (Silver, Leung, & Cai, 1992), and learners' ability to verbalize their mathematical understanding (Stigler, Fernandez, & Yoshida, 1992).

Researchers have identified several likely contributors to the achievement gap:

9.33

Research indicates that American teachers have much less preparation time than their Asian counterparts (Stevenson, 1992). How might this explain why instruction in these classrooms is more complex?

- Lessons in these countries emphasize problem solving and are taught in a reflective, relaxed, and nonauthoritarian manner (Perry, Venderstoep, & Yu, 1993).

- High levels of interaction take place in lessons, and teachers guide learners' thinking rather than dispensing information. Compared to American students, they spend much less time doing seatwork (Fernandez, Yoshida, & Stigler, 1992; Lappan & Ferrini-Mundy, 1993).

- Mathematics is more strongly related to students' lives than it is in this country (Stigler & Stevenson, 1991).

- Asian students are on-task for a greater percentage of their instructional time than American students (Stevenson, 1992).

Instruction in these countries is more consistent with cognitive views of learning. For instance, from our study of Chapter 8, we see that problem solving is grounded in both information processing and constructivism. Constructivism also helps us understand why high levels of interaction are important and how relating mathematics to students' lives makes their tasks more nearly authentic.

Cognitive Views of Learning: Implications for Instruction

Like the changes in views of both reading and writing, Gena Evans's work with her students reflects attempts to move instruction in mathematics away from a behaviorist orientation and toward a framework guided by cognitive views of learning.

These attempts are endorsed by the professional leadership in mathematics. Most significant has been the work of the National Council of Teachers of Mathematics (1989) with the publication of the *Curriculum and Evaluation Standards for School Mathematics.* The *NCTM Standards,* as they're commonly called, contain ambitious goals. At a societal level, they call for reform resulting in mathematically literate workers, increased participation of historically underrepresented groups in the study of mathematics, lifelong learners, and an informed electorate.

At the school and classroom levels the *NCTM Standards* assert that

- Mathematics is a problem-solving activity, not the application of rules and procedures.
- Math involves reasoning (with heavy emphasis on estimation) more than memorization.
- Studying mathematics should make sense.
- Math is communication.
- Math should relate to the real world.

9.34

What are some different ways that teachers could emphasize "math is communication"? Give at least one specific, concrete example.

At the same time, the *NCTM Standards* de-emphasize proceduralized aspects of instruction, such as memorizing facts and relationships, using clue words to determine which operation to use, performing paper and pencil computations, practicing routine problems and skills out of context, and teaching by telling. We can see the shift from behaviorism to cognitive views of learning reflected in the changing emphasis. (The *NCTM Standards* are undergoing revision; revised standards will be available for 2000/2001.)

Characteristics of Effective Math Instruction

To examine math instruction based on cognitive views of learning, let's look again at Gena Evans's lesson. Some of its characteristics were

- a focus on problem solving,
- real-world application,
- emphasis on reasoning, and
- high levels of interaction.

A Focus on Problem Solving. Gena's lesson focused on problem solving, the activity took several days, and the problem was nonroutine. (You recall from Chapter 8 that a routine problem is one for which a ready-made procedure for finding the solution exists, such as the problem with the buses.) Like Laura Hunter's students in Chapter 8, Gena's students had to devise their own strategies for solving the problem, and the problem could be solved in different ways. No single strategy was necessarily better than others.

Real-World Application. Not only did Gena's lesson focus on problem solving, but it also emphasized a real-world problem that was intrinsically motivating. This application provided context for some important concepts and procedures. For instance, the students learned the concept of *average* and were given practice in finding averages. They also dealt with finding the fraction or percentage of the fruits that were peel, and they dealt with consumer issues. Each concept was more meaningful because it was studied in the context of a real-world problem.

If students were provided with enough experience in solving problems such as the one in Gena's lesson, some of their unproductive beliefs, such as *math learned in school has nothing to do with the real world, solving a math problem shouldn't take more than a few minutes, math consists primarily of rules and procedures to be memorized,* and *math has nothing to do with other content areas* would eventually be dispelled.

Emphasis on Reasoning.   Reasoning was at the heart of Gena's lesson. For instance, realizing that the peels from the fruits would vary in thickness and concluding that they would need to average several samples required reasoning. Reasoning was also required to determine how much of the fruit was peel and what proportion of the total cost was paid for peel.

Gena helped promote reasoning by guiding the students as they discussed possible solutions instead of simply explaining how the problem should be solved and having the students try to perform operations presented in the explanation.

High Levels of Interaction.   Gena also emphasized interaction as she guided the students' progress. High levels of peer and teacher student interaction were used to analyze the problem.

Interaction is critical to learning math, and cognitive views of learning help us understand why. Interaction puts learners in an active role, and activity is at the core of cognitive learning theory. Interaction also allows learners to describe their current understanding and it requires the use of language—characteristics that are consistent with constructivism, particularly Vygotsky's views.

In addition, a knowledge of students' thinking is essential if teachers are to provide the scaffolding necessary to guide learning (Fennema, Carpenter, & Franke, in

9.35

Think back to Jenny Newhall's lesson in Chapter 7. Explain how her lesson illustrated each of the characteristics described here.

Problem-based learning helps students connect abstract math concepts to the real world.

press). In order to understand students' thinking, we must interact with them and listen as they interact with each other.

Cognitive Views of Learning: Experimental Programs

The emphasis on cognitive views of learning has resulted in a series of experimental programs, all consistent with the positions taken by the NCTM. Four are outlined in Table 9.2.

While a detailed discussion of these approaches is beyond the scope of this text, we want to highlight important similarities. Each focuses on problem solving, all are based on the belief that mathematics should make sense, all emphasize real-world application, and in all, the teacher's role is to guide learning rather than to lecture and explain.

Research examining these approaches has been positive. Compared to control students, students in CGI classrooms, for example, solved problems more effectively and

9.36

Identify one other characteristic that all the approaches have in common.

Table 9.2 Experimental approaches in the reform of mathematics

Experimental Approach	Characteristics
Cognitively Guided Instruction (CGI) (Fennema, Carpenter, & Peterson, 1989)	• Primary grades • Focus on solving word problems • Applications to students' lives • Strategy development • Guided discovery and modeling • Emphasis on understanding learner thinking as a route to teacher development
Teaching for Understanding (Lampert, 1989)	• Intermediate grades • Emphasis on processes, dialogue, relationships, and multiple methods • Involving learners in problems that matter to them • Teacher guides instruction
Anchored Instruction (Cognition and Technology Group at Vanderbilt, 1990, 1994)	• Emphasis on authentic problems • Problem situations presented in story form (instructional anchors) • All information needed to solve problems are embedded in the anchors • Supported by technology • Teacher guides and coaches learners
Heuristic Problem Solving (Schoenfeld, 1987, 1992a)	• Emphasis on real world problems • Focus on strategic aspects of problem solving • Emphasis on metacognition • Teacher guides whole-class and small-group discussion

were more confident in their mathematical ability, and their computational skills were comparable (Villasenor & Kepner, 1993). Similar results occurred for students in anchored instruction (Van Haneghan, Barron, Young, Williams, Vye, & Bransford, 1992), heuristic problem solving (Schoenfeld, 1992a), and teaching for understanding (Lampert, 1992).

Putting Reform into Perspective

Gena Evans's lesson was consistent with cognitive views of learning, as well as teaching as emphasized in the *NCTM Standards* and the models described above. These approaches are demanding, and they're not without their critics. Let's consider some of these perspectives.

First, implementing reforms is difficult and won't happen quickly (Ball, 1996). Lessons like Gena's are time consuming and require high levels of organization and teacher expertise. A great deal of content and pedagogical content knowledge is required—knowledge that teachers often lack (Graeber & Tirosh, 1988; Lampert, 1989; Simon, 1993).

Reform efforts have also been criticized by conservative critics who assert that

- basic skills are being abandoned at the expense of "fuzzy" mathematics where estimates replace right answers,

- the "new" math is a misguided attempt to promote self-esteem at the expense of learning, and

- the reform efforts are one more example of widespread "dumbing down" of the curriculum.

To put both the reforms and the criticisms into perspective, we want to make three points. First, when teachers are faced with change, they sometimes tacitly come to believe that everything they've done to that point should be abandoned. For instance, since problem solving is being emphasized, teachers sometimes conclude that they should forget about facts and basic skills. This isn't the case. Children need to know basic math facts, and most children won't learn the facts as incidental aspects of problem solving; they must be practiced to automaticity (Weinert & Helmke, 1995). This is consistent with information-processing theory, and reformers don't disagree. Reformers argue, instead, that the excessive amount of time students now spend in drill and seatwork activities isn't the best way to produce meaningful learning.

Second, reformers aren't suggesting that learners be allowed to believe that any answer they get is as good as any other answer. "Anything goes" is a misinterpretation resulting from a superficial understanding of the reform efforts.

Third, the success of any reform depends on teachers; teacher knowledge is critical. Our goal in writing this chapter is to increase teachers' knowledge bases, so they can make decisions that result in the most learning possible for their students.

Classroom Connections

Helping Students Understand Mathematics

1. Embed operations and processes in the context of real-world problems.
   - A fourth-grade teacher whose class is working on addition and substraction of two-digit numbers gives her students problems such as, "You've gone to a convenience store, bought a soda for 79 cents, and a pack of gum for 35 cents. You give the clerk $2.00. He gives you back three quarters, a dime, and a penny. Did you get ripped off?"
   - A first-grade teacher has each of the children put 9 counters under one hand and, without looking, move 5 of them into view. She asks, "How could I figure out how many are left under my hand?"

2. Promote learner reasoning and emphasize that answers in mathematics must make sense.
   - The teacher who presented the problem with the convenience store purchases has students describe their thinking as they try to determine whether or not the clerk took advantage of them.
   - The first-grade teacher working with counters emphasizes "sense making" with questions, such as,
     "How do we know that our answer will be less than 9?"

"How do we know that our answer will be more than 1?" and after they get an answer,
"How do you know that your answer is correct?"
"How could we check to be sure our answer makes sense?"

3. Require students to provide estimates before they perform calculations.
   - A seventh-grade teacher working on percents and decimals has the students solve problems such as, "A jacket that sold for $40 is marked down 20%. How much is the sale price?" Before solving the problem, she requires an estimate.

4. Promote high levels of interaction in math lessons.
   - The teacher who presented the problem with the convenience store purchase has the students work in groups for five minutes to discuss their solutions to the problem and their reasoning. She then guides a whole-group discussion of the problem.
   - The teacher who presented the problem with the jacket requires several students to explain how they arrived at their estimate. She also has them explain how they arrived at the discount price.

Learning and Teaching Science

To begin this section of the chapter, let's look again at Hannah Brown's students in the chapter's opening case. In response to her question about why the moon is completely round sometimes, a half moon at others, and only a crescent at still others, the students gave answers such as, "Clouds," "The atmosphere," and ". . . something to do with the sun, like solar flare-ups." The students obviously had some misconceptions about the moon's phases and what causes them.

Now let's change the subject and try a couple of simple exercises. Imagine that you're playing catch, and you've just thrown a baseball to your partner. The drawing below represents the path of the ball while it's in the air. Point A is just after the ball has left your hand, Point B is the top of the arc, and Point C is just before your friend catches it. Draw arrows at A, B, and C to illustrate the direction of the forces on the ball at each of these points. (Assume air resistance is negligible and can be ignored.)

As a second example, imagine that you have a tennis ball tied to a string, and you whirl the ball in a circular path around your head. Suppose you let go of the string. Which of the drawings below best illustrates the path of the ball after it's been released?

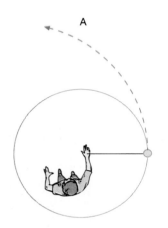
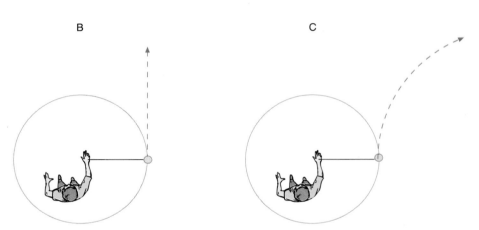

Now let's see how you did. In the first activity, if air resistance is ignored, the only force acting on the baseball at each of the three points is gravity, which means you should have drawn one arrow pointing downward at each of the points.

If you didn't respond this way, you're not alone. In tasks similar to yours, researchers found that more than two thirds of the participants failed to correctly describe the forces, including those who had taken a college physics course (Clement, 1983; Osborne & Freyberg, 1985).

In a task similar to the second activity, researchers found that a third of the college students in their study, again including those who had taken a physics course, selected Choice A, indicating that the ball would continue to travel in a curved path (McCloskey, Caramazza, & Green, 1980). Newton's law of inertia, however, states that a moving object continues moving *in a straight line* unless a force acts on it, so Choice B is most valid.

In looking at these examples, we see that learners commonly have a number of misconceptions about the way the world works. This was illustrated in Hannah's students' thinking about the phases of the moon and in the results we just saw. Why do learners think this way, and what does cognitive learning theory have to offer us in trying to explain it? We examine these questions in the sections that follow.

Difficulties in Learning Science

Students often find that science is more difficult to learn than other subjects. This is true for at least three reasons. First, science courses typically introduce a great many new concepts very quickly. In fact, some researchers argue that middle- and high-school science texts introduce more new vocabulary per page than foreign language texts (Carey, 1986). More important, however, are two other factors:

- Life experiences often lead to naive theories and beliefs, and
- Curricula and instruction fail to confront learners' current understanding.

Let's examine them.

Life Experiences and Naive Theories

Let's look again at the activities that you did. In the first one, typical suggestions for the forces operating on the ball are illustrated in the following drawing:

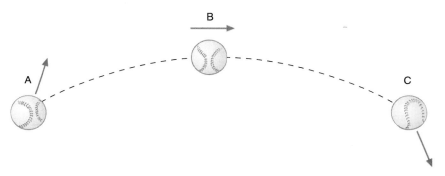

Intuitively, they make sense. For instance, at Point A the ball is traveling both up and foreword, so it makes sense that there would be a force in this direction. The same applies at Points B and C.

In the second activity, since the ball is traveling in a circle, it also makes sense that it will continue in a curve once released. In fact, that probably makes more sense than concluding that the ball will suddenly begin to travel in a straight line. Once released, however, it does go straight, as evidenced by slings such as the one David used to slay Goliath.

Naive theories are *intuitive understandings learners construct based on their day-to-day experiences* (Anderson & Roth, 1989; Glynn, Yeany, & Briton, 1991; Smith & Anderson, 1984). Many well-documented examples exist. For instance, students commonly believe that green plants, rather than manufacturing their own food, get their food from outside sources, just as animals do. This makes intuitive sense. We feed ourselves and other animals. We water plants, and we even buy containers of plant food to sprinkle on them. So the misconception about green plants is sensible; in fact, probably more sensible than the idea that plants manufacture their own food.

Naive Theories: Theoretical Explanations. Cognitive views of development and learning help us understand why learners form and retain naive theories. First, all cognitive theories view learners as actively trying to make sense of the world. This means that they don't passively respond to the environment as behaviorists assume, nor do they

9.37

Some people believe that the earth is closer to the sun in the summer (our northern hemisphere summer), and this is the reason our summers are warmer than our winters. In fact, the earth is slightly farther from the sun in summer. Identify at least one common life experience that could lead to this invalid conclusion.

9.38

If a car is traveling along a highway at a steady rate of 60 mph, most people believe that the force pushing the car forward is greater than the forces holding it back. In fact, the forces forward and backward are equal. Explain why people think as they do.

Hands-on science activities allow learners to construct meaningful science concepts.

9.39

Which view of learning—behaviorism, information processing, or constructivism—best explains why learner understanding varies dramatically, even though all learners in a class have heard the same accurate explanation of a topic?

simply absorb information in the form it is presented. They construct understanding that makes sense to them and, as we saw in the previous section, many naive theories are more intuitively sensible than the accepted theories. So naive theories allow learners to establish and maintain equilibrium, which is the cornerstone of Piaget's theory, as we learned in Chapter 2.

Once formed, naive theories form all or parts of *schemas,* which we described in Chapter 7 as *organized networks of connected information.* These schemas are stored in long-term memory and retrieved when needed to help learners understand new experiences. Changing a misconception requires that schemas be modified; i.e., the network of connected information must be reorganized. This reorganization is demanding and disrupts a learner's equilibrium; it's easier to simply retain the misconception. That is exactly what learners will do unless a new conception is more sensible to the learner than his or her previous understanding.

Curriculum and Instruction

As we saw in our discussions of constructivism in Chapters 2, 7, and 8, learners tend to interpret new experiences based on their existing understanding. They use any naive theories they have to interpret new information, which means that additional understanding will be even further distorted.

Unfortunately, curriculum developers and teachers generally fail to confront learners' existing ideas. Information is commonly presented in general and imprecise terms, allowing learners to interpret new information on the basis of their naive theories (Anderson & Smith, 1987). For instance, in our example with the baseball, physics texts discuss in detail the forces that initially propel the ball, the height the ball travels, and the distance it travels. Precise descriptions of the forces on the ball *in flight* are rare, however. This is typical for much of science curricula.

Teachers also fail to confront learners' existing conceptions, falling into one of three categories, none of which is very successful in leading to valid and deep understanding of the topics being studied (Smith & Anderson, 1984):

- Activity-driven teachers focus on learner involvement in hands-on activities, assignments, and demonstrations. They tacitly assume that student engagement in the activity equals learning.

- Expository-directed teachers present information with their own naive belief that accurate presentation of content equals similarly accurate learner understanding.

- Discovery-oriented teachers allow students to continue interpreting new information on the basis of their existing ideas, even if those ideas aren't valid. Such teachers are guided by the belief that teacher intervention in learning activities is ineffective.

Unfortunately, each of these teaching approaches has shortcomings. In the first case, simply having students do a hands-on activity will do little to change naive theories; learners simply interpret the experience based on their current understanding. As we saw in Chapter 7, "hands-on" activities are not necessarily "minds-on" activities.

Second, expository instruction is consistent with the view that learners *record* rather than *construct* understanding, a view of learning that is being increasingly discredited. Finally, research confirms that "pure" discovery learning is often inefficient and frustrating for learners (Hardiman, Pollatsek, & Weil, 1986; Schauble, 1990).

So what do we do about learners' lack of understanding in science? Cognitive learning theory can help us find some answers.

9.40

Research indicates that naive theories must be directly confronted if learners are to develop more mature understanding. Using Piaget's work as a basis, explain why this is so.

Helping Learners Understand Science

Deeper learner understanding of science requires two critical changes (Anderson & Roth, 1989):

- adapting the curriculum and
- refocusing instruction.

Adapting the Curriculum

Programs effective in increasing learners' understanding of science adapt the curriculum in two ways. First, they reduce technical vocabulary to those terms that are absolutely essential for explaining other ideas (Anderson & Roth, 1989). Second, they emphasize depth over breadth, something that American science courses haven't historically done. Program developers must make decisions about what topics are most important to teach, teach them in depth, and eliminate less important topics.

> Parsimony is essential in setting out educational goals. Schools should pick the most important concepts and skills to emphasize so that they can concentrate on the quality of understanding rather than on the quantity of information presented. (Rutherford & Algren, 1990, p. 185)

The National Research Council, in presenting its *National Science Education Standards* (1996), suggests less emphasis should be placed on "covering many science topics," and more emphasis should be placed on "studying a few fundamental science concepts" (p. 113).

This shift in emphasis has important implications for science teachers. Textbooks and curriculum guides are likely to present an overwhelming array of information. In using these materials, teachers must identify critical topics to be covered in depth, others to be examined less thoroughly, and still others to eliminate completely.

Refocusing Instruction

We saw that none of the three traditional approaches to instruction—activity-driven, expository-directed, or discovery-oriented—are very successful in promoting valid and deep understanding of science in learners. So how can instruction be refocused to increase learning?

Fortunately, research provides some answers (Anderson & Roth, 1989; Driver, Asoko, Leach, Mortimer, & Scott, 1994; Nussbaum & Novick, 1982; Pintrich, Marx, & Boyle, 1993). Figure 9.7 summarizes these results, which are discussed below.

Figure 9.7 A model for effective science instruction

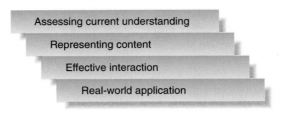

Assessing current understanding

Representing content

Effective interaction

Real-world application

Accessing Current Understanding. Our study of cognitive learning theory helps us understand why learners form naive theories and beliefs. It also helps us understand why learners are reluctant to give them up—a reluctance confirmed by research.

To directly confront learners' naive theories and beliefs, we must first understand what they are. This means that we must assess learners' current understanding. To do so, Nussbaum and Novick (1982) suggest that lessons begin with an *exposing event*—a problem or demonstration that requires explanation. Hannah's question, "What makes the moon look like that?" was such an event, and the students' answers revealed major misconceptions about the phases of the moon. The questions we asked about the forces on a baseball in flight or the path of the tennis ball are also examples. As learners offer their explanations, their present understanding is revealed. Once revealed, teachers are in a position to directly confront learners' existing understanding. We consider learners' current understanding again in the section "Effective Interaction."

Representing Content. In Chapter 8 we saw that concept learning requires high-quality examples, and representing problems is an essential step in successful problem solving. Promoting meaningful learning in science is similar: *multiple, concrete* representations of topics are essential. For instance, suppose you're trying to understand Bernoulli's Principle, which says that as the speed of air over a surface increases, the force the air exerts on the surface decreases (the principle that explains why airplanes are able to fly). At this point, the principle is probably not meaningful to you, so let's go on. Hold two pieces of paper as shown in the following drawing, lean over, blow between them, and observe what happens to the papers.

You likely saw that they came together at the bottom. Your blowing between the two pieces of paper and seeing them come together is a representation of Bernoulli's Principle. It is a single, concrete representation, illustrating the second element of the model in Figure 9.7.

You probably can't construct a valid understanding of the principle based on this single representation, however, so additional ones are necessary (Brenner, et al., 1997; Spiro, Feltovich, Jacobson, & Coulson, 1992). For instance, take one of the papers, hold it as shown in the following sketch, and blow vigorously over the top. This is a second, concrete representation. In this case, the paper rose up as you blew.

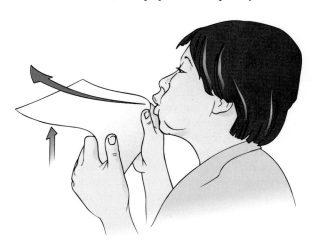

9.41

Using our discussion of cognitive learning theory as a basis, explain why more than one representation is necessary in order for learners to construct understanding of the topics they study.

The two representations we just examined are concrete examples of Bernoulli's Principle. While concrete representations are desirable beginning points—and should be used if available—other alternatives exist. Models, sketches, mathematical formulas, and even verbal descriptions can serve as representations.

Effective Interaction.   We saw earlier that involvement in an activity won't necessarily produce learning; neither will representations of content. But, as we saw in Chapter 7, learning *is* facilitated by social interaction. Unfortunately, typical science instruction is often teacher-centered, lacking adequate opportunities for teacher and student dialogue.

Social interaction promotes meaningful science learning in at least five ways:

- When combined with high-quality representations it allows teachers to assess learners' current understandings.
- It helps create cognitive conflict.
- It promotes a community of learners.
- It allows teachers to provide scaffolding for learners.
- It helps learners develop an understanding of the nature of science.

Think again about the two pieces of paper and, before reading further, write a brief description that explains why the papers came together at the bottom. Include a sketch with your explanation. The explanation and sketch will reflect your current understanding about Bernoulli's Principle.

If your explanation is typical, you suggested that as you blew, the air curled around the papers at the bottom and pushed the pieces of paper together, as shown in the following sketch.

9.42

What label would Nussbaum and Novick (1982) use to describe you blowing between the two pieces of paper? What is the purpose in having learners perform an activity such as this?

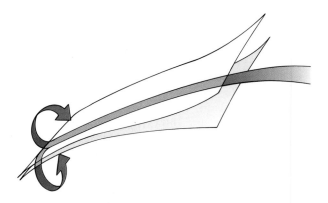

As we've said repeatedly, one of the characteristics of constructivism is that new learning depends on current understanding. We've also said that science is sometimes difficult for learners because they bring naive theories and beliefs to the learning experience. This leads us to the role of cognitive conflict.

Cognitive conflict *occurs when learners are no longer satisfied with their existing understanding,* and consequently struggle to develop understanding that makes more sense to them. In the absence of cognitive conflict, learners remain satisfied with what they currently know. Promoting learning in science requires identifying learners' current understandings, so naive theories and beliefs can be directly confronted (Anderson & Roth, 1989; Bruning, et al., 1995). Confronting naive or incomplete conceptions is important, because learners won't change their thinking until their current understanding is demonstrated to be implausible.

Introducing cognitive conflict requires a teacher's skilled guidance in a supportive community of learners (Anderson & Roth, 1989). In a **community of learners** *the teacher and students work together to develop understanding of the topics they're studying.* In a learning community, teachers introduce problems (such as why the two papers came together at the bottom), students offer explanations based on their current understanding, and the merits of these explanations are examined in small- and large-group discussions.

9.43

What concept from constructivism is the teacher applying when she asks timely questions and helps students arrive at valid understandings of the topic?

The teacher's role in these discussions is critical. She must guide students so discussions don't wander unproductively, ask timely questions that cause students to reconsider their current thinking, and ultimately help students arrive at a valid understanding of the topic. Simply explaining, or intervening too soon, robs learners of the chance to develop their own understanding. Not intervening soon enough can detract from learning because time is wasted and learners become uncertain and frustrated.

As an example of this process, let's look at how Clarice Torres, a fourth-grade teacher, guides her students toward an understanding of Bernoulli's Principle.

Kathy:	I . . . think air . . . kinda . . . like curled around the bottom and then pushed the papers together.
Clarice:	What evidence do we have for that?
Kathy:	They . . . went together. Something had to do it.
Clarice:	Does everyone agree . . . ?
Devon:	I . . . I'm not so sure. . . . Why would the air just go around . . . like that?
Kathy:	I dunno. . . . . It just did.

Clarice:	(After waiting several seconds in which no one talked) What do any objects that are moving want to do? . . . Anyone?
Devon:	Go straight . . . They want to go straight.
Clarice:	So what does the air want to do?
Tiffany:	Go . . . straight? . . . It . . . wants to go straight . . . I . . . guess.

As the discussion continues, Clarice asks students to analyze the forces on the papers and consider where the air is moving more rapidly. Gradually, they conclude that the faster-moving air (resulting from blowing) between the papers must have reduced the force between them, so the papers are pushed together by the slower-moving (still) air outside them.

This brief case illustrates the characteristics of effective interaction that we outlined earlier in this section. First, the discussion—together with students' direct experience—led to cognitive conflict. Their original thinking was becoming less plausible to them.

Second, Clarice didn't simply explain why the papers came together; instead she guided students' thinking as their understanding evolved. This occurred within a supportive community of learners.

Third, Clarice's guidance provided a form of scaffolding. Without this scaffolding it is unlikely that the students—on their own—could have arrived at an understanding of the principle. Her scaffolding was a critical part of the process.

Finally, as learners acquire experience in science learning activities like this, they learn that conclusions are made on the basis of evidence, figure out how to gather the best evidence possible, and develop a tolerance for ambiguity. These are characteristic of science as a way of understanding the world.

Real-World Application. Learning science can be intrinsically motivating, because much of what students learn in science can be directly applied to the real world. We saw earlier that Bernoulli's Principle helps us understand how airplanes are able to fly—a very real-world application. Studying inertia helps us understand why cars sometimes can't negotiate curves, why seatbelts and airbags are important safety features, and how the spin cycle works in an automatic washer. Understanding that green plants make their own food helps us understand producers, consumers, and food chains. Examples could be given for nearly every topic learners study. As learners acquire experience, they come to believe that science is, in fact, an integral part of their lives.

Social interaction provides opportunities for students to work collectively on developing their understanding of science concepts.

Classroom Connections

Helping Learners Understand Science

1. Access learners' current understanding.
   - A first-grade teacher places two large, deflated balloons on a balance to demonstrate they have the same mass. To demonstrate that air has mass, she then inflates one of the balloons and puts it back on the balance. When the children see that the side of the balance with the inflated balloon on it goes down, she asks them to explain why they think it happened.
   - To demonstrate *convection* as a method of heat transfer, a fifth-grade teacher places a covered baby food jar full of hot, colored water into a beaker of cold water. She pokes a hole in the cover, allowing a stream of colored water to rise from the baby food jar to the top of the cold water. She then asks the students to explain why they think the colored water rose to the top.

2. Provide as many concrete representations of topics as possible.
   - A third-grade teacher burns paper, puts vinegar into baking soda, and shows the students a piece of rusted iron to demonstrate chemical changes. She contrasts these examples with crumpled and torn paper, melting ice, and brewing coffee to illustrate physical changes.
   - A chemistry teacher demonstrates Charles' Law by putting one balloon in ice water and another in hot water to demonstrate changes in volume resulting from different temperatures. She links the demonstration to the relationship $T_1/V_1 = T_2/V_2$ and has the students solve problems using the equation.
   - A life-science teacher illustrates the concept of *camouflage* by scattering different colored toothpicks on measured areas of grass on the school grounds and has the students find as many as possible in 2 minutes. She also shows colored slides of snakes, insects, fish, and mammals in their natural habitats to illustrate how they are protected by their coloration.
   - A sixth-grade teacher helps her students understand *adaptation* by displaying a cactus (very small leaves—needles—to prevent loss of moisture) and a broad-leafed plant and showing pictures of plants in their natural habitats. She also shows pictures of Arctic hares with small ears (so they won't lose too much heat) and Southwestern desert rabbits with large ears. She has the students consider why elephants have such large ears, why antelope have long legs, and why alligators' eyes are near the tops of their skulls—all to illustrate how organisms adapt to their environments.

3. Promote high levels of interaction in your teaching.
   - The fifth-grade teacher teaching *convection* has the students explain why they think the colored water rose to the top of the cold water. During the discussion she helps them see relationships between heat, expansion, density, and flotation, and links each of these ideas to the concept of *convection.*
   - A sixth-grade teacher has her students work in groups to determine what factors would influence how fast aspirin tablets would dissolve. She monitors their work as they discuss and consider factors such as the volume and temperature of the liquid in which the aspirin are placed, the type of liquid, and whether or not the aspirin is left whole or is crushed. She then has the teams discuss their findings in a whole-group discussion.

4. Make tasks and problems as authentic as possible.
   - The chemistry teacher whose class is studying Charles' Law presents problems such as, "You have this balloon here at room temperature, and we're going to put it in the freezer. In 4 hours what will the volume of the balloon be?"

To solve the problem, the students estimate the volume of the balloon and measure the temperature in the room and the freezer. They then calculate the balloon's volume in the freezer.

- The teacher whose students examined the dissolving rates of aspirin has them discuss reasons why the experiments' results would provide useful knowledge, such as how quickly pain reliever would be absorbed into a person's system.

Looking Across the Content Areas

As we've seen in this chapter, the different content areas pose unique learning and teaching challenges. Despite these differences, however, some common elements and issues exist across the disciplines. Let's look at them.

Common Threads in Learning and Teaching

The following elements all influence learning in each of the content areas:

- Learners' background knowledge
- The use of learning strategies
- Language and dialogue
- Multiple representations of content and authentic tasks

Learners' Background Knowledge

Background knowledge influences learning in each of the content areas, but it does so in different ways. In reading, it serves as a foundation for comprehension. In writing, it acts as a storehouse for ideas. Learners' combined procedural and declarative knowledge help them identify and solve different types of problems in math. Naive conceptions often hamper learning in science. But in each of the content areas, new understanding builds on existing learner schemas.

Effective teachers assess learners' background knowledge and use this information to adapt their instruction. Questioning, quizzes, short writing assignments, and other activities such as concept mapping can all be used to assess learners' current understanding.

The Use of Learning Strategies

All four content areas require active strategic learners. Effective readers attack text strategically. Effective writers frame their writing with goals and sub-goals. Math and science both require learners to become actively involved in making sense of new information.

Effective teachers provide explicit instruction in strategy use by explaining and modeling strategies (Rosenshine, 1997). They describe their thinking as they model, and they give learners many opportunities to practice strategies in a variety of contexts and receive feedback.

Language and Dialogue

Sharing and comparing ideas with language and dialogue also facilitate learning in all four content areas. The foundations of linguistic knowledge are found in dialogue, and student interaction is central to reciprocal teaching. The use of clear language is the central focus of writing, and both math and science learning are enhanced by opportunities to discuss and analyze our own and others' ideas.

Teachers promote the use of language by creating supporting learning environments in which students are willing to take risks. Teachers encourage learners to speculate, predict, share ideas, and analyze others' thinking in a supportive and nonthreatening way (Hiebert & Raphael, 1996). Teachers create these classrooms by establishing standards for acceptable behavior, modeling, promoting the involvement of all students with questioning, and encouraging learners as they struggle with difficult ideas.

Multiple Representations of Content and Authentic Tasks

Learning in all four content areas is enhanced when ideas are represented in a variety of ways and tasks are embedded in realistic activities. Comprehension is enhanced when learners are required to read from a variety of realistic sources—books from different content areas, magazines, newspapers, and other sources. Writing improves when learners write about a variety of topics that are personally meaningful to them. Learning in math and science best occurs when problems and applications are linked to real-world examples.

In all four areas we saw movement away from abstract, detached disciplinary learning toward more functional and applied approaches. The creation of meaningful and applied learning tasks benefits learning, motivation, and transfer (Pintrich & Schunk, 1996; Shuell, 1996; Wittrock & Mayer, 1996).

Summary

Learning to Read and Teaching Reading

Learning to read occurs in two stages. The first emphasizes deriving meaning from symbols and requires background and linguistic knowledge. The second emphasizes the use of strategies to gain information from text.

Code-emphasis approaches target decoding skills, such as translating the sounds of letters into words. Phonics, a code-emphasis approach, stresses letter–sound relations and rules for sounding out words. Meaning-emphasis approaches stress the functional nature of printed words and reading as one element of the communication process.

In the middle elementary grades the emphasis shifts to reading to learn. Through self-regulatory processes, such as summarizing and self-questioning, readers learn to monitor their comprehension and improve the amount they learn from reading.

Learning To Write and Teaching Writing

Learning to write requires understanding of task requirements and background and discourse knowledge. In the planning stage, writers generate and organize ideas. During translation, they put ideas on paper, and in the final stage—revising—they correct errors, clarify ideas, and restructure the piece to make it more organized and cohesive.

Writing instruction has shifted toward a process emphasis, where communication and problem solving are emphasized over rule-driven procedures. A cognitively-oriented writing classroom emphasizes creating a community of writers and teaches writing strategies within the context of meaningful tasks.

The Challenge of Diversity in Learning to Read and Write

Different background knowledge, lack of linguistic knowledge in English, and lack of confidence in their ability to use English effectively are obstacles for cultural minorities. Teachers help overcome these obstacles by creating supportive and language rich environments that include concrete experiences, linguistic scaffolds, and meaningful learning activities. Most important are caring teachers who welcome and embrace all students.

Learning and Teaching Mathematics

Learning mathematics requires a shift in emphasis away from mastery of procedures and rules to an understanding of the reasons behind these rules. Effective teachers create a classroom culture in which traditional beliefs about math are challenged and replaced with strategies that allow learners to attack problems in meaningful ways. Effective math instruction focuses on real-world problem solving, emphasizes multiple solutions to problems, and forges connections to other content areas.

Learning and Teaching Science

Learning and teaching science are complicated by the naive theories that learners bring to learning experiences. Based on life experiences, naive theories often conflict with accepted scientific explanations.

Increasing learner understanding requires change in both science curriculum and instruction. The curriculum needs to emphasize depth over breadth, focusing on key ideas. Instruction needs to represent content more effectively, encourage thoughtful dialogue about content, and apply content to real-world applications.

Important Concepts _____

background knowledge (p. 349)

classroom culture (p. 375)

code-emphasis approaches (p. 352)

cognitive conflict (p. 388)

community of learners (p. 388)

conceptually driven views (p. 354)

data-driven models (p. 354)

discourse knowledge (p. 362)

emergent literacy (p. 349)

language experience (p. 351)

linguistic knowledge (p. 349)

meaning-emphasis methods (p. 351)

naive theories (p. 383)

phonics (p. 352)

planning stage (p. 362)

reading (p. 349)

reciprocal teaching (p. 358)

revising stage (p. 365)

task environment (p. 361)

translation stage (p. 364)

whole language (p. 351)

"We better get moving," Susan urged Jim as they approached the door of Kathy Brewster's classroom. "The bell is gonna ring, and you know how Brewster is about this class. She thinks it's *so* important."

"Did you finish your homework?" Jim asked and then stopped himself. "What am I talking about? You've done your homework in every class since I first knew you."

"I don't mind it all that much. Actually, it bothers me when I don't get something, and sometimes it's even sorta fun. My dad helps me quite a bit. He says he wants to keep up with the world," Susan explained with a laugh.

"In some classes, I just do enough to get a decent grade, but not in here," Jim responded. "I used

to hate history, but it's sorta interesting the way Brewster's always telling us about the way we are 'cuz of something that happened a zillion years ago. Besides, you miss a homework assignment in this class, and you're dead," He grinned wryly. "Nobody messes with Brewster."

"Gee, Mrs. Brewster, that assignment was impossible," Harvey grumbled as he walked in.

"That's good for you," Kathy smiled back. "I know it was a tough assignment, but it makes you think. It's hard for me, too, when I'm studying and trying to put together new ideas, but if I hang in, I feel like I can usually get it."

"Aw, c'mon, Mrs. Brewster. I thought you knew everything."

"I wish. I have to study every night to keep up with you people,

and the harder I study, the smarter I get," Kathy continued with a smile.

"But you make us work so hard," Harvey continued in feigned complaint.

"Yes, but look how good you're getting at writing," Kathy smiled again, pointing her finger at him. "I think you hit a personal best on your last one. You've become a very good writer."

She watched as Harvey smiled slightly on his way to his desk.

Kathy turned to Jennifer as she walked in, and said quietly, "I pulled your desk over here, Jenny," motioning to a spot in the middle of the second row. "You've been a little quiet lately. . . . I almost considered calling your Mom, to see if everything's okay," and she touched Jennifer's arm, motioning her to the spot.

She finished taking roll and then pulled down a map in the front of the room. "Let's look again at the map and review for a moment to see where we are. We began our discussion of the Crusades yesterday. What was significant about them? . . . Greg?"

"You came in . . . with pictures . . . of Crusaders and asked us to imagine what it'd be like to be one of 'em. . . . Antonio said he didn't think he'd like iron underwear," Greg grinned as the rest of the class giggled.

"All right, that's true." Kathy smiled back. "Now, how did we start the lesson? . . . Kim?"

". . ."

"Remember, we started by imagining that we all left Lincoln High School and that it was taken over by people who believed that all extracurricular activities should be cut out. We then asked what we should do about it. What did we decide we should do?"

"We decided . . . uhh, . . . we'd talk to them . . . and try and change their minds," Kim responded hesitantly.

"Right. Exactly, Kim. Very good. We said that we would be on a 'crusade' to try to change their minds."

"Now, what were the actual Crusades all about? . . . Selena?"

". . . The Christians wanted to get the Holy Land back from the Muslims."

"About when was this happening?"

". . . I . . . I . . . I'm not sure."

"Look up at our time line."

". . . Oh . . . yeah, about 1100," Selena answered peering at the time line.

"Good, and why did they want them back? . . . Becky?"

". . . They . . . were . . . the Holy Lands were important for the Christians. I s'pose . . . they just wanted them because of that."

"Yes. Good, Becky," Kathy smiled. "Indeed, that was a factor. What else? . . . Anyone?"

After surveying the class and seeing uncertainty on students' faces, Kathy said, "You might not see what I'm driving at. . . . Let's look at this," and she then displayed a map that illustrated the extent of Muslim influence in the Middle East, North Africa, and Europe.

"What do you see here? . . . Cynthia?"

Cynthia scanned the map for several seconds and then said, "It looks like the Muslims are getting more and more . . . like . . . territory."

"Yes, very good. So, what implication did this have for the Europeans?"

". . . They prob'ly were . . . scared . . . like afraid the Muslims would take over their land," Scott volunteered.

"That's a good thought, Scott," Kathy responded. "They certainly were a military threat. In fact, the conflict occurring in Bosnia is a present-day reminder of the clash between Christians and Muslims. How else might they have been threatening?"

"Maybe . . . like economically," Brad added. "You're always telling us how economics rules the world," he added with a grin.

"Brilliant, Brad," Kathy laughed. "I've taught you well. Indeed, economics was a factor. In fact, this is

a little ahead of where we are, but we'll see that the military and economic threats of the Muslims, together with the religious issue, were also factors that led to Columbus's voyage to the New World. . . . Think about that. The Muslims in 1000 A.D. have had an influence on us here today."

"Now," Kathy said, "let's get back on track. Why do we study the Crusades? Like, who cares, anyway? . . . Toni?"

"They were . . . important in Europe, . . . like its development, . . . it affected its development in the Middle Ages, you know . . . like fashion and war strategies and stuff, . . . like all the way up to today. The Renaissance wouldn't have been the same without them."

"Excellent, Toni! Very good analysis. Now, for today's assignment, you were asked to write a paragraph answering the question, 'Were the Crusades a success or a failure?' You could take either position. We want to learn how to make and defend an argument, so the quality of your paragraph depends on how you defended your position, not on the position itself. Remember, this is a skill that goes way beyond a specific topic like the Crusades. This applies in everything we do.

"So, let's see how we made out. Go ahead. . . . Nikki?"

"I . . . said they were a failure. They didn't . . ."

"Wait a minute!" Joe interrupted. "How about the new fighting techniques they learned?"

"Joe," Kathy began firmly, "what is one of the principles we operate on in here?"

"We don't have to agree with someone . . . their point, but we . . . have to listen. . . . Sorry."

"Go on, Nikki," Kathy continued.

"That's okay," Nikki continued nodding to Joe. "It seemed to me that . . . like militarily, at least, they failed 'cuz the Europeans didn't accomplish . . . what they were after, . . . you know, to get the Holy Land back for Christianity," Nikki said. "There were a bunch of . . . well, several Crusades, and after only one did they get sort of a foothold, and it only lasted a short time, like about 50 years, . . . I think."

"Okay. That's good, Nikki," Kathy responded. "You made your point and then supported it. That's what I wanted you to do in your paragraph."

"Now, go ahead, Joe. You were making a point," Kathy said, turning back to him.

"I said they were a success because the Europeans learned new military . . . like strategies that they used on the Natives in the . . . like here, the Americas, and they were good at it. If it hadn't been for the Crusades, they prob'ly wouldn't have learned the stuff, . . . tech-niques, at least not for a long time. Like then, only the . . . Japanese could do that stuff, you know, like attacking techniques the Crusaders learned when they went to the Middle East. It even changed our ideas about like guerrilla warfare."

"Also good, Joe," Kathy responded, nodding. "This is exactly what we're after. Nikki and Joe took opposite points of view in their paragraphs, but they each provided several details to support their positions. Again, we're more concerned with the support you provide than the actual position you take.

"Let's look at one more," she went on. "What was your position, Anita?"

"I said they . . . were a success," Anita responded. "Europe, you know, like Western Europe took a lot from their culture, their culture in the Middle East. Like, some of the spices we eat today first came to Europe then."

"Now isn't that interesting!" Kathy waved energetically. "See, here's another case where we see ourselves today finding a relationship to people who lived 1,000 or more years ago. That's what history is all about."

"Brewster loves this stuff," David whispered to Kelly, smiling slightly.

"Yeah," she replied. "History has never been my favorite subject, but it's sure a relief to be in here after sitting in Orr's class."

"Okay. One more," Kathy continued, giving David a knowing look, "and we'll move on."

The class reviewed another example, and then Kathy told the students to revise their paragraphs in light of what they had discussed that day and to turn in a final product the following day.

When the period was nearly over, Kathy said, "Excuse me, everyone, but the bell is about to ring. I just want to remind you that for those of you who are making group presentations on the Renaissance, we start next Wednesday and finish on Thursday. You need to decide what groups will be on each day. For those who chose to write the paper on the Middle Ages, remember that your papers are due next Friday. Remember, in both cases you have to identify any relationships you think exist between the Crusades and the period you chose, and how our lives have been affected by both."

I n ideal classrooms, students pay attention, ask questions, and want to learn. They do their assignments without complaint and study without being coaxed or cajoled. But teachers don't teach in an ideal world. They often have students who are not motivated; more accurately, students don't seem motivated to work on the tasks their teachers set out for them.

Teachers contribute a great deal to students' desires to learn and to take responsibility for their own learning. They won't be successful with every student, but with a positive, proactive approach to motivation, they can influence many (Stipek, 1996).

In this chapter we examine theory and research on student motivation, together with teacher characteristics, classroom climate variables, and instructional factors that can help increase students' desires to learn.

After you've completed this chapter, you should be able to meet the following objectives:

- Explain learner motivation on the basis of behavioral, cognitive, and humanistic theories.
- Explain the role of motivation in developing self-regulation.
- Explain how teacher personal characteristics promote student motivation.
- Describe how classroom climate variables promote student motivation.
- Identify instructional factors that promote student motivation.

"Children's motivation to learn lies at the very core of achieving success in schooling. Given rapid technological advances, an ever-changing knowledge base, and shifting workplace needs, a continuing motivation to learn may well be the hallmark of individual accomplishment across the lifespan" (Weinstein, 1998, p. 81).

Motivation is *a force that energizes, sustains, and directs behavior toward a goal* (Baron, 1992; Schunk, 1990). Researchers have found a strong, positive correlation between motivation and achievement (Pintrich & Schunk, 1996; Wang, Haertel, & Walberg, 1993). Motivated students typically have positive attitudes toward school, cause fewer management problems, and describe school as satisfying. Motivated learners approach tasks eagerly, exert high levels of effort, and persist in the face of difficulty (Stipek, 1996). They are, not surprisingly, a primary source of job satisfaction for teachers.

Our job as teachers is to try to increase learners' inclination to perform meaningful learning tasks, and this is our frame of reference in this chapter.

Extrinsic and Intrinsic Motivation

Two students sit next to each other in a class. They look alike and are similar in ability but act very differently. One studies primarily to get high grades and seldom joins in discussions unless there is some payoff; the other jumps into assignments, eagerly participates, and seems to enjoy learning. Why the difference?

Motivation can be described in two broad categories. **Extrinsic motivation** *refers to motivation to engage in an activity as a means to an end,* whereas **intrinsic motivation** *is motivation to engage in an activity for its own sake* (Pintrich & Schunk, 1996). For example, extrinsically motivated learners may study hard for a test because they believe studying will lead to a high test score, teacher compliments, or some other end. In contrast, intrinsically motivated learners study because they view studying as worthwhile in itself. These relationships are illustrated in Figure 10.1.

Although we tend to think of extrinsic and intrinsic motivation as two ends of a continuum (meaning the higher the extrinsic motivation, the lower the intrinsic motivation and vice versa), they are actually on separate continuua (Pintrich & Schunk, 1996). A person might study hard, for example, both because it is enjoyable *and* because he or she wants a good grade in a class. Another person might study only to receive the good grade. The first is high in both extrinsic and intrinsic motivation, whereas the second is high in extrinsic motivation but low in intrinsic motivation.

Figure 10.1 Extrinsic and intrinsic motivation

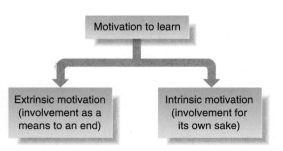

Extrinsic and intrinsic motivation also vary with the situation, and can change over time. Jim, in the opening case study, for example, appeared to be extrinsically motivated in other classes ("In some classes, I just do enough to get a decent grade . . .") but intrinsically motivated in Kathy's history class ("I used to hate history, but it's sorta interesting the way Brewster's always telling us about the way we are 'cuz of something that happened a zillion years ago.").

Ideally, students will be intrinsically motivated, and much of a teacher's effort is aimed at promoting intrinsic motivation. Research indicates that intrinsically motivated students achieve higher than those who are only extrinsically motivated (Gottfried, 1985). Jim's comments demonstrate how important teachers can be in promoting intrinsic motivation.

Theories of Motivation

In Chapters 6, 7, and 8, we examined different views of learning. These theories can also help in understanding motivation. In fact, some researchers argue that learning and motivation are so interrelated that a person can't fully understand learning without considering motivation (Pintrich, Marx, & Boyle, 1993). We examine these views in the following sections.

Behaviorism: Motivation as Reinforcement

In your study of behaviorism in Chapter 6, you learned that reinforcement results in an increase in behavior. Praise, high test scores, and grades are all reinforcers that can cause this increase. Because they are ends that result from student effort, they are potential extrinsic motivators. Jim's comment, "You miss a homework assignment in this class, and you're dead" is another example. Working to avoid the consequences for failing to do his homework suggests extrinsic motivation.

Effective Reinforcers

The effectiveness of behavioral approaches to motivation depends on effective reinforcers. Although the use of reinforcers is controversial (Harter & Jackson, 1992; Kohn, 1992, 1996), it is still quite common, especially in elementary classrooms. Examples of reinforcers used in elementary classrooms are listed in Table 10.1.

Reinforcers aren't as effective for middle- or high-school students or for underachievers. Adult influence on middle school students declines in favor of peers and peer approval, and reinforcers provided by adults aren't as effective as they are with younger students. This problem is compounded by the impersonal structure of middle, junior high, and high schools, where a teacher sees a student for only 50 minutes a day in classes of 30 or more. These conditions make using personalized reinforcers difficult.

Criticisms of a Behavioral Approach to Motivation

Although the use of rewards is common in schools, behaviorism as an approach to motivation is controversial. (Rewards are *intended* reinforcers; they become reinforcers only if the behaviors they follow increase.) Some of the opposition is philosophical, focusing on the belief that schools should cultivate intrinsic interest in learning (Anderman &

10.1

On the basis of the information in the case study, would you describe Susan as being high in both extrinsic and intrinsic motivation, or high in one and low in another? Explain.

10.2

Jim demonstrated intrinsic motivation in Kathy's class, but his comment about missing a homework assignment implies extrinsic motivation. Are these two examples inconsistent? Explain.

Table 10.1 Potential reinforcers in elementary classrooms

Source	Examples
Consumable	M & M's
	Popcorn
	Soft drinks
Entertainment	Watching a favorite videotape
	Listening to the radio during project work
Independence	Free time
Adult approval	Teacher praise
	Comments on written work
Peer approval	Selection for teamwork
	Classmates asking for help
Competition	Highest grade in the class
	First to finish assignment correctly
Privilege or responsibility	Class monitor
	Directing class play

Maehr, 1994). Other criticisms are more pragmatic, arguing that using rewards is unwieldy and inefficient. Let's look at these arguments.

10.3

The research cited in this section suggests that the *offer* of a reward is more significant than the reward itself in decreasing intrinsic motivation. Explain these research results.

Rewards Decrease Intrinsic Motivation. As we saw in Chapter 6, research indicates that *offering* rewards for engaging in intrinsically motivating tasks decreases interest in the tasks (Deci & Ryan, 1987; Kohn, 1993; Schwartz, 1990). For instance, fourth- and fifth-graders who were offered rewards for participating in an already interesting math task chose the task less often in free time than students who weren't rewarded (Greene, Sternberg, & Lepper, 1976), and students who were rewarded for correct solutions to problems chose less difficult problems than those who were offered no rewards (Harter, 1978).

Rewarding students for simply completing tasks, such as giving all students A's for merely turning in a paper, also detracts from motivation, because it communicates that any level of performance is acceptable and minimal effort will do (Cameron & Pierce, 1994; Chance, 1992; Dickinson, 1989).

Learners' Focus Is Narrowed. Rewards also tend to narrow learners' focus. Students in lower grades say they engage in learning tasks to master the content; students in higher grades more often cite grades as motivators (deCharms, 1980). All teachers have been asked, "Will this be on the test?", and although this question is unavoidable to a certain extent, emphasizing test scores and grades as reasons for studying exacerbates the problem (Ames, 1992; Crooks, 1988).

Rewards Present Logistical Problems. Using rewards as motivators also creates logistical problems. Dispensing rewards requires time and energy, and rewards given to some students may cause resentment in those who don't receive them. Behavior modification, a widely used strategy in the 1960s, lost popularity partially because of these

Identifying effective reinforcers that are grade-level appropriate can increase student motivation.

factors. Now "token economies," in which tokens or tickets can be exchanged for prizes at the end of a designated period, are most commonly used with students having learning exceptionalities, or to reward groups rather than individuals.

Finally, as you found in Chapter 6, constant and effusive praise or a barrage of positive comments on papers loses credibility with students, and their effectiveness as reinforcers is sharply reduced.

Rewards Ignore Student Cognitions.   Probably the biggest shortcoming of behaviorism as an approach to motivation is the fact that it considers only the application of rewards and ignores learners' perceptions and beliefs. Learners don't merely respond to rewards; they assess the teacher's motives in giving the rewards, how consistently rewards are administered, and what the rewards suggest about their ability. These cognitions are unavoidable, because learners don't passively respond to the environment; they actively attempt to make sense of their experiences.

Cognitive Theories of Motivation

"C'mon, let's go," Melanie urged her friend Yelena as they were finishing a homework assignment.

"Just a sec," Yelena muttered. "I just can't seem to figure this out. I don't know why I missed this one. I thought I did the whole thing right, and it all made sense, but the answer turned out wrong."

"Let's work on it tonight. Everybody's leaving," Melanie urged.

"Go ahead, I'll catch up to you in a minute. I've gotta figure this out. . . . I just don't get it. This is the darndest problem I've ever seen."

10.4

What concept from behaviorism best explains why constant and effusive praise becomes ineffective as a reinforcer?

10.5

On the basis of behaviorism, how would a teacher know whether praise acts as a reinforcer?

As we examine this brief exchange, we find that we can't explain Yelena's behavior very well on the basis of behaviorism. Although getting the right answer would be reinforcing, it doesn't account for Yelena's effort to understand why the problem made sense but still came out wrong. Behaviorism also doesn't help us understand why Yelena persisted in her efforts to solve the problem even though she is struggling with it.

Cognitive Theories: The Need to Understand

Cognitive theories of motivation *focus on learners' needs for order, predictability, and an understanding of events.* "Children are seen as naturally motivated to learn when their experience is inconsistent with their current understanding or when they experience regularities in information that are not yet represented by their schemata" (Greeno, Collins, & Resnick, 1996, p. 25). For example, why do young children so eagerly explore their environments? Why is the "play" of puzzles completely engrossing for a four-year-old (and many adults)? Why was Yelena unable to leave until she solved the problem? Cognitive theorists suggest that each is motivated by the need to understand and make sense of the world.

Piaget's concept of *equilibrium,* discussed in Chapter 2, is an example of this need, and it is a cornerstone of his theory. When people are unable to explain experiences with their existing schemes, they are motivated to modify the schemes, and this process results in development. Piaget (1952) also argued that humans are naturally inclined to practice their developing schemes. This inclination explains why children open and close doors repeatedly with no apparent desire to examine the contents inside, and why they want the same story read over and over to the point of parental exasperation.

Cognitive theories help us explain a variety of other phenomena, such as

- why people are intrigued by brain teasers and other problems with no practical application,
- why people are curious when something occurs unexpectedly,
- why students ask questions about incidental and unrelated aspects of lessons,
- why people persevere on activities and then quit after they've mastered the task, and
- why people want feedback about their performance, even if it's negative feedback.

The items on the list all relate to a basic desire to simply understand "the way the world works."

Cognitive Theories: The Development of Self-Efficacy

You saw in Chapter 6 that social cognitive theory examines behavior, the environment, and personal factors in the learner. With respect to motivation, social cognitive theorists focus on two personal factors: expectations and beliefs.

The role of expectations can be explained with **expectancy × value theories** (Atkinson, 1964; Feather, 1982), *which suggest that learners are motivated to work on a task to the extent that they (a) expect to succeed on the task and (b) value task achievement or other potential outcomes.* If both are present, learners may develop a sense of **self-efficacy,** *which is learners' beliefs about their capability of succeeding on specific tasks* (Schunk, 1994). To feel a sense of self-efficacy, learners must believe they are mak-

10.6

A father, reading his son a familiar story, sees that the child is getting sleepy, so he decides to skip a few pages. His son immediately corrects him and demands that all the pages be read. Explain the child's behavior on the basis of the information in this section.

10.7

Think about the concept of *self-esteem,* presented in Chapter 3. Describe specifically how self-efficacy and self-esteem are different.

ing genuine progress toward a worthwhile goal, not merely trying hard, doing as well or better than others, or succeeding on a trivial task.

Self-efficacy is a positive emotional experience. It can be exhilarating, for example, to solve a difficult algebra problem on your own, to make it to the bottom of a ski slope for the first time without falling, or to repair your car. This feeling of self-efficacy results in an eagerness to work on other problems, to try a more difficult slope, or to tackle another repair job.

Influence of Self-Efficacy on Behavior and Cognition. Self-efficacy affects several aspects of learner behavior and cognition, which are summarized in Table 10.2 (Bandura, 1993; Schunk, 1994). Learners high in self-efficacy have more positive beliefs, approach learning activities more willingly, expend greater effort, persist longer in the face of difficulty, use strategies more effectively, and perform higher than their low-efficacy peers, even when ability is similar. What can teachers do to increase self-efficacy?

Factors Influencing Self-Efficacy. Four factors influence people's beliefs about their capability to perform (Bandura, 1986):

1. Past performance
2. Modeling
3. Verbal persuasion
4. Psychological state

As you would expect, past performance on similar tasks is the most important factor. A history of success in giving oral reports, for example, increases a person's self-efficacy for giving future reports. Modeling, such as observing others deliver excellent reports, can also increase self-efficacy. Seeing others succeed raises expectations, provides information about how a skill is performed, and is motivating (Bandura, 1986).

Although limited in its effectiveness, verbal persuasion, such as a teacher commenting, "I know you will give a fine report," can increase self-efficacy. It may improve self-efficacy indirectly by encouraging students to engage in demanding tasks: if they're successful, efficacy increases.

10.8

Research indicates that praising students for performance on an easy task can lower intrinsic motivation (Stipek, 1996). Using the concept of *self-efficacy* as the basis for your explanation, explain why this could happen.

10.9

What kind of peer model—one perceived to be of higher ability, of similar ability, or of lower ability—would increase an individual's self-efficacy the most? Explain.

Table 10.2   The influence of self-efficacy on behavior and cognition

	High Self-efficacy Learners	Low Self-efficacy Learners
Task orientation	Accept challenging tasks	Avoid challenging tasks
Effort	Expend high effort when faced with challenging tasks	Expend low effort when faced with challenging tasks
Persistence	Persist when goals aren't initially reached	Give up when goals aren't initially reached
Beliefs	Believe they will succeed	Focus on feelings of incompetence
	Control stress and anxiety when goals aren't met	Experience anxiety and depression when goals aren't met
	Believe they're in control of their environment	Believe they're not in control of their environment
Strategy use	Discard unproductive strategies	Persist with unproductive strategies
Performance	Perform higher than low-efficacy students of equal ability	Perform lower than high-efficacy students of equal ability

Finally, factors such as fatigue or hunger can reduce efficacy even though they're unrelated to the task, and emotional arousal, such as anxiety, can reduce efficacy by filling working memory with thoughts of failure.

What can teachers do to help students increase their self-efficacy?

Darren is a low achiever in Laura Cossey's seventh-grade math class. As Laura monitored the students during seatwork, she saw that Darren had made little progress on the word problems.

"Come on, Darren. I know you can do this work," Laura whispered. "Read the problem carefully a few times. Then break the problem into parts and try drawing a picture of each part. I'm going to come back here in a few minutes to see how you're doing."

In a few minutes, Laura returned, leaned over Darren, and said, "What do we have?"

Darren was still somewhat uncertain, but he obviously had gone over the problem and tried to get started. He pointed to the problem and said, "They want to know the overall percentage decrease in the cost."

"Good," Laura smiled. "Now, what else do you know?"

As Darren began explaining his understanding of the problem, Laura asked only as many questions as necessary to keep him on the right track. Finally, as he arrived at a solution, she said, "That's excellent thinking, Darren. . . . Now, look at the problem again to see whether it all makes sense. I'll be back in a minute to see your final solution. You be ready to explain to me exactly how you did it. Okay?" She smiled and moved on to another student.

10.10

What concept does "provided only enough guidance to be sure that he made genuine progress toward the solution—essentially on his own" best describe?

In this brief episode, we see how teachers can influence learners' self-efficacy. First, using verbal persuasion, Laura expressed her belief that he could solve the problem. Second, although she offered a strategy, she provided only enough guidance to be sure that he made genuine progress toward the solution—essentially on his own. Most importantly, through her guidance, Darren saw evidence of his own learning progress.

This example illustrates how important teachers can be in the development of student self-efficacy. Imagine the impact on Darren's self-efficacy if Laura had said, "Here, let me help you; I know this is hard for you." Suppose she had simply explained how to do the problem while Darren looked on passively, or had provided "false" success by praising minimal effort. These attempts to be helpful, though done in good faith, would have decreased Darren's self-efficacy. He might have concluded, perhaps unconsciously, "Mrs. Cossey doesn't think I can do this on my own, so she has to do it for me," or, "She must not think I'm very smart if she compliments me for that." Social cognitive theory helps us understand the important influence teachers have on learner beliefs and expectations.

Humanistic Views of Motivation

10.11

Cognitive and humanistic views of motivation both have the notion of *needs* at their centers. Which of the two approaches views needs more broadly? Explain.

In Chapter 7, you saw that cognitive learning theory developed in the mid-1950s in response to the shortcomings of behaviorism. At about the same time, another movement called **humanistic psychology** began, *which views motivation as people's attempts to fulfill their total potential as human beings* (Hamachek, 1987). This perspective on motivation is still popular, because of its emphasis on learner growth and potential.

Humanistic Psychology: Development of the Whole Person

The first half of the twentieth century was dominated by two major forces: behaviorism and psychoanalysis. As you know, behaviorism explains learning and motivation by using concepts such as *reinforcers* and *punishers*. Psychoanalysis, most heavily influenced by Sigmund Freud (1856–1939), focuses on unconscious drives and internal instincts, and has contributed familiar concepts such as the *id, ego,* and *superego*. Humanistic psychology is a reaction against the kind of thinking that reduces human behavior to either a response to the environment or to internal instincts. Instead, it examines the total person—physical, emotional, interpersonal, and intellectual—and how these elements interact to affect learning and motivation. It focuses on individuals' perceptions, responses to internal needs, and the drive for "self-actualization," or becoming all that one can be (Maslow, 1968, 1954/1970). This new orientation became known as a "third force" during the 1950s, alongside behaviorism and psychoanalysis.

Motivation as Growth

Humanistic views of motivation assume that learners seek fulfilling experiences. This view argues that people have an innate, biological tendency to fully develop their inherited talents, and that learners are motivated to grow and enhance themselves (Graham & Weiner, 1996; Maslow, 1971; Rogers, 1963). According to the humanistic view, there is no such thing as an unmotivated learner. The inattentive seventh-grader who pokes the person in front of her is motivated; her motivation is just directed at nonacademic activities.

Promoting Growth: Implications for Teaching. Humanistic views of motivation emphasize the personal and emotional side of learning and teaching. According to this view, learner motivation depends on how learners view themselves as people and how they see the school contributing to their growth. If classes are personally meaningful, students are motivated to learn; if not, they aren't. Good teaching is "the process of inviting students to see themselves as able, valuable, and self-directing, and of encouraging them to act in accordance with these self-perceptions" (Purkey & Novak, 1984, p. xiii).

Two elements of the teaching–learning process are essential to humanistic psychologists: the *student–teacher relationship* and *classroom climate* (Hamachek, 1987). Carl Rogers (1967), prominent thinker in the humanistic movement, suggests that effective teachers have three qualities that promote the student–teacher relationship:

- They are genuine, *real* people, without fronts or facades, who embrace their feelings as their own.
- They are accepting, viewing students as worthy individuals in their own right.
- They are empathetic, able to consider teaching–learning experiences from students' points of view.

Classroom climate is an outgrowth of the collective student–teacher relationships that form over time. Humanistic classrooms are safe environments where students believe they can learn and are expected to do so. Standards remain high but attainable. Each person is valued because he or she is an innately valuable human being.

An emerging body of research supports these assertions. Connell and Wellborn (1991) argue that "relatedness" is one of three basic human needs (along with competence and autonomy). They describe relatedness as the need to feel connected to others in a social environment and to feel worthy and capable of love and respect. Additional research indicates that teachers rated highly in *affection* for, *understanding* of, *sympathy* with, and *availability* to students had students who were more engaged in classroom activities than those rated lower in these areas (McCombs, 1998; Skinner &

10.12

Identify an example in Kathy Brewster's lesson where the student–teacher relationship was illustrated. Then identify an example in which she promoted a positive classroom climate.

Belmont, 1993). Further, students' interest in and assessment of the importance of their class work is related to their sense of belonging and personal support from their teachers (Goodenow, 1993). Collectively, these findings suggest that an accepting and supportive classroom environment—where each student is valued regardless of academic ability or performance—is important for both learning and motivation (Stipek, 1996).

Classroom Connections

Applying Behavioral Approaches to Motivation in Your Classroom

1. Praise students appropriately for accomplishments.
   - A fifth-grade teacher praises students when they demonstrate clear understanding of a topic or problem solution. She praises trivial accomplishments sparingly.
   - An English teacher underlines well-written passages in her students' essays, comments positively about them, and explains why the sections warrant the praise.

Applying Cognitive Approaches to Motivation in Your Classroom

2. Begin lessons with challenging questions and discrepant events.
   - A third-grade teacher drops an ice cube into a cup of alcohol (which the students initially think is water), and the ice cube drops to the bottom of the cup. "We know that ice floats on water," she says. "How can we explain what just happened?"
   - A math teacher has a "problem of the week." Once a week, the students are required to bring in a challenging, everyday problem for the class to solve.

3. Explain the reasons for dealing with the topics being studied.
   - A life science teacher introducing a unit on body systems says, "Understanding each of our body systems can help us lead healthier lives, and being healthy allows us to enjoy things more than if we're sick or hurt."

4. Provide clear and prompt feedback on assignments and tests.
   - A math teacher returns all tests and quizzes the following day and discusses frequently missed problems.
   - An elementary teacher writes comments on students' papers, suggesting revisions. The originals and the revisions are then checked and placed in students' portfolios.

5. Establish clear expectations for your students.
   - A geography teacher writes a letter to parents at the beginning of the school year. The letter tells parents how learning activities will be conducted, describes the procedures for turning in work, and states that all students in her class are expected to be involved and successful.

6. Develop self-efficacy by giving students only as much help as they need to make progress on challenging goals.
   - After displaying a problem, a fifth-grade teacher asks students to suggest ways of solving it. Each strategy offered is taken seriously and discussed in detail.
   - An English teacher returns students' essays with suggestions for improvement. After students make revisions, the essays are reviewed by peers, revised again, and turned in. The teacher makes comments identifying areas where the essays have been improved.

Applying Humanistic Approaches to Motivation in Your Classroom

7. Display a caring and empathetic manner with students.

- A sixth-grade teacher spends time with students before and after school each day, helping them with problems and assignments.
- An algebra teacher conducts a help session twice a week after school. He stays as long as any student wants to remain. Sometimes, conversations turn to school policy, and he listens intently when students express their views.

8. Create a supportive classroom climate for learners.

- A fifth-grade teacher demands that all students treat each other with respect. Personal criticisms and sarcasm are forbidden. She carefully models these behaviors for students.
- A first-grade teacher encourages and accepts all students' comments and questions. He tells students that mistakes are a part of learning and treats them that way in learning activities.

Personal Factors in Motivation

In the first section of the chapter, we looked at motivation from three theoretical perspectives. Now we turn to personal, or individual, factors that influence motivation: arousal, needs, beliefs, goals, and self-regulation. As we examine these factors we'll see that some are related to cognitive theories, while others more closely fit humanistic views. We begin with the concept of arousal.

Motivation and Arousal

As students, we've all had the experience of sitting nervously as an instructor hands out a test. Our blood pressure rises, our breath comes a little faster, and our hands may even sweat. We are alert and wide awake. Our motivation is high, and we are in a state of **arousal,** which is *a physical and psychological state of excitement in reaction to the environment.* Great coaches have reputations for being effective motivators because they are able to induce high levels of arousal in their players.

To be effective, arousal needs to be at an optimal level (Morris, 1988); too little or too much decreases performance. If we're exhausted coming into the test or if we have personal problems, for example, our level of arousal may be too low and we won't be at our best. On the other hand, if we're aroused to the point of anxiety, our performance may also suffer.

Anxiety, Motivation, and Performance

Anxiety is *arousal to the point of general uneasiness and tension,* and its relationship with motivation and performance is complex. For example, relatively high anxiety improves performance on simple, well-practiced tasks but lowers performance on new or difficult assignments (Covington & Omelich, 1987).

Anxiety results from a variety of factors including the difficulty of a task as well as personal factors (Wolf, Smith, & Birnbaum, 1997). With respect to personal factors, some students are anxious because they are poorly prepared; others prepare but use ineffective strategies; still others study diligently but "choke" on tests. (In Chapter 14, we offer suggestions to teachers for reducing test anxiety in their students.)

Our study of information-processing in Chapter 7 helps us understand the relationship between motivation, arousal, and performance. If the task is difficult and arousal high (to the point of anxiety), thoughts such as "I'll never get this stuff" and "I can't do this" lower performance by occupying working memory space, leaving less to devote to the task. On the other hand, simple tasks require limited working memory space, so arousal increases performance.

Capitalizing on Arousal: Curiosity Motivation

"**Curiosity** *is elicited by activities that present students with information or ideas that are discrepant from their present knowledge or beliefs and that appear surprising or incongruous*" (Pintrich & Schunk, 1996, p. 277). Curiosity induces arousal and can be a powerful source of intrinsic motivation (Lepper & Hodell, 1989).

Teachers can capitalize on curiosity motivation by asking paradoxical questions ("If Rome was such a powerful and advanced civilization, why did it fall apart?") or by using demonstrations with seemingly contradictory events (a bimetallic rod bends downward the first time when heated and upward the second, seemingly defying gravity). These discrepant events are designed to induce curiosity and pull students into the lesson.

Motivation and Needs

A **need** *is a real or perceived lack of something necessary.* Needs can be simple and obvious, such as the need for food as signaled by hunger. They can also be complex and abstract, such as the need for order and understanding—a cornerstone of cognitive theories of motivation. Here, the need is to eliminate uncertainty; while eliminating uncertainty isn't necessary for survival, it makes people feel more comfortable.

In this section, we begin with a humanistic perspective on needs as we consider Maslow's hierarchy, then we turn to cognitive needs.

Motivation as a Hierarchy of Needs: The Work of Maslow

Abraham Maslow (1968, 1954/1970), the father of the humanistic movement, described needs as existing in two groups: the first consisting of basic needs, such as survival and safety, and the second based on the desire for self-fulfillment and self-actualization.

His work resulted in the hierarchy shown in Figure 10.2.

Deficiency Needs. The bottom four categories of Maslow's hierarchy are called **deficiency needs,** which are needs that, when unfulfilled, *energize or move people to meet them*. Until a lower need is met, people aren't likely to move to a higher one. This assertion suggests that a person who doesn't feel safe, for example, won't be concerned with belonging, self-esteem, or any other higher need.

Growth Needs. If all deficiency needs are met, an individual can focus on the top three levels, which are called growth needs. According to Maslow, people respond to growth needs differently than they do to deficiency needs. **Growth needs** are never "met" in the same sense as are the bottom four; rather, they *expand and grow as people have experiences with them*. For instance, as people's understanding of an area such as literature increases, their desire to learn and study actually increases, rather than decreases. This explains why some people seem to have an insatiable desire for learning and are constantly involved in growth activities, or why an individual never tires of quality art or music.

Figure 10.2 Maslow's hierarchy of needs

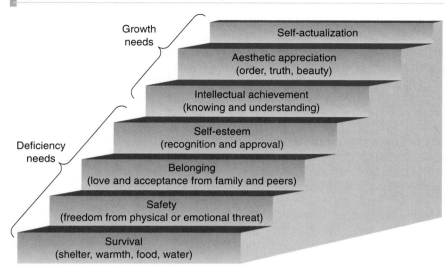

Growth needs
- Self-actualization
- Aesthetic appreciation (order, truth, beauty)
- Intellectual achievement (knowing and understanding)

Deficiency needs
- Self-esteem (recognition and approval)
- Belonging (love and acceptance from family and peers)
- Safety (freedom from physical or emotional threat)
- Survival (shelter, warmth, food, water)

Source: Adapted from *Motivation and Personality* 2nd Edition by Abraham H. Maslow. Copyright 1954 by Harper & Row, Publishers, Inc. Copyright © 1970 by Abraham H. Maslow. Reprinted by permission of HarperCollins Publishers Inc.

In an attempt to understand self-actualization, Maslow studied individuals he believed to be self-actualized, such as Thomas Jefferson, Albert Einstein, and Eleanor Roosevelt. As his work progressed, he began to see patterns in the characteristics of these people (see Figure 10.3). Although fewer than 1% of all people ever reach this level (Maslow, 1968), everyone strives for self-actualization, and Maslow concluded that it is reached by first satisfying deficiency needs so that one is free to reach for the higher ones.

10.14

On the basis of Maslow's work, would you conclude that people with high need for aesthetic appreciation have high self-esteem? Have they met their need for intellectual achievement? Explain in each case.

Figure 10.3 Characteristics of self-actualized individuals

- They have a clear perception of reality.
- They accept themselves, others, and the world for what they are.
- They are spontaneous in act and thought.
- They are problem-centered rather than self-centered.
- They are autonomous and independent.
- They are sympathetic to the condition of other human beings and seek to promote the common welfare.
- They have a democratic perspective of the world.
- They are creative.
- They establish deep and meaningful relationships with a few people rather than superficial bonds with a large number of people.
- They have peak experiences that are marked by feelings of great excitement, happiness, and insight.

Maslow's work has been criticized because his descriptions are imprecise and people don't always behave as would be predicted from the hierarchy. Michelangelo, for example, lay on his back for four years in enormous discomfort to create his masterpiece on the ceiling of the Sistine Chapel, a triumph of aesthetics at the expense of lower needs. At a more immediate level, we've all heard of people who put themselves in grave danger to protect a loved one or defend a principle. In Maslow's hierarchy, however, you can see the interrelationship of physical, emotional, intellectual, and aesthetic needs; together, these describe the needs of the "whole person" emphasized by humanistic thinkers.

Implications of Maslow's Work for Teachers.   Maslow's work has important implications for education. When children come to school tired, hungry, or—in extreme cases—abused, their desire to learn is certainly diminished. The hot breakfast and free lunch programs in schools are efforts to meet these deficiency needs, and teachers are now trained to identify evidence of abuse so that counselors can respond immediately.

Kathy Brewster was aware of Maslow's work, and consciously applied it in her teaching. Concerned that Jennifer might feel left out, she attempted to increase her feeling of belonging by moving her into the middle of the class. This concern for students' emotional well-being lies at the core of the humanistic emphasis in teaching. When a deficiency need is met, it diminishes, and the individual is freed to move to the next level on the hierarchy.

Maslow's work also suggests that teachers need to create learning environments where students are free from physical or emotional threat. Students who are threatened by potential embarrassment or who work in an otherwise unsafe and disorderly environment are less motivated to learn and achieve less than those whose learning situations are safe and stable (Blumenfeld, 1992; Brophy & Good, 1986; McCombs, 1998).

Cognitive Learning Needs

Although Maslow's work, with its emphasis on the whole person, has humanistic psychology as its theoretical foundation, other needs can best be explained using a cognitive framework. We consider these needs in this section.

The Need for Competence.

> Larry, crying, ran into the house. He had fallen off his bike again. His mother sympathetically put a bandage on his scraped knee and told him to wait and she would help him with the bike as soon as she finished writing a report for work. In a few minutes, however, Larry was back outside making another attempt at learning to ride a bike.

White (1959), in a classic paper, explains Larry's behavior as a response to the need for competence, and he argued that **competence motivation** *is an innate need in human beings that energizes people to master tasks and skills.* With increasing competence, an individual is more capable of coping with the environment and, according to White, this increasing capability is the source of competence motivation.

Teachers capitalize on competence motivation when they emphasize improvement and provide students with feedback suggesting they are increasing their skills. It is a strong endorsement for a learning-focused classroom, which we discuss in the last section of the chapter.

10.15

Explain competence motivation, using cognitive theories of motivation.

The Need for Control and Self-Determination.   Another cognitive perspective links motivation to *control* and *self-determination*. According to this view, people have a need to control their environment, to be "origins" of their fate, rather than "pawns" to external forces (deCharms, 1968).

The need for control is a form of intrinsic motivation evidenced in both industrial settings and the classroom (Lepper & Hodell, 1989). Studies of stress in the workforce reveal that jobs having little autonomy or control, such as assembly line work, induce more stress in people than those with responsibility and freedom.

Teachers can address this need by allowing student input in classroom decisions, such as the development of classroom rules or choices in learning activities (Ames, 1990). Kathy Brewster understood learners' need for self-direction and applied her understanding when she gave students the choice of making a group presentation on the Renaissance or writing a paper about the Middle Ages. Opportunities such as these arise more often than we think. When students feel in control of and responsible for their own learning, classroom climate improves and motivation to learn increases.

The Need to Achieve.   Student responses to the photograph on this page and questions in the caption are used to assess **achievement motivation,** *which is a drive to excel in learning tasks and the capacity to experience pride in accomplishment* (Atkinson, 1980, 1983). Achievement motivation is important in classrooms because it both directs students toward accomplishments and reduces the need to avoid failure. (The need to avoid failure causes students to experience anxiety in testing situations and avoid challenging tasks.)

To understand how achievement motivation operates, let's return to the photograph and questions in the caption. A student with a high need to achieve might respond to the questions in this way:

> "He's concerned about the C. He knows he can do better and should have studied harder."

In contrast, a student with a high need to avoid failure might decide:

> "He's not very good at science, and it was a hard test. He maybe shouldn't have taken this class."

These responses reveal differences in the need to achieve and the need to avoid failure. Students with a high need for achievement tend to be motivated by challenging assignments, high grading standards, explicit feedback, and opportunities to try again. In contrast, students with a high need to avoid failure tend to experience anxiety in testing situations and avoid challenging tasks. They're motivated by liberal reinforcement for success, small clear steps in assignments, easy grading, and protection from embarrassment for failure.

Attribution Theory.   Three students eagerly waited as their teacher handed back a test.

> "How'd you do, Bob?" Anne asked.
> "Terrible," Bob answered somewhat sheepishly. "I just can't do this stuff. I'm no good at writing the kind of essays she wants."
> "I didn't do so good either," Anne replied, "but I knew I wouldn't. I just didn't study hard enough. I knew I was going to be in trouble."
> "Unbelievable!" Ronnie added. "I didn't know what the heck was going on, and I got a B+. I don't think she read mine."

10.16

In this section, we said that control is *another* source of intrinsic motivation. What is the first source that Lepper and Hodell (1989) identified?

10.17

Provide an explanation for achievement motivation from a behaviorist point of view. How would behaviorists measure achievement motivation?

10.18

Suppose a competitive diver was a failure-avoiding learner. How would this likely affect both her progress and her selection of dives to perform in competition?

Questions such as, "What is happening here?" "What happened in the past?" and "What is going to happen?" are used to measure students' achievement motivation.

Earlier, we said that cognitive views of motivation assume that people have a need for order and understanding. This view suggests that the students in the example have an innate desire to understand why they got the grades they did. In response to that desire, they created *explanations (perceived causes) for their successes and failures,* which are called **attributions.** Bob suggested he wasn't good enough (lack of ability), Anne thought she hadn't tried hard enough (lack of effort), and Ronnie essentially wrote the issue off to luck. In addition to ability, effort, and luck, learners may also attribute successes and failures to difficulty of the task, effective or ineffective strategies, mood, help, interest, unfair teacher practices, clarity of instructions, or other factors. Ability, effort, luck, and task difficulty are most common (Weiner, 1990).

The tendency to search for attributions is common in people's everyday lives. In response to something as simple as a headache, people say things such as, "I wonder if I'm coming down with something," or "Maybe it's something I ate." People instinctively search for an explanation for the headache. They may even ask, "What do you attribute that to?" in response to a person's description of some occurrence.

Attribution theory *is an attempt to systematically describe explanations for success and failure in classroom situations.* Attributions can be described on three different dimensions (Weiner, 1992, 1994a, 1994b). The first is *locus:* whether or not the cause is inside (I) or outside (O) the learner. Ability and effort are inside, for example, whereas luck and task difficulty are outside. The second is *stability* (S or US): whether the cause stays the same or can change. Effort and luck are unstable, because they can change, whereas ability stays the same. (In the next section we'll see that young children and some adults believe that ability can change with effort.) The third is the extent to which students accept *responsibility* for their successes or failures, i.e., whether or not they *control* (C or UC) the learning situation. Learners control their effort, for example, whereas they have no control over luck or task difficulty.

Attributions are important because they affect learner reactions to success and failure. Locus, for example, influences the sense of pride and self-esteem related to the experience, whereas stability leads to expectations for future performance. Table 10.3 presents a summary of students' attributions and reactions to success and failure.

Impact of Attributions on Behavior. Let's look at the students' attributions again. Both Anne and Bob feel bad about their low scores, because both effort and ability are internal; but Anne thinks she has control over her results, and she would be apt to try harder the next time. Attributing failure to lack of effort is likely to improve performance (Weiner, 1994a). In contrast, since Bob thinks he has no control, he's likely to think, "What's the use? I won't do any better anyway." Attributing failure to lack of ability decreases future performance (Weiner, 1994a).

In the extreme, Bob's attributions can lead to **learned helplessness,** *the feeling that no amount of effort can lead to success* (Seligman, 1975). This perspective leads to

> **10.19**
>
> Why is attributing failure to effort more desirable than attributing it to ability?

Table 10.3 Cognitive and affective reactions to attributions

When Learners Are Successful			
Attribution	**Example**	**Affective Reaction**	**Cognitive Reaction**
Effort (I, US, C)	"I studied hard for this test."	Increased pride	Expectation of different performance
Ability (I, S, UC)	"I'm good at math."	Increased pride	Expectation of similar performance
Task difficulty (E, S, UC)	"The test was easy."	Decreased pride	Expectation of similar performance
Luck (E, US, UC)	"I guessed right."	Decreased pride	Expectation of different performance
When Learners Fail			
Attribution	**Example**	**Affective Reaction**	**Cognitive Reaction**
Effort (I, US, C)	"I didn't study enough."	Increased shame	Expectation of different performance
Ability (I, S, UC)	"I'm not good at math."	Increased shame	Expectation of similar performance
Task difficulty (E, S, UC)	"The test was hard."	Decreased shame	Expectation of similar performance
Luck (E, US, UC)	"I guessed wrong."	Decreased shame	Expectation of different performance

overwhelming feelings of shame and self-doubt that result in giving up without even trying. At-risk students with histories of failure are susceptible to learned helplessness. In more recent work, Seligman (1995) recommends "immunizing" children against pessimism by providing them with successful mastery experiences.

Ronnie's situation is different. Although he was successful, his pride in his accomplishment was reduced. He can't expect similar results in the future, because luck is unstable and external. If he thinks the world is capricious, his motivation won't increase because he isn't in control. His motivation would be greater if he could attribute his success to an internal source, such as effort or ability.

Attribution Training. Research indicates that learners can improve the effectiveness of their attributions through training. In a pioneering study, Dweck (1975) provided students who demonstrated learned helplessness with successful and unsuccessful experiences. When the students were unsuccessful, the experimenter specifically stated that the failure was caused by lack of effort. Comparable students were given similarly successful experiences but no training. After 25 sessions, the learners who were counseled about their lack of effort responded more appropriately to failure, persisted longer, and adapted their strategies more effectively. Subsequent research has corroborated Dweck's findings (Forsterling, 1985).

Motivation and Beliefs

To this point, we have discussed two personal factors in motivation: arousal and needs. Individual beliefs can also influence motivation. You saw in our discussion of social cognitive theory that beliefs are basic to the concept of *self-efficacy*. We extend this discussion now.

> **10.20**
>
> What evidence do you have that Anne has high self-efficacy? Use her comments and the characteristics of self-efficacy to provide an answer.

Beliefs About Ability

Attribution theory views ability as a stable entity, and this is the way it is described in Table 10.3. Other research, however, indicates that young children (Nicholls & Miller, 1984) and some adults (Dweck & Bempechat, 1983) view ability as a skill and thus incremental; this view suggests that ability is alterable and controllable. This **incremental view of ability** *holds that ability can be improved with effort*. Others retain an **entity view of ability,** believing *that ability is stable and uncontrollable.*

Beliefs About Ability and Effort

Developmental differences exist in beliefs about ability. Young children tend to have an optimistic view of their ability, hold high expectations for success, and be quite resilient to failure. Through the early elementary grades, children tend to view effort and ability as synonymous. "They assume that smart people try hard and trying hard makes you smart. . . . If a person succeeds, then he must have tried hard and he must be smart. If he fails, he must not have tried and he must not be smart" (Stipek, 1998, p. 93).

Unfortunately, as learners get older, they are more likely to view ability as a stable entity. They differentiate between effort and ability and begin to perceive an inverse relationship between the two; i.e., high effort indicates low ability and vice versa (Nicholls & Miller, 1984). Further, as learners grow older, being perceived as having high ability becomes increasingly important to them, they react more strongly and more negatively to failure, and their perceptions of their ability tend to be more influenced by teachers' responses to them (Ames, 1990; Anderman & Maehr, 1994). We examine these responses in more detail in the next section.

How Teachers Influence Learners' Achievement-Related Beliefs

The way teachers respond to learners can strongly influence learners' beliefs about their ability. In this section, we consider four ways that this can happen:

- Attributional statements
- Praise and criticism
- Emotional displays
- Offers of help

Attributional Statements. The *statements teachers make to students about the causes of their performance*—**attributional statements**—can influence students' beliefs about their own competence.

For instance, suppose a teacher is talking to a student who has failed to solve a problem correctly. Which of the following is the more desirable statement?

"That's a very good effort. I know that these problems are difficult for you."
"I believe if you tried a little harder, you'd be able to solve this problem."

Based on our discussion of attribution theory, the second statement is clearly better. Attributing failure to lack of effort communicates that the learner has the ability to complete the task. The first statement attributes failure to lack of ability and, while the

10.21

On the basis of the information in this section, which student—Anne or Bob (p. 411)—is more likely to have an incremental view of ability? Explain.

Student beliefs about their own ability as students can be enhanced by experiences in which challenging tasks are successfully accomplished.

teacher may in good faith be concerned about the learner's feelings, it undermines beliefs about competence (Stipek, 1996).

Now suppose the learner has been successful in solving the problem. Which of the following statements is more desirable?

"Well done. I see that you've been working hard on this."
"You're good at this."

While attributing failure to lack of effort is desirable, attributing success to effort may actually detract from beliefs about competence, because learners tend to believe that success requiring high effort indicates lower ability than success achieved with less effort (Nicholls & Miller, 1984; Schunk, 1983a).

Attributions of effort are further complicated by skill level. When learners are initially learning a skill, attributing progress to effort is desirable, but as their skills improve, they are likely to react better to attributions of ability. We saw this illustrated in Kathy Brewster's interaction with Harvey in our opening case study. When he complained, "But you make us work so hard," Kathy suggested that his hard work was increasing his ability when she said, "Yes, but look how good you're getting at writing. I think you hit a personal best on your last one. You've become a very good writer."

Praise and Criticism. Praising students appears to be straightforward: simply praise students for desired behavior.

The use of praise isn't that simple, however. Older students may perceive praise as reward for effort, rather than for accomplishment, or interpret praise for performance on easy tasks as an indication that the teacher believes they have low ability (Graham, 1991; Stipek, 1996).

Criticism also appears to be straightforward: we should avoid it. However, research indicates that criticism can have a positive effect on learners' self-concepts of ability (Parsons, Kaczala, & Meece, 1982). Learners interpret criticism as an indication that the teacher believes they have high ability.

These interpretations are developmental. Learners younger than about age 11 are less likely to view effort and ability as inversely related (Barker & Graham, 1987).

Emotional Displays. Teachers' emotional reactions to learners' successes and failures can also affect their attributions and expectations for success. For example, when teachers express anger in response to learner failure, learners are likely to attribute their failure to lack of effort, whereas failing learners who receive sympathy from teachers are more likely to attribute their failure to lack of ability (Graham, 1984). The teacher's expression of emotion influenced learners' perceptions of the causes of their failures and their expectations for future success (Stipek, 1996).

Helping. Offering students unsolicited help can also be pernicious. For instance, researchers have found that children as young as 6 rated a student offered unsolicited help lower in ability than another offered no help (Graham & Barker, 1990). Further, learners offered help may feel negative emotions, such as incompetence, anger, worry, or anxiety (Meyer, 1982).

None of these research results suggests that teachers should not praise students, express sympathy, offer help, or encourage effort. Rather, they remind us that the context in which these actions occur is important. We must continually ask ourselves how our actions will be interpreted by learners. As always, the way we respond to students requires sensitivity and careful judgment.

The Need to Protect Self-Worth

Covington (1992) asserts that self-worth is a basic need, and that all individuals instinctively strive to protect their self-worth when it is threatened, such as in the case of public failure. Covington suggests further that students' self-worth is determined, in part, by their academic achievements.

We saw earlier that older learners perceive an inverse relationship between effort and ability, and that perceptions of high ability become increasingly important to them. As a result, exerting effort can be risky, because failure after working hard suggests that one is "dumb." As a result, students may engage in "self-handicapping" behavior to protect their self-worth (Pintrich & Schunk, 1996). This can occur in several ways: making a point of not trying ("Oh sure, I would get grades as good as yours if I studied half as hard as you do"), procrastinating ("I could have done a lot better, but I didn't start studying until midnight last night"), or blaming lack of performance on anxiety (Covington & Omelich, 1987; Mantzicopoulos, 1989). "From the students' points of view, failure without effort doesn't reflect on their ability. What they have achieved is 'failure with honor'" (Ames, 1990, p. 413). These self-handicapping behaviors are more common among low achievers, who often choose to not seek help when it's needed (Middleton & Midgley, 1997). The problem may be exacerbated in classrooms that are competitive, ability focused, and difficult (Midgley, Arunkumar, & Urdan, 1996).

Students with high need for achievement, though, are more likely to see ability as incremental. Challenging tasks allow them to improve their skills, and improved skills mean they're "getting smarter." Failure is less likely to threaten their sense of competence or self-worth, because it merely means that more work is needed. This pattern leads to sustained, successful learning (McClelland, 1985).

10.22

A student named Billy, seeing a C on a test, says, "That isn't bad, considering how little I studied. I didn't crack a book." Explain Billy's behavior on the basis of Covington's self-worth theory.

Motivation and Goals

We introduced the topic of goals in Chapter 6 and examined them again when we discussed matching cognitive strategies to goals in Chapter 8. For example, skimming a passage would be an effective strategy if the goal was to get an overview of the material, whereas summarizing would be a better strategy if the goal was comprehension.

Goals have been widely used to motivate workers and improve performance in the business world. They increase learner motivation and self-efficacy in at least three ways (Locke & Latham, 1990):

1. They give learners a standard against which to measure their progress; use of this measuring stick results in tangible evidence of learning.
2. They increase effort and persistence.
3. They encourage the development of new strategies when old ones are unsuccessful.

Despite these advantages, research indicates that many students—including those in college—study without clear goals in mind (Morgan, 1985). Students copy and reorganize their notes, for example, but don't consider whether or not these tasks contribute to their understanding. They seem to tacitly think that spending time equals learning. After they are taught to set effective goals, achievement increases (Morgan, 1987).

Characteristics of Effective Goals

Effective goals have three characteristics:

1. Specific (vs. broad and general)
2. Immediate or close at hand (vs. distant)
3. Moderately difficult (vs. too easy or too hard) (Jagacinski, 1997; Schunk, 1994)

Consider those characteristics as you examine the following goals:

1. To try harder on all my assignments
2. To learn algebra
3. To solve and explain algebra equations with one unknown

The problem with the first is that it is distant and not specific; it doesn't tell the student what to do next. The same is true for the second. In contrast, the third goal is specific, moderately difficult, and can be attacked immediately. Effective goals motivate students by providing concrete and challenging but achievable targets.

Learning versus Performance Goals

For goals to work, learners must be committed to them (Pintrich & Schunk, 1996). One way of increasing commitment is to guide students in setting their own goals, rather than to impose goals on them (Ridley, McCombs, & Taylor, 1994). In guiding students as they set goals, however, the distinction between *learning oriented* and *performance oriented goals* is important (Ames & Archer, 1988; Dweck, 1985). To illustrate these differences, consider the following goals:

1. To get at least a B on my essay

Actively involving students in their own learning takes advantage of personal factors, such as goals, needs, and beliefs, in motivation.

10.23

You are a sixth-grade math teacher working with a student who has very low self-efficacy. On the basis of the information in this section, offer a specific suggestion as to how you might try to improve his self-efficacy.

2. To score in the top fourth of the class on the next test
3. To identify a new example of every bold-faced topic in the next section of the chapter
4. To explain how I solved each of the problems on this assignment

doing for grades, status

The first and second are **performance goals,** which *focus on demonstrating high ability and avoiding failure.* In a performance orientation, learning isn't viewed as a goal in itself, but rather as a means to an end, such as a high test score or good grade. Performance goals lead to "getting by" or playing the game, instead of genuine understanding.

Performance goals can also lead to feelings of anxiety about success and failure, loss of self-worth after failure (Dweck & Leggett, 1988), and an *ego orientation,* in which students are concerned about looking smarter or performing better than others, rather than about learning and understanding (Nicholls, 1984).

learn for understanding

The third and fourth goals on the list, in contrast, are **learning goals,** or *goals that focus on the challenge and mastery of a task* (Pintrich & Garcia, 1991; Stipek, 1996). Learning goals lead to a *task orientation,* in which students focus on understanding and don't worry about failure or comparisons with others (Nicholls, 1984). A task orientation can lead to selecting more challenging activities, sustaining interest even after formal instruction has been completed, using "deep processing" strategies such as comprehension monitoring and elaboration, and increasing self-efficacy (Ames, 1990; Maehr, 1976). Performance goals and an ego orientation can result in avoiding challenging activities, not asking for help when it's needed, limiting effort, and using surface strategies, such as rehearsal (Meece, Blumenfeld, & Hoyle, 1988).

The difference between learning goals and performance goals is subtle but important. For example, the focus in the fourth goal on the list is in *explaining* how each problem was solved. Merely solving a number of problems isn't a true learning goal because it doesn't focus on a deep understanding of the problems. Focus on understanding is important both for achievement and for increased self-efficacy (Schunk, 1994). The same is true for the third goal. Identifying a new example is a powerful learning strategy that can increase understanding, and with it, self-efficacy.

Although helping students set effective goals is not a panacea, it can reduce many of the problems involved with beliefs about ability and effort that we discussed earlier. Research indicates that students who adopt learning goals persist in the face of difficulty; attribute success to internal, alterable causes; take risks and accept academic challenges; and focus on personal mastery (Bruning, Schraw, & Ronning, 1995). Teachers can help students develop this orientation by stressing content mastery and understanding, de-emphasizing grading and competition, and modeling their own search for understanding as they teach (Urdan, Pajares, & Lapin, 1997).

Motivation and Self-Regulated Learning

As teachers, we all should be trying to help learners become self-regulated. Self-regulation involves three components: metacognitive awareness, effective strategy use, and motivational control (Bruning et al., 1995). Learners demonstrate metacognitive awareness when they try to make sense of the task, select and adapt strategies to help them encode information meaningfully (self-monitoring), and compare their present performance to their goals (self-assessment) (Ridley et al., 1994).

Effective strategy use depends on having a repertoire of strategies, as we saw in Chapter 8. In this section, we complete the picture by discussing how motivational control contributes to self-regulated learning. The relationships among metacognition, strategy use, and motivational control are outlined in Figure 10.4.

Motivational Control

Motivation is an essential part of self-regulation. Learners demonstrate **motivational control** *when they set goals, believe they are capable of achieving them (self-efficacy), and adjust to the demands of studying and learning* (Bruning et al., 1995).

Motivational control can be enhanced through self-monitoring (Schunk, 1997; Wolters, 1997). For example, a student who monitors the amount of time spent "studying" may find that she is actually spending less time than she thought on the task and more on activities that don't contribute to learning, such as changing the volume of the stereo, getting something to drink, and reorganizing notes without actually learning from them. This realization can motivate her to change her habits. If she tries to change and believes that the change will increase her learning, her motivation is likely to be sustained (Schunk, 1997).

Self-monitoring can also increase self-efficacy. As students see themselves making progress toward learning goals, their self-efficacy increases; we all feel good when we accomplish something. These feelings of efficacy then enhance learning. "Students who feel efficacious about learning choose to engage in tasks, select effective strategies, expend effort, and persist when difficulties are encountered" (Schunk, 1994, p. 2). The development of motivational control through goal setting and self-monitoring enhances both immediate learning and the development of self-regulation.

This discussion has a number of implications for us as we teach. First, we should set clear goals and communicate them to students. Second, we should help our students

> **10.24**
> In Chapter 6, you saw that self-regulated learning involved goal setting, self-observation, and self-assessment. To which component of self-regulation in Figure 10.4 does goal setting most closely relate? To which component do self-observation and self-assessment most closely relate? Explain.

Figure 10.4 Components of self-regulation

learn to set their own goals and encourage a learning rather than a performance orientation. This requires that we collaborate with our students, helping them to construct their own learning goals (Ridley et al., 1994). Third, we should help them select strategies and teach them to monitor their progress toward the goals. As learners become aware of these processes and their competence develops, self-regulation increases.

To this point in the chapter, we've examined theoretical views of motivation—behavioral, cognitive, and humanistic—together with personal factors that affect people's motivation—arousal, needs, beliefs, goals, and self-regulation. In the next section, we combine these elements in a classroom model for promoting student motivation.

Classroom Connections

Applying an Understanding of Motivation and Arousal in Your Classroom

1. Begin classes with discrepant or eye-catching activities.
   - A third-grade teacher begins a study of animals with exoskeletons by bringing a lobster to class. She asks the students to compare the way the lobster feels and the way their own arms and legs feel.
   - A Spanish teacher periodically begins lessons with slides he's taken on trips to Mexico, emphasizing vocabulary and culture in each presentation.

Applying an Understanding of Motivation and Needs in Your Classroom

2. Attend to students' deficiency needs.
   - A seventh-grade teacher asks two of the more popular girls in her class to introduce a new girl to some of the other students and to take her under their wings until she gets acquainted.
   - A fifth-grade teacher calls on all students in her class to be certain they all feel that they're a part of the activity. She makes them feel safe by helping them respond correctly when they are initially unable to answer.

3. Model growth needs with your students.
   - A social studies teacher brings in a newspaper columnist's political opinion piece and asks students for their opinions on the issue.
   - An English teacher comments to his class on an interesting television special about environmental issues and asks students what they think could be done about some of them.

4. Promote feelings of control by allowing students a voice in decision making.
   - A middle-school teacher has students suggest classroom rules. He makes it a point to include some of them on his list.
   - A geography teacher allows students to decide the order in which they will study different cultural units.

Applying an Understanding of Motivation and Beliefs in Your Classroom

5. Help students attribute initial achievement to effort and growing expertise to ability.
   - As they initially work on word problems, a second-grade teacher carefully monitors student effort in seatwork. When she sees assignments that indicate effort, she makes comments to individual students, such as, "Your work is improving all the time" or "Your hard work is paying off, isn't it?"
   - As students' understanding of balancing equations increases, a chemistry teacher comments, "You people are getting smarter all the time. You've really gotten good at this stuff."

6. Describe ability as incremental.
   - A sixth-grade English teacher comments, "I wasn't good at grammar for a long time. But I kept trying, and I found that I can do it. I'm good at grammar and writing now. You can get better at it too, but you have to work at it."

The Classroom: A Model for Promoting Student Motivation

The earlier sections of the chapter provided you with the conceptual background to understand your students' motivation to learn. Our goal for this section is to present a model—synthesized from the information you've studied in the earlier sections—that teachers can use to promote motivation to learn in their classrooms. The model (see Figure 10.5) is not a set of rules to be applied without thinking, nor is it a list of teacher actions to be checked off. When implemented with professional judgment, the components of the model can significantly increase student motivation.

Class Structure: Creating a Learning-Focused Framework for Motivation

To be most effective, the model for promoting student motivation must be embedded in a learning-focused framework that emphasizes a task orientation (versus performance or ego), improvement and evidence of progress (versus social comparisons), and an incremental (versus entity) view of ability. Differences between a learning-focused and a performance-focused classroom are outlined in Table 10.4.

Let's look at some of the things Kathy Brewster did to promote a learning-focused classroom.

   • She promoted a climate of cooperation rather than competition, and avoided comparisons of performance among her students.

Figure 10.5 A model for promoting student motivation

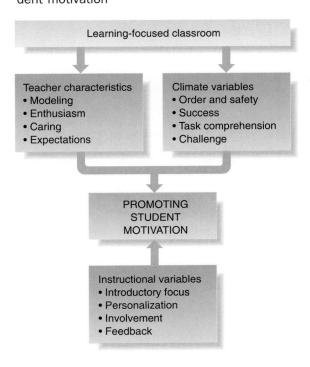

- She demonstrated an incremental view of ability, as indicated by her comment to Harvey, "I think you hit a personal best on your last [essay]. You've become a very good writer."

- She personalized her instruction by using a "crusade" to win back the school as context for her discussion of the Crusades.

- She gave her students the choice of either making a group presentation or writing a paper about the Renaissance.

In contrast, if she were performance focused, her emphasis would be on giving students high grades, comparing students' performances with each other, and attempting to motivate students with reminders of upcoming tests and threats of failure. Displays of grade distributions on the chalkboard, and comments such as, "C'mon, there were only two A's on the last test," and "If you people don't get going, you'll be repeating this course next year," characterize this orientation.

Within this learning-oriented framework, the model for promoting student motivation has three parts:

1. *Teacher characteristics:* The teacher's personal orientations toward students, teaching, and learning
2. *Climate variables:* Teacher and classroom characteristics that promote feelings of security, understanding, and challenge
3. *Instructional variables:* Specific actions teachers can take to promote student motivation in learning activities.

A teacher's goal in applying the model is to increase learners' self-efficacy and help learners develop self-regulation. Let's turn now to the model's specific components.

Teacher Characteristics: Personal Qualities that Increase Motivation

That teachers make a difference in student learning is a theme of this text, and it is certainly true for motivation. Teachers create learning environments, implement instruction, and establish learning-oriented or performance-oriented classrooms. None of the other

10.25

A teacher says, "Excellent job on the last test, everyone. Over half the class got an A or a B." On the basis of the information in this section, how appropriate is this comment? Explain.

Table 10.4   Comparisons of learning-focused and performance-focused classrooms

	Learning-Focused	Performance-Focused
Definition of success	Improvement, progress, mastery	High grades, performance compared with that of others
Reasons for effort	Learn something new	High grades, demonstrate ability
Basis for satisfaction	Progress, challenge, mastery	Doing better than others, success with minimum effort
Evaluation criteria	Evidence of progress	Social comparisons
Interpretation of errors	Information, part of the learning process	Failure, lack of ability
Concept of ability	Incremental, improves with effort	Entity, fixed

Source: From *Transforming the school culture to enhance motivation.* Paper presented at the Annual Meeting of the American Educational Research Association, San Francisco, April, 1992. By M. Maehr. Adapted by permission.

Groupwork within learning-focused classrooms provides opportunities for students to experience success in challenging tasks.

components of the model are effective if the teacher characteristics—modeling, enthusiasm, caring, and positive expectations—are lacking. These characteristics are highlighted in Figure 10.6.

Teacher Modeling

Teachers' attitudes and beliefs about teaching and learning are communicated through modeling. Student motivation is virtually impossible if teachers model distaste or lack of interest in the topics they teach. Statements such as the following serve no useful purpose and are devastating for motivation:

"I know this stuff is boring, but we have to learn it."
"I know you hate proofs."
"This isn't my favorite topic either."

In contrast, even the most mundane topics can be made more palatable to students if the teacher models interest in them.

Modeling affects motivation in other ways as well. For example, Kathy modeled an incremental view of ability in saying, "I have to study every night to keep up with you people, and the harder I study, the smarter I get." She also modeled effort attributions and high self-efficacy by saying, ". . . but if I hang in, I feel that I can usually get it." Other than direct experience, modeling is the most powerful factor affecting learners' self-efficacy (Bruning et al., 1995).

> **10.26**
>
> Explain why or how a statement such as, "It's hard for me, too, when I'm studying and trying to put together new ideas," demonstrates effective modeling.

Teacher Enthusiasm: Communicating Genuine Interest

Research indicates that teachers who present information enthusiastically increase learners' self-efficacy, attributions of effort and ability, self-confidence, and achievement more than do less enthusiastic teachers (Perry, 1985; Perry, Magnusson, Parsonson, & Dickens, 1986).

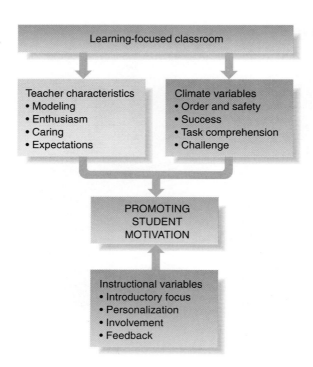

In the opening case study, you saw the effect of enthusiasm on David's and Kelly's behavior after Kathy commented, "Now isn't that interesting! . . . That's what history is all about." David's reaction was, "Brewster loves this stuff," and perhaps more significantly, Kelly's reaction was, "History has never been my favorite subject, but it's sure a relief to be in here. . . ."

The most significant aspect of Kathy's enthusiasm was that she demonstrated her own interest in the topic. It didn't include a pep talk or unnecessary theatrics; rather, it clearly identified the reasons why she found the topic interesting and meaningful, and she communicated those reasons to her students. A teacher's goal in projecting enthusiasm is to induce in students the feeling that the information is valuable and worth learning, not to amuse or entertain them (Good & Brophy, 1997).

10.27

Which theoretical approach to motivation best explains the positive effects of enthusiasm? Offer an explanation based on that theoretical approach.

Teacher Caring

- A first-grader calls her teacher "Mom."
- A fifth-grade teacher walks out on the playground during recess to talk with his students.
- A high-school teacher makes a special effort to make sure that Ngen Kao, a new student, feels welcome.

We saw earlier in the chapter that a growing body of research confirms the importance of learners' relationships with their teachers in promoting motivation (Stipek, 1996). "Learners' natural motivation to learn can be elicited in safe, trusting, and supportive environments characterized by . . . quality relationships with caring adults that see their unique potential" (McCombs, 1998, p. 399). The teacher caring emphasized in humanistic views of motivation reminds us that we don't teach math, science, or language arts; we teach people. We should focus on the learner as a whole person, including emotional and social needs as well as intellectual ones.

Caring refers to *teachers' abilities to empathize with and invest in the protection and development of young people* (Chaskin & Rauner, 1995). It's more than warm, fuzzy feelings that make people kind. In addition to understanding how students *feel,* caring teachers are committed to their students' growth and competence. They're attempting to do their very best for the people under their care (Noddings, 1995).

The importance of caring is captured in a fourth-grader's comment, "If a teacher doesn't care about you, it affects your mind. You feel like you're a nobody, and it makes you want to drop out of school" (Noblit, Rogers, & McCadden, 1995, p. 683).

Communicating Caring.   How do teachers communicate caring to students? Although the ways are highly individual, research has identified several characteristics, which are outlined in Table 10.5.

In examining these characteristics, the thread we see running through them is *time.* We all react positively when someone is willing to spend time with us. Willingness to spend personal time with students communicates better than anything else that teachers care. Helping students who have problems with an assignment or calling a parent after school hours communicates that teachers care about student learning. Spending personal time to ask a question about a baby brother or compliment a new hairstyle communicates caring about a student as a human being.

> **10.28**
>
> Research indicates that a negative emotional climate results in lowered student achievement. Using the information presented in this chapter, explain why this result could happen.

Table 10.5   Characteristics of caring teachers

Category	Description
Showing respect and politeness	Teachers are polite, treat students with respect, listen to their comments and questions, and are responsive to legitimate needs for second chances and extra help.
Valuing individuality	Teachers know students as human beings, noticing and commenting on changes in dress, habits, and behavior.
Helping with personal problems	Teachers are willing to listen to students' concerns about interpersonal relationships and nonacademic questions and problems.
Helping with schoolwork	Teachers are willing to help students, continually encourage students to do their best, and spend time in and out of class trying to explain material in understandable ways.
Going the "extra mile"	Teachers are willing to spend time with students to provide guidance in personal matters, help with difficult classwork, and work with students on extracurricular activities.

Source: Based on work by Bosworth (1995). Adapted with permission.

Teacher Expectations

"This is a new idea we've been working on, and it will be challenging, but I know you can all do the assignment. I want you to start right in while the ideas are still fresh in your mind. I'll be around in a moment to answer any questions. When you're done, you can choose a game until recess."

"This material is hard, but we've got to learn it. I want everyone to start right away, and no fooling around. Jesse, did you hear me? Some of you will have problems with this, and I'll be around as soon as I can to straighten you out. No messing around until I get there."

Teacher expectations for student behavior and achievement are communicated subtly (and not so subtly) every day. The first teacher acknowledged that the assignment was difficult, but she expected students to successfully complete it. The second, in contrast, implied that some students were less able than others and presented the entire assignment in a negative frame of reference.

How Teachers Form Expectations.   Research examining the ways teachers form expectations is controversial (Good & Brophy, 1997). Several studies indicate that test scores, information about ability grouping, physical appearance, socioeconomic status (SES), race, and gender affect teacher expectations (Clifton, Perry, Parsonson, & Hryniuk, 1986; Jones, 1990; Jussim, 1989; Trujillo, 1986).

These studies, however, were based on data from fictional student records; the teachers had no opportunity to interact with real students. Other research indicates that teachers' perceptions of students are based primarily on the students' participation in learning activities and their performance on assignments and tests, rather than physical appearance or status (Good & Brophy, 1997). These studies indicate that teachers' perceptions of students are quite accurate, sometimes more accurate than predications based on test data (Helmke & Schrader, 1987; Short, 1985).

How Expectations Affect Teacher Behavior.   The effects of expectations on the ways teachers treat students can be grouped into four categories: emotional support, teacher effort and demands, questioning, and feedback and evaluation. They are summarized in Table 10.6.

Table 10.6   Characteristics of differential teacher expectations

Characteristic	Teacher Behavior Favoring Perceived High Achievers
Emotional support	Have more interactions; interact more positively; give more smiles; make more eye contact; stand closer; orient body more directly; seat students closer to teacher
Teacher effort and demands	Give clearer and more thorough explanations; give more enthusiastic instruction; ask more follow-up questions; require more complete and accurate student answers
Questioning	Call on more often; allow more time to answer; give more encouragement; do more prompting
Feedback and evaluation	Give more praise; give less criticism; offer more complete and lengthier feedback and more conceptual evaluations

Source: Based on reviews by Good (1987a, 1987b) and Good and Brophy (1997).

We see from the information in the table that teachers can be discriminatory, treating students they perceive to be high achievers more favorably than those they perceive to be low achievers. Students are sensitive to this discrimination, and children as young as first grade are aware of differential treatment of high and low achievers (Stipek, 1996). In one study, researchers concluded that, "After ten seconds of seeing and/or hearing a teacher, even very young students could detect whether the teacher talked about or to an excellent or a weak student and could determine the extent to which that student was loved by the teacher" (Babad, Bernieri, & Rosenthal, 1991, p. 230).

The impact of teacher expectations on student motivation can be best explained on the basis of which theory of motivation? Provide an explanation based on this theory.

Teacher Expectations: Implications for Motivation. What does this research suggest to teachers? First, when teacher expectations are realistic, such as those based on student performance, they pose little problem. When they are based on something other than student performance, however, or are lower than past performance warrants, they can reduce both motivation and achievement.

Second, expectations tend to be self-fulfilling. "Such low expectations can serve as self-fulfilling prophecies. That is, the expression of low expectations by differential treatment can inadvertently lead children to confirm predictions about their abilities by exerting less effort and ultimately performing more poorly" (Weinstein, 1998, p. 83). As a result, healthy attributions for both success and failure are harder to develop. High expectations, in contrast, communicate that the teacher cares enough to make every possible effort on their behalf; ultimately, motivation and self-worth are enhanced.

The goal of this section is to *increase awareness*. Expectations are subtle and often out of teachers' conscious control. As you saw in Chapter 4, teachers often don't realize

Positive teacher expectations communicate that all students can learn to their fullest potential.

that they hold different expectations for their students. With awareness and effort, teachers will do their best to treat all students as fairly and equitably as possible. We examine specific strategies to promote equitable treatment in Chapter 11.

Climate Variables: Creating a Motivating Environment

As students spend time in classrooms, they get feelings about whether they're safe and welcome and whether the classroom is a desirable place to learn. **Classroom climate** refers to *teacher and classroom characteristics that promote students' feelings of safety and security, together with a sense of success, challenge, and understanding* (see Figure 10.7).

Climate is important because it creates an environment that encourages both motivation and achievement (Raviv, Raviv, & Reisel, 1990). Students learn best in a safe and orderly environment that promotes success on meaningful and challenging tasks. In a healthy climate, students are treated as competent people. They understand the requirements of learning tasks, perceive them as challenging, and believe they will succeed if they make reasonable effort (Brophy, 1987b; Clifford, 1990). Let's look at specific ways to influence classroom climate.

Order and Safety: Classrooms as Secure Places to Learn

Effective schools are places of trust, order, cooperation, and high morale (Rutter, Maughn, Mortimore, Ouston, & Smith, 1979). For students to be motivated to learn, schools must be physically and psychologically safe places. In fact, safety is so important that it is addressed specifically in the *Learner-Centered Psychological Principles* (Alexander & Murphy, 1998; American Psychological Association Board of Educational Affairs, 1995), which we introduced in Chapter 1 and discuss in detail in Chapter 13.

Both cognitive and humanistic views of motivation provide rationales for establishing a safe and orderly learning environment. From a cognitive perspective, order helps create a sense of equilibrium in learners; from a humanistic view, only survival precedes safety as a need in Maslow's hierarchy.

How does this idea translate into classroom practice? First, the teacher sets the tone by modeling respect and courtesy. "Teachers who . . . avoid such negative practices as criticism of student behavior, screaming, sarcasm, scolding, and ridicule facilitate student learning" (Murphy, Weil, & McGreal, 1986, p. 86). Students who are criticized for venturing personal or creative thoughts about a topic are unlikely to take the risk a second time.

Success

Once a safe and orderly environment is established, student expectation for success is the most important climate variable. This is the expectancy component of expectancy × value theory. (Note here that we're referring to the learners' expectation for success, not teacher expectations as we discussed earlier.)

Teachers promote positive student expectations by using instructional strategies that maximize opportunities for success and minimize failures. For example:

- Begin lessons with open-ended questions. Build on students' existing understanding.

10.30

Explain the negative effects of criticism; use behaviorism as a basis for your explanation. Then explain using social cognitive theory.

10.31

Identify a specific example in Kathy Brewster's lesson in which she promoted feelings of safety in her students.

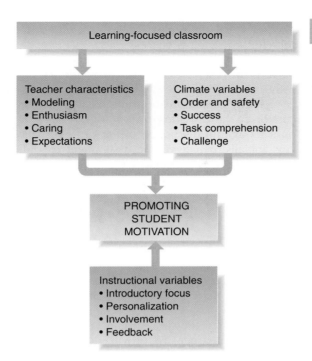

Figure 10.7 Climate variables in the model for promoting student motivation

- Use a variety of high-quality examples and demonstrations to promote understanding.
- Prompt students when they have difficulty answering questions.
- Provide scaffolded practice before students are put on their own.

Success—like many aspects of teaching and learning—isn't as simple as it appears. Our goal in promoting success is to help learners develop self-efficacy, which means the success must be on tasks learners perceive to be meaningful and worthwhile. Success on trivial tasks does little to create feelings of competence and self-efficacy. Without challenge, learners experience "artificial success," and apathy results (Clifford, 1990). Let's examine challenge further.

Challenge

Why do children persist in learning to ride a bicycle even though they fall repeatedly, and why does intrinsic interest in the skill decrease once it's been mastered? Children will stop riding a bicycle for its own sake, for example, and from that point on use it only to be with friends or ride to someone's house.

In the previous section, we emphasized that students need to be successful. This emphasis doesn't imply, however, that *constant* success is necessary or even desirable. In fact, to promote motivation, success should occur in moderately difficult or challenging tasks, and it should be explained in terms of personal effort, increasing ability, and well-chosen strategies (Clifford, 1990). A sense of challenge is needed if students are to experience feelings of satisfaction, competence, persistence, and control (Baron, 1998; Kloosterman, 1997; Wasserstein, 1995).

The importance of challenge is supported by White's (1959) concept of *competence motivation,* Piaget's (1952) work, the concept of *self-efficacy,* and goal theory.

10.32

You are teaching a lesson on "living things" to your first-graders and you display for them a live hamster and a stone from the playground. Describe two open-ended questions you could use to begin the lesson.

10.33

In this section we focused on cognitive interpretations of challenge. How would behaviorists explain the positive influence of challenge? How would humanistic thinkers explain it?

According to White and Piaget, only increasing competence is emotionally satisfying, self-efficacy requires success on tasks of worth and substance, and moderate difficulty is one characteristic of effective goals (Schunk, 1994). Some researchers believe *challenge* is an essential component of intrinsically motivating activities (Lepper & Hodell, 1989).

Kathy capitalized on the motivating features of challenge. She didn't limit her discussion of the Crusades to meaningless dates, times, and other facts, but instead focused on a thoughtful discussion of the Crusades' success or failure. Some students, like Harvey, initially perceived the assignment as difficult, but it was more satisfying than a hashing of the facts would have been. In pursuit of these challenging goals, Kathy provided enough scaffolding to ensure that her students could meet the challenge.

Task Comprehension

From expectancy × value theory, we know that, to be motivated, learners must expect to succeed and must believe that what they're learning is important and valuable. Challenge helps promote a sense of value. Value is also enhanced when *students understand both what they're supposed to be learning and why they're learning it* (Anderson, 1989; Blumenfeld, 1992; Good & Brophy, 1997). This understanding is called **task comprehension.**

The "why they're learning it" aspect of task comprehension is critical for both teacher and learner. To provide an appropriate rationale for objectives and learning activities, teachers must think about what they want students to learn and why it is important. If students are to be motivated to learn, activities should teach things that are worth learning (Good & Brophy, 1997).

From learners' perspectives, understanding what they're learning and why is critical in the development of self-regulation. Understanding "what" and "why" allows them to identify appropriate goals, select effective strategies, and maintain their effort in the face of difficulty.

Kathy focused explicitly on the reasons for studying the Crusades when she asked, "Why do we study the Crusades? Who cares, anyway?" Later, she commented, "We want to learn how to make and defend an argument, so the quality of your paragraph depends on how you defended your position, not on the position itself. Remember, this is a skill that goes way beyond a specific topic like the Crusades. This applies in everything we do." Questions and comments such as these help students understand why they are studying a topic. Further, when they see a link among the Crusades, the Renaissance, and their lives today, for example, they are more likely to believe that what they're learning is worthwhile. This belief increases the "value" component of expectancy × value theory.

Compare Kathy's comments with the following statements actually made by teachers.

> Today's lesson is nothing new if you've been here.
> Get your nose in the book; otherwise, I'll give you a writing assignment.
> This test is to see who the really smart ones are. (Brophy, 1987a, p. 204)

How motivated would you be if the teacher told you that you weren't going to learn anything new, that the rationale for an activity is to avoid a different assignment, or that a low score on a test means you aren't smart?

You can see how climate variables are interdependent. Kathy's challenging assignment was an effective motivator because the other variables were present. If her classroom had been emotionally threatening or if the students had been unable to succeed, the positive effects of challenge would have been lost. On the other hand, if her topic

10.34

Research indicates that activities that are too challenging might lower student motivation. What concept from this chapter best explains why this might be the case? Provide an explanation based on the concept.

10.35

On the basis of our earlier discussion of class structure, explain specifically why a statement such as, "This test is to see who the really smart ones are," could decrease motivation.

had been a dry coverage of facts or if the students hadn't known why they were studying it, no level of success or safety would have motivated them.

Instructional Variables: Developing Interest in Learning Activities

Teacher and climate variables form a general framework for motivation. Within this context, the teacher can do much in specific learning activities to enhance learner motivation. These factors are illustrated in Figure 10.8.

From an instructional perspective, a motivated student can be viewed as, ". . . someone who is actively engaged in the learning process" (Stipek, 1996, p. 85). But how do we promote and maintain active engagement? Teachers often think about engagement using the concept of *interest* (Zahorik, 1996), and a body of research examining interest is beginning to emerge (Alexander & Murphy, 1998). Interest is important because it, like engagement, has been linked to learner attention, comprehension, elaboration, and the seeking of additional information (Krapp, Hidi, & Renninger, 1992).

Certain topics seem to be universally interesting to students—death, danger, chaos, power, money, sex, and romance (Wade, 1992). Unfortunately, little of the school curriculum focuses on these topics, leaving teachers with the question, "What can you do to increase learner interest?"

To increase interest, our goal is to initially capture students' attention and then maintain their involvement in the learning activity. The instructional variables in Figure 10.8 are intended to accomplish these goals.

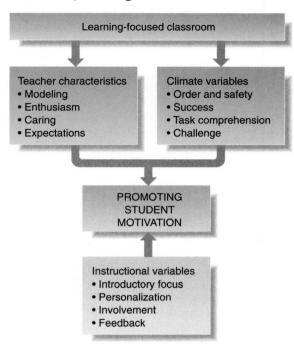

Figure 10.8 Instructional variables in the model for promoting student motivation

Introductory Focus: Attracting Students' Attention

As an introduction to the topic of cities and their locations, a social studies teacher hands out a map of a fictitious island. On it are physical features such as lakes, rivers, mountains, and bays. Also included is information about altitude, rainfall, and average seasonal temperature. The teacher begins, "Our class has just been sent to this island to settle it. We have this information about its climate and physical features. Where should we make our first settlement?"

A science teacher passes a baseball and a golf ball around the room and has the students feel them. After confirming that the baseball feels heavier, he climbs up onto his desk, holds the two balls in front of him, and, as he prepares to drop them, says, "I'm going to drop these balls at the same time. What do you predict will happen?"

By beginning their lessons in these ways, the teachers were attempting to increase interest by capitalizing on **introductory focus,** *which attracts student attention and provides a framework for the lesson.* In our discussion of curiosity motivation, we saw that learners are motivated by unique, attractive, eye-catching, or discrepant experiences, and—according to cognitive views of motivation—by a desire to *understand* events. Introductory focus capitalizes on the effects of curiosity and the desire for understanding.

10.36

Introductory focus performs two important functions. What are they?

Unfortunately, conscious planning for lesson introductions occurs infrequently; only 5% of teachers in one study made an explicit effort to draw students into the lesson (Anderson, Brubaker, Alleman-Brooks, & Duffy, 1984). Providing for effective introductory focus need not be difficult, however. All that is required is some conscious effort to connect the content of the lesson to students' backgrounds and interest. Some examples are provided in Table 10.7.

Once learners are attracted to the lesson and a conceptual framework is provided, the lesson has to maintain their attention. This can be accomplished through personalization, involvement, and feedback.

Personalization: Links to Students' Lives

One way to make learning tasks interesting is through personalization (Cordova & Lepper, 1996). Let's look again at Kathy Brewster's lesson. Early in the process, she said, "Remember, we started by imagining that we all left Lincoln High School and that it was taken over by people who believed that all extracurricular activities should be cut out." She then used this example as a framework and an analogy to introduce her students to the Crusades. As another example, when introducing the topic of genetics, a teacher might say, "Once we understand genetics, we'll be able to figure out why Reeanne has blue eyes and Edward has brown."

10.37

Look again at the example with Reeanne, Edward, and eye color. Explain how it might be used as an example of both introductory focus and personalization. Then describe how it might be used only as personalization.

These are both examples of personalization, or *personal meaningfulness*. **Personalization** *attempts to make topics meaningful by using intellectually and/or emotionally relevant examples.* Kathy used her school; she combined both intellectually and emotionally relevant examples. In the case with genetics, the teacher used two students in her class.

"Most motivation theorists encourage the development of tasks that have some personal meaning for students" (Stipek, 1996; p. 101). A survey of experienced teachers corroborates these views; they described personalization as one of the most important ways to promote student interest in learning activities (Zahorik, 1996).

The value of *personalization* can be explained in several ways. First, relating content to students personally is a core element of humanistic views of motivation. Second, you saw in Chapter 7 that meaningfulness enhances learning; personalization is one way of increasing meaningfulness. Third, anything people can relate to personally is more concrete for them than distant or abstract information; you saw in Chapter 2 that concrete experiences were an essential component of Piaget's work.

When direct personalization is difficult, analogies can be used. As an example, let's look at the way a teacher introduced *Julius Caesar,* a classic play about power, ambition, friendship, and denial. Its message is as important today as when it was written more than 300 years ago.

> *Julius Caesar* is basically a play about an internal conflict, a moral decision for which there is really no wrong or right answer. If we kill this man, we might save our republic but we endanger ourselves. If we don't kill him, we could be endangered. [It focuses on one] man's struggle with a moral decision, the consequences of his actions, and how people turn against him.
>
> And so . . . . I gave them an artificial scenario. I said, "You are the first officer on the Starship Enterprise.
>
> "Captain Kirk has been getting out of hand. He's a good captain; he's been made Commander of the Fleet. But you, his closest friend, and your fellow officers have been noticing that he's been getting too risky, a little big-headed. You're afraid that he's going to endanger the Federation Fleet and might just seek glory in some farcical campaign."

Table 10.7 Types and examples of introductory focus

Type	Example
Problems and questions	A literature teacher shows a picture of Hemingway and says, "Here we see 'Papa' in all his splendor. He seemed to have everything—fame, adventure, romance. Yet, he took his own life. Why would this happen?"
	A science teacher asks students to explain why two pieces of paper come together at the bottom (rather than move apart) when students blow between them.
Inductive sequences	Students see the following sentences "I had a ton of homework last night!" "That's the ugliest outfit ever!" "She's the most gorgeous girl in the world!"
	They find a pattern and develop a concept of *hyperbole.*
Attractive examples	A literature teacher shows the class a picture of Ernest Hemingway.
	An elementary teacher begins a unit on amphibians by bringing in a live frog.
Objectives and rationales	A math teacher begins, "Today, we want to learn about unit pricing. This will help us decide which product is a better buy. It will help us all save money and be better consumers."

And they really took off on that . . . they said they found out there really wasn't a right answer. They argued back and forth. You couldn't just kill him because the whole fleet likes him. If you kill him, it's your head on the chopping block, too. But you also have a moral obligation to your country and you can't let him go on. What they finally came up with was that it's a pretty tough decision to make. (Wilson, Shulman, & Richert, 1987, p. 112)

By comparing *Julius Caesar* to characters on the Starship Enterprise, the teacher was able to relate the Shakespearean story to *Star Trek*—something real in students' lives.

Involvement

Introductory focus and personalization pull students into lessons but, unless a lesson or topic is particularly intriguing or timely, neither one alone nor the two in combination will sustain motivation. The key to maintaining motivation is **involvement,** *students actively participating in the learning activity.*

Think about your experience at lunch or a party. When you're talking and actively listening, you pay more attention to the conversation than you do when you're on its fringes. The same applies in classrooms. Conscious teacher efforts to promote involvement result in increased participation and learning (Blumenfeld, 1992; Pratton & Hales, 1986). Let's look at two specific strategies for increasing student involvement: open-ended questioning and hands-on activities.

> **10.38**
>
> Is the concept of *involvement* the same as the concept of *activity* as we discussed it in Chapter 7? If not, how are they different?

Effective teachers maintain students' motivation by by actively involving them in lessons.

Using Open-Ended Questioning to Promote Involvement.   Questioning is the most generally applicable tool the teacher has to maintain involvement. Student attention is at a peak when teachers ask questions but drops during teacher monologues (Lemke, 1982).

We discuss questioning in detail in Chapter 11, but we introduce one strategy here, because it is particularly effective in improving involvement and motivation. This strategy is open-ended questioning (Kauchak & Eggen, 1998). **Open-ended questions** *are those for which a variety of answers are acceptable.* For instance, in a lesson on amphibians, a teacher might begin by showing the students a frog or picture of a frog and asking,

"Look at the frog. What do you see in the picture?"

In the case of *Julius Caesar,* the teacher might ask,

"What has happened so far in the play?"

"What are some of the major events?"

"What is one thing you remember about the play?"

These ask for simple observations of the topic. A second type of open-ended question asks for comparisons. For instance,

"How is the frog similar to a lizard?"

"How are the frog and a toad similar or different?"

"How are Brutus and Marc Antony similar? How are they different?"

"How does the setting for Act I compare with that for Act II?"

Because many answers are acceptable, open-ended questions are safe and virtually ensure success—two of the climate variables we discussed earlier. By combining safety and success, even the most reluctant student can be encouraged to respond without risk or fear of embarrassment.

Also, because they can be asked and answered quickly, open-ended questions can help solve the problem of involving 30 or more members of a class during a single lesson. Without the use of at least some open-ended questions, calling on reluctant responders often enough to increase their level of attention and interest can be difficult.

We caution, however, that "artificial" open-ended questions don't work. If students are asked to observe or compare but the teacher has a particular answer in mind, students quickly perceive that the questions aren't truly open-ended, and their effectiveness is reduced.

10.39

What climate variable must exist before students will be willingly involved? Explain.

Involving Students: Hands-On Activities.   Using hands-on activities is another effective way of promoting involvement and student interest (Zahorik, 1996). When students are working with manipulatives in math, concrete materials in science, maps and globes in geography, or computers as they write essays, their level of interest increases significantly. In addition, hands-on activities add variety in learning activities, and variety has been found to create learner interest (Zahorik, 1996).

Additional ways of promoting involvement and interest are illustrated in Table 10.8. Improvement drills add an element of game-like arousal to otherwise routine activities, and seeing improvement can increase self-efficacy. Using chalkboards is similar to having students solve problems on paper at their desks, but the chalkboards are more hands-on, and students often will use them even when they won't try if only paper is used.

Groupwork, in which students work together toward common learning goals, can also promote motivation (Baron, 1998; West, 1997). David Shelton, Jenny Newhall, and

Table 10.8   Strategies to promote involvement

Technique	Example
Improvement drills	Students are given a list of 10 multiplication facts on a sheet. Students are scored on speed and accuracy, and points are given for individual improvement.
Games	The class is divided equally according to ability, and the two groups respond in a game format to teacher questions.
Individual work spaces	Students are given their own chalkboards on which they solve math problems and identify examples of concepts. They hold the chalkboards up when they've solved the problem or when they think an example illustrates a concept. They also write or draw their own examples on the chalkboards.
Student groupwork	Student pairs observe a science demonstration and write down as many observations of it as they can.

Sue Southam in Chapter 7 and Laura Hunter and Sue Brush in Chapter 8 all used groupwork to promote student involvement and interest.

Feedback

Let's return to Kathy's lesson once more. In addition to everything else she did, Kathy gave students specific information about progress on their paragraphs. Research indicates that feedback used to improve future performance has powerful motivational value (Clifford, 1990). In fact, the influence of feedback is so powerful that it could be called a principle of learning and motivation.

Feedback is particularly motivating when combined with clear student goals. Feedback gives learners information about the extent to which goals are being attained and, if they're falling short, they can try harder or use a different strategy. If they have met or exceeded the goal, they get a feeling of accomplishment and increased self-efficacy.

10.40

On the basis of the information in this section, what should a teacher do after scoring a test and returning it to students?

The need for feedback can be explained using cognitive theories of motivation. Not having a sense of how you're doing interferes with equilibrium, and a feeling of self-efficacy is impossible if you're not sure how you're performing. In our discussion of attribution theory, you also found that learners have a need to understand and explain why they are performing the way they are. Feedback helps them form accurate explanations.

When teachers provide feedback about performance, the emphasis should be on progress and mastery of the content, rather than on social comparisons (Crooks, 1988; Maehr, 1992; Schunk, 1994). This is especially important for less able students.

Combining Elements of the Model for Promoting Student Motivation

We have now examined the class structure and each of the 12 components of the model for promoting student motivation. We described them separately for the sake of clarity, but we want to emphasize the benefits of combining as many components as possible in your teaching. For instance, one middle-school teacher did the following:

> In beginning a unit on folktales, the teacher wrote three folktales about the school principal and two other teachers in the school. She began the lesson by telling the students that they would be given some brief stories and that they were to read them and find a pattern in them. The purpose was to give them some practice in becoming good thinkers. She then asked the students to make observations about the stories by comparing them and looking for characteristics they had in common.

The teacher in this case capitalized on several elements of the model. She presented the folktales as a form of introductory focus, and her purpose and rationale for the lesson helped promote task comprehension. She used open-ended questioning to promote safety, success, and involvement, and her folktales capitalized on personalization. In this simple example, the teacher employed six features of the model, and it would have been easy to change the wording of her introduction slightly to increase the element of challenge. Assuming she has motivating personal characteristics, most of the model is employed in one simple yet creative lesson.

One of the most important messages we want to send in writing this chapter is that teachers' roles involve much more than simply delivering content. One of those aspects is a conscious attempt to promote student motivation to learn.

Classroom Connections

Demonstrating the Personal Characteristics of the Model for Promoting Student Motivation in Your Classroom

1. Show students you care by giving them your personal time.
   - A geography teacher calls parents as soon as he sees a student having even minor academic or personal problems. He solicits their help in monitoring the student and solving the problem.

2. Display enthusiasm in your teaching.
   - During quiet reading time, a fourth-grade teacher comments on a book she's interested in and reads while the students are reading.

3. Model incremental views of ability.
   - An English teacher comments, "I've really studied a lot since I started teaching this class, and I'm a lot smarter in American literature than I've ever been before."

4. Maintain appropriately high expectations for all students.
   - A second-grade teacher makes a conscious attempt to treat all students in her class as equally as possible, distributing her questions to them equally, and demanding as much as she can from each.

Applying the Climate Variables of the Model for Promoting Student Motivation in Your Classroom

5. Carefully describe objectives and rationales for your assignments.
   - A junior-high English teacher carefully describes his assignment and due dates. Each time, he explains why the assignment is important.

6. Promote challenge and success in learning activities.
   - A fifth-grade teacher comments, "We're really getting good at percentages. I have a problem that is going to make us all think. It will be tough, but I think we can do it."

   - A language-arts teacher always has the class practice three or four homework exercises as a whole group and discusses them before students begin to work independently.

Applying the Instructional Variables of the Model for Promoting Student Motivation in Your Classroom

7. Plan lesson introductions to attract students' attention and provide an umbrella for the lesson.
   - A middle-school science teacher begins each class with a question or problem that leads into the lesson. She began one lesson on local geology by asking students to imagine what their area looked like 1 million, 10 million, and 100 million years ago.
   - A fifth-grade teacher introduces concepts, principles, and rules inductively by beginning with examples, asking students to describe and compare the examples and find patterns that lead to each idea.

8. Promote involvement by eliciting responses from all students.
   - A language-arts teacher randomly calls on all her students whether or not they raise their hands. At the beginning of the year, she explains that this is her practice, that her intent is to encourage participation, and that they will soon get over any uneasiness about being "put on the spot." Whenever students are unable to answer, she gives them extra support in the form of cues and prompts.

9. Personalize content.
   - A history teacher begins a unit on World War II by commenting that many of the students' grandparents and great-grandparents were probably directly involved in it. As an alternative assignment, he asks students to interview their grandparents about their memories of and experiences of the War.

- A fifth-grade teacher begins a lesson on percentage by bringing in an advertisement for toys from a local newspaper. The ad says "10% to 25% off marked prices." After discussing how to compute percentage discounts, she returns to the ad and asks students to compute their savings on various items.

10. Provide prompt and informative feedback on student performance.
   - A fourth-grade teacher discussed the most frequently missed items on all her quizzes, asking students to explain why the correct answers are correct and considering the questions from different perspectives whenever possible.
   - A seventh-grade teacher writes on a student paper, "You have some very good ideas. Now you need to rework your essay so that it is grammatically correct. Look carefully at the notes I've made on your paper."

Motivation and Diversity

When we examine the research on the school success of ethnic minorities, we see a pattern. On most measures of school success—achievement test scores, retention in grade, and drop-out rates—many ethnic minorities in the United States perform less well than their majority counterparts (Macionis, 1994; Mullis, Dossey, Foertsh, Jones, & Gentile, 1991). Although some differences can be linked to SES, troubling disparities remain. Many minority students leave school unprepared to participate in and benefit from today's technologically-oriented and skill-demanding world.

Educators have turned to motivational research in an attempt to address these problems. Unfortunately, the picture remains cloudy. For example, researchers have attempted to explain why the achievement of African American students is lower than expected by hypothesizing deficits in need for achievement, internal locus of control, expectations for success, and academic self-concept—all motivational factors linked to achievement. In a comprehensive review of this literature, however, Graham (1994) concluded that deficits don't exist and that African American students "maintain a belief in personal control, have high expectance, and enjoy positive self-regard" (p. 55). Researchers have also found that African American and Latina mothers have strong interest in their children's schooling, are enthusiastic about education, and hold high expectations for their children's future (Stevenson, Chen, & Uttal, 1990).

The picture is made more complex by research suggesting that motivation varies not only between minority groups but also within groups. For example, researchers have identified differences in the way African American parents approach the task of motivating their children (Steinberg, Dornbusch, & Brown, 1992), and similar differences have been identified in Asian and Latino families. Peer groups within minority cultures also influence motivation differently, sometimes complementing school achievement, at other times detracting from it (Goodenow, 1992b; Steinberg et al., 1992). In addition, researchers have pointed out the considerable differences that exist among different African American communities: motivational issues in an inner-city African American community are different from those in suburban or rural ones (Graham, 1994; Slaughter-Defoe, Nakagawa, Takanashi, & Johnson, 1990).

10.41

From your study of the classroom model for promoting student motivation, what are some teacher characteristics, climate variables, and instructional variables that could influence minority students' motivation?

Motivational Problems: Student Perspectives

In attempting to understand how schools influence minority students' motivation and achievement, researchers have focused on students' perceptions of their school experiences and have identified the following problems:

- Lack of connection between classroom content and students' lives
- Alienation from school
- Disengagement and lack of involvement in classes
- Distant and inflexible teachers

Students report feeling alienated from school, like outsiders at a party. This feeling results from factors such as cultural discontinuities, language barriers, and academic problems (Ogbu 1992; Wong-Fillmore, 1992). In one study, researchers asked about connections between school and students' personal happiness:

Interviewer:	What do you really like about school? What makes you happy?
Diane:	Nothing really. I just come because I have to. Because I don't want to grow up being stupid.
Interviewer:	There's nothing you look forward to?
Diane:	Ummm . . . (defiantly stares; challenges.) Getting an education?
Interviewer:	Do you think there's a way to get an education without coming to school?
Diane:	(shakes her head no)
Interviewer:	It has to be this way?
Diane:	(softly; no eye contact) Yeah.

(Kramer & Colvin, 1991, p. 6)

Another student, who was discussing his decision to leave school at age 16, describes his alienation as follows:

Student:	I wouldn't go to nobody.
Interviewer:	Not even a counselor?
Student:	No.
Interviewer:	That seems funny. Don't you work in the office?
Student:	Yeah, but I don't *talk* to them [student emphasis].

(Kramer-Schlosser, 1992, p. 132)

Disengagement is another problem. Teachers report that students don't come to class or that when they do, they are reluctant to participate.

> They'll try to sit at the edges or the back of the classroom and they actually try to become less visible to me, or they'll act up so they get sent out of the classroom and there's less time, less chance I'll call on them or hold them accountable. . . . Usually they don't join the class. (Kramer & Colvin, 1991, p. 12)

Adding to these problems are student perceptions that teachers just don't care. One student described her teachers this way:

Nichole:	People here don't have many people to talk to. I don't. The teachers . . . some of them don't care about their students.

10.42

How does student disengagement relate to the concept of *involvement* discussed earlier? What questioning strategy suggested in this chapter and other parts of this text would be effective in increasing the involvement of cultural minorities?

	They say, "They [administrators] want me to teach and I'm going to do it no matter what." I don't like that. I like them to say, "I'm here to teach and help you because I care." That's what I like. But a lot of them are just saying, "I'm here to teach so I'm gonna teach." I don't think that's right.
Interviewer:	Do they actually say that?
Nichole:	It's more an attitude, and they do say it. Like Ms. G. She's like . . . she never says it, but you know, she's just there and she just wants to teach, but she doesn't want to explain the whole deal.
Interviewer:	How do you know that?
Nichole:	I could feel it. The way she acts and the way she does things. She's been here seven years and all the kids I've talked to that have had her before say, "Oooh! You have Ms. G.!" Just like that.
Interviewer:	But a teacher who really cares, how do they act?
Nichole:	Like Mr. P. He really cares about his students. He's helping me a lot and he tells me, "I'm not angry with you, I just care about you." He's real caring and he does teach me when he cares.

(Kramer & Colvin, 1991, p. 13)

The pattern we see is a lack of connection to both school and classes. Students attend school, sit in classes, but don't feel a part of them. They question whether anyone cares about them and, from their perspective, the classes have little meaning for their daily lives.

Motivational Problems: Possible Solutions

Research suggests some possible solutions to student alienation and disengagement. Students must feel that they belong and can contribute to the classroom community. They need to value the classes they take and find them meaningful.

Teachers are critical to the success of this process. Research indicates that those who are effective at motivating at-risk and minority students have the following characteristics:

- They are enthusiastic, supportive, and have high expectations for student achievement.
- They create learner-centered classrooms with high levels of student involvement.
- They make a special effort to connect classroom content to students' lives (Kramer & Colvin, 1991; Kramer-Schlosser, 1992).

Teachers need to make a special effort to make all students feel welcome and to demonstrate that they sincerely care. They also need to communicate that they hold positive expectations and that they'll work with learners if students try. One teacher identified as effective in working with minority and at-risk students described his efforts in this way:

I believe that marginal students who begin the year poorly and improved did so because they knew I would do all I could to help them to be a success in school. I told them I would explain, and explain, and explain until they understood. They were worth every moment it would take. No one ever has to fail. (Kramer-Schlosser, 1992, p. 137)

Because a focus on learners is a theme of this text, we emphasize two characteristics of teachers who support learners in their classrooms. First, they attempt to connect the topics they teach to the lives and concerns of students. Second, they create learning activities that promote high levels of student involvement. Teacher questioning, hands-on activities, groupwork, and discussions replace lectures and other teacher-centered approaches. They literally take the content to students, rather than say, "Here it is. Come and get it if you want it."

Teacher characteristics such as *caring, enthusiasm,* and *high expectations*—important for all students—are critical for minority and at-risk learners. Other motivational elements, such as *order and safety, challenge, success,* and *feedback,* make classrooms accessible and inviting for students on the margins. Conscious attention to these variables are important for all students and especially so for motivating diverse learners.

Classroom Connections

Capitalizing on Diversity in Your Classroom

1. Communicate positive expectations for student success through your words and teaching strategies.

   - A math teacher responsible for basic math classes stresses at the beginning of the school year that she expects all students to succeed. She collects and grades homework every day and talks with students and their parents when it isn't handed in. She tests and quizzes frequently and gives detailed feedback to students about their performance.

2. Create learning environments that involve students in meaningful learning.

   - A social-studies teacher supplements his units with student group projects. For example, in their study of the Civil Rights Movement of the 1960s, he asks students to interview older neighbors, relatives, and friends about their memories of the Movement and has groups report on their findings on a class sharing day.

   - An English teacher redesigned his writing class to address issues that were important to his students. At the beginning of the term, he spent some time identifying issues that students wanted to talk and write about (e.g., dress codes, cafeteria food). He encouraged students to debate issues before writing about them and arranged with the school newspaper to publish some of the better ones in a pro and con editorial section.

3. Communicate caring by spending time with students, on both academic and personal topics.

   - A middle-school science teacher in an inner-city school helps organize an after-school science club. Students work on projects, take field trips, and have different professionals in the scientific community come in to talk about their jobs. Whenever possible, she recruits minorities and females for these professional visits.

   - An elementary teacher regularly calls parents and other caregivers, both to discuss attendance or academic problems and to congratulate them on special achievements or improvements by their children.

Windows on Classrooms

At the beginning of the chapter, you saw how Kathy Brewster applied an understanding of student motivation in her teaching. She maintained high expectations for her students, accommodated their personal needs, promoted self-efficacy, and maintained a high level of student involvement in a safe and orderly learning environment.

We turn now to a case study that describes another teacher presenting the same topic to a different group of students. As you read this classroom episode, compare the approach with Kathy Brewster's work with her students.

"What are we up to today, Mr. Marcus?" Joe asked as he came into Damon Marcus's classroom Thursday morning.

"You'll see in a minute," Damon nodded and smiled. "Now, quickly, get to your seat so that we can get started."

Damon watched as students took their seats, and then announced, "Listen, everyone, I have your tests here from last Friday. Liora, Ivan, Lynn, and Segundo, super job on the test. They were the only A's in the class."

After handing back the tests, Damon moved to the chalkboard and wrote the following:

A-4
B-7
C-11
D-4
F-3

"You people down here better get moving," Damon commented, pointing to the D's and F's on the chalkboard. "This wasn't that hard a test. Remember, we have another test in 2 weeks. Let's have some improvement. C'mon, now. I know you can do better. Let's give these four a run for their money.

"You can look over your papers, but be sure to turn them in by the end of the class period," Damon continued, as he turned to the day's lesson.

"Now let's get going. We have a lot to cover today. . . . As you'll recall from yesterday, we began talking about the Crusades and said that they were an attempt by the Christian powers of Western Europe to wrest control of the traditional holy lands of Christianity away from the Muslims. Now when was the First Crusade?" Damon asked, looking over the classroom.

"About 1500, I think," Clifton volunteered.

"No, no," Damon shook his head. "Remember that Columbus sailed in 1492, which was before 1500, so that doesn't make sense. It was well before 1500. . . . Wynetta?"

"It was about 1100, I think."

"Excellent, Wynetta. Now, remember, everyone, you need to know these dates, or otherwise you'll get confused just as Clifton did here. I know that learning dates and places isn't the most pleasant stuff, but you might as well get used to it because that's what history is about and they'll be on the next test."

While this was going on, Brad whispered to Donna, "Let me look at your test a sec. I got one point on this one, and I don't get it." Donna handed Brad her test, and he carefully read her answer and then read his own again.

"I still don't get it," he whispered and shrugged as he handed back her paper.

"Ask him about it," Donna suggested.

Damon continued, "The First Crusade was in 1095, and it was called the 'People's Crusade.' There were actually seven Crusades in all, ranging from the one in 1095 to the point where enthusiasm for them ended by 1300."

"The Fourth Crusade was particularly notorious," he continued. "In it, the Crusaders sacked Constantinople in 1203, and the Greek Byzantine Church hated the Crusaders forever after that."

Damon continued, "The Crusades weren't just religiously motivated. The Muslim world was getting stronger and stronger, and it was posing a threat to Europe. For example, it had control of much of northern Africa, had expanded into southern Spain, and even was moving into other parts of southern Europe. So it was a threat economically and militarily, as well as religiously. This was also a factor in the Crusades."

Damon continued presenting information about the Crusades, including facts such as Richard the Lionheart's capture of Cyprus and the sponsorship of later Crusades by the French.

Seeing that about 20 minutes were left in the period, Damon then said, "Now I want you to write a summary of the Crusades that outlines the major people and events and tells why they were important. You should be able to finish by the end of the class period. If you don't, turn them in tomorrow at the beginning of the class period. You may use your notes. Go ahead and get started while I come around and collect your tests."

As Damon started to collect the tests, Brad came up to his desk and said, "Mr. Marcus, I don't get this. I only got 1 out of 5 on this one. But Donna got a 4 and the answers say almost the same thing."

"Let me look at Donna's," Damon requested.

Brad went back and got Donna's test. Damon looked at both tests, and turned to Brad, "Donna's answer was better organized and clearer than yours."

He continued down the aisles, collecting students' tests. As he went by, he saw that Jeremy hadn't written anything on his paper. Damon finished collecting the papers and then went back to Jeremy's desk. Jeremy's paper was still blank.

"C'mon back here," Damon motioned to a table at the back of the room.

"Are you having trouble getting started?" Damon asked sympathetically. "I know you have a tough time with written assignments. Let me help you."

Damon then took a blank piece of paper and started writing as Jeremy watched. He wrote several sentences on the paper and then said, "See how easy that was? That's the kind of thing I want you to do. Go ahead—that's a start. Keep that so you can see what I'm looking for. Go back to your desk and give it another try."

Questions for Discussion and Analysis

Compare Damon's lesson with Kathy's. In making your comparison, consider the following questions. In each case, be specific and take information directly from the case studies.

1. Compare the two teachers' attempts to capitalize on the motivating effects of arousal. How were they alike and different?

2. Would Damon's handling of the lesson likely appeal to students with a high need for achievement? How appealing would the lesson be for students with a high need to avoid failure? Explain in both cases.

3. Assess Damon's lesson in terms of Maslow's hierarchy. How well did he meet needs at each level?

4. Would Damon's teaching more likely promote learning goals or performance goals? a task orientation or an ego orientation? Explain.

5. On the basis of Damon's remarks after he turned back the test, describe some possible attributions for students who did well on the test and some possible attributions for students who did poorly on the test.

6. Assess the effectiveness of Damon's lesson for students from diverse backgrounds. Make specific suggestions for improvement in instances for which you believe his teaching could be improved.

7. Assess Damon's instruction on the basis of each element of the model for promoting student motivation. In instances in which you believe he could have improved, offer specific suggestions for improvement.

Summary

Extrinsic and Intrinsic Motivation

Motivation is a force that energizes, sustains, and directs behavior toward a goal. Extrinsic motivation—the desire to engage in a task as a means to an end—comes from outside the learner in the form of high test scores, grades, and teacher compliments. Intrinsic motivation—the desire to engage in a task for its own sake—is a response to needs within the learner, such as curiosity, a desire for competence, or the feeling of being able to accomplish a goal. Fostering intrinsic motivation should be a goal of all teaching.

Theories of Motivation

Behaviorism suggests that motivation results from using reinforcers effectively. Critics of behavioral approaches to motivation contend that reinforcers detract from intrinsic motivation and cause learners to focus on the reinforcers instead of learning.

Cognitive views of motivation emphasize that people have an innate need for order and predictability. Closely related to Piaget's concept of *equilibrium,* cognitive theories suggest that learners are motivated to resolve cognitive conflict when experiences don't make sense to them.

Humanistic views of motivation focus on the learner as a whole person and examine the relationships among physical, emotional, intellectual, and aesthetic needs. Classroom climate and the teacher–student relationship are central to the humanistic view.

Personal Factors in Motivation

Arousal is a physical or psychological reaction to the environment. Extreme arousal can result in anxiety, which is both a cause and a result of poor performance. Teachers can capitalize on the positive effects of arousal by using eye-catching or discrepant events in their teaching.

A need is a real or perceived lack of something necessary. From a humanistic perspective, Maslow described a hierarchy beginning with survival and safety needs, progressing through belonging and esteem needs, and ending with intellectual and aesthetic needs. Cognitive needs include needs for competence, control, and achievement. Attribution theory describes people's desire to understand and explain their performance on tasks.

Motivation is an important element of self-regulation. Self-regulated learners set challenging goals, persist in the face of difficulty, and adjust when strategies are ineffective. Learners high in self-efficacy also display characteristics of self-regulation.

A Classroom Model for Promoting Student Motivation

Within a learning-focused rather than a performance-focused classroom, teachers can do much to increase student motivation to learn. Teacher characteristics, including modeling, enthusiasm, caring, and high expectations, combine with classroom climate and instructional variables to enhance motivation.

Motivation is increased when students work in a safe and orderly classroom, experience success, understand tasks and the reasons for them, and experience optimal challenge. Teachers can increase motivation in their lessons by preparing attractive lesson beginnings, involving students, personalizing content, and providing informative feedback.

Important Concepts _____

achievement motivation (p. 411)

anxiety (p. 407)

arousal (p. 407)

attribution theory (p. 412)

attributional statements (p. 414)

attributions (p. 412)

caring (p. 425)

classroom climate (p. 428)

cognitive theories of motivation (p. 402)

competence motivation (p. 410)

curiosity (p. 408)

deficiency needs (p. 408)

entity view of ability (p. 414)

expectancy × value theories (p. 402)

extrinsic motivation (p. 398)

growth needs (p. 408)

humanistic psychology (p. 404)

incremental view of ability (p. 414)

intrinsic motivation (p. 398)

introductory focus (p. 431)

involvement (p. 433)

learned helplessness (p. 412)

learning goals (p. 418)

motivation (p. 398)

motivational control (p. 419)

need (p. 408)

open-ended questions (p. 434)

performance goals (p. 418)

personalization (p. 432)

self-efficacy (p. 402)

task comprehension (p. 430)

Creating Productive Learning Environments

CHAPTER OUTLINE

"What are you doing with those cake pans?" Jim Barton jokingly asked his wife, Shirley, as he walked into the kitchen and saw her hard at work constructing some cardboard cake pans.

"What do you think?" she grinned at him. "Do they look like cake?" she asked, holding up rectangular cardboard pieces drawn to resemble two cakes cut into pieces.

"Actually, they almost do," he responded, a bit impressed with her work.

"My students didn't score as well as I would have liked on the fractions part of the Stanford Achievement Test last year, and I promised myself that they were going to do better this year."

"But you said the students aren't as sharp this year."

"That doesn't matter. I'm pushing them harder. I think I could have done a better job last year, so I swore I was really going to be ready for them this time."

Jim walked back into the living room with a smile on his face, mumbling something about thinking that teachers who have taught for 11 years were supposed to burn out.

The next day, Shirley met with her 28 fifth-graders, and they began their day, which usually follows this schedule:

8:30–10:00	Language arts (spelling, writing, grammar)
10:00–10:55	Math
10:55–11:05	Break
11:05–11:35	Science
11:35–12:00	Lunch
12:00–1:30	Reading
1:30–2:00	Social Studies
2:00–3:00	Rotating subjects (art, music, P.E., computer)

As Shirley walked up and down the aisles, she put two pieces of paper on each student's desk and stopped periodically to comment on someone's work or offer reassurance as the class completed a writing assignment. When she glanced at her watch and saw that it was 9:58, she announced, "Quickly turn in your writing and get out your math homework. We're running a little late today." As she walked by Brad, she touched him on the arm and pointed to his folder, reminding him to return from his window-gazing.

Her students stopped their writing and passed the papers forward, each putting his or her paper on top of the stack. Shirley collected them from the first person in each row and, as she walked by Shelli, she paused and asked, "How are you feeling today, Shelli? Is your cold better?"

"A lot better," Shelli replied. "I've just got some sniffles now."

Shirley put the papers into a folder and stepped to the chalkboard as she watched the students put their reading materials away and pull out their math books. She wrote the following problems on the chalkboard:

$$\frac{3}{8} + \frac{2}{8} = \qquad \frac{3}{7} + \frac{4}{7} =$$

$$\frac{5}{12} + \frac{6}{12} =$$

At 10:01, the students had their math books out and were waiting.

"Now," she began as she pulled out two drawings designed to look like pizzas, each cut into eight parts, "We've been adding fractions, so for a moment, let's look again at what we've been doing. What does the 8 mean in the first problem? . . . Dean?"

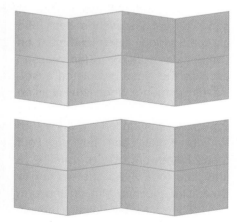

"We have eight parts of something altogether."

"Parts of what?"

". . . Supposed to be pizza."

"And what kind of parts? . . . Emerson?"

". . . ."

"How do the parts compare with each other?"

". . . They're all equal."

As soon as Shirley walks past him, Kevin sticks his foot across the aisle, tapping Alison on the leg with his shoe while he watches Shirley's back from the corner of his eye. "Stop it, Kevin," Alison mutters, swiping at him with her hand.

Shirley turns, comes back up the aisle, and continues, "Good, Emerson," and standing next to Kevin, she asks, "How do we know they're equal? . . . Kevin?" looking directly at him.

". . . I . . . I can see them. . . . They look equal."

"Okay. Good," Shirley smiled. "We have two pizzas, both cut into eight equal parts."

Shirley continued, asking Nel what the top numbers meant in the first problem. She then asked, "How much pizza did we eat altogether? . . . Gayle?"

"Five pieces."

"What part of a whole pizza did we eat?"

"I . . . . think . . . 5/8 of it."

"Good. And how did Gayle get that? . . . Estella?"

". . . She added them up."

"How might we prove that adding them up is the thing to do? . . . Anyone?"

After a short pause, Natasha finally said, "We have three pieces there (pointing to the first drawing), and if we had two more pieces, we would have five altogether, so it would be 3/8 and 2/8, which would be 5/8 altogether."

"What do the rest of you think about that?" Shirley queried.

"I don't think so," Adam shook his head. "It looks like 5/16 to me."

"No, look," Natasha countered, pointing to the drawing. "We have only eight pieces altogether."

"What about the other drawing?"

"We're not on the other drawing. We're on this one. I said put two more pieces on this one."

Shirley watched as other students joined the discussion, moved over to Sondra, who had been whispering and passing notes to Sherrill across the aisle, and said quietly, "Move up here," nodding to a desk at the front of the room.

"What did I do?" Sondra protested.

"When we talked about our rules at the beginning of the year, we agreed that it was important to listen when other people are talking," Shirley whispered to her.

"I was listening," Sondra protested.

"We don't learn as much when people aren't paying attention, and I'm uncomfortable when we don't learn. Move quickly now," Shirley said evenly as she watched the progress of the discussion.

Her students continued discussing the pizza problem for several more minutes, finally agreeing that Natasha's "proof" seemed to make sense.

Shirley then continued with the second and third problems on the chalkboard and concluded by saying, as she tapped her knuckle on the chalkboard, "Now, let's think about these problems. What is similar about them? Like, pretend that they're all pizzas and we're adding pieces of them."

". . . They all have the same pieces," Karen noted.

"I'm not sure what you mean," Shirley queried.

". . . Like 8 and 8, 7 and 7, and 12 and 12."

"Ahh, I see," Shirley nodded. "Each of these problems has the same denominator." She pointed respectively to the 8s, the 7s, and the 12s. "Yes," she said raising her voice, "let's keep that in mind as we study some more problems.

"Now," she continued as she strode vigorously across the front of the room, "we're going to shift gears because I've got another, different kind of problem." She pulled out the two cardboard cake rectangles that she had made the night before, one divided into thirds and the other divided in half.

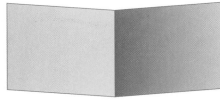

"Now we have cakes instead of pizza," she smiled, "and I'm still hungry, so I eat this piece," she said, pointing to the third. "Then I go sort of wild and eat this piece too," pointing to the half. "How much cake have I eaten?"

"A third of one and a half of the other," Tenisha volunteered.

"Makes sense, . . . but is that more than a whole cake, a whole cake, or what part of a cake?"

". . . I'm pretty sure less," Adam offered, peering at the two cakes.

"How do you think we could find out for sure?" Shirley wondered. She paused and then said, "To help us, take two of the pieces of paper from the copying room that I put on your desks while you were working on your writing and carefully fold them like our cakes here."

The students quickly took the papers from their desks and began folding. Shirley helped some of them who had trouble folding their papers into thirds.

"Now we have two whole papers, which we'll pretend are our cakes. Let's think about our problem again. If we eat a third of one and a half of the other one, how much have we eaten altogether? . . . How can we figure that out?"

". . . Let's lay one on top of the other," Jan suggested, after thinking for several seconds.

"Good idea. . . . Go ahead and try it."

". . . It's less than a whole cake," Tanya offered after peering carefully at the papers.

"How much less?"

Tanya thought about it and gestured and shrugged an 'I don't know.'

"Any other ideas? . . . Anyone?"

The students offered a few uncertain suggestions, and Shirley then asked, "Let's think about the work we've been doing. What did we just review?" pointing at the chalkboard.

"Adding up the pizzas," Juan offered.

"And what do we know about them?"

". . . They weren't like the cakes," Bryan added.

"In what way?" Shirley asked with a quizzical shrug.

"They were the same. . . . They had the same-size parts. . . . And . . . these are different," he pointed to the cakes.

"Maybe we need to cut them different so they're the same," Enrico suggested.

This response prompted additional discussion, after which Shirley offered, "Let me make a suggestion how we can get them to be the same, using Enrico's idea."

She continued, "How much cake do we have here? . . . Tim?"

". . . A third."

"Fine," Shirley smiled. "Now, let's all fold our 'cakes' this way," and she folded the cardboard in half along the opposite axis as she watched the students. "How many pieces do I have altogether now? . . . Karen?"

". . . It looks like six," she responded uncertainly.

"Yes. Good, Karen. I saw you actually counting them," Shirley noted and then counted the six squares again out loud. "So what portion is now shaded? . . . Jon?"

". . . Two sixths."

"Excellent, Jon!" and she moved to the chalkboard and wrote 1/3 and 2/6 alongside each other with an equal sign between.

"Now, how do we know that the 1/3 and 2/6 are equal?"

"It's the same amount of cake," Dan shrugged.

Shirley then continued by having the students fold the second 'cake' into thirds so that it appeared as follows:

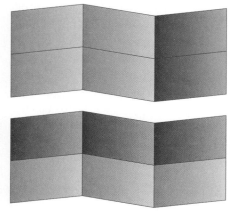

"Now, what do we see here?"

". . . They both have the same number of pieces," Lorraine noted.

"And all the pieces are the same size," Crystal added.

"Ooh, ooh, I know!" Adam said excitedly. "We've eaten 5/6 of the cake."

"That's an interesting thought, Adam. Would you explain that for us please?"

". . . It's like the pizza. We have two pieces there, and three pieces there, so it's 5/6 of the pizza, ah cake."

"I don't get that," Mike shook his head.

". . . What if we cut them out, to see how many we have," Gail suggested.

"Good thought, Gail," Shirley nodded. "Let's do it. . . . Everybody cut out these pieces," she said, pointing to the marked pieces in the 'cake' on the top.

She watched as the students took out scissors from their desks and cut out the pieces.

"Now, go ahead and lay them over the other 'cake.' . . . What do you see there?"

"There are five pieces covered," John observed. "We ate 5/6 of the cake alright."

"Now, let's think about what we did," Shirley continued. "What was our problem?"

". . . We were trying to figure out how much cake we ate," Lakesha offered.

"Why was that a problem?"

"The pieces weren't the same size."

"So what did we do about it? . . . Karen?"

". . . We fixed them so they were the same size."

"And exactly how did we do that? . . . Bryan?"

". . . We made the 1/3 of a cake into 2/6, and we made the 1/2 a cake into 3/6, and then we could just add them up."

Shirley then said with a grin, "You're all pretty clever. . . . Let's see how you do now," and she pulled out two more pieces of cardboard, one of which was divided into thirds and the other into fourths. She then guided the students' analysis of the second problem in the same way she had done with the first.

They then reviewed the problem as they did the first one, and Shirley said, "Tomorrow, I'll show you how we can figure out a little more quickly how to make the parts equal, so that we don't have to work as hard as we did with the 1/3 and 1/4."

Finally, seeing that it was 10:52, Shirley said, "Yikes! It's nearly time for science. Put your math books and materials away, and we'll have our break."

Both teachers and the public at large believe that creating classroom environments that are orderly and focus on learning is essential. From 1968 until 1986, those surveyed by the Gallup polls identified school discipline as the most important problem teachers face. From 1986 to 1992, discipline ranked third only to drugs and inadequate funding as the biggest educational problem. In 1994 and 1995 it surfaced again as the number one problem (Elam & Rose, 1995). This is a particularly acute problem for pre-service and beginning teachers, who typically feel ill-prepared to deal with issues related to classroom management and discipline (Kher-Durlabhji, Lacina-Gifford, Jackson, Guillory, & Yandell, 1997).

Commonly overlooked in discussions of management and discipline is the role of effective instruction. Research indicates that it is virtually impossible to maintain an orderly classroom in the absence of effective instruction and vice versa.

In this chapter, we examine the results of this research and analyze the relationship between effective instruction and classroom management.

After you've completed this chapter, you should be able to meet the following objectives:

- Explain how instruction and classroom management contribute to productive learning environments.
- Identify essential teaching skills that help create productive learning environments.
- Explain how effective planning can prevent management problems.
- Identify differences between cognitive and behavioral approaches to management.
- Describe how effective intervention techniques can eliminate management problems.

Productive Environments and Learning-Focused Classrooms

Let's stop at this point and consider Shirley's classroom. It typifies conditions that many teachers face every day: her class is too large, her students differ in many ways, and she never has enough time.

Despite her less-than-ideal conditions, Shirley's students had the opportunity to learn as much as possible. She was well organized and expert in her instruction. Her students were involved yet orderly, and she handled minor disruptions quickly and efficiently. Shirley created and maintained a **productive learning environment,** which is *one that is orderly and focuses on learning.* In it students feel safe, both physically and emotionally, and the day-to-day operations—including the language, values, expectations, learning experiences, and unspoken rules and conventions—are all designed to help students learn as much as possible (Tishman, Perkins, & Jay, 1995).

In productive learning environments, classroom order and effective instruction are interdependent (Doyle, 1986). As we said in the introduction to the chapter, it is virtually impossible to maintain an orderly learning environment in the absence of effective instruction and vice versa.

Because instruction is so important in the creation of productive learning environments, we begin our discussion with it.

> **11.1**
>
> In Chapter 9, we saw that Japanese students spend less time doing seatwork than their American counterparts. Based on the research cited in the chapter, would the American learning environment be considered more or less productive than the Japanese environment? Explain.

Creating Productive Learning Environments: Effective Teaching

Suppose you sit in the back of any classroom, regardless of grade level or topic being taught. What would you expect to see the teacher doing? Just as we're familiar with the basic skills in reading, writing, and math that all learners need, there are **essential**

teaching skills, which are *the abilities that all teachers should have to promote order and learning,* even in their first year of teaching. Each of the essential teaching skills is correlated with increased student achievement and is derived from an extensive body of research literature that emerged in the 1970s and 1980s (Gage, 1985; Good & Brophy, 1986, 1997; Shuell, 1996). (Expert teachers go well beyond these essential skills as they create experiences that maximize learning for their students. We examine these approaches to instruction in Chapters 12 and 13.) The essential teaching skills are outlined in Figure 11.1.

Essential Teaching Skills

For the sake of clarity, we'll discuss the skills separately, but they are interdependent; none is as effective alone as it is in combination with the others. The balance and interaction of these skills are critical.

Attitude

Admittedly, "attitude" is not a skill, but we want to discuss it at the beginning of our coverage of essential teaching skills in order to emphasize that positive attitudes are fundamental to effective teaching. To see why, let's look again at Shirley Barton's general orientation toward teaching and her students.

High-Efficacy Teachers.   Shirley believed that she could influence her students' learning and that it was her responsibility to do so. She was able and willing to conclude, "I could have done a better job last year," and she expected to improve this year. Shirley was high in **personal teaching efficacy,** which is *the belief that teachers can have an important positive effect on students* (Bruning, Schraw, & Ronning, 1995). Teachers high in personal efficacy increase student achievement by accepting students and their ideas, using praise rather than criticism, persevering with low achievers, and using their time effectively. In contrast, low-efficacy teachers are less student-centered, spend less time on learning activities, "give up" on low achievers, and use criticism more than do high-efficacy teachers (Kagan, 1992a). High-efficacy teachers also tend to be more flexible, adopting new curriculum materials and changing strategies more readily than low-efficacy teachers (Poole, Okeafor, & Sloan, 1989).

11.2

Figure 11.1 identifies questioning as one of the essential teaching skills. How would the questioning of an *expert* teacher differ from the questioning of a *novice?* Explain. (Hint: Think about the characteristics of expertise that were discussed in Chapter 8.)

Figure 11.1   Essential teaching skills

- Attitudes
- Use of time
- Organization
- Communication
- Focus
- Feedback
- Questioning
- Review and closure

Democratic Teachers. Students in productive learning environments accept responsibility for their own learning and behavior, acquire learning strategies, and understand the reasons for classroom rules and procedures. This acceptance of the responsibility for learning isn't innate; it's something students learn, and it's best learned in a democratic environment.

Rudolph Dreikurs (1968), a psychiatrist known for his work in student discipline, argues that democratic teachers are both caring and firm. They listen and try to see things from learners' perspectives, they create physically and emotionally safe classrooms, and they help learners understand the reasons for school work (Rogers, 1991). At the same time, they view students as responsible and hold them accountable for their actions. Dreikurs argues that a teacher who doesn't stand firm when a student breaks a rule communicates that the rule has no real purpose and actions don't have consequences. These messages confuse students who are trying to make sense of the world.

Use of Time

In addition to having positive attitudes about students' capabilities and using democratic practices to promote student responsibility, effective teachers promote learning by using their time effectively. Time is a valuable resource; efforts at reform have suggested lengthening the school year, school day, and even the amount of time devoted to certain subjects (Karweit, 1989). However improving learning through increased time isn't as simple as it appears on the surface because, as we see in Table 11.1, different levels of classroom time influence learning in different ways.

As one moves from allocated time to academic learning time, the relationship with learning becomes stronger (Nystrand & Gamoran, 1989). In classrooms where students are engaged and successful, high levels of learning occur, and learners feel good about themselves and the material they're learning (Fisher et al., 1980).

Our goal as teachers should be to increase each of the levels to the point where it's as close to allocated time as possible. Shirley's students, for instance, having made a quick and smooth transition from reading, had their math books out and were waiting at 10:01. The class lost only one minute of their allocated time at the beginning of the class, and they continued until 10:52. Of the 55 minutes allocated to math, Shirley devoted 52 minutes to instruction.

11.3

William Glasser (1985) argues that all students come to school with innate needs, one of which is belonging, and that disruptive behavior reflects unmet belonging needs. Predict how Glasser believes a caring teacher responds to disruptive behavior.

11.4

What is the allocated time for the class you're now in? Of this time, how much does your instructor typically devote to instruction?

11.5

You found in Chapter 10 that another factor, in addition to success, is necessary for students to feel good about themselves and the material they're learning. What is this factor? Why is it important?

Table 11.1   Levels of classroom time

Level	Description
Allocated time	The amount of time a teacher or school designates for a content area or topic
Instructional time	The amount left for teaching after routine management and administrative tasks are completed
Engaged time	The amount of time students are actively involved in learning activities
Academic learning time	The amount of time students are actively involved in learning activities *during which they're successful*

Organization

One way of maximizing instructional time is through efficient organization. How many times do you put something away and later can't locate it? Have you ever said, "I've simply got to get organized," or, "If he'd just get organized, he could be so effective"? Teacher organization affects learning because it determines how efficiently time is used (Bennett, 1978; Rutter, Maughan, Mortimer, Ouston, & Smith, 1979).

Organization includes *the set of teacher actions that increase instructional time.* These characteristics are outlined in Table 11.2.

Shirley's organization allowed as much class time as possible to be devoted to instruction and, equally important, it saved her energy. Teachers who have their mate-

Table 11.2   Characteristics of effective organization

Dimension	Example
Starting on time	Shirley's students had their math books out and were waiting by 10:01.
Preparing materials in advance	Shirley had her cardboard "cakes" prepared and waiting.
Established routines	At Shirley's signal, the students passed their papers forward without having to be told specifically to do so.

rials prepared and have established efficient routines can devote their working memory space and physical energy to thinking about and guiding student learning. This is essential if they are going to regularly conduct engaging and meaningful learning activities.

Organization is also important from the learners' perspective. Well-established routines are predictable and give learners a sense of order and equilibrium, all of which contribute to a productive learning environment.

Communication

The link between effective communication, student achievement, and student satisfaction with instruction is well established (Cruickshank, 1985; Snyder et al., 1991). Also, research indicates that the way teachers interact with students influences their motivation and attitudes toward school (Pintrich & Schunk, 1996). In this section, we examine four aspects of effective communication: (a) precise terminology, (b) connected discourse, (c) transition signals, and (d) emphasis.

Precise Terminology. **Precise terminology** *means that teachers eliminate vague terms* (*e.g.,* perhaps, maybe, might, and so on, usually) *from their language.* When teachers use these seemingly innocuous terms in their explanations and responses to students' questions, students are left with a sense of uncertainty about the topics they're studying, and this uncertainty detracts from learning (Smith & Cotten, 1980). For example, suppose you asked, "What do high-efficacy teachers do that promotes learning?" and your instructor responded, "Usually, they use their time somewhat better and so on," in comparison with, "They believe they can increase learning, and one of their characteristics is the effective use of time." The first response contains uncertainty, whereas the second is clear and precise.

11.6

To which level of classroom time in Table 11.1 does precise terminology most closely relate?

Connected Discourse: Making Relationships Clear. **Connected discourse** *means the teacher's lesson is thematic and leads to a point.* If the point of the lesson isn't clear, if it is sequenced inappropriately, or if incidental information is interjected without indicating how it relates to the topic, the classroom discourse becomes "disconnected" or "scrambled." Effective teachers keep their lessons on track and spend less time on matters unrelated to the topic than their less effective counterparts (Coker, Lorentz, & Coker, 1980; Smith & Cotten, 1980).

11.7

Does the information in this section imply that teachers should avoid interjecting additional material into lessons? Explain.

Transition Signals. **Transition signals** *are verbal statements indicating that one idea is ending and another is beginning.* When Shirley said, "Now, we're going to shift gears because I've got another, different kind of problem," or if an American government teacher said, "We've been talking about the Senate, which is one house of Congress. We're going to turn now to the House of Representatives," they were *signaling a transition.* Because not all students are at the same place mentally, a transition signal alerts them that they are making a conceptual shift—moving to a new topic—and allows them to prepare for it.

Emphasis: Signaling Important Ideas. **Emphasis,** a fourth aspect of effective communication, *alerts students to important information in a lesson and is communicated through verbal and vocal cues and repetition.* For example, Shirley raised her voice—a form of vocal emphasis—in saying, "Let's keep that in mind as we study some more problems." When teachers say, "Now remember, everyone, this is very important . . . ," or, "Listen carefully now," they're using verbal emphasis.

11.8

Think about your study of Chapter 7. What concept is being illustrated when learners link new to past information or create new links in what they already understand?

11.9

Focus relates most closely to which level of classroom time discussed earlier?

11.10

Identify one important difference between introductory and sensory focus.

11.11

Social cognitive theory can also be used to explain the importance of feedback. Using social cognitive theory, explain why feedback is important.

Repeating a point—redundancy—is also a form of emphasis. For instance, "What did we say earlier that these problems had in common?" reminds students of an important feature in the problems and helps them link new to past information. Redundancy is particularly helpful when reviewing abstract rules, principles, and concepts (Brophy & Good, 1986; Shuell, 1996).

Focus

You saw in Chapter 10 that **introductory focus** *attracts students' attention and provides a framework for the lesson.* In addition to attracting attention, it is designed to enhance motivation by arousing curiosity and making lesson content interesting.

Shirley provided introductory focus for her students by showing them the two "cakes" and saying, ". . . I've got a problem," and, "How much cake have I eaten?" Her "cakes," together with her problem, attracted students' attention and provided a context for the rest of the lesson.

Shirley's "cakes" also acted as a form of **sensory focus,** which is *the use of stimuli—concrete objects, pictures, models, materials displayed on the overhead, and even information written on the chalkboard—to maintain attention.* Her "cakes" gave students something to look at and provided a mental model to help them conceptualize an abstract idea. Jenny Newhall's demonstration with the cup and water in Chapter 2, Jenny's balances in Chapter 7, and Suzanne Brush's graph in Chapter 8 all provided forms of sensory focus. Sensory focus serves as a continual reminder of the lesson's topic and direction.

Feedback

The importance of feedback in promoting learning is well documented (Weinert & Helmke, 1995). In Chapter 6 we saw that **feedback** is *information about the accuracy or appropriateness of a response.* It gives students information about the extent to which they are accomplishing learning goals. We know that effective feedback increases learning by providing *immediate, specific, and corrective information* for *learners* (Brophy & Good, 1986; Rosenshine & Stevens, 1986), and it has a *positive emotional tone* (Murphy, Weil, & McGreal, 1986). Information-processing theory and constructivism both help us understand why. Feedback gives students information they can use to check the accuracy of their background knowledge, and it helps them elaborate on their existing understanding.

As we saw in Chapter 10, feedback also increases motivation to learn by helping satisfy learners' intrinsic need to understand how they're progressing and why (Clifford, 1990).

Verbal Feedback. Teachers provide verbal feedback in question-and-answer sessions in ways ranging from a simple acknowledgment of an answer, such as "Okay" and "Good," to extended responses about the accuracy of the answers. The most important aspect of this feedback is the information it provides. For instance, suppose a teacher displays the following sentence:

Running is a very good form of exercise.

and this exchange takes place:

> *T:* How is the word *running* used in the sentence? . . . Mylan?
> *M:* It's a verb.
> *T:* Not quite, Mylan. Can someone help him out?

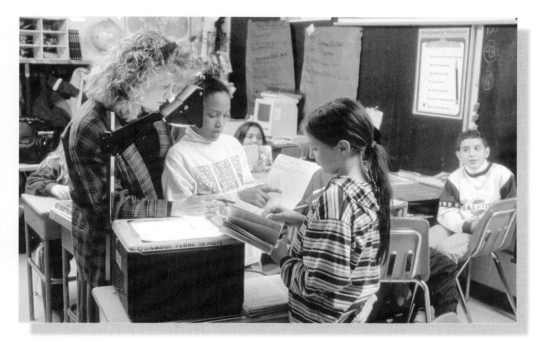

Teachers provide continual feedback to learners through their interactions in the classroom.

The feedback was immediate, but it wasn't specific and it gave Mylan no additional information. Contrast that response with the following:

T: How is the word *running* used in the sentence? . . . Emilio?
E: It's a verb.
T: Look again, Emilio. Running is the topic of the sentence. So how is it used?
E: . . . It's the subject.

In the second example, the teacher provided information that both helped Emilio understand why his first answer was incorrect and allowed him to answer correctly.

Written Feedback. Teachers also provide valuable feedback through the notes and comments they write on student work. Because time and effort are required to write detailed comments, providing written feedback can be demanding and, as a result, feedback becomes brief and sketchy, giving students little useful information (Bloom & Bourdon, 1980).

An acceptable solution to this problem is to provide model responses to written assignments. For instance, to help students evaluate their answers to an essay item, the teacher could write an ideal answer and share it with the class, allowing students to compare their answers with the model. The model answer, combined with discussion and time available for individual help after school, provides adequate feedback yet is manageable for the teacher.

> **11.12**
>
> Research indicates that the emotional tone of feedback is important. On the basis of the model for promoting student motivation (in Chapter 10), explain why a positive emotional tone is important.

Questioning

As instruction has become more learner-centered in response to the cognitive revolution in general and constructivism in particular, teachers are increasingly being asked to guide learning rather than to simply deliver information.

Questioning is the most important tool teachers have for guiding students as they construct their understanding (Wang, Haertel, & Walberg, 1993). A teacher skilled in questioning can assess student background knowledge, cause learners to rethink their ideas, help them form relationships, involve shy or reticent students, recapture students' attention, promote success, and enhance self-esteem. Questioning is also a tool to maintain the pace and momentum of a lesson, and research indicates that lesson momentum is an important factor in keeping students engaged (Kounin, 1970).

Becoming skilled in questioning is difficult. To avoid overloading their own working memories, teachers need to practice questioning strategies to the point that they are essentially automatic, leaving working memory space available to monitor students' thinking and assess learning progress. Although the process is demanding, with effort and experience teachers can and do become expert at questioning (Kerman, 1979; Rowe, 1986).

Effective questioning has four characteristics, which are outlined in Table 11.3.

Shirley skillfully applied these characteristics in her teaching. She asked many questions; in fact, she developed her entire lesson around questioning. She practiced **equitable distribution,** *the practice of calling on all students—both volunteers and nonvolunteers—as equally as possible;* she addressed her students by name; and she never strayed from the goal of her lesson.

Equitable distribution can be a powerful motivational tool. In a study involving thousands of students and hundreds of teachers, researchers found that when equitable distribution was widely practiced, learning increased for both high and low achievers, classroom management problems decreased, and the absentee rate went down: more evidence that instruction and classroom order are interdependent (Kerman, 1979). Equitable distribution also works at the college level; the expectation of being called on resulted in increased student preparation for class, greater retention of information, and greater confidence in what they learned (McDougall & Granby, 1996).

Also, as a pattern, Shirley asked the question first and selected the student second. All students knew that they could be called on and, as a result, were more attentive. If students are selected before the question is asked, the rest of the class know they are "off the hook," as soon as a student is identified, and attention can suffer.

At this point, you might wonder, "I'm supposed to call on all the students, but what do I do if they can't answer?" One solution is **prompting,** which is *the process of*

11.13

Why are equitable distribution and calling on students by name important? To which of the teacher characteristics discussed in Chapter 10 does equitable distribution most closely relate?

Table 11.3   Characteristics of effective questioning

Characteristic	Description
Frequency	The number of questions teachers ask
Equitable distribution	A pattern in which all students in the class are called on as equally as possible
Prompting	A teacher question or cue that elicits a response after a student has failed to answer or has given an incorrect or incomplete answer
Wait-time	The period of silence before or after a student response

helping students respond by providing cues after an incorrect or incomplete answer or silence. For example, when Shirley first asked Emerson, "And what kind of parts?" and he was unable to answer, she continued, "How do the parts compare with each other?" which elicited his answer, "They're all equal." Her prompt took little time, pointed out relationships in the content being considered, and helped ensure a successful response. Prompts facilitate learning, probably helping other students think through the question as much as they help the individual being prompted (O'Flahavan, Hartman, & Pearson, 1988).

Finally, learning is enhanced when students are provided with **wait-time,** a *period of silence before or after a student is asked a question.* It increases learning by giving students time to think. In most classrooms—regardless of grade or ability levels—wait-times are very short, often less than one second (Rowe, 1986). Increasing wait-time to about three to five seconds increases learning in at least three ways:

- The length and quality of student responses improve.
- Failures to respond are reduced and voluntary participation increases.
- Equitable distribution and participation from minority students improve. (Rowe, 1986; Tobin, 1987)

Cognitive Levels of Questions. The kinds of questions teachers ask also influence learning. Which are better: low-level questions that require mere recall, or questions that demand considerable student thought? The cognitive levels of teacher questions have been widely researched but, surprisingly, the results are mixed. Both low-level questions (such as *knowledge* on the Bloom taxonomy [Bloom, Englehart, Furst, Hill, & Krathwohl, 1956]) and high-level questions (such as *application* and *synthesis*) correlate positively with achievement, depending on the teaching situation (Good & Brophy, 1997).

These seemingly contradictory results can be explained on the basis of the teacher's goals. If the goal is automaticity with basic skills, low-level questions may be most effective. On the other hand, if the goal is for students to analyze factors leading up to the Revolutionary War, for example, high-level questions are more effective. Teachers' first concerns should be what they are trying to accomplish—their goals—not the level of questions they choose to ask. When goals are clear, appropriate questions follow.

Review and Closure

Lessons are more coherent when review and closure are used to summarize and pull ideas together. **Review** *summarizes previous work and helps students link what has been learned to what is coming.* It can occur at any point in a lesson, although it is most common at the beginning and end. Effective reviews emphasize important points and encourage elaboration; in Shirley's lesson, students reviewed adding fractions with like denominators and then used this information to understand the need for making the pieces of "cake" equal, as a step toward learning to add fractions with unlike denominators. Effective reviews involve more than simple rehearsal; they shift the learner's attention away from verbatim details to deeper conceptual connections in the material being studied (Dempster, 1991).

Closure is *a form of review occurring at the end of a lesson;* in it, topics are summarized, structured, and integrated. The notion of closure is common and intuitively sensible; it pulls content together and signals the end of a lesson. When concepts, principles, generalizations, and rules are being taught, an effective form of closure is to have

11.14
Most teachers, instead of prompting, turn the question to another student, and the student initially asked the question becomes even more reluctant to respond. What concept from behaviorism explains this increasing reluctance?

11.15
When would it be appropriate—even desirable—to keep wait-times shorter than three to five seconds? Give at least two examples.

11.16
Describe Shirley's closure in her lesson.

Review provides opportunities for teachers to emphasize important points and to help students organize information in meaningful ways.

students state a definition of the concept or state the principle, generalization, or rule in their own words. This leaves them with the essence of the topic, providing a foundation for subsequent lessons.

This completes our discussion of instructional factors that contribute to productive classroom learning environments. In the next section, we turn our attention to classroom management and how it influences productive learning environments.

Classroom Connections _____

Demonstrating Professional Attitudes in Your Classroom

1. Demonstrate teaching efficacy by having high expectations for your students and showing them you are committed to their learning.
   - A geometry teacher, knowing that her students initially have trouble with proofs, offers help sessions twice a week after school.
   - A third-grade teacher calls a student's parents and solicits their help as soon as the student fails to turn in an assignment or receives an unsatisfactory grade on a quiz or test.

2. Commit yourself to being a role model for students.
   - A seventh-grade teacher displays the statement "I will always try to behave in the way I expect you to behave in this class" on the bulletin board, and she uses it as a guiding principle in her class.

Maximizing Instructional Time in Your Classroom

3. Carefully plan and organize materials to maximize instructional time. Avoid spending class time gathering and displaying materials.

   • A first-grade teacher has several boxes filled with frequently used science materials, such as soft drink bottles, balloons, matches, baking soda, vinegar, funnels, and a hot plate. The night before a science demonstration, she spends a few minutes selecting her materials from the boxes and sets them on the shelf near her desk so that she'll have everything ready at the beginning of the lesson.

4. Begin lessons on time; give students a short assignment or problem while you conduct your beginning routines.

   • An English teacher displays a paragraph on the overhead at the beginning of the class period and asks students to identify and correct all the mechanical errors in it.

   • An algebra teacher gives students a problem that is slightly more difficult than their homework assignment and has them solve it while she takes roll.

Demonstrating Essential Teaching Skills in Your Classroom

5. Monitor your communication to be certain your presentations are clear and concise.

   • A second-grade teacher videotapes a lesson she conducts with her students and then studies the tape to check her language and nonverbal communication.

   • A ninth-grade American government teacher asks colleagues to visit his class and check whether he emphasizes the important points in the lesson, sequences the presentation logically, and communicates changes in topics clearly.

6. Use problems, demonstrations, and displays to provide introductory and sensory focus during lessons.

   • A science teacher dealing with the concept of *kindling temperature* soaks a cloth in a water–alcohol mix, ignites it, and asks, "Why isn't the cloth burning?"

   • A second-grade teacher introducing the concept of *verb* has a student walk across the room, writes "Kelly walked across the room" on the chalkboard, and begins her lesson from that point.

   • A life-science teacher beginning a study of arthropods brings a live lobster to class and builds the lesson around the lobster's characteristics.

7. Begin and end each class with a short review.

   • An English teacher begins, "We studied pronoun–antecedent agreement yesterday. Give me an example that illustrates the idea and explain why it is correct."

   • A fifth-grade teacher whose class is studying different types of boundaries says, "We've looked at three kinds of boundaries between the states so far today. What are the three?"

Creating Productive Learning Environments: Classroom Management

We said earlier that in productive learning environments, effective instruction and classroom order are interdependent. In the previous sections we discussed ways that teachers aid learning through their attitudes and beliefs and actions. In this section of the chapter we examine how classroom management contributes to a productive learning environment.

Classroom Management and Discipline

Some of the most basic research examining teachers' abilities to create and maintain orderly classrooms was done by Jacob Kounin (1970). His research indicated that the key to orderly classrooms is *the ability to prevent behavior problems from occurring* rather than handling misbehavior once it happens. This led to separating the concepts of **classroom management,** which refers to *teachers' strategies that create and maintain an orderly learning environment,* and **discipline** which involves *teacher responses to student misbehavior.* We will focus on the concept of *management* and examine discipline in that context.

The relationship between classroom management and learning is well documented (Blumenfeld, Pintrich, & Hamilton, 1987; Evertson, 1987). A comprehensive review of research on the topic concluded "Effective classroom management has been shown to increase student engagement, decrease disruptive behaviors, and enhance use of instructional time, all of which results in improved student achievement" (Wang et al., 1993, p. 262). Additional research has identified effective management as one of the key characteristics of an effective school (Purkey & Smith, 1983).

Effective classroom management also increases learner motivation (Radd, 1998). In Chapter 10, we saw that order and safety are necessary to promote student motivation, and Brophy (1987a) identified classroom management as an "essential precondition for motivating students" (p. 208). Further, by seeking student input on instructional and management issues, the teacher can promote student ownership and involvement, both of which increase learner motivation (McLaughlin, 1994).

Cognitive Approaches to Management: Developing Learner Responsibility

In contrast with behavioral approaches to management, which emphasize compliance with rules based on reinforcers and punishers, cognitive approaches to management focus on learner understanding and treat learners as thinking, feeling individuals. They understand that learners' expectations, beliefs, and emotional needs all influence the learning process. Rules are important but, instead of focusing on mere compliance, they are treated as guidelines based on a need to promote order and learning.

Cognitive approaches to management are based on both information-processing and constructivist views of learning. From an information-processing perspective, classroom management can contribute to self-regulation by being "one vehicle for the enhancement of student self-understanding, self-evaluation, and the internalization of self-control" (McCaslin & Good, 1992, p. 8). Self-understanding, self-evaluation, and self-control are metacognitive, and the development of metacognition provides students with powerful learning tools.

Just as learners construct understanding of concepts, principles, and other forms of content, they must, from a constructivist perspective, construct understanding of what it means to be responsible, why rules and procedures are necessary, and what their role is in contributing to a productive learning environment. This understanding evolves from discussions of reasons for rules and procedures, and examples of appropriate and inappropriate behavior (Blumenfeld et al., 1987). This constructivist-based responsibility orientation can contribute to ethical development (DeVries & Zan, 1995; Kohn, 1996). Learners are more likely to obey rules when they understand that rules exist to protect their rights and the rights of others.

11.17

What are at least three ways in which orderly classrooms contribute to learning?

11.18

Think again about your study of theories of motivation in Chapter 10. Use your understanding of these theories to explain why a well managed classroom is more motivating than a poorly managed one.

11.19

It says in this section that cognitive approaches to management "treat learners as thinking, feeling individuals." How do behaviorist approaches to management treat learners?

Planning for Effective Classroom Management

Often, we visit classrooms in which management doesn't seem to exist. The atmosphere is calm but not rigid, movement and interaction are comfortable, and students work quietly. The teachers hardly seem aware of management as an issue. They give few directions that focus on behavior, they reprimand students infrequently, and the reprimands they do give rarely intrude on others' learning. Are these ideal situations? Of course. Are they impossible to achieve? No.

Obviously, some classes are tougher to manage than others and, in a few cases, it may be difficult to reach the ideal described in the previous paragraph. In most instances, an orderly classroom is attainable, but it doesn't happen by accident. It requires careful planning, and beginning teachers often underestimate the amount of planning and work it takes (Bullough, 1989; Weinstein, Woolfolk, Dittmeier, & Shankar, 1994).

The cornerstone of an effective management system is a well conceived and administered set of procedures and rules (Emmer, Everston, Clements, & Worsham, 1997; Evertson, Emmer, Clements, & Worsham, 1997). In planning procedures and rules, teachers must consider both the characteristics of their students and the physical environment of their classrooms. The relationship among these factors is illustrated in Figure 11.2.

Figure 11.2 Planning for an orderly classroom

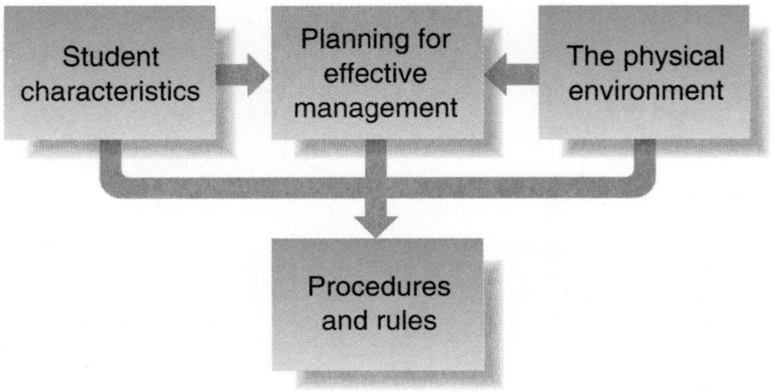

Student Characteristics

Sam Cramer had completed his first semester's observation and tutoring in a high school, and it had been a terrific experience. He had taught several lessons and, except for the occasional rough spot, they had gone well. Students were interested and responded when involved. Management was not a problem.

For his second semester, Sam moved to a junior high. It seemed like a different planet. Students were bubbling with excess energy. Giggling, whispering, and note passing were constant distractions. His first lesson was a disaster. They wouldn't let him teach!

From your study of Chapters 2 and 3, you know that students think, act, and feel different at different stages of intellectual, psychosocial, and moral development. As Sam found out the hard way, students at different grade levels interpret and respond to rules and procedures differently, and teachers must anticipate these differences as they plan. These stages and related characteristics are outlined in Table 11.4.

Keep in mind that these are general characteristics and individual students will vary. As a pattern, however, we see increasing independence and self-regulation as learners develop. They retreat somewhat from their reliance on and affection for teachers and become more likely to question authority. The process peaks during early adolescence, when students' responses to their own physical, emotional, and intellectual changes are most uncertain. During the high-school years, self-regulation develops, students begin to behave like young adults, and they respond well to being treated as such. Students of all ages, however, need the emotional security of knowing that their teachers are genuinely interested in them as people and sincerely care about their learning.

11.20

Explain differences in student characteristics for different ages using Piaget's and Erikson's work in Chapters 2 and 3 as a basis for your explanation.

Table 11.4   Learner characteristics affecting classroom management

Stage	Student Characteristics
Stage 1: Kindergarten through grade 2	• are compliant, eager to please teachers • have short attention span, tire easily • are restless, wander around room • require close supervision • break rules because they forget • need rules and procedures to be explicitly taught, practiced, and reinforced
Stage 2 Grades 3 through 6	• are increasingly independent, but still like attention and affection from teachers • respond well to concrete incentives (e.g., stickers, free time), as well as praise and recognition • understand need for rules and accept consequences; enjoy participating in rule-making process • know how far they can push • need rules to be reviewed and consistently and impartially enforced
Stage 3: Grades 7, 8, and 9	• attempt to test independence; are sometimes rebellious and capricious • need firm foundation of stability; explicit boundaries and predictable outcomes are critical • need rules clearly stated and administered
Stage 4: Grades 10 and above	• behave more stably than in previous stage • communicate effectively adult to adult • respond to clear rationales for rules

Source: Learning from Teaching: A Developmental Perspective, by J. Brophy and C. Evertson, 1976, Boston: Allyn & Bacon. Copyright 1976 by Allyn & Bacon. Adapted with permission. Brophy, J., and Evertson, C. 1978. "Content Variables in Teaching," *Educational Psychologist, 12,* 310–316.

The Physical Environment

"I can't see the board."

"Fred tripped me."

"What? I can't hear."

Few classrooms are ideal. Classes are too large, storage space is limited, and, when used, maps or overhead projector screens cover half the chalkboard. For many teachers, arranging the desks and furnishings is a compromise between what they would like and what is possible.

Three aspects of the physical environment that should be considered when teachers plan are (Evertson, 1987):

- Visibility—the room must be arranged so that all students can see the chalkboard, overhead projector, or other displays.

- Accessibility—the room should be designed so that access to high-traffic areas, such as the pencil sharpener and places students put papers, are kept clear and separated from each other.

- Distractibility—desks should be arranged so that potential distractions, such as movement visible through classroom windows, are minimized.

11.21

Beginning teachers' writing on the board is often too small for students— particularly those at the back of the room—to see. Many beginning teachers seem to be unaware of this possibility. Using your understanding of Chapter 7 as a basis, explain why beginning teachers may have this tendency.

Research indicates that no single room arrangement works for all situations. One study found that behavior improved and quantity of work increased when learners were seated in rows (Bennett & Blundel, 1983). For discussions, a semicircle was most effective (Rosenfield, Lambert, & Black, 1985). Teachers should consider desk arrangement when they plan and then experiment to see what works best for them.

Establishing Procedures

Having considered the characteristics of your students and your classroom environment, you're now ready to plan the procedures and rules for your classroom. **Procedures** establish *the routines students will follow in their daily activities,* such as how students pass in papers, sharpen their pencils, and make transitions from one activity to another. **Rules** provide *standards for acceptable behavior,* such as "Listen when someone else is talking."

Let's look again at Shirley's work with her students. She told the students to turn in their writing, and they passed the papers forward, each putting his or hers on the top of the stack without being told to do so. It was a well-practiced procedure.

Expert teachers, to a much greater extent than novices, plan and teach procedures until they're essentially automatic routines, and these routines help the day flow fluidly by providing a sense of regularity and equilibrium (Borko & Putnam, 1996). For example, teaching students what they are expected to do after completing assignments and how late or missing homework will be handled are important. These procedures may seem minor, but they affect the efficiency of the classroom and communicate that learning is the primary purpose of school.

11.22

What procedures govern the class in which this text is being used? Were these procedures explicitly discussed or implicitly assumed? Why do you think so?

Creating Effective Rules

Rules that provide standards for student behavior are essential, and research confirms their value in creating an orderly environment (Emmer et al., 1997; Evertson et al., 1997); "Evidence exists indicating that clear, reasonable rules, fairly and consistently enforced, not only can reduce behavior problems that interfere with learning but also can promote a feeling of pride and responsibility in the school community" (Purkey & Smith, 1983, p. 445). Students in effective schools see rules and teachers as fair and necessary even if they don't like some individual rules and penalties (Wayson & Lasley, 1984).

Some guidelines for establishing rules are outlined in Figure 11.3 and discussed in the sections that follow (Evertson, 1987).

Provide Rationales for Rules. The successful development of responsibility and self-regulation requires that learners understand the reasons for rules. Providing rationales is important for at least three reasons:

- Rules are often abstract, and discussions of rationales help learners construct understanding of them.

- Rationales help students understand that rules aren't arbitrary, and discussing the need for a particular rule helps students think about rights and responsibilities, which helps in the development of self-regulation and moral reasoning.

Classroom rules establish standards for behavior that allow learning to take place.

Figure 11.3   Guidelines for preparing rules

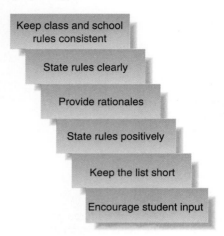

Keep class and school rules consistent

State rules clearly

Provide rationales

State rules positively

Keep the list short

Encourage student input

- Students who understand reasons for rules are more likely to obey them.

Allow Student Input.   A responsibility orientation also requires that students are provided with some voice in the rule-making process. Cooperative rule-setting has at least four benefits:

- It promotes a feeling of ownership, which increases the likelihood that students will obey the rules.
- It emphasizes internal versus external control.
- It helps students see the values, such as respect and responsibility, behind rules.
- It treats students as moral thinkers and promotes moral development (DeVries & Zan, 1995; Kohn, 1996; Lickona 1991).

Glasser (1969, 1985) advocates the use of periodic classroom meetings to establish, monitor, and improve classroom rules. The meetings emphasize problem solving and stress that students are responsible for making the classroom a livable place.

One teacher who tried this at the beginning of the year commented:

> The rules the students came up with are the ones I wanted anyway and, besides, they're often tougher on themselves than I would be. Actually, they handle it pretty well, so as I see it, I have nothing to lose by giving them a say in the process. They feel good about it.

Keep Class and School Rules Consistent.   This self-evident suggestion reminds teachers that they should review district and school rules before creating their own. For example, if the school requires hall passes when students are out of classrooms, individual teachers are obligated to enforce the rule.

11.23

How does the rule "Listen when someone else is talking" illustrate the idea of students' rights and responsibilities? How did the way Shirley handled the infraction of this rule help students understand the rationale behind it?

State Rules Clearly.   If rules are stated clearly, an inordinate amount of class time isn't used to interpret them. Researchers found that one ineffective manager had the rule "Be in the right place at the right time" (Emmer, Evertson, & Anderson, 1980). How much help would that rule be to a third-grader wanting to do the right thing? As another example, contrast "Bring all needed materials to class each day" with "Always be prepared." In the latter case, students are left uncertain; even in the former, the teacher needs to carefully discuss, explain, and illustrate the rule.

State Rules Positively.   "Listen when someone else is talking" is preferable to "Don't interrupt." Rules stated positively create a climate of positive expectations and encourage responsibility. Although the difference is subtle, rules stated negatively can contribute to an adversarial climate. Also, positively stated rules specify desired behavior; rules stated negatively only identify what students are not to do.

11.24

We said students must instantly know when they break a rule. "Instantly knowing" relates to what concept from your study of information processing in Chapter 7?

Keep the List Short.   For rules to be effective, students must be constantly aware of them and must instantly know when they break one. The most common reason students break rules is that they simply forget! Although this is particularly true for young children, it applies to older ones as well.

Making Rules and Procedures Work

So far we've found that instruction and classroom order are interdependent, effective teachers more often prevent rather than solve management problems, and planning is critical in this process. Now we turn to putting these plans into practice. As we make the transition, we emphasize three important points:

- Behavior patterns are established in the first few days of school.
- Rules and procedures must be carefully taught.
- Rules and procedures must be constantly monitored.

Beginning the School Year

Research consistently indicates that the patterns of behavior for the year are established in the first few days of school (Doyle, 1986; Evertson et al., 1997). Evertson (1987) stresses the precedent-setting nature of the first day:

> The first day of school has special significance for both teachers and students. It is at this time that rules, routines, and expectations are established. Students' first impressions about their classrooms, their teachers, and what standards are expected can have a lasting effect on their attitudes and on the ways they will engage in classroom tasks. (p. 69)

Effective teachers realize this and are ready to go from the first bell of the first day.

> Vicki Williams is organizing her handouts on the first day of class. Her eighth-graders come into the room; some take their seats while others mill around talking in small groups. As the bell rings, she looks up and says over the hum of the students, "Everyone take your seats, please," and she turns back to finish organizing her materials.
>
> Donnell Alexander is waiting at the door for her eighth-graders and has also prepared handouts. As the students come in, she smiles and says, "Take your seats quickly, please. You'll find your name on the desk. The bell is going to ring in less than a minute, and everyone must be at his or her desk and quiet when it does. Please read the handout while you're waiting." She is standing at the front of the room, surveying the class as the bell rings. When it stops, Donnell begins, "Good morning, everyone."

In the first few minutes of the year, Vicki's and Donnell's students each learned some important ideas about the way their classes would be run. From Vicki they learned, "Being in your seat at the beginning of the period isn't important," whereas Donnell's clear message was, "Be ready to start when the bell rings." Students quickly understand these differences and, unless Vicki reverses her pattern, she will soon have problems—not dramatic problems perhaps, but chronic and low grade problems that, like nagging sniffles, won't go away. Some guidelines for the first few days of school are summarized in Table 11.5.

Teaching Rules and Procedures

We said earlier that a cognitive approach to classroom management treats rules and procedures as abstract guidelines for behavior. As with any abstraction, learners construct understanding of the guidelines from concrete examples and discussions (Jones, 1987).

Table 11.5   Guidelines for beginning the school year

Guideline	Examples
Establish expectations	• Explain requirements and grading systems, particularly with older students.
	• Emphasize that learning and classroom order are interdependent.
Plan structured instruction	• Plan with extra care during this period.
	• Conduct eye-catching and motivating activities.
	• Use the first few days to assess learners' skills and background knowledge.
	• Use large- rather than small-group instruction.
	• Minimize transitions from one activity to another.
Teach rules and procedures	• Begin teaching rules and procedures the first day.
	• Frequently discuss and practice rules and procedures during the first few days.
	• Intervene and discuss every infraction of rules.
Begin communication with parents	• Send a letter to parents that states positive expectations for the year.
	• Call parents after the first or second day to nip potential problems in the bud.

Helping young students understand rules and procedures is especially important because they lack experience, and rules and procedures are often somewhat abstract. Let's see how one first-grade teacher, Martha Oakes, taught one of her procedures.

11.25

You want to teach the rule "Listen when others are talking" on the first day of school. Describe precisely how you would teach this rule to a group of third-graders. How would you teach it to a group of seventh-graders?

I put each of their names, as well as my own, on a cubby hole in a storage place on the wall of my room. I did a very short worksheet myself and literally walked it over and put it in my storage spot, thinking aloud as I went. "Hmm, I'm finished with my worksheet. . . . What do I do now? . . . I need to put it in my storage space. If I don't put it there, my teacher can't check it, so it's very important. . . . Now, I start on the next assignment." I then gave each of them the worksheet, directing them to take it to their file, quietly and individually, as soon as they were finished. After we had done one, I asked them why we did that. Then I gave them another, asked them what they were going to do and why, and had them do it. I asked them to think what would happen if we didn't put papers where they belong. I asked them whether they had ever lost anything and how this was similar. After we had practiced a few times, I only had to remind them periodically.

Martha understood the developmental characteristics of her first-graders, realizing that unless she explicitly taught her procedures, students were unlikely to understand or follow them. Her planning, modeling, dry runs, and actual practice helped make her classroom function like a well-oiled machine. Older students may not need a dry run, but clear explanations of procedures, reasons for them, and examples are no less important.

Notice that Martha emphasized the reason for the procedure. This helps students understand that it exists to help the class run smoothly, and it makes sense to follow it, because they'll learn more if they do. This is consistent with cognitive approaches to management.

Monitoring Rules and Procedures

Constructivism helps us understand that learners construct understanding that makes sense to them, and this understanding depends on their existing background knowledge. We also know that understanding evolves over time through a process that isn't smooth or linear.

This means that no matter how good a job you do of "teaching" rules and procedures, monitoring and discussing them will be necessary as the students' understanding of them increases (Emmer et al., 1997; Evertson et al., 1997). Effective teachers react to misbehavior immediately, refer students to the rule that was broken, and discuss the reasons why the rule is important and the behavior inappropriate. Shirley did this in stopping Sondra's whispering and note passing. It was an example of effective rule monitoring because she called Sondra's attention to the rule and reminded her of its rationale as she enforced it.

As understanding of a rule increases, students are more likely to obey it, regardless of consequences, because it makes sense and they've had a voice in its creation. It becomes a social contract—Stage 5 in Kohlberg's descriptions of moral reasoning. Other students will obey the rules because they know the teacher monitors them. Understanding, combined with the knowledge that rules are being monitored, prevents many off-task and disruptive behaviors.

> **11.26**
>
> Think about our discussion of concept teaching in Chapter 8. Based on the suggestions for teaching concepts, explain why Martha was effective in teaching her students procedures.

> **11.27**
>
> To what stage of moral development does obeying rules because they know the teacher is monitoring them most closely relate? Explain.

Classroom Connections

Planning Procedures and Rules in Your Classroom

1. Carefully plan your classroom procedures and rules before the year begins.

   - A third-grade teacher prepares a handout for his students and their parents that describes how papers should be prepared, how grades are determined, and procedures for making up work.

   - A seventh-grade math teacher prepares a written list of rules before she starts class on the first day. She then asks students to suggest additional rules that will help make the classroom a positive place to learn.

2. Consider the developmental level of your students in preparing and teaching rules and procedures.

   - A first-grade teacher reviews her procedures for entering class in the morning for a few minutes each day until the students are able to follow the procedure without directions.

   - At the beginning of the school year, an eighth-grade teacher tries to establish a positive classroom climate by conducting a daily review of the rule requiring students to speak to each other respectfully and by discussing the reasons for the rule.

3. Consider your physical environment in planning procedures and rules.

   - A sixth-grade teacher arranges students' desks so that they are facing away from the classroom window, which looks out on the physical education field.

- A geometry teacher has the custodian move her projection screen into the corner of the room so that it doesn't cover the chalkboard.

Making Rules and Procedures Work

4. Be prepared for the first day of class.
   - A kindergarten teacher greets the children as they come to the door of her room. She takes each by the hand and walks with him or her to a seat at a table with the student's name on it. Crayons and other materials are waiting, and the students use these materials until everyone arrives.
   - An eighth-grade science teacher is standing at the door as the students file into the room on the first day. "Move to your seats quickly please," she says, "and begin reading the paper that's on your desk. We'll begin discussing it as soon as the bell rings."

5. Explain and have the students practice your classroom procedures.
   - A first-grade teacher has his students practice his procedures several times in dry runs during the first few days of school. He has them continue to practice until they follow the procedures without being told.
   - An eighth-grade physical-science teacher takes a full class period to describe and explain safe lab procedures. She distributes a handout describing them to each student, models correct procedures, and explains the reasons behind each.
   - A fifth-grade teacher goes through the rules one by one. She asks the students to give her an example of following each rule and another example of not following the rule. In each case, she asks them why the rule is important and they discuss the reasons.

Dealing with Misbehavior: Cognitive Approaches to Intervention

Our focus to this point has been on preventing management problems. We have emphasized the interdependence of instruction and classroom management, the importance of planning, the role of carefully taught and monitored rules and procedures, and the need to communicate with parents.

Despite teachers' best efforts, however, management problems occur, and teachers must intervene in cases of disruptive behavior or chronic inattention. In this section, we examine cognitive approaches to intervention; in the next, we look at intervention from a behaviorist perspective.

We said earlier that cognitive approaches to management focus on learner understanding rather than mere compliance, and this applies to intervention as well. As we examine these approaches we consider:

- The way teachers talk to learners
- Guidelines for successful intervention
- Logical consequences

Classroom Interventions: Talking to Students

We said earlier that management seems to be a non-issue in some classrooms. The atmosphere is calm, but not rigid, and discipline rarely intrudes on the learning environment. Creating a classroom in which students feel free to express their ideas, yet respect the rights of others requires a sensitive and skilled teacher. The way we talk to students is important in creating this atmosphere. Experts identify three aspects of this process:

Effective interventions require both clear verbal and congruent nonverbal communication.

- Verbal–nonverbal congruence
- I-messages
- Active listening

Verbal–Nonverbal Congruence.

Professor: How do you know when your teacher really means what she says?

Third-grader: Well, her eyes get big and round, and she looks right at us. She doesn't move and her voice is a little louder, but she talks kinda slowly. Sometimes she stands over us and looks down at us.

Professor: What happens then?

Third-grader: The class does what she wants!

(Woolfolk & Brooks, 1985, p. 514)

11.28

Explain why verbal–nonverbal congruence is consistent with cognitive views of learning. Be specific in your explanation.

When we think about communication, we typically think of a conversation, in which two or more people have some kind of discussion. However, much of a receiver's perception of a message is derived from the way words are said and the way the speaker appears when saying them, rather than the words themselves. This is the source of the maxim, "It's not what you say, but how you say it." This channel of communication, called **nonverbal,** includes *the tone of voice and the body language people use to convey unspoken messages*. Essential elements of nonverbal communication are listed in Table 11.6. Let's see how it works in a classroom.

Karen Wilson's tenth-graders are working on their next day's English homework as she circulates among them. She is helping Jasmine when Jeff and Mike begin whispering loudly behind her.

11.29

Of the nonverbal behaviors in Table 11.6, which are easiest or most unobstrusive to use? Which are more difficult?

Table 11.6 Characteristics of nonverbal communication

Nonverbal Behavior	Example
Proximity	A teacher moves close to an inattentive student. In another case, a teacher moves to a student and touches her on the shoulder.
Eye contact	A teacher looks an off-task student directly in the eye when issuing a directive.
Body orientation	A teacher directs himself squarely to the learner, rather than over the shoulder or sideways.
Facial expression	A teacher frowns slightly at a disruption, brightens her face at a humorous incident, and smiles approvingly at a student's effort to help a classmate.
Gestures	A teacher puts her palm out (Stop!) to a student who interjects as another student is talking.
Vocal variation	A teacher varies the tone, pitch, and loudness of his voice for emphasis and displays energy and enthusiasm.

"Jeff. Mike. Stop talking and get started on your homework," she says, glancing over her shoulder.

The two slow their whispering, and Karen turns back to Jasmine. Soon, though, the boys are whispering as loudly as ever.

"I thought I told you to stop talking," Karen says over her shoulder again, this time with irritation in her voice.

The boys glance at her and quickly resume whispering.

Isabel Rodriguez is in a similar situation with her ninth-grade algebra class. As she is helping Vicki, Ken and Lance begin horsing around at the back of the room.

Isabel quickly excuses herself from Vicki, turns, and walks directly to the boys. Looking Lance in the eye, she says pleasantly but firmly, "Lance, we have plenty to do before lunch, and noise disrupts others' work. Begin your homework now," and then looking directly at Ken, she continues, "Ken, you too. Quickly now. We have only so much time, and we don't want to waste it." She waits until they're working quietly, and then she returns to Vicki.

11.30

Early in the chapter we saw that democratic teachers are caring yet firm. Describe nonverbal behaviors that communicate caring. Then describe nonverbal behaviors that communicate firmness.

The intent of both teachers' words was similar, but the messages were very different. Karen's communicated, "I want you to stop, but I'm not committed to being sure you do." She issued her directive over her shoulder, didn't check to see if the boys actually did stop, and became irritated when they didn't. Isabel, in contrast, communicated, "I want you to stop, and it's important that you do." When the horseplay began, she responded immediately, faced the students directly, emphasized the relationship between classroom order and learning, and made sure they were on-task before she went back to Vicki.

Karen's communication was incongruent. Her words said one thing, but her body language said another. Incongruent communication confuses students who are trying to understand the culture of the classroom. In these cases, words are the least credible part of the message. Fifty-five percent of a message's credibility is communicated with body language; 38% with the tone, pitch, and variation in voice quality; and a meager 7% through the actual words (Mehrabian & Ferris, 1967). Research in classrooms corroborates the importance of nonverbal communication: Direct eye contact and proximity both influence management messages (Houten & Doleys, 1983). In talking to students, teachers need to keep their nonverbal behavior consistent with their words, or their words lose credibility.

I-Messages.   Despite the importance of nonverbal communication, the clarity and tone of our words impacts their effectiveness. Let's look again at how Shirley handled Sondra's whispering and note passing in our opening case study. When Sondra asked, "What did I do?" Shirley responded, "When we talked about our rules at the beginning of the year, we agreed that it was important to listen when other people are talking." When she protested, Shirley said, "We don't learn as much when people aren't paying attention, and I'm uncomfortable when we don't learn . . ." Shirley sent an **I-message,** which is *a three-part statement that: (a) addresses behavior rather than personal characteristics, (b) describes the effects on the sender, and (c) identifies feelings generated in the sender.*

The way Shirley talked to Sondra had both short- and long-term consequences (Gordon, 1974). First, by referring to the rule, Shirley addressed Sondra's behavior rather than her character or personality. When teachers say, "You're driving me up the wall," they're blaming students and implying weaknesses in their characters. Focusing on the incident communicates that students' intrinsic worth is unchanged, but the behavior is unacceptable. This approach takes learners' beliefs and needs into account.

Shirley then demonstrated the second and third parts of an I-message by saying, "We don't learn as much when people aren't paying attention, and I'm uncomfortable when we don't learn. . . ." This describes the effect on the sender and the feelings it generates. The intent in the message is to help students understand the effects their actions have on others—a step toward responsible behavior and self-regulation.

Active Listening.   "Communication is a two-way street" is another time-honored maxim. Teachers who effectively communicate with their students are also good listeners (Gordon, 1974). When students believe that teachers are listening rather than evaluating what they say, they begin to trust the teacher and feel free to communicate openly. For example,

> Gayle goes to Mrs. Cortez after class and says, "Mrs. Cortez, I don't think I should have gotten a zero on that last assignment."
>
> Mrs. Cortez sits down, focuses her attention on Gayle, and says evenly, "You don't think the grade was fair?"
>
> "No," Gayle says, squirming slightly.
>
> "Tell me why."
>
> "I was absent the day you assigned it, and I didn't know that it was due today."
>
> "I understand how you feel, Gayle," Mrs. Cortez responds, leaning forward. "I would feel bad, too, if I got a zero on an assignment. But I told you the day you got back that the assignment had been given and that it was due today. In the future, I would suggest that you write assignments down in your notebook so that you're less likely to forget them."

Mrs. Cortez sat down, *gave Gayle her full attention, and responded to both the intellectual and emotional content of the message.* These are essential characteristics of **active listening** (Sokolove, Garrett, Sadker, & Sadker, 1990). Notice also that Mrs. Cortez didn't acquiesce to Gayle's implication of unfairness. Active listening doesn't imply that standards are sacrificed or that rules and procedures are violated. Mrs.

11.31

This section focuses on cognitive approaches to intervention. In what way does it also relate to humanistic views of learners? Be specific in your explanation.

11.32

A student stops after class and comments, "Gee, Mrs. Taylor. That test was too hard. I studied for three days and still did terrible." The teacher glances up from her papers, smiles, and says, "It was designed to be challenging. I'm sure you'll do better on the next one," and then returns to her work. Is the teacher demonstrating the characteristics of active listening? Explain.

Cortez's willingness to take time to listen without defensiveness is the essence of active listening.

Guidelines for Successful Intervention

Intervening in classroom management problems is never easy. If it were, classroom management wouldn't remain a persistent problem. Some basic guidelines can help in the process.

Withitness. An essential component of successful interventions is monitoring the classroom and understanding the dynamics of student behavior. This capability, called **withitness** (Kounin, 1970), *means the teacher knows what is going on in all parts of the classroom all the time and communicates this knowing verbally and nonverbally.* Kounin described it as "having eyes in the back of the head." The label is intuitively sensible. We've all known people who seem oblivious to the world around them, and we may even have used the phrase, "He needs to get with it." Let's compare two teachers who vary in their withitness.

> Ron Ziers is explaining the procedure for finding percentages of numbers to his seventh-graders. As he illustrates the procedure, Kareem, in the second desk from the front of the room, is periodically poking Katilyna, who sits across from him. She retaliates by kicking him in the leg. Bill, sitting behind Katilyna, pokes her in the arm with his pencil. Ron doesn't respond to the students' actions. After a second poke, Katilyna swings her arm back and catches Bill on the shoulder. "Katilyna!" Ron says sternly. "We keep our hands to ourselves! . . . Now, where were we?"
>
> Karl Wickes, a seventh-grade life-science teacher in the same school, has the same group of students. He puts a transparency displaying a flowering plant on the overhead. As the class discusses the information, he notices Barry whispering something to Julie, and he sees Kareem poke Katilyna, who kicks him and loudly whispers, "Stop it." As Karl asks, "What is the part of the plant that produces fruit?" he moves to Kareem's desk, leans over, and says quietly but firmly, "We keep our hands and materials to ourselves in here." He then moves to the front of the room, watches Kareem out of the corner of his eye, and says, "Barry, what other plant part do you see in the diagram?"

Karl demonstrated three features of withitness

- He *identified the misbehavior immediately;* he went at once to Kareem. Ron did nothing until the misbehavior had spread to other students.

- He *correctly identified the right student;* he knew that Kareem was the original cause of the incident. Ron reprimanded Katilyna, leaving the students with a sense that the teacher doesn't know what's going on.

- He saw two incidents of misbehavior, and *he responded to the more serious infraction first.* Since Kareem's poking was more disruptive than Barry's whispering, he responded to Kareem first, and he then simply called on Barry, which got him back into the activity, making further intervention unnecessary.

Withitness goes beyond dealing with misbehaving students. It also includes *checking students' verbal and nonverbal behavior for evidence of learning progress.* Alert teachers notice inattentive students and walk over to them or call on them to bring them back into the lesson. They also respond to quizzical looks and other nonverbal behaviors with questions such as, "I see uncertain looks on some of your faces. Do you want

---

11.33

Using your study of information processing in Chapter 7 as a basis, explain why some teachers lack withitness; i.e., seem oblivious to what is going on in their classroom as they teach.

11.34

Use your understanding of social cognitive theory from Chapter 6 to explain why failure to intervene when a student is disruptive might lead to the misbehavior spreading.

11.35

Identify an instance in Shirley Barton's teaching in which she demonstrated withitness. Cite the example directly from the case study.

11.36

Kounin (1970) describes a concept called **overlapping** which is *a teacher's ability to attend to two incidents at the same time without focusing exclusively on either one.* Identify an example of overlapping in the examples with Karl Wickes.

Withit teachers constantly monitor the classroom for signs of learning progress and problems.

me to rephrase that question?" Teachers in productive learning environments are sensitive to student learning progress (Duffy, Roehler, Meloth, & Vavrus, 1985; O'Keefe & Johnston, 1987).

Preserve Student Dignity.   A basic principle for any intervention is to preserve a student's dignity. Loud reprimands in front of the class, public criticism, and sarcasm all detract from a sense of safety and a learning-focused classroom environment. For example,

> "Janet, what are you doing?"
> "Nothing."
> "Yes you were. Speak up so that everyone can hear."
> ". . ."
> "You were talking. What's the rule about talking without permission?"
> ". . ."
> "Let's hear it. I want to hear you say the rule."
> ". . . We don't talk until we're recognized."
> "That's right. Do you understand that?"
> ". . . Yes."

This prolonged encounter was unnecessary and unproductive. If we recognize students as thinking, feeling beings, we must know that Janet understood what she was doing. Asking a student to state a rule makes sense, but the tone was negative, and Janet was forced into a humiliating position. Her only alternatives were to acquiesce or lash out; she loses either way, and she's likely to resent the teacher's abuse of power. Instead, the teacher could have had her identify the rule, asked or explained why it is important, enlisted compliance with it, and moved on with the lesson or spoken with the student privately (in the hall or after class).

11.37

Put yourself in the role of the teacher and describe how you might later use Gordon's I-messages to deal with Janet.

Creating Productive Learning Environments   **475**

Be Consistent.   "Be consistent" is advised so often that it's a cliché. The need for consistency is obvious, but achieving complete consistency in the real world of teaching is virtually impossible. In fact, research indicates that our interventions *should* be contextualized; they depend on the specific student and situation (Doyle, 1986).

For example, most classrooms have a rule "Speak only when recognized by the teacher." Suppose you're monitoring seatwork, and a student innocently asks a work-related question of another student then quickly turns back to work. Do you intervene, reminding her that talking is not allowed during seatwork? Failing to do so is technically inconsistent, but you don't intervene and you shouldn't. A student who repeatedly turns around and whispers, though, becomes a disruption, warranting an intervention.

This example illustrates one of the advantages of cognitive versus behavioral approaches to management. A cognitive approach assumes that students can and should be expected to understand the difference in the two incidents. A behavioral approach focuses only on the behavior and consequences.

Follow-Through.   To illustrate the principle of follow-through, think again about the examples with Karen Wilson and Isabell Rodriguez in our discussion of nonverbal communication. Karen told Jeff and Mike to stop whispering but turned back to Jasmine before she made certain they complied. Isabell, in contrast, made sure Ken and Lance were working quietly before she turned back to Vicki.

While follow-through is difficult, it is critical. Without follow-through, a management system breaks down because students learn that teachers aren't fully committed to maintaining an orderly classroom environment. This confuses them and detracts from the process of developing responsibility. This is another reason that the first few days of the school year are so important. If you follow through carefully during this period, management becomes much easier during the rest of the year.

Keep Interventions Brief.   Keep all interventions as brief as possible. Researchers have documented a negative relationship between time spent on discipline and student achievement; long interventions break the flow of the lesson and detract from instructional time (Crocker & Brooker, 1986; Evertson, Anderson, Anderson, & Brophy, 1980).

Let's see how Shirley applied this principle in her work with her fifth-graders. First, she simply touched Brad on the arm. She used nonverbal communication to stop Kevin and she spoke quietly to Sondra. In each case, she kept the encounter short and minimized its impact on the rest of the class.

Avoid Arguments.   Finally, whenever possible, avoid arguing with students, because teachers never "win" arguments. They can exercise their authority, but resentment is often the outcome, and the encounter may expand into a major incident. Shirley handled this problem skillfully in her encounter with Sondra. She simply referred to the rule, restated her request, and ensured that it was followed. In comparison, consider an alternative scenario.

> "I wasn't *speaking*."
>> "You were whispering."
>> "It doesn't say *no whispering*."
>> "You know what the rule means. We've been over it again and again."
>> "Well, it's not fair. I wasn't speaking. You don't make other students move when they whisper."
>> "You were whispering, so move."

11.38

What concept from Piaget's work (in Chapter 2) relates to consistency? Explain how it is related.

11.39

Describe how Shirley demonstrated follow-through in dealing with Sondra in our opening case study.

11.40

The statement that "long interventions break the flow of the lesson" relates to what concept discussed earlier in the chapter?

The student, of course, knew what the rule meant and was simply playing a game with the teacher, who allowed herself to be drawn into an argument. Shirley didn't, and the incident was disarmed almost immediately.

Logical Consequences

Logical consequences *treat misbehaviors as problems and help learners see a meaningful link between their actions and the consequence.*

Let's look at a classroom example.

The kindergarten boys found a lovely mud puddle on the playground during recess. They had much fun running and splashing and then came back into the room wet and dripping, and they left muddy footprints all over the room.

Their teacher called them aside for a conference. "Boys, we have two problems here. One is that the classroom is all dirty and it needs to be fixed so that the other children don't get wet and dirty. What can you do to fix it?"

One little boy suggested that they could mop the floor.

"Good idea," said the teacher. "Let's find our custodian, Mrs. Smith, and you can get a mop from her and mop the floor. Now what about our other problem, your dirty clothes?"

"We could call our mothers and ask them to bring us clean clothes!" suggested one boy.

"Another good idea," said the teacher. "But what if your mothers are not home?"

This was a tougher problem. Finally, one boy said, "I know, we could borrow some clean clothes from the lost and found box!"

"Good thinking," said the teacher. "And what can we do so that you don't lose so much time from class again?"

"Stay out of mud puddles!" was the reply in unison. (McCarthy, 1991, p. 19)

In this incident, the teacher helped the children see the link between their behavior and the consequence, and she also put the students in a problem-solving role. As a result, the immediate problem was solved and the children also learned to take responsibility for their behavior. Research indicates that children who learn to understand the effects of their actions on others become more altruistic and are more likely to take action to make up for their misbehavior (Berk, 1994).

11.41

Using Piaget's theory as a basis, explain why children need to *learn* that their actions affect others.

Designing and Maintaining a Cognitive Management System

Designing a management system based on cognitive views of learning emphasizes understanding and individual responsibility. As procedures and rules are planned, the focus is on rationales for, and learner input into, their creation. Time is spent during the first few days of school in class meetings (Glasser, 1990). The class is treated as a learning community and the goal in the meetings is to create a productive learning environment. Teachers emphasize that rules are social contracts, and all learners are responsible for adhering to them.

Rules and procedures are treated as abstract ideas, the understanding of which is constructed through concrete examples and discussions. When learners break rules, they are reminded of the social contract they agreed upon and that the rules exist to promote learning and protect the rights of everyone. Misbehaviors are treated as problems, and consequences are the logical outcomes of the problems' solutions.

The way we talk to students, the guidelines we've suggested, and logical consequences all treat learners as responsible, thinking individuals. Assuming they're responsible and treating them as such is the most desirable way to intervene when incidents occur. However, alternatives exist, as we'll see in the next section.

Dealing with Misbehavior: Behavioral Approaches to Intervention

Applications of behaviorism, although controversial, can initiate and maintain desired behaviors. While behaviorism is being discredited as a basis for designing learning activities, it remains popular as an approach to classroom management (Reynolds, Sinatra, & Jetton, 1996).

Decisions About Behavioral Systems

Cindy Daines's first-graders were sometimes frustrating. Although she tried alerting the groups and having the whole class make transitions at the same time, every transition took four minutes or more.

In an effort to improve the situation, she made some "tickets" from construction paper, bought an assortment of small prizes, and displayed the items in a fishbowl on her desk the next day. She then explained, "We're going to play a little game to see how quiet we can be when we change lessons. . . . Whenever we change, such as from language arts to math, I'm going to give you two minutes and then I'm going to ring this bell," she continued, ringing the bell as a demonstration. "Students who have their books out and are waiting quietly when I ring the bell will get one of these tickets. On Friday afternoon, you can turn these in for prizes you see in this fishbowl. The more tickets you have, the better the prize will be."

During the next few days, Cindy moved around the room, handing out tickets and making comments such as, "I really like the way Merry is ready to work," "Ted already has his books out and is quiet," and "Thank you for moving to math so quickly."

She knew it was working when she heard "Shh" and "Be quiet!" from the students, and she moved from the prizes to allowing the students to "buy" free time with their tickets, to finally giving them Friday afternoon parties as group rewards when the class had accumulated enough tickets. She gradually was able to space out the group rewards as the students' self-regulation developed.

Two decisions must be made when behavioral approaches are considered. First, will the system emphasize reinforcers for desired behavior or punishers for undesirable behavior? Second, will the consequences be individually or group administered?

Reinforcers or Punishers? Reinforcers, as you saw in Cindy's system, can be effective in initiating new behaviors (McCaslin & Good, 1992). In planning a reinforcement system, teachers identify the desired behaviors, link them to reinforcers, and communicate both to the students. Cindy followed this process by explaining what students had to do to earn prizes.

Punishers, in contrast, focus on eliminating undesired behavior. Guidelines for using punishers are outlined in Figure 11.4.

Punishers can suppress undesirable behaviors, but they don't teach desired ones, so they shouldn't form the core of a management system. Emphasizing desired behaviors is much more effective than attempting to eliminate unwanted ones (Alberto & Troutman, 1990).

Individual or Group Consequences? A second planning decision involves individual versus group consequences. Individual consequences are useful when focusing on

11.42

Cindy's comments, such as, "Ted already has his books out and is quiet," are an application of what concepts from your study of behaviorism and social cognitive theory in Chapter 6?

11.43

Even though emphasizing positive behaviors is preferred, many teachers largely ignore them and focus instead on undesirable behaviors. Why do you think this happens?

Figure 11.4 Guidelines for using punishers

- Use punishers as infrequently as possible to avoid negative emotional reactions.
- Apply punishers immediately and directly to the behavior.
- Apply punishers only severe enough to eliminate the behavior.
- Avoid using seatwork as a punisher.
- Apply punishers logically, systematically, and dispassionately—never angrily.
- Explain and model appropriate alternative behaviors.

behaviors displayed by one or a few students, such as a behavior modification system designed for a single, chronically misbehaving student (Alberto & Troutman, 1990). They concentrate efforts where they're most needed but are very demanding for teachers.

Group systems link consequences to the behavior of the whole group. Cindy Daines's parties are examples: the class was given parties when they had accumulated enough points. The influence of peer pressure and the ease of administration are two advantages of group systems.

As Cindy found, logistics can be demanding when using a behavioral system. She managed hers by first using individual tokens and then switching to group rewards. Food, privileges, praise, stars, free time, and displays of work are all examples of rewards for desired behavior. Some are controversial, and careful judgment should be used in choosing them.

Although the use of group rewards can be effective, the effect of group punishment is different. Punishing the group for the misbehavior of a few leads to anger and resentment and is generally ineffective. If the problem lies with a small group of students and punishment is required, it should be administered individually.

Assertive Discipline: A Structured Approach to Consequences

Lee and Marlene Canter (1992) have created an approach to management called **assertive discipline** that *emphasizes carefully stating rules and describing specific reinforcers and punishers.* Assertive discipline has been popular because it clearly specifies consequences for breaking and following rules, eliminating the need for split-second decisions by the teacher (see Table 11.7).

Assertive discipline is controversial. Critics charge that it is punitive, pits teachers against students, and stresses obedience and conformity at the expense of learning and self-control (Curwin & Mendler, 1988; McLaughlin, 1994). The Canters disagree, contending that its emphasis on positive reinforcement is effective (Canter, 1988). Despite this controversy, the program has been widely used. It is difficult to find a school district in the country that hasn't had at least some exposure to assertive discipline; estimates suggest that more than 750,000 teachers have been trained in the program (Hill, 1990).

Designing and Maintaining a Behavioral Approach to Management

On the surface, designing a behavioral approach to management appears to be similar to designing a cognitive system. It typically involves the following steps:

Table 11.7 Sample consequences in implementing assertive discipline

Consequences for Breaking Rules	
First infraction	Name on list
Second infraction	Check by name
Third infraction	Second check by name
Fourth infraction	Half-hour detention
Fifth infraction	Call to parents

Consequences for Following Rules
A check is removed for each day that no infractions occur. If only a name remains, and no infractions occur, the name is removed.
All students without names on the list are given 45 minutes of free time Friday afternoon to do as they choose. The only restrictions are that they must stay in the classroom, and they must not disrupt the students who didn't earn the free time.

- Prepare a list of specific rules. The rules should represent observable behaviors (e.g., speak only when recognized by the teacher).
- Specify punishers for breaking rules and reinforcers for obeying each rule (such as the consequences in Table 11.7).
- Display the rules and procedures, and explain the consequences to the students.
- Consistently apply consequences.

A behavioral system doesn't preclude providing rationales or creating the rules with learner input, of course. The focus, however, is on the application of consequences that are intended to modify observable behavior, in contrast with a cognitive system, which emphasizes the development of learner understanding and responsibility.

In designing their management systems, teachers will likely use elements of both cognitive and behavioral approaches. Behavioral systems have the advantage of immediate applicability; it takes time to develop learner responsibility and self-control. Behavioral systems are effective in initiating desired behaviors, particularly with young students, and they're useful in suppressing chronic misbehavior. A behavioral approach, however, focuses on external control, so it isn't effective in helping learners develop self-regulation.

Keeping both cognitive and behavioral approaches to management in mind, let's consider a series of intervention options.

An Intervention Continuum

Disruptions vary widely, from an isolated incident (such as a student briefly whispering to a neighbor during quiet time) to chronic infractions (such as someone repeatedly poking, tapping, or kicking other students). Because infractions vary, teachers' reactions

11.44

Explain, from a cognitive perspective, how ignoring inappropriate behavior could be effective. Then explain how it might be effective from a behavioral perspective.

11.45

A teacher praising Jimmy for working quietly is trying to implement two concepts from social cognitive theory. What are they? Explain.

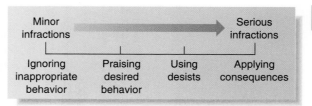

Figure 11.5 An intervention continuum

should also vary. To maximize instructional time and minimize disruptions, our goal is to keep interventions as unobtrusive as possible. A continuum designed to reach this goal is described in Figure 11.5.

Ignoring Inappropriate Behavior

The least obtrusive intervention is to simply ignore the behavior. This is appropriate if a student asks a quick question about a seatwork problem, for example. It is also appropriate if two students briefly whisper about something that isn't school related. If brief, the incident can be ignored.

Praising Desired Behavior

Teachers are urged to "catch 'em being good," which is particularly effective as a method of prevention. Elementary teachers effectively use statements like, "I really like the way Jimmy is working quietly," and middle and secondary teachers will quietly comment to students after class, "I'm extremely pleased with your work this last week. You're getting better and better at this stuff. Keep it up." The combination of praise and ignoring misbehavior can be very effective with minor disruptions (Pfiffer, Rosen, & O'Leary, 1985; Rosen, O'Leary, Joyce, Conway, & Pfiffer, 1984).

Using Desists

A **desist** *occurs when a teacher tells a student to stop a behavior* (Kounin, 1970). "Glenys, we don't leave our seat without permission," "Glenys!", a finger to the lips, and a stern facial expression are all desists, and are the most common teacher reaction to misbehavior (Humphrey, 1979; Sieber, 1981).

Clarity and tone are important in the effectiveness of desists. For example, "Randy, what is the rule about touching other students in this class?" or, "Randy, how do you think that makes Willy feel?" are clearer than "Randy, stop that," because they link the behavior to a rule or the consequences of the behavior. Students react to these subtle differences, preferring rule and consequence reminders to teacher commands (Nucci, 1987).

The tone of desists should be firm but not angry. Kounin (1970) found that kindergarten students handled with rough desists actually became more disruptive and that older students were uncomfortable in classes in which rough desists were used. Borg and Ascione (1982) found that gentle reprimands, together with the suggestion of alternative behaviors and effective questioning techniques, reduced time off-task by 20 minutes a day.

Clear communication (including congruence between verbal and nonverbal behavior), an awareness of what's happening in the classroom (withitness), and the characteristics of effective instruction are critical in using desists to stop misbehavior. However, even when these critical elements are used, simple desists alone sometimes don't work.

11.46

Nucci (1987) found that learners prefer rule and consequence reminders to teacher commands. Does a cognitive or a behavioral view better account for this preference? Why?

11.47

On the basis of your study of social cognitive theory in Chapter 6, explain why rough desists might result in students becoming more disruptive. What other explanations might there be?

Clarity and a positive tone make desists opportunities for student learning.

Applying Consequences

Careful planning and effective instruction will eliminate much misbehavior before it starts. Some minor incidents can be ignored, and simple desists will stop others. When these strategies don't stop disruptions, however, you must apply consequences that are related to the problem.

Logical consequences are preferable because they treat misbehaviors as problems and demonstrate a link between the behavior and the consequence. Classrooms are busy places, however, and it isn't always possible to solve problems with logical consequences. In these instances, behavioral consequences offer an alternative:

> Jason is an intelligent and active fifth-grader. He loves to talk and seems to know just how far he can go before Mrs. Aguilar gets exasperated with him. He understands the rules and the reasons for them, but his interest in talking seems to take precedence. Ignoring him isn't working. A call to his parents helped for a while, but soon he was back to his usual behavior—never quite enough to require a drastic response, but always a thorn in Mrs. Aguilar's side.
>
> Finally, she decides that she will give him one warning. At a second disruption, he is placed in time-out from regular instructional activities. She meets with Jason and explains the new rules. The next day, he begins to misbehave almost immediately.
>
> "Jason," she warns, "you can't work while you're talking, and you're keeping others from finishing their work. Please get busy."
>
> He stops, but five minutes later, he's at it again. "Jason," she says quietly as she moves back to his desk, "I've warned you. Now please go back to the time-out area."
>
> A week later, Jason is working quietly and comfortably with the rest of the class.

Jason's behavior is common, particularly in elementary and middle schools; it is precisely this behavior that drives teachers up the wall. Students like Jason cause more teacher stress and burnout than threats of violence and bodily harm. His behavior is disruptive so it can't be ignored; praise for good work helps to a certain extent, but much of his reinforcement comes from his buddies. Desists work briefly, but teachers burn out constantly monitoring him. Mrs. Aguilar had little choice but to apply consequences.

The key to handling students like Jason is consistency. He understands what he is doing, and he is capable of controlling himself. When he can, with absolute certainty, predict the consequences of his behavior, he'll quit. He knew that his second infraction would result in time-out and, when it did, he quickly changed his behavior. There was no argument, little time was used, and the class wasn't disrupted.

Serious Management Problems: Violence and Aggression

Class is disrupted by a scuffle. You look up to see that Ron has left his seat and gone to Phil's desk, where he is punching and shouting at Phil. Phil is not so much fighting back as trying to protect himself. You don't know how this started, but you do know that Phil gets along well with other students and that Ron often starts fights and arguments without provocation. (Brophy & Rohrkemper, 1987, p. 60)

This morning several students excitedly tell you that on the way to school they saw Tom beating up Sam and taking his lunch money. Tom is the class bully and has done things like this many times. (Brophy & Rohrkemper, 1987, p. 53)

What would you do in these situations? What would be your immediate reaction? How would you follow through? What long-term strategies would you employ to ensure that these problems do not recur? These questions were asked of teachers identified by their principals as effective in dealing with serious management problems (Brophy & McCaslin, 1992). In this section, we consider their responses, together with other research examining violence and aggression in schools.

Problems of violence and aggression require both immediate actions and long-term solutions. In the short term, the behavior must be stopped and the victim must be protected. Long-term strategies place the problem in a larger context and attempt to deal with possible causes.

Short-Term Strategies

Experts recommend an immediate and assertive response to aggressive acts. Students must be confronted immediately, told clearly that violence or aggression will not be allowed, and helped to understand the severity of their actions. It is important to communicate that students are accountable for their actions (Brophy, 1996). In the incident with the lunch money, for example, Tom must be told that his actions were reported, that they're unacceptable and that they won't be tolerated. In the case of the classroom scuffle, participants should be separated immediately and told that this kind of behavior is not permitted.

Long-Term Solutions

Expert teachers and their less effective counterparts differ in their long-term solutions (Brophy & McCaslin, 1992). Strategies of expert teachers are comprehensive and instructional; in addition to stopping the immediate behavior, they focus on long-term solutions. Less effective teachers depend more on threats and coercion than systematic long-term strategies.

11.48

Suppose Mrs. Aguilar has just begun implementing her system with Jason and she saw him briefly talk to one of his buddies. Should she ignore the behavior or apply a consequence? Provide a rationale for your response.

11.49

Where on the intervention continuum would short-term actions be? Why would other interventions be skipped?

As a long-term strategy, students need to be taught alternatives to fighting. Students must learn how to control their tempers and cope with frustration. One approach uses problem-solving simulations to teach aggressive youth to understand the motives and intentions of other people. Research indicates that aggressive youth often respond the way they do because they misread others' intentions as being hostile (Hudley, 1992). Following problem-solving sessions, aggressive students were less hostile in their interpretation of ambiguous situations and were rated as less aggressive by their teachers.

Other approaches include teaching aggressive students to express anger verbally instead of physically and to solve conflicts through communication and negotiation rather than fighting (Lee, Pulvino, & Perrone, 1998). One form of communication and negotiation is learning to make and defend a position—to *argue* effectively (Rancer, Goff, Kosberg, & Avtgis, 1997). Researchers found that students taught to make effective arguments—strongly emphasizing that arguing and verbal aggression are very different—became much less combative when encountering others with whom they disagreed. Learning to argue also has incidental benefits: skillful arguers of any age are seen by their peers as intelligent and credible.

Experts also suggest the involvement of parents and other school personnel (Brophy, 1996; Moles, 1992). Research indicates that a large majority of parents (88%) want to be notified immediately if school problems occur (Harris, Kagay, & Ross, 1987). In addition, school counselors, school psychologists, social workers, and principals have all been trained to deal with these problems and can provide advice and assistance. Experienced teachers can also provide a wealth of information about how they've handled similar problems. No one should face persistent or serious problems of violence or aggression alone.

In conclusion, we want to put problems of school violence and aggression into perspective. Though they are possibilities—and you should understand options for dealing with them—the majority of your management problems will be issues of cooperation and motivation. Many can be prevented, others can be dealt with quickly, and some require individual attention. We all hear about students carrying guns to school and incidents of assault on teachers in the news. Statistically, however, considering the huge numbers of students that pass through schools each day, these incidents remain infrequent.

11.50

Suppose you have just broken up a fight between two junior-high boys. One of the boys has been in four fights in the past two months. Describe specifically what you might do to help change this behavior.

Classroom Connections

Using Successful Interventions in Your Classroom

1. In talking to students, be sure your verbal and nonverbal messages are congruent.
   - In response to an underachiever's attempts to answer a question, the teacher orients her body directly toward him, looks directly at him, and nods reassuringly.
   - In directing two students to quit whispering and begin working, a teacher moves close to them, looks them in the eye, and remains standing in front of them until they comply.

2. Use problem-solving strategies and logical consequences to help students develop responsibility.
   - A second-grade teacher uses Friday afternoons to do classroom chores. Two students begin a tug-of-war over a cleaning rag and knock over a potted plant. The teacher talks to the students and they agree that the mess should be cleaned up. They write a note to their parents

explaining that they will be working in the classroom before school the next two mornings to pay for the cost of a new pot.

3. Use positive reinforcers to initiate and teach desirable behaviors.

   • A first-grade teacher, knowing that the times after recess and lunch are difficult for many students, institutes a system in which the class has one minute to settle down and get out their materials after a timer goes off. When the class meets the requirement, they earn points toward free-time activities.

   • To encourage students to clean up quickly after labs, a junior-high science teacher offers them a free five minutes of talk in their seats if the lab is cleaned up in time. Students who don't clean up in time are required to finish in silence.

4. Keep discipline encounters with students brief, clear, and to the point. Hold discussions regarding fairness or equity after class and in private.

   • After having been asked to stop whispering for the second time in ten minutes, a student protests that he was asking about the assigned seatwork. The teacher reminds him of the two incidents in ten minutes and that his whispering is disruptive. The teacher then removes a slip from his packet without further discussion. The teacher sits down with him after class to discuss the problem and work toward a solution.

   • A first-grade teacher tries to make interventions instructional. When she uses nonverbal cues to discipline, she points to the appropriate rule on the chalkboard. If students seem confused, she either bends down and talks to them quickly in private or makes a general reminder about the rule and its reason, such as "Class, there's too much noise in here, and I'm having trouble thinking."

5. Follow through consistently in cases of disruptive behavior.

   • A teacher separates two boys who disrupt lessons with their horseplay, telling them the new seat assignments are theirs until further notice. The next day, they sit in their old seats as the bell is about to ring. "Do you know why I moved you two yesterday?" the teacher says immediately. After a momentary pause, both students nod. "Then move quickly now, and be certain you're in your new seats tomorrow. You come talk with me when you're ready to solve this horseplay problem."

   • A high-school teacher reminds students about being seated when the bell rings. As the bell rings the next day, two girls are standing, having a conversation. The teacher turns to them and says, "I'm sorry, but you must not have understood me yesterday. To be counted on time, you need to be in your seats when the bell rings. Please go to the office and get a late admit pass. Please do it now . . . and if you want to talk with me about this, come in after class. Now, class, yesterday we were talking. . . ."

Accommodating Diversity in Productive Learning Environments

We saw earlier that a productive learning environment involves a combination of order and effective instruction. However, involving all learners can be a challenge in classrooms with diverse student populations.

Accommodating Diversity: Teacher Expectations

In our discussion of teacher expectations in Chapter 10, we found that, because teachers expect more of high achievers, teachers often call on such students more often, give them more time to answer, and prompt and encourage them more. This practice is inconsistent with the concept of *equitable distribution,* discussed earlier in this chapter, and it correlates with lowered achievement. "Teachers who restrict their questions primarily to a small group of active (and usually high-achieving) students are likely to communicate undesirable expectations . . . and generally to be less aware and less effective" (Good & Brophy, 1997, p. 378). Unfortunately, cultural minorities are often called on less frequently than non-minorities.

Consider Shirley Barton's questioning. By calling on her students as equally as possible and using open-ended questions she communicated, "I don't care if you're African American, Latino, Asian, white, boy, or girl. I don't care if you're gifted or have a learning disability. I expect you to participate, and I expect you to learn." Nothing better communicates that the teacher and all the students are "in this together," and that all students are expected to be successful learners.

To be a successful strategy, the practice of calling on all students must be the norm. Calling on cultural minorities or low achievers only occasionally can leave the impression that they're being singled out, and they may be embarrassed or even resentful.

Establishing a pattern of equitable distribution is difficult. However, if you persevere, it can be accomplished, and the results—both in terms of achievement and learner motivation—can be striking.

Accommodating Diversity: Communication with Parents

Productive learning environments invite all students into the classroom and communicate that students and their parents are partners in learning. In a comprehensive review of variables affecting student learning, researchers concluded,

> Because of the importance of the home environment to school learning, teachers must also develop strategies to increase parent involvement in their children's academic life. This means teachers should go beyond traditional once-a-year parent/teacher conferences and work with parents to see that learning is valued in the home. Teachers should encourage parents to be involved with their children's academic pursuits on a day-to-day basis, helping them with homework, monitoring television viewing, reading to their young children, and simply expressing the expectation that their children will achieve academic success. (Wang et al., 1993, pp. 278–279)

Communication with parents or other primary caregivers is not an appendage to the teaching process; it is an integral part of the teacher's job. It is even more critical when working with students from diverse backgrounds.

Benefits of Communication

Research indicates that students benefit from home–school cooperation in at least four ways:

- Higher long-term academic achievement
- More positive attitudes and behaviors
- Better attendance rates
- Greater willingness to do homework (Cameron & Lee, 1997; Epstein, 1990).

These outcomes likely result from parents' increased participation in school activities, their more positive attitudes about schooling, and teachers' increased understanding of learners' home environments (Weinstein & Mignano, 1993). Responding to a student's disruptive behavior is easier, for example, when his teachers learn that his mother or father has lost a job, his parents are going through a divorce, or there's a serious illness in the family. In addition, parents can help develop and reinforce behavior management plans. One teacher reported:

> I had this boy in my class who was extremely disruptive. He wouldn't work, kept "forgetting" his homework, distracted other children, wandered about the room. You name it; he did it. The three of us—the mother, the boy and I—talked about what we could do, and we decided to try a system of home rewards. We agreed that I would send a note home each day, reporting on the boy's behavior. For every week with at least three good notes, the mother added one Christmas present. In this way, what the child found under the tree on Christmas Day was directly dependent on his behavior. By Christmas, he had become so cooperative, I couldn't believe he was the same child! After Christmas, I observed some backsliding, so we all agreed to reverse the system: The mother took away one present each time a majority of the week's reports were negative. She didn't have to take many away! (Weinstein & Mignano, 1993, p. 226)

While some may criticize this approach because it's based on behaviorism, it worked; more importantly, it was the result of collaboration between the parent and teacher. This collaboration can have long-term benefits that are hard to assess based on a single incident. For example, teachers who encourage parental involvement report more positive feelings about teaching and their school. They also rate parents higher in helpfulness and follow-through and have higher expectations for parents (Epstein, 1990).

11.51

In addition to benefits to parents, what are at least two specific ways in which increased parental involvement can result in positive benefits to students?

Barriers to Parental Involvement

Involving parents in the education of their children is a desired goal, but it doesn't happen automatically. Economic, cultural, and language barriers are often difficult to overcome. Understanding is a first step in resolving these difficulties.

Teachers can involve parents in their children's learning through active communication strategies that express caring and concern.

Economic Barriers. Communication and involvement take time, and economic commitments often come first. First among these is employment; half the parents in one study indicated that their employment prevented them from helping their youngsters with homework (Ellis, Dowdy, Graham, & Jones, 1992). Other parents lack economic resources (such as child care, transportation, and telephones) that would allow them to participate in school activities. Most parents want to be involved in their children's schooling, but schools need to be flexible and provide help and encouragement (Epstein, 1990).

Cultural Barriers. Discontinuities between students' home cultures and the culture of the school can also be barriers to home–school cooperation (Delgado-Gaiton, 1992; Harry, 1992). Students may come from homes where the parents experienced schools that were very different from the ones their children have to cope with. Also, some parents may have only gone through the elementary grades or may have had negative school experiences. One researcher described the problem this way:

> Underneath most parents is a student—someone who went to school, sometimes happily, sometimes unhappily. What often happens when the parent-as-adult returns to school, or has dealings with teachers, is that the parent as child/student returns. Many parents still enter school buildings flooded with old memories, angers, and disappointments. Their stomachs churn and flutter with butterflies, not because of what is happening today with their own children, but because of outdated memories and past behaviors. (Rich, 1987, p. 24)

11.52

Explain the feelings of the parents in the Rich (1987) quote; base your answer on our study of classical conditioning in Chapter 6.

Parents like these will require encouragement and support to become involved.

In many Asian and Latino families, parents respect the teacher's authority so much that they hesitate to become involved in matters they believe are best handled by the school (Harry, 1992). This deference to authority implies, "You're the teacher; do what is best," but it is often interpreted by teachers as apathy.

Teacher authority and management style can also be a source of cultural conflict. A study of Puerto Rican families found that parents thought U.S. schools were too impersonal—that teachers didn't "worry about" their children enough. One parent explained, "In the U.S., the teachers care about the education of the child, but they don't care about the child himself and his problems" (Harry, 1992, p. 479). These parents wanted teachers to act more like parents, providing both warmth and structure for their children.

Language Barriers. Language can be another potential barrier to effective home–school cooperation. Parents of bilingual students often do not speak English; this makes home–school communication more difficult. In these situations, the child often has the responsibility of interpreting the message. Homework poses a special problem because parents are unable to interpret assignments or provide help (Delgado-Gaiton, 1992).

11.53

Identify at least two specific things you as a teacher could do to overcome cultural and language barriers in communicating with the parents of your students.

Schools also often compound the problem by using educational jargon when they send letters home. The problem is especially acute in special education, where legal and procedural safeguards can be bewildering. For example, studies indicate that parents often don't understand Individual Education Plans (Harry, 1992) or even remember that they've signed one (Stein, 1983). Other research indicates that many parents feel ill-prepared to assist their children with school-related tasks, but that suggestions from school describing specific strategies in the home can be effective in bridging the home–school gap (Gorman & Balter, 1997; Hoover-Dempsey, Bassler, & Burow, 1995).

Strategies for Involving Parents

Virtually all schools have formal communication channels, such as interim progress reports, that tell parents about their youngster's achievement at the midpoint of each grading period: open houses (during which teachers introduce themselves and describe general guidelines and procedures), parent–teacher conferences, and, of course, report cards. Although these processes are schoolwide and necessary, as an individual teacher, you can do more to enhance the communication process.

Early Communication. Earlier in the chapter we said that teachers should open lines of communication in the first few days of school. This is particularly important in working with learners from diverse backgrounds. Let's see how one teacher handled this:

> Joan Williams, an eighth-grade English teacher, began the process of communicating with parents on the first day of school by soliciting students' input. With their help, she prepared a description of her rules and procedures. On the second day, she had a letter prepared for her students to take home for their parents' signature. Because she had several Spanish-speaking students in her class, she enlisted the aid of another teacher and sent a copy written in Spanish to the parents of those students. The letter appears in Figure 11.6.

Joan's letter accomplished several things. Although she is not a Spanish-speaker, the fact that she prepared a letter in Spanish communicated caring to her students and their parents. Joan's letter also included specific suggestions for parents. Even if parents cannot read a homework assignment, for example, asking their children to show it to them and explain it is valuable.

Further, the letter was written in the form of a contract; the parents' signatures symbolize a commitment to working with the teacher. Also, because students had input into the content of the letter, they felt ownership of the process and encouraged their parents to work with them in completing their homework.

Regardless of the approach, early and positive communication is essential. Don't wait until management problems arise to establish communication links with parents. Their support in the home will mean a better learning environment in the classroom.

Maintaining Communication. Early and positive communication helps get the year off to a good start, and continuing communication can maintain the momentum. Melissa Bolden, a sixth-grade teacher, took the following step.

> At the beginning of each grading period, Melissa sends a letter home to parents or caregivers that describes the topics that will be covered, the tests and the approximate times they will be given, and any special projects that are required for the period. Because she speaks no language other than English, she asks students whose parents do not speak English to rewrite the letter in their native languages. She reports that the students take pride in writing the letters and even offer suggestions for changes that will better communicate with their parents or other caregivers. She asks students to read the letters to their parents; this forms a link between home and school and better ensures that the message was understood.

Although Melissa's communique required considerable effort the first year, she reported that it became much easier. She had the letters in a computer file, which she briefly edited in her second year. Now in her third year, she reports that the response of both her students and their parents makes the effort more than worthwhile.

11.54

How can teachers find out whether the letters and notes they are sending home make sense to parents? (Hint: Think back to Chapters 7 and 8 and the strategies teachers use to check comprehension.)

11.55

How does Joan Williams's approach, together with a letter like the one in Figure 11.6, demonstrate that the teacher is democratic?

Figure 11.6 Letter to parents

August 22, 1996

Dear Parents,

I am looking forward to a productive and exciting year, and I am writing this letter to encourage your involvement and support. You always have been and still are the most important people in your youngster's education. We cannot do the job without you.

For us to work together most effectively, some guidelines are necessary. With the students' help, we prepared the ones listed here. Please read this information carefully and sign where indicated. If you have any questions, please call me at Southside Junior High School (441-5935), or at home (221-8403) in the evenings.

Sincerely,

Joan Williams

AS A PARENT, I WILL TRY MY BEST TO DO THE FOLLOWING:
1. I will ask my youngsters about school every day. (Evening meal is a good time.) I will ask them about what they're studying and try to learn about it.
2. I will provide a quiet time and place each evening for homework. I will set an example by also working at that time or reading while my youngster is working.
3. Instead of asking if their homework is finished, I will ask to see it. I will have them explain some of the information to see if they understand it.

Parent's Signature_____

CLASSROOM GUIDELINES:

1. I will be in class and seated when the bell rings.
2. I will follow directions the first time they are given.
3. I will bring covered textbook, notebook, paper, and two sharpened pencils to class each day.
4. I will raise my hand for permission to speak or leave my seat.
5. I will keep my hands, feet, and objects to myself.

HOMEWORK GUIDELINES:

1. Our motto is I WILL ALWAYS TRY. I WILL NEVER GIVE UP.
2. I will complete all assignments. If an assignment is not finished or ready when called for, I understand that I get no credit for it.
3. If I am absent, it is my responsibility to come in before school in the morning (8:15–8:45) to make it up.
4. I know that I get one day to make up a test or turn in my work for each day I'm absent.
5. I understand that extra credit work is not given. If I do all the required work, extra credit isn't necessary.

Student's Signature_____

Many teachers also send packets of students' work home, requiring that parents sign and return them. This maintains the link between home and school and gives parents an ongoing record of their children's learning.

As it continues to expand, technology will provide another channel for improving communication. A voice mail system, for example, can result in improved quality and quantity of teacher–parent communication (Cameron & Lee, 1997).

11.56

In addition to initial classroom meetings, how might teachers communicate to parents that they care about their children?

Classroom Connections

Capitalizing on Diversity in Your Classroom

1. Maintain high but attainable expectations for all your students.
   - A second-grade teacher begins as many of her learning activities as possible with a concrete object, picture, written passage, or demonstration. To capitalize on equitable distribution and open-ended questions, she begins the activity by asking a number of the students to make observations of what they see.
   - A literature teacher begins her discussion of assigned readings by asking students to tell one fact about the story or one impression they had of it.
   - A sixth-grade teacher responds to incorrect answers or silence from her students by rephrasing her initial question; if they still don't answer, she asks them to describe what is displayed before them.

2. Establish communication links between school and home during the first few days of school.
   - A kindergarten teacher makes a personal telephone call to the parents of each of her students during the first week of school. She tells the parents how happy she is to have their children in her class, encourages them to contact her at any time, and gives them her home phone number.

3. Maintain communication links throughout the year.
   - A fourth-grade teacher sends home a "class communicator" each month. It briefly describes the topics the students will be studying and gives suggestions parents might follow in helping their children. The students are required to write personal notes to their parents on the communicator, describing their efforts and progress.
   - A teacher calls a parent during the first week of school to report that her daughter didn't turn in her first two homework papers. "I want to catch these things early," she says on the phone. "Monica is a capable student, and I want her to get off to a good start."

4. Communicate in straightforward language. Avoid technical terms and educational jargon.
   - A second-grade teacher goes over a letter to parents with her students. She has them explain to her what each part of the letter says, and she then asks the students to read and explain the letter to their parents.

Windows on Classrooms

At the beginning of the chapter, you saw the interdependence of instruction and classroom management in the way Shirley Barton conducted her lesson and dealt with classroom management.

Let's look now at a case study illustrating two ninth-grade teachers working with their students on the same topic. As you read, look for similarities and differences in the two teachers' approaches to instruction and classroom management.

Judy Harris is a ninth-grade geography teacher whose class is involved in a cultural unit on the Middle East. She has 32 students in a room designed for 24, so the students are sitting within arm's reach across the aisles.

As Ginger comes into the room, she sees a large map projected high on the screen at the front of the room. She quickly slides into her seat just as the bell stops ringing. Most students have already begun studying the map and the accompanying directions on the chalkboard: "Identify the longitude and latitude of Cairo and Damascus."

Judy takes roll and hands back a set of papers as students busy themselves with the task. As she hands Jack his paper, she touches him on the arm and points to the overhead, reminding him to return from his window-gazing.

She waits a moment for students to finish, then pulls down a large map in the front of the classroom and begins by saying, "We've been studying the Middle East, and you just identified Damascus here in Syria," she notes, pointing at the map. "Now, think for a moment and make a prediction about the climate in Damascus."

Judy pauses, surveys the class, and says, "Bernice?" as she walks down one of the rows.

". . . Damascus is about 34° North latitude, I think."

As soon as Judy walks past him, Darren reaches across the aisle, tapping Kendra on the shoulder with his pencil while he watches Judy's back from the corner of his eye. "Stop it, Darren," Kendra mutters, swiping at him with her hand.

Judy turns, comes back up the aisle, and continues, "Good, Bernice. It's very close to 34°." Standing next to Darren, she asks, "What would that indicate about its temperature at this time of the year? . . . Darren?" she asks, looking directly at him.

". . . I'm not sure."

"Warmer or colder than here?"

". . . Warmer, I think."

"Okay. Good prediction, Darren. And why might that be the case? . . . Jim?"

"Move up here," Judy says quietly to Rachel, who has been whispering and passing notes to Deborah across the aisle. Judy nods to a desk at the front of the room as she waits for Jim to answer.

"What did I do?" Rachel protests.

Judy leans over Rachel's desk and points to a rule displayed on a poster:

LISTEN WHEN SOME-
ONE ELSE IS TALKING.

"Quickly, now." She motions to the desk.

". . . Damascus is south of us and also in a desert," Jim responds.

"I wasn't doing anything," Rachel protests.

"I get frustrated when I'm watching people who aren't paying attention. I'm uncomfortable when I'm frustrated. Please move," Judy says evenly, looking Rachel in the eye.

"Good analysis, Jim. Now let's look at Cairo," she continues as she watches Rachel move to the new desk.

Now, let's turn to another teacher, Janelle Powers. Like Judy's classroom, Janelle's room is crowded; she has 29 students.

Shiana came through the classroom doorway just as the tardy bell rang.

"Take your seat quickly, Shiana," Janelle directed. "You're just about late. All right. Listen up, everyone," she continued. "Ali?"

"Here."

"Gaelen?"

"Here."

"Chu?"

"Here."

Janelle finished taking the roll, and she then walked around the room and handed back a set of papers as she went.

"You did quite well on the assignment," she commented. "Let's keep up the good work. . . . Howard and Manny, please stop talking while I'm returning the papers. Can't you just sit quietly for one minute?"

The boys, who were whispering, turned back to the front of the room.

"Now," Janelle continued, after handing back the last paper and returning to the front of the room, "we've been studying the Middle East, so let's review for a moment. . . . Look at the map and identify the longitude and latitude of Cairo. Take a minute and figure it out right now."

The students began as Janelle went to her file cabinet to get out some transparencies.

"Stop it, Damon," she heard Leila blurt out behind her.

"Leila," Janelle responded sternly, "we don't talk out like that in class."

"He's poking me, Mrs. Powers."

"Are you poking her, Damon?"

". . ."

"Well?"

". . . Not really."

"You did too," Leila complained.

"Both of you stop it," Janelle warned. "Another outburst like that, Leila, and your name goes on the chalkboard."

As the last students were finishing the problem, Janelle looked up from the materials on her desk to an example on the overhead and heard Howard and Manny talking and giggling at the back of the room.

"Are you boys finished?"

"Yes," Manny answered.

"Well, be quiet then until everyone is done," Janelle directed, and went back to rearranging her materials.

"Quiet, everyone," she again directed as she looked up once more in response to a hum of voices around the room. "Is everyone finished? . . . Good. Pass your papers forward. . . . Remember, put your paper on the top of the stack. . . . Roberto, wait until the papers come from behind you before you pass yours forward."

Janelle collected the papers, put them on her desk, and then began, "We've talked about the geography of the Middle East and now we want to look at the climate a bit more. It varies somewhat. For example, Syria is extremely hot in the summer but is actually quite cool in the winter. In fact, it will snow in some parts.

"Now, what did we find for the latitude of Cairo?"

". . . 30°," Miguel volunteered.

"North or south, Miguel? . . . Wait a minute. Howard? . . . Manny? . . . This is the third time this period that I've had to say something to you about your talking and the period isn't even 20 minutes old yet. Get out your rules and read me the rule about talking without permission. . . . Howard?"

". . ."

"It's supposed to be in the front of your notebook."

". . ."

"Manny?"

". . . 'No speaking without permission of the teacher,'" Manny read from the front page of his notebook.

"Howard, where are your rules?"

". . . I don't know."

"Move up here," Janelle directed, pointing to an empty desk at the front of the room. "You've been bothering me all week. If you can't learn to be quiet, you will be up here for the rest of the year."

Howard got up and slowly moved to the desk Janelle had pointed out. After Howard was seated, Janelle began again, "Where were we before we were rudely interrupted? . . . Oh yes. What did you get for the latitude of Cairo?"

"30° North," Miguel responded.

"Okay, good. . . . Now, Egypt also has a hot climate in the summer, in fact very hot. The summer temperatures will often go over 100° Fahrenheit. . . . Egypt is also mostly desert, so the people have trouble making a living. Their primary source of subsistence is the Nile River, which floods frequently. Most of the agriculture of the country is near the river."

Janelle continued presenting information to the students for the next several minutes.

"Andrew, are you listening to this?" Janelle interjected as she saw Andrew put his head down on his folded arms.

". . . Yes," he responded, lifting up his head.

"I hope so, because all this will be on the next test, which is only a week away."

Janelle then continued with her presentation.

Let's compare Janelle's classroom environment to Judy's. In analyzing the two classes, you may want to consider the following questions. In each case, be specific and take information directly from the case study in making your comparisons.

1. What would you infer about Janelle's planning for classroom management, compared with Judy's? What seemed to be different about the two?

2. Although you don't have a lot of specific evidence about either teacher's rules, how do they compare on the basis of the evidence you do have?

3. Compare the two teachers' application of essential teaching skills. Be sure to provide evidence when the presence or absence of the skill is inferred rather than observed.

4. Compare the way the teachers talked to their students when they intervened. Identify specific behaviors in the case study in making your comparison.

5. Using the information from this chapter as the basis for your assessment, assess Janelle Powers's overall management effectiveness. Consider your answers to Questions 1 through 4 as you make your analysis.

6. Like most classrooms, Janelle's class contains learners with diverse backgrounds. How effective would her management and instruction be for these students?

Summary

Productive Environments and Learning-Focused Classrooms

In productive learning environments, the classroom culture—which includes the language, values, learning experiences—is focused on learning. In productive learning environments, classroom order and effective instruction are interdependent. It is very difficult to maintain an orderly classroom in the absence of effective teaching, and it is also impossible to teach effectively in a classroom that lacks order.

Creating Productive Learning Environments: Effective Teaching

Essential teaching skills are teaching behaviors that promote student learning and contribute to productive learning environments. Effective teachers are high in efficacy; they believe they are responsible for student learning and can increase it. They are caring and enthusiastic, they are good role models, and they have high expectations for their students.

Effective teachers are well organized, know what's going on in their classrooms, use their time well, and communicate clearly. They represent content in attention-getting ways, provide clear and informative feedback to students, and review important ideas.

Effective teachers use effective questioning strategies. They ask many questions, prompt students who don't answer successfully, employ equitable distribution, and give students time to think about their answers.

Creating Productive Learning Environments: Classroom Management

Well-planned procedures and rules help establish and maintain orderly classrooms. An effective list of rules should be short, clear, and positive and include reasons for the rules' existence. Allowing student input into rules promotes understanding, gives the students a sense of control, and contributes to responsibility and self control.

Procedures organize daily classroom routines. Like any concept or skill, rules and procedures must be carefully taught, monitored, and reviewed.

Rules and procedures should be taught in the same way that any abstraction is taught: Learners construct understanding of them as they see and discuss examples.

The first few days of the school year are critical in establishing expectations. Communication with parents should begin as soon as school opens and continue throughout the year.

Effective managers keep their interventions brief, preserve student dignity, and follow through consistently on management decisions. Focusing on positive behavior, ignoring misbehavior, and employing simple desists can eliminate minor disruptions. Logical consequences help students see the connection between their behaviors and the effects of their behaviors on others.

More lengthy interventions are sometimes necessary when misbehavior persists or occurs frequently. In cases of chronic or serious misbehavior, it is necessary to intervene immediately and hold students accountable.

Important Concepts _____

active listening (p. 473)

assertive discipline (p. 479)

classroom management (p. 462)

closure (p. 459)

connected discourse (p. 455)

desist (p. 481)

discipline (p. 462)

emphasis (p. 455)

equitable distribution (p. 458)

essential teaching skills (p. 451)

feedback (p. 456)

I-message (p. 473)

introductory focus (p. 456)

logical consequences (p. 477)

nonverbal communication (p. 471)

organization (p. 454)

overlapping (p. 474)

personal teaching efficacy (p. 452)

precise terminology (p. 455)

procedures (p. 465)

productive learning environment (p. 451)

prompting (p. 458)

review (p. 459)

rules (p. 465)

sensory focus (p. 456)

transition signals (p. 455)

wait-time (p. 459)

withitness (p. 474)

12
Teacher-Centered Approaches to Instruction

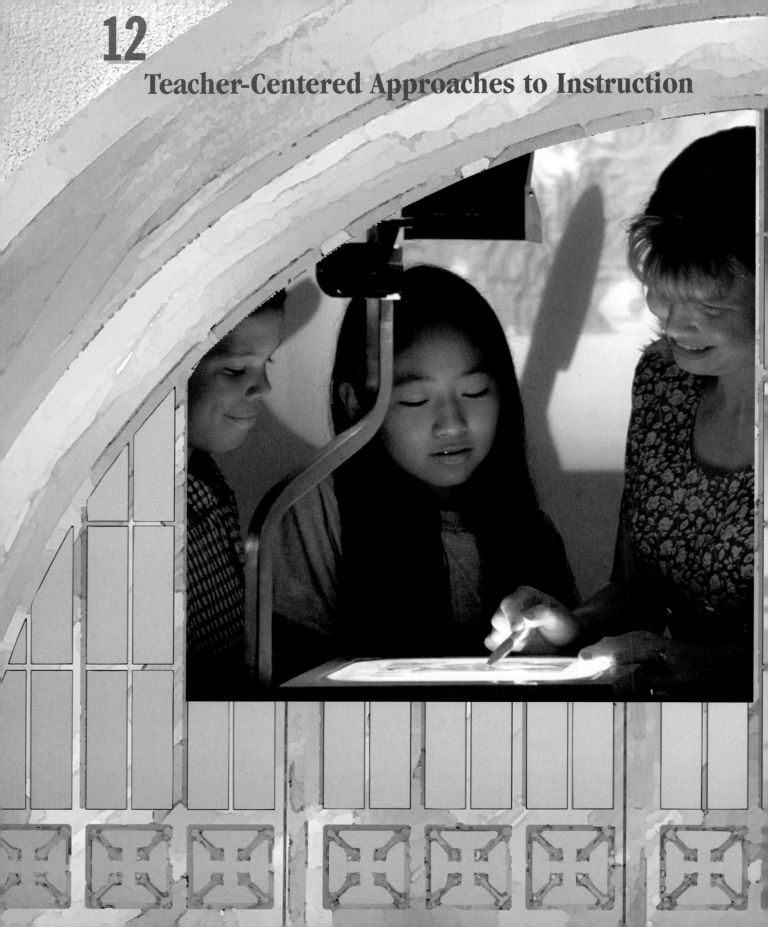

CHAPTER OUTLINE

Sam Barnett is a first-year second-grade teacher who is working with his students in a unit on addition. Because he is a beginning teacher and he is teaching a lesson on addition that he knows will be difficult for his second-graders, he plans in detail. His plan for the next set of lessons appears as shown in the figure on the next page.

With his plan on his desk, Sam began math by saying, "Okay, class, today we are going to go a step farther with our work in addition so that we'll be able to solve problems like this," displaying the following on the overhead.

Jana and Patti are friends. They
were saving special soda cans to
get a free compact disc. They can
get the disc if they save 35 cans.
Jana had 15 cans and Patti had 12.
How many did they have together?

After pausing briefly to give students a chance to read the problem, Sam continued. "Now, why do you think it's important to know how many Jana and Patti have together?"

". . . So, they . . . can know . . . how much they get, like . . . so they can get their CD," Devon answered haltingly.

"Sure," Sam smiled. "If they know how many they have, they'll know how close they're coming to getting their CD. . . . If they don't, they're stuck. That's why it's important."

"We'll come back to the problem in a minute," Sam continued, "but before we do, let's review. Everyone take out your counter sticks and beans and do this problem."

Sam then put the following on the chalkboard and watched as students used their sticks and beans to demonstrate their answer.

$$8$$
$$+7$$

"Very good," Sam smiled as most of the students laid a stick with 10 beans glued on it and 5 more beans on the centers of their desks. Others laid out 15 beans, and Sam showed them how they could exchange 10 of them for a stick with 10 glued on it.

Sam had the students do two more problems with their counters and then continued, "Let's begin by looking at our problem again."

Turning on the overhead again he said, "Everyone look up here. Good. Now what does the problem ask us? . . . Shalinda?"

". . . How many . . . they have together?" Shalinda responded hesitantly.

"And how many does Jana have? Abdul?"

Unit: Addition of two-digit numbers

Objectives:
To understand addition of two-digit numbers:

1. Recognize that word problems require addition.
2. Add two-digit numbers that don't require regrouping.
3. Add two-digit numbers that require regrouping.

To understand place value:

1. Add numbers so places values are accurate.
2. Explain the difference between a numeral in the ones place and a numeral in the tens place.

Rationale: Being able to add two-digit numbers is a basic skill all students must possess. Understanding place value is critical for understanding all number operations.

Procedure:

1. Present problem requiring addition of two-digit numbers.
2. Explain that these problems are important and that we must be able to solve them quickly and easily.
3. Distribute beans and bean sticks to the students.
4. Review single-digit addition. Have students represent solutions with their materials.
5. Demonstrate the solution to a two-digit problem.
6. Have the students represent the solution with their materials.
7. Have the students explain the difference between a numeral in the tens place and a numeral in the ones place (such as 27 compared to 12).
8. Give practice problems and discuss them.
9. Assign problems on worksheet.

Assessment:
Give the students a series of word problems, some of which require two-digit addition, and have them solve the problems.

Materials:
Text, problem worksheet.

"Ummh . . . fifteen?"

"Good, Abdul. And how many does Patti have? Celinda?"

"Twelve."

"Okay, so let's put the problem on the chalkboard like this," Sam continued, writing the following:

$$\begin{array}{r} 15 \\ +12 \\ \hline \end{array}$$

"Now, I'd like everyone to show me how to make a 15 at your desk by using your sticks and beans."

Sam paused as the class worked at their desks.

"Does everyone's look like this?" Sam asked as he demonstrated at the flannel board.

They did the same with the 12, and Sam continued, "Now, watch what I do here. . . . When I add 5 and 2, what do I get? Hmm, let me think about that . . . 5 and 2 are 7. Let's put a 7 up on the chalkboard," Sam said as he walked to the chalkboard and added a 7.

$$\begin{array}{r} 15 \\ +12 \\ \hline 7 \end{array}$$

"Now show me that with your beans," and he watched as the students combined seven beans on their desks.

"Now, we still have to add the 10s. What do we get when we add two 10s? Hmm, that should be easy. One 10 and one 10 is two 10s. Now, look where I have to put the 2 up here. It is under the 10s column because the 2 means two 10s." With that, he wrote the following on the chalkboard.

$$
\begin{array}{r}
15 \\
+12 \\
\hline
27
\end{array}
$$

"So, how many cans did Jana and Patti have together? . . . Alesha?"

". . . 27?"

"Good, Alesha. They had 27 altogether. Now, with your beans, what is this 7?" he asked, pointing to the 7 on the chalkboard. . . . Carol?"

". . . It's this," she said, motioning to the seven beans on her desk.

"Good, yes it is. It's the seven individual beans. . . . Now, . . . what is this 2? . . . Jeremy?" Sam went on, pointing to the numeral on the chalkboard.

". . . It's . . . these," Jeremy answered, holding up the two sticks with the beans glued on them.

"Now, we saw that I added the 5 and the 2 before I added the two 1s. Why do you suppose I did that? . . . Anyone?"

". . . Maybe . . . you have to find out how many . . . like ones . . . you have . . . to see if we can make . . . a 10 . . . or something," Callie offered.

"That's excellent thinking, Callie. That's exactly right. We'll see why again tomorrow when we have some problems in which we'll have to regroup, and that will be just a little tougher, but for now let's remember what Callie said.

"Now, who can describe in words for us one more time what the 2 means. . . . Leroy?"

"It's . . . two, . . . ah, two . . . bunches or something like that of 10 beans."

"Yes, that's correct, Leroy. It's two groups of 10 beans or, in the case of Jana and Patti, it's two groups of 10 soda cans."

"So let's look again. There is an important difference between this 2," pointing to the 10s column, "and this 2," pointing to the 2 in the 12. What is this difference? . . . Katrina?"

". . . That 2 . . . is . . . two . . . groups of 10, and that one is just 2 . . . by itself."

"Yes, that's good thinking, Katrina. Good work, everyone. . . . Show me this 2," pointing to the 10s column.

The students held up two sticks with the beans glued on them.

"Good, and show me this 2," pointing to the 2 in the 12, and the students held up two beans.

"Great," Sam nodded. "Now, let's try another one," he continued, displaying the following on the chalkboard.

$$
\begin{array}{r}
23 \\
+12 \\
\hline
\end{array}
$$

Sam watched as students used their beans and sticks to make 35, and again they discussed the problem. They did two more, and then Sam gave the students an assignment of 10 more problems to do for homework.

Conducting high-quality instruction is at the heart of what teachers do. As we have seen, it requires an understanding of learners, knowledge about the way learning occurs, and insight into what motivates students to learn. Using these elements as a framework, we now turn to two chapters examining instruction in depth. In this chapter we consider teacher-centered approaches and in Chapter 13 we turn to instruction from a learner-centered perspective.

When you've completed your study of this chapter you should be able to meet the following objectives:

- Describe the characteristics of teacher-centered instruction.
- Explain how teacher-centered planning occurs.

- Identify the elements of direct instruction
- Describe the elements of effective lectures and lecture–discussions.

Characteristics of Teacher-Centered Instruction

To begin this section, let's think about Sam Barnett's work with his second-graders. His planning and instruction illustrated four aspects of teacher-centered instruction:

- During his planning, Sam identified specific objectives for the lesson and designed learning activities to help students meet the objectives.
- The lesson remained focused on the objectives.
- His objectives were designed to have students learn a well-defined body of information (the skill of adding two-digit numbers).
- Sam took primary responsibility for guiding the learning (by modeling and explaining a specific procedure for the skill.)

When teachers are teaching well-defined content that all students are expected to master, teacher-centered instruction can be effective. Nevertheless, teacher-centered instruction is sometimes criticized; we examine some of these criticisms at the end of the chapter. When teacher-centered instruction *is* effective, expectations are clear, lessons are highly structured and predictable, and learners receive ample opportunities for practice and feedback.

Let's turn now to a detailed discussion of planning and conducting teacher-centered learning activities.

Planning for Teacher-Centered Instruction

On the surface, planning for teacher-centered instruction seems simple: specify objectives, design learning activities to help students reach the objectives, and assess the extent to which the objectives have been reached. It isn't as simple as it appears on the surface, however. Planning and conducting effective lessons require that teachers have at least three kinds of prerequisite knowledge.

Prerequisites to Effective Planning

The relationship between planning and instruction is complex and interconnected. As you have seen in other parts of this book, *knowledge* is important for most aspects of learning and teaching; the same is true for planning. Effective planning requires at least three kinds of teacher knowledge:

- Knowledge of content
- Pedagogical content knowledge
- Knowledge of learners and learning

Knowledge of Content

We can't teach what we don't understand ourselves. To be effective, teachers must thoroughly understand the content they're teaching (Jetton & Alexander, 1997).

Knowledge of content has important implications for planning because teachers can't be expert in every topic they teach and because they don't want to limit their instruction to only those topics they know well. When they're uncertain, they need to spend more time studying and planning.

Pedagogical Content Knowledge

Knowledge of content alone, however, is not enough. As you saw in Chapter 1, teachers must also have **pedagogical content knowledge** (Shulman, 1986), or *knowledge of ways to represent topics for learners, plus an understanding of what makes topics difficult or easy for them to learn.* Sam demonstrated pedagogical content knowledge by helping the students represent two-digit numbers with their beans and sticks. The beans and sticks were concrete representations of the numbers, and he understood that these representations would help make the numbers more meaningful for his second-graders.

Knowledge of Learners and Learning

Understanding learning and the factors that influence learning is an important goal for this book. We know, from our study of Piaget's and Vygotsky's work in Chapter 2 and cognitive views of learning in Chapters 7 and 8, that more learning occurs when learners are active than when they're passive. Sam understood this and attempted to put his students in an active role as they learned math. Sam also knew that second-graders' thinking tends to be concrete operational, so he prepared concrete ways to represent his content. And because he understood the role language plays in learning and development, he provided scaffolding, through interactive questioning for his students. Sam's knowledge of learners and learning guided his planning and the conduct of his lesson.

A Teacher-Centered Planning Model

The most common teacher-centered approach to planning is based on work done by Ralph Tyler and described in his book *Basic Principles of Curriculum and Instruction*, first published in 1950. This text is a classic; over the years, it has had more impact on the way teachers are taught to plan and organize instruction than any other work.

Tyler described the relationship between planning and instruction in four logical and sequential steps, outlined in Figure 12.1.

Sam Barnett used this model in his planning, and this likely reflects his recent teacher-education experience. Tyler's model was so influential that literally hundreds of thousands of teachers and educational leaders have been trained in its use. Let's look more closely at the components of the model.

12.1

Consider some of the other teachers you've studied throughout the book, such as Karen Johnson at the beginning of Chapter 2, and Shirley Barton in Chapter 11. Describe their pedagogical content knowledge in each case.

12.2

Could teachers have thorough knowledge of content and inadequate pedagogical content knowledge? How? Could teachers have pedagogical content knowledge without knowledge of content? Explain.

12.3

Tyler's model of planning has been called *linear rational*. Explain the terms *linear* and *rational* using Figure 12.1.

Figure 12.1 A teacher-centered planning model

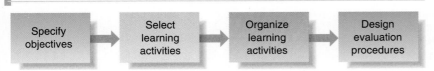

Specify objectives → Select learning activities → Organize learning activities → Design evaluation procedures

Specifying Objectives

The planning process begins with teachers specifying objectives. The most useful form for stating objectives is "to express them in terms which identify both the kind of behavior to be developed in the student and the content or area of life in which this behavior is to operate" (Tyler, 1950, p. 46). **Behavioral objectives**—*statements that specify learning outcomes in terms of observable student behaviors*—provide focus and direction for both teachers and learners.

Mager's Behavioral Objectives.   Another powerful teacher-training influence was the publication of Robert Mager's *Preparing Instructional Objectives* in 1962. In his short and highly readable book, Mager suggested that an objective ought to describe "what the student will be doing when demonstrating his achievement and how you will know he is doing it" (p. 53). **Mager's behavioral objectives** have three parts:

1. An observable behavior
2. The conditions under which the behavior will occur
3. Criteria for acceptable performance

Examples of objectives written according to Mager's format are listed in Table 12.1.

Gronlund's Instructional Objectives.   A popular alternative approach to preparing objectives is suggested by Norman Gronlund (1995). **Gronlund's instructional objectives** include *a general objective, such as* know, understand, *or* apply, *followed by specific learning outcomes that operationally define what is meant by* knows, understands *or* applies. Objectives written according to Gronlund's format are illustrated in Table 12.2.

Gronlund's objectives, in contrast with Mager's, don't include *conditions* and *criteria*. These ". . . are especially useful for programmed instruction and for mastery testing in simple training programs. When used for regular classroom instruction, however, they result in long cumbersome lists that restrict the freedom of the teacher" (Gronlund, 1995, p. 10). Experience supports Gronlund's position. Rarely do teachers specify conditions and criteria in their objectives, although thinking about them can help teachers

12.4

You want your students to understand the main ideas in a passage. Using Mager's format, write an objective that would reflect this goal.

12.5

Using Gronlund's format, rewrite the objective you formulated in Margin Note 12.4.

Table 12.1   Objectives using Mager's approach

Objective	Condition	Performance	Criteria
Given a list of sentences, the student will identify the adjective in each.	given a list of sentences	identify	each
Given 10 problems involving subtraction with regrouping, the student will correctly solve 7.	given 10 problems	solve	7 of 10
Given a ruler and compass, the student will construct the bisector of an angle to within 1°.	given a ruler and compass	construct	within 1°

Table 12.2 Objectives using Gronlund's format

General Objective	Specific Learning Outcome
Understands concepts	1. Writes definitions of concepts 2. Identifies examples of concepts 3. Generates examples of concepts 4. Identifies coordinate concepts
Solves problems	1. Identifies information relevant to the problem 2. Describes problem qualitatively 3. Translates qualitative description into numerical symbols 4. Estimates answer 5. Generates solution to problem

design effective assessments. Mager's work is significant because of its historical impact, but most curriculum materials use Gronlund's approach or a modification of it.

Objectives in the Cognitive Domain.   Let's look at three specific learning outcomes using Gronlund's format.

- Defines adjectives
- Identifies adjectives in sentences
- Makes writing attractive by creatively using adjectives

All these outcomes have "understands adjectives" as the general objective, so they fit in the **cognitive domain,** which *focuses on knowledge and understanding of facts,*

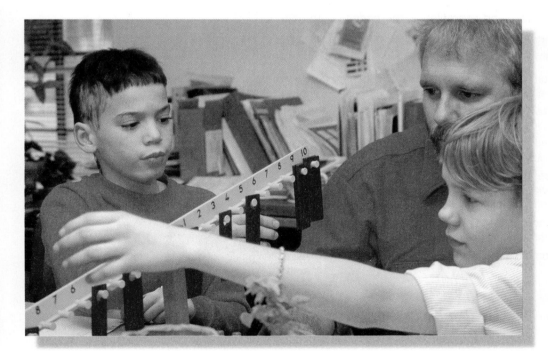

The different levels of the cognitive domain help teachers design learning activities that emphasize problem solving and critical thinking.

concepts, principles, rules, skills, and problem solving. The outcomes vary, however, in their demands on learners, how they should be taught, and how they would be assessed.

In response to these differences, researchers developed a system to classify different kinds of learning outcomes and assessments (Bloom, Englehart, Furst, Hill, & Krathwohl, 1956). The results of this effort are referred to as **Bloom's taxonomy,** *a classification system developed to help teachers think about the objectives they write, the learning activities they design, and the assessments they prepare*. It has six levels ranging from memory to higher-order operations, which are outlined in Table 12.3.

A primary value of the taxonomy is to remind us that we want our students to learn more than knowledge of the topics we teach, and that we must make conscious efforts to help students reach higher levels. This goal is even more important as we move into the twenty-first century, with increased emphasis on student thinking, decision making, and problem solving.

Objectives in the Affective Domain. In schools, most of the explicit focus is on objectives in the cognitive domain. Teachers often have many implicit objectives that don't fit there, however. For example, while they rarely write them as objectives, science and math teachers typically want students to like these subjects and appreciate their importance in today's world. In these cases, teachers have outcomes that fit into the **affective domain,** which *focuses on attitudes and values and the development of students' personal and emotional growth*.

Objectives in the affective domain can also be classified into levels, and a taxonomy similar in structure to the one in the cognitive domain has been developed (Krathwohl, Bloom, & Masia, 1964). The guiding principle behind the affective domain is *internalization*, or the extent to which an attitude or value has been incorporated into

12.6

Classify each of the three outcomes for the general objective "understands adjectives" into one of the levels of the taxonomy in Table 12.3.

12.7

A science teacher says, "One of the things I'm after is for them to get over their fear of science. Otherwise they'll take only what's required in high school." At what level in the affective taxonomy would you classify this goal?

Table 12.3   Levels, outcomes, and examples in the cognitive domain

Level	Outcome	Example
Knowledge	Knows terms, facts, rules, classifications, generalizations, principles, algorithms, and methods	States the definition of figurative language
Comprehension	Translates, interprets, predicts, generalizes, explains, identifies examples	Identifies statements that are similes and metaphors
Application	Applies rules, methods, and principles to unique situations	Rewrites a passage and increases expressiveness using figurative language
Analysis	Breaks communication into parts, determines point of view, recognizes bias, specifies implications, identifies theme	Identifies author intent in use of figurative language
Synthesis	Creates new products, methods, and patterns, from constituent elements	Creates an original work using figurative language
Evaluation	Judges on the basis of evidence and criteria	Assesses quality of a piece of writing in which the author has used figurative language

Source: Taxonomy of Educational Objectives: Book 1: Cognitive Domain edited by Benjamin S. Bloom. Copyright © 1956, 1984 by Longman Publishing Group.

Table 12.4 Levels, outcomes, and examples in the affective domain

Level	Outcome	Example
Receiving	Is willing to listen, open-minded	Pays attention in science class
Responding	Demonstrates new behavior, volunteers involvement	Volunteers answers, asks questions
Valuing	Shows commitment, maintains involvement	Reads ahead in text, watches science-oriented programs on television
Organizing	Integrates new value into personal structure	Chooses to take 4 years of science in high school because of interest in science
Characterizing by value	Gains open, firm, and long-range commitment to value	Chooses a branch of science as a career field

Source: Taxonomy of Educational Objectives: Handbook II: Affective Domain by D. Krathwohl, B. Bloom, and B. Masia, 1964, New York: David McKay. Copyright 1964 by David McKay. Adapted by permission.

a student's total value structure. The affective domain is outlined in Table 12.4 and illustrated with an example from science.

While much of teachers' focus in the affective domain is implicit, they sometimes focus on it explicitly. For example, many multicultural lessons have as their goal increased awareness of and appreciation for other cultures' values and customs. Likewise, learning about disabilities helps students develop more positive attitudes toward

Fostering growth in the affective domain promotes personal and emotional development that leads to student self-regulation.

Growth in the psychomotor domain contributes to healthy self-concepts and increases physical well-being in students.

people with exceptionalities (Hardman, Drew, & Egan, 1996). The taxonomy reminds us that affective dimensions of learning are important, and we should keep them in mind when we plan and teach.

Objectives in the Psychomotor Domain. A third type of learning, called the **psychomotor domain,** *focuses on the development of students' physical abilities and skills.* It has, historically, received less emphasis than the cognitive or effective domains, except in physical education. Taxonomies for the psychomotor domain weren't even developed until the 1970s (Harrow, 1972; Simpson, 1972). However, schools are increasing their emphasis on physical development as its role in overall development becomes better understood. For instance, kindergarten children practice tying their shoes, and classrooms often have a puppet whose coat they button and unbutton. In the early school years, the ability to physically manipulate a pencil is considered in assessing a child's readiness for writing. In addition, science requires using equipment such as microscopes and balances, geometry courses require constructions with compasses and rulers, word processing and driver's training require physical skills, and fine motor movements are critical in art and music. These are all goals in the psychomotor domain.

Table 12.5 presents a description and illustration of the psychomotor taxonomy using Harrow's (1972) conception as a framework.

Considering the psychomotor domain provides us with a more complete picture of our students as developing human beings. In addition to helping them grow cognitively and affectively, we want them to develop healthy bodies that they can use throughout their lives. In areas where physical skills are necessary and potentially underdeveloped, an understanding of the psychomotor taxonomy can help teachers as they make planning decisions.

12.8

How does emphasis on the psychomotor domain change over the span of the K–12 curriculum?

Table 12.5   Levels, outcomes, and examples in the psychomotor domain

Level	Outcome	Examples
Reflex movements	Involuntary responses	Blinking, knee jerks
Basic fundamental movements	Innate movements, combinations of reflexes	Eating, running, physically tracking an object
Perceptual abilities	Movement following interpretation of stimuli	Walking a balance beam, skipping rope, writing *p* and *q*
Physical abilities	Endurance, strength, flexibility, agility	Pull-ups, toe touching, distance bicycling
Skilled movements	Efficiency in complex movement tasks	Hitting a tennis ball, jazz dancing
Nondiscursive communication	Communication with physical movement, body language	Pleasure, authority, warmth, and other emotions demonstrated with body language

Source: A Taxonomy of the Psychomotor Domain: A Guide for Developing Behavioral Objectives by A. Harrow, 1972. New York: David McKay. Copyright 1972 by David McKay. Adapted by permission.

Preparing Learning Activities

Once objectives have been specified, teachers next prepare learning activities designed to help learners reach them. For instance, Sam wanted his students to understand the addition of two-digit numbers with and without grouping. He planned to help students reach his goal by demonstrating how to solve problems and having students practice both with their beans and sticks and with paper and pencil. These were his learning activities.

Organizing Learning Activities

Merely selecting learning activities isn't enough. The activities must be organized and sequenced to be most effective. For instance, Sam began by reviewing single-digit addition. He then moved to the addition of two-digit numbers and, finally, took up a discussion of place value. This progression from simple to complex was intended to accommodate the developmental characteristics of his students. Teachers consciously sequence and organize learning activities to help students reach specific objectives.

12.9

You want your first-graders to improve their awareness of whether or not they're paying attention in lessons. Describe how you would prepare and organize learning activities to reach this objective.

Task Analysis: A Behavioral Planning Tool

Kelly Ryan stared at the second-grade math book and didn't know where to start. Her assignment in her methods class was to identify a topic in the area of math, plan a lesson, and teach it to a small group of second-graders. She had met with Mrs. Ramirez, her cooperating teacher, and they had identified two-digit subtraction with regrouping as a topic that needed more work. Mrs. Ramirez had even given her some worksheets with subtraction problems:

$$
\begin{array}{ccccc}
98 & 27 & 25 & 72 & 45 \\
-19 & -18 & -16 & -13 & -36 \\
\hline
\end{array}
$$

Kelly sat, a bit bewildered, not knowing where to begin.

Task analysis, which is *the process of breaking content down into its component parts* (Gardner, 1985; Merrill, 1983), can be a helpful planning tool when teachers are uncertain about how to sequence and organize elements involved in understanding a topic. Breaking a complex skill into subskills helps teachers think in terms of prerequisites, and helps learners by allowing them to practice simpler skills before moving to more complex ones. Basic steps in doing a task analysis are outlined in Figure 12.2.

Teachers begin a task analysis by specifying the *terminal behavior*—what students will be able to demonstrate when the lesson is finished. This is stated in the form of an objective, such as "converting fractions to decimals" or "solving two-digit subtraction problems that require regrouping."

Teachers then *identify the prerequisite skills* needed to reach the objective. Some prerequisite skills for performing two-digit subtraction with borrowing include:

- Knowing basic subtraction facts (e.g., $7 - 5$)
- Understanding place value (e.g., 15 is really 1 ten plus 5 ones)
- Being able to do two-column subtraction with no regrouping when the bottom number is a single digit (e.g., $15 - 4$)

We see the influence of behaviorism in this process: the emphasis is on discrete, observable behaviors that are to be mastered before complex behaviors are tackled.

Once identified, subskills must be sequenced from simple to complex. Gagne (1985) describes this process as a learning hierarchy, and presents evidence that learning prerequisite skills facilitates learning target skills (Gagne & Dick, 1983). The sequence in Kelly Ryan's case is straightforward: students must first know basic facts and place value, then one-digit from two-digit subtraction, and two-digit from two-digit subtraction without regrouping before they can master subtraction with regrouping.

Having sequenced skills, teachers determine which ones students lack, usually through a pretest at the beginning of a unit. Kelly's instruction will depend, for example, on whether or not her students understand subtraction without regrouping. If they don't, the topic will need to be reviewed or even formally retaught before she moves to regrouping (Rosenshine & Stevens, 1986).

Whether teachers adhere to a behavioral view of learning or not, task analysis has value in the planning process. By forcing teachers to think about goals and specific outcomes in concrete terms, task analysis helps shift teachers' attention away from content to students: what they already know and what kinds of learning activities can be designed to build on this knowledge.

Assessing Learner Understanding

The final phase of the Tyler model calls for specifying assessment procedures. Sam followed the model by stating in his lesson plan how his students would be assessed. Specifying objectives during the planning process provides both a blueprint for learning

12.10

Suppose you want your students to be able to write sentences using adverbs properly. Design a brief task analysis for this skill.

Figure 12.2   Performing a task analysis

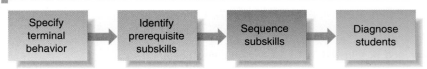

activities and a focus for assessing learning. We discuss this idea further in Chapter 14 when we describe assessment procedures in detail.

The Tyler model is a logical, sequential framework for planning instruction. It makes sense to first consider what you want students to learn, then to select ways of helping them learn it, and finally to determine whether or not the learning has taken place.

Instructional Alignment: A Key to Learning

One outcome of careful planning is **instructional alignment,** which is *the match between goals, learning activities, and assessment.* You saw alignment in Sam Barnett's planning. His objective was for his second-graders to be able to add two-digit numbers, his learning activities focused on this skill, and his assessment was designed to determine the extent to which they could perform the skill.

Alignment is critical if teaching is to be effective and learning is to be maximized. However, it is surprisingly easy for instruction to be out of alignment. For instance, if a teacher's goal is for students to be able to write effectively, yet instruction focuses on isolated grammar skills, the instruction is out of alignment. Similarly, a teacher who wants her students to be able to apply math concepts and attempts to teach it by having students practice computation problems is also having problems with alignment. The

Instructional alignment ensures a match between goals, learning activities, and assessment.

question instructional alignment encourages us to ask is, "What does my goal (such as "apply math concepts") actually mean, and do my learning activities actually point to the goal?"

This completes our discussion of planning for teacher-centered instruction. Next, we turn to an examination of three teacher-centered approaches: direct instruction, lectures, and lecture–discussions.

Classroom Connections _____

Using Taxonomies to Select Objectives

1. Consciously plan for goals in the affective domain and, where appropriate, in the psychomotor domain.

   - A physics teacher plans her initial presentation of vector problems around soccer players kicking the ball and moving to it. "I want them to appreciate science and see that vectors apply to 'where they live,'" she says.

   - A music teacher dislikes rock music but plans to begin her unit on different musical forms with songs by prominent rock stars. "Students appreciate the classics once they find out that a lot of rock stars first got their ideas from them," she notes.

2. In the cognitive domain, carefully consider the level of your instruction. Make an effort to focus your goals on meaningful activities that encourage student thinking.

   - A fourth-grade teacher comments after giving a quiz on body parts, "I give them a drawing and have them identify the parts in the drawing. It's much better than having them just memorize the definitions."

   - In a geography lesson, the teacher wants her students to understand how climate is influenced by the interaction of a number of variables. She does this by giving students a map of a fictitious island, together with longitude, latitude, topography, and wind direction. She then gears her instruction around the conclusions they can make about the climate of the island.

Using Instructional Alignment to Make Your Teaching Effective

3. Be sure that your goals, learning activities, and assessments are consistent. Keep the need for alignment in mind as you plan.

   - A geometry teacher wants her students to experience the intellectual rigor involved in geometric proofs. She then spends much of her planning time creating problems and examples to help the students practice doing proofs and seeing the logic involved in them.

   - A middle-school teacher wants her students to become persuasive writers. With this goal in mind, she has them write letters to local politicians and school board members taking positions on issues they feel strongly about, such as the building of a new park or a proposed student dress code. They discuss and analyze the letters before mailing them.

Direct Instruction

Earlier we said that teacher-centered instruction involves objectives and learning activities specified by the teacher, lessons that remain focused on the objectives, well-defined content, and teachers taking primary responsibility for guiding the learning. **Direct**

instruction (Rosenshine, 1979) is *a teacher-centered strategy designed to help students learn procedural skills.*

Procedural Skills

Procedural skills *have three essential characteristics:*

- *They have a specific set of identifiable operations or procedures* (which is why they're called procedural skills).
- *They can be illustrated with a large and varied number of examples.*
- *They are developed through practice* (Doyle, 1983).

Adding two-digit numbers, as we saw in Sam Barnett's lesson, is a procedural skill. Others include adding fractions with unlike denominators, punctuating sentences, finding the longitude and latitude of cities, balancing chemical equations, and solving percent mixture problems. Each has an unlimited number of examples, each follows specific procedures, and each enables students to develop facility through practice.

12.11

What similarities and differences are there between procedural skills and concepts, discussed in Chapter 8?

Models of Direct Instruction

A great deal of research was conducted in the 1970s and 1980s to identify essential steps in effective direct instruction lessons (Good, Grouws, & Ebmeier, 1983; Hunter, 1982; Rosenshine & Stevens, 1986). Different authors describe the steps differently, but the steps themselves are similar in all models. Table 12.6 illustrates the essential elements of three of these models.

Table 12.6   Models of direct instruction

Teaching functions (Rosenshine & Stevens, 1986)	Missouri Mathematics Program (Good, et al., 1983)	Hunter Mastery Teaching (Hunter, 1982)
Review Review homework, prior learning, prerequisite skills	**Opening** Review skills, collect homework	**Anticipatory set** Present problem or question to attract learners' attention; explain purpose of lesson
Presentation Specify goal; teach in small steps; use examples	**Development** Provide examples; model processes; rapid pace; high learner involvement	**Input and Modeling** Present information; provide examples; model processes
Guided Practice Practice problems; teacher questioning; high success; feedback; reteach if needed	**Seatwork** Successful practice; student accountability	**Structured practice** Practice examples; check for learner understanding; provide feedback
Independent Practice Learners practice; teacher monitors work	**Homework** Homework every day but Friday; review problems each day	**Independent Practice** Learners practice; teacher monitors; provide feedback

Figure 12.3 Steps in direct instruction

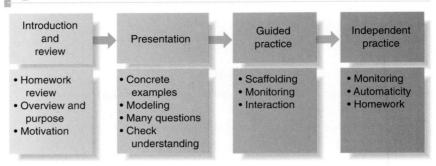

Introduction and review	Presentation	Guided practice	Independent practice
• Homework review • Overview and purpose • Motivation	• Concrete examples • Modeling • Many questions • Check understanding	• Scaffolding • Monitoring • Interaction	• Monitoring • Automaticity • Homework

Steps in Direct Instruction

In analyzing the different models, we see that direct instruction can be described in four essential steps, illustrated in Figure 12.3 and discussed in the sections that follow.

Though originally developed by observing the actions of effective teachers, direct instruction can be analyzed using the information-processing model discussed in Chapter 7. Table 12.7 identifies the steps in direct instruction and the corresponding element from information-processing theory.

Introduction and Review

12.12

Explain why review is important using information-processing theory as a basis for your explanation. Also explain why introduction and review are important using motivation theory as a basis.

Direct instruction begins with a review of the previous day's work, including a discussion of students' homework. The teacher then attempts to capture students' attention and motivate them to learn by describing the objective and explaining why studying the topic is important. Although this procedure may seem obvious, 21% of all skills lessons begin with little or no introduction (Brophy, 1982). Sam expanded this phase by asking students why *they* thought it was important, placing learners in a more active role and allowing him to check their understanding of the problem.

Presentation

The second step in direct instruction involves presenting information so that it can be processed into learners' working memories and helping learners connect it with infor-

Table 12.7 Direct instruction and information processing

Direct Instruction Step	Information-Processing Element
Introduction and review	Attract and focus learner attention. Activate background knowledge.
Presentation	Input information into working memory.
Guided practice	Check perception. Begin encoding into long-term memory.
Independent practice	Complete encoding. Develop automaticity.

mation already in long-term memory. Sam's presentation used both modeling and hands-on experiences to help students understand the procedure for adding two-digit numbers. Modeling provided a specific set of actions students could follow, examples provided concrete experiences, and Sam proceeded in short steps to avoid overloading students' working memories.

Knowing that putting learners in active roles increases learning, Sam also encouraged interaction in his lesson. He asked students to verbally explain what the 7 and 2 meant, he had them demonstrate each with their sticks and beans, and he also asked them to explain the difference between the 2 in 27 and the 2 in 12. Discussing and explaining procedures is a very important part of learning activities, and one that teachers sometimes miss. They often involve learners in a hands-on activity but then fail to make the connection between it and the abstractions represented (Ball, 1992).

12.13

Explain the role of discussion and interaction from a constructivist perspective.

Guided Practice

Guided practice applies the concept of *scaffolding,* discussed in Chapters 2, 8, and 9, and helps learners encode information into long-term memory. After the initial presentation, students practice under the watchful eye of the teacher, who applies enough scaffolding to ensure success, but not so much that students' sense of challenge and accomplishment is reduced (Rosenshine & Meister, 1992). Sam had his students work a problem, and they discussed it carefully while Sam monitored their progress. He had them work on their own only after he was sure they were ready.

Independent Practice

In the independent practice phase, teacher support (scaffolding) is gradually reduced and responsibility is shifted to the students. At this point, students are expected to perform the skill on their own—perhaps with some initial hesitancy, but later with ease and fluency. The goal is automaticity, intended to free working memory to focus on application, such as solving complex word problems.

Teacher monitoring is still important during independent practice. Effective teachers carefully monitor the students to be certain that they understand what they're doing. Less effective teachers are more likely to merely check to see that students are on task (e.g., on the right page, following directions).

12.14

Which phase of direct instruction is most important in ensuring successful independent practice? Why?

Effective direction instruction provides opportunities for students to actively encode information during guided and independent practice.

Table 12.8 Characteristics of effective homework

Characteristic	Rationale
Extension of classwork	The teacher teaches; homework reinforces.
High success rates	Success is motivating. Success leads to automaticity. No one is available to provide help if students encounter problems.
Part of class routines; assignments written on chalkboard	Becomes a part of student expectations, increases likelihood of students completing assignments.
Graded	Increases accountability and provides feedback.

Source: Based on work by Cooper (1989), Berliner (1984), and Walberg, Paschal, & Weinstein, (1985).

Homework

Homework is a common form of independent practice, and its effect on learning is positive, especially when it is aligned with classroom work and when teachers grade and comment on it. The effects of homework are especially strong at the high-school and junior-high level. Research also indicates that frequency is important. For example, 5 problems every night are more effective than 25 once a week (Cooper, 1989; Dempster, 1991).

Effective homework has four essential characteristics, which are outlined in Table 12.8.

Instructional alignment—important in planning and teaching—is essential to homework. Homework should be an extension of instruction and, although grading homework can be time-consuming, some mechanism for providing feedback on it is critical if students are to take it seriously and use it as a learning tool.

12.15

Using social cognitive theory as a basis, explain why assigning but not collecting homework is ineffective practice.

Lectures and Lecture–Discussion

Organized Bodies of Knowledge

In the last section, we examined direct instruction and emphasized its use in teaching procedural skills—content, such as adding two-digit numbers, that can be illustrated with a variety of examples and developed by practicing a specified set of operations.

But the goals for an English teacher involved in a unit on twentieth-century American literature, for example, are different. A specific relationship, set of characteristics, or procedures doesn't exist. The topic can't be illustrated with precise examples. Instead, the teacher's goal might be for students to understand how concepts (such as *plot, setting,* and *character development*) interact in a work, or for students to be able to generalize that "Authors' works are influenced by their personal experiences." The term *organized bodies of knowledge* is often used to describe this type of content (Calfee, 1986; Rosenshine, 1986). **Organized bodies of knowledge** are *topics that examine facts, concepts, generalizations, and principles, and the relationships among them.*

12.16

Think about some of the case studies in other chapters in this text. Identify two of these in which an organized body of knowledge was being taught.

Because organized bodies of knowledge can't be illustrated with precise examples, practice and feedback—effective in skills instruction—can't be used to help learners encode information and develop automaticity. As a result, different approaches to instruction are required. Most common among them are lectures and lecture–discussions.

Lectures

The prevalence of the lecture as a teaching method is paradoxical. Although it is, and historically has been, the most widely criticized of all teaching methods, it continues to be one of the most commonly used (Cuban, 1984). Three reasons are given for its durability:

- Lectures are efficient for the teacher; planning time is limited to organizing content.
- Lectures are flexible; they can be applied to virtually any content area.
- Lectures are seemingly simple; all of teachers' working memory space can be devoted to organizing and presenting content.

Despite their widespread use, lectures have a major disadvantage. Lecturing puts students in a passive mode, which is inconsistent with cognitive theories of learning, such as information processing and constructivism. Constructing understanding and encoding information into long-term memory require active learners. Lectures are especially problematic for young learners because of their short attention spans and limited vocabularies.

The ineffectiveness of lecture as a teaching method is well documented. In seven comparisons of lecture to discussion, discussion was superior in all seven on measures of retention and higher-order thinking. In addition, discussion was superior in seven of nine studies on measures of student attitude and motivation (McKeachie & Kulik, 1975).

It isn't that lectures, in themselves, are always inappropriate; it is that they are often ineffectively or inappropriately used. As with all aspects of instruction, the key is clear goals. Ausubel (1963) argued that effective lectures provide students with information that would take them hours to find on their own. Lectures are appropriate if the teacher's goals include:

- To acquire information not readily accessible in other ways
- To integrate information from a variety of sources
- To understand different points of view (Henson, 1988; McMann, 1979)

If teachers are clear about their goals and if their goals can be met with lectures, their occasional use may be appropriate.

Lecture–Discussions

One of the most effective ways to overcome the weaknesses of lectures is to use **lecture–discussions,** *a combination of short lectures supplemented with teacher questioning* (Kauchak & Eggen, 1998).

Lecture–discussions include three essential elements that occur in repeated cycles:

- Presenting information—the teacher begins by providing the students with some information about the topic.
- Comprehension monitoring—after a brief presentation, the teacher asks a series of questions designed to assess the students' understanding of the information.

During lecture–recitations, teachers monitor student comprehension through frequent questions.

• Integration—the teacher asks additional questions designed to help students identify conceptual links in the content.

Let's look in on an American History class in which lecture–discussion is being used. Darren Anderson is discussing the events leading up to the American Revolutionary War. We join her as she introduces the topic.

12.17

Which of the essential teaching skills that were discussed in Chapter 11 is best illustrated by Darren's description, "When we're finished today, we'll see . . . and even all the way to today?" Explain.

Pointing to a timeline above the chalkboard, she began, "About where are we now in our progress? . . . Anyone?"

". . . About . . . there," Adam responded uncertainly, pointing to about the middle of the 1700s on the timeline.

"Yes, good," Darren smiled. "That's about where we are. However, I would like for us to understand what happened before that time, so we're going to back up a ways. . . . Actually, all the way to the early 1600s. When we're finished today, we'll see that the Revolutionary War didn't just happen; there were events that led up to it that made it almost inevitable. . . . That's the most fun part of history. To see how something that happened at one time affected events at another time, . . . and even all the way to today . . . Okay, let's go.

"We know that the Jamestown Colony was established in 1607," she continued, "and it was founded by the British, but we haven't really looked that carefully at French expansion into the New World. Let's look again at the map," she went on, pulling a map down in the front of the room.

"Here we see Jamestown, . . . but at nearly the same time, a French explorer named Champlain came down the St. Lawrence River and formed Quebec City here," again pointing to the map. "And, . . . over the years, at least 35 of the 50 states were discovered or mapped by the French, and several of our big cities, such as Detroit, St. Louis, New Orleans, and Des Moines were founded by the French. It began with French fur traders and continued from there. A string of French forts were built along the Ohio and Mississippi Valleys," she continued pointing to a series of locations she had marked on the map.

"Now, what do you notice about the location of the two groups . . . or what does it suggest to us?"

After thinking a few seconds, Alfredo offered, "The French had a . . . lot of Canada, and . . . it looks like this country too . . . sort of all that," waving to the north and west on the map.

"It looks like the east was, . . . like British, and the west was like French," Troy added.

"Yes, and remember, this was all happening at about the same time," Darren continued. "Also, the French were more friendly with the Native Americans than the British, and the Iroquois nation, the biggest Native American group, was actually more powerful than either the French or the British at that time.

"Also, the French had what they called a seigniorial system, where the settlers were given land if they would serve in the military. . . . So, . . . what does this suggest about the military power of the French?"

". . . Prob'ly . . . good," Josh suggested. "The people got land if they did it, . . . I mean, . . . went in the army."

"And the Native Americans probably helped, . . . 'cuz the French, . . . they were friendly with the French," Tenisha added.

"Now, what else do you notice here?" Darren asked moving her hand up and down the width of the map.

". . . Mountains?" Danielle answered uncertainly.

"Yes, exactly," Darren smiled. "Why are they important? What do mountains do? . . . Anyone?"

"Ummh . . . The British were sort of fenced in, maybe. . . . and the French were home free, . . . I mean, . . . they could expand and do as they pleased."

"Good. And now the plot thickens. The British needed land and wanted to expand. So they headed west over the mountains and guess who they ran into? Sarah?"

"Uhh, the French?" Sarah offered haltingly.

"And conflict broke out. Now, when the French and British were fighting, why do you suppose the French were initially more successful than the British? . . . What do you think? . . . Dan?"

". . . Well, . . . they had that signor . . . you know . . . system, so they were more motivated to fight, 'cuz of the land and stuff."

"Other thoughts? . . . Bette?"

". . . I think that the Native Americans were part of it. The French got along better with them, so they helped the French."

"Okay, good thinking everyone, . . . now let's think about the British. . . . Let's look at some of their advantages."

Let's stop now and take a look at Darren's work with her students. She began by trying to capture learners' attention and increase their interest in the lesson by saying that events in the past influence the way we live today. She then presented information about Jamestown, Quebec, and French settlements in the present-day United States and, after a brief presentation, involved students in the lesson. Let's look back at some of the dialogue.

Darren:	Now, what do you notice about the location of the two groups . . . or what does it suggest to us?
Alfredo:	The French had a . . . lot of Canada, and . . . it looks like this country too . . . sort of all that (pointing to the north and west on the map).
Troy:	It looks like the east was, . . . like British, and the west was like French.

Darren's question was intended to check student understanding of the presentation to that point and actively involve them in the lesson. After hearing their responses, she went back to presenting information when she said, "Yes, and remember, this was all happening at about the same time," and she continued by briefly describing the French seigniorial system and pointing out that the French and Native Americans were friendly.

She then turned the lesson back to students a second time.

> *Darren:* So, . . . what does this suggest about the military power of the French?
> *Josh:* . . . Prob'ly . . . good. The people got land if they did it, . . . I mean, . . . went in the army.
> *Tenisha:* And the Native Americans probably helped, . . . 'cuz the French, . . . they were friendly with the French," Tenisha added.

While the segments appear to be similar, there is an important distinction between the two. In the first, by asking, "Now, what do you notice about the location of the two groups . . . or what does it suggest to us?" Darren asked students to paraphrase or summarize what she presented. As we saw in Chapters 8 and 9, summarizing is a powerful form of comprehension monitoring.

In the second, she was attempting to promote deeper understanding of the topic by encouraging students to find links—integration—between the seigniorial system, the relationship between the French and the Native Americans, and the French military power. Darren's goal for the entire lesson was broad integration—an understanding of the cause and effect relationships between the French and Indian Wars and the American Revolutionary War.

12.18

Describe specifically how Darren, in later lessons, might broaden the integration even further. To what might the French and Indian Wars and the American Revolutionary War be linked?

Lecture–Discussion: A Theoretical Analysis

Earlier in the chapter we saw that the effectiveness of direct instruction can be explained by information-processing theory. The same is true for lecture–discussion, and there are strong parallels between the two. For example, Darren began her lesson by trying to attract learners' attention and increase their interest in the topic. When she *presented information,* information was made available for input into learners' working memories. When she *monitored comprehension,* she put the students in active roles, allowing her to check their perceptions and encourage the process of encoding information into long-term memory. Her attention to *integration* extended the process of encoding and increased the meaningfulness of the content.

Teacher questioning is integral to the effectiveness of lecture–discussions and consistent with four aspects of cognitive theories of learning:

- It allows teachers to assess student background knowledge.
- It encourages students to become active and involved in lessons.
- It promotes integration and meaningfulness, which encourage elaboration and encoding.
- It allows teachers to monitor learning progress and adapt accordingly.

Teacher-centered lectures provide none of these opportunities.

12.19

At least five of the essential teaching skills discussed in Chapter 11 were illustrated in Darren's lesson. Identify those skills and explain how they were used.

Classroom Connections

Using Direct Instruction Effectively in Your Classroom

1. Introduce lessons with a demonstration, question, or problem to promote student interest.

   - A sixth-grade teacher comes into class and writes on the chalkboard, "The animal most likely to survive on Earth is the INSECT!" He then says, "Let's keep this statement in mind as we begin our study of insects today."
   - A math teacher beginning a unit on percentages and decimals comments that the star quarterback for the state university has a completion rate of 58%. "What does that mean?" she asks. "How can we figure it out?"

2. Maintain high levels of student involvement during the presentation phase of direct instruction lessons.

   - A seventh-grade geography teacher helps his students locate the longitude and latitude of a series of locations by "walking them through" the process, using a map and a series of specific questions.
   - A third-grade teacher helps her students understand the concept *adjective* by showing a paragraph with several italicized adjectives in it, explaining what adjectives do, and asking questions to help the students see how adjectives are used in sentences.

3. Provide as much guided practice as necessary to ensure students' successful transition from your presentation to independent practice.

   - A fifth-grade teacher, wanting students to understand similes and metaphors, makes the transition from teacher presentation to guided practice by saying, "All right. Everyone write a sentence with at least one simile or metaphor in it." She then circulates around the class, examining students' sentences. She has several students share their sentences by writing them on the chalkboard. The class discusses whether these are similes or metaphors and then continues writing and sharing others until the teacher is sure the students can proceed on their own.

4. Monitor students during independent practice.

   - A first-grade teacher has assigned a series of problems involving addition and subtraction for homework. As students begin to work on the problems, he walks up and down the rows to check each student's progress. He periodically stops and offers suggestions as he checks their work.

Using Lecture–Discussions Effectively in Your Classroom

5. Incorporate as many examples as possible in the lesson and relate these to students' experiences.

   - An American-history teacher discussing immigration in the nineteenth and early twentieth centuries compares these immigrant groups with the Cuban population in Miami, Florida, and Mexican immigrants in San Antonio, Texas. He examines the difficulties immigrants encounter when they first come to the United States.

6. Keep the presentation of information short, review frequently, and examine relationships among items of information.

   - A biology teacher is presenting information related to transport of liquids in and out of cells, identifying and illustrating several of the concepts in the process. About five minutes into the presentation, she stops and asks, "Suppose a cell is in a hypotonic solution in one case and a hypertonic solution in another. What's the difference between the two? What would happen to the cell in each case?"

Accommodating Learner Diversity: Classroom Interaction

As we've seen throughout this chapter, cognitive learning theory views learners as active processors or constructors of knowledge: if teacher-centered instruction is to be successful, learners must be put in active roles. Direct instruction attempts to capitalize on active learner involvement during teacher presentation, as well as in guided practice and independent practice. Lecture–discussion does the same in the comprehension monitoring and integration phases.

Students interacting with the teacher and with each other are the most common and effective forms of activity, so understanding the interaction patterns of different learners is critical if interactive teacher-centered lessons are to be effective.

Classroom Interaction: Research Findings

Classroom interaction patterns are amazingly homogeneous across the United States, both over time and across grade levels (Cazden, 1986; Cuban, 1984):

12.20

What theory of learning is implied in this quote? Explain and document your explanation with information taken from the quote.

> [T]he dominant form of interaction is the teacher-directed lesson in which the instructor is in control, determining the topics of discussion, allocating turns at speaking, and deciding what qualifies as a correct response. Verbal participation is required of students. Implicitly, teaching and learning are equated with talking, and silence is interpreted as the absence of knowledge. Students are questioned in public and bid for the floor by raising their hands. They are expected to wait until the teacher awards the floor to one of them before answering. Speaking in turn is the rule, unless the teacher specifically asks for choral responses. Display questions prevail. Individual competition is preferred to group cooperation. Topics are normally introduced in small and carefully sequenced steps, with the overall picture emerging only at the end of the teaching sequence. (Villegas, 1991, p. 20)

Although this form of interaction may work for some students, it is inappropriate for others. Many students come from cultures in which adults and children interact in ways that differ from the patterns found in most American classrooms. Let's look at these differences and see how teachers might accommodate them in the classroom.

Accommodating Diversity: Experimental Programs

KEEP: The Kamehameha Early Education Program

Teachers working with Native Hawaiian students have found that these learners don't interact effectively in environments like those described in the quote above. Often they don't participate at all, or they participate in disruptive ways, breaking in and interrupting other students (Au, 1992; Tharp, 1989). These patterns are associated with lowered achievement and lowered self-esteem.

Researchers, attempting to understand this problem, went into Hawaiian homes and observed the children interacting with adults, siblings, and peers. They discovered a conversational style incompatible with traditional instruction. Typically, Hawaiian children jumped into conversations in their homes, contributing freely as an adult or other child spoke. There were no clear turns marked by pauses; instead, several people talked at once, and overlapping speech was common. School felt strange to the children because teachers didn't allow them to join in whenever they wanted.

Working with these differences, researchers helped teachers adjust their questioning strategies to the Hawaiian students. Here's how one group reading lesson sounded. (The brackets indicate people speaking at the same time.)

Teacher: Why do you think the author wrote this story? What did he want—what did he want you to learn from it?

Chad: About moths

Teacher: About moths. What—what else?

Natasha: ⎡Caterpillars

Kamalu: ⎣You can't keep things in⎦

you can't keep things ⎡forever

Chad: ⎣in jars⎦

Kamalu: They have to come ⎡like moths

Darralyn: ⎣how to take care of it⎦

Kamalu: ⎡You can't keep them in a glass jar forever⎤

Natasha: ⎣You can keep a dog or cat forever⎦

but like insects you cannot keep 'em ⎡forever⎤

Teacher: ⎣Okay⎦

Natasha: they have to be ⎡free⎤

Chad: ⎣Hey, once⎦

I kept one lizard forever

Keala: ⎡Born to be free⎤

Teacher: ⎣Excuse me⎦

Is there anything else that they were telling us?

⎡she was trying to tell us⎤

Keala: ⎣Yeah⎦

Teacher: about? (Au, 1992, pp. 10–11)

Notice how the interaction patterns overlapped, with students joining in to contribute to each other's thoughts. Also, many interchanges were student to student. The teacher intervened only when necessary to clarify a point. These adjustments made the classroom interaction more like the conversation patterns in learners' homes, and resulted in increased student achievement. "Hawaiian children in regular classrooms are among the lower achieving minorities in the United States; in Kamehameha School's KEEP classrooms, they approach national norms on standard achievement tests" (Tharp, 1989, p. 350).

Wait-Time: Working with Native American Students

Similar efforts to make questioning strategies compatible with Native American interaction patterns have also been successful (Tharp, 1989). Researchers noticed differences between the wait-times of Anglo and Navajo teachers. Anglo teachers would interpret pauses in a Navajo student's response as a sign of a completed answer, not realizing that long pauses (by Anglo standards) and silences were a regular part of Navajo conversation. Interrupted in this way, Navajo students felt unappreciated and uncomfortable and became less willing to participate. Adjusting wait-times produced expected results; in one study of Pueblo Indian children, students in longer wait-time classes participated twice as frequently as those in shorter wait-time classes (Winterton, 1977).

12.21

Research with low-achieving students in small reading groups found a positive correlation between call-outs and achievement. How might you explain this finding and the one from the KEEP project?

12.22

What was described as a desirable amount of wait-time in Chapter 11? How long might desirable wait-times be in the situations described in this section?

Research with Hawaiian and Native American students is valuable because it reminds us that students come to our classes with very different patterns of interaction. It's impossible to understand all these patterns in advance, which means we must try to learn as much about our students as we can when we begin to work with them. We can gather information about our students' interaction patterns in at least three different ways:

- Listen to the way they interact when they're unlikely to be influenced by academic expectations: in extracurricular activities, nonacademic discussions outside of class, or during lunch.

- Listen to the way they talk as they participate in lessons and in small groups.

- See if any patterns exist in their reluctance to respond or in the way they behave when they're unable to answer questions.

Opening lines of communication with parents and talking with colleagues from other cultures can also provide insights into ways to make our classroom interactions more culturally compatible. This insight is important; research indicates that teachers who understand their students' speech patterns accept and use student responses more frequently than those who lack this understanding (Washington & Miller-Jones, 1989). Both direct instruction and lecture–discussion are heavily dependent on student interaction for their success. Understanding different patterns of interaction can increase teacher effectiveness.

Understanding patterns of interaction has an additional benefit. The better teachers understand their students' typical patterns, the more capable they are of helping students gradually acquire interaction patterns that can increase their school success.

> All of us, regardless of class or cultural background, have to acquire literacies that go beyond our home-based ways of making sense and using language. . . . The key challenge for schools is to introduce and enculturate students into these school-based discourses without denigrating their culturally specific values and ways of using language. (Michaels & O'Connor, 1990, p. 18)

This should be our ultimate goal, one that is consistent with Ogbu's (1987) concept of *accommodation without assimilation*.

Classroom Connections _____

Capitalizing on Diversity in Your Classroom

1. Be sensitive to different interaction patterns during instruction.
   - A fourth-grade teacher waits several seconds as a Native American student haltingly responds to a question. He admonishes other students who jump in and answer questions when the response is slow in coming.

- A middle-school teacher doesn't correct the language of his students, instead offering substitute descriptions that build upon students' responses.

2. Learn about the interaction patterns of your students.
   - A fourth-grade teacher invites the parents, guardians, or caregivers of her students to a

special evening session of her class. She asks the students to introduce the adult with them and to tell something about each. In turn, she asks each adult to say something about the child in his or her care.

- A junior-high teacher volunteers to cosponsor a school club. He uses the club meetings to observe the way different students interact with each other.

3. Help learners develop school-based interaction patterns.

- In learning activities, a first-grade teacher liberally praises students who listen to each other and wait their turn to speak. She reminds them that the way we talk and listen in class doesn't have to be the same as the way we talk and listen at home or on the playground.

- A middle-school teacher establishes the following rule at the beginning of the school year, "Listen respectfully while others have the floor." He discusses why the rule is important both from an interpersonal and learning perspective. He explains that he understands that everyone talks differently at lunch, in the halls and at home, but that his classroom is a place where everyone gets an opportunity to express themselves.

Putting Teacher-Centered Instruction into Perspective

The increasing interest in constructivist views of learning and the increasing emphasis on learner-centered education has led to considerable criticism of teacher-centered instruction in general and direct instruction in particular (Marshall, 1992; Stoddart, Connell, Stofflett, & Peck, 1993). Critics argue that direct instruction, for example, focuses on lower-level objectives and breaks content into small pieces. They charge that the process is based on behaviorism and emphasizes *performance* instead of *understanding*.

The following classroom example illustrates these criticisms. A teacher is attempting to teach place value to her third-graders. On the basis of directions given in the teacher's manual, she begins by putting 45 tally marks on the chalkboard and circling four groups of 10, and asks,

Teacher:	How many groups of 10 do we have there, boys and girls?
Children:	4.
Teacher:	We have 4 groups of 10, and how many left over?
Children:	5.
Teacher:	We had 4 tens and how many left over?
Beth:	4 tens.
Sarah:	5.
Teacher:	5. Now, can anybody tell me what number that could be? We have 4 tens and 5 ones. What is that number? Ann?
Ann:	(Remains silent)
Teacher:	If we have 4 tens and 5 ones, what is that number?
Ann:	9.
Teacher:	Look at how many we have there (points to the 4 groups of ten) and 5 ones. If we have 4 tens and 5 ones we have? (slight pause) 45.
Children:	45.
Teacher:	Very good. (Wood, Cobb, & Yackel, 1992, p. 180)

Effective teachers adapt their questioning strategies to the interaction styles of their students.

Unquestionably, Ann, and probably many others, didn't understand place value, and the teacher did little to increase their understanding. Once they gave the desired response, the teacher reinforced them with "Very good" and moved on.

This pattern of focusing on student verbalization or overt performance at the expense of understanding is typical in many classrooms (Goodlad, 1984; Stodolsky, 1988), and critics charge that direct instruction is inherently to blame.

Those who defend teacher-centered instruction argue that this doesn't have to be the case, however, and further argue that some present criticisms of direct instruction are made on political grounds, direct instruction not being "politically correct or romantically correct" (Rosenshine, 1997, p. 2). As we saw earlier, both Sam Barnett and Darren Anderson were conducting teacher-centered lessons, yet were successful in involving students in their lessons and emphasizing understanding over performance.

As with much of instruction, it isn't the strategy, per se, that's to blame; it's that the strategy isn't being effectively implemented. No strategy, curriculum, program, or process is any better or worse than the quality of the person implementing it. This is why we believe educational psychology is so important. As your knowledge of learning and learners increases, your ability to implement and adapt teaching strategies that result in the most learning possible for all your students will improve, and your teaching effectiveness will grow.

12.23

Describe specifically what the teacher might have done to increase students' understanding of place value in this lesson.

Windows on Classrooms

Like Shirley Barton, in Chapter 11, Robin Voss is a fourth-grade teacher preparing for her next day's math lesson.

"What's up?" Darcie Towers, her colleague from the next room, asked as she entered Robin's room.

"Just getting ready for tomorrow," Robin replied, looking up from her work.

"This class is so slow," she continued with a wry smile. "I love them to death, but it takes them forever to get anything. My kids last year were so sharp. What a pleasure they were."

"I know what you mean," Darcie smiled back. "When I take them for science we struggle with some of the concepts. They eventually get the ideas, but it takes time."

"Yeah, if we only had more time . . .," Robin nodded. "My class is too big, and they aren't as well behaved as last year, besides not being as sharp. . . . Oh well. We do our best."

Robin has 29 students in her class. She usually schedules her day as follows:

8:30–10:00	Language Arts (Spelling, writing, grammar)
10:00–11:00	Math
11:00–11:10	Break
11:10–11:45	Science
11:45–12:10	Lunch
12:10–1:40	Reading
1:40–1:50	Break
1:50–2:15	Social Studies
2:15–3:00	Resource (Art, music, P.E., computer)

At 10 A.M. Robin looked up from her desk, where she had been grading some papers while the students were working on their language arts homework assignment. "Time to put your language arts materials away," she announced. "Have your paper ready to turn in first thing tomorrow. Now you need to get out your math books and your assignment for today. Hurry now."

Since she had only two more papers to score, she finished them while her students put their language arts materials away and got out their math books and papers.

When they finished, she stood up and moved to the front of the room. "Ready to go?" she smiled at the class. "Tim? . . . Faye? You should have your math books on your desks by now."

At 10:09 she began, "Everyone ready? . . . Good. Now look. I'm going to put some problems on the board, and I want you to solve them."

"Do you want our math papers for today?" Brett asked from the back of the room.

"Oh, yes. Thank you, Brett, for reminding me. . . . Everyone, pass in your math assignment for today."

The students then began passing their papers forward.

"Be sure to put yours on top of the stack," Robin reminded them as she watched.

She then collected the papers from the first person in each row,

bound them with a rubber band, and began.

At 10:12 she moved to the board and wrote the following:

$$3/9 + 4/9 = ?$$
$$2/5 + 1/5 = ?$$
$$5/12 + 4/12 = ?$$

"We've been adding fractions, so let's review for a moment," she continued. "Joyce, what's the answer to the first problem?"

". . . Seven ninths."

"Okay. Very good. And the second one. . . . John?"

"Three fifths."

"Excellent Kay, the third?"

". . . Nine . . . twenty . . . fours?" Kay responded hesitantly.

"No, no, sweetheart. What do we do when we add fractions?"

". . ."

"What's our rule?"

". . ."

"Gloria?"

"We add the numerators, . . . but the denominators stay the same."

"Very good, Gloria. Please repeat that, Kay."

". . . Add the numerators, but the denominators stay the same."

"Good, Kay, now remember that. . . . Remember that, everyone.

"Now, today we're going to look at some different kinds of problems. We're going to learn to add fractions when the denominators are not the same. Look back up here again," she said pointing at

Teacher-Centered Approaches to Instruction **525**

the review problems on the chalk-board. "See, these problems all have the same denominators, so that's why our rule of adding the numerators but leaving the denominators alone works. But when the denominators are not the same we can't do that. That's what we're going to discuss today.

"Let me show you some examples," she continued, writing the following on the board:

$$1/3 + 1/6 = ? \qquad 2/3 + 1/4 = ?$$
$$1/3 + 1/2 = ? \qquad 1/6 + 4/9 = ?$$

"Here we see that the denominators in each problem are different. The 3 and 6 are different, the 3 and 4, the 3 and 2, and the 6 and 9," she noted, pointing to the respective problems. "So, what do you suppose we have to do with the problems? . . . What do you think? . . . Anyone?"

". . ."

"I know this is tough, and you might not see it right off. We have to get the denominators to be the same. Then once they're the same we can do what? . . . Kathy?"

". . ."

"What did we do in those problems?" she asked pointing to the review problems.

". . . Added."

"Added what?"

"Added . . . the top numbers," Kathy said quickly after remembering the rule.

"Good, Kathy. So, what can we do once we get the denominators to be the same?

"Add the top numbers."

"Yes! Super, Kathy. That's very good."

"And what is the top number in a fraction called?"

"Numerator," the class responded in unison. "And the bottom number?"

"DENOMINATOR!" they answered, anticipating the question.

"Good," Robin smiled. "So, let's review for a second. What are we going to do? . . . Quentin?"

". . ."

"What did I just say a few minutes ago? . . . about the denominators . . . being . . . the same?"

"They're the same," Quentin nodded.

"Good. So, I'm going to show you how to get the denominators to be the same. Then, all we have to do is add the numerators the way we did before. Seems easy enough. What do you think . . .?"

The students nodded, and Robin then wrote the following on the board:

1. *See if one denominator will divide into the other. If it will, divide it and multiply the result by the numerator.*
2. *If one denominator won't divide into the other, find a number that both will go into. Then follow Step 1 for each number.*

"Read Step 1 for us, . . . Neva," she directed after she finished writing.

Neva read the first step, and Robin then had Janelle read the second step.

"Now, let me show you how to follow the steps," she continued.

"Let's look at the first problem," she said pointing at the board. "I'm looking at the denominators and seeing that the 3 will divide into the 6. . . . So, I will do that. Three into 6 is 2, and 2 times 1 is 2, so 1/3 equals 2/6," and

she then wrote the 2/6 on the board, so it appeared as follows:

$$(2/6) \; 1/3 + 1/6 = ?$$

"The 1/3 and the 2/6 are equal, so we call them equivalent fractions," she continued and she then wrote "equivalent fractions" on the board in large letters.

"Now, since they're equivalent, we can use the 2/6 in place of the 1/3 and ta da, we have fractions where the denominators are the same. . . . That's what we wanted," she finished with a wave of her hand.

She then erased the parentheses and the 1/3, so the problem appeared as follows:

$$2/6 + 1/6 = ?$$

"So, what is our answer now? . . . Horace?

". . ."

"What do we do when we add fractions when the denominators are the same?"

"Add."

"Good. So, what's the answer?"

"Three . . . Tw . . . Sixths," Horace responded, changing when he saw Robin shaking her head as he started to say "twelfths."

"Excellent, Horace," Robin smiled, pleased that Horace gave the correct response.

"That's good, everyone," Robin added. "Now, let's look at the next one. What's a little funny about this one? . . . Anyone?"

". . ."

"Look at the denominators."

". . ."

"They're different," Alex volunteered.

"Well, yes, but what's more important than that?"

"We can't just add the numerators," Erin added.

"Yes, but we already know that, too. Come on, everybody, think. . . . Look at the steps on the board."

The students all looked at the board and read the two steps again.

"Okay," Robin said after giving the students a chance to finish. "We know that the 3 and 4 are different, *and* . . ." she paused emphasizing the *and,* "the 3 will not go into the 4. . . . That's what I wanted you to realize. . . . So, . . . we need a number that both will go into. . . . Give me a number that both 3 and 4 will go into, . . . someone."

". . . Eight," Robbie offered.

"No, no. Will 3 go into 8? Think about it for a second."

"Twelve," Monica offered.

"Excellent, Monica. Yes, both 3 and 4 will go into 12. So, . . . now we do what we did with the first problem. Watch carefully . . ."

She then continued, "Three into 12 is 4, . . . times 2 is 8, . . . so, 2/3 is the same as 8/12. . . . What do we call 2/3 and 8/12?"

". . ."

"What kind of fractions?"

". . ."

"Look up here."

"EQUIVALENT FRACTIONS!" the class said in unison.

"Very good. . . . And, we do the same thing with the 1/4."

Robin then illustrated and described the process for finding the equivalent fraction for 1/4, writing on the board:

$$(8)/(12)\ 2/3 + 1/4\ (3)/(12) = ?$$

"So, again we erase the 2/3 and the 1/4 . . ."

"Why did we do that, Mrs. Voss?" David asked from the middle of the room.

"Because they're equivalent fractions," Robin answered. "Eight twelfths and 2/3 are equivalent, and 1/4 and 3/12 are equivalent. . . .

"So, what's the answer to the problem? . . . David?"

". . . Eleven . . . Tw . . . Twelves," David answered seeing Robin nodding as he began to say "Twelves."

"Excellent, David. Good thinking," Robin smiled. "Yes, our answer is 11/12.

"Now, let's try the next one," Robin continued after hesitating for a few seconds. "Look again at the steps on the board for a second and think about what you should do."

Robin went through the next two problems as she had done with the others, then gave students two additional problems, discussed them with her students, and assigned ten problems for homework.

"Are there any questions?" she asked. "Okay, good. Get started, and I'll be around to check on you after I've looked at your assignment for today."

Robin then began looking through the previous night's homework papers while students began their new homework.

"Good," she thought to herself as she scored them. "Most of them did okay. A few added both the numerators and the denominators, but they're the slowest ones in the class."

"Just a second," she smiled at Elliot, who had his hand raised as she glanced up from her desk. "Be patient for a moment, and I'll be right there."

She got out her grade book, opened it in preparation for recording the grades, and then went back to Elliot.

She continued this process—responding to students' questions and recording scores—until math time was over.

Questions for Discussion and Analysis

Let's analyze Robin's planning and conduct of her lesson. In doing your analysis you may want to consider the following questions. In each case, be specific and use information taken directly from the case study as evidence in responding to each question.

1. Robin's lesson was an application of direct instruction. How effectively did she implement the direct instruction model in her teaching?

2. As conducted, was Robin's application of direct instruction based more on an information processing view of learning or more on a behaviorist view of learning?

3. Consider the essential teaching skills that were discussed in Chapter 11. How effectively did Robin apply these skills in her teaching?

4. Shirley Barton at the beginning of Chapter 11, Sam Barnett at the beginning of this chapter, and Robin were all teaching procedural skills. Which of the three did the best job of helping the students apply their understanding in the real world? Which did the poorest job?

5. As in most classrooms, Robin's class comprises learners with diverse backgrounds. How effective would the lesson be for these students?

6. What suggestions do you have for improving Robin's lesson based on the information in Chapter 12? Again, be specific.

Summary

Characteristics of Teacher-Centered Instruction

Teacher-centered instruction is characterized by clearly specified objectives, lessons that remain focused on those objectives, well-defined content, and teachers taking primary responsibility for teaching the content.

Teacher-centered approaches to planning involve identifying objectives, preparing and organizing learning activities consistent with the objectives, and designing assessments that match both the objectives and learning activities.

Direct Instruction

Direct instruction is a teacher-centered strategy effective for teaching procedural skills, which are developed through practicing a set of identifiable operations or procedures on many and varied examples. It involves an introduction and review, teacher presentation, guided practice and independent practice. In each phase, attempts are made to put learners in active roles.

Lectures and Lecture–Discussions

Because of their simplicity, lectures are widely used, in spite of evidence suggesting they are less than effective because they place students in passive learning roles.

Lecture–discussions consist of teachers making short presentations followed by questions designed to monitor learners' comprehension and help learners' integrate new with existing understanding. Lecture–discussions are designed to overcome some of the weaknesses in lectures by putting learners in active roles through interactive questioning.

Accommodating Learner Diversity: Classroom Interaction

Teacher–student and student–student interaction are the most common ways that learners are put in active roles. To capitalize on classroom interaction, teachers need to understand learners' interaction patterns, which can both help them accommodate learner diversity in classroom activities and help learners develop effective classroom interaction capabilities.

Putting Teacher-Centered Instruction into Perspective

Critics of teacher-centered instruction argue that it is based on a behavioral view of learning, focuses on low-level objectives and emphasizes performance instead of understanding. Proponents argue that teacher-centered instruction often isn't effectively implemented, arguing that the effectiveness of any approach depends on the ability of the teacher to adapt it to the learning needs of students.

Important Concepts

affective domain (p. 504)

behavioral objectives (p. 502)

Bloom's taxonomy (p. 504)

cognitive domain (p. 503)

direct instruction (p. 510)

Gronlund's instructional objectives (p. 502)

instructional alignment (p. 509)

lecture–discussions (p. 515)

Mager's behavioral objectives (p. 502)

organized bodies of knowledge (p. 514)

pedagogical content knowledge (p. 501)

procedural skills (p. 511)

psychomotor domain (p. 506)

task analysis (p. 508)

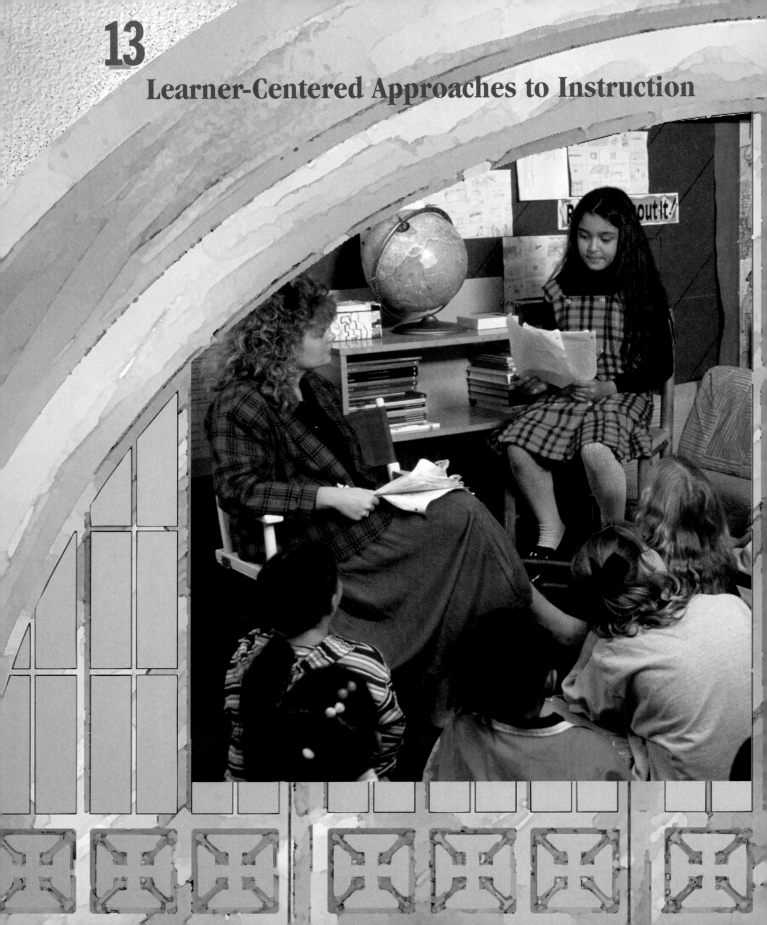

CHAPTER OUTLINE

Scott Sowell, a seventh-grade science teacher, sits at his desk planning for next week's classes. Looking at his notes he thinks to himself, "Scientific method, experimenting, controlling variables. . . . They're still having problems with this stuff. . . . Funny, we did the plant experiment as a whole class, and they seemed to get it. I explained it so carefully. . . . Why are they still having trouble? . . . Maybe they just need some more practice. . . . Actually, I'm sure they need more practice. I think I'll have them do the pendulum problem."

The next Monday Scott begins by demonstrating a simple pendulum, explaining frequency as the number of swings in a certain time period, and asking for some common examples. The students identify a metronome and a pendulum clock, and Scott then asks them what might affect the frequency of the pendulum. They offer length, weight, and angle of release as possibilities.

Scott continues, "Okay, here's your job. . . . Your job as a group is to design your own experiment. Think of a way . . . to test how each one of these affects the frequency of swing. Your job is to use the equipment you have at your desk to design and carry out the experiment. That's your job. Go to it."

We look in now on one group of four—Marina, Paige, Wensley, and Jonathan. They tie a string to a ring stand and measure its length, as shown in the following sketch.

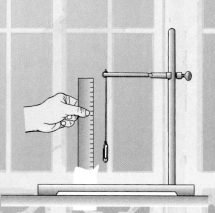

"49, 49 centimeters," Wensley notes, measuring the string.

Video Case

"And what we can do, and the frequency is the . . . the frequency is the number, . . . the frequency is the seconds and the . . . the frequency is the seconds and the what?" Marina turns to Scott as he comes by the group.

"The frequency is the number of swings in some time period. What time period are you using?" Scott responds.

The group agrees to use 15 seconds and then prepares to do their first test.

"Go," Jonathan says, as he begins timing.

Wensley releases the pendulum, and Marina counts for 15 seconds.

"Stop," Jonathan directs.

"21," Marina notes.

Scott again walks by the group,

looks at Jonathan's results, and says, "Tell me exactly what you're doing right now. Explain to me what you're doing."

"We measured the length as 49. . . . The height was 25," Wensley explains.

"So you've done one test so far. . . . What are you going to do for your next test?"

"Make it heavier," "We could make it shorter," Wensley and Marina suggest almost simultaneously amid comments from Paige and Jonathan.

"I'm going to come back after your next test and look at it," Scott comments, moving on to another group.

"You want to make it shorter and add more weight?" Wensley wonders.

They briefly discuss whether the angle will be accurate, since they're determining what the angle will be by measuring the distance from the top of the table to the end of the pendulum, as shown in the following sketch.

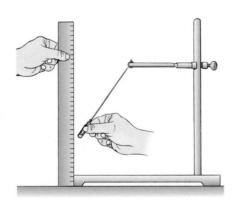

They then prepare to conduct their second test by shortening the string and adding a second paper clip to the end of the first one.

They again release the pendulum and count the number of swings, this time getting 25 in 15 seconds.

Simultaneously, the students blurt out:

Marina:	The shorter it is the longer it lasts.
Paige:	The faster.
Wensley:	The shorter, the shorter, the weight makes it go this way, it makes it go faster.
Jonathan:	Yeah, it makes it go faster.

"Mr. Sowell, we found out that the shorter it is and the heavier it is the faster it goes," Marina says to Scott as he returns to the group.

"So tell me how you found out that the length affected it," Scott queries as he kneels down in front of the group.

"We made it long, and then we shortened it a little more, and then we made it heavier, and that showed . . .," Marina explains.

"So in Test 1, the length was 49, and the frequency was 21, and on the same test the weight was one paper clip?" Scott queries.

"And the height . . . ," Wensley begins.

"The height was . . . ?" Scott repeats.

"The, the, the angle," Wensley breaks in.

"Ohh, okay, the angle was 25, the weight was 1, your length was 49. . . . What did you change dif-ferent between Test 1 and Test 2?" Scott continues.

"The amount of paper clips," Marina explains.

"So you changed the weight? What else did you change?"

"The length," Wensley notes.

"The length, so you changed the weight and the length."

"And the angle," Marina adds.

"So, you changed all three between the two tests. . . . Which caused that higher frequency?"

"The length," Paige responds.

"I think weight, the weight," Marina counters.

"What do you think?" Scott goes on, looking at Wensley. "Marina thinks weight."

"Weight," Wensley answers.

"What do you think?" he asks turning to Jonathan.

"The weight."

"What do you think, Paige?" Scott asks.

"The length."

"So, you think weight," pointing at Marina, "you think weight," turning to Jonathan, "you think weight," looking at Wensley, "and you think length," pointing at Paige. "Why can't you look at these two sets of data and decide? . . . Take a look at your two tests. I want you to take a look at your two tests. This had one paper clip; this had two paper clips; this had 49 length; this had 27 length. . . . You should be able to look at these two and tell something. . . . But why can't you all come to a conclusion by looking at the numbers? . . . Think about that. Why can't you look at these numbers and come to a conclusion?"

"Well, like the length, and the height, and the weight was always changed. None of them ever stayed the same in any of them, so it has to be different," Marina offers.

"What was the first thing you said?"

"Everything changed," Wensley and Jonathan offer simultaneously.

"Think about that," Scott directs as he gets up and moves to another group.

"Everything needs to stay the same except for one thing," Jonathan offers as the group starts back to work.

"Okay, I know," Paige suggests. "Add one more, like this one except keep the length 49 and . . ."

"Is that what the first one was, length was 49?" Wensley asks as he begins measuring the string.

"So what are we going to keep the same and what are we going to change?" Jonathan asks.

"We're going to change the paper clip weight," Wensley answers.

"Back to one or back to two?" Marina asks.

"Back to two."

"Okay do the same length," Paige directs.

"I know, I'm trying to get it right there," Wensley returns.

"Make it 49," Paige continues.

Measuring the string at 49, the group prepares to do their next test.

"Make it be 56 centimeters, the height," Paige goes on.

Wensley then attaches a second paper clip to the end of the first one as shown in the following sketch, pulls the paper clip to the side, and counts the swings.

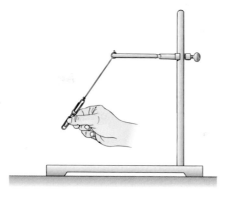

"21," Marina notes.

"One paper clip?" Jonathan asks.

"Two," Marina and Wensley return simultaneously.

"Okay and compare it to the second test now," Paige proposes.

"Okay, the same height, the same paper clips, except the length is different," Paige observes.

"Let's try it one more time to see what we get," Wensley suggests.

"We compare this test to that test," Paige notes.

"Mr. Sowell?" Marina asks as Scott walks over to the group. "Okay, we did this test and we compared it to that test. . . . Everything was the same except for the length, and the shorter it is the faster it goes. Do we need to test it again?"

"Yeah, you need to come up with a conclusion about length, you need to come up with a conclusion about weight, and a conclusion about angle," and he moves over to another group.

"Now we know that the shorter it is, the faster it goes," Marina

concludes again.

The students discuss their results to this point and then decide to test the weight.

"We're going to keep the same height," Marina suggests.

"56," Paige adds.

"And the same length, 49," Wensley puts in.

"The weight will be . . . two?" Paige wonders.

"No, three," Marina responds.

"So we're testing weight here," Wensley comments.

"We're doing that now," Marina adds.

Measuring the height to be 56, and adding three paper clips, they then conduct the next test.

"20," Marina counts after Jonathan says, "Stop."

"Have you done two tests on the weight?" Scott asks as he returns to the group.

"Okay, let's look at weight," he adds.

"For both of them it's 20, but this is three and this is two," Paige notes.

"So what does that tell you about weight?" Scott asks and then turns to another group.

As the group continues working on their experiment, Scott circulates around the room, finally announcing, "Let's take three or four more minutes, do one or two more tests, conclude the things you want to conclude, and then we're going to stop and talk."

The students briefly discuss their results, and then Marina says, "So now let's look at angle, I mean height . . . Make the height . . ."

"Taller or shorter?" Paige asks.

"How about . . . taller," Marina suggests.

"So the height is 62, no 63," Wensley says, measuring it with his meter stick.

"Go," Jonathan says, and they again count the number of swings.

"21," Marina counts as Jonathan says, "Stop."

"It's the same as that one," Paige notes observing that the frequencies were the same when the angles were different.

"It's the same because, remember, the weight changed," Marina responds, concluding that the difference in weight accounts for the frequency being the same when the angles were different. "The weight changed."

"What did you find out?" Scott asks as he returns to check on their progress.

"Okay, for this one," Marina began. "Okay, Mr. Sowell, so this is what we did. . . . So, here we figured out that we changed the length. And the longer it is the shorter, the shorter the frequency is, . . . and for right here, the heavier it is the . . . the faster the frequency is. And then the height, . . . or the angle right here, so . . . it was the same as that one."

"This is good," Scott said, pointing to their paper. "See how you ch . . . remember the problem we originally came . . ."

"We only changed each time what we're testing," Paige breaks in.

"Right, right," Scott confirms. "But now when I look at this data, I see two different weights and two different heights."

"Yeah, but in the first one the height was 56 and the weight was 3, and it came out to 21, and in the second one the height was higher and the weight was lower, so it was the same thing, so that's what we showed," Marina notes, again concluding that the change in weight explains why the frequency was the same when the heights were different.

Scott prompts the students to think about the way they dealt with two different variables for an earlier test and to try and think about their present test in the same way.

"Okay, run another test, and then we're going to stop," he suggests, moving over to another group.

The group does two more tests, making the height greater in one and the weight greater in the next. Both come out to 21 swings and the group concludes that the weight influenced the results in one and the height in the other. Scott returns and asks them to summarize their results.

"Let's do it out loud before you write it," Scott suggests as he listens to the students work. "Okay, talk to me about length."

"The lower it is, the lower the frequency," Marina responds.

"Rephrase that," Scott requests.

"The longer the string is, the slower the frequency is," Wensley adds.

"The angle?" Scott asks.

"The higher the angle is the fast . . . the more the frequency is," Wensley continues.

"What about weight?"

"The heavier it is, the faster it goes," Marina adds.

"I want to look at these again. . . . Write those down for me."

The students write their conclusions, as Scott walks to the front of the room and rings a bell to call the class together.

"Okay, now, we've done the experiments, some groups maybe got further than others; that's fine, you've all come to some type of conclusion. You may not all have the same conclusions and that's fine; you've used different methods, you should expect different results.

"When I call your group, I want the speaker of your group to report your findings to the class," he continues, turning back to the class as a whole.

A spokesperson for each group then comes to the front of the room to report their findings. In general, the groups conclude that each variable—the length, weight, and angle—affected the frequency.

Scott then asks the students to explain how they tested each of the variables. After they describe their procedures, he asks them to offer reasons why the different groups' results varied and what they could do to improve the results.

Among their ideas was the suggestion that they do repeated tests.

Scott confirms that their suggestions are good ones, and says, "Let's take a look at something here," as he takes a ring stand and puts it on his demonstration table. He attaches a paper clip, puts the pendulum in motion, asks one of the students to count, adds a second paper clip, and again has the students count, to demonstrate that weight doesn't affect the frequency.

He has a student state the conclusion and writes it on the board. Then he does a second demonstration to show that angle also has no effect on the frequency, and again asks a student to make a conclusion.

After the demonstrations, he says, "Now I want someone to give me a conclusion about what we learned about designing experiments and how we work our variables. . . . Who wants to talk about that? . . . Wensley? Tell me what we learned about how to set up an experiment. What did we get from this?"

"Each time, each time you do a different part of the experiment, only change one of the variables," Wensley explains.

"Why is that?"

"You're only checking one thing at a time. If you do two, there might be an error in the experiment."

"Okay, . . . keep talking, . . . if you change more than one thing at one time, why would it be difficult?"

"Because, . . . because . . . ah, it's easy to do one thing, cuz that's the only thing you're doing, but if you do two things you got to see, see the way it turns out to, because two things, two different things you can't work with as much as one."

"Good, okay, for example, if you were testing weight and length, okay, your group had to finally decide that we can't change weight at the same time as we change length, because when we test it . . ."

"It came out, . . . it was different," Wensley interjects.

"Right, and what else, you couldn't, you couldn't tell what?"

"You couldn't compare them," Marina adds.

"Right, you couldn't compare them. You couldn't tell which one was causing it, could you? . . . It might go faster, but all of a sudden you'd say, well is it the weight or is it the length?"

"So, that's the two things we've learned, okay. Does anyone have any questions about anything we've done? . . . Okay!" Scott says as he dismisses the students.

In Chapter 12, we discussed teacher-centered approaches to instruction, and saw that they can be effective for learning procedural skills and other forms of knowledge that all students should master.

Teacher-centered instruction may be less effective for more complex goals that emphasize higher-order thinking and problem solving, however. In these cases learner-centered approaches may be more desirable. We consider these approaches in this chapter.

When you've completed your study of this chapter, you should be able to meet the following goals:

- Identify differences between teacher-centered and learner-centered approaches to planning.
- Describe the elements of learner-centered planning.
- Discuss the relationship between cognitive views of learning and learner-centered instruction.
- Describe features of different learner-centered approaches to instruction.

Characteristics of Learner-Centered Instruction

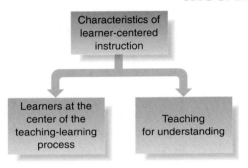

Figure 13.1 Characteristics of learner-centered approaches to instruction

As we better understand learning, we begin to appreciate how complex it is, with social interaction and differences in learner background knowledge, motivation, beliefs, expectations, and emotions all influencing the process (Alexander & Murphy, 1998; Nuthall & Alton-Lee, 1993; Pintrich, Marx, & Boyle, 1993).

The foundations of learner-centered approaches to instruction are cognitive views of learning in general and constructivism in particular. According to these views, errors and misconceptions are learners' expressions of their current understanding, and meaningful learning develops over long periods of time, often occurring after periods of confusion and conflict (Brooks & Brooks, 1993; Clements & Battista, 1990).

Grounded in cognitive views of learning, two characteristics of learner-centered instruction are illustrated in Figure 13.1 and discussed below. Let's look at them.

Learners at the Center of the Learning Process

The expanding influence of cognitive learning theory, ongoing research examining the thinking of experts, and growing criticisms of direct instruction have resulted in increased emphasis on the role of the student in learning. This emphasis has resulted in a number of learner-centered initiatives, among them the American Psychological Association's *Learner-Centered Psychological Principles,* which originally appeared in 1993 (Presidential Task Force on Psychology in Education, 1993) and have since been modified (American Psychological Association Board of Educational Affairs, 1995). These "principles" are outlined in Table 13.1.

Learner-Centered Psychological Principles

Researchers have distilled these principles into five generalizations about learning and teaching (Alexander & Murphy, 1998), which can be found in Figure 13.2.

The generalizations in Figure 13.2 remind us that the learner is the central figure in the learning process. We need to consider learners' background knowledge, their cognitive and affective thoughts, their development, and their social environment when we teach.

Implications of Student-Centered Learning for Teachers

Placing students at the center of learning requires important shifts in our teaching. Teachers no longer merely present and explain topics. Instead, they guide learners' efforts to develop their own understanding. This makes the teacher's role more complex and demanding. Some of this complexity was illustrated in Scott's lesson; for example, after he assigned the problem and the students conducted one test, they decided to make the pendulum both shorter and heavier, indicating that they didn't understand how to control variables. Scott recognized the problem and intervened.

13.1

What two theories of motivation are most reflected in the learner-centered psychological principles? What theory of motivation is not reflected in the principles? Explain, citing evidence from the principles themselves.

Table 13.1   APA learner-centered psychological principles

Cognitive and Metacognitive Factors

Principle	Description
1. Nature of the learning process	The learning of complex subject matter is most effective when it is an intentional process of constructing meaning from information and experience.
2. Goals of the learning process	The successful learner, over time and with support and instructional guidance, can create meaningful, coherent representations of knowledge.
3. Construction of knowledge	The successful learner can link new information with existing knowledge in meaningful ways.
4. Strategic thinking	The successful learner can create and use a repertoire of thinking and reasoning strategies to achieve complex learning goals.
5. Thinking about thinking	Higher-order strategies for selecting and monitoring mental operations facilitate creative and critical thinking.
6. Context of learning	Learning is influenced by environmental factors, including culture, technology, and instructional processes.

Motivational and Affective Factors

Principle	Description
7. Motivational and affective influences on learning	What and how much is learned is influenced by the learner's motivation. Motivation to learn, in turn, is influenced by the individual's emotional states, beliefs, interests and goals, and habits of thinking.
8. Intrinsic motivation to learn	The learner's creativity, higher order thinking, and natural curiosity all contribute to motivation to learn. Intrinsic motivation is stimulated by tasks the learner perceives to be of optimal novelty and difficulty, relevant to personal interests and providing for personal choice and control.
9. Effects of motivation on effort	Acquisition of complex knowledge and skills requires extended learner effort and guided practice. Without learner's motivation to learn, the willingness to exert this effort is unlikely without coercion.

Developmental and Social Factors

Principle	Description
10. Developmental influences on learning	As individuals develop, there are different opportunities and constraints for learning. Learning is most effective when differential development within and across physical, intellectual, emotional, and social domains is taken into account.
11. Social influences on learning	Learning is influenced by social interactions, interpersonal relations, and communication with others.

Individual Differences

Principle	Description
12. Individual differences in learning	Learners have different strategies, approaches, and capabilities for learning that are a function of prior experience and heredity.
13. Learning and diversity	Learning is most effective when differences in learners' linguistic, cultural, and social backgrounds are taken into account.
14. Standards and assessment	Setting appropriately high and challenging standards and assessing the learner as well as learning progress—including diagnostic, process, and outcome assessment—are integral parts of the learning process.

Figure 13.2 Five general statements related to the learner-centered principles

1. The knowledge base	One's existing knowledge serves as the foundation of all future learning by guiding organization and representations, by serving as a basis of association with new information, and by coloring and filtering all new experiences.
2. Strategic processing and control	The ability to reflect and regulate one's thoughts and behaviors is essential to learning and development.
3. Motivation and affect	Motivational or affective factors, such as intrinsic motivation, attributions for learning, and personal goals, along with the motivational characteristics of learning tasks, play a significant role in the learning process.
4. Development and individual differences	Learning, although ultimately a unique adventure for all, progresses through various common stages of development influences by both inherited and experiential/environmental factors.
5. Situation or context	Learning is as much a socially shared undertaking as it is an individually constructed enterprise.

Marina:	Mr. Sowell, we found out that the shorter it is and the heavier it is, the faster it goes.
Scott:	So, tell me how you found out that the length affected it.
Marina:	We made it long, and then we shortened it a little more, and then we made it heavier, and that showed . . .
Scott:	So, in Test 1, the length was 49, and the frequency was 22, and on the same test the weight was one paper clip?
Wensley:	And the height . . .
Scott:	The height was . . . ?
Wensley:	The, the, the angle.
Scott:	Ohh, okay, the angle was 25, the weight was 1, your length was 49. . . . What did you change different between Test 1 and Test 2?
Marina:	The amount of paper clips.
Scott:	So you changed the weight? What else did you change?
Wensley:	The length.
Scott:	The length, so you changed the weight and the length.
Marina:	And the angle.
Scott:	So, you changed all three between the two tests . . . . Which caused that higher frequency?"

Learner-centered instruction actively involves learners in their quest for understanding.

Paige:	The length.
Marina:	I think weight, the weight.
Scott:	What do you think? (looking at Wensley) Marina thinks weight.
Wensley:	Weight.
Scott:	What do you think? (looking at Jonathan)
Jonathan:	The weight.
Scott:	What do you think, Paige?
Paige:	The length.
Scott:	So, you think weight (pointing at Marina); you think weight (turning to Jonathan), you think weight (looking at Wensley), and you think length (pointing at Paige). Why can't you look at these two sets of data and decide? . . . Take a look at your two tests. . . . I want you to take a look at your two tests. This had one paper clip; this had two paper clips; this had 49 length; this had 27 length. . . . You should be able to look at these two and tell something. . . . But why can't you all come to a conclusion by looking at the numbers? . . . Think about that. Why can't you look at these numbers and come to a conclusion?"
Marina:	Well, like the length, and the height, and the weight was always changed. None of them ever stayed the same in any of them, so it has to be different.
Scott:	What was the first thing you said?
Wensley: *Jonathan:*	[Everything changed.]
Scott:	Think about that.

Two aspects of learner-centered instruction are illustrated in this excerpt. First, the students' understanding evolved from their efforts and experiences, not Scott's explanations. Second, Scott carefully monitored and guided the process to be sure it remained meaningful for them. He didn't intervene so soon that the students weren't allowed to struggle with the problem themselves, but he didn't wait so long that they became confused and frustrated.

This is extremely sophisticated instruction. As we saw in the lesson, intervention and guidance are often necessary to help students make progress and prevent or eliminate misconceptions, but too much intervention hampers their initiative and prevents them from developing their own understanding. Unfortunately, no rules exist to tell teachers whether or not they should intervene, or how extensive the intervention should be. Further, when teachers work with one group, other groups may go off task, so they can't stay with any group too long.

Whole-group discussions aren't much easier. When two students are involved in dialogue, other students may not be understanding or even paying attention. If they're not, the teacher must do something to bring them back into the lesson. It's easy to see why teacher-centered approaches, which are much easier to implement, have been popular for so long.

13.2

Think back to your study of information processing in Chapter 7. What characteristic of teachers' information processing systems makes learner-centered instruction difficult for teachers? What can be done to help overcome this difficulty? Explain.

13.3

What process and what subprocesses from the basic processes in thinking (in Table 8.5 on p. 331) does "justifying thinking" best illustrate? Explain.

Teaching for Understanding

The phrase "teaching for understanding" seems like a paradox; no teacher consciously teaches for lack of understanding. As you saw in the example with place value at the end of Chapter 12, however, understanding doesn't always result from instruction, and "teaching for understanding" isn't as simple as it appears. Understanding involves thought-demanding processes, such as explaining, finding evidence, justifying thinking, providing additional examples, generalizing, and relating parts to wholes (Knapp, Shields, & Turnbull, 1995; Perkins & Blythe, 1994). We saw these elements in Scott's lesson.

Let's consider "understanding" a bit more. By the end of the lesson, how well did Paige, Marina, Wensley, and Jonathan grasp the idea of controlled variables? Let's look at an interview following the lesson to give us some insight into their understanding.

The interviewer asked the students to write down three conclusions they made about the experiment, and they responded by saying that the length influenced the frequency, but that the angle and weight made no difference.

Interviewer:	Now I don't really believe that. I'm not sure about that business about the weight. Now, you told me that the weight doesn't matter, but I'm not convinced. Can you describe how we could test that, so I will believe you when you tell me that the weight doesn't matter?
Marina:	Okay, first you can do it with one or two, it doesn't matter how many times you test frequency . . .
Interviewer:	So, we're going to put on one paper clip (reaching for the end of the pendulum as shown in the following sketch).

Video Case

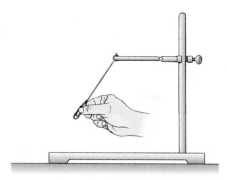

And then what are we going to do, Wensley . . . ? We have on the one paper clip. Remember now, you're trying to convince me that the weight doesn't matter, since you all four said that. Okay, now what am I going to do? I have the one paper clip hanging here. Now what am I going to do?

Wensley: Set it at an angle that you want.

Interviewer: Set it at some angle. What angle?

Wensley: About here (pointing to what would be about a 45-degree angle).

Interviewer: Okay, anything else I ought to do, Jonathan?

Jonathan: Time how long we want to do it.

Interviewer: Time how long we want to do it, okay.

They decide to time the pendulum for ten seconds, and they then conduct the test.

Interviewer: So, it went back and forth 14 times in 10 seconds. So, what should we do now? What do we need to do now, Jonathan?

Jonathan: Keep the same paper clip, but shorten it to see the difference.

Marina: No, we're doing the weight.

Wensley: We're doing the weight.

Jonathan: Ohh, oh yeah, put two paper clips on.

Interviewer: Put two paper clips on. (He then begins to attach a second paper clip to the end of the first one, in effect also changing the length of the pendulum.)

Marina: No, no, inside the knot, inside the knot, inside the knot. If you put it there it changes the length.

Wensley: No, you have to put it here (standing up and pointing to the knot).

Interviewer: I can't do this?

All: No!

Interviewer: Now, explain to me why I can't do this. . . . Paige?

Paige: When you do that, it's longer.

Interviewer: Why do I care? We're testing the weight. We put on more weight. Why do I care if it's here (attached to the end of the first paper clip) or up here (in the knot)?

Wensley: Because you can't have . . . it's easier to do one variable at a time.

Interviewer: Now, what is the variable we're dealing with here?

All: The weight.

Interviewer:	So, I don't want to do this. (Increase the length.) Tell me again why I don't want to do this, Wensley.
Wensley:	Cuz, your variables would change. You'd have two of them instead of only one. And you're only doing one variable, and that would be the weight.
Interviewer:	What other variable would I be changing by doing this?
Wensley:	The length.
Interviewer:	So, what do I need to do?
Marina:	Put the paper clip into the knot, next to the other one.
Interviewer:	So tell me one more time why we did this, Paige.
Paige:	So we could change the weight.
Interviewer:	So we could change the weight?
Paige:	But not make it longer.
Interviewer:	And not make it longer. So what is the word we use for the length. What are we doing with the length? We are . . .
Wensley:	Controlled variable?
Interviewer:	The length is a what?
Wensley:	Controlled variable.
Interviewer:	The length is a controlled variable. . . . So when you control a variable, what do you do?
Marina:	It doesn't change.
Interviewer:	It doesn't change . . . So what do I do now, Jonathan?
Jonathan:	Swing it.
Interviewer:	(Pulls the pendulum to an angle of 90 degrees)
Marina:	No, swing it from the same place where you started.
Interviewer:	Excuse me?
Marina:	Preferably from the same place as last time.
Interviewer:	Okay, about here. . . . Why do I want to do that?
Marina:	It would also be another variable if you started from another angle. . . . You'd be dealing with two variables, angle and weight. . . . You want to be dealing with just one variable, like Wensley said.

During the lesson we saw confusion and uncertainty. But the interview suggests that the students understood the idea of controlled variables when they were finished. By focusing on understanding and placing students in the center of the process, teachers help students learn to take responsibility for constructing and verifying their own conclusions. Taking responsibility leads to self-regulated learning, a concept we've emphasized throughout this book.

Misconceptions About Learner-Centered Instruction

Teachers sometimes misinterpret learner-centered instruction when they attempt to apply it in their classrooms. We consider three misinterpretations in this section.

- Clear goals and careful preparation are less important in learner-centered than in teacher-centered approaches.

- If students are involved in discussions and other forms of social interaction, learning is automatically taking place.

- Teachers have less important roles in student-centered learning than in traditional instruction.

Because students are constructing their own understanding, teachers might infer that clear goals are less important when using learner-centered approaches. Nothing

Clear goals allow teachers to design learning tasks that match students' needs.

could be further from the truth. In fact, clear goals are even more important, because they give teachers points of focus as they guide the class. Teachers may modify their goals as learners build on their current understanding, but they begin with clear goals in mind.

Concluding that discussions and other forms of social interaction automatically lead to learning is equally inaccurate. As we saw in Scott's lesson, teachers must carefully monitor discussions, and if students head down blind alleys or develop misunderstandings about the topic, teachers must intervene and redirect the discussion (Brown & Campione, 1994). We want students to become self-regulated and construct understandings that make sense to them, but their understandings must be valid. Allowing his students to continue experimenting without controlling variables would have been counterproductive in Scott's lesson, as would allowing students to conclude that both the weight and the angle influenced the frequency.

Finally, because teachers are not lecturing and explaining, it might appear that they have a less important role in learner-centered approaches than in teacher-centered approaches. As we've already seen, their role is both more important and more difficult. If they understand a topic, most teachers can learn to adequately explain it. *Guiding* learners so *the learners* develop a deep understanding of the topic is much more sophisticated and much more difficult.

With these characteristics of learner-centered instruction in mind, let's examine the planning process.

13.4

What advantages are there to placing students in groups to promote student interaction? disadvantages?

13.5

What evidence do we have from the first paragraph of the case study that *explaining* doesn't necessarily result in learner understanding?

Planning for Learner-Centered Instruction

Learner-centered planning is embedded in a **contextual planning model,** which *considers the traditional questions of teaching (such as goals, learning activities, and assessment) but focuses on guiding learners' constructions of understanding and helping them*

Figure 13.3 Learner-centered planning model

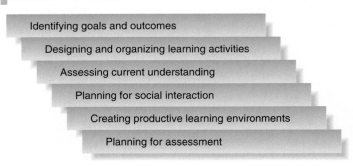

- Identifying goals and outcomes
- Designing and organizing learning activities
- Assessing current understanding
- Planning for social interaction
- Creating productive learning environments
- Planning for assessment

monitor their own learning, rather than simply transmitting knowledge (Bransford, 1993; Resnick & Klopfer, 1989). These planning elements are illustrated in Figure 13.3 and discussed in the sections that follow.

Identifying Goals and Outcomes

In planning for learner-centered instruction, goals and outcomes are as—or even more—important than they are in teacher-centered approaches, but stating them is more complex. The teacher isn't thinking of specific, discrete behaviors that can be practiced to mastery, such as Sam Barnett was when his students were working on subtraction. Rather, goals in learner-centered lessons focus on understanding that is complex and sometimes ill-defined. For example, Scott's goal was for students to understand how to design and conduct experiments. Reaching the goal required collaboration, an understanding of controlled and experimental variables, the ability to design effective tests, and logical interpretation of the results—tasks not effectively learned through direct instruction.

Scott's lesson also illustrates the need for teacher flexibility. Students' responses and their current understanding may require that goals be altered, sometimes in the middle of a lesson (Brooks & Brooks, 1993). For example, Scott's students couldn't design an experiment until they understood how to control variables, so he modified his original goal, intervened, and guided the students until they saw that controlling variables was essential.

The need for flexibility was also illustrated in Tracey Stoddard's lesson in Chapter 2. Her students' current understanding required that she change the direction of her lesson to conduct a series of experiments that helped them understand that coats and sweaters trap rather than generate heat.

Finally, learner-centered instruction attempts to increase students' awareness of and control over their own thinking as they work. This important goal is woven through all learning activities. Content outcomes are only part of our goal; the cognitive processes the students use to get there and the depth of their understanding are equally important.

Designing and Organizing Learning Activities

Learner-centered instruction emphasizes learning activities that have two characteristics: authentic tasks and multiple representations of content.

13.6

To what concept does students becoming "aware of and developing control over their own thinking" refer? To what theory of learning does the concept most closely relate?

Authentic Tasks

Authentic tasks are *learning activities that require an understanding similar to the understanding that would be used in the world outside the classroom* (Needels & Knapp, 1994). As teachers plan, they embed learning activities in real-world tasks. This is both intuitively sensible and consistent with cognitive views of learning. Designing and conducting experiments (as we've discussed throughout this chapter), finding the area of a classroom (as Laura Hunter's students did in Chapter 8), or having students write opinion columns about a public issue are all real-world tasks. Leading history students to understand why Quebec is French-speaking or helping geography students understand why the Great Basin in Nevada and Utah is so dry require real-world understanding. Tasks and understandings such as these are the focus of learner-centered activities.

Multiple Representations of Content

Placing students at the center of the learning process acknowledges that the construction of understanding is a personal process. Ensuring individual understanding requires multiple representations of topics (Brenner et al., 1997), or "criss-crossing a conceptual landscape" (Spiro, Feltovich, Jacobson, & Coulson, 1992), as we discussed in Chapter 8. Certain ways of representing ideas will be meaningful to some students, and different representations will be meaningful to others. Providing an array of representations acknowledges the uniqueness of students and provides multiple paths for making ideas meaningful.

To illustrate the idea of multiple representations, think back to the goals and representations of some of the teachers you've studied so far, which are outlined in Table 13.2. In each instance, the teacher capitalized on the powerful influence that demonstrations and concrete illustrations have on learning (Nuthall & Alton-Lee, 1993).

13.7

If a teacher cannot prepare a learning activity that involves an authentic task, does this imply that the activity or goal to which it is related is inappropriate? Explain.

13.8

Consider the concept of *transfer,* which you studied in Chapter 8. To what feature that promotes transfer does the concept of *multiple representations of content* most closely relate?

Authentic learning tasks help students connect abstract ideas to the real world.

Table 13.2 Multiple representations of content

Teacher and Chapter	Goal	Representations
Karen Johnson Chapter 2	To understand *density* Eighth grade	Cotton balls in drinking cup Wooden cubes Water and vegetable oil Population density Screen-door screen
Jenny Newhall Chapter 2	To understand that air takes up space First grade	Demonstration with cup and paper towel Releasing air bubble Hands-on experience
Diane Smith Chapter 4	To understand comparative and superlative pronouns Fifth grade	Pencils of different lengths Different student hair colors
Jenny Newhall Chapter 7	To understand the relationship between length and weight on a balance beam Fourth grade	Manipulating a balance beam with a variety of lengths and weights
Suzanne Brush Chapter 8	To understand how data can be rep- resented in graphs Second grade	Data from jelly bean survey Graphical representations Hands-on activities
Kathy Brewster Chapter 10	To understand the impact of the Crusades High school	School "crusade" Information from actual Crusades Learner essays
Shirley Barton Chapter 11	To understand equivalent fractions Fourth grade	Four concrete equivalent fractions Numerical examples
Scott Sowell Chapter 13	To understand controlled variables Seventh grade	Simple pendulums of different lengths, weights, and angles

Preparing different ways of representing content is perhaps the most difficult planning task facing a teacher. It requires both a thorough knowledge of the topic and extensive pedagogical content knowledge.

Assessing Current Understanding

13.9

Assessing current understanding on the basis of students' comments is time-efficient and relatively simple. However, this process can easily lead to erroneous conclusions on the part of the teacher. Explain why.

The influence of current understanding on new learning is at the core of all cognitive learning theories, and the third learner-centered principle (see Table 13.1) stresses the importance of linking new to existing information. This means teachers must plan to assess learners' current understanding.

Current understanding can be assessed in at least two ways. One way is to give formal pretests related to the topic, and the other is to begin a lesson and informally assess understanding on the basis of students' comments and responses to questions. Scott, for example, assigned the task and observed the students as they worked. In monitoring their efforts, he learned that they didn't understand controlled variables. This process is sometimes called *dynamic assessment,* and it involves gathering information about students' understanding while they're involved in authentic learning tasks (Spector, 1992).

Multiple representations of content provide learners opportunities to view ideas from different perspectives.

Planning for Social Interaction

Social interaction has an important role in cognitive views of learning, and it is also emphasized in the eleventh learner-centered principle in Table 13.1. Teachers should consciously plan to capitalize on the social nature of learning.

Too often, planning for social interaction simply means "put the students into groups." It isn't that simple, however. If groupwork isn't carefully planned, it can result in confusion and wasted time. Effective groupwork requires specifying tasks clearly, learning how to work together, and careful monitoring by the teacher. Scott's students worked well together, his task was clear, and he closely monitored the progress of the groups. (We discuss characteristics of effective groupwork later in the chapter.)

In whole-group activities, social interaction is facilitated by teacher questioning. The questioning skills we discussed in Chapter 11 are critical. If teachers don't have these skills, discussions tend to revert to mini-lectures, and the benefits of social interaction are lost.

The quality of the representations teachers use influences student interaction. Clear and meaningful representations provide students with concrete referents, so they can talk about and exchange ideas. If the representations are ineffective, virtually no amount of teacher guidance will result in meaningful discussions.

> **13.10**
>
> What are "clear" and "meaningful" knowledge representations? Illustrate your explanation with at least two different examples.

Creating Productive Learning Environments

In Chapter 11 we found that productive learning environments are safe, orderly, and learning focused. A productive learning environment is particularly critical if learner-centered instruction is to be successful. Learner-centered instruction requires that students feel free to take risks and offer conclusions, conjectures, and evidence without fear of criticism or embarrassment. It also requires students who are willing to listen to each other, wait their turn, and consider and reconsider their own ideas while others are talking. Students may not have these abilities or inclinations when learner-centered instruction is first introduced. When this happens, teachers need to help students develop as independent learners and assist them in accepting responsibility for their own behavior. Conscious planning helps identify the specific skills to be developed and the strategies, such as modeling, that will be used to teach them.

Planning for Assessment

Learner-centered instruction also has implications for assessing learning. Rather than answer questions about abstract and isolated problems, students demonstrate their understanding in realistic, lifelike contexts. Scott's students, for example, could be asked to design an experiment to determine which type of dog food would make puppies grow better. In addition to assessing students' ability to apply the information they've

Social interaction provides opportunities for teachers to assess learner understanding and foster the exchange of ideas between students.

Classroom Connections _____

Planning for Effective Learner-Centered Instruction

1. Identify what you want your students to understand or be able to do after you're finished with a lesson or unit and let this be your guide for planning.

   - A social-studies teacher is planning a unit on the Great Depression and how it influenced people's lives. She remains focused on the influence of the Depression on people as she plans the unit and gathers materials.
   - A third-grade teacher wants her students to understand the difference between physical and chemical changes. She keeps this goal in mind as she designs learning activities.

2. Prepare a variety of representations of the content you want students to understand.

   - The social studies teacher working on the Great Depression has the students read excerpts from *The Grapes of Wrath,* finds a video of people standing in bread lines, finds statistics on the rash of suicides after the stock market crash, and selects descriptions of Franklin D. Roosevelt's back-to-work programs.
   - The third-grade teacher doing a unit on chemical and physical change plans to have the students melt ice, crumple paper, dissolve sugar, break toothpicks, and make Kool-Aid to illustrate physical change. She also plans to have them watch a laser disc that describes physical change. She plans to have them melt sugar, burn paper, pour vinegar into baking soda, and chew soda crackers to illustrate chemical change.

3. Plan for social interaction.

   - A geography teacher involved in a lesson on the geographies and economies of different regions in the United States plans to have students work in groups of three to identify similarities and differences in the regions. As students work in groups, they develop a chart comparing the different regions, and these charts form the basis for a whole-class discussion.

learned, teachers can gather information about students' thinking in the process. (We discuss alternative or authentic assessments in detail in Chapter 14.)

In summary, when teachers plan for learner-centered instruction, they identify goals, organize and sequence learning activities, and assess learning, just as they would when using teacher-centered approaches. Learner-centered approaches, however, require more care in the way content is represented, as well as conscious planning for social interaction and the learning environment. In addition, teachers need to be more flexible in their planning, adapting goals and strategies as instruction unfolds.

13.11

Explain why planning based on a behaviorist approach would be simpler than learner-centered planning.

Types of Learner-Centered Instruction

To this point in the chapter we've considered the characteristics of learner-centered instruction, and we also discussed planning for learner-centered activities. We now want to examine several learner-centered strategies. They are:

- Discovery learning
- Inquiry

- Discussions
- Cooperative learning
- Individualized instruction
- Technology

Discovery Learning

Discovery learning is *a strategy that provides students with information they use to construct understanding.* Discovery learning was first made popular by Jerome Bruner (1960, 1966, 1971), who argued persuasively in the 1960s and 1970s for student autonomy and initiative. Many of his views about learning are similar to those held by constructivists today.

Types of Discovery

Discovery learning generated a considerable amount of research that helped clarify some of the issues involved, such as the distinction between unstructured and guided discovery (Keislar & Shulman, 1966). Pure discovery, or **unstructured discovery,** *occurs in a natural setting where learners construct understanding on their own,* such as a scientist making a unique discovery in a research project. According to some, Piaget's work implies a pure discovery approach, suggesting that ". . . educators get out of the way so that children can do their natural work . . ." (Resnick & Klopfer, 1989, p. 4). **Guided discovery** occurs *when the teacher identifies a content goal, arranges information so that patterns can be found, and guides students to the goal.*

Research on Discovery Learning

Research indicates that unstructured discovery is less effective than more guided approaches (Anastasiow, Bibley, Leonhardt, & Borish, 1970; Hardiman, Pollatsek, & Weil, 1986; Schauble, 1990). In unstructured discovery activities, students often become lost and frustrated, and this confusion can lead to misconceptions (Brown & Campione, 1994). As a result, unstructured discovery is rarely used in classrooms today, except in student projects and investigations.

Guided discovery is another matter. It is consistent with cognitive views of learning in general and constructivism in particular (Bransford, 1993; Brown & Campione, 1994), and its effectiveness is documented with research. For example, a meta-analysis of research on writing instruction indicated that students taught with a guided-discovery approach showed three times more improvement than those taught through unstructured discovery and four times more improvement than those taught with a traditional expository approach (Hillocks, 1984).

A more recent study found that guided discovery resulted in more transfer and greater long-term retention of science concepts and principles than did direct instruction (Bay, Staver, Bryan, & Hale, 1992). In comparing the two, researchers found that teachers spent less time lecturing and explaining and more time asking questions during guided discovery than they did during direct instruction. In addition, they found that students were more involved and had more opportunities to practice higher-order thinking—both important elements of learner-centered instruction (Alexander & Murphy, 1994; Marshall, 1997).

13.12

On the basis of the information in this section, what principle of "making information meaningful" from Chapter 7 is applied more effectively by guided discovery than it is by direct instruction?

Through guided discovery, teachers use constructivist learning principles to help students form concepts through hands-on experiences.

Guided Discovery: An Application

Let's see what guided discovery might look like in the classroom.

Judy Nelson is beginning the study of longitude and latitude in social studies with her sixth-graders. In preparation, she buys a beach ball, finds an old tennis ball, and checks her wall maps and globes.

She begins by having the students identify where they live on the wall map and then says, "Suppose you were hiking in the wilderness and got lost and injured. You have a cellular phone, but you need to describe exactly where you are. How might you do that? You have a map of the area with you but it's a topographic map showing rivers and mountains." As students discuss the problem, they realize that typical ways of locating themselves—such as cities and street signs—won't work.

She continues, "It looks as if we have a problem. We want to be able to tell rescuers exactly where we are, but we don't have a way of doing it. Let's see whether we can figure this out."

She then holds up the beach ball and globe and asks her students to observe and compare the two. In the process, they identify north, south, east, and west on the beach ball, and she draws a circle around the center of the ball, which they identify as the equator. They do the same with the tennis ball, which she then cuts in half, allowing them to see that the ball is in two hemispheres.

Judy continues by drawing other horizontal lines on the beach ball and saying, "Now, compare the lines with each other."

". . . They're all even," Kathy volunteers.

"Go ahead, Kathy. What do you mean by *even?*" Judy encourages.

". . . They don't cross each other," Kathy explains, motioning with her hands.

"Okay," Judy nods, smiling.

Judy asks for and gets additional comparisons, such as, "The lines all run east and west," and, "They get shorter as they move away from the equator." Judy writes them on the chalkboard. After the class is done making comparisons, Judy introduces the term *latitude* to refer to the lines they have been discussing.

She continues by drawing vertical lines of longitude on the beach ball and identifies them as shown below:

Let's look now at some of the dialogue that follows:

Judy:	How do these lines compare with the lines of latitude?
Tricia:	. . . They go all around the ball.
Judy:	Good. And what else?
Elliot:	. . . Length, . . . they're all as long, long as each other, same length.
Thomas:	Lengths of what?
Elliot:	The up-and-down lines and the cross ones.
Judy:	What did we call the cross ones?
Elliot:	. . . Latitude.
Jime:	We said that they got shorter. . . . So how can they be the same length?
Tabatha:	I think those are longer (pointing to the longitude lines).
Judy:	How might we check to see about the lengths?
Jime:	. . . Measure . . . them, the lines, like a tape or string or something.
Judy:	What do you think of Jime's idea?

The students agree that it seems to be a good idea, so Judy helps hold pieces of string in place while Jime wraps them around the ball at different points, and the class compares the lengths.

Chris:	They, they're the same (holding up two "longitude" strings).
Nicole:	Not these (holding two "latitude" strings).

After comparing the strings, Judy then asks students to work in pairs to summarize what they found. They make several conclusions, which Judy helps them rephrase. Then she writes the conclusions on the board:

Longitude lines are farthest apart at the equator; latitude lines are the same distance apart everywhere.

Lines of longitude are the same length; latitude lines get shorter north and south of the equator.

Lines of longitude intersect each other at the poles; lines of latitude and longitude intersect each other all over the globe.

Judy continues, asking, "Now, how does this help us solve our problem of identifying an exact location?" With some guidance from her, the class concludes that location can be pinpointed by where the lines cross. She notes that this is what they'll focus on the next day. (Eggen & Kauchak, 1996, adapted with permission)

This lesson illustrated several characteristics of learner-centered instruction. First, the students were at the center of the learning process. They constructed their own understanding of longitude and latitude; Judy didn't simply "explain" it to them. Second, she focused on *understanding* instead of definitions or problems with little meaning for the students. Third, Judy's planning provided for multiple representations of content; she used the beach ball, tennis ball, globe and strings, and planned to use maps the following day.

Finally, the learning activity emphasized social interaction. Undoubtedly, this approach took more time than direct instruction, but without this time and effort, students like Elliot would probably leave the lesson with incomplete understandings.

Several of the case studies you've already read used guided discovery to varying degrees, such as Jenny Newhall and Tracy Stoddard in Chapter 2, Diane Smith in Chapter 4, Suzanne Brush in Chapter 8, and Shirley Barton in Chapter 11. You may want to refer again to these case studies to further develop your understanding of guided discovery.

Inquiry

Closely related to guided discovery, **inquiry** is *a strategy in which facts and observations are used to answer questions and solve problems* (Kauchak & Eggen, 1998). Inquiry typically includes the following steps:

- Identifying a question or problem
- Forming an hypothesis to answer the question or solve the problem
- Gathering data to test the hypothesis
- Drawing conclusions from the data
- Generalizing on the basis of the conclusions

Scott's students were involved in an inquiry activity. They were presented with the problem of determining how the length, weight, and angle affect the frequency of a simple pendulum. While the problem could have been presented more generally, such as, "What influences the frequency of a simple pendulum," Scott chose to narrow the problem to make it more manageable for the students.

In Scott's lesson, the students didn't form hypotheses; instead they moved directly to gathering data. Understanding and applying the processes needed to gather meaningful data were the lesson's primary goals; understanding the relationships between length, weight, angle, and frequency were secondary. This emphasis on process is characteristic of inquiry activities (Eggen & Kauchak, 1996; Kauchak & Eggen, 1998).

Conclusions and generalizations were made both in small groups and as part of the whole-class discussion. Again, much of the discussion focused on the process of controlling variables.

13.13

In the dialogue, Judy said, "It looks like we have a problem. We want to be able to tell rescuers exactly where we are, but we don't quite have a way of doing it. Let's see whether we can figure this out." What essential teaching skill from Chapter 11 does this statement best illustrate?

13.14

Your use of the case studies to develop your understanding of guided discovery illustrates one characteristic of learner-centered planning. Identify this characteristic. Explain how it is illustrated.

13.15

Based on Scott's and Judy Nelson's lessons, explain how guided discovery and inquiry are similar and different. Explain how Scott could have planned and conducted his lesson so that it would have been guided discovery. In doing so, how would his goals have been different? Explain why it would have been difficult for Judy Nelson to conduct her lesson in an inquiry format.

Discussions

Discussions are *strategies designed to stimulate thinking, challenge attitudes and beliefs, and develop interpersonal skills* (Oser, 1986). These thinking and interpersonal skills include:

- learning to listen to others
- developing tolerance for dissenting views
- learning democratic processes
- critically examining one's understanding, attitudes, and values, as well as those of others

Like guided discovery, discussions incorporate characteristics of learner-centered instruction: learners are at the center of the learning process and deep understanding of the topic is a goal. Discussions are consistent with cognitive views of learning, since learners are active in developing their understanding, and they emphasize the social aspects of learning.

To illustrate discussions and to see how teacher-centered and learner-centered instruction can be used to complement each other, let's return to Darren Anderson and her work with her American History students in Chapter 12. She used lecture–discussion to help her students acquire background related to the conflicts between the French and

Discussions provide opportunities for learners to share ideas and develop their interpersonal communication skills.

British prior to the Revolutionary War. Now she wants her students to further analyze certain aspects of the conflict.

She begins, "Today we're going to pull together some ideas we've been thinking about related to the Revolutionary War. To do that, I'd like to present an idea and have us talk about it. Some historians, reviewing all the facts about the war, suggest that, on paper, the British 'should' have won. When they say this, they're not saying 'should' like 'ought' but rather that the British had important advantages but wasted them. What do you think? . . . Anyone? . . . Well, think about it while I put this statement on the board."

She then wrote

"The British advantages during the Revolutionary War should have ensured victory"

on the chalkboard.

"Okay," she went on. "Now that you've had time to think, does anyone want to take a stab at this? . . . Shirley, go ahead."

". . . I . . . I agree," Shirley began after pausing for several seconds. "They had lots of soldiers and guns and stuff, and, and, and like equipment. They should have won."

"I agree too," Martha added. "They had more . . . soldiers and they were . . . like real soldiers. And . . ."

"But they, they, the soldiers were in the wrong place . . . most of the time," Hank interjected.

"Hold on a second, Hank. That's a good idea, but please give Martha a chance to finish," Darren admonished gently, gesturing to Hank.

She continued, "Anything else, Martha?"

"Well, . . . I was just going to say that because they were real soldiers, they were better trained."

"Yeah, but the British started the war. You know we talked about all the taxes, like on tea, and the people here, . . . in the colonies, got mad, cuz it wasn't fair, and . . . ," Ed added.

"Not really," Joan countered. "I think the Colonists started it. They shot first."

"That is an interesting issue," Darren smiled, "but what is the question we're examining here? Ken?"

". . . If the British should . . . should have won the war . . . or not."

"Yes, good, Ken. Let's keep that in mind, everyone. On the other hand, if you want to argue that the issue of who started the war is relevant, please go ahead."

After hesitating briefly, both Ed and Joan nodded that they didn't want to pursue the issue, so Darren continued.

"Now, Hank, what were you saying?"

"Well, even though they, you know, . . . the British, had more, . . . had more soldiers, it, it didn't . . . always help them."

"Why do you say that, Hank?"

". . . Well, like we talked about Saratoga, you know, you showed us on the map. That one, that general . . . Burgoyne went to Philadelphia, 'er sent a bunch of his soldiers to Philadelphia and wasted them, well at least sort of wasted them. He was s'posed to go up, up to Albany. So, that's what I mean, like they didn't seem to be too smart about the way they fought, or like they had bad strategy or something."

"That's an interesting thought, Hank. Jeremy, do you have something to add?"

"Just, like, . . . also the British had . . . what . . . I can't remember, you know, like those ones that were paid, were paid to fight . . ."

"Mercenaries," Darren said.

"Yeah, mercenaries, they were just being paid to fight, so they didn't fight very hard."

"So, what exactly are you saying?"

". . . Well, having lots of soldiers isn't necessarily the most important. Like if they didn't really want to fight all that hard, . . . that would matter. . . . The colonies, the people in the colonies, like they lived here, so they fought really hard . . . I think."

"Okay! Very good, everyone. Now, return to our question on the board. What other advantages or disadvantages did the British have that influenced the outcome of the war?"

Characteristics of Effective Discussions

Using Darren's lesson as context, let's look now at four characteristics of effective discussions:

13.16

When effectively done, direct instruction, lecture–discussion, guided discovery, and discussions have an important element in common. What is this element?

- Focus
- Student background knowledge
- Emphasis on understanding
- Student–student interaction

Focus.   Teachers provide focus in discussions by posing a question or problem, such as whether or not the British should have won the Revolutionary War. Teachers maintain this focus through questions and comments (Krabbe & Polivka, 1990). Students have a tendency to wander and, without intervention, an animated discussion can develop over an irrelevant issue. The following excerpt from her lesson illustrates how Darren intervened.

Ed:	Yeah, but the British started the war. You know we talked about all the taxes, like on tea, and the people here, . . . in the colonies, got mad, cuz it wasn't fair, and . . .
Joan:	Not really. I think the Colonists started it. They shot first.
Darren:	That is an interesting issue, but what is the question we're examining here? Ken?
Ken:	. . . If the British should, should have won the war . . . or not.
Darren:	Yes, good, Ken. Let's keep that in mind, everyone. On the other hand, if you want to argue that the issue of who started the war is relevant, please go ahead.

Keeping students focused and helping them recognize when they are making irrelevant arguments is an important part of the teacher's role as a facilitator.

Student Background Knowledge.   Background knowledge is critical in discussions. Discussions should follow lessons in which background has been developed, such as the lecture–discussion we saw Darren conduct in Chapter 12. If students' backgrounds are insufficient, discussions are ineffective, disintegrating into random conjectures, uninformed opinions, and "pooled ignorance." We've probably all been in situations where we've been asked to discuss a problem or issue with limited background. It is a waste of time at best.

Emphasis on Understanding.   Discussions are best used to explore relationships, integrate ideas, and develop thinking and interpersonal skills. They're not effective for developing initial understanding. Successful discussions invite students to identify links between ideas and construct understanding that makes sense to them. Uncertainty, conjecture, and healthy disagreement are all part of this process. This is the reason background knowledge is so important.

Student–Student Interaction. Student interaction is integral to discussions (Dillon, 1987; Krabbe & Polivka, 1990). Student–student interaction helps students learn to challenge others' thinking and explain and defend their own reasoning, both consistent with the idea of constructing understanding. In addition, students learn to respect others' opinions and right to speak, to wait their turn, and to remain open-minded in the face of new evidence. Development of these communication skills is often as important as the content students are learning.

Research on effective discussion reveals that teachers have a difficult time shifting from an information-giving role to that of facilitator (Dillon, 1987). They tend to dominate discussions, turning them into mini-lectures (Cazden, 1986; Cuban, 1984). To be successful discussion leaders, teachers need to intervene only when necessary and ask questions that encourage students to think and interact with the content and each other, not with the teacher.

13.17

In what ways might Scott's lesson be described as a discussion? In what ways did his lesson not illustrate the characteristics of a discussion?

Cooperative Learning

While a great deal of instruction is conducted in whole-class settings, teachers sometimes have goals that can't be met in large groups. In large groups, it's easy for quiet or less confident students to go unnoticed. Students learn that opportunities for participation are limited and some drift off, even in stimulating discussions. Individual students don't get many chances to construct, defend, and share their conclusions with others. To reach goals not effectively met in large groups and to encourage the involvement of all learners, *cooperative learning* offers an effective alternative.

Though researchers don't agree on a single definition, most agree that **cooperative learning** *consists of students working together in groups small enough so that everyone can participate in a clearly assigned task* (Cohen, 1994). Slavin (1995), a leading authority in cooperative learning, defines cooperative learning as *students working together to help each other learn,* and Johnson and Johnson (1994) define it as *students working together to accomplish shared goals.* Different views of cooperative learning share at least four common features:

- Students are placed in small groups (typically 2 to 5).
- Goals direct the groups' activities.
- Social interaction is emphasized.
- Learners must depend on each other to reach the goals.

The fourth characteristic is critical and is sometimes called *positive interdependence* (Johnson & Johnson, 1994) or *reciprocal interdependence* (Cohen, 1994). Interdependence encourages students to work collectively toward some common goal.

We saw these features in Scott's lesson. His students were placed in groups of four; their goal was to determine how length, weight, and angle affected the frequency of a simple pendulum; a great deal of interaction took place in the groups; and learners collaborated in designing, implementing, and interpreting the experiment.

Many of the teachers in the cases you've studied in earlier chapters used cooperative learning as an integral part of their instruction. In addition to Scott Sowell in this chapter, Jan Davis in Chapter 1, Jenny Newhall in Chapter 7, Sue Southam in Chapter 7, and Laura Hunter and Suzanne Brush in Chapter 8 all used cooperative learning in their instruction.

Introducing Cooperative Learning

Effectively introducing students to cooperative learning requires organization. Materials must be readily available and quickly distributed to each group, and students must be able to get into and out of groups easily. If the process isn't well organized, instructional time is lost in transitions. Also, goals and directions must be clear to prevent activities from disintegrating into aimless "bull sessions."

Suggestions for initially planning and organizing cooperative learning activities include the following:

- Introduce your students to cooperative learning with short, simple tasks.
- Have students practice moving into and out of groups quickly. Group members can be seated together prior to the activity to make the transition from the whole-class activity to student groups and back again with little disruption.
- Give students a clear and specific task to accomplish in the groups.
- Specify the amount of time students are allowed to accomplish the task (and keep it short).
- Require that students produce a product as a result of the cooperative learning activity.
- Monitor the groups while they work.

We saw these characteristics in Scott's lesson. His students were used to working in groups, so they were able to collaborate effectively on a complex task. He had the groups seated together, the task was clear and specific, he required that they write down their conclusions, and, perhaps most significantly, he carefully monitored the progress of the groups. Because of the complexity of the task, they worked on it for most of the period.

Specific Approaches to Cooperative Learning

Different models of cooperative learning are designed to accomplish different goals. Let's examine two of these.

Student Teams Achievement Divisions (STAD). Created by Robert Slavin (1995), **STAD** *implements cooperative learning by using a structured system of rewards to promote concept, procedural skill, and fact learning.* STAD typically follows a direct instruction format, but in place of solitary independent practice, *team study* is used. During team study, students complete exercises on teacher-prepared worksheets and compare their results with those of their teammates. The teacher intervenes only if team members are unable to resolve disagreements about answers. Team study is complete when all teammates understand and can explain the problems or exercises.

Team study is followed by quizzes, which are scored as they would be in any other situation. If individuals score higher on a quiz than their average to that point in the class, they are awarded *improvement points,* and individual improvement points contribute to team awards. Improvement points contributing to team awards is the mechanism designed to promote positive interdependence.

Two elements are critical to STAD: (a) individual accountability, and (b) group awards (Slavin, 1995). Individuals are accountable because they take the quizzes alone and they contribute to group awards if their quiz score is higher than their average at

---

13.18

A teacher places her third-graders in groups of three, gives each group magnets and a packet including a dime, spoon, aluminum foil, rubber band, wooden pencil, paper clip, and nails. She tells the groups to experiment with the magnets and items for ten minutes and write their observations on paper. As they work, she answers questions and makes comments. The class as a whole group discusses the results. How effectively did the teacher introduce cooperative learning to her students? Cite evidence from the example to support your conclusion.

Cooperative learning involves students in small-group learning activities that teach both content and interpersonal skills.

that point in the grading period. Although rewards are used with STAD, teams do not compete with each other. All groups can achieve the highest group awards if they improve enough or have high enough averages.

Jigsaw II. **Jigsaw II** is *a form of cooperative learning in which individual students become experts on subsections of a topic and teach that subsection to others.* In contrast with STAD, which is most effective for teaching procedural skills, Jigsaw II is designed to teach organized bodies of knowledge. In a unit on Central America, for instance, a social studies teacher may have one student from each team focus on the geography, another on the climate, a third on the economy, and a fourth on the political system of each country. Individuals study their topics and then attend "expert meetings," in which all students assigned to a particular topic (e.g., the climate) meet, compare notes, and clarify their understanding. "Experts" then teach the other members of their teams. Each member contributes a different piece of the knowledge puzzle, thus the name "Jigsaw." All members are held accountable for the content of each area.

> **13.19**
>
> Positive or reciprocal interdependence is one characteristic of cooperative learning. How is interdependence accomplished with STAD? How is it accomplished with Jigsaw II? Explain.

Cooperative Learning: Theory and Research

Cooperative learning is consistent with constructivist views of learning, advocates arguing that learners co-construct more powerful understandings than individuals can construct alone (Linn & Burbules, 1993; O'Donnell & O'Kelly, 1994). Vygotsky's influence, particularly, can be seen in the emphasis on social interaction. Cooperative learning is most effective when learners in cooperative groups are in their zones of proximal development, able to benefit from the support they receive from their peers (O'Donnell & O'Kelly, 1994).

Advocates argue that cooperative learning benefits learners in three ways: (a) increased achievement and cognitive skills, (b) improved social skills, and (c) the development of workplace skills, such as learning to be both a leader and a follower in teams, dealing with "difficult" associates, and accommodating the norms of groups (Linn & Burbules, 1993).

Research supports the first suggested benefit: cooperative learning methods have been effective in increasing achievement—including higher-level outcomes, such as problem solving—in a variety of content areas on both teacher-made and standardized tests at all grade levels (Johnson & Johnson, 1989; Cohen, 1994; O'Donnell & Dansereau, 1992; Quin, Johnson, & Johnson, 1995; Slavin, 1995).

Research also indicates that cooperative learning can improve social skills, fostering the acceptance of mainstreamed students with exceptionalities and promoting friendships and positive attitudes among students who differ in achievement, ethnicity, and gender (Slavin, 1995).

Development of workplace skills is more controversial. Some researchers argue that groups in the workplace are often dysfunctional, with authoritarian styles of interaction, subtle coercion to adopt group norms, and lack of risk-taking all common. In addition, because the workplace is changing rapidly, specific workplace objectives may be obsolete by the time students are out of school (Linn & Burbules, 1993). Rather than attempting to develop workplace skills, they argue, schools should focus on cognitive objectives and broad social dispositions.

Effectively using cooperative learning isn't as simple as it appears on the surface. Its effectiveness depends on careful planning and implementation; merely putting students in groups doesn't guarantee learning (Sherman, 1988; Tingle & Good, 1990). To be effective, four factors must operate:

- Task goals must be appropriate, and learners must have adequate background knowledge.
- Social norms must be positive, and group members must have equal status.
- The type and amount of interaction must be appropriate.
- Learners must be held accountable.

With respect to the first factor, if the goal is to generate as many ideas as possible (brainstorming), group activities are productive (Linn & Burbules, 1993). On the other hand, individual work is often more effective for aspects of problem-solving that require coordinating several ideas (Lammers, 1986). Also, if learners lack the background knowledge needed to attack a problem, cooperation leads nowhere (Basili & Sanford, 1991).

Second, social norms can interfere with group effectiveness. For example, groups may use sarcasm to embarrass an individual into agreement, students may feel pressure from the group to move along instead of offering dissenting views, and ideas from the highest-status or most dominant member of the group are the ones often accepted (Linn

& Burbules, 1993). We saw some evidence of this in Scott's lesson. Marina was the most dominant member of the group, and in at least one case Paige deferred to her, even though Paige's idea was more nearly correct. On the other hand, both Paige and Marina contributed as much or more to the group than Wensley or Jonathan, which runs counter to research indicating that boys tend to dominate groupwork (Linn & Burbules, 1993; O'Donnell & O'Kelly, 1994).

Third, the amount and type of interaction are critical. For example, when learners are given problems with no single right answers (such as designing and completing the experiment in Scott's lesson), achievement depends on the amount of reciprocal interaction; i.e., all members of the team contribute about equally to completing the task (Cohen, 1994). On the other hand, if the task involves well-defined procedures, such as practicing procedural skills, interaction is not reciprocal, and the students benefitting most are the ones who provide explanations (scaffolds), not the ones receiving them (Webb, 1991; Webb & Palinscar, 1996).

Finally, as we saw in our discussion of STAD, Slavin (1995) argues that individual accountability and group awards are critical if cooperative learning is to increase academic achievement. Without them, one or two members of the group may do most of the work, while the others go along for the ride (Cohen, 1994; O'Donnell & O'Kelly, 1994; Slavin, 1995). This both decreases learning and causes resentment in those doing the work (Salomon & Globerson, 1989).

This discussion suggests two things: (a) cooperative learning isn't a panacea (which teachers are sometimes led to believe) and (b) its effective implementation requires careful thought and organization (which is true of all aspects of teaching).

13.20

How will individual accountability in cooperative learning most commonly be accomplished? What does this imply about students receiving group grades (all students in the group receiving the same grade)?

Cooperative Learning: A Tool for Capitalizing on Diversity

We saw earlier that cooperative learning, if properly implemented, can be effective for promoting friendships and positive attitudes toward students who differ in achievement, ethnicity, gender, and exceptionality (Slavin, 1995). Let's see how a teacher uses cooperative learning to improve interpersonal relations among a group of students from diverse backgrounds.

As Maria Sanchez watched her third-graders bent over their work, she was simultaneously pleased and uneasy. They had made huge strides in their math and reading abilities since the beginning of the year, but the class still didn't feel like a cohesive group. There was little mixing among her minority and nonminority students, she worried about the six ESL students who were still struggling with English, and there were four resource students who left her class every day for extra help. She could tell they felt different from the others and didn't want to leave.

Maria decided to try cooperative learning to see if she could help the class become more cohesive. Over the weekend, she used suggestions from their previous year's teacher, their performance on her tests, and her own judgment to organize the students into groups of four, with equal numbers of high- and low-ability readers in each group. She also mixed the students by race and gender, and she put each ESL student and each student with an exceptionality into different groups. Then she gathered materials that she would use with the groups.

On Monday, she organized the groups and explained how they were to work together. She sat with one group and modeled cooperation and being helpful for the rest of the students.

Then she sent each group to a different part of the room to begin working on specific tasks to help them become better acquainted. In reading, one student from each group would read a paragraph, and another would ask questions of the other group members, using stems that Maria had provided. As they worked, Maria moved around the room, promoting cooperation, ensuring that all students were involved, and preventing individuals from dominating the groups.

After a demanding but fairly successful first session, Maria sent her students outside for recess.

"Phew," she thought to herself as she surveyed the classroom. "This sure isn't any easier, but it already seems a little better."

As we saw earlier, effective cooperative learning requires careful planning and monitoring, particularly when students are first introduced to the process. Groups need to be carefully organized and trained to function effectively, tasks must be structured to promote interaction, and group progress must be monitored (Cohen, 1994). Let's look at these elements.

Grouping.   As you saw in Maria's case, cooperative learning groups should have equal numbers of high- and low-ability students, boys and girls, ethnic minorities, and students with exceptionalities, particularly when the goal is to promote positive relationships among students.

Training.   Effective group interaction doesn't just happen; it must be planned and taught. Effective "helping" behaviors can be taught, and these skills are especially valuable for minority students, who are often hesitant about seeking and giving help (Webb & Farivar, 1994). Effective group interaction skills include:

- *Listening and questioning skills:* Helping other students verbalize and express their ideas and learning to listen to others' ideas without judging them

- *Checking for understanding:* Asking for elaboration when answers are incomplete

- *Staying on-task:* Making sure the discussion remains focused and time limits are met

- *Emotional support:* Supportive comments for incorrect answers (e.g., "That's okay. I don't always get it the first time either.") (Kagan, 1994; Webb & Farivar, 1994)

Role playing, teacher modeling, and videotapes of effective groups are all effective in teaching these skills (Fitch & Semb, 1992).

Learning Tasks.   To be successful in promoting acceptance of diversity, cooperative learning tasks must require cooperation and communication (Cohen, 1994; Good, McCaslin, & Reys, 1992). Maria accomplished this by providing question stems for each group and by having students take turns reading paragraphs and asking and answering questions. By rotating students through these roles, Maria encouraged participation from all group members and helped prevent higher-status or more aggressive students from dominating the activity. Other tasks that can be used to encourage communication and cooperation include presenting and checking math problems, practicing spelling and grammar exercises in which students take turns as students and tutors, and providing open-ended problems (Cohen, 1994; Quin et al., 1995).

Monitoring.   As Maria found, groups need constant monitoring and support, especially initially. As we saw earlier, student achievement is related to the amount and quality of interaction in groups, which also influence group cohesion and intragroup relations

---

13.21

Provide a specific explanation for why students are more likely to develop positive attitudes toward students different from themselves in cooperative learning groups than in whole-group activities.

13.22

Describe an open-ended problem from your content area that might be effective with a diverse group of students.

Teacher monitoring ensures that cooperative learning groups function effectively.

(Cohen, 1994). Teachers should deal with problems in individual groups. If the problems persist, they can reconvene the class for discussion, additional modeling, and role playing.

Classroom Connections _____

Capitalizing on Diversity in Your Classroom

1. Use the composition of cooperative learning groups to capitalize on the strengths of diverse students.

   • A first-grade teacher waits until several weeks into the school year to form cooperative learning groups in her classroom. She uses this time to observe her students and gather data about student interests, talents, and

   friendships. She uses this information in making decisions about group membership.

2. Design learning tasks that require group interaction and cooperation.

   • A sixth-grade math teacher uses cooperative learning groups to provide practice and feedback in his class. When he assigns word problems, he asks students to work in pairs and compare and explain their answers to the other student in the pair. They may ask for help only when they're unable to resolve disagreements.

- An English teacher uses cooperative learning as a way to provide student reactions and responses to each other's writing. Students in each group take turns reading and reacting to each other's works on the basis of style and clarity. They then make suggestions for revision.

3. Use warm-up, introductory, and team-building exercises to promote interaction within groups.

- A social-studies teacher encourages group solidarity by having members interview each other about such things as their favorite food, hobby, song, or vacation. Each interviewer then presents this information to other members of the group.
- A high-school teacher starts her cooperative learning activities with an icebreaker called "Truth and Lies." Each person in the group says four things about himself or herself, three of which are true and one of which is a lie. The others try to guess which one is the lie.

4. Provide feedback to students about their interactions within the group.

- An English teacher monitors reader response sessions and joins in with students during the activities. Comments such as, "I really like the way you used examples from his writing to tell him what you liked," help students understand how to give constructive feedback.
- A kindergarten teacher sometimes interrupts cooperative learning activities when she detects problems, such as students arguing about who gets to perform a certain task. She tells them they must learn to cooperatively solve their problem, and she models cooperation in simulations and think-alouds.

5. Evaluate cooperative learning groups to determine their effectiveness.

- A fourth-grade teacher asks her students to fill out evaluation forms after cooperative group activities. On the half-sheet of paper, she asks students to tell her:
  a. What I learned
  b. What I liked about working in the group
  c. How the group could help me learn better

Individualized Instruction

So far, we've examined guided discovery, discussions, and cooperative learning, which represent a trend from whole-group to small-group instruction. We examine the trend in this section with a discussion of individualization.

Individualization is *a form of instruction adapted to meet the specific learning needs of each student.* Three ways of individualizing are (a) varying time available for learning, (b) varying learning activities, and (c) varying instructional materials.

Varying Time Available for Learning

Learners differ in the amount of time needed to master a topic, with high achievers needing less time than low achievers (Slavin, 1987). Teachers often accommodate this difference by giving common assignments and then providing extra instruction for small groups while the majority of the students work on seatwork or enrichment activities.

In skill areas, a technique called *team-assisted individualization* (Slavin, 1985) keeps objectives constant but varies the time and resources available to students. In it, students work on individualized learning materials in mixed-ability teams. It differs from STAD primarily in that teachers provide direct instruction to small groups (they don't with STAD).

Varying Learning Activities

Varying learning activities provides a second way of individualizing. For instance, an English teacher might allow students to write a paper, give an oral report, or prepare a multimedia presentation about an author. A science teacher may allow students to prepare written reports or conduct an investigation. Allowing students choices in learning activities provides opportunities for students to pursue topics of individual interest and learn in different ways; both can greatly increase motivation.

Varying Instructional Materials

Individualization has become easier in recent years, with the increased availability of audiovisual materials (audio- and videotaped instruction, filmstrips, and computer software) (Good & Brophy, 1997). If these materials are not available, reading passages can be made more accessible by providing study guides and by conducting prereading discussions that focus on key ideas (Anderson & Armbruster, 1984).

Research on Individualized Instruction

Research results examining individualized instruction are mixed. Individualization appears to be most effective when assessment is frequent and opportunities for student choice, self-regulation, and peer cooperation exist (Good & Brophy, 1997). Although acknowledging that some students need more time and instruction than others, Good and Brophy (1997) conclude, "It seems more appropriate to develop high-quality instructional materials and methods intended for all students than to set out from the beginning to develop different materials and methods for various students" (pp. 320–321). Further, they note, although individualization is well suited for practice on basic skills, it is not effective for developing higher-order thinking and problem solving.

Learner-Centered Instruction: Utilizing Technology

Technology is changing the way we live as well as the ways we learn and teach. Different forms of technology, including computers, videodiscs, videotape, the Internet, and educational television all have the potential to improve learning and teaching.

Putting hardware into classrooms doesn't automatically increase learning, however. In this section we examine some of the issues related to technology and how technology can be used most effectively.

Good and Bad Reasons for Using Technology

Like all aspects of education, the effective use of technology requires clear thinking and careful organization. Since using technology requires extra time and expense, it must produce benefits that justify the effort. At least two reasons exist for integrating technology into the learning and teaching environment.

First, learning about technology in schools prepares students for life in a technological society. Learners are growing up in a world that will increasingly require technological literacy, so experience with technology is virtually required.

Second, technology can increase learner motivation. Using computers and other forms of technology has been shown to increase engaged time on certain academic tasks (Pask-McCartney, 1989; Summers, 1990–1991). In other cases, learning has been

13.23

Identify a topic area in which student choice would be effective and desirable, and identify another topic area in which it wouldn't be advisable.

13.24

Based on the cognitive learning theories you've studied in this text, explain why individualization is not well suited to higher-order thinking and problem solving.

13.25

In order to effectively integrate technology into the existing curriculum, what is the first thing teachers should consider? Explain.

13.26

Identify two other sources of intrinsic motivation that were discussed in Chapter 10. Describe examples of how technology could be used to capitalize on these sources. Be specific in your examples.

Learners can use technology to organize data, problem-solve, and interact with others.

made more meaningful by having learners create their own technology-based products, such as word-processing documents, hypermedia, and computer generated art (Buchholz, 1991; Franklin, 1991; Volker, 1992). Additional research indicates that using technology can increase students' perceptions of being in control of their learning (Arnone & Grabowski, 1991; Relan, 1992), which we found in Chapter 10 to be one of the sources of intrinsic motivation.

However, if teachers are using technology because it's trendy, because they're competing with other teachers, because they're trying to impress their principals, or simply "because it's there," they're implementing it for the wrong reasons (Roblyer, Edwards, & Havriluk, 1997).

Using Technology to Improve Learning

If technology is to be used effectively, educators must first be clear about the goals they expect to accomplish with it (Harrington-Lueker, 1997). Vague notions of "surfing the 'Net," or giving kids access to computers are not adequate, and can even be counterproductive.

Assuming that goals are clear, technology appears promising in at least five areas.

- Representing difficult-to-teach topics
- Creating and using databases
- Facilitating interaction among learners

- Developing problem-solving skills
- Drill and practice

Let's look at them.

Representing Difficult-to-Teach Topics.   Many of the abstract topics we teach are difficult to represent, and this difficulty is what makes them hard to learn. For these topics, technologically based simulations have been found to be effective (Alessi & Trollip, 1991). We can simply drop a paper clip and a ball of clay, for example, to demonstrate that objects of different weights fall at the same rate, but it's virtually impossible to illustrate the actual acceleration of a falling object. Here, technology can be a powerful tool. For example, Figure 13.4 illustrates the position of a falling ball at uniform time intervals. We see that the distance between the images is greater and greater, indicating that the ball is falling faster and faster. This presents a semi-concrete example of acceleration, which is virtually impossible to represent in any other way.

As another example, learners can use computer software to simulate a frog dissection, rather than cut up an actual frog. While the simulation has the disadvantage of not allowing students the hands-on experience, it has at least three advantages: (a) it is less expensive, since it can be used over and over, (b) it is more flexible, because the frog can be "reassembled," and (c) the simulation avoids sacrificing a frog for science (Roblyer et al., 1997).

Other simulations give students a sense of what it would be like to walk on the moon or see how personnel work together in an emergency room. As the quality of software improves, representations will become more sophisticated and the simulations will be more interactive, further increasing learner motivation and understanding.

Creating and Using Databases.   "**Databases** are *computer programs that allow users to store, organize, and manipulate information, including both text and numerical data*" (Roblyer et al., 1997, p. 141).

> In developing a database, students are engaged in activities that contribute to the development of organizational skills and higher-order thinking skills. They refine a specific vocabulary. They research information on a given topic. They verify the accuracy of data, note the similarities and differences among data examined, and explore relationships. They classify information discovered. They consider how information might be communicated effectively to others. (Forcier, 1996, pp. 180–181)

Designing databases is consistent with cognitive views of learning. In preparing them, learners are faced with meaningful tasks, and the process is often facilitated by working with others. For example, a teacher working on a unit involving factors that influence economic growth might have students develop a database that includes the population and population density, gross national product, defense budget, literacy rate, and personal income of several countries. Once constructed, learners can compare the countries and form conclusions about the countries' economies and their potential for growth.

Learners can also create databases about themselves. For example, one second-grade class placed information such as height, eye color, favorite activity, favorite foods, and month of birth in a database and used it to create a class yearbook (Roblyer et al., 1997).

Facilitating Interaction.   When we think of interaction, we typically mean learners talking face-to-face. However, with technological advances such as e-mail and the

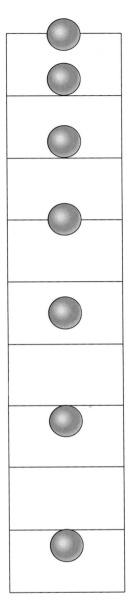

Figure 13.4

Illustration of a falling ball

13.27

To what concept from Chapter 7 does making simulations more "interactive" most closely relate? How does this increase learner understanding?

13.28

What kinds of content—concepts, rules, generalizations, principles, or organized bodies of knowledge—are most commonly represented in databases? Think back to your study of Chapter 7 and explain how databases help make information meaningful for learners.

Internet, students can now communicate and work with people thousands of miles away.

One application is to link students with a partner or penpal from another country. As they communicate, learners can compare school experiences, leisure activities, and other aspects of their different cultures. Learners can communicate directly, or they can send diary or journal entries. Writing to communicate with other people is an authentic task, which encourages students to write more, write more clearly and creatively, and use better grammar and spelling (Roblyer et al., 1997).

In addition to simple communication, students can collaborate with their penpals on group projects, send samples of work back and forth for feedback and evaluation, and provide information not easily accessed in other ways (Peha, 1995).

Developing Problem Solving Skills.   One of the difficulties in teaching problem solving is the creation of authentic problems that are not cut and dried. Problems are usually well defined and routine, the numbers needed to solve the problem (and only those numbers) are included, and even the computational operation is often suggested (Cognition and Technology Group at Vanderbilt, 1992).

These aren't the kinds of problems people typically encounter. Real-world problems are often ill-defined, and their solution isn't as routine as the problems students usually encounter in school. Technology can help learners acquire experience with more authentic problems. For example,

> Jasper has just purchased a new boat and is planning to drive it home. The boat consumes 5 gallons of fuel per hour and travels at 8 mph. The gas tank holds 12 gallons of gas. The boat is currently located at mile marker 156. Jasper's home dock is at mile marker 132. There are two gas stations on the way home. One is at mile marker 140.3 and the other is at mile marker 133. They charge $1.10 and $1.25 respectively. They don't take credit cards. Jasper started the day with $20. He bought 5 gallons of gas at $1.25 per gallon (not including a discount of 4 cents per gallon for paying cash) and paid $8.25 for repairs to his boat. It's 2:35. Sundown is at 7:52. Can Jasper make it home before sunset without running out of fuel? (Williams, Bareiss, & Reiser, 1996, p. 2)

This problem is part of a video-based series called *The Adventures of Jasper Woodbury,* developed by the Cognition and Technology Group at Vanderbilt (1992). Each segment begins with a brief adventure or story called an *anchor.* The problem you read has been condensed; the actual problem contains more detail, including a considerable amount of irrelevant information. The problem is purposely left ill-defined, allowing students the opportunity to identify, represent, and solve authentic problems.

13.29

Word processing is often compared to a typewriter, and databases are sometimes compared to file cabinets or Rolodex files. To what would a spreadsheet be best compared? Explain.

Students can also develop problem-solving skills with **spreadsheets** which are *programs that organize and manipulate numerical data* (Roblyer et al., 1997). For instance, students are faced with the question of what size pizzas (small, medium, or large) divided into different portions (such as four, six, or eight pieces) are most cost-effective. Are two small pizzas of four portions each, for example, more cost effective than one large pizza cut into eight pieces? They gather data from pizza companies, look at what kinds of calculations are necessary to solve the problem, offer hypotheses, enter data and formulas into the spreadsheet, and calculate the cost for pizzas of different radii. The process requires a great deal of higher-order thinking, and the spreadsheet helps them efficiently organize and examine the data and results (Paul, 1995).

Drill and Practice.   Drill and practice programs provide exercises that students work, usually one at a time, and feedback about the students' answers. Drill and practice activities vary in sophistication and the amount of feedback they provide.

Technology provides teachers with opportunities to interact with students as they work on realistic problems.

Drill and practice activities were among the first uses of computers in schools; they are still used extensively. They're controversial, however. Critics argue they're overused and used inappropriately; for example, as a way of introducing concepts and skills rather than reinforcing familiar ones. In addition, drill and practice is often criticized as behaviorist, emphasizing isolated skills at the expense of understanding.

Drill and practice activities have proven effective in one primary area, however—the development of automaticity. They are particularly effective for students with exceptionalities (Okolo, 1992; Higgins & Boone, 1993).

For example, research indicates that students with mild learning disabilities depend heavily on finger-counting strategies in computing math problems; this becomes a bottleneck when they move to more complex skills. Computer programs can be used to remediate this problem. They typically begin by pretesting to determine students' entry skills. They then build on the skills by introducing new math facts at a pace that ensures high success rates. When students fail to answer correctly, the programs provide the answer and retest that fact. To develop automaticity (and discourage finger counting), presentation rates are timed, and students' response times are shortened as their proficiency increases. Results are encouraging; experimental students outperformed comparable students who didn't use the programs, performed almost as well as nonhandicapped students, and maintained their gains over a four-month summer break (Hasselbring, Goin, & Bransford, 1988).

Programs that adjust to student background knowledge, success rates, and response times are a marked improvement over what some critics call "electronic flashcard machines" (Carlson & Silverman, 1986). These are valid criticisms. If computers are little more than flash cards on a screen, time, energy, and a great deal of money are being wasted.

Well-designed drill and practice programs should meet three criteria:

13.30

In this section we said that finger-counting strategies become a bottleneck when more complex skills are required, and automaticity is necessary. Why is automaticity important?

- *Control over the presentation rate.* Students should have as much time as they need to answer questions and study the feedback.

- *Appropriate feedback for correct answers.* Brief, attractive, positive feedback should be provided for correct answers.

- *Better reinforcement for correct answers.* Some programs inadvertently provide more attractive or interesting feedback for wrong answers, which encourages learners to answer incorrectly, so they can see the feedback. (Roblyer, et al., 1997)

Properly designed drill and practice activities have three advantages over traditional paper and pencil exercises. First, they provide learners with immediate feedback, often impossible otherwise. Second, they can be motivating. Third, they save teachers' time; students can be working on them while teachers attend to other students' needs.

Like all aspects of education, the effective use of technology requires thoughtful planning and wise teacher decisions. We hope that this section has provided information that will help in making those decisions.

Putting Learner-Centered Instruction into Perspective

In Chapter 12 we attempted to present a balanced look at teacher-centered approaches to instruction, and we tried to do the same in this chapter with learner-centered approaches. We end this chapter with three final reminders.

First, teachers need to keep in mind that all approaches to instruction are intended to help students reach goals; they are not goals in themselves. This statement may seem self-evident, but instructional strategies sometimes take on a life of their own—the strategy becomes the goal. For example, putting students into cooperative groups is not an appropriate goal. A valid goal might be to help students develop interpersonal skills and if that's the case, cooperative learning can be effective. Cooperative learning for the sake of cooperative learning, however, is inappropriate.

Second, regardless of approach, effective instruction is clearly aligned. Teachers must be clear about their goals and design learning activities to reach them. Learner-centered approaches do not in any way reduce the need for instructional alignment. Scott Sowell began his lesson with a problem and used a hands-on cooperative learning activity to help his students design and conduct experiments in order to understand the effect (or lack of effect) of length, weight, and angle on the frequency of a simple pendulum. He chose this approach because it was aligned with his goal. He didn't use a hands-on cooperative learning approach for its own sake.

Third, as we said in Chapter 12, no strategy—teacher-centered or learner-centered—is any better or worse than the ability of the person implementing it. The crucial issue is not the effectiveness of direct instruction, guided discovery, or cooperative learning, for example; it is the expertise of the teacher using them. For some goals, a teacher-centered approach like direct instruction may be most effective; for others, a learner-centered approach like guided discovery may be better (Airasian & Walsh, 1997).

In the past, experts and researchers tried to develop "teacher proof" methods and curricula. They were unsuccessful. We would be better served trying to prepare teachers capable of exercising sound judgment, flexibility, and sensitivity (Michaels & O'Connor, 1990). This is why we believe that understanding learners and learning is so important. This is the understanding we hope you acquire by studying educational psychology.

Classroom Connections

Using Learner-Centered Approaches to Instruction in Your Classroom

1. Use a variety of examples and representations of the topics you teach.

   • A teacher beginning a unit on folktales writes a series of "folktales" about the school principal and other teachers. She also has students read folktales about characters such as Paul Bunyan and Pecos Bill and provides a matrix linking folktales to true historical events. She then discusses some contemporary figures who have been described in the media as "folk heroes" and how they may have achieved that status. Finally, she has the students write their own "folktales" about anyone they choose.

2. Use guided-discovery approaches to instruction to develop deep understanding of ideas.

   • A fourth-grade teacher embeds examples of possessive pronouns and singular and plural possessive nouns in the context of a paragraph. He then guides students' discussion as they develop explanations for why sentences (such as "The girls' and boys' accomplishments in the middle school were noteworthy, as were the children's feats in the elementary school") were punctuated the way they were.

   • A first-grade teacher begins a unit on reptiles by bringing a snake and turtle to class. She also includes colored pictures of lizards, alligators, and sea turtles. She has students describe the live animals and the pictures and then guides them to the essential characteristics of reptiles.

Conducting Effective Discussions in Your Classroom

3. Ensure that students have a solid background of information before conducting discussions.

   • A biology teacher is planning a discussion of global warming. Before the discussion, she presents information about the depletion of the Amazon rain forest, U.S. data on carbon dioxide emissions, and Eastern European countries' records on air emissions.

4. Begin discussions with a clear issue or problem and keep the discussion focused on the issue.

   • A history teacher involved in a discussion of the efficacy of the U.S. involvement in Vietnam asks simply, "Considering the historical context, was America's decision to go into Vietnam a wise one?" He then keeps the students focused on America's initial decision to enter the conflict. When they discuss the war's outcome, he refocuses them on the original decision.

Using Cooperative Learning Effectively in Your Classroom

5. Introduce students to cooperative learning by using simple tasks.

   • A second-grade teacher begins the school year by having cooperative learning groups work on simple, convergent tasks. She keeps the time limits short and discusses group problems immediately. Later she gives groups more complex and open-ended problems to solve.

Using Individualization Effectively in Your Classroom

6. Vary objectives and learning activities.

   • To increase students' interest in art, a kindergarten teacher provides watercolors and clay and allows students to work on individual projects with these different media.

   • A social-studies teacher uses a unit on American immigrants to allow her students to explore their own cultural and ethnic backgrounds. After introducing the topic, she has students work individually or in groups, exploring the history of their ethnic group in the United States as well as their own family histories. At the end of the unit, students share their findings.

Using technology effectively in your classroom.

7. Use technology to reach goals that cannot be reached more efficiently in other ways.
   - A middle-school teacher uses a computer program called *Oregon Trail* to develop students' problem solving skills. While using the simulation, students work in groups to make decisions about routes, supplies, and rates of travel.
   - To help her students understand the need to write coherently, a fifth-grade teacher has them use word processing programs to scramble sentences, share the scrambled sentences with partners, and have the partners put them back together in ways that make sense.

Windows on Classrooms

At the beginning of this chapter, you saw how Scott Sowell planned and conducted his lesson in an effort to actively involve his students in learning and to place them at the center of the learning process.

Let's look now at a teacher working with a class of ninth-grade geography students. As you read the case study, consider the extent to which the teacher applied the information you've studied in this chapter in her lesson.

Judy Holmquist, a ninth-grade geography teacher at Lakeside Junior High School, is involved in a unit on climate regions of the United States. To begin the unit, she divided the class into groups, and each group gathered information about the geography, economy, ethnic groups, and future issues in Florida, California, New York, and Alaska. She then put the information the students had gathered (see p. 573) into the matrix.

Judy began the day's lesson by referring the class to information they had gathered and put on the chart and reminded them they would be looking for similarities and differences in the information.

Focusing their attention on the information in the first column, she began by saying, "What I want you to do is get with your partner and write down three differences and similarities on just the geography portion of the chart. I want three, and I want them written down on paper, and I want you to each write them down so that if I call on one or the other of you, you've got the information right in front of you. . . . So get together with your partner."

As Judy moved among the groups, offering help and answering questions, Chris raised his hand and said, "I don't understand exactly what we're supposed to do."

"Okay, take a look at the geography column. . . . You give me three things that are alike and three things that are different," Judy explained quietly.

Video Case

"In all four of them or in two of them?" Matt continued.

"In all four of the regions. Yes. From all four of the regions. Yes. You got it," she confirmed, as they went to work.

"Three things that are similar; three differences," she repeated in response to a question from another group, and she repeated it

	Geography	Economy	Ethnic Groups	Future Issues
F L O R I D A	Coastal plain Florida uplands Hurricane season Warm ocean currents Dec. 69 1.8 (Temp. Moisture) March 72 2.4 June 81 9.3 Sept. 82 7.6	Citrus industry Tourism Fishing Forestry Cattle	Native Americans Spanish Cubans Haitians African American	Population explosion Immigration problems Pollution Tax revisions Money for education
C A L I F O R N I A	Coastal ranges Cascades Sierra Nevadas Central Valley Desert Dec. 54 2.5 (Temp. Moisture) March 57 2.8 June 66 T Sept. 69 .3	Citrus industry Wine/vineyards Fishing Lumber Television/Hollywood Tourism Computers	Spanish Mexican Asian African American	Earthquakes Deforestation Population explosion Pollution Immigration problems
N E W Y O R K	Atlantic Coastal Plain New England uplands Appalachian Plateau Adirondack Mts. Dec. 37 3.9 (Temp. Moisture) March 42 4.1 June 72 3.7 Sept. 68 3.9	Vegetables Fishing Apples Forestry Light manufacturing Entertainment/TV	Dutch Native Americans Italians French Polish Puerto Rican African American English Irish Russian	Industrial decline Decaying urban areas Waste disposal Crime Homelessness Crowded schools
A L A S K A	Rocky Mountains Brooks Range Panhandle area Plateaus between mountains Islands/treeless Warm ocean currents Dec. −7 .9 (Temp. Moisture) March 11 .4 June 60 1.4 Sept. 46 1.0	Mining Fishing Trapping Lumbering/forestry Oil/pipeline Tourism	Eskimo (Inuit) Native Americans Russian	Unemployment Cost of living Oil spills Pollution

a second and a third time in response to other questions, in the process reminding the class that they had four minutes to complete the task.

"The temperature like in September in New York and California. Can I put that down as the same, cuz they're like 68 in California and 69 in New York?" Kiki asked as they were working.

"Yes," Judy nodded, "and you might think about why, too," reminding the class that they could use the climate and physical maps in their books as additional sources of information.

"Like for similarities, do they have to be alike in all of them?"

"Not necessarily, no. It could be in just two of them."

"Okay," Ann said brightly.

Judy continued to respond to questions as students worked, gave them another minute, and then called them back together.

"You look like you're doing a good job. . . . Okay, I think we're ready."

"Give me a piece of information, Jackie, from the geography column," Judy began, pointing to the overhead.

"Mmm, they all have mountains except for Florida."

"Okay, they all have mountains except for Florida," Judy repeated and wrote it under "Similarities" on the chalkboard.

"Give me something else. . . . Jeff?"

"They all touch the oceans in places."

"Okay, what else? Give me something else. Go ahead, Todd."

"They're all in four corners."

"Okay, we have four corners."

"What else? . . . Missy?"

"New York and Florida both have coastal plains."

"Okay, New York and Florida both have coastal plains," she again repeated, writing the information on the chalkboard.

"Okay, you two in the back. I can hear you. Scott, give me something."

"They all have cold weather in December."

"Aha," Judy chuckled, "We're going to look at that one. Cold weather in December."

"Okay. . . . Tim?"

"All the summer temperatures are above 50% . . . er 50°," Tim answered to some laughter from the rest of the class.

"What else can you tell me? How about some differences?" Judy encouraged. "Okay, Chris?"

"The temperature ranges a lot."

"All right. . . . John?"

"Different climate zones."

"Alaska gets below zero. It's the only . . . is the only one that gets below zero."

"It's the only one that gets below zero in winter. Is that what you said?" Judy asked to confirm Kiki's response, and Kiki nodded.

"Okay, let's have a little bit more. I know you've got some more. I see it written on your paper."

"Carnisha, do you have anything to add?"

"All except Alaska have less than 4 inches of moisture in the winter," Carnisha offered.

"Okay, have we exhausted your lists? Anyone else have anything more to add?"

Judy waited a few seconds and then said, "Okay, now I want you to look at the economy, and I want you to write down three similarities and

three differences in terms of the economy. You have three minutes."

As students again returned to their groups, Judy monitored them as she had done earlier.

After they finished, she again called for and received a number of similarities and differences based on the information in the economy column.

She then shifted the direction of the lesson, saying, "Okay, great. . . . Now, let's see if we can link geography and economics. For example, why, in terms of a similarity, do they all have fishing?" she asked, waving her hand across the class as she walked toward the back of the room. "John?"

"They're all near the coast."

"Okay, why do they all have forestry? . . . Okay, Jeremy?"

"They all have lots of trees," he answered to smiles from the rest of the class.

"Now, if they have lots of trees, what does this tell you about their climate?"

"It's warm enough for them to grow."

"But along with being warm enough, it has . . . ?"

"Fertile soil."

"And?"

"Moisture."

"Great, Okay.

"Now, let's take a look. We have fruit in California and Florida. Why do we have the citrus industry there?"

"Okay, Jackie, good," she said, seeing Jackie's raised hand.

"Never mind."

"Pardon?"

"Never mind."

"Oh, you know," Judy encouraged.

"No."

"Why do we grow oranges down here?"

"It's the climate."

"All right, because of the climate. Okay, now. Jackie says it's because of the climate. What kind of climate allows the citrus industry? . . . Tim?"

". . . Humid subtropical."

"Okay, humid subtropical. Humid subtropical means that we have what? . . . Go ahead."

"Long humid summers, short mild winters," he replied, reading from the book.

"Okay. Let's look at tourism. Why does each area have tourism?" Judy continued. "Okay, Lance?"

"Because they're all spread out. They're each at four corners,

and they have different seasons that they're popular in."

Seeing that the period was nearing a close, Judy said, "Okay, let's deal with one issue. I want you to summarize . . . Listen up. I want to know what effect climate has on the economy of those regions."

She gave the class one minute to work again in their pairs, announcing that she expected to hear from as many people as possible.

"Let's see what you've got for an answer," she said after the minute had passed. "Braden, you had one. . . . Okay, I want to know what effect, . . . listen up, excuse me, Brooks, . . . I want to know what effect geography, which is cli-

mate and landforms, has on the economy," she said, pointing at Braden.

"If you have mountains in the area, you can't have farmland," he responded.

"Okay, what else? . . . Becky?"

"The climate affects like what's grown and like what's done inside the section."

"Okay, great. Climate affects what's grown and what was the last part of that?"

"Like what's done," Becky repeated as the bell rang.

Judy waved, "Okay, great. Class dismissed," as students began gathering their materials to move to their next class period.

Questions for Discussion and Analysis

Analyze Judy's lesson in the context of the information in this chapter. In doing your analysis, you may want to consider the following questions. In each case, be specific and take information directly from the case study.

1. How effectively did Judy apply the characteristics of learner-centered instruction in her lesson? Explain, using information taken directly from the case study.

2. Of the learner-centered strategies described in the chapter, which did Judy use, or most nearly use? Explain.

3. How effectively did Judy use cooperative learning to meet the goals of her lesson? Assess her use of cooperative learning, using the following criteria: (a) clearly specified task, (b) concrete product, and (c) teacher monitoring.

4. Think back to the essential teaching skills discussed in Chapter 11. Which of these did Judy Holmquist demonstrate in her lesson? Confirm your conclusions with information taken directly from the case study.

5. Provide an overall assessment of the lesson. Use evidence taken from the case study in making your assessment. What could Judy have done to make the lesson more effective? Be specific in making your suggestions.

Summary

Characteristics of Learner-Centered Instruction

Learner-centered instruction, grounded in cognitive views of learning, places learners at the center of the learning process and emphasizes thought-demanding processes such as explaining, finding evidence, providing examples, and generalizing in an effort to acquire deep understanding of the topics being studied. Learner-centered instruction is based on learner-centered psychological principles, which view learners as intrinsically motivated, active seekers of knowledge who work with others to socially construct meaning.

Planning for Learner-Centered Instruction

Planning for learner-centered instruction involves identifying goals, designing learning activities to reach the goals, and constructing appropriate assessments. In addition, teachers planning for learner-centered activities consider how to make tasks authentic, represent content in a variety of ways, accommodate learners' current understanding and social interactions, and create and maintain productive learning environments.

Types of Learner-Centered Instruction

Learner-centered approaches include guided discovery, inquiry, discussions, cooperative learning, individualization, and interactive applications of technology.

Teachers using guided discovery help learners reach goals by helping them identify patterns in information that has been provided. Inquiry helps students learn to solve problems by making and testing hypotheses with data. Discussions promote social and higher-order cognitive abilities by providing opportunities for learners to interact with each other. Cooperative learning develops thinking as well as collaborative social skills through structured small-group activities. Individualization tailors instruction to the unique needs of each student by varying time, learning activities, or instructional materials. Technology can be used to support each of the other approaches.

Putting Learner-Centered Instruction into Perspective

The approach to instruction that teachers use should depend on their goals. Effective teachers have clear goals and present learning activities that are aligned with them. Effective teachers remember that the approach to instruction is a means to reaching the goal; it isn't the goal itself.

Important Concepts

authentic tasks (p. 545)

contextual planning model (p. 543)

cooperative learning (p. 557)

databases (p. 567)

discovery learning (p. 550)

discussions (p. 554)

guided discovery (p. 550)

individualization (p. 564)

inquiry (p. 553)

Jigsaw II (p. 559)

spreadsheets (p. 568)

STAD (p. 558)

unstructured discovery (p. 550)

14

Assessing Classroom Learning

Chapter Outline

Kathy Stevens walked among the desks of her seventh-graders as they worked on their seatwork assignment. "Check that one again," she whispered as she passed Kim. Checking each student's work as she walked by, she continued this process for another five minutes. She then called for the students' attention.

"Let me hand back your quizzes," she announced. "You did fine on today's. You seem to understand when you explain your solutions, and you're doing okay on your home-work, so we're going to have our test Thursday. We'll review a little more tomorrow to be sure you understand the word problems," she smiled.

"Now, let's take a look at several items that a few of you missed on the quiz," she continued as she handed the papers back to students.

Later, as Kathy worked on her test in the faculty lounge, Ken Allen, another math teacher, walked by. "How's your new system working?" he asked.

"Good," she replied. "Since I've been giving the short quiz every day, they're more conscientious about their homework, and they did better on the last test."

"Mmm. . . . Tell me again exactly what you're doing."

"I just give them a problem or two every day that's based on their homework. I score it while they begin the next day's assignment, and I hand it back at the end of the period. If we have an extra-tough topic, I don't get a quiz in every day, but they get at least three a week."

Quizzes, tests, and other assessments have a powerful affect on student learning. One review of research on classroom evaluation practices put it this way:

> Here is something approaching a law of learning behavior for students: namely that the quickest way to change learning is to change the assessment system. (Elton & Laurillard, 1979, p. 100)

Despite its importance, teachers often feel ill-prepared to deal with the complexities of classroom assessment (Linn, 1990). Experienced teachers express concerns about their ability to write individual assessment items, to construct valid assessments, and to assign grades (Crooks, 1988; Haertel, 1986). Beginning teachers also express concerns about their ability to assess student progress (Lomax, 1994), ranking this problem fourth after classroom management, motivation, and dealing with individual differences (Veenman, 1984).

In this chapter, we address these concerns by examining the effects of assessment on learning and motivation, analyzing teachers' assessment patterns, and describing ways to design effective classroom assessments.

After you've completed this chapter, you should be able to meet the following objectives:

- Explain basic assessment concepts.
- Describe classroom teachers' assessment patterns.
- Analyze assessment items for factors that detract from their validity.
- Construct alternative assessments in your content area or grade level.
- Apply effective assessment procedures in your own classroom.

Classroom Assessment

The case study at the beginning of the chapter illustrates the process of assessment, one of the most basic and difficult tasks teachers face in their work. **Classroom assessment** *includes all the processes involved in making decisions about students' learning progress* (Airasian, 1997). It includes observations of students' written work, their answers to questions in class, and performance on teacher-made and standardized tests. It includes authentic assessments, such as watching first-graders print, observing a word-processing class type a letter, or having auto mechanics students repair an engine. It also involves decisions, such as assigning grades, reteaching a topic, and providing additional instruction. When combined, *these elements make up a teacher's* **assessment system.** In Kathy's case, her system included monitoring her students' learning progress by using their homework, her quizzes, and her tests.

Functions of Classroom Assessment

In addition to gathering information and making decisions about learning progress, assessment accomplishes two other important goals: (a) increasing learning and (b) increasing motivation (Crooks, 1988).

The relationship between learning and assessment is strong and robust. Students learn more in classes where assessment is an integral part of instruction than in those where it isn't, and brief, frequent assessments are more effective than long, infrequent ones (Bangert-Drowns, Kulik, & Kulik, 1991; Dempster, 1991; Kika, McLaughlin, & Dixon, 1992).

Implying a link between testing and motivation is controversial because some critics argue that assessment can detract from motivation. In the real world, however, evidence runs counter to this argument (Crooks, 1988; Eggen, 1997). Think about your own experiences. In which classes did you learn the most and for which did you study the hardest? For most students, they're the ones in which they're thoroughly assessed and given frequent feedback. As we saw in Chapter 10, learners have a need to understand what they are supposed to learn, why they are learning it, and how they are progressing. Assessment gives them information about their progress, exerting a powerful influence on the amount and ways students study (Airasian, 1997; Stiggins, 1997).

Measurement and Evaluation

Two basic processes are involved in assessment: **measurement,** *which includes all the information teachers gather as part of the assessment process,* and **evaluation,** *which is the decisions teachers make on the basis of the measurements.*

Effective teachers use a range of measurement tools to capture different aspects of student learning. Some, as listed in Figure 14.1, use traditional paper-and-pencil formats, whereas others employ alternative formats to assess higher-order thinking and problem-solving ability.

Formal and Informal Measurement

Informal measurements are *measurements gathered incidentally,* such as listening to students' comments and answers to questions, noticing puzzled looks, or seeing that a student isn't paying attention. In contrast, *the process of systematically gathering information is called* **formal measurement.** Tests and quizzes are formal measurements, as are performance observations, such as a physical education teacher observing the number of sit-ups a student can do.

Figure 14.1 Traditional and alternative measurement formats

Traditional Measurement Formats	Alternative Measurement Formats
True–false	Specific performance task
Multiple choice	Timed trial
Matching	Exhibition of work
Fill in the blank	Reflective journal entry
Short, open-ended answer	Open-ended oral presentation
Paragraph response to specific question	Oral response to specific question
Paragraph response to open-ended question	Collaborative group project
Essay	Audiovisual presentation
	Debate
	Simulation

Source: Adapted from Cheek (1993).

14.1

How would a behaviorist explain the advantage of frequent, announced quizzes over those given infrequently? (Hint: Think about the concept of *reinforcement schedules* from Chapter 6.)

14.2

Should you describe for your students precisely what your tests will cover? Why or why not? Should you go over tests item by item once they've been taken and scored? Again, why or why not?

14.3

Identify an important similarity and an important difference between traditional and alternative measurement formats. Also identify an advantage and a disadvantage of each.

14.4

Identify an example of an informal measurement in the case study illustrating Kathy Stevens's work with her students.

The Need for Systematic Assessment

Informal measurements are essential in helping teachers make the frequent instructional decisions required in every class. Kathy used them to help her decide when to stop seatwork and when to schedule a test. Teachers also use informal measurements to decide how fast they can teach a topic, whom they should call on next, and when they should stop one activity and move on to the next.

Informal measurements have a drawback, however. Because teachers don't obtain the same information from each student, they don't know about individual students' progress. Concluding that the whole class understands an idea on the basis of responses from only a few can be a mistake.

Without realizing it, teachers sometimes make decisions as important as assigning grades on the basis of informal measurements. Students who respond readily and have engaging personalities are often awarded higher grades than their less outgoing peers. Further, students who are physically attractive are often judged more favorably by teachers than their less attractive peers (Ritts, Patterson, & Tubbs, 1992). Gathering systematic information about each student's progress is one way to prevent these biases.

Systematic assessment is particularly important in the lower elementary grades, where teachers often rely on performance assessments, such as handwriting samples and verbal identification of written numerals, to make evaluation decisions. The question "Could I defend and document this decision to a parent if necessary?" is a helpful guideline in this process.

Validity: Making Appropriate Evaluation Decisions

Validity *means that the assessment measures what it is supposed to measure.* It involves "the adequacy and appropriateness of the interpretations made from assessments, with

14.5

What would be an example of a systematic assessment in the class you're in now? What makes it systematic? What would be an example of an assessment that is not systematic?

Gathering systematic information about each student and keeping current records about student's learning progress help ensure accurate assessment.

regard to a particular use" (Gronlund & Linn, 1995, p. 47). Validity describes the link between the information gathered and the decisions made from that information (Shepard, 1993). From an instructional point of view, validity is the extent to which a measurement is congruent or aligned with goals and instruction.

The concept of *validity* is at the heart of many controversies in assessment. For example, critics argue that standardized tests are culturally biased and, as a result, are invalid for minority students (Helms, 1992). Other critics assert that questions measuring isolated and decontextualized skills—such as standardized tests—give an incomplete and therefore invalid picture of student understanding. This assertion has contributed to the movement toward "alternative" or "authentic" assessment (Herman, Aschbacher, & Winters, 1992; Moss, 1992). We examine authentic assessment in detail later in the chapter.

In classrooms, validity suffers when assessment decisions are made on the basis of personality, appearance, or other factors not related to learning goals. Also, teachers who give lower scores on essay items because of messy handwriting are using invalid criteria. Unfortunately, these actions are usually unconscious; without realizing it, teachers often base their assessments on appearance, rather than on substance.

None of this implies, however, that teachers are doomed to use invalid assessments. Teachers who continually look for ways to improve their assessments, analyze patterns in student responses, and revise their measurements will increase the validity of their assessment system. These actions are a part of the reflective attitude toward teaching that we emphasize throughout this text.

Reliability: Consistency in Measurement

Reliability, an intuitively sensible concept, *describes the extent to which measurements are consistent.* For instance, if your bathroom scale's readings vary whether your weight does or not, it is not reliable. We are aggravated by people who are unreliable because we can't count on them to follow through on what they agree to do. Your old scale and those people are inconsistent. Unreliable measurements cannot be valid, even if the measurements are congruent with the teacher's goals.

The influence of scoring consistency on reliability can be illustrated with essay tests, which are often unreliable. Studies indicate that different instructors with similar backgrounds, ostensibly using the same criteria, have awarded grades ranging from excellent to failure on the same essay (Gronlund, 1993). When inconsistency in scoring occurs, lack of reliability makes the item invalid.

Similarly, informal measurements are often unreliable, because not all students respond to the same question. Uncertainty on one student's face doesn't mean the other students are confused; likewise, a quick, confident answer from one student doesn't necessarily mean the entire class understands the topic. One solution is the use of formal, more reliable assessments.

Traditional Assessment

The way teachers historically have assessed learning, and the way much of learning will continue to be assessed, is through the use of teacher-made tests. When well designed and constructed, these tests provide valid assessments of many aspects of student learning (Gronlund & Linn, 1995). In this section, we examine teachers' assessment patterns

14.6

Describe an example of a measurement that might be invalid for a student from a minority group. Why would it be invalid?

14.7

A junior-high teacher gave her students the following writing assignment: "Describe a room in your home. Check to make sure your writing is correct in terms of grammar and punctuation." When she returned the papers, they had two grades: one for creativity and one for punctuation and grammar. Are both of these grades valid? Explain.

14.8

Research indicates that increasing the length of a test increases reliability, but studies of child development indicate that attention spans of young children are limited. How can teachers reconcile these two findings?

and discuss ways of constructing measurement items to make them as valid and reliable as possible.

Teachers' Assessment Patterns

Laura Brinson's second-graders are working on subtracting one-digit from two-digit numbers with regrouping. She put a series of problems on the chalkboard, and her students are now busily solving them as Laura circulates.

"Check this one again, Kelly," she says, seeing that Kelly had written

$$
\begin{array}{r}
24 \\
-9 \\
\hline
25
\end{array}
$$

on her paper.

"I think I'll take a grade on this one," Laura says to herself. She collects the papers after the students finish, scores them, and writes "90" in her grade book for Kelly because she missed one of the 10 problems from the chalkboard.

Laura's assessment of her second-graders is typical of elementary teachers, particularly at the primary level (see Table 14.1). She relies heavily on informal measures versus formal, teacher-made tests. In addition, elementary teachers tend to use commercially prepared items, such as those that come with textbook series, and they emphasize affective goals (Marso & Pigge, 1992; Stiggins & Conklin, 1992).

Middle-school and senior-high teachers' assessment practices differ from those of elementary teachers in at least two ways. They depend more on traditional tests than on performance measures, and they prepare their own items instead of relying on published tests. Table 14.2 summarizes characteristics of these teacher-made items (Boothroyd, McMorris, & Pruzek, 1992; Frary, Cross, & Weber, 1992; Marso & Pigge, 1992).

14.9

Why do elementary teachers tend to rely on performance measures to a greater extent than middle or secondary teachers?

Table 14.1   Elementary teachers' assessment patterns

Characteristic	Description
Performance measures	Primary teachers rely heavily on actual samples of student work (e.g., the ability to form letters or write numerals) to evaluate student learning (Marso & Pigge, 1992).
Informal measurements	Measurement is often informal, as was the case in Laura's class. She comments, "I take a grade a few times a week. I don't really have a regular schedule that I follow for grading." Further, teachers sometimes give social and background characteristics greater emphasis than ability (Marso & Pigge, 1992; Salmon-Cox, 1981).
Commercially prepared tests	When they do test, elementary teachers depend heavily on commercially prepared and published tests. Teachers in the primary grades rarely prepare their own formal tests, instead using informal assessments or using exercises from texts or teachers' editions.
Emphasis on affective goals	Primary teachers emphasize affective goals, such as "Gets along well with others" (Salmon-Cox, 1981). In one analysis of kindergarten progress reports sent home to parents, over a third of the categories were devoted to intrapersonal or interpersonal factors (Freeman & Hatch, 1989).

Table 14.2 Characteristics of teacher-made test items

1. Teachers commonly use test items containing many technical errors.
2. Teachers rarely use techniques such as item analysis and tables of specifications to improve the quality of their items. Once items are constructed, teachers tend to reuse them without revision.
3. Even though teachers state that higher order objectives are important, over three fourths of all items are written at the knowledge/recall level, and most of those above the knowledge level are in math and science. In other areas, 90% to 100% of the items are written at the knowledge level.
4. About 1% of all teacher-made test items use the essay format. This figure is higher in English classes.
5. The short-answer format is used most frequently, such as:
   a. Which two countries border on Mexico? _____

   _____
   b. Why does a cactus have needles, whereas an oak tree has broad leaves? _____

   _____
6. Matching items are common, for example:
   _____ A quadrilateral with one pair of opposite equal sides
   _____ A three-sided plane figure with two sides equal in length
   _____ A quadrilateral with opposite sides equal in length

   a. Parallelogram
   b. Pentagon
   c. Rhombus
   d. Scalene triangle
   e. Square
   f. Isosceles triangle

Several factors help explain the patterns in Table 14.2. First, teachers' jobs are complex and demanding, and teachers respond by simplifying their work (Stiggins, Conklin, & Bridgeford, 1986). Reusing an item is simpler than revising it, for example. Essay items are easy to write but difficult and time-consuming to score; multiple-choice items are just the opposite. The simplest alternatives are the completion and matching formats, which are most popular with teachers. Further, knowledge and recall items are easy to construct, score, and defend.

In addition, teachers lack confidence in their ability to write good test items and to improve test quality (Marso & Pigge, 1992). Because of inadequate training, teachers have difficulty writing unambiguous test items at a level above knowledge and recall (Carter, 1984; Fleming & Chambers, 1983).

These findings indicate a need for better quality assessments, "particularly items that are less ambiguous and require more of students than the simple recall of facts and information" (Stiggins et al., 1986, p. 9).

14.10

Explain why most test items written above the knowledge level are in math and science.

Designing Valid Test Items

We introduced the concept of *validity* earlier and we reexamine it now, focusing on specific test items. An item is valid if students who understand the content answer the item correctly and those who don't understand it get the item wrong. For instance, if you've given a multiple-choice item with *a* as the answer but most of the class chose *c*, the results may indicate a general misconception, a difficult idea, or a lack of good teaching—or, the item may have been misleading. If a question is misleading, it's invalid; the other alternatives are not problems with validity. One way to discern where the trouble lies is to discuss the item with your class and determine why so many people selected the incorrect choice.

If clues to the correct answer are included in the item, students may answer correctly without understanding the topic; this, too, makes the item invalid. Learners as young as fifth- and sixth-graders can use item clues to identify correct choices (Sudweeks, Baird, & Petersen, 1990). Teachers confess they have trouble writing effective items but believe many of these problems could be eliminated through training (Carter, 1986). Our goal for this section is to help you write better, more valid items.

Using the concept of *validity* as our framework, we now turn to a discussion of specific item formats. Item formats can be classified as *selected-response formats*—multiple-choice, true–false, or matching—which require learners to choose the correct answer from a list of alternatives, or *supply formats*—completion and essay—which require learners to produce their own answers (Stiggins, 1997). Items can also be classified as *objective,* which are those on which equally competent learners will obtain the same scores (e.g., multiple-choice), or *subjective,* where the scores are influenced by the judgment of the person doing the scoring (e.g., essay) (Gronlund & Linn, 1995). Let's examine objective, selected-response formats first.

Multiple-Choice Items

The multiple-choice format is one of the most effective for preparing valid and reliable items at different levels of thinking; most standardized tests use this format. Gronlund (1993) suggests that teachers should try writing multiple-choice items first and then switch to another format only if the objectives or content require it.

Multiple-choice items *contain a stem, which consists of a question or incomplete statement, and several alternative choices; students choose the best one.* The incorrect alternatives are called **distracters** *because they are designed to distract students who don't understand the content being measured in the item.*

Items may be written so that only one choice is correct, or they may be in a "best-answer" form, in which more than one choice is partially correct but one is clearly bet-

Table 14.3 Guidelines for preparing multiple-choice items

1. Present one clear problem in the stem of the item.
2. Make all distracters plausible and attractive to the uninformed.
3. Vary the position of the correct choice randomly. Be careful to avoid overusing choice *c*.
4. Avoid similar wording in the stem and the correct choice.
5. Avoid phrasing the correct choice in more technical terms than distracters.
6. Keep the correct answer and the distracters similar in length. A longer or shorter answer should usually be used as an incorrect choice.
7. Avoid using absolute terms (e.g., *always, never*) in the incorrect choices.
8. Keep the stem and distracters grammatically consistent.
9. Avoid using two distracters with the same meaning.
10. Emphasize *negative wording* by underlining if it is used.
11. Use "none of the above" with care, and avoid "all of the above" as a choice.

Source: How to Construct Achievement Tests, 4th ed., by N. Gronlund, 1988. Upper Saddle River, NJ: Prentice Hall. Copyright 1988 by Prentice Hall. Adapted by permission.

ter than the others. The best-answer form is more demanding, promotes higher-level thinking, and measures more complex achievement. Guidelines for preparing multiple-choice items are summarized in Table 14.3.

14.13

What is the simplest and most effective way to correct Item 2 in Figure 14.2?

The Stem. The stem should pose one question or problem for students to consider. With this guideline in mind, analyze the items in Figure 14.2.

The first item is essentially a series of true–false statements linked only by the fact that they fall under the same stem. The second item presents two problems. If students select choice *b*, for example, it could be they don't know that veins are part of the circulatory system, or it could be they don't realize that veins carry blood back to the heart rather than away from it. The third item, in comparison, presents a single, clearly stated problem, with the distracters providing possible alternatives.

Distracters. Although carefully written stems are important, good distracters are critical for effective multiple-choice items. Distracters should target students' misconceptions so that these mistaken views can be identified and remediated. One way to generate effective distracters is to first include the stem on a test as a short answer or fill-in-the-blank item. As students respond, you can use incorrect answers as distracters for future tests, knowing that these are viable alternatives for some students (Stiggins, 1997).

Many problems with faulty multiple-choice items involve clues in distracters that allow students to answer the question correctly without knowing the content. Figure 14.3 contains six items with faulty distracters. See if you can identify features in them that are inconsistent with the guidelines. Then turn to the discussion that follows.

What kinds of problems did you find with the distracters? In Item 1, you can see that forms of the term *circulate* appear in both the stem and the correct answer.

In Item 2, the correct choice is written in more technical terms than the distracters. Teachers fall into this trap when they take the correct choice directly from the text and then make up the distracters. Their informal language appears in the distracters, whereas text language appears in the correct answer.

Figure 14.2 Multiple-choice items of differing quality

1. The circulatory system is the system that
   *a. transports blood throughout the body
   b. includes the lungs
   c. protects the vital organs of the body
   d. turns the food we eat into energy
2. Which of the following is a part and function of the circulatory system?
   *a. The blood vessels that carry food and oxygen to the body cells
   b. The blood veins that carry blood away from the heart
   c. The lungs that pump blood to all parts of the body
   d. The muscles that help move a person from one place to another
3. Which of the following describes the function of the circulatory system?
   *a. It moves blood from your heart to other parts of your body.
   b. It turns the sandwich you eat into energy you need to keep you going throughout the day.
   c. It removes solid and liquid waste materials from your body.
   d. It protects your heart, brain, and other body parts from being injured.

Figure 14.3   Constructing distracters for multiple-choice items

1. Which of the following is a function of the circulatory system?
    a. to support the vital organs of the body
   *b. to circulate the blood throughout the body
    c. to transfer nerve impulses from the brain to the muscles
    d. to provide for the movement of the body's large muscles
2. Of the following, the definition of *population density* is
    a. the number of people who live in your city or town
    b. the number of people who voted in the last presidential election
   *c. the number of people per square mile in a country
    d. the number of people in cities compared to small towns
3. Of the following, the most significant cause of World War II was
    a. American aid to Great Britain
    b. Italy's conquering of Ethiopia.
    c. Japan's war on China
   *d. the devastation of the German economy as a result of the Treaty of Versailles.
4. Which of the following is the best description of an insect?
    a. It always has one pair of antennae on its head.
   *b. It has three body parts.
    c. None lives in water.
    d. It breathes through lungs.
5. The one of the following that is not a reptile is a
    a. alligator.
    b. lizard.
   *c. frog.
    d. turtle.
6. Which of the following illustrates a verb form used as a participle?
    a. Running is good exercise.
   *b. I saw a jumping frog contest on TV yesterday.
    c. Thinking is hard for many of us.
    d. All of the above.

In Item 3, the correct choice is significantly longer than the incorrect choices; a similar clue is given when the correct choice is shorter than distracters. If one choice is significantly longer or shorter than others, it should be a distracter.

In Item 4, choices *a* and *c* are stated in absolute terms, which alerts test-wise students. Absolute terms, such as *all, always, none,* and *never,* are usually associated with incorrect answers. If used, they should be in the correct answer, such as "All algae contain chlorophyll."

The stem in Item 5 is stated in negative terms without being emphasized. Also, choice *a* is grammatically inconsistent with the stem. One solution to the problem is to end the stem with *a(n),* thereby preserving grammatical consistency.

In Item 6, choices *a* and *c* are automatically eliminated because both are gerunds and only one answer can be correct. Also, Item 6 uses "all of the above" as a choice; it can't be correct if *a* and *c* are eliminated. That makes *b* the only possible choice. A student could get the item right and have no idea what a participle is.

14.14

Rewrite each of the six items in Figure 14.3 so that they are consistent with the guidelines.

As you can see, preparing good multiple-choice items requires thought and care. With effort and practice, however, you can become skilled at it, and when you do, you have a powerful learning and measurement tool.

Measuring Higher-Level Learning. Although most of the examples presented to this point measure low-level outcomes, the multiple-choice format can be effectively used to assess higher-order thinking as well. In an "interpretive exercise," students are presented with material similar, but not identical, to information presented in class and are asked to analyze it in some way (Gronlund, 1993). The material may be in the form of a graph, chart, table, map, picture, or case study. Figure 14.4 contains an example from the area of science.

In this case, the teacher's goal was for science students to be able to apply information about heat, expansion, mass, volume, and density to a familiar but unique situation. This type of exercise promotes transfer, helps develop critical thinking, and can increase learner motivation.

Figure 14.4 Interpretive exercise used with the multiple-choice format

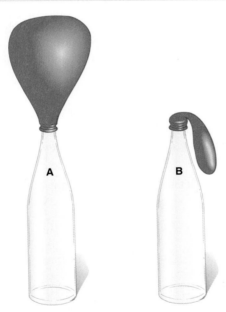

Look at the drawings above. They represent two identical soft drink bottles covered with identical balloons sitting side-by-side on a table. Bottle A was then heated. Which of the following is the most accurate statement?
  a. The density of the air in Bottle A is greater than the density of the air in Bottle B.
 *b. The density of the air in Bottle A is less than the density of the air in Bottle B.
  c. The density of the air in Bottle A is equal to the density of the air in Bottle B.
  d. We don't have enough information to compare the density of the air in Bottle A to the density of the air in Bottle B.

True–False Items

14.15

Using teachers' assessment patterns as a frame of reference, what is another problem that the four sample items have in common?

The **true–false format** *involves statements of varying complexity that learners have to judge as being correct or incorrect.* Because they usually measure lower-level outcomes, and because students have a 50–50 chance of guessing the correct answer, true–false items should be used sparingly (Gronlund & Linn, 1995). As with the multiple-choice format, guidelines can help teachers improve their effectiveness (see Figure 14.5).

Look at the examples presented below, and based on the guidelines, see if you can identify problems with the items. Then turn to the discussion that follows.

1. Mammals are animals with four-chambered hearts that bear live young.
2. Most protists have only one cell.
3. Negative wording should never be used when writing multiple-choice items.
4. All spiders have exoskeletons.

Item 1 contains two ideas: (a) mammals have four-chambered hearts, and (b) they bear live young. The first is true, but the second is not true in all cases—some mammals, such as the duck-billed platypus, are egg layers. Therefore, the item is false, potentially confusing students. If both ideas are important, they should be written in separate items.

In Item 2, we see the qualifying word *most,* which is a clue that the statement is true. In comparison, Item 3 uses the term *never.* As you saw in the previous section, negative wording should be used with caution in multiple-choice items, but to say *never* is a false statement. In general, true–false items should be free of qualifying terms such as *may, most, usually, possible,* and *often,* and absolutes such as *always, never, all,* and *none.* If qualifiers are used, they're most appropriate in false statements, and absolutes are most effective in true statements. For instance, Item 4 uses the absolute *all,* but the statement is true.

Matching Items

The **matching format** is *a variation on multiple-choice questions and is most effective when the same alternatives are used in a series of items* (Stiggins, 1997). For instance, consider the following items:

1. The statement, "Understanding is like a light bulb coming on in your head" is an example of:
   *a. simile.
   b. metaphor.
   c. hyperbole.
   d. personification.

Figure 14.5 Guidelines for preparing true–false items

1. When using the format, write slightly more false than true statements. (Teachers tend to write more true than false statements, and students tend to mark answers they're unsure of as "true.")
2. Make each item one clear statement.
3. Avoid clues that may allow students to answer correctly without fully understanding the content.

2. "That's the most brilliant comment ever made" is a statement of:
   a. simile.
   b. metaphor.
   *c. hyperbole.
   d. personification.

Combining the items into a single matching format is more efficient than writing a series of multiple-choice items, as the following example illustrates.

Match the following statements with the figures of speech by writing the letter of the appropriate figure of speech in the blank next to each statement. Each figure of speech may be used *once, more than once,* or *not at all.*

_____ 1. Understanding is like a light bulb coming on in your head

_____ 2. That's the most brilliant comment ever made.

_____ 3. His oratory was a belch from the bowels of his soul.

_____ 4. Appropriate attitudes are always advantageous.

_____ 5. Her eyes are limpid pools of longing.

_____ 6. He stood as straight as a rod.

_____ 7. I'll never get this stuff, no matter what I do.

_____ 8. The colors of his shirt described the world in which he lived.

a. alliteration
b. hyperbole
c. metaphor
d. personification
e. simile

At least four characteristics of effective matching items are illustrated in the example. First, the material is homogeneous; all the statements are figures of speech, and only figures of speech are given as alternatives. Other topics appropriate for matching items include persons and their achievements, historical events and dates, terms and definitions, authors and their works, and principles and their illustrations (Gronlund & Linn, 1995). Homogeneity is necessary to make all alternatives plausible.

Second, effective matching items have more statements than possible alternatives (to prevent getting the right answer by process of elimination). Third, the alternatives can be used more than once or not at all. Finally, the entire item fits on a single page. Items with more than ten statements should be broken into two items, and items that appear on parts of two pages require students to flip back and forth, increasing the likelihood of accidental error.

14.16

What are some other topics with homogeneous material that could be appropriately measured with the matching format?

Completion Items

1. What is an opinion _____?
2. What is the capital of Canada _____?

Completion items *include a question or an incomplete statement that requires the learner to supply appropriate words, numbers, or symbols.* As you saw earlier, the completion format is popular with teachers, probably because questions seem easy to construct. This advantage is misleading, however, because completion items have two serious disadvantages.

First, it is very difficult to phrase a question so that only one possible answer is correct. A number of defensible responses could be given to Question 1, for example.

14.17

Rewrite the two sample completion items so that only one defensible response can be given.

Overuse of the completion format puts students in the position of trying to guess the answer the teacher wants, rather than giving the one they think is most correct. Second, unless the question requires solving a problem, completion formats usually measure knowledge-level outcomes. Because of these weaknesses, completion formats should be used sparingly (Gronlund, 1993). Table 14.4 presents guidelines for preparing items using this format.

Essay Items: Measuring Complex Outcomes

Often the ability to organize ideas, the ability to make and defend an argument, or the ability to express ideas are desired outcomes. Essay items provide an effective way to measure these goals.

Essay items *require students to make extended written responses to questions or problems.* Essay questions are valuable for two reasons. First, organizing, expressing, and defending ideas require higher-order critical thinking. Second, the essay format is often the only way these goals can be measured (Stiggins, 1997). Also, when students study for an essay exam, they are more likely to organize information in a meaningful way (Foos, 1992).

Despite their value, essay items have several disadvantages:

- Scoring is very time-consuming.
- Scoring is subjective and can be unreliable.
- Essay items are strongly influenced by writing skill. If writing skill is a desired outcome, this influence is appropriate. If not, it detracts from the validity of the items.
- Grammar, spelling errors, and handwriting tend to artificially influence scores (Airasian, 1997; McDaniel, 1994).

Because essay items appear to be easy to write, they are often ambiguous, leaving students uncertain about how to respond. The result is that the student's ability to interpret the teacher's question is often the outcome measured.

14.18

Your written response to an essay item contains several grammatical errors and a number of misspelled words. Your instructor takes off points for these errors. Is he or she making a valid decision in doing so? Why or why not?

Table 14.4   Guidelines for preparing completion items

Guideline	Rationale
1. Use only one blank and relate it to the main point of the statement.	Several blanks are confusing, and one answer may depend on another.
2. Use complete sentences followed by a question mark or period and place the blanks to the left of the question statements.	Complete sentences allow students to more nearly grasp the full meaning of the statement. Scoring is easier when all responses are to the left.
3. Keep blanks the same length. Use "a(an)" at the end of the statement or eliminate indefinite articles.	A long blank for a long word or a particular indefinite article commonly provides clues to the answer.
4. For numerical answers, indicate the degree of precision and the units desired.	Degree of precision and units clarify the task for students and prevent them from spending more time than necessary on an item.

Table 14.5   Guidelines for preparing and scoring essay items

1. Elicit higher order thinking by using such terms as *explain* and *compare*. Have students defend their responses with facts.
2. Write a model answer for each item. This can be used both for scoring and for providing feedback.
3. Require all students to answer all items. Allowing students to select particular items prevents comparisons and detracts from reliability.
4. Prepare criteria for scoring in advance.
5. Score all students' answers to a single item before moving to the next item.
6. Score all responses to a single item in one sitting if possible. This increases reliability.
7. Score answers without knowing the identity of the student. This helps reduce the influence of past performance and expectations.

In light of these limitations, essay items should be reserved for complex, high-level learning outcomes that cannot be measured with other formats (Gronlund, 1993). Table 14.5 presents guidelines for preparing and scoring essay items.

Using Rubrics to Improve the Scoring of Essays.   Probably the most essential component in scoring essays is to establish grading criteria in the form of a scoring rubric. A **rubric** *is a scoring tool that lists the criteria for grading* (Goodrich, 1996/97). Criteria should be prepared prior to scoring and applied uniformly throughout the process. Figure 14.6 is an example that links points to criteria.

This rubric is content-free, referring to general, organizational criteria. Similar rubrics can be constructed that focus on specific concepts or topics. Using rubrics when scoring essays can increase reliability.

Figure 14.6   Rubric for scoring essay items

High Score	5	The response is clear, focused, and accurate. Relevant points are made with good support (derived from the content to be used, again as spelled out in the exercise). Good connections are drawn, and important insights are evident.
	3	The answer is clear and somewhat focused, but not compelling. Support of points made is limited. Connections are fuzzy and lead to few important insights.
Low Score	1	The response either misses the point, contains inaccurate information, or otherwise demonstrates a lack of mastery of the material. Points are unclear, support is missing, and/or no insights are included.

Source: Adapted from Stiggins (1997, p. 169).

As you saw earlier, many teachers depend on the tests included in textbooks, teachers' guides, and other commercially prepared curriculum materials. Although using these tests obviously saves time, they should be used with caution for at least three reasons:

1. *Goals:* The goals of the curriculum developers may not be the same as the goals you have for your students. If items don't reflect the goals and instruction in your course, they are invalid.
2. *Emphasis:* The tests reflect the emphasis of the curriculum developers and, even if your goals are similar to theirs, the emphasis reflected on the commercially prepared test may not parallel yours.
3. *Quality:* This factor is perhaps most important. Many commercially prepared tests are of low quality and are written at low levels, tapping student memorization rather than higher-order thinking.

These problems suggest that teachers should exercise caution in using tests supplied by textbook publishers (Airasian, 1997). They often are little, if any, better than items teachers prepare themselves, and are less likely to be congruent with teachers' goals and instruction than teacher-prepared items. Although writing quality test items is demanding, the benefits make it worth the effort.

> **14.19**
>
> We identified three problems with the use of commercially prepared tests: goals, emphasis, and quality. Which do these problems affect more—validity or reliability? Explain.

Authentic Assessment

Traditional assessments, most commonly in the form of multiple-choice tests, have come under increasing criticism over the last several years (Herman et al., 1992; Reckase, 1997). In response to these criticisms, the use of authentic assessments, or "direct examination of student performance on significant tasks that are relevant to life outside of school" (Worthen, 1993, p. 445), is growing in importance. The terms **alternative assessment, authentic assessment,** and **performance assessment** are used interchangeably to describe *assessments that directly measure student performance through "real life" tasks* (Wiggins, 1996/97; Worthen, 1993). Examples include:

- Writing a persuasive essay
- Designing menus for a week's worth of nutritionally balanced meals
- Identifying and fixing the problems with a lawn mower engine that won't start
- Creating an original piece of pottery
- Designing and conducting an experiment to measure the effects of different levels of exercise on hamsters

In addition to products, such as the essay, menu, or piece of pottery, teachers using authentic assessments are also interested in the processes students use to prepare the products, and as a result, they emphasize higher-order thinking (Gronlund, 1993). Insights into these processes provide teachers with opportunities to build upon student knowledge and correct student misconceptions (Parke & Lane, 1996/97). For example, a structured interview might be used to gain insight into students' thinking as they design science experiments.

Because of the emphasis on applied, higher-level tasks, authentic assessments have the potential to change both instruction and learning (Pomplun, Capps, & Sundbye, 1997). Authentic assessments are consistent with constructivist views of learning, which recognize that learning is holistic and should be contextualized within authentic tasks (Camp, 1992).

Let's look at two forms of authentic assessments: performance assessments and portfolios.

Performance Assessments

A middle-school science teacher notices that her students have difficulty applying scientific principles to everyday events. In an attempt to improve this ability, she focuses on everyday problems (e.g., why an ice cube floated in one cup of clear liquid but sank in another), which students have to solve in groups and discuss as a class. On Fridays, she presents another problem (e.g., why two clear liquids of the same volume, when put on a balance, don't have the same mass), and the students have to solve it in groups. As they work, she circulates among them, taking notes that will be used for assessment and feedback.

A health teacher reads in a professional journal that the biggest problem people have in applying first aid is not the mechanics *per se,* but knowing what to do and when. In an attempt to address this problem, the teacher periodically has unannounced "catastrophe" days. Students entering the classroom encounter a catastrophe victim with an unspecified injury. With each victim they must first diagnose the problem and then apply first-aid interventions.

These teachers are using performance assessments to gather information about students' abilities to apply information in realistic settings. **Performance assessments** are tasks on which *"students are required to demonstrate their level of competence or*

14.20

Construct an authentic assessment for Shirley Barton in our opening case study on teaching fractions in Chapter 11. What makes it "authentic"?

14.21

Are essay items performance assessments? Defend your answer, using the information from this section.

Performance assessments measure students' ability to demonstrate skills similar to those required in real-world settings.

knowledge by creating a product or a response" (Valencia, Hiebert, & Afflerback, 1994, p. 11). They attempt to increase validity by placing students in as lifelike a situation as possible and evaluating their performance against preset criteria (Feuer & Fulton, 1993). The label "performance assessment" originated in content areas such as science, where students were required to demonstrate a skill in a hands-on situation rather than recognizing a correct answer on a teacher-made or standardized test (Hiebert & Raphael, 1996).

Designing Performance Assessments

Experts have identified four steps in designing classroom performance assessments (Gronlund, 1993): (a) specifying desired outcomes, (b) selecting the focus of evaluation, (c) determining the appropriate degree of realism, and (d) selecting evaluation procedures.

Specifying Desired Outcomes. The first step in designing any assessment is to develop a clear idea of what you're trying to measure. A clear description of the skill or process helps students understand what is required and helps the teacher design appropriate instruction. An example in the area of speech is outlined in Figure 14.7 (based on work by Gronlund, 1993).

Selecting the Focus of Evaluation. Having specified performance outcomes, teachers must next decide whether assessment will focus on processes or products. Processes are often the initial focus, with a shift to products after procedures are mastered (Gronlund, 1993). Examples of both processes and products as components of performance assessments are found in Table 14.6.

Determining the Appropriate Degree of Realism. The value of performance assessments lies in their link to realistic tasks: ultimately teachers want students to use the skill in the real world. Time, expense, and safety may prevent the "real thing," however, and intermediate steps might be necessary.

For example, in driver education the goal is to produce safe drivers. However, putting students in heavy traffic to assess how well they function behind the wheel is both unrealistic and unsafe. Figure 14.8 contains evaluation options ranging from low to high realism to assess driver education skills.

Figure 14.7 Performance outcomes in speech

Oral Presentation
1. Stands naturally.
2. Maintains eye contact.
3. Uses gestures effectively.
4. Uses clear language.
5. Has adequate volume.
6. Speaks at an appropriate rate.
7. Topics are well organized.
8. Maintains interest of the group.

Table 14.6   Processes and products as components of performance

Content Area	Product	Process
Math	Correct answer	Problem-solving steps leading to the correct solution
Music	Performance of a work on an instrument	Correct fingering and breathing that produces the performance
English Composition	Essay, term paper, or composition	Preparation of drafts and thought processes that produce the product
Word Processing	Letter or copy of final draft	Proper stroking and techniques for presenting the paper
Science	Explanation for the outcomes of a demonstration	Thought processes involved in preparing the explanation

Simulations provide opportunities for teachers to measure performance with intermediate degrees of realism in cases in which high realism is impossible. For instance, a geography teacher wanting to measure students' understanding of the impact of climate and geography on the location of cities might display the information shown in Figure 14.9. Students would be asked to identify the best location for a city on the island and the criteria they used in determining the location. The criteria provide the teacher with insight into the students' understanding and thought processes.

14.22

How does realism influence validity and reliability? Explain, using the driver education example as a frame of reference.

Selecting Evaluation Procedures.   The final step in designing performance assessments is to select (or construct) evaluation procedures. Reliability is a primary concern. While it is difficult, acceptable levels of reliability can be achieved if care is taken (Nystrand, Cohen, & Dowling, 1992).

Well-defined criteria in the form of scoring rubrics, similar to those used with essay items, increase both reliability and validity. Clearly written criteria provide models of excellence and clear performance targets for students (McTighe, 1996/1997). Effective criteria have four elements (Herman et al., 1992; Messick, 1994):

1. One or more dimensions that serve as a basis for assessing student performance
2. A description of each dimension
3. A scale of values on which each dimension is rated
4. Definitions of each value on the scale

Figure 14.8   Continuum of realism on performance tasks

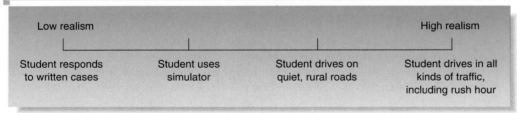

Low realism ———————————————————————— High realism

| Student responds to written cases | Student uses simulator | Student drives on quiet, rural roads | Student drives in all kinds of traffic, including rush hour |

Figure 14.9 Simulation in geography

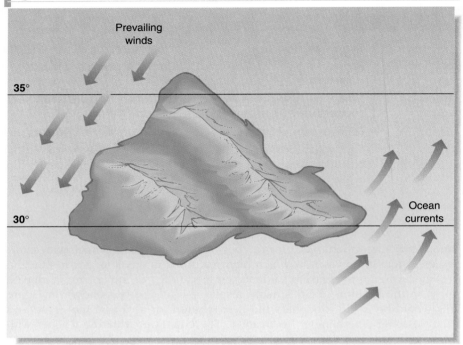

Let's look now at three ways to evaluate learner performance: (a) systematic observation, (b) checklists, and (c) rating scales.

Ways to Evaluate Performance

Teachers observe students in classroom settings all the time. Observations typically are not systematic, however, and records are rarely kept. **Systematic observations** are designed to solve these problems by *encouraging teachers to specify criteria and take notes* based on the criteria. For example, a science teacher attempting to teach her students scientific problem-solving might establish the following criteria.

1. States problem or question
2. States hypotheses
3. Identifies independent, dependent, and controlled variables
4. Describes the way data will be gathered
5. Orders and displays data
6. Evaluates hypotheses based on the data

The teacher's notes would then refer directly to the criteria, making them consistent for all groups. The notes could be used to give learners feedback and provide information that could be used in future planning.

Checklists extend systematic observation by specifying important aspects of performance and by sharing them with students. **Checklists** are *written descriptions of dimensions that must be present in an acceptable performance*. When checklists are

Systematic observation incorporating checklists and rating scales allows teachers to access accurately and to provide valuable information to students about their performance.

used, the desired performances are typically "checked off" rather than described in notes, as they would be with a systematic observation. For example, the science teacher wanting to assess scientific problem-solving ability might use a checklist such as the one in Figure 14.10. Notes could be added to each dimension, to combine the best of checklists and systematic observations.

Checklists are useful when a criterion can be translated into a yes-or-no answer, such as "Specifies values for controlled variables," because students either did or did not

Figure 14.10   Checklist for evaluating experimental technique

DIRECTIONS: Place a check in the blank for each step performed.
_____ 1. Writes problem at the top of the report.
_____ 2. States hypothesis(es).
_____ 3. Specifies values for controlled variables.
_____ 4. Makes at least two measurements of each value of the dependent variable.
_____ 5. Presents data in a chart.
_____ 6. Draws conclusions consistent with the data in the chart.

specify the values. In other cases, however, such as "Draws conclusions consistent with the data in the chart," the results aren't cut-and-dried. Conclusions aren't literally consistent or inconsistent with the data; some conclusions are more thorough or insightful than others. Rating scales address this problem.

Rating scales are *written descriptions of evaluative dimensions and scales of values on which each dimension is rated.* Rating scales can be constructed in descriptive, graphic, or numerical formats, as shown in Figure 14.11. They allow more precise information to be gathered than is possible with checklists, and the increased detail gives the learner more specific feedback and the teacher and class more opportunity to evaluate and discuss the performance.

14.23

Create a rating scale that would allow you to assess someone's performance in creating high-quality multiple-choice test items.

14.24

How do systematic observations, checklists, and rating scales influence validity and reliability? Explain.

Portfolio Assessment: Involving Students in Authentic Assessment

The use of portfolios, another form of alternative assessment, has the additional advantage of involving students in the design, collection, and evaluation of learning products. **Portfolios** are *collections of work that are reviewed against preset criteria to judge learning progress* (Stiggins, 1997). Because they are cumulative, connected, and occur over a period of time, they can provide a "motion picture" of learning progress versus the snapshots provided by disconnected tests and quizzes (Ziomek, 1997). The portfolio is *not* the assessment; it is a collection of students' products, such as essays, journal entries, artwork, and videotapes. The assessments are the students' and teacher's judgments of learning progress.

Two features distinguish portfolios from other forms of assessment:

1. Portfolios collect work samples over time, reflecting developmental changes.
2. Portfolios involve students in design, collection, and evaluation.

Portfolios promote self-regulation by involving students in the assessment of their own learning progress. Portfolios have been used in teacher education to help candidates reflect on their growth as professionals, identify strengths and weaknesses, and document professional skills during job-seeking (Guillaume & Rudney, 1997). Examples of portfolio assessments in different content areas are found in Table 14.7.

Portfolios are designed to reflect student growth. For example, writing samples can document the changes that occur over a term or course. This documentation can then be used as a basis for communicating with parents and for helping students observe their own progress.

Two questions are involved when portfolio assessments are used. First, who decides what goes into the portfolio? Second, on what criteria will the students' work be evaluated? Student involvement in selecting portfolio content provides opportunities for students to reflect on their own learning progress. One seventh-grade language-arts teacher shared her experience in involving students:

> I introduced the idea that their portfolios might present a broader picture—how students have changed or improved, what their particular interests are, and areas where they still have difficulties. This comment led my students to suggest including the following items: an early and a later piece of writing, a rewrite of something, examples of what they like and don't like, a list of books they like and don't, and reading logs that show how their thinking about books has changed. (Case, 1994, p. 46)

Criteria were also jointly established and included (a) how well students explained why they selected particular pieces, (b) the actual pieces, (c) clarity and completeness

Figure 14.11   Three rating scales for evaluating oral presentations

Numerical Rating Scale

Directions: Indicate how often the pupil performs each of these behaviors while giving an oral presentation. For each behavior circle **1** if the pupil **always** performs the behavior, **2** if the pupil **usually** performs the behavior, **3** if the pupil **seldom** performs the behavior, and **4** if the pupil **never** performs the behavior.

Physical Expression

   A. Stands straight and faces audience.

       1   **2**   **3**   **4**

   B. Changes facial expression with change in the tone of the presentation.

       1   **2**   **3**   **4**

Graphic Rating Scale

Directions: Place an **X** on the line which shows how often the pupil did each of the behaviors listed while giving an oral presentation.

Physical Expression

   A. Stands straight and faces audience.

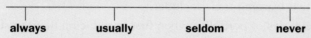

     always   **usually**   **seldom**   **never**

   B. Changes facial expressions with change in tone of the presentation.

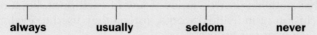

     always   **usually**   **seldom**   **never**

Descriptive Rating Scale

Directions: Place an **X** above the statement which best describes the pupil's performance on each behavior.

   Physical Expression

   A. Stands straight and faces audience.

stands straight, always looks at audience	**weaves, fidgets, eyes roam from audience to ceiling**	**constant, distracting movements, no eye contact with audience**

B. Changes facial expressions with change in tone of the presentation.

matches facial expressions to content and emphasis	**facial expressions usually appropriate, occasional lack of expression**	**no match between tone and facial expression; expression distracts**

Source: From P. Airasian, *Classroom Assessment,* p. 229. Copyright 1997 by McGraw-Hill Company. Reproduced with permission of the McGraw-Hill Company.

Table 14.7 Portfolio samples in different content areas

Content Area	Example
Elementary Math	Homework, quizzes, tests, and projects completed over time.
Writing	Drafts of narrative, descriptive, and persuasive essays in various stages of development. Samples of poetry.
Art	Projects over the course of the year collected to show growth in an area like perspective or in a medium like painting.
Science	Lab reports, projects, classroom notes, quizzes, and tests compiled to provide an overview of learning progress.

of the cover letter describing the contents, and (d) neatness and organization. As learners considered what to put in the portfolio, the issue of including only their best work versus pieces demonstrating growth came up. One student commented, "We could all just turn in the papers that got the best grades. But we already got those grades, so what would be the point of making a portfolio?" (Case, 1994, p. 46)

By involving students in these decisions, teachers help them understand options in assessing their own growth and promote self-regulation. Some guidelines that can help make portfolios effective learning tools include:

- Provide examples of portfolios when first introducing them to students.

- Involve students in the selection and evaluation of their work.

- Require that students provide an overview of each portfolio, a rationale for the inclusion of individual works, criteria they used to evaluate, and an overall summary of progress.

Portfolios foster self-regulation by providing opportunities for students to become actively involved in assessing their own learning progress.

- Provide students with frequent and detailed feedback about their decisions.

Putting Traditional and Authentic Assessment into Perspective

The idea of authentic assessment is not new (Worthen, 1993). Oral exams; art exhibits; performances in music, athletics, and business education; proficiency testing in language; and hands-on assessments in vocational areas have been used for years to assess learners' abilities to perform complex tasks. Increased interest in authentic assessments in recent years likely results from at least three sources.

First, traditional assessments have been increasingly criticized. Some of these criticisms include:

- They focus on low-level knowledge, discrete content, and skills.
- Objective formats, such as multiple-choice, don't measure learners' ability to apply understanding in the real world
- They measure only outcomes, providing no insight into the processes learners' use to arrive at their conclusions (Herman et al., 1992).

Authentic assessments respond to these criticisms by attempting to tap higher-level thinking and problem-solving skills, emphasizing real-world applications, and focusing on the processes learners use to produce their products (Herman et al., 1992; Newman, Secado, & Wehlage, 1995).

Second, critics argue that traditional test formats are grounded in behaviorism; they "assume a theory of learning incompatible with current understanding—one that is componential, hierarchical, and unidimensional" (Camp, 1992, p. 243), whereas alternative assessment is more consistent with constructivist views of learning.

Third, the authentic assessment movement is designed to increase access to higher education for learners with diverse backgrounds (Hiebert & Raphael, 1996).

On the other hand, difficulties have been encountered in trying to implement and use authentic assessments. First, while proponents claim that authentic assessments do a better job of measuring higher-order thinking, little evidence exists to support these claims (Terwilliger, 1997).

Second, implementation is difficult. Research indicates that without extensive staff development, teachers are unlikely to systematically implement authentic assessments (Hiebert & Raphael, 1996), and the process is very time consuming, even with support (Valencia & Place, 1994).

Access is a third factor. Little evidence indicates that access to higher education for learners with diverse backgrounds has been improved as the result of the authentic assessment movement. While the efforts have been directed at increasing access for low income students in particular, "those performance assessments on which data have been reported to the public indicate that the majority of students are performing poorly" (Hiebert & Raphael, 1996, p. 567).

Finally reliability remains an issue. As we said earlier, obtaining acceptable levels of reliability is possible if care is taken (Nystrand et al., 1992), but in practice this has been a problem. For example, the state of Vermont in a widely publicized movement implemented a Portfolio Assessment Program in 1992, but research on the program indicates that scorers assessing the same portfolio often gave very different ratings (Koretz, Stecher, & Diebert, 1993). Additional research on portfolios has identified similar problems (Herman & Winters, 1994).

14.25

A teacher wants to use portfolio assessment in a fifth-grade math class. Identify at least three types of items that might be included in the portfolio.

At the classroom level, allowing students to determine portfolio content also raises the reliability issue. When students choose different items to place in their portfolio, cross-student comparisons are difficult and reliability in assessing the portfolios suffers. Experts suggest supplementing portfolios with traditional, standard measures to obtain the best of both processes (Reckase, 1997).

As with virtually all aspects of learning and teaching, assessment isn't as simple as it appears on the surface; effective measurement and evaluation require sensitive and intelligent teachers. A combination of traditional and authentic assessment—carefully considered and wisely implemented—is likely to be most effective (Terwilliger, 1997).

Classroom Connections

Creating Valid and Reliable Assessments in Your Classroom

1. Be sure objectives and tests are congruent.
   - A life-science teacher compares items on his tests to the objectives in the curriculum guide and his unit plan to be sure all the appropriate objectives are covered.

2. Write individual test items soon after material has been presented. Make a special effort to write items above the knowledge/recall level.
   - A social-studies teacher writes a draft of one test item at the end of each day to be certain the emphasis on her tests is consistent with her instruction. She reports that she can now write a good item in less than five minutes.

3. Analyze test items after they have been written to make sure they measure intended outcomes.
   - A fourth-grade teacher rereads the items she has written to eliminate wording that might be confusing or too advanced for her students.

4. Construct scoring rubrics for essay items. Score essays by using the rubric as the criterion.
   - A high-school economics teacher writes an "ideal" response to each essay item she prepares. She then awards points to students for each element of the model demonstrated in their answers.

5. Use commercially prepared items with caution.

   - A third-grade teacher comments, "I look at the tests they send with the book. I find the good items and use them. Then I make up the rest of the items myself."

6. Use alternative assessments to increase validity.
   - A fifth-grade math teacher assigns his students the task of going to three supermarkets and comparing prices on a list of five household items. They are required to determine which store provided the best bargains and what the difference was among the stores on each item.
   - A fourth-grade teacher uses portfolios to evaluate students' writing progress during the school year. Students are required to keep a weekly journal describing their work and noting accomplishments.

7. Use portfolios and performance assessments to develop learner self-regulation.
   - A middle-school language-arts teacher uses portfolios as a central organizing theme for his curriculum. Students collect pieces of work over the course of the year and share and evaluate these with other members of their writing teams.
   - A fifth-grade teacher asks each student to compile a portfolio of work and present it at parent–teacher conferences. Prior to the conference, the teacher meets with students and helps them identify individual strengths and weaknesses.

Effective Assessment Practices

In the previous sections, we examined both traditional and alternative assessment. Though good items and authentic measures are essential, there is more to effective assessment. To maximize learning, individual items must be combined into tests; authentic assessments must be designed; students need to be prepared; and assessments must be administered, scored, and discussed. We look now at four processes in effective assessment: (a) designing assessments, (b) preparing students, (c) administering assessments, and (d) analyzing results.

Designing Assessments

In designing assessments, the first task is to be sure they are consistent with your goals and instruction. This seems obvious but, because tests are usually prepared some time after instruction is completed, it often doesn't occur. For example, a topic given little emphasis in class might have several items related to it, whereas another, given much greater emphasis, is covered less thoroughly on the test. A topic may be discussed in class at the applied level, but test items are at a knowledge level. A goal may call for an observable performance, but the assessment consists of multiple-choice questions. Each of these factors reduces the validity of a test.

Tables of Specifications: Increasing Validity Through Planning

One way to help ensure that goals and tests are consistent is to prepare a table of specifications or a behavior–content matrix. A **table of specifications** is *a matrix derived from the teacher's objectives that classifies topics measured on the test by cognitive level or specific outcomes.* For example, a geography teacher based her instruction in a unit on the Middle East on the following list of objectives:

Understands location of cities

1. States location
2. Identifies historical factors in settlement

Understands climate

1. Identifies major climate regions
2. Explains reasons for existing climates

Understands influence of physical features

1. Describes topography
2. Relates physical features to climate
3. Explains impact of physical features on location of cities
4. Analyzes impact of physical features on economy

Understands factors influencing economy

1. Describes economies of countries in the region
2. Identifies characteristics of each economy
3. Explains how economies relate to climate and physical features

Table 14.8 presents a table of specifications for a cognitive-level matrix based on the objectives for a topic. The teacher has a mix of items, with more emphasis placed

14.26

Two teachers were arguing about the best time to construct a table of specifications—during planning, before teaching a unit, or after a unit. What are the advantages and disadvantages of each approach? Explain.

Table 14.8 Sample table of specifications

Content	Outcomes		
	Knowledge	Comprehension	Higher-Order Thinking and Problem-Solving
Cities	4	2	2
Climate	4	2	2
Economy	2	2	
Physical features	4	9	7
Total items	14	15	11

on physical features than other items. This emphasis reflects the teacher's objectives, which emphasize the influence of physical features on the location of cities, the climate, and the economy of the region. In addition, this emphasis presumably also reflects the time and effort spent in class on each area. Ensuring this match among goals, instruction, and assessment is a primary function of a table of specifications.

For authentic assessments, establishing criteria as discussed in the section on systematic observations, checklists, and rating scales serves a function similar to that of tables of specifications. The criteria identify performance, determine emphasis, and attempt to ensure congruence between goals and assessments.

Preparing Students for Assessments

Let's begin this section by looking at a brief case study in which a teacher prepares her students for an upcoming test.

> Tanya Erickson is making the transition from reading to math on a Wednesday. She is standing in front of the room with a transparency in her hand at 10:02 as her students get out their math books.
>
> "Get out your chalkboards and chalk," she reminds them, referring to small individual chalkboards she had made for each of them at the beginning of the year.
>
> "Look up here at the chalkboard," she begins, pointing to the chalkboard at the front of the room. "I just want to remind you again that we're having a test tomorrow on finding equivalent fractions and adding fractions with unlike denominators, and we decided that the test will go in your math portfolios. On the test, you will have to add some fractions in which the denominators are the same and others in which the denominators are different. There will also be word problems in which you will need to do the same thing. I'll give the test back Friday, and if we all do well, we won't have any homework over the weekend."
>
> "YEAH!" the students shout in unison, as Tanya smiles at their response.
>
> She holds up her hand, they quiet down, and she continues. "I have some problems on the test that are going to make you think," she smiles. "But we've all been working hard, and we're getting so smart, we'll be able to do it. You're my team, and I know you'll come through," she continues energetically.
>
> "To be sure we're okay," she goes on, "I have a few problems that are just like those on the test, so let's see how we do. Write these first two on your chalkboards."

14.27

A teacher closely follows her curriculum guide, checks off objectives, and writes at least one test item related to each objective as soon as she's finished covering it with her students. Is she being consistent with the idea of tables of specifications by using this procedure? Why or why not?

$$1/3 + 3/4 = ?\quad 2/7 + 4/7 = ?$$

Tanya watches as they work on the problems and hold their chalkboards up when they're finished. Seeing that three of the students miss the first problem, she carefully goes through it with the class, comparing it with the second problem. She then displays the following three problems:

$$2/3 + 1/6 = ?\quad 4/9 + 1/6 = ?\quad 2/9 + 4/9 = ?$$

Two students miss the second one, so again she goes through this problem carefully.

"Now, let's try one more," she continues, displaying the following problem on the overhead.

> You are at a pizza party with five other people, and you order two pizzas. The two pizzas are the same size, but one is cut into four pieces and the other is cut into eight pieces. You eat one piece from each pizza. How much pizza do you eat altogether?

Again, Tanya watches as students work on the problem, discusses it, and reviews the solution with them when they are finished. In the process, she asks questions such as, "What information in the problem is particularly important, and how do we know?" "What do we see in the problem that's irrelevant?" and, "What should we do first in solving the problem?"

She displays two more word problems for them and then says, "The problems on the test are like the ones we practiced in here today." She responds to additional questions from the students and concludes her review by saying,

"All right, when we take a test, what do we always do?"

"WE READ THE DIRECTIONS CAREFULLY!" the students shout in unison.

"Okay, good," Tanya smiles. "Now, remember, what will you do if you get stuck on a problem?"

"Go on to the next one so we don't run out of time."

"And what will we be sure not to do?"

"We won't forget to go back to the one we skipped."

In preparing students for tests, teachers have long- and short-term goals. Long term, they want students to understand test-taking procedures and strategies and to enter testing situations with a minimum of anxiety. Short term, they want students to understand the test format and the content being tested. By preparing students, teachers increase the probability that test scores accurately reflect achievement, thus increasing validity.

Teaching Test-Taking Strategies

Teachers can improve students' test-taking strategies by helping them understand the importance of:

- using time efficiently and pacing themselves,
- reading directions carefully,
- identifying the important information in questions,
- understanding the demands of different testing formats, and
- Finding out how questions will be scored.

14.28

Identify at least two specific examples of things Tanya Erickson did to promote test-taking skills in her students.

To be most effective, students should be reminded of the strategies throughout the school year, concrete examples should be linked to the strategies, and students should be given practice with a variety of formats and testing situations. Research indicates that strategy instruction significantly improves test-taking performance and that young, low-ability, and minority students who have limited test-taking experience benefit the most (Anastasi, 1988; Walton & Taylor, 1996/97).

Reducing Test Anxiety

'Listen my children and you shall hear. . . . Listen my children and you shall hear'. . . . Rats! I knew it this morning in front of Mom.

14.29

Using classical conditioning as a basis, explain the emotional component—such as feelings of dread—of test anxiety. Using information processing as a basis, explain how the cognitive component of test anxiety can lower test performance.

Like this student, many of us have experienced the negative effects of anxiety in a testing situation. For most of us, the adverse effects of pressure are momentary and minor, with little impairment of performance. For a portion of the school population, however (estimates run as high as 10%), anxiety during testing situations is a serious problem (Hill & Wigfield, 1984; Williams, 1992).

Test anxiety is *a relatively stable, unpleasant reaction to testing situations that lowers performance.* Most theories of test anxiety suggest that it consists of two components (Pintrich & Schunk, 1996). Its *emotional component* can include physiological symptoms, such as increased pulse rate, dry mouth, and headache, as well as feelings of dread and helplessness and sometimes "going blank." Its *cognitive,* or *worry component* involves thoughts, such as worrying about failure (e.g., parents being upset, having to retake the course) and being embarrassed by a low score. During tests, test-anxious students tend to be preoccupied with test difficulty and are often unable to focus on the individual items.

Test anxiety is triggered by testing situations that (a) involve pressure to succeed, (b) are perceived as difficult, (c) impose time limits, and (d) contain unfamiliar items or formats (Wigfield & Eccles, 1989). Unannounced or surprise tests, particularly, can trigger adverse amounts of test anxiety (Saigh, 1984).

Teachers can do much to minimize test anxiety (Everson, Tobias, Hartman, & Gourgey, 1991), and the most successful of these efforts are usually aimed at the worry component (Pintrich & Schunk, 1996). Suggestions include:

14.30

You have an extremely test-anxious student in your class. State specifically what you would do to reduce her anxiety. What should you do if you think her anxiety is a danger to her emotional health?

- Use criterion-referenced measures to minimize the competitive aspects of tests.
- Avoid social comparisons, such as public displays of test scores and grades.
- Increase the frequency of quizzes and tests.
- Discuss test content and procedures prior to testing.
- Give clear directions and be sure students understand the test.
- Teach students test-taking skills.
- Use a variety of measures, including authentic assessments, to measure students' understanding and skills.
- Provide students with ample time to take tests.

Specific Test-Preparation Procedures

Before any test, teachers want to be as sure as possible that learners understand test content and procedures and expect to succeed on the exam. In preparing students for her test, Tanya Erickson did three important things:

1. She specified precisely what would be on the test.
2. She gave students a chance to practice the items under test-like conditions.
3. She established positive expectations in her students and encouraged them to link success and effort.

Clarifying test format and content establishes structure for students; this structure, in turn, reduces test anxiety (Szafran, 1981). Research indicates that providing this structure leads to higher achievement for all students, particularly those of low ability (Carrier & Titus, 1981).

Merely specifying the content often isn't enough, however, particularly with elementary students, so Tanya actually gave students practice exercises and presented them in a way that paralleled the way they would be presented on her test. In learning math skills, for instance, her students first practiced adding fractions with like denominators, then learned to find equivalent fractions, and finally added fractions with unlike denominators, each in separate lessons. On the test, however, the problems were mixed, and Tanya gave students a chance to practice integrating these skills prior to the test. The benefits of this practice are particularly important for young (Kalechstein, Kalechstein, & Doctor, 1981) and minority (Dreisbach & Keogh, 1982) students. Finally, Tanya clearly communicated that she expected the students to do well on the test. The benefits of establishing positive expectations have been confirmed by decades of research (Good, 1987b).

Tanya also encouraged attributions of effort and ability for success and she modeled an incremental view of ability by saying, "But we've all been working hard, and we're getting so smart, we'll be able to do it." From our study of motivation in Chapter 10, you know that encouraging the belief that ability is incremental benefits both performance and long-term motivation.

Administering Assessments

Let's return again to Tanya Erickson and her class at 10:00 the next morning.

Tanya had opened a window before school started, but shuts it because delivery trucks are driving back and forth outside. She had considered rearranging the desks in the room but decided to wait until after the test.

"Okay, everyone," she calls. "Let's get ready for our math test." With that, the students put their books under their desks.

She waits a moment, sees that everyone's desk is clear, and says, "When you're finished with the test, turn it over, and I'll come and get it. Now, look at the chalkboard. After you're done, work on the assignment listed there until everyone else is finished. Then, we'll start reading."

As she hands out the tests, she says, "If you get too warm, raise your hand, and I'll turn on the air conditioner. I shut the window because of the noise outside.

"Work carefully," she says after everyone has a copy of the test. "We've all been working hard, and I know you will do well. You have as much time as you need. Now go ahead and get started."

The students quickly begin working, and Tanya stands near the door, watching their efforts.

After several minutes, she notices Dean doodling at the top of his paper and periodically glancing around the room. She goes to him, puts an arm around his shoulders, and says, "It looks like you're doing fine on these problems," and she points to some near the top of the paper. "Now concentrate a little harder. I'll bet you can do most of the others." She smiles reassuringly and again stands near the door.

Tanya moves over to Abdul in response to his raised hand. "The lead on my pencil broke, Mrs. Erickson," he whispers.

"Take this one," Tanya responds, handing him one. "Come and get yours after the test."

As students finish, Tanya picks up their papers, and they begin the assignment written on the chalkboard.

Let's analyze how Tanya administered the test. First, she arranged the environment to be comfortable, free from distractions, and similar to the way it was when the students learned the content. Distractions can depress test performance, particularly in young or low-ability students (Trentham, 1975).

Second, Tanya gave precise directions about taking the test, collecting the papers, and spending their time afterward. These directions helped maintain order in the room and prevented distractions for late-finishing students.

Finally, Tanya carefully monitored the test during the entire time students worked on it. This not only allowed her to encourage students who became lost or distracted but also discouraged cheating. In the real world, unfortunately, some students will cheat if given the opportunity. However, classroom climate, such as the emphasis on learning versus performance, and external factors, such as the teacher leaving the room, influence cheating more than whether students are inherently inclined to do so (Bushway & Nash, 1977; Newstead, Franklyn-Stokes, & Armstead, 1996). Teacher monitoring during tests also helps students learn to monitor their own test-taking behaviors.

In Tanya's case, monitoring was more a form of giving support than of being a watchdog. When she saw that Dean was distracted, she quickly intervened, offered him encouragement, and urged him to increase his concentration. This encouragement is particularly important for underachieving and test-anxious students, who tend to become distracted and have lapses in their effort (Nottelman & Hill, 1977).

Analyzing Results

Let's return to Tanya's class once more as she hands back the tests on Friday morning.

"Do you have our tests finished, Mrs. Erickson?" the students ask as they get out their math books.

"Of course!" she smiles at them, handing back their papers.

"Overall, you did very well on the test, and I'm very proud of you. I knew all that hard work would pay off."

"There are a few items I want to go over, though," she continues. "Five of you had trouble with Number 8, and you all made nearly the same mistake, so let's take a look at it."

She waits a moment while the students read the problem and then asks, "Now, what are we given in the problem? . . . Hannah?"

"There's a drawing of two cakes. One is cut into 12 pieces, and the other is cut into 6 pieces."

"Okay. Good. And what else do we know? . . . Shareef?"

Tanya continues the discussion and explanation of the problem. She then carefully discusses two other problems that were frequently missed. In the process, she makes notes at the top of her copy, identifying the problems that were difficult. She writes "Ambiguous" by one problem and underlines some of the wording in it. By another, she writes, "Teach them how to draw diagrams of the problem." Finally, she puts her copy of the test in a file folder, lays it on her desk to be filed, and turns back to the class.

Tanya's efforts didn't end with administering the test. She scored it and returned it the next day, discussed the results, and provided students with feedback as quickly as possible. This process is important for both achievement and motivation (Bangert-

14.31

In an effort to keep his students informed about the amount of time left during a test, a teacher reminds them of the time every ten minutes. Is this a good idea? How will it affect test anxiety? If at all possible, what should teachers do in scheduling the amount of time students have to take a test?

Monitoring student progress during assessment allows teachers to answer questions and clear up misunderstandings.

Drowns, Kulik, Kulik, & Morgan, 1991). Feedback allows learners to correct common misconceptions and, as you saw in Chapter 10, knowledge of results is one variable that promotes student motivation. Virtually all teachers provide feedback after a test, and many take up to half a class period to do so (Haertel, 1986). Because student motivation is high, many teachers believe that the instruction in these postmortems is more valuable than the original instruction.

In addition, Tanya made positive comments about the performance of the class on the test. In a study examining this factor, students who were told they did well on a test performed better on a subsequent measure than those who were told they did poorly, even though the two groups did equally well on the first test (Bridgeman, 1974). Research also supports the benefits of individual feedback on tests; students who receive comments such as, "Excellent! Keep it up!" and, "Good work, keep at it!" do better on subsequent work (Page, 1992). The effects of these short, personalized comments justify the extra work involved.

Finally, Tanya made notes on her copy of the test and filed the copy. Her notes reminded her that the wording on one of her problems was misleading, so she could revise the problem before she gave it again. This, plus other information taken from the test, will assist her in future planning for both instruction and assessment.

Accommodating Diversity in Classrooms: Reducing Bias in Assessment

When teachers assess their students, they gather data to make decisions about student progress and help them in improving their instruction. Learner diversity, however, often

14.32

Explain why knowledge of results is important for motivation from a behaviorist, then a cognitive, and finally from a humanistic view of motivation.

complicates this process. In this section, we examine strategies to accommodate this diversity.

Minority students may lack experience with general testing procedures, different test formats, and test-taking strategies, and they may not understand the purpose of assessments. Also, because most assessments are strongly language-based, language may present another obstacle, so the effective testing practices we discussed in the previous section are particularly important for minority students (Land, 1997). In addition, teachers can respond to diversity in assessment in at least three other ways: (a) being careful with wording in assessment items, (b) making provisions for non-native English speakers, and (c) accommodating diversity in scoring.

Being Careful with Wording in Assessment Items

14.33

Is content bias more a problem with validity or reliability? Explain.

Content bias is always a possibility when assessing students with diverse backgrounds. For example, minority learners can have difficulties with items containing information uncommon in their culture, such as transportation (e.g., ambulances, cable cars, garbage trucks), sports (e.g., football, hockey, skiing, surfing), and musical instruments (e.g., banjo, guitar, harmonica) (Cheng, 1987). In addition, holidays such as Thanksgiving or historical figures such as Abraham Lincoln and Franklin Roosevelt, which most people in American culture take for granted, may be unfamiliar to them. When these terms and events are included in assessment items, teachers are measuring both the intended topic and students' understanding of American vocabulary and culture.

There is no easy solution to this problem, but teacher awareness and sensitivity are starting points. In addition, encouraging students to ask questions and discussing tests thoroughly after they're given can help uncover unintended bias.

Making Provisions for Non-Native English Speakers

How would you do if your next exam in this class were presented in Spanish, French, or German? This prospect gives you some idea of the problems facing non-native English-speaking students during tests. Ways to accommodate language differences include modifying the test or test procedures (see Table 14.9). Of these modifications, simplifying test language appears most promising (Abedi, 1997). Unfortunately, little additional research

Table 14.9 Modifications to accommodate language diversity

Modifications of the Test	Modifications of the Test Procedures
Assessment in the native language	Extra assessment time
Changes in vocabulary or linguistic complexity	Oral directions in the native language
Addition of visual supports or extra example items	Use of dictionaries
Use of glossaries in native languages or in English	Reading aloud of questions in English
Linguistic modifications of test directions	Directions read aloud or explained

Source: Adapted from Butler & Stevens, 1997

exists that has examined the effectiveness of different modifications on test performance (Butler & Stevens, 1997).

Accommodating Diversity in Scoring

As you saw earlier, essay exams and authentic assessments can be effective for measuring students' ability to organize information, think analytically, and apply their understanding to real-world problems. However, they also place an extra burden on students who are wrestling with both content and language.

What can teachers do? Valid assessment often requires the use of essays and alternative formats, and teachers cannot ignore students' grammatical errors. One solution is to evaluate essays and performance assessments with two grades: one for content and another for grammar, spelling, and punctuation (Hamp-Lyons, 1992; Scarcella, 1990). **Multiple trait scoring** *creates different criteria for different dimensions of a product.* For example, an item in science that asks students to propose a solution to the problem of water pollution might be scored on three criteria: (a) solution to the problem, (b) understanding of content, and (c) way the ideas are developed (Hamp-Lyons, 1992). Breaking the score into three areas allows the teacher to discriminate among understanding of content, problem solving, and ability to use language. Each of these suggestions is designed to ensure, as much as possible, that test scores reflect differences in achievement and not cultural bias related to background knowledge, vocabulary, or testing sophistication.

Classroom Connections _____

Capitalizing on Diversity in Your Classroom.

1. Be continually aware of the effect that diversity can have on assessment.
   - At the beginning of the school year, a math teacher in an inner-city school carefully explains her grading system and what it requires of students. She emphasizes that it is designed to promote learning.
   - A first-grade teacher takes extra time and effort during parent–teacher conferences to explain how she arrives at grades for her students. She saves students' work samples and shares them with the parents during conferences.

2. Adapt testing procedures to meet the needs of all students.
   - A history teacher encourages her students to ask her about any terms on the test that they don't understand. Unless their understanding of the term is part of what she is measuring, she defines and illustrates the term for students.
   - A second-grade teacher adjusts her testing procedures for her non-native English speakers. She arranges to give the students extra time, and she provides an older student to act as a translator for those whose command of English is still rudimentary.

3. Thoroughly discuss results after tests have been scored and returned.
   - A science teacher discusses all of the frequently missed items on his tests. He asks students why they responded as they did and what their thinking was. He writes notes during the discussion to revise items that may have been ambiguous or that required knowledge not all students should be expected to know.

Grading and Reporting: The Total Assessment System

To this point, we have discussed the preparation of traditional test items, the design of alternative assessments, and the assessment process itself, which includes preparing students, administering assessments, and analyzing results. Designing a total assessment system requires considering additional issues:

- How many tests and quizzes should be given?
- How will authentic assessments be used?
- How will homework be counted?
- How is missed work made up?
- How are affective dimensions, such as cooperation and effort, reported in the overall assessment?
- How is performance reported (e.g., letter grade, percentage, descriptive statement)?

These decisions are largely the teacher's responsibility, and this is significant for beginning teachers, who have no experience to fall back on. Merely knowing that the decisions are the teacher's, however, removes some of the uncertainty in the process. We examine these decisions and offer some suggestions in the following sections.

Designing a Grading System

Designing a grading system is an important task because it influences both student learning and teacher workload. Some guidelines can help in this process:

1. Your system should be consistent with school and district policies.
2. Your system should be designed to gather frequent and systematic information from each student.
3. In most situations, homework should be an integral part of the assessment system.
4. You should be able to confidently defend the system to a parent or administrator if necessary.

With these guidelines in mind, let's look at elements of an effective system.

Formative and Summative Evaluation

14.34

Think about the effects of formative evaluation on elementary, junior high, and high school students. With which group would formative evaluation be most important? least important? Explain why this would be the case.

The way a teacher uses quizzes and tests influences learning. Although we often think of giving tests and quizzes to assign grades, they can also be given to provide the teacher and students with feedback about learning progress—perhaps a more important function. In this case, they are given, scored, and discussed just as any other quiz or test would be, but they are not included in any grading decision. This process is called **formative evaluation** because *it is used only to provide feedback to the learner.*

Tests, quizzes, homework, and authentic assessments used to make grading decisions, however, are part of the process called **summative evaluation,** which is *evaluation used for grading purposes.* In public schools, most assessments are used for summative evaluations, but formative evaluations can be helpful in making instructional decisions and in providing incentives for student effort (Stipek, 1996).

Norm-Referenced and Criterion-Referenced Evaluation

Assigning value to students' work is an important assessment role. This task is as diverse as giving smiley faces, writing comments on papers, and assigning grades. Norm-referenced and criterion-referenced evaluations are two ways to assign value to student performance. **Norm referencing** means that *decisions about students' work are based on comparisons with their peers;* **criterion referencing** means that *a decision is made according to a predetermined standard.* A comparison of norm and criterion referencing is found in Table 14.10.

Criterion-referenced evaluation has two important advantages. First, because it reflects the extent to which goals are met, it more effectively describes content mastery. Second, criterion referencing de-emphasizes competition, which can discourage students from helping each other, threaten peer relationships, detract from intrinsic motivation, and encourage students to attribute success and failure to ability rather than to effort (Ames, 1992; Maehr, 1992; Stipek, 1996). Although criterion referencing alone won't eliminate all these problems, it is usually preferable to norm referencing.

14.35

Is the assessment system for the class you're in norm referenced or criterion referenced? What makes it that way?

Tests and Quizzes

For teachers in upper-elementary, middle, and secondary schools, tests and quizzes form a cornerstone of the grading system. Some teachers add tests and quizzes together and count them as a certain percentage of the overall grade. Others weigh them differently in assigning grades. However it is done, frequent monitoring of progress with feedback to students is important for both achievement and motivation (Dempster, 1991; Stipek, 1996).

Authentic Assessments

If you're using authentic assessments, they should be included in your grading system. To do otherwise communicates that they are less important than the traditional measures you're using. If you rate student performance on the basis of well-defined criteria, scor-

Table 14.10   A comparison of norm referencing and criterion referencing

	Examples	Characteristics
Norm referencing	Grading on the curve: 15% of students get *A*s	Compares students' performances to each other
	15% get *B*s	Creates a competitive environment
	40% get *C*s	
	15% get *D*s	
	15% get *F*s	
Criterion referencing:	94–100 = A 86–93 = B	Reflects extent to which course goals are being met
	Performance assessments (e.g., recognizes shapes, knows rhyming sounds, knows directions)	Reduces student competitiveness

ing will have acceptable reliability and alternative assessments can then be an integral part of the total assessment system.

Homework

In Chapter 12, you found that properly designed homework contributes to learning. To be most effective, homework should be collected, scored, and included in the grading system (Cooper, 1989). Beyond this point, however, research provides little guidance as to how it should be managed. Accountability, feedback, and your own workload all influence this decision. Table 14.11 outlines some options.

As you can see, each option has advantages and disadvantages. The best strategy is one that results in learners making the most consistent and conscientious effort on their homework without costing you an inordinate amount of time.

Assigning Grades: Increasing Learning and Motivation

Having made decisions about tests, quizzes, alternative assessments, and homework, you are now ready to design your total grading system. At this point, you must make two decisions: (a) what to include and (b) the weight to assign each component. Tests, quizzes, alternative assessments, and homework should each be included in most cases. Some teachers build in additional factors, such as effort, class participation, and attitude. This practice, though common in classrooms, is discouraged by assessment experts (Gronlund & Linn, 1995). Gathering systematic information about affective variables is difficult, and assessing them is highly subjective. Factors such as effort, coop-

> **14.36**
> Using social cognitive theory, explain why it is important that homework be scored and included in the grading system. What can you do about the possibility that students will copy their homework from others?

Table 14.11 Homework assessment options

Option	Advantages	Disadvantages
Grade it yourself	Promotes learning. Allows diagnosis of students. Increases student effort.	Is very demanding for the teacher.
Grade samples	Reduces teacher work, compared with first option.	Doesn't give the teacher a total picture of student performance.
Collect at random intervals	Reduces teacher workload.	Reduces student effort unless homework is frequently collected.
Change papers, students grade	Provides feedback with minimal teacher effort.	Consumes class time. Doesn't give students feedback on their own work.
Students score own papers	Is the same as changing papers. Lets students see their own mistakes.	Is inaccurate for purposes of evaluation. Lets students not do the work and copy in class as it's being discussed.
Students get credit for completing assignment	Gives students feedback on their work when it's discussed in class.	Reduces effort of unmotivated students.
No graded homework, frequent short quizzes	Is effective with older and motivated students.	Reduces effort of unmotivated students.

eration, preparedness, and class attendance should be reflected in a separate section of the report card.

Here are two teachers' systems for assigning grades:

Sun Ngin		Lea DeLong	
Tests and Quizzes	50%	Tests	45%
Homework	20%	Quizzes	45%
Observation	20%	Homework	10%
Projects	10%		

We see that the systems are quite different. Sun Ngin, an eighth-grade physical-science teacher, emphasizes both homework and alternative assessments, which include projects and what he calls "observation." Traditional tests and quizzes count only 50% in his system. Lea DeLong emphasizes tests and quizzes much more heavily; they count 90% in her system. The rationale in each case was straightforward. Sun indicated that homework was important to student learning and believed that unless it was emphasized, students wouldn't do it. He also included projects as an important part of his grades. In his judgment, projects involved his students in the study of science, and he used systematic observation to chart their progress as they worked on projects and other hands-on activities. Lea, a secondary Algebra II teacher, thought that students fully understood the need to do their homework in order to be successful on the tests and quizzes. She gave a weekly quiz and three tests during a nine-week grading period.

In order to be effective in promoting learning, your assessment system must be understood by students (Thorkildsen, 1996). Even young students will understand the relationship between effort and grades if they are quizzed frequently and if their homework is scored and returned quickly. On the other hand, even high school students have problems understanding a grading system if it is too complex (Evans & Engelberg, 1988).

Raw Points or Percentages?

In assigning scores to assignments, quizzes, or tests, teachers have two options. In a percentage system, they convert each score to a percentage and then average the percentages as the grading period progresses. In the other system, they accumulate raw points and convert to a percentage only at the end of the period.

To illustrate these options, let's think back to Laura Brinson's work with her second-graders, first presented in our discussion of teachers' assessment patterns. Kelly, one of her students, missed 1 of 10 problems on a seatwork assignment. As is typical of many teachers, Laura used a percentage system and, because 9 correct out of 10 is 90%, she wrote 90 for Kelly on this assignment. This is a straightforward and simple process.

Suppose now that students are graded on another assignment; this time, it is five items long and Kelly gets three of the five correct. Her grade on this assignment would be 60. Teachers then typically average the assignments, meaning that Kelly's average at this point is 75 because the average of 90 and 60 is 75.

This process is flawed, however. By finding the percentage for each assignment and averaging the two, they are given equal weight. In fact, on the two assignments, Kelly has correctly responded to 12 of 15 problems. If Laura had recorded Kelly's raw points for each assignment, her average at that point would be 80 ($12/15 \times 100$), 5 points higher than the average gotten by using a percentage system.

If averaging percentages is flawed, why is it so common? The primary reason is simplicity. In addition to being simpler for teachers to manage, it is easier to communicate to students and parents. Many teachers, particularly those in the elementary and middle schools, have attempted point systems and later gone back to percentage systems because of pressure from students, who better understand percentage systems.

Recent research shows that computer grade-keeping systems facilitate the use of point systems (Feldman, Kropkf, & Alibrandi, 1996). These researchers also found the use of a point system in which students are given points for turning in assignments and compiling projects can undermine motivation by tacitly communicating that the goal in class is completing tasks versus learning. To avoid this, teachers need to grade on both quality and quantity and continually emphasize the role that instructional tasks play in learning.

As with most aspects of teaching, the option is your choice. A percentage system is fair if assignments are similar in length, tests are also similar in length, and tests are given more weight than quizzes and assignments. On the other hand, a point system can work if the teacher simply has the students keep a running total of their points and then communicates the number they must have for an A, a B, and so on at any point in the grading period.

14.37

What kind of grading system is used in the class you're taking? Is it a point, percentage, or some other system? Is the system clear? Do you know where you stand at all times during the semester or quarter?

Classroom Connections

Using Effective Assessment in Your Classroom

1. Be explicit about what will be covered on assessments.
    *   A social-studies teacher shares her table of specifications with her students prior to the test. In addition she explains, "On Thursday's test, you will be asked to explain in an essay question how the characteristics of the northern, middle, and southern colonies affected the economy of each region." The test the next day closely follows this blueprint.

2. Provide practice for your students under test-like conditions.
    *   As she prepares her class for an essay exam, a social-studies teacher displays the following question on the overhead: "The southern colonies were primarily agricultural rather than industrial. Using the characteristics of the region, explain why this would be the case."

She gives the students a few minutes to respond. She then discusses the item and appropriate responses to it, reminding students that this is the type of question they will have on the test.

3. Prepare and keep a test-item file.
    *   A fourth-grade teacher writes items for science and social studies and stores them in a computer file, classified according to topic. When he begins to prepare a test, he goes back into the file to retrieve and review the items.

4. Do an analysis of test items.
    *   After giving a test, a sixth-grade teacher surveys the distribution of student responses. She then revises items that are misleading or that have ineffective distracters. The revisions are stored in the computer for next time.

5. Hand back tests, discuss them, and collect them for later use.

- A second-grade teacher discusses problems that a significant number of students missed on a math test and then asks the students to rework the problems and hand them back in.

6. Consider the effects of the total assessment system on learning and motivation.

- A history teacher gives frequent quizzes between major tests. He notices a decrease in test anxiety, as well as an increase in the amount of time students spend studying for his classes.

Windows on Classrooms

At the beginning of the chapter, you saw how Kathy Stevens used her understanding of assessment to help increase both her students' achievement and motivation. In studying the chapter, you've seen how assessment, in both traditional and alternative forms, can help teachers make strategic decisions about their students' learning progress.

Let's look now at another teacher working with a group of students. As you read the case study, compare the teacher's approach with the suggestions you've studied in the chapter.

Ron Hawkins is a tenth-grade English teacher at Brentwood High School. He teaches three sections of standard English and two sections of English Honors II.

We look in now at his third period on Monday as he begins a unit on pronoun cases with one of his standard classes.

The tardy bell rang at 9:10 as Ron began, "All right, listen, everyone. . . . Today, we're going to begin a study of pronoun cases. Everybody turn to page 484 in your text. . . . We see at the top of the page that we're dealing with pronoun cases. This is important in our writing because we want to be able to write and use Standard English correctly, and this is one of the places where people often get mixed up. So, when we're finished with our study here, you'll all be able to use pronouns correctly in your writing."

He then wrote the following on the chalkboard:

> Pronouns use the nominative case when they're subjects and predicate nominatives.
>
> Pronouns use the objective case when they're direct objects, indirect objects, or objects of prepositions.

"Let's review briefly," Ron continued. "Give me a sentence that has both a direct and indirect object in it. . . . Anyone?"

"Mr. Hawkins gives us too much homework," Amato offered jokingly.

Ron wrote the sentence on the chalkboard amid laughter from the students and then continued, smiling, "Okay, Amato. Good sentence, even though it's incorrect. I don't give you *enough* work. . . . What's the subject in the sentence?"

" . . . "

"Go ahead, Amato."

"Oh, I'm sorry. . . . *Mr. Hawkins.*"

"Yes, good. *Mr. Hawkins* is the subject," Ron replied as he underlined *Mr. Hawkins* in the sentence.

"Now, what's the direct object? . . . Helen?"

". . . Homework."

"All right, good. And what's the indirect object? . . . Anya?"

". . . *Us.*"

"Excellent, everybody." Ron proceeded by reviewing predicate nominatives and objects of prepositions.

He then continued, "Now let's look at some additional examples. Look at the overhead."

He then displayed an overhead with ten sentences written on it. Here are the first four.

1. Did you get the card from Esteban and (I, me)?
2. Will Meg and (she, her) run the concession stand?
3. They treat (whoever, whomever) they hire very well.
4. I looked for someone (who, whom) could give me directions to the theater.

"Okay, look at the first one. Which is correct? . . . Omar?"

". . . Me."

"Good, Omar. How about the second one? . . . Lonnie?"

". . . Her."

"Not quite, Lonnie. Listen to this. . . . Suppose I turn the sentence around a little and say, 'Meg and her will run the concession stand.' See, that doesn't sound right, does it? *Meg and she* is a compound subject, and when we have a subject, we use the nominative case. . . . Are you okay on that, Lonnie?"

Lonnie nodded and Ron went on, "Look at the third one. . . . Cheny."

". . . I don't know. . . . *whoever,* I guess."

"This one is tricky all right," Ron nodded. "When we use *whoever* and *whomever, whoever* is the nominative case and *whomever* is the objective case. In this sentence, *whomever* is a direct object, so it is the correct form."

Ron then continued with the rest of the sentences as he had with the first four. After he finished, he gave the students another list of sentences in which they were to select the correct form of the pronoun.

On Tuesday, Ron first went over the exercises the students had completed for homework and then continued with some additional examples of using *who, whom, whoever,* and *whomever.* He then discussed the rules for pronoun–antecedent agreement (Pronouns must agree with their antecedents in gender and number) and again had students work examples as he had done with pronoun cases. He continued with pronouns and their antecedents on Wednesday and began a discussion of indefinite pronouns as antecedents for personal pronouns—*anybody, either, each, one, someone*—and had students work examples as he had done before.

Near the end of class on Thursday, Ron announced, "Tomorrow, we're going to have a test on this material—pronoun cases, pronouns and their antecedents, and indefinite pronouns. You have your notes, so study hard . . . Are there any questions? . . . Good. I expect you all to do well. I'll see you tomorrow."

On Friday morning as the students filed into class and the bell rang, Ron picked up a stack of tests from his desk.

"Everybody ready?" he asked, and amid some mock groans and murmurs each student took a test copy and began working.

The test comprised 30 sentences, ten of which dealt with case, ten with antecedents, and ten with indefinite pronouns. The final part of the test directed the students to write a paragraph.

The following are some sample items from the test: For each of the items below, mark A on your answer sheet if the pronoun case is correct in the sentence, and mark B if it is incorrect. If it is incorrect, supply the correct pronoun.

1. Be careful who you tell.
2. Will Rennee and I be in the outfield?
3. My brother and me like water skiing.

Write the pronoun that correctly completes the sentence.

11. Arlene told us about _____ visit to the dentist to have braces put on.
12. The Wilsons planted a garden in _____ backyard.
13. Cal read the recipe and put _____ in the file.
14. Each of the girls on the team wore _____ school sweater to the game.
15. None of the brass has lost _____ shine yet.
16. Few of the boys on the team have taken _____ physicals yet.

The directions for the final part of the test were as follows:

Write a short paragraph that contains at least

two examples of pronouns in the nominative case and two examples of pronouns in the objective case. Include also at least two examples of pronouns that agree with their antecedents. Remember!! The paragraph must make sense. It cannot just be a series of sentences.

Ron watched as his students worked, periodically walking up and down the aisles. Seeing that 15 minutes remained in the period and that some students were only starting on their paragraphs, he announced, "You only have 15 minutes left. Watch your time and work quickly. You must be finished by the end of the period."

He then continued monitoring the students, again reminding them to work quickly when 10 minutes were left and again when 5 minutes were left.

Luis, Simao, Moy, and Rudy were hastily finishing the last few words of their tests as the bell rang. Luis finally turned in his paper as Ron's fourth-period students were filing into the room.

"Here," Ron said. "This pass will get you into Mrs. Washington's class if you're late. . . . How did you do?"

"Okay, I think," Luis said over his shoulder as he scurried out of the room, "except for the last part. It was hard. I couldn't get started."

"I'll look at it," Ron said. "Scoot now."

On Monday, Ron returned the tests, saying, "Here are your papers. You did fine on the sentences, but your paragraphs need a lot of work. Why did you have so much trouble with them, when we had so much practice?"

"It was hard, Mr. Hawkins."

"Not enough time."

"I hate to write."

Ron listened patiently and then said, "Be sure you write your scores in your notebooks. . . . Okay. . . . You have them all written down? . . . Are there any questions?"

"Number 8," Enrique asked.

"Okay, let's look at 8. It says, 'I didn't know to (who, whom) to give the letter.' There, the pronoun is the object of a preposition, so it's *whom.*

"Any others?"

A sprinkling of questions came from around the room, and Ron responded, "We don't have time to go over all of them. I'll discuss three more."

He responded to the three students who seemed to be most urgent in waving their hands. He then collected their tests and began a discussion of adjective and adverb clauses.

Questions for Discussion and Analysis

Analyze Ron's lesson now in the context of the information in this chapter. In doing your analysis, consider the following questions. In each case, be specific and take information directly from the case study in making your comparison.

1. Alternative or authentic assessments were discussed in the chapter. How "authentic" was Ron's assessment?

2. How well were Ron's curriculum and assessment aligned? Explain specifically. What could he have done to increase curricular alignment?

3. In the section on effective testing practices, we discussed preparing students for tests, administering tests, and analyzing results. How effectively did Ron perform each task? Describe specifically what he might have done to be more effective in these areas.

4. Like most classes, Ron's class is composed of learners with diverse backgrounds. How effective was his teaching and assessment for these students?

5. What were the primary strengths of Ron's teaching and assessment? What were the primary weaknesses? If you think Ron's teaching and assessment could have been improved on the basis of information in this chapter, what suggestions would you make? Be specific.

6. Was Ron's teaching primarily behaviorist in its orientation, or was it more constructivist? Explain. How might he change his orientation?

Summary

Classroom Assessment

Classroom assessment includes the data teachers gather through tests, quizzes, homework, and classroom observations, as well as the decisions teachers make about student progress. Effective assessment results in increased learning, as well as improved motivation.

Teachers informally measure student understanding during classroom activities and discussions. Formal measurements are attempts to systematically gather information for grading and reporting.

Validity involves the appropriateness of interpretations made from measurements. Reliability describes the extent to which measurements are consistently interpreted. Both concepts provide standards for effective assessment.

Traditional Assessment

Teachers in elementary schools rely on performance measures and commercially prepared items and focus on affective goals more than teachers of older students. Teachers of older students tend to use completion items more than other formats, and their assessments overemphasize memory and low-level outcomes.

Teachers can improve the effectiveness of their assessments by keeping validity and reliability issues in mind when they construct items. Multiple-choice, true–false, matching, completion, and essay items all have strengths and weaknesses that can be addressed through thoughtful item writing.

Authentic Assessment

Authentic assessments, including performance assessments and portfolios, ask students to perform complex tasks similar to those found in the real world. In designing alternative assessments, teachers attempt to place students in realistic settings, asking them to perform high-level tasks involving problem solving in various content areas. Portfolio assessment involves students in the construction of a collection of work samples that documents learning progress. The reliability of alternative assessments can be improved through careful application of predetermined criteria and the use of systematic observation, checklists, and rating scales to evaluate products.

Effective Assessment Practices

Effective assessments are congruent with goals and instruction, and effective teachers communicate what will be covered on assessments, allow students to practice on items similar to those that will appear on tests, teach test-taking skills, and state positive expectations for student performance. Increasing testing frequency, using criterion referencing, providing clear information about tests, and giving students ample time help reduce test anxiety.

Grading and Reporting: The Total Assessment System

Grading and reporting are important functions of an assessment system. Formative evaluation provides feedback about learning, whereas summative evaluations are used for grading purposes. Norm-referenced evaluation compares a learner's performance with that of peers, whereas criterion-referenced evaluation compares students' performance with a standard.

Important Concepts _____

alternative assessment (p. 594)

assessment system (p. 580)

authentic assessment (p. 594)

checklists (p. 598)

classroom assessment (p. 580)

completion items (p. 591)

criterion referencing (p. 615)

distracters (p. 586)

essay items (p. 592)

evaluation (p. 581)

formal measurement (p. 581)

formative evaluation (p. 614)

informal measurements (p. 581)

matching format (p. 590)

measurement (p. 581)

multiple-choice items (p. 586)

multiple trait scoring (p. 613)

norm referencing (p. 615)

performance assessment(s) (pp. 594, 595)

portfolios (p. 600)

rating scales (p. 600)

reliability (p. 583)

rubrics (p. 593)

summative evaluation (p. 614)

systematic observations (p. 598)

table of specifications (p. 605)

test anxiety (p. 608)

true–false format (p. 590)

validity (p. 582)

Appendix

Standardized Tests

Teachers ask a number of questions about students' progress that are difficult to answer on the basis of teacher-made instruments alone. They include: How do the students in my class compare with students across the country?, How well is our curriculum preparing students for college or future training?, and How does a particular student compare with other students of similar ability? **Standardized tests,** or *assessment instruments given to large samples of students (in many cases, nationwide) under uniform conditions and scored according to uniform procedures,* are designed to answer those questions. The scores people make on a standardized test are compared with the scores of a **norming group,** who are *people similar in age, grade level, and background who have taken the same test.* A student's performance on the test is then reported in comparison with this norming group.

The influence of standardized testing can hardly be overstated. The fact that students in other industrialized countries, such as Japan and Germany, score higher than U.S. students on some of these tests has alarmed many in this country (Stedman, 1997). The "reform movement" that began in the early 1980s was largely a by-product of standardized test results. Few of the concerns voiced about students' learning progress have been made without information gathered from standardized tests. Standardized tests also influence individual students. "The results of a morning's testing often become a powerful factor in decisions about the future of each student" (Gardner, 1992, p. 77).

Standardized testing is also controversial. In a given year, 127 million students take state-mandated tests at a cost of between $725 million and $915 million annually (National Commission on Testing and Public Policy, 1990). In addition, standardized tests are often used to compare students' performance in different schools, districts, states, and even countries. Many teachers believe that standardized testing is overemphasized and adversely affects a balanced school curriculum (Herman et al., 1994; Urdan & Paris, 1991). To place these concerns in perspective, let's look at some uses of standardized tests.

Functions of Standardized Tests

Standardized tests serve several functions. They can be used to gather information about learning progress, to diagnose an individual student's strengths and weaknesses, and to make selection and placement decisions in instructional programs. They also help school personnel in measuring the effectiveness of specific programs.

Student Assessment

Probably the most common function of standardized testing is to provide an external, objective picture of student progress. Parents, teachers, and school administrators often want to know how individual students or groups of students compare with other students at their grade level. Standardized tests provide one means of comparison and, when combined with teacher-made assessments and other measures of classroom performance, they can help provide a complete picture of student progress.

Diagnosis

Standardized tests are also used to diagnose student strengths and weaknesses. For example, if a student scores low on the math section of an achievement test, a more detailed diagnostic test could be used to gather additional information about specific strengths and weaknesses in math.

Placement and Selection

Placing students and selecting students for programs where the number of available slots are limited are two other uses of standardized tests. For instance, a math faculty will have students coming to their high school from "feeder" middle schools, private schools, and schools outside the district. Scores from the math section of a standardized test can help place students in classes that will best match their backgrounds and capabilities.

Standardized test results can also be used to place students in advanced programs, such as programs for the gifted, and they are used as one basis for university selection. Most of us, for instance, took either the *Scholastic Aptitude Test (SAT)* or the *American College Testing Program (ACT)* during our junior or senior year in high school. These are standardized tests, the results of which played an important part in determining whether we were accepted by the college of our choice. Because college students come from different parts of the country and because their backgrounds are diverse, these tests provide a basis for uniform comparison.

Program Evaluation and Improvement

Standardized tests can also provide valuable information about instructional programs. For example, an elementary school has moved from a traditional reading program to one that emphasizes writing and children's literature. To assess the effectiveness of this change, the faculty use teacher-made assessments, student work samples, and the perceptions of teachers and parents. However, the faculty still don't know how the students' performance compares with their performance when the old curriculum was in place or with the performance of peers in other reading programs. Standardized test results can help answer these questions.

Accountability

Increasingly, schools and teachers are being held responsible for student learning (Darling-Hammond & Snyder, 1992). Parents, school board members, state officials, and decision makers at the federal level are demanding evidence that tax dollars are being used efficiently. Standardized test scores provide one indicator of this effectiveness.

The accountability movement has resulted in the creation of a controversial testing program called the National Assessment of Educational Progress (Jones, 1996). Critics contend that misuse of standardized test scores can result in narrowing the curriculum and give an inaccurate picture of student learning (E. Baker, 1989). Proponents claim that standardized tests can provide valuable information about the relative performance of different states, districts, and schools.

Types of Standardized Tests

Achievement Tests

Achievement tests, the most widely used type of standardized tests, *are designed to measure and communicate how much students have learned in different content areas.* Although most common in reading and math, they also measure learning in science, social studies, computer literacy, and other content areas. Popular achievement tests include the *Iowa Test of Basic Skills,* the *California Achievement Test,* the *Stanford Achievement Test,* the *Comprehensive Test of Basic Skills,* and the *Metropolitan Achievement Test,* as well as individual statewide assessments and minimum-level skills tests.

Standardized achievement tests serve several purposes:

- Determining how well students have mastered a content area
- Comparing the performance of students with others across the country
- Tracking student progress over time
- Determining whether students have the background knowledge to begin instruction in particular areas
- Identifying learning problems

Most standardized achievement tests come as batteries of specific tests administered over several days. These tests are intended to reflect a curriculum common to most schools, and thus will assess some, but not all, of the goals of a specific school. This is both a strength and a weakness. Because they are designed for a range of schools, they can be used in a variety of locations. On the other hand, this "one size fits all" approach may not accurately measure achievement for a specific curriculum. For example, one study found that only 47% to 71% of the math content measured on commonly used standardized achievement batteries was the same as content covered in popular elementary math textbooks (Berliner, 1984). In a worst-case scenario, this means that students might have had opportunity to learn less than half the content measured on the test.

Schools and teachers should be cautious in selecting and interpreting standardized achievement tests for their students. When selecting a test, it is important to go beyond the name and to examine the specific contents described in the testing manual's table of specifications. Comparing the content of the test with your curriculum objectives helps decide whether the test is valid for your use.

Diagnostic Tests

Whereas achievement tests measure students' progress in a variety of curriculum areas, **diagnostic tests** *provide a detailed description of learners' strengths and weaknesses in specific skill areas.* They are common in the primary grades, where instruction is designed to match the developmental level of the child, especially in the area of math and reading. Diagnostic tests are usually administered individually and, compared to achievement tests, they include a larger number of items, use more subtests, and report scores in more specific areas (Gronlund & Linn, 1995). A diagnostic test in reading, for example, might target letter recognition, word analysis skills, sight vocabulary, vocabulary in context, and reading comprehension. Commonly used diagnostic tests include the *Metropolitan Achievement Tests,* the *Detroit Test of Learning Aptitude,* the *Durrell Analysis of Reading Difficulty,* and the *Stanford Diagnostic Reading Test.*

Intelligence Tests

In Chapter 4, we discussed **intelligence** in the context of individual differences and defined it as *the capacity to acquire knowledge, the ability to think and reason in the abstract, and the capability for solving problems.* **Intelligence tests** are designed to measure those abilities. Attempts to measure intelligence in a valid and reliable way were among the first standardized tests.

A Short History of Intelligence Tests

Standardized intelligence tests originated in the early 1900s when Alfred Binet was asked by the French minister of public instruction to assist in developing an instrument to be used in the education of students with mental disabilities. He selected a number of school-related skills, such as defining words and making change, and with his partner, Theodore Simon, developed a series of tests based on these skills. They gave the tests to heterogeneous groups of children, eliminating items so difficult that no students passed or so easy that all did. The result was an objective instrument, essentially independent of social class or the person administering the test, that could be passed by the average child of a given age.

Although intelligence tests were first developed to measure the capabilities of learners with disabilities, they were later broadened to describe the performance of a broad spectrum of people. Initially, performance was described as a mental age; for example, a child succeeding on tasks designed for a typical eight-year-old had a mental age of eight years.

To overcome problems with older populations—describing a 20-year-old as functioning like a 30-year-old wasn't meaningful, for example—the mental age (M.A.) was divided by the chronological age (C.A.) and multiplied by 100, resulting in the familiar ratio IQ (intelligence quotient). For example, a six-year-old with an M.A. of an eight-year-old would have an IQ of 133 ($8/6 = 1.33 \times 100 = 133$).

The importance of Binet and Simon's pioneering work is hard to overstate. For the first time, educators had an objective way of predicting school success; students who performed well on the test usually did well in school and vice versa. The predictions weren't perfect, but they were a vast improvement over people's intuition. The test was translated and brought to the United States by Lewis Terman, a professor at Stanford, and it then became the famous Stanford–Binet. The updated version is one of the two most widely used intelligence tests in schools today.

The Stanford–Binet

The Stanford–Binet is an individually administered instrument comprising subtests, much like Binet's original. It comes in a kit that includes a box of standard toy objects for young children, booklets of printed cards for older students, a large picture of unisex and multicultural dolls, a recording booklet, and a test manual. Earlier versions heavily emphasized verbal tasks, but the most recent edition is more diverse, including performance items not requiring verbal skills (Thorndike, Hagen, & Sattler, 1986). Table A.1 presents descriptions of some sample subtests in the latest revision.

The Stanford–Binet is a technically sound instrument second only to the Wechsler scales (described in the next section) in popularity. It has been revised and renormed a number of times over the years, most recently in 1986, using 5,000 schoolchildren in 47 states and Grades 3 through 12, stratified by economic status, geographic region, and community size. Members of the White, African American, Hispanic, Asian, and Asian/Pacific Islander subcultures were all represented in proportion to their membership in the total U.S. population. Teachers should consider the norming population for a test because similarities between that population and their own influences test validity.

The Wechsler Scales

Developed by David Wechsler over a period of 40 years, the Wechsler scales are the most popular intelligence tests in use today (Salvia & Ysseldyke, 1988). The three Wechsler tests, aimed at preschool–primary, elementary, and adult populations, have two main parts: verbal and performance. The Wechsler Intelligence Scale for Children–Third Edition (WISC–III; Wechsler, 1991) is an individually administered intelligence test with 13 subtests, of which six are verbal and seven are performance (Table A.2 presents some sample subtests). The performance sections were added because of dissatisfaction with the strong verbal emphasis of earlier intelligence tests. Like the Stanford–Binet, the Wechsler scales are technically sound (Anastasi, 1988; Kaplan & Saccuzzo, 1993).

The Wechsler's two subtests, yielding separate verbal and performance scores, are an asset. For example, a substantially higher score on the performance compared with the verbal subtest could indicate a language problem related to poor reading or language-based cultural differences (Kaplan & Saccuzzo, 1993). Because these subtests demand a minimum of verbal ability, performance tasks are helpful in studying students who resist school-like tasks, learners with disabilities, and persons with limited education (Maller, 1994).

Table A.1 Sample subtests from the revised (4th edition) Stanford–Binet

Subtest	Example/Description
Comprehension (Verbal reasoning)	Students are asked to explain facets of everyday life (e.g., "Why do people wear sunglasses?" or "Why do we go to the doctor?"). This subtest measures the ability to use and reason with words.
Number series (Quantitative reasoning)	Students are presented with a numerical sequence such as 1, 4, 7, and are expected to provide the next number. This subtest measures students' ability to find abstract patterns in numbers.
Abstract/visual reasoning (Copying)	Pictures of block designs are shown to students, and they are asked to copy them either with blocks (young children) or with paper and pencil (older children). This subtest measures students' ability to visualize and reproduce abstract patterns.

Source: Adapted with permission of The Riverside Publishing Company from *Stanford–Binet Intelligence Scale Technical Manual: Fourth Edition* by R. L. Thorndike, E. P. Hagen, and J. M. Sattler. The Riverside Publishing Company, 8420 W. Bryn Mawr Avenue, Chicago, IL 60631. Copyright 1986.

Table A.2   Sample items from the WISC–III

Verbal Section	
Subtest	**Description/Examples**
Information	This subtest taps general knowledge common to American culture: a. How many minutes are there in an hour? b. Who was the first president of the United States?
Arithmetic	This subtest is a test of basic mathematical knowledge and skills, including counting and addition through division: a. Ted had three cookies but gave one to his friend. How many did he have then? b. There were six balls to play with and two teams. How many balls could each team have?
Similarities	This subtest is designed to measure abstract and logical thinking through use of analogies: a. How are a dog and a tree alike? b. How are books and newspapers alike?

Performance Section	
Subtest	**Description/Examples**
Picture completion	Students are shown a picture with elements missing, which they are required to identify. This subtest measures general knowledge as well as visual comprehension.
Block design	This subtest focuses on a number of abstract figures. Designed to measure visual-motor coordination, it requires students to match patterns displayed by the examiner.

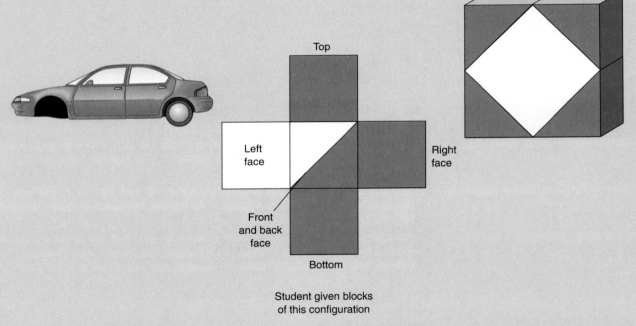

Top

Left face

Right face

Front and back face

Bottom

Student given blocks of this configuration

Individual versus Group Intelligence Tests

Individually administered intelligence tests have significant advantages over group ones. Because both the directions and responses are oral, no opportunity for an error on an answer sheet exists, and the test administrator can seek clarification of uncertain answers and spot signs of fatigue, worry, or anxiety. Also, by observing carefully, the test administrator can often determine why the student gave the answer he or she did. These factors are important in interpreting a student's score. Experts emphasize that attentiveness, motivation, and anxiety can all have powerful effects on intelligence test performance (Snyderman & Rothman, 1987).

In contrast with individually administered tests, group tests are heavily weighted toward verbal skills, and are susceptible to motivational, test-taking, and language problems. Because test data are so important in decision making and because individual tests are clearly superior, the use of group intelligence tests for individual diagnosis and placement is questionable.

Aptitude Tests

Although *aptitude* and *intelligence* are often used synonymously, aptitude is only one characteristic of intelligence—the capacity to acquire knowledge. **Aptitude tests** *are designed to predict the potential for future learning and to measure general abilities developed over long periods of time*. Aptitude tests are commonly used in selection, placement, and assessment decisions, and correlate highly with achievement tests (Popham, 1995). The concept of *aptitude* is intuitively sensible; for example, people will say, "I just don't have any aptitude for math," implying that their potential for learning math is limited.

The two most common aptitude tests at the high-school level are the SAT and the ACT. They are designed to measure a student's potential for success in college. This potential is heavily influenced by previous experience, however; classroom-related knowledge, particularly in language and mathematics, is critical for success on the tests. But because the tests are objective and reliable, they eliminate teacher bias and the unevenness of grades from different teachers and different schools. In this regard, they add valuable additional information in predicting future success.

The SAT I is a revised version of the original Scholastic Aptitude Test (SAT) containing six subsections: three verbal and three math. The verbal subtests include analogies, sentence completion (vocabulary and sentence structure), and critical reasoning; math subtests include standard computation, estimation, and student-produced response questions. Calculators are now allowed for use during the test.

The American College Testing Program (ACT) consists of tests in four areas: English, math, reading, and science reasoning. The total test takes about three hours, and calculators are not allowed.

Evaluating Standardized Tests: Validity Revisited

Wendy Klopman was a little nervous. She had been asked to serve on a district-wide committee to select a new standardized achievement test battery for the elementary grades. Her task was to get feedback from the faculty at her school about two options, the Stanford Achievement Test and the California Achievement Test.

After giving a brief overview of the two tests during a faculty meeting, Wendy opened the floor for questions.

"How much do the two tests cover problem solving?" a fifth-grade teacher asked.

"We're moving our language arts curriculum more in the direction of writing. How do the tests cover this topic?" a first-grade teacher wondered.

As the discussion continued, a confused and exasperated colleague asked, "Which one is better? That's really the bottom line. How about a simple answer?"

Wendy couldn't offer a simple answer, not because she was unprepared, but because she was asked to make a judgment about validity.

In Chapter 14, you saw that validity involves "the adequacy and appropriateness of the interpretations made from assessments, with regard to a particular use" (Gronlund & Linn, 1995, p. 47), and we emphasized the importance of matching assessments and goals. For teacher-made tests, validity is influenced by the kinds of assessments teachers construct and how the assessments are used.

In the case of standardized tests, determining validity is different because the tests have already been constructed. Here, the teacher is asked to judge the suitability of a test for a specific purpose. Validity resides in the appropriate use of a test, not in the test itself (Messick, 1989; Shepard, 1993).

Experts describe three kinds of validity: (a) content, (b) predictive, and (c) construct, and each provides a different perspective on the issue of appropriate use.

Content Validity

Content validity *represents the overlap between what is taught and what is tested.* Content validity is determined by comparing test content with curriculum objectives and is a primary concern when considering standardized achievement tests. The questions Wendy was asked about which test was "better" and whether they covered problem solving and writing addressed content validity. The "better" test is the one with the closer match between a school's goals and the content of the test.

Predictive Validity

Often, educators use standardized tests to predict how students will do in a future course or program of study. **Predictive validity** *is an indicator of a test's ability to gauge future performance.* It is central to the SAT and the ACT; these tests are designed to measure a student's potential to do college work. Predictive validity is also the focus of tests that gauge students' readiness for academic tasks in kindergarten and first grade.

Predictive validity is usually quantified by correlating a test and some other criterion, such as grades. A perfect correspondence or correlation between two variables would be 1.0; in testing, most correlations are substantially less than that. For example, a correlation of .42 exists between the SAT and college grades (Shepard, 1993). High school grades are the only predictor that is better (a correlation of .48).

Why isn't the correlation between tests and college performance higher? The primary reason is that the SAT is designed to predict "general readiness" for college; other factors, such as motivation, study habits, and specific content background, also affect performance.

Construct Validity

Construct validity *is an indicator of the logical connection between a test and what it is designed to measure.* It is somewhat abstract but important in understanding the total concept of *validity* (Messick, 1989; Shepard, 1993). It answers the question, Do these items actually measure the ideas the test is designed to measure? For instance, in examining the SAT, many of the items do indeed tap the ability to do abstract thinking about words and numbers—tasks that students are likely to face in their college experience. Because of this, the test has construct validity.

Understanding and Interpreting Standardized Test Scores

We said earlier that standardized tests are given to literally thousands of students. To deal with the vast amounts of information gathered and to describe individuals' performances compared with others', statistical methods are used in summarizing test information.

Descriptive Statistics

To illustrate the use of statistics in summarizing information, examine Table A.3, which contains scores made by two classes of 31 students on a 50-item test. (As you examine this information, keep in mind that a standardized test would have a sample much larger than 31 and would probably contain a larger number of items. We use a class-size example here for the sake of illustration.)

The scores for the two classes are ranked from the highest to the lowest score and also include the mean, median, and mode. (We discuss the mean, median, and mode in the sections that follow.) As you can see, the simple array of scores can be cumbersome and uninformative, even when scores are ranked. An efficient way of summarizing information is needed.

Frequency Distributions

One way of summarizing test data is to simply count the number of people who obtained each score; this is called a **frequency distribution,** which can be represented as a graph with the possible scores on the horizontal *(x)* axis and the frequency, or the number of students who got each score, on the vertical *(y)* axis. The frequency distributions for the two classes are shown in Figure A.1.

This information is still in rough form, but we can already begin to see differences between the two classes. For instance, the scores from the first class are spread out over a wider range than the second class, and there is a greater grouping of scores near the middle of the second distribution. Beyond this qualitative description, however, the distribution isn't particularly helpful. A more quantitative summary of the information is needed.

Measures of Central Tendency

Measures of central tendency—*the mean, median, and mode—are quantitative descriptions of how the group performed as a whole.* The **mean** is *the average score,* the **median** is *the middle score in the distribution,* and the **mode** is *the most frequent score.*

Table A.3   Scores of two classes on a 50-item test

Class 1	Class 2
50	48
49	47
49	46
48	46
47	45
47	45
46	44 ⎤
46	44
45	44 mode
45	44
45	44 ⎦
44 ⎤	43
44	43
44 mode	43
44 ⎦	43
43—median	42—median & mean
42—mean	42
41	42
41	42
40	41
40	41
39	41
39	40
38	40
37	39
37	39
36	38
35	38
34	37
34	36
33	35

To obtain a mean, simply add the scores and divide by the number of scores. As it turns out, both distributions have 1,302/31 = 42. The class average or mean of 42 is one indicator of how each group performed as a whole.

The median for the first distribution is 43 because half the scores (15) fall equal to or above 43 and the other half are equal to or below 43. Using the same process, we can find that the median for the second distribution is 42.

Figure A.1 Frequency distributions for two classes on a 50-item test

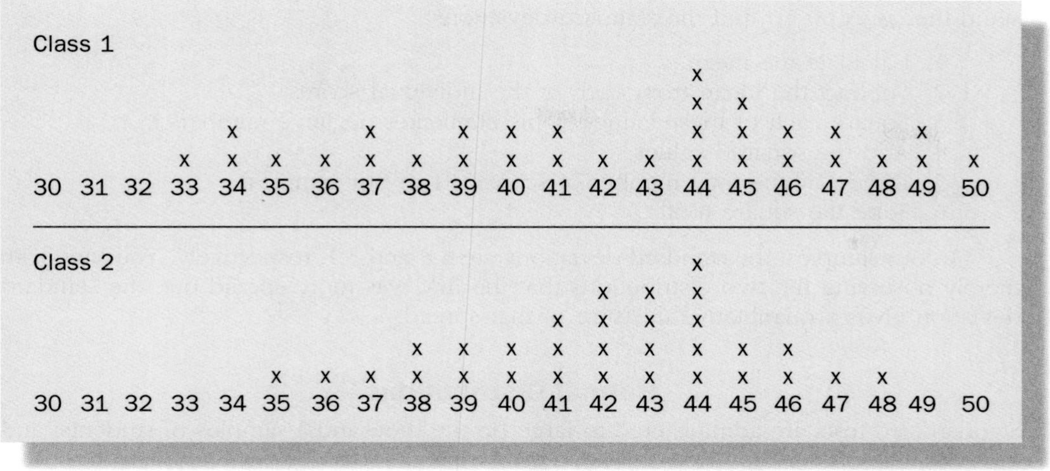

```
Class 1
                                          x
                                          x   x
           x         x     x   x   x      x   x   x   x         x
       x   x   x   x   x   x   x   x   x   x   x   x   x   x   x   x   x
      30  31  32  33  34  35  36  37  38  39  40  41  42  43  44  45  46  47  48  49  50
   ─────────────────────────────────────────────────────────────────────────────────
Class 2
                                                  x
                                          x   x   x
                                      x   x   x   x
                          x   x   x   x   x   x   x   x   x
                  x   x   x   x   x   x   x   x   x   x   x   x   x
      30  31  32  33  34  35  36  37  38  39  40  41  42  43  44  45  46  47  48  49  50
```

The median is useful when extremely high or low scores skew the mean and give a false picture of the sample. For example, you commonly hear or read demographic statistics such as "The median income for families of four in this country went from . . . in 1988 to . . . in 1998." The *median* income is used because just a few people like Bill Gates would make the average (mean) income quite high and give an artificial indicator of typical families' standards of living. The median, in contrast, is not affected by these extremes and gives a more realistic picture of the typical American family's economic status.

Looking once more at the two samples, you can see that the most frequent score for each is 44, which is the mode. Small samples, such as here, will often have more than one mode, resulting in "bimodal" or even "trimodal" distributions.

Using our measures of central tendency, you can see that the two samples are very much alike: the same mean, nearly the same median, and the same mode. As you saw from examining the frequency distribution, however, this doesn't give a complete picture of the two. A measure of their variability or "spread" is also needed.

Measures of Variability

To get a more accurate picture of the samples, you need to find out how much the scores in the sample vary, or what the spread is. One measure of variability is the **range**—*the distance between the top and bottom scores*. In the first class, the range is 17; in the second class, the range is 13. This finding confirms what you saw earlier in the frequency distribution. Although simple to compute, the range suffers from the problem of being overly influenced by one or more extreme scores. Another measure of variability that minimizes the problem is the **standard deviation,** which is *a statistical mea-*

sure of the spread of scores. With the use of computers, teachers rarely have to calculate a standard deviation manually, but we describe the procedure here to help you understand the concept. To find the standard deviation:

1. Calculate the mean.
2. Subtract the mean from each of the individual scores.
3. Square each of these values. (This eliminates negative numbers.)
4. Add the squared values.
5. Divide by the total number of scores (31 in our samples).
6. Take the square root.

In our samples, the standard deviations are 4.8 and 3.1, respectively. You saw from merely observing the two distributions that the first was more spread out; the standard deviation gives a quantitative measure of that spread.

Normal Distributions

Standardized tests are administered to large (in the thousands) samples of students, and the distribution of scores often approximates a normal distribution. To understand this concept, look again at our two distributions of scores and then focus specifically on the second one. If you drew a line over the top of the frequency distribution, it would appear as shown in Figure A.2.

Now imagine a very large sample of scores, such as you would find from a typical standardized test. The curve would approximate the one shown in Figure A.3. This is a **normal distribution,** which is *a distribution of scores in which the mean, median, and mode are all the same score, and the scores distribute themselves in a bell-shaped curve.* Many large samples of human characteristics, such as height and weight, tend to distribute themselves in this way, as do the large samples of most standardized tests.

Our sample has both a mean and median of 42 but a mode of 44, so its measures of central tendency don't quite fit the normal curve. Also, as you can see from Figure A.3, 68% of all the scores fall within one standard deviation from the mean, but in our distribution, about 71% of the scores are within one standard deviation above and below the mean. You can see from these illustrations that the samples aren't quite normal distributions; this is typical of smaller samples found in most classrooms.

Interpreting Standardized Test Results

Using our two small samples, we have illustrated techniques to summarize standardized test score results. Again, keep in mind that data gathered from standardized tests come from literally thousands of students, rather than from the small number we used

Figure A.2   Frequency distribution for the second class

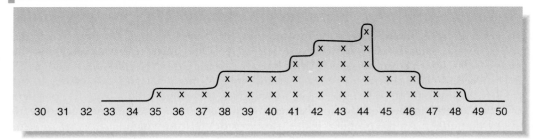

Figure A.3   Normal distribution

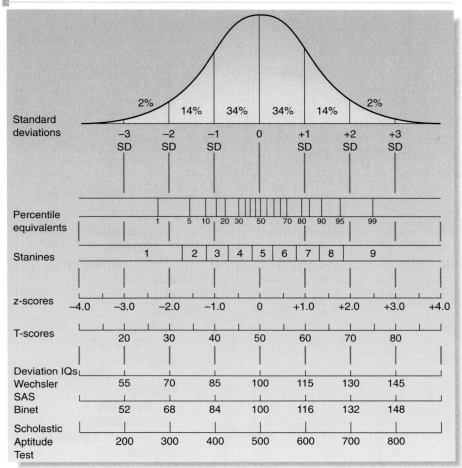

in our illustrations. A goal for standardized test users is to compare individual students with other students from around a state, a nation, or even the world. To make these comparisons, test makers use raw scores, percentiles, stanines, and grade equivalents. Some of these scores are illustrated in Figure A.4 on a Stanford Achievement Test Report.

Raw Scores

All standardized tests begin with and are based on raw scores. A **raw score** is simply *the number of items the individual answered correctly*. For example, in Figure A.4, you can see that David's raw score for reading comprehension was 43: Of a possible 54 items, David answered 43 of them correctly. But what does this mean? Was the test easy or difficult? How did he do, compared with others taking the exam? As you can see, this score doesn't tell us much until we compare it with others. Percentiles, stanines, grade equivalents, and standard scores help us do that.

Figure A.4 Stanford Achievement Test Report

STANFORD

ACHIEVEMENT TEST SERIES, EIGHTH EDITION

TEACHER:	DANNY CHAVEZ		1988 NORMS:	STANFORD GRADE 4	OLSAT GRADE 4	STUDENT SKILLS ANALYSIS FOR DAVID PALMER
SCHOOL:	LAKESIDE ELEMENTARY	GRADE: 4 TEST DATE:	SPRING LEVEL:	NATIONAL INTER 1	NATIONAL E	
DISTRICT:	NEWTOWN	4/96	FORM:	J	1	

TESTS	NO. OF ITEMS	RAW SCORE	NATL PR-S	LOCAL PR-S	GRADE EQUIV	NATIONAL GRADE PERCENTILE BANDS
Total Reading	94	70	65–6	75–6	5.6	
Vocabulary	40	27	54–5	59–5	5.0	
Reading Comp.	54	43	72–6	80–7	6.7	
Total Math	118	58	28–4	29–4	4.2	
Concepts of No.	34	14	20–3	21–3	3.6	
Computation	44	22	28–4	29–4	4.0	
Applications	40	22	37–4	38–4	4.3	
Total Language	60	47	64–6	60–6	5.8	
Lang. Mechanics	30	21	41–5	38–4	4.4	
Lang. Expression	30	26	80–7	75–6	9.7	
Spelling	40	22	37–4	37–4	4.2	
Study Skills	30	21	53–5	55–5	5.2	
Science	50	31	60–6	80–7	5.5	
Social Science	50	42	88–7	90–8	8.7	
Listening	45	25	34–4	35–4	3.9	
Using Information	70	35	24–4	25–4	3.5	
Thinking Skills	101	45	27–4	30–4	3.5	
Basic Battery	387	243	44–5	45–5	4.6	
Complete Battery	487	316	52–5	55–5	5.1	

National Grade Percentile Bands scale: 1 10 30 50 70 90 99

AGE 10 YRS 2 MOS	READING GROUP	LANGUAGE ARTS GROUP	MATHEMATICS GROUP	COMMUNICATIONS GROUP
(H) REGULAR INSTRUCTION		SPELLING	CONCEPTS	LISTENING

COPY XX

PROCESS NO. X–(SSAI)–X REVISED 09/29/89

Source: Stanford Achievement Test: 8th Edition. Copyright © 1989 by The Psychological Corporation. Reproduced by permission. All rights reserved.

Percentiles

Percentile is one of the most commonly reported scores on standardized tests. The **percentile rank (PR)** *is a ranking that compares an individual's score with the scores of all the others who have taken the test.* For instance, David's raw score of 43 in reading comprehension placed him in the 72nd percentile nationally and the 80th percentile locally. That means his score was as high or higher than 72% of the scores of people who took the test across the nation and 80% of the scores of students who took the test in his district.

Parents and students often confuse percentiles with *percentages.* Percentages reflect the number correct compared with the total number possible. Percentile rank, in contrast, tells how a student did in comparison with other students taking the test.

Percentiles are used because they are simple and straightforward. One thing should be kept in mind, however: These are *rankings,* and differences between the ranks are not equal. For instance, in our first distribution of 31 students, a score of 48 would be in the 90th percentile, 46 in the 80th, 44 in the 60th, and 43 in the 50th percentile. You can see that the difference between the 90th and 80th percentiles is twice as great (2 points) in our sample as the difference between the 60th and 50th percentiles (1 point). With large samples, this difference can be even more pronounced. Students who score at the extremes in the sample vary more from their counterparts than do those who score near the middle of the distribution. This finding is confirmed in Figure A.3, where you can see that the range of scores from the 50th to the 60th percentile is much smaller than the range from the 90th to the 99th percentile.

Percentile bands *describe standardized test score performance in percentile ranges, rather than as precise percentiles.* Their advantage is they acknowledge the possibility of measurement error by presenting a range of percentile scores (Lyman, 1991). In this respect, percentile bands function somewhat like stanines.

Stanines

The stanine is another score that can be derived from David's achievement test results. For example, his reading comprehension score placed him in Stanine 6 nationally and Stanine 7 locally. We obtained these by comparing his percentile scores to the stanine ranges in Figure A.3. The **stanine (S),** or **standard nine,** *describes a range of scores.* Stanine 5 is in the center of the distribution and includes all the scores within one fourth of a standard deviation on either side of the mean (see Figure A.3). Stanines 4, 3, and 2 are each a band of scores half a standard deviation in width extending below Stanine 5, and Stanines 6, 7, and 8 are also a half standard deviation in width extending above Stanine 5. Stanines 1 and 9 cover the tails of the distribution. A student with a score that falls one standard deviation above the mean will have a stanine score of 7, and a score two standard deviations above the mean will have a stanine score of 9.

The stanine is widely used because it is simple and because it encourages teachers and parents to interpret scores based on a range instead of fine distinctions that may be artificial. For instance, a score in the 57th percentile may be the result of one or two extra points on a subtest, compared with a score in the 52nd percentile, and the student may have guessed the answer correctly, so the difference between the two wouldn't be meaningful. Both scores would fall in Stanine 5, which is probably a more realistic indicator of performance. Reducing the scores to a simple nine-point band, however, sacrifices considerable information. For instance, in our first distribution, with a standard deviation of 4.8, a score of 40 would be in Stanine 4 because 40 is slightly more than one-fourth standard deviation below the mean. A score of 44 would be in Stanine 6 because it is slightly more than one-fourth standard deviation above the mean. However, a 40 is at the 35th percentile, and a 44 is at the 65th, a considerable difference. It is important to keep the advantages and disadvantages of stanines in mind as you help parents and students interpret standardized test scores.

Grade Equivalents

A third commonly reported score is called the grade equivalent. **Grade equivalents** *compare an individual's score with those of a particular age group.* For example, David's grade equivalent for total reading is 5.6. This means he scored as well on the test as the average score for those students taking the test who are in the sixth month of the fifth grade.

Reporting results in this way can be misleading because it oversimplifies results and suggests comparisons that are not necessarily valid. They tell that David is somewhat advanced in reading. They do not suggest that he should be promoted to fifth grade, nor do they suggest that he should be reading with fifth-graders. Other factors, such as maturity, psychosocial development, and motivation, must be considered in making decisions about students. Because of these limitations and the possibility for misinterpretation, grade equivalents should be used cautiously and never in isolation from other measures (Mehrens & Lehmann, 1987).

Standard Scores

As you saw in our discussion of percentiles, differences in raw scores don't result in comparable differences in the percentile rank. For instance, you saw that it took only one raw score point difference—43, compared with 42—to move from the 50th to the 60th percentile but that it took a two-point difference—48, compared with 46—to move from the 80th to the 90th percentile in our first distribution in Figure A.2. To deal with this discrepancy, standard scores were developed.

Standard scores *express test performance in standard deviation units* (Gronlund & Linn, 1995). Standardized test makers use the mean and standard deviation to report standard scores.

One type of standard score is the **z-score,** which is *the number of standard deviation units from the mean.* A z-score of 2 is two standard deviations above the mean, for example, and a z-score of −1 is one standard deviation below the mean. The **T-score,** *with the mean defined as 50 and the standard deviation defined as 10, is another standard score.* A T-score of 70 would be two standard deviations above the mean and would correspond to a z-score of 2. The SAT has a mean defined as 500 and a standard deviation defined as 100. A score of 550 on the verbal part would mean that you scored one-half deviation above the mean, or at the 68th percentile for this subtest.

Standard scores are useful because they make comparisons convenient. Because they are based on equal units of measurement throughout the distribution, intergroup and intertest comparisons are possible (Lyman, 1991).

Standard Error of Measurement

Although standardized tests are technically sophisticated, they still contain measurement error; scores only reflect an approximation of a student's "true" score. If we gave a student the same test over and over, for example, the scores would vary. If you averaged those scores, you would have a good estimate of the student's "true" score. Although it's impractical to give a person the same test repeatedly, you can get an estimate of the true score by using the **standard error of measurement,** *which describes a range of scores within which a person's true score is likely to fall.* This range is sometimes termed the *confidence interval, score band, or profile band.* For example, suppose Ben has a raw score of 46 and Kim has a raw score of 52 on a test with a standard error of 4. This means that Ben's true score is between 42 and 50 and that Kim's is between 48 and 56. At first glance, Kim appears to have scored significantly higher than Ben, but considering the standard error, their scores may be equal, or Ben's true score may even be higher than Kim's. Understanding the concept of *standard error* is important when you make decisions based on standardized tests. For instance, it would be unwise to place Ben and Kim in different ability groups solely on the basis of the results illustrated here.

References

AAAMR Ad Hoc Committee on Terminology and Classification. (1992). *Mental retardation: Definition, classification, and systems of support* (9th ed.). Washington, DC: American Association on Mental Retardation.

Abedi, J. (1997, March). The impact of the linguistic features of the NAEP test items on students' performance on NAEP assessments. Paper presented at the annual meeting of the American Educational Research Association, Chicago.

Aboud, F., & Skerry, S. (1984). The development of ethnic identity: A critical review. *Journal of Cross-Cultural Psychology, 15,* 3–34.

Adams, A., Carnine, D., & Gersten, R. (1982). Instructional strategies for studying content area texts in the intermediate grades. *Reading Research Quarterly, 18,* 27–53.

Adams, M. (1989). Thinking skills curricula. *Educational Psychologist, 24,* 25–77.

Adams, M. (1990). *Beginning to read.* Cambridge, MA: MIT Press.

Adamson, H. (1993). *Academic competence, theory, and practice: Preparing ESL students for content courses.* White Plains, NY: Longman.

Airasian, P. (1997). *Classroom assessment* (3rd ed.). New York: McGraw-Hill.

Airasian, P., & Walsh, M. (1997). Constructivist cautions. *Phi Delta Kappan, 78* (6), 444–449.

Alberto, P., & Troutman, A. (1990). *Applied behavior analysis for teachers* (2nd ed.). Upper Saddle River, NJ: Merrill/Prentice Hall.

Alberto, P., & Troutman, A. (1995). *Applied behavior analysis for teachers* (3rd ed.). Upper Saddle River, NJ: Merrill/Prentice Hall.

Alessi, S., & Trollip, S. (1991). *Computer-based instruction: Methods and development.* Upper Saddle River, NJ: Prentice Hall.

Alexander, P., & Murphy, P. (1994, April). *The research base for APA's learner-centered psychological principles.* Paper presented at the Annual Meeting of the American Educational Research Association, New Orleans.

Alexander, P., & Murphy P. (1998). The research base for APA's learner-centered psychological principles. In N. Lambert & B. McCombs (Eds.), *How students learn: Reforming schools through learner-centered education* (pp. 25–60). Washington, DC: American Psychological Association.

Allen, V. (1992). Teaching bilingual and ESL children. In J. Flood, J. J. Jensen, D. Lapp, & J. Squire (Eds.), *Handbook of research on teaching the English language arts* (pp. 356–364). New York: Macmillan.

Allermatt, E., Jovanovic, J. & Perry, M. (1997, March). *Bias or Sensitivity? Gender and Achievement Level Effects on Teachers' Classroom Questioning Practices.* Paper presented at the Annual meeting of the American Educational Research Association, Chicago.

American Association for the Advancement of Science (AAAS). (1993). *Benchmarks for science literacy.* Washington, DC: Author.

American Association of University Women. (1992). *How schools shortchange girls.* Annapolis Junction, MD: Author.

American Psychiatric Association. (1994). *Diagnostic and Statistical Manual of Mental Disorders.* Washington DC: Author.

American Psychological Association Board of Educational Affairs. (1995). *Learner-centered psychological principles: A framework for school redesign and reform* [On-line]. Available: http://www.apa.org/ed/lcp.html

Ames, C. (1990). Motivation: What teachers need to know. *Teachers College Record, 91,* 409–421.

Ames, C. (1992). Classrooms: Goals, structures, and student motivation. *Journal of Educational Psychology, 84*(3), 261–271.

Ames, C., & Archer, J. (1988). Achievement goals in the classroom: Students' learning strategies and motivation processes. *Journal of Educational Psychology, 80,* 260–267.

Anastasi, A. (1988). *Psychological testing* (6th ed.). New York: Macmillan.

Anastasiow, N., Bibley, S., Leonhardt, T., & Borish, G. (1970). A comparison of guided discovery, discovery, and didactic teaching of math to kindergarten poverty children. *American Educational Research Journal, 7,* 493–510.

Anderman, E., & Maehr, M. (1994). Motivation and schooling in the middle grades. *Review of Educational Research, 64,* 287–309.

Anderson, C., & Roth, K. (1989). Teaching for meaningful and self-regulated learning in science. In J. Brophy (Ed.), *Advances in research on teaching* (Vol. 1, pp. 265–309). Greenwich, CT: JAI Press.

Anderson, C., & Smith, E. (1987). Teaching science. In V. Richardson-Koehler (Ed.), *Educators' handbook*. New York: Longman.

Anderson, J. (1990). *Cognitive psychology and its implications* (3rd ed.). New York: Freeman.

Anderson, J. (1995). *Cognitive psychology and its implications* (4th ed.). New York: Freeman.

Anderson, J., Reder, L., & Simon, H. (1995). *Applications and misapplications of cognitive psychology to mathematics education.* Unpublished manuscript. (Accessible at http://www.psy.cmu,edu/~mm4b/misapplied.html)

Anderson, J., Reder, L., & Simon, H. (1996). Situated learning and education. *Educational Researcher, 25*(4), 5–10.

Anderson, L. (1989). Learners and learning. In M. Reynolds (Ed.), *Knowledge base for the beginning teacher* (pp. 85–100). New York: Pergamon Press.

Anderson, L., Brubaker, N., Alleman-Brooks, J., & Duffy, G. (1984). *Making seatwork work* (Research Series No. 142). East Lansing: Michigan State University, Institute for Research on Teaching.

Anderson, L., Evertson, C., & Brophy, J. (1979). An experimental study of effective teaching in first-grade reading groups. *Elementary School Journal, 79,* 193–223.

Anderson, M., Nelson, L., Fox, R., & Gruber, S. (1988). Integrating cooperative learning and structured learning: Effective approaches to teaching social skills. *Focus on Exceptional children, 20*(9), 1–8.

Anderson, R., Hiebert, E., Scott, J., & Wilkinson, I. (1985). *Becoming a nation of readers.* Washington, DC: National Institute of Education.

Anderson, T., & Armbruster, B. (1984). Studying. In D. Pearson (Ed.), *Handbook of reading research* (pp. 657–679). White Plains, NY: Longman.

Applebee, A., Langer, J., Mullis, I., & Jenkins, L. (1990). *The writing report card, 1984–88: Findings from the Nation's Report Card.* Washington, DC: U.S. Department of Education, Office of Educational Research and Improvement.

Arias, M., & Casanova, U. (Eds.). (1993). *Bilingual education: Politics, practice, and research. Ninety-second yearbook of the National Society for the Study of Education, Part 2.* Chicago: University of Chicago Press.

Armstrong, T. (1994). Multiple intelligences: Seven ways to approach curriculum. *Educational Leadership, 52*(3), 26–27.

Arnold, D., Lonigan, C., Whitehurst, G., & Epstein, J. (1994). Accelerating language development through picture book reading: Replication and extension to a videotape learning format. *Journal of Educational Psychology, 86*(2), 235–243.

Arnone, M., & Grabowski, B. (1991). *Effects of variations in learner control on children's curiosity and learning from interactive video.* Proceedings of Selected Research Presentations at the Annual Convention of the AECT (ERIC Document Reproduction No. ED 334972).

Arter, J. (1996). Designing performance tasks: Introduction. In R. Blum, & J. Arter (Eds.), *Student performance assessment in an era of restructuring.* Alexandria, VA: ASCE.

Ashcraft, M. (1989). *Human memory and cognition.* Glenview, IL: Scott, Foresman.

Atkinson, J. (1964). *An introduction to motivation.* Princeton, NJ: Van Nostrand.

Atkinson, J. (1980). Motivational effects in so-called tests of ability and educational achievement. In L. Fyans (Ed.), *Achievement motivation: Recent trends in theory and research.* New York: Plenum Press.

Atkinson, J. (1983). *Personality, motivation, and action.* New York: Praeger.

Atkinson, R., & Shiffrin, R. (1968). Human memory: A proposed system and its control processes. In K. Spence & J. Spence (Eds.), *The psychology of learning and motivation: Advances in research and theory* (Vol. 2). San Diego: Academic Press.

Atwell, N. (1987). *In the middle: Writing, reading and thinking with adolescents.* Portsmouth, NH: Heinemann.

Au, K. (1992, April). *"There's almost a lesson here": Teacher and students' purposes in constructing the theme of a story.* Paper presented at the Annual Meeting of the American Educational Research Association, San Francisco.

August, D., & Pease-Alvarez, L. (1996). *Attributes of effective programs and classrooms serving English language learners.* University of California, Santa Cruz: National Center for Research on Cultural Diversity and Second Language Learning.

Ausubel, D. (1963). *The psychology of meaningful verbal learning.* New York: Grune & Stratton.

Babad, E., Bernieri, F., & Rosenthal, R. (1991). Students as judges of teachers' verbal and nonverbal behavior. *American Educational Research Journal, 28*(1), 211–234.

Baker, D., & Stevenson, D. (1986). Mothers' strategies for children's school achievement: Managing the transition to high school. *Sociology of Education, 59,* 156–166.

Baker, E. (1989). Mandated tests: Educational reform or quality indicator? In B. Gifford (Ed.), *Test policy and test performance: Education, language, and culture* (pp. 3–23). Boston: Kluwer.

Baker, L. (1989). Metacognition, comprehension monitoring, and the adult reader. *Educational Psychology Review, 1,* 3–38.

Baker, L., & Anderson, R. (1982). Effects of inconsistent information on text processing: Evidence for comprehension monitoring. *Reading Research Quarterly, 17,* 281–293.

Baker, L., & Brown, A. (1984). Metacognitive skills of reading. In D. Pearson (Ed.), *Handbook of reading research.* White Plains, NY: Longman.

Ball, D. (1992, Summer). Magical hopes: Manipulatives and the reform of math education. *American Educator,* pp. 28–33.

Ball, D. (1996). Teacher learning and the mathematics reforms: What we think we know and what we need to learn. *Phi Delta Kappan, 77,* 500–508.

Ballantine, J. (1989). *The sociology of education.* Upper Saddle River, NJ: Prentice Hall.

Bandura, A. (1977). *Social learning theory.* Upper Saddle River, NJ: Prentice Hall.

Bandura, A. (1986). *Social foundations of thought and action: A social cognitive theory.* Upper Saddle River, NJ: Prentice Hall.

Bandura, A. (1989). Social cognitive theory. In R. Vasta (Ed.), *Annals of child development* (Vol. 6, pp. 1–60). Greenwich, CT: JAI Press.

Bandura, A. (1993). Perceived self-efficacy in cognitive development and functioning. *Educational Psychologist, 28*(2), 117–148.

Bangert-Drowns, R., Kulik, C., Kulik., J., & Morgan, M. (1991). The instructional effect of feedback in test-like events. *Review of Educational Research, 61*(2), 213–238.

Bangert-Drowns, R., Kulik, J., & Kulik, C. (1991). Effects of frequent classroom testing. *Journal of Educational Research, 85,* 89–99.

Banks, J. (1997). Multicultural Education: Characteristics and Goals. In J. Banks and C. Banks (Eds.), *Multicultural Education: Issues and Perspectives,* (3rd ed.) (pp. 3–32). Boston: Allyn & Bacon.

Barbetta, P., & Heron, T. (1991). Project Shine: Summer home instruction and evaluation. *Intervention in School and Clinics, 26,* 276–281.

Baringa, M. (1997). New insights into how babies learn language. *Science, 277,* 641.

Barker, G., & Graham, S. (1987). Developmental study of praise and blame as attributional cues. *Journal of Educational Psychology, 79,* 62–66.

Barkley, R. (1994). Impaired delayed responding: A unified theory of attention-deficit hyperactivity disorder. In R. Barkley (Ed.), *Disruptive behavior disorders in children* (pp. 11–57). New York: Plenum.

Baron, J. (1998). Using learner-centered assessment on a large scale. In N. Lambert & B. McCombs (Eds.), *How students learn: Reforming schools through learner-centered education* (pp. 211–240). Washington, DC: American Psychological Association.

Baron, R. (1992). *Psychology* (2nd ed.). Needham Heights, MA: Allyn & Bacon.

Basili, P., & Sanford, J. (1991). Conceptual change strategies and cooperative group work in chemistry. *Journal of Research in Science Teaching, 28,* 293–304.

Bay, M., Staver, J., Bryan, T., & Hale, J. (1992). Science instruction for the mildly handicapped: Direct instruction versus discovery teaching. *Journal of Research in Science Teaching, 29,* 555–570.

Beane, J. (1991). Sorting out the self-esteem controversy. *Educational Leadership, 49*(1), Sept. 25–30.

Bech, K. (1996) *The segmentation of moral judgments of adolescent students in Germany—Findings and problems.* Paper presented at the Annual meeting of the American Educational Research Association, New York.

Bee, H. (1989). *The developing child* (5th ed.). New York: Harper & Row.

Behrend, D., Rosengren, K., & Perlmutter, M. (1992). The relation between private speech and parental interactive style. In R. Díaz & L. Berk (Eds.), *Private speech: From social interaction to self-regulation* (pp. 85–100). Hillsdale, NJ: Erlbaum.

Benard, B. (1993). Fostering resilience in kids. *Educational Leadership, 51*(3), 44–48.

Benard, B. (1994). *Fostering resilience in urban schools.* San Francisco: Far West Laboratory.

Bennett, N., & Blundel, D. (1983). Quantity and quality of work in rows of classroom groups. *Educational Psychology, 3,* 93–105.

Bennett, S. (1978). Recent research on teaching: A dream, a belief, and a model. *British Journal of Educational Psychology, 48,* 27–147.

Bereiter, C., & Scardamalia, M. (1987). *The psychology of written composition.* Hillsdale, NJ: Erlbaum.

Berk, L. (1994). *Child development* (3rd ed.). Needham Heights, MA: Allyn & Bacon.

Berk, L. (1996) *Infants, children, and adolescents* (2nd ed.). Boston: Allyn & Bacon.

Berk, L. (1997). *Child development* (4th ed.). Boston: Allyn & Bacon.

Berkowitz, M. (1997, March). *Integrating structure and content in moral education*. Paper presented at the Annual meeting of the American Educational Research Association, Chicago.

Berliner, D. (1984). *Making our schools more effective: Proceedings of three state conferences*. San Francisco: Far West Laboratory.

Berliner, D. (1987). Simple views of effective teaching and a simple theory of classroom instruction. In D. Berliner & B. Rosenshine (Eds.), *Talks to teachers* (pp. 93–110). New York: Random House.

Bernardo, A. (1994). Problem-specific information and the development of problem-type schemata. *Journal of Experimental Psychology: Learning, Memory & Cognition, 20*(2), 379–395.

Berninger, V., Vaughan, K., Abbott, R., Abbott, S., Rogan, L., Brooks, A., Reed, E., & Graham, S. (1997). Treatment of handwriting problems in beginning writers: Transfer from handwriting to composition. *Journal of Educational Psychology, 89*, 652–666.

Beyer, B. (1984). Improving thinking skills: A practical approach. *Phi Delta Kappan, 65*, 556–560.

Beyer, B. (1988). Developing a scope and sequence for thinking skills instruction. *Educational Leadership, 45*(7), 26–30.

Binfet, J., Schonert-Reicht, K., & McDougal, P. (1997, March). *Adolescents' perceptions of the moral atmosphere of school: Motivational, behavioral, and social correlates*. Paper presented at the Annual meeting of the American Educational Research Association, Chicago.

Bixby, J. (1997, March). *School Organization as Context for White Teachers' Talk About Race and Student Achievement*. Paper presented at the Annual meeting of the American Educational Research Association, Chicago.

Bloom, B. (1981). *All our children learning*. New York: McGraw-Hill.

Bloom, B. (1984). The search for methods of group instruction as effective as one-to-one tutoring. *Educational Leadership, 41*(8), 4–17.

Bloom, B., & Bourdon, L. (1980). Types and frequencies of teachers' written instructional feedback. *Journal of Educational Research, 74*, 13–15.

Bloom, B., Englehart, M., Furst, E., Hill, W., & Krathwohl, O. (1956). *Taxonomy of educational objectives: The classification of educational goals: Handbook 1. The cognitive domain*. White Plains, NY: Longman.

Blumenfeld, P. (1992). Classroom learning and motivation: Clarifying and expanding goal theory. *Journal of Educational Psychology, 84*(3), 272–281.

Blumenfeld, P., Pintrich, P., & Hamilton, V. L. (1987). Teacher talk and students' reasoning about morals, conventions, and achievement. *Child Development, 58*, 1389–1401.

Boothroyd, R., McMorris, R., & Pruzek, R. (1992, April). *What do teachers know about measurement, and how did they find out?* Paper presented at the Annual Meeting of the National Council on Measurement in Education, San Francisco.

Borg, W., & Ascione, F. (1982). Classroom management in elementary mainstreaming classrooms. *Journal of Educational Psychology, 74*, 85–95.

Borko, H., & Putnam, R. (1996). Learning to teach. In D. Berliner & R. Calfee (Eds.), *Handbook of educational psychology* (pp. 673–708). New York: Simon & Schuster Macmillan.

Bosworth, K. (1995). Caring for others and being cared for: Students talk about caring in school. *Phi Delta Kappan, 76*, 686–693.

Bower, G., Clark, M., Lesgold, A., & Winzenz, D. (1969). Hierarchical retrieval schemes in recall of categorized word lists. *Journal of Verbal Learning and Verbal Behavior, 8*, 323–343.

Bowie, R., & Bond, C. (1994). Influencing future teachers' attitudes toward Black English: Are we making a difference? *Journal of Teacher Education, 45*(2), 112–118.

Boyes, M. & Allen, S. (1993). Styles of parent-child interaction and moral reasoning in adolescence. *Merrill-Palmer Quarterly, 39*, 551–570.

Braddock, J. (1990). Tracking the middle grades: National patterns of grouping for instruction. *Phi Delta Kappan, 71*(6), 445–449.

Bradley, D. & Switlick, D. (1997) The past and future of special education. In D. Bradley, M. King-Sears and D. Tessier-Switlick (Eds.), *Teaching Students in Inclusive Settings* (pp. 1–20). Boston: Allyn & Bacon.

Bradley, L., & Bryant, P. (1991). Phonological skills before and after learning to read. In S. Brady, & D. Shankweiler (Eds.), *Phonological processes in literacy* (pp. 37–45). Hillsdale: NJ: Erlbaum.

Brady, P. (1990). Improving the reading comprehension of middle school students through reciprocal teaching and semantic mapping strategies. Unpublished doctoral dissertation, University of Oregon, Eugene.

Brandes, A. (1995, April). *Barriers to conceptual change in a sixth-grade classroom*. Paper presented at the Annual Meeting of the American

Educational Research Association, San Francisco.

Bransford, J. (1993). Who ya gonna call? Thoughts about teaching problem solving. In P. Hallinger, K. Leithwood, & J. Murphy (Eds.), *Cognitive perspectives on educational leadership* (pp. 2–30). New York: Teachers College Press.

Bransford, J., Goldman, S., & Vye, N. (1991). Making a difference in people's abilities to think: Reflections on a decade of work and some hopes for the future. In L. Okagaki & R. Sternberg (Eds.), *Directors of development* (pp. 147–180). Hillsdale, NJ: Erlbaum.

Bransford, J., & Johnson, M. (1972). Contextual prerequisites for understanding: Some investigations of comprehension and recall. *Journal of Verbal Learning and Verbal Behavior, 11,* 717–726.

Bransford, J., & Stein, B. (1984). *The IDEAL problem solver.* New York: Freeman.

Brenner, M., Mayer, R., Moseley, B., Brar, T., Durán, R., Reed, B., & Webb, D. (1997). Learning by understanding: The role of multiple representations in learning algebra. *American Education Research Journal, 34* (4), 663–689.

Bridgeman, B. (1974). Effects of test score feedback on immediately subsequent test performance. *Journal of Educational Psychology, 66,* 62–66.

Brody, N. (1992). *Intelligence* (2nd ed.). San Diego: Academic Press.

Brooks, J. (1990). Teachers and students: Constructivists forging connections. *Educational Leadership, 47* (5), 68–71.

Brooks, J., & Brooks, M. (1993). *In search of understanding: The case for constructivist classrooms.* Alexandria, VA: Association for Supervision and Curriculum Development.

Brooks, L., & Dansereau, D. (1987). Transfer of information: An instructional perspective. In S. Cormier & J. Hagman (Eds.), *Transfer of learning: Contemporary research and applications.* San Diego: Academic Press.

Brophy, J. (1981). On praising effectively. *Elementary School Journal, 81,* 269–278.

Brophy, J. (1982). *Fostering student learning and motivation in the elementary school classroom.* East Lansing: Michigan State University, Institute for Research on Teaching.

Brophy, J. (1986). Research linking teacher behavior to student achievement: Potential implications for instruction of Chapter 1 students. In B. Williams, P. Richmond, & B. Mason (Eds.), *Designs for Compensatory Education Conference proceedings and papers* (pp. IV-121–IV-179). Washington, DC: Research and Evaluation Associates.

Brophy, J. (1987a). On motivating students. In D. Berliner & B. Rosenshine (Eds.), *Talks to teachers* (pp. 201–245). New York: Random House.

Brophy, J. (1987b). Syntheses of research on strategies for motivating students to learn. *Educational Leadership, 45* (2), 40–48.

Brophy, J. (1990). Teaching social studies for understanding and higher order applications. *Elementary School Journal, 90,* 351–418.

Brophy, J. (1992). Probing the subtleties of subject-matter teaching. *Educational Leadership, 49* (7), 4–8.

Brophy, J. (1996). *Teaching problem students.* New York: Guilford Press.

Brophy, J., & Good, T. (1986). Teacher behavior and student achievement. In M. Wittrock (Ed.), *Handbook of research on teaching* (3rd ed.) (pp. 328–375). New York: Macmillan.

Brophy, J., & McCaslin, M. (1992). Teachers' reports of how they perceive and cope with problem students. *Elementary School Journal, 93* (1), 3–68.

Brophy, J., & Rohrkemper, M. (1987). *Teachers' strategies for coping with hostile-aggressive students.* East Lansing: Michigan State University, Institute for Research on Teaching.

Brown, A. (1994). The advancement of learning. *Educational Researcher, 23,* 4–12.

Brown, A., Bransford, J., Ferrara, R., & Campione, J. (1983). Learning, remembering, and understanding. In J. Flavell & E. Markman (Eds.), *Handbook of child psychology: Vol. 3. Cognitive development* (4th ed., pp. 77–166). New York: Wiley.

Brown, A., & Campione, J. (1986). Psychological theory and the study of learning disabilities. *American Psychologist, 41,* 1059–1068.

Brown, A., & Campione, J. (1994). Guided discovery in a community of learners. In K. McGilly (Ed.), *Classroom lessons: Integrating Cognitive theory and classroom practice* (pp. 229–270). Cambridge: MIT Press.

Brown, A., & Palincsar, A. (1987). Reciprocal teaching of comprehension strategies: A natural history of one program for enhancing learning. In J. Borkowski & J. Day (Eds.), *Cognition in special education: Comparative approaches to retardation, learning disabilities, and giftedness.* Norwood, NJ: Ablex.

Brown, A. & Smiley, S. (1977). Rating the importance of structural units of prose passages: A problem of metacognitive development. *Child Development, 48,* 1–8.

Brown, A. & Smiley, S. (1978). The development of strategies for studying texts. *Child Development, 49,* 1076–1088.

Brown, J., Collins, A., & Duguid, P. (1989). Situated cognition and the culture of learning. *Educational Researcher, 18,* 32–42.

Brown, R., & McNeill, D. (1966). The "tip-of-the-tongue" phenomenon. *Journal of Verbal Learning and Verbal Behavior, 5,* 325–337.

Bruer, J. (1993). *Schools for thought: A science of learning for the classroom.* Cambridge: MIT Press.

Bruner, J. (1960). *Process of education.* Cambridge, MA: Harvard University Press.

Bruner, J. (1966). *Toward a theory of instruction.* New York: Norton.

Bruner, J. (1971). *Relevance of education.* New York: Norton.

Bruner, J. (1985). Vygotsky: A historical and conceptual perspective. In J. Wertsch (Ed.), *Culture, communication, and cognition: Vygotskian perspectives* (pp. 21–34). New York: Cambridge University Press.

Bruning, R., Schraw, G., & Ronning, R. (1995). *Cognitive psychology and instruction* (2nd ed.). Upper Saddle River, NJ: Prentice Hall.

Buchholz, W. (1991). A learning activity for at-risk ninth through twelfth grade students in creating a computer-generated children's storybook design. Master's thesis, New York Institute of Technology (ERIC Document Reproduction No. ED 345695).

Bullough, R. (1989). *First-year teacher.* New York: Teachers College Press.

Bushway, A., & Nash, W. (1977). School cheating behavior. *Review of Educational Research, 47,* 623–632.

Busmeyer, J., & Myung, I. (1988). A new method for investigating prototype learning. *Journal of Experimental Psychology: Learning, Memory & Cognition, 14,* 1292–1302.

Butler, F., & Stevens, R. (1997). Test accommodations: What are they? *CRESSTLINE, 2,* 8.

Butler-Por, N. (1987). *Underachievers in school: Issues and interventions.* New York: Wiley.

Buzzelli, C., & Johnston, B. (1997, March). *Expressive morality in a collaborative learning activity: The creation of moral meaning.* Paper presented at the Annual Conference of the American Educational Research Association, Chicago.

Byrne, B. (1984). The general/academic self-concept nomological network: A review of construct validation research. *Review of Educational Research, 54,* 427–456.

Byrne, B., & Gavin, D. (1996). The Shavelson Model revisited: Testing for the structure of academic self-concept across pre, early, and late adolescents. *Journal of Educational Psychology, 88* (2), 215–228.

Byrnes, J. (1988). Formal operations: A systematic reformulation. *Developmental Review, 8,* 66–87.

Caccamise, D. (1987). Ideas generation in writing. In A. Matsushashi, (Ed.), *Writing in real time: Modeling production processes* (pp. 224–253). Norwood NJ: Ablex.

Calderhead, J., & Robson, M. (1991). Images of teaching: Student teachers' early conceptions of classroom practice. *Teaching and Teacher Education, 7,* 1–8.

Calfee, R. (1986, April). *Those who can explain teach.* Paper presented at the Annual Meeting of the American Educational Research Association, San Francisco.

Calfee, R. (1994). Critical literacy: Reading and writing for a new millennium. In N. Ellsworth, C. Hedley, & A. Baratta (Eds.), *Literacy: A redefinition* (pp. 19–38). Hillsdale, NJ: Erlbaum.

Cameron, C., & Lee, K. (1997). Bridging the gap between home and school with voice-mail technology. *Journal of Educational Research, 90,* 182–190.

Cameron, J., & Pierce, D. (1994). Reinforcement, reward, and intrinsic motivation: A meta-analysis. *Review of Educational Research, 64,* 363–423.

Camp, R. (1992). Assessment in the context of schools and school change. In H. Marshall (Ed.), *Redefining student learning: Roots of educational change* (pp. 241–263). Norwood, NJ: Ablex.

Canter, L. (1988). Let the educator beware: A response to Curwin and Mendler. *Educational Leadership, 46* (2), 71–73.

Canter, L., & Canter, M. (1992). *Assertive discipline.* Santa Monica, CA: Lee Canter & Associates.

Caplan, N., Choy, M., & Whitmore, J. (1992). Indochinese refugee families and academic achievement. *Scientific American, 266* (2), 36–42.

Carey, S. (1986). Cognitive science and science education. *American Psychologist, 41,* 1123–1130.

Carlson, S., & Silverman, R. (1986). Microcomputers and computer assisted instruction in special classrooms: Do we need the teacher? *Learning Disability Quarterly, 9,* 105–110.

Carpenter, T., Fennema, E., & Franke, M. (in press). Cognitively guided instruction: A knowledge base for reform in primary mathematics instruction. *Elementary School Journal.*

Carpenter, T., Levi, L., Fennema, E., Ansell, E., & Franke, M. (1995, April). *Discussing alternative strategies as a context for developing understanding in primary grade mathematics classrooms.* Paper presented at the Annual Meeting of the

American Educational Research Association, San Francisco.

Carrier, C., & Titus, A. (1981). Effects of notetaking pretraining and text mode expectations on learning from lectures. *American Educational Research Journal, 18,* 385–397.

Carrol, J. (1963). A model of school learning. *Teachers College Record, 64,* 723–733.

Carrol, W. (1994). Using worked examples as an instructional support in the algebra classroom. *Journal of Educational Psychology, 86* (3), 360–367.

Carter, K. (1984). Do teachers understand the principles for writing tests? *Journal of Teacher Education, 35* (6), 57–60.

Carter, K. (1986). Test-wiseness for teachers and students. *Educational Measurement: Issues and Practice, 5* (6), 20–23.

Carter, K. (1990). Teachers' knowledge and learning to teach. In R. Houston (Ed.), *Handbook of research on teacher education* (pp. 291–310). New York: Macmillan.

Case, S. (1994). Will mandating portfolios undermine their value? *Educational Leadership, 52* (2), 46–47.

Cattell, R. (1963). Theory of fluid and crystallized intelligence: A critical experiment. *Journal of Educational Psychology, 54,* 1–22.

Cattell, R. (1971). *Abilities: Their structure, growth, and action.* Boston: Houghton Mifflin.

Catterall, J., & Cota-Robles, E. (1988). *The educationally at-risk: What the numbers mean.* Palo Alto, CA: Stanford University Press.

Cazden, C. (1986). Classroom discourse. In M. Wittrock (Ed.), *Handbook of research on teaching* (3rd ed., pp. 432–464). New York: Macmillan.

Cazden, C. (1988). *Classroom discourse.* Portsmouth, NH: Heinemann.

Ceci, S. (1990). *On Intelligence . . . More or less.* Englewood Cliffs, N.J.: Prentice Hall.

Cermak, L., & Craik, F. (1979). *Levels of processing in human memory.* Hillsdale, NJ: Erlbaum.

Chall, J. (1967) *Learning to read: The great debate.* New York: McGraw-Hill.

Chall, J., Jacobs, V., & Baldwin, L. (1990). *The reading crisis: Why poor children fall behind.* Cambridge, MA: Harvard University Press.

Chance, P. (1992). The rewards of learning. *Phi Delta Kappan, 74* (3), 200–207.

Chance, P. (1993). Sticking up for rewards. *Phi Delta Kappan, 74,* 787–790.

Chapman, J. (1988). Learning-disabled children's self-concept. *Review of Educational Research, 58,* 347–371.

Chaskin, R., & Rauner, D. (1995). Youth and caring: An introduction. *Phi Delta Kappan, 76,* 667–674.

Cheek, D. (1993). Plain talk about alternative assessment. *Middle School Journal, 25* (2), 6–10.

Chekley, K. (1997). The first seven . . . and the eighth. *Educational Leadership, 55,* 8–13.

Cheng, L. R. (1987). *Assessing Asian language performance.* Rockville, MD: Aspen.

Cheung, K. (1995). On meaningful measurement: Issues of reliability and validity from a humanistic constructivist information-processing perspective. *Educational Research and Evaluation, 1,* 90–107.

Chi, M., Bassok, M., Lewis, M., Reimann, P., & Glaser, R. (1989). Self-explanations: How students study and use examples in learning to solve problems. *Cognitive Science, 5,* 121–152.

Chinn, C. (1997, March). *Learning strategies and the learner's approach to understanding some science concepts.* Paper presented at the Annual Meeting of the American Educational Research Association, Chicago.

Chinn, C., & Brewer, W. (1993). The role of anomalous data in knowledge acquisition: A theoretical framework and implications for science instruction. *Review of Educational Research, 63,* 1–49.

Choate, J. (Ed.) (1997) *Successful inclusive teaching.* Boston: Allyn & Bacon.

Chomsky, N. (1972). *Language and mind* (2nd ed.). Orlando, FL: Harcourt Brace.

Chomsky, N. (1976). *Reflections on language.* London: Temple Smith.

Chomsky, N., & Miller, G. (1958). Finite-state languages. *Information and Control, 1,* 91–112.

Clark, J., & Paivio, A. (1991). Dual coding theory and education. *Educational Psychology Review, 3,* 149–210.

Clark, K., & Clark, M. (1939). The development of consciousness of self and the emergence of racial identification in Negro preschool children. *Journal of Social Psychology, 10,* 591–599.

Clay, M. (1975). *What did I write?* Portsmouth, NH: Heinemann.

Clement, J. (1983). A conceptual model discussed by Galileo and used intuitively by physics students. In D. Gentner & A. Stevens (Eds.), *Mental models* (pp. 206–251). Hillsdale, NJ: Erlbaum.

Clements, B., & Evertson, C. (1982, March). *Orchestrating small-group instruction in the elementary school classroom.* Paper presented at the Annual Meeting of the American Educational Research Association, New York.

Clements, D., & Battista, M. (1990). Constructivist learning and teaching. *Arithmetic Teacher, 38,* 34–35.

Clifford, M. (1990). Students need challenge, not easy success. *Educational Leadership, 48* (1), 22–26.

Clifton, R., Perry, R., Parsonson, K., & Hryniuk, S. (1986). Effects of ethnicity and sex on teachers' expectations of junior high school students. *Sociology of Education, 59,* 58–67.

Clinkenbeard, P. (1992, April). *Motivation and gifted adolescents: Learning from observing practice.* Paper presented at the Annual Meeting of the American Educational Research Association, San Francisco.

Cobb, P. (1994). Where is the mind? Constructivist and sociocultural perspectives on mathematical development, *Educational Researcher, 23.*

Cognition and Technology Group at Vanderbilt. (1990). Anchored instruction and its relationship to situated cognition. *Educational Researcher, 19,* 2–10.

Cognition and Technology Group at Vanderbilt. (1992). The Jasper Series as an example of anchored instruction: Theory, program description, and assessment data. *Educational Psychologist, 27,* 291–315.

Cognition and Technology Group at Vanderbilt. (1994). Multimedia environments for enhancing student learning in mathematics. In S. Vosniadou, E. De Corte, & H. Handl (Eds.), *Technology-based learning environments: Psychological and educational foundations* (NATO ASI Series F: Computers and Systems Sciences, Vol. 137, pp. 167–173). Berlin: Springer.

Cohen, E., (1994). Restructuring the classroom: Conditions for productive small groups. *Review of Educational Research, 64,* 1–35.

Cohen, E. (1991). Strategies for creating a multiability classroom. *Cooperative Learning, 12* (1), 4–7.

Coker, H., Lorentz, C., & Coker, J. (1980, April). *Teacher behavior and student outcomes in the Georgia study.* Paper presented at the Annual Meeting of the American Educational Research Association, Boston.

Cole, M. (1991). Conclusion. In L. Resnick, J. Levine, & S. Teasley (Eds.), *Perspectives on socially shared cognition* (pp. 398–417). Washington, DC: American Psychological Association.

Collins, A., Brown, J., & Holum, A. (1991). Cognitive apprenticeship: Making thinking visible. *American Educator, 15,* 38–46.

Collins, A., Brown, J., & Newman, S. (1989). Cognitive apprenticeship: Teaching the crafts of reading, writing, and mathematics. In L. Resnick (Ed.), *Knowing, learning, and instruction: Essays in honor of Robert Glaser* (pp. 453–494). Hillsdale, NJ: Erlbaum.

Conger, R., Conger, K., Elder, G., Lorenz, F., Simons, R., & Whitbeck, L. (1992). A family process model of economic hardship and adjustment of early adolescent boys. *Child Development, 63,* 526–541.

Connell, J., & Wellborn, J. (1991). Competence, autonomy, and relatedness: A motivational analysis of self-system processes. In M. Gunnar & L. Sroufe (Eds.), *Self processes in development. Minnesota Symposia on Child Psychology: Vol. 23* (pp. 43–77). Chicago: University of Chicago Press.

Consortium for Longitudinal Studies. (1983). *As the twig is bent: Lasting effects of preschool programs.* Hillsdale, NJ: Erlbaum.

Cooper, H. (1989). Synthesis of research on homework. *Educational Leadership, 47* (3), 85–91.

Copeland, W., & Decker, D. (1995, April). *Video cases and the development of meaning making in preservice teachers.* Paper presented at the Annual Meeting of the American Educational Research Association, San Francisco.

Cordova, D., & Lepper, M. (1996). Intrinsic motivation and the process of learning: Beneficial effects of contextualization, personalization, and choice. *Journal of Educational Psychology, 88* (4), 715–730.

Cormier, S. (1987). The structural processes underlying transfer of training. In S. Cormier & J. Hagman (Eds.), *Transfer of learning: Contemporary research and applications.* San Diego: Academic Press.

Cortes, C. E. (1986). The education of language-minority students: A contextual interaction model. In *Beyond language: Social and cultural factors in schooling language-minority students* (pp. 299–343). Los Angeles: California State University, Evaluation, Dissemination, and Assessment Center.

Cotton, K., & Savard, W. (1981). *Instructional grouping: Ability grouping.* Portland, OR: Northwest Regional Laboratory.

Council of Chief State School Officers. (1993). *State indicators of science and mathematics education.* Washington, DC: Author.

Covington, M. (1992). *Making the grade: A self-worth perspective on motivation and school reform.* Cambridge, MA: Harvard University Press.

Covington, M., & Omelich, C. (1987). "I knew it cold before the exam": A test of the anxiety blockage hypothesis. *Journal of Educational Psychology, 79,* 393–400.

Cowan, S. (1988). Coping strategies of university students with learning disabilities. *Journal of Learning Disabilities, 21,* 161–164.

Craik, F., & Lockhart, R. (1972). Levels of processing: A framework for memory research. *Journal of Verbal Learning and Verbal Behavior, 11,* 671–680.

Crocker, R., & Brooker, G. (1986). Classroom control and student outcomes in grades 2 and 5. *American Educational Research Journal, 23,* 1–11.

Crooks, T. (1988). The impact of classroom evaluation practices on students. *Review of Educational Research, 58,* 438–481.

Cruickshank, D. (1985). Applying research on teacher clarity. *Journal of Teacher Education, 35* (2), 44–48.

Cruickshank, D. (1987). *Reflective teaching: The preparation of students of teaching.* Reston, VA: Association of Teacher Educators.

Crystal, D., & Stevenson, H. (1991). Mothers' perceptions of children's problems with mathematics: A cross-national comparison. *Journal of Educational Psychology, 83,* 372–376.

Cuban, L. (1984). *How teachers taught: Constancy and change in American classrooms: 1890–1980.* White Plains, NY: Longman.

Cummins, J. (1991). Interdependence of first and second-language proficiency in bilingual children. In E. Bialystol (Ed.), *Language Processing in Bilingual Children* (pp. 70–89). Cambridge: Cambridge University Press.

Curwin, R., & Mendler, A. (1988). Packaged discipline programs: Let the buyer beware. *Educational Leadership, 46*(2), 68–71.

Cushner, K., McClelland, A., & Safford, P. (1992). *Human diversity in education.* New York: McGraw-Hill.

Dansereau, D. (1985). Learning strategy research. In J. Segal, S. Chipman, & R. Glaser (Eds.), *Thinking and learning skills* (Vol. 1, pp. 209–239). Hillsdale, NJ: Erlbaum.

Darling-Hammond, L., & Snyder, J. (1992). Reframing accountability: Creating learner-centered schools. In A. Lieberman (Ed.), *The changing contexts of teaching* (pp. 3–17). Chicago: University of Chicago Press.

Darling-Hammond, L., Wise, A., & Pease, S. (1983). Teacher evaluation in the organizational context: A review of the literature. *Review of Educational Research, 53,* 285–328.

Davis, G. (1989). Testing for creative potential. *Contemporary Educational Psychology, 14,* 257–274.

Davis, G., & Rimm, S. (1993). *Education of the gifted and talented* (3rd ed.). Upper Saddle River, NJ: Prentice Hall.

Davis, R. (1989). The culture of mathematics and the culture of schools. *Journal of Mathematical Behavior, 8,* 143–160.

de Bono, E. (1976). *Teaching thinking.* London: Temple Smith.

deCharms, R. (1968). *Personal causation.* San Diego: Academic Press.

deCharms, R. (1980). The origins of competence and achievement motivation in personal causation. In L. Fyans (Ed.), *Achievement motivation: Recent trends in theory and research.* New York: Plenum Press.

Deci, E., & Ryan, R. (1987). The support of autonomy and the control of behavior. *Journal of Personality and Social Psychology, 53,* 1024–1037.

De Corte, E., Greer, B., & Verschaffel, L., (1996). Mathematics teaching and learning. In D. Berliner & R. Calfee (Eds.), *Handbook of educational psychology* (pp. 491–549). New York: Simon & Schuster Macmillan.

Delgado-Gaiton, C. (1992). School matters in the Mexican American home: Socializing children to edu-

cation. *American Educational Research Journal, 29* (3), 495–516.

De Lisi, R., & Straudt, J. (1980). Individual differences in college students' performance on formal operations tasks. *Journal of Applied Developmental Psychology, 1,* 201–208.

Delisle, J. (1984). *Gifted children speak out.* New York: Walker.

Delpit, L. (1995). *Other people's children: Cultural conflict in the classroom.* New York: The New Press.

Dempster, F. (1991). Synthesis of research on reviews and tests. *Educational Leadership, 48* (7), 71–76.

Derry, S. (1992). Beyond symbolic processing: Expanding horizons for educational psychology. *Journal of Educational Psychology, 84,* 413–419.

Deshler, D., & Schumaker, J. (1993). Strategy mastery by at-risk students: Not a simple matter. *Elementary School Journal, 94* (2), 153–166.

DeVries, R. (1997). Piaget's social theory. *Educational Researcher, 26* (2), 4–18.

DeVries, R., & Zan, B. (1995, April). *The sociomoral atmosphere: The first principle of constructivist education.* Paper presented at the Annual Meeting of the American Educational Research Association, San Francisco.

Diaz, R. (1983). Thought and two languages: The impact of bilingualism. In Z. Gordon (Ed.), *Review of research in education* (Vol. 10). Washington, DC: American Educational Research Association.

Diaz, R. (1990). Bilingualism and cognitive ability: Theory, research, and controversy. In A. Barona & E. Garcia (Eds.), *Children at risk: Poverty, minority status, and other issues of educational equity* (pp. 91–102). Washington, DC: National Association of School Psychologists.

Dickinson, A. (1989). The detrimental effects of extrinsic reinforcement on intrinsic motivation. *Behavior Analyst, 12,* 1–15.

Dillon, D. (1989). Showing them that I want them to learn and that I care about who they are: A microethnography of the social organization of a secondary low-track English reading classroom. *American Educational Research Journal, 26* (2), 227–259.

Dillon, J. (1987). *Questioning and discussion: A multidisciplinary study.* Norwood, NJ: Ablex.

Dole, J., Duffy, G., Roehler, L., & Pearson, D. (1991). Moving from the old to the new: Research on reading comprehension instruction. *Review of Educational Research, 61,* 239–264.

Dolgins, J., Myers, M., Flynn, P., & Moore, J. (1984). How do we help the learning disabled? *Instructor, 93* (7), 29–36.

Doyle, D. (1997). Education and character. *Phi Delta Kappan, 78* (6) 440–443.

Doyle, R. (1989). The resistance of conventional wisdom to research evidence: The case of retention in grade. *Phi Delta Kappan, 71,* 215–220.

Doyle, W. (1983). Academic work. *Review of Educational Research, 53,* 159–199.

Doyle, W. (1986). Classroom organization and management. In M. Wittrock (Ed.), *Handbook of research on teaching* (3rd ed., pp. 392–431). New York: Macmillan.

Dreikurs, R. (1968). *Psychology in the classroom* (2nd ed.). New York: Harper & Row.

Dreisbach, M., & Keogh, B. (1982). Test-wiseness as a factor in readiness test performance of young Mexican American children. *Journal of Educational Psychology, 74,* 224–229.

Driscoll, M. (1994). *Psychology of learning for instruction.* Needham Heights, MA: Allyn & Bacon.

Driver, B., Asoko, H., Leach, J., Mortimer, E., & Scott, P. (1994). Constructing scientific knowledge in the classroom. *Educational Researcher, 23,* 5–12.

Duffy, G. (1992, April). *Learning from the study of practice: Where we must go with strategy instruction.* Paper presented at the Annual Meeting of the American Educational Research Association, San Francisco.

Duffy, G., Roehler, L., Meloth, M., & Vavrus, L. (1985, April). *Conceptualizing instructional explanation.* Paper presented at the Annual Meeting of the American Educational Research Association, Chicago.

Dunkle, M., Schraw, G., & Bendixon, L. (1995, April). *Cognitive processes in well-defined and ill-defined problem solving.* Paper presented at the Annual Meeting of the American Educational Research Association, San Francisco.

Dweck, C. (1975). The role of expectations and attributions in the alleviation of learned helplessness. *Journal of Personality and Social Psychology, 31,* 674–685.

Dweck, C. (1985). Motivation. In R. Glaser & A. Lesgold (Eds.), *Handbook of psychology and education.* Hillsdale, NJ: Erlbaum.

Dweck, C., & Bempechat, J. (1983). Children's theories of intelligence: Consequences for learning. In S. Paris, G. Olson, & H. Stevenson (Eds.), *Learning and motivation in the classroom* (pp. 239–255). Hillsdale, NJ: Erlbaum.

Dweck, C., & Leggett, E. (1988). A social-cognitive approach to motivation and personality. *Psychological Review, 95,* 256–273.

Eccles, J., Jacobs, J., & Harold, R. (1990). Gender-role stereotypes, expectancy effects, and parents' role in the socialization of gender differences in self-perceptions and skill acquisition. *Journal of Social Issues, 46,* 183–201.

Eggen, P. (1997, March). *The Impact of Frequent Assessment on Achievement, Satisfaction with Instruction, and Intrinsic Motivation of Undergraduate University Students.* Paper presented at the Annual Meeting of the American Educational Research Association, Chicago.

Eggen, P., & Kauchak, D. (1996). *Strategies for teachers: Teaching content and thinking skills* (3rd ed.). Needham Heights, MA: Allyn & Bacon.

Eggen, P., Kauchak, D., & Kirk, S. (1978). Hierarchical cues and the learning of concepts from prose materials. *Journal of Experimental Education, 46* (4), 7–10.

Eggen, P., & McDonald, S. (1987, April). *Student misconceptions of physical science concepts: Implications for science instruction.* Paper presented at the Annual Meeting of the National Association for Research in Science Teaching, Washington, DC.

Elam, S., & Rose, L. (1995). The 27th annual Phi Delta Kappa/Gallup poll. *Phi Delta Kappan, 77* (1), 41–49.

Elliot, S., & Busse, R. (1991). Social skills assessment and intervention with children and adolescents. *School Psychology International, 12,* 63–83.

Ellis, S., Dowdy, B., Graham, P., & Jones, R. (1992, April). *Parental support of planning skills in the context of homework and family demands.* Paper presented at the Annual Meeting of the American Educational Research Association, San Francisco.

Elton, L., & Laurillard, D. (1979). Trends in research on student learning. *Studies in Higher Education, 4,* 87–102.

Emmer, E. (1988). Praise and the instructional process. *Journal of Classroom Interaction, 23,* 32–39.

Emmer, E., & Evertson, C. (1981). Synthesis of research on classroom management. *Educational Leadership, 38,* 342–347.

Emmer, E., Evertson, C., & Anderson, L. (1980). Effective classroom management at the beginning of the school year. *Elementary School Journal, 80,* 219–231.

Emmer, E., Evertson, C., Clements, B., & Worsham, M. (1997). *Classroom management for secondary teachers* (4th ed.). Needham Heights, MA: Allyn & Bacon.

Emmer, E., Evertson, C., Sanford, J., Clements, B., & Worsham, M. (1994). *Classroom management for secondary teachers* (3rd ed.). Upper Saddle River, NJ: Prentice Hall.

Englert, C., Raphael, T., Anderson, L., Anthony, H., & Stevens, D. (1991). Making strategies and self-talk visible: Writing instruction in regular and special education classrooms. *American Educational Research Journal, 28,* 337–372.

Epstein, J. (1990). School and family connections: Theory, research, and implications for integrating sociologies of education and family. In D. Unger & M. Sussman (Eds.), *Families in community settings: Interdisciplinary perspectives* (pp. 99–126). New York: Haworth Press.

Ericcson, K., & Kintsch, W. (1995). Long-term working memory. *Psychological Review, 102,* 211–245.

Ericsson, K., Krampe, D., & Tesch-Romer, R. (1993). The role of deliberate practice in the acquisition of expert performance. *Psychological Review, 100,* 363–406.

Erikson, E. (1968). *Identity: Youth and crisis.* New York: Norton.

Erikson, E. (1980). *Identity and the life cycle* (2nd ed.). New York: Norton.

Esquival, G. (1995). Teacher behaviors that foster creativity. Educational Psychological Review, 7(2), 185–202.

Evans, E., & Engelberg, R. (1988). Student perceptions of school grading. *Journal of Research and Development in Education, 21*(2), 45–54.

Everson, H., Tobias, S., Hartman, H., & Gourgey, A. (1991, April). *Text anxiety in different curricular areas: An exploratory analysis of the role of subject matter.* Paper presented at the Annual Meeting of the American Educational Research Association, Chicago.

Evertson, C. (1987). Managing classrooms: A framework for teachers. In D. Berliner & B. Rosenshine (Eds.), *Talks to teachers* (pp. 54–74). New York: Random House.

Evertson, C., Anderson, C., Anderson, L., & Brophy, J. (1980). Relationship between classroom behaviors and student outcomes in junior high mathematics and English classes. *American Educational Research Journal, 17,* 43–60.

Evertson, C., Emmer, E., Clements, B., & Worsham, M. (1997). *Classroom management for elementary teachers* (4th ed.). Needham Heights, MA: Allyn & Bacon.

Eysenck, M., & Keane, M. (1990). *Cognitive psychology: A student's handbook.* Hillsdale, NJ: Erlbaum.

Fan, X., Chen, M., & Matsumata, A. (1997). Gender difference in mathematics achievement: Findings from the National Education Longitudinal Study of 1988. *Journal of Experimental Education, 65* (3), 229–242.

Faw, T., & Belkin, G. (1989). *Child psychology.* New York: McGraw-Hill.

Feather, N. (Ed.). (1982). *Expectations and actions.* Hillsdale, NJ: Erlbaum.

Feldhusen, J. (1989). Synthesis of research on gifted youth. *Educational Leadership, 46* (6), 6–11.

Feldman, A., Kropkf, A., & Alibrandi, M. (1996, April). *Making grades: How high school science teachers determine report card grades.* Paper presented at the Annual Meeting of the American Educational Research Association, New York.

Fennema, E. (1987). Sex-related differences in education: Myths, realities, and interventions. In V. Richardson-Koehler (Ed.), *Educators' Handbook* (pp. 329–347). White Plains, NY: Longman.

Fennema, E., Carpenter, T., & Franke, M. (in press). A longitudinal study of learning to use children's thinking in mathematics instruction. *Journal for Research in Mathematics Education.*

Fennema, E., Carpenter, T., & Peterson, P. (1989). Learning mathematics with understanding. In J. Brophy (Ed.), *Advances in research on teaching.* Vol. 1: *Teaching for meaningful understanding and self-regulated learning.* Greenwich, CT: JAI Press.

Fennema, E., & Franke, M. (1992). Teachers' knowledge and its impact. In D. Grouws (Ed.), *Handbook of research in mathematics teaching and learning* (pp. 147–164). New York: Macmillan.

Fennema, E., & Koehler, M. (1983). Expectations and feelings about females' and males' achievement in mathematics. In E. Fennema (Ed.), *Research on relationship of spatial visualization and confidence of male/female achievement in grades 6–8* (Final Report, National Science Foundation Project No. SED78-17330). Washington, DC: National Science Foundation.

Fennema, E., & Peterson, P. (1987). Effective teaching for girls and boys: The same or different? In D. Berliner & B. Rosenshine (Eds.), *Talks to teachers* (pp. 111–125). New York: Random House.

Fernald, L. (1989). Tales in a textbook: Learning in the traditional and narrative modes. *Teaching of Psychology, 16*(3), 121–124.

Fernandez, C., Yoshida, M., & Stigler, J. (1992). Learning mathematics from classroom instruction: On relating lessons to pupils' interpretations. *Journal of the Learning Sciences, 2,* 333–365.

Feuer, M., & Fulton, K. (1993). The many faces of performance assessment. *Phi Delta Kappan, 74* (6), 478.

Fielding, L., & Pearson, P. (1994). Reading comprehension: What works. *Educational Leadership, 51*(5), 62–68.

Finn, C., Dulberg, L., & Reis, J. (1979). Sex differences in educational attainment: A cross-national perspective. *Harvard Educational Review, 49,* 477–503.

Fisher, C., Berliner, D., Filby, N., Marliave, R., Cohen, K., & Dishaw, M. (1980). Teaching behaviors, academic learning time, and student achievement: An overview. In C. Denham & A. Lieberman (Eds.), *Time to learn* (pp. 7–32). Washington, DC: National Institute of Education.

Fitch, M., & Semb, M. (1992, April). *Peer teacher learning: A comparison of role playing and video evaluation for effects on peer teacher outcomes.* Paper presented at the Annual Meeting of the American Educational Research Association, San Francisco.

Fitzgerald, J. (1987). Research on revision in writing. *Review of Educational Research, 57,* 481–506.

Fitzgerald, J. (1995). English-as-a-second-language learners' cognitive

reading processes: A review of research in the United States. *Review of Educational Research, 65*(2), 145–190.

Fitzgerald, J., & Markman, L. (1987). Teaching children about revision in writing. *Cognition and Instruction, 41,* 3–24.

Flavell, J. (1985). *Cognitive development* (2nd ed.). Upper Saddle River, NJ: Prentice Hall.

Flavell, J., Friedrichs, A., & Hoyt, J. (1970). Developmental changes in memorization processes. *Cognitive Psychology, 1,* 324–340.

Flavell, J., Miller, P., & Miller, S. (1993). *Cognitive development* (3rd ed.). Englewood Cliffs, NJ: Prentice Hall.

Fleming, M., & Chambers, B. (1983). Teacher-made tests: Windows on the classrooms. In W. Hathaway (Ed.), *Testing in the schools: New directions for testing and measurement* (No. 19). San Francisco: Jossey-Bass.

Foos, P. (1992). Test performance as a function of expected form and difficulty. *Journal of Experimental Education, 60* (3), 205–211.

Forcier, R. (1996). *The computer as a productivity tool in education.* Upper Saddle River, NJ: Prentice Hall.

Forman, E. (1996). Learning mathematics as participation in classroom practice: Implications of sociocultural theory for educational reform. In L. Steffe & P. Nesher (Eds.), *Theories of mathematics learning* (pp. 115–130). Mahwah, NJ: Erlbaum.

Forsterling, F. (1985). Attributional retraining: A Review. *Psychological Bulletin, 98,* 495–512.

Fowler, R. (1994, April). *Piagetian versus Vygotskian perspectives on development and education.* Paper presented at the Annual Meeting of the American Educational Research Association, New Orleans.

Franklin, S. (1991). Breathing life into reluctant writers: The Seattle Public Schools laptop project. *Writing Notebook, 8,* 40–42.

Franklin, W. (1997, March). *African-American Youth At Promise.* Paper presented at the Annual meeting of the American Educational Research Association, Chicago.

Frary, R., Cross, L., & Weber, L. (1992, April). *Testing and grading practices and opinions in the nineties: 1890s or 1990s?* Paper presented at the Annual Meeting of the American Educational Research Association, San Francisco.

Freeman, E., & Hatch, J. (1989). What schools expect young children to know: An analysis of kindergarten report cards. *Elementary School Journal 89,* 595–605.

Fuchs, D., Fuchs, L., Mathes, P., & Simmons, D. (1997). Peer-assisted learning strategies: Making classrooms more responsive to diversity. *American Educational Research Journal, 34*(1), 174–206.

Fuchs, L., Fuchs, D., Bentz, J., Phillips, N., & Hamlett, C. (1994). The nature of student interactions during peer tutoring with and without prior training and experience. *American Educational Research Journal, 31*(1), 75–103.

Gage, N. (1985). *Hard gains in the soft sciences: The case of pedagogy.* Bloomington, IN: Phi Delta Kappa.

Gage, N., & Berliner, D. (1989). Nurturing the critical, practical, and artistic thinking of teachers. *Phi Delta Kappan, 71,* 212–214.

Gagne, E., Yekovich, C., & Yekovich, F. (1993). *The cognitive psychology of school learning* (2nd ed.). New York: HarperCollins.

Gagne, R. (1985). *The conditions of learning and a theory of instruction* (4th ed.). New York: Holt, Rinehart & Winston.

Gagne, R., & Dick, W. (1983). Instructional psychology. In M. Rosenzweig & L. Porter (Eds.), *Annual review of psychology*. Palo Alto, CA: Annual Reviews.

Gall, M. (1984). Synthesis of research on teachers' questioning. *Educational Leadership, 42* (3), 40–47.

Garber, H. (1988). *Milwaukee Project: Preventing mental retardation in children at risk*. Washington, DC: American Association on Mental Retardation.

Gardner, H. (1983). *Frames of mind: The theory of multiple intelligences*. New York: Basic Books.

Gardner, H. (1992). Assessment in context: The alternative to standardized testing. In B. Gifford (Ed.), *Changing assessments: Alternate views of aptitude, achievement, and instruction* (pp. 77–119). Boston: Kluwer.

Gardner, H. (1993). *Creating minds: An anatomy of creativity seen through the lives of Freud, Einstein, Picasso, Stravinsky, Elliot, Graham, and Gandhi*. New York: Basic Books.

Gardner, H. (1995). Reflections on multiple intelligences: Myths and messages. *Phi Delta Kappan, 77,* 200–209.

Gardner, H., & Hatch, T. (1989). Multiple intelligences go to school. *Educational Researcher, 18*(8), 4–10.

Gardner, M. (1985). Cognitive psychological approaches to instructional task analysis. In E. Gordon (Ed.), *Review of research in education* (Vol. 12, pp. 157–195). Washington, DC: American Educational Research Association.

Garner, R., Alexander, P., Gillingham, M., Kulikowich, J., & Brown, R. (1991). Interest and learning from text. *American Educational Research Journal, 28,* 643–659.

Gay, B. (1997) Educational equality for students of color. In J. Banks & C. Banks (Eds.) *Multicultural Education: Issues and Perspectives* (3rd ed.), 195–228. Boston: Allyn & Bacon.

Gaziel, H. (1997) Impact of school culture on effectiveness of secondary schools with disadvantaged students. *Journal of Educational Research, 90*(5), 310–318.

Gelfand, D., Jenson, W., & Drew, C. (1988). *Understanding child behavior disorders* (2nd ed.). New York: Holt, Rinehart & Winston.

Gelman, R., Meck, E., & Merkin, S. (1986). Young children's numerical competence. *Cognitive Development, 1,* 1–29.

Genishi, C. (1992, April). *Oral language and communicative competence*. Paper presented at the Annual Meeting of the American Educational Research Association, San Francisco.

Gentile, J. (1996). Setbacks in the "Advancement of learning?" *Educational Researcher, 25,* 37–39.

Gersten, R. (1996). The double demands of teaching English language learners. *Educational Leadership, 52*(5), February, 18–21.

Gersten, R., & Woodward, J. (1995). A longitudinal study of transitional and immersion bilingual education programs in one district. *Elementary School Journal, 95*(3), 223–239.

Gilligan, C. (1982). *In a different voice: Psychological theory and women's development*. Cambridge, MA: Harvard University Press.

Gilligan, C., & Attanucci, J. (1988). Two moral orientations: Gender differences and similarities. *Merrill-Palmer Quarterly, 34,* 223–237.

Gladney, L., & Greene, B. (1997, March). *Descriptions of motivation among African American high school students for their favorite and least favorite classes*. Paper presented at the Annual Meeting of the American Educational Research Association, Chicago.

Glaser, R., & Chi, M. (1988). Overview. In M. Chi, R. Glaser, & M. Farr (Eds.), *The nature of expertise* (pp. xv-xxviii). Hillsdale, NJ: Erlbaum.

Glasser, W. (1969). *Schools without failure*. New York: Harper & Row.

Glasser, W. (1985). *Control theory in the classroom*. New York: Perennial Library.

Glasser, W. (1990). *The quality school: Managing students without coercion*. New York: Harper & Row.

Glick, M., & Holyoak, K. (1987). The cognitive basis of knowledge transfer. In S. Cormier & J. Hagman (Eds.), *Transfer of learning: Contemporary research and applications*. San Diego: Academic Press.

Glickman, C., & Bey, T. (1990). Supervision. In R. Houston (Ed.), *Handbook of research on teacher education* (pp. 549–568). New York: Macmillan.

Glover, J., Ronning, R., & Bruning, R. (1990). *Cognitive psychology for teachers*. New York: Macmillan.

Glynn, S., Yeany, R., & Briton, B. (Eds.). (1991). *The psychology of learning science*. Hillsdale, NJ: Erlbaum.

Gollnick, D., & Chinn, P. (1986). *Multicultural education in a pluralistic society* (2nd ed.). New York: Merrill/Macmillan.

Gollnick, D., & Chinn, P. (1994). *Multicultural education in a pluralistic society* (4th ed.). New York: Merrill/Macmillan.

Good, T. (1987a). Teacher expectations. In D. Berliner & B. Rosenshine (Eds.), *Talks to teachers* (pp. 159–200). New York: Random House.

Good, T. (1987b). Two decades of research on teacher expectations:

Findings and future directions. *Journal of Teacher Education, 37*(4), 32–47.

Good, T., & Brophy, J. (1986). School effects. In M. Wittrock (Ed.), *Handbook of research on teaching* (3rd ed.) (pp. 570–604). New York: Macmillan.

Good, T., & Brophy, J. (1997). *Looking in classrooms* (7th ed.). New York: HarperCollins.

Good, T., Grouws, D., & Ebmeier, H. (1983). *Active mathematics teaching.* New York: Longman.

Good, T., & Marshall, S. (1984). Do students learn more in heterogeneous or homogeneous groups? In P. Peterson, L. Wilkinson, & M. Hallinan (Eds.), *The social context of instruction: Group organization and group process* (pp. 15–38). San Diego: Academic Press.

Good, T., McCaslin, M., & Reys, B. (1992). Investigating work groups to promote problem solving in mathematics. In J. Brophy (Ed.), *Advances in Research on Teaching* (Vol. 3, pp. 115–160). Greenwich, CT: JAI Press.

Goodenow, C. (1992a, April). *School motivation, engagement, and sense of belonging among urban adolescent students.* Paper presented at the Annual Meeting of the American Educational Research Association, San Francisco.

Goodenow, C. (1992b). Strengthening the links between educational psychology and the study of social contexts. *Educational Psychologist, 27*(2), 177–196.

Goodenow, C. (1993). Classroom belonging among early adolescent students: Relationships to motivation and achievement. *Journal of Early Adolescence, 13,* 21–43.

Goodlad, J. (1984). *A place called school.* New York: McGraw-Hill.

Goodland, J., Soder, R., & Sirotnik, K. (Eds.) (1990). *The moral dimen-sion of teaching.* San Francisco: Jossey-Bass.

Goodrich, H. (1996/97). Understanding rubrics. *Educational Leadership, 54*(4), 14–17.

Gordon, T. (1974). *Teacher effectiveness training.* New York: Wyden.

Gorman, J., & Balter, L. (1997). Culturally sensitive parent education: A critical review of quantitative research. *Review of Educational Research, 67,* 339–369.

Gottfried, A. (1985). Academic intrinsic motivation in elementary and junior high students. *Journal of Educational Psychology, 82,* 525–538.

Graeber, A., & Tirosh, D. (1988). Multiplication and division involving decimals: Preservice elementary teachers' performance and beliefs. *Journal of Mathematical Behavior, 7,* 263–280.

Graham, S. (1984). Communicating sympathy and anger to black and white children: The cognitive (attributional) consequences of affective cues. *Journal of Personality and Social Psychology, 47,* 14–28.

Graham, S. (1991). A review of attribution theory in achievement contexts. *Educational Psychology Review, 3*(1), 5–39.

Graham, S. (1994). Motivation in African Americans. *Review of Educational Research, 64*(1), 55–117.

Graham, S., & Barker, G. (1990). The downside of help: An attributional-developmental analysis of helping behavior as a low ability cue. *Journal of Educational Psychology, 82,* 7–14.

Graham, S., & Johnson, L. (1989). Teaching reading to learning disabled students: A review of research-supported procedures. *Focus on Exceptional Children, 21*(6), 1–9.

Graham, S., & Weiner, B. (1996). Theories and principles of motivation. In D. Berliner & R. Calfee (Eds.), *Handbook of Educational Psychology* (pp. 63–84). New York: Macmillan.

Grant, L. (1984). Black females' "place" in desegregated classrooms. *Sociology of Education, 57,* 98–111.

Grant, L., & Rothenberg, J. (1986). The social enhancement of ability differences: Teacher-student interactions in first- and second-grade reading groups. *Elementary School Journal, 87,* 29–49.

Graves, D. *A fresh look at writing.* Portsmouth, NH: Heinemann.

Greene, D., Sternberg, B., & Lepper, M. (1976). Overjustification in a token economy. *Journal of Personality and Social Psychology, 34,* 1219–1234.

Greenleaf, C. (1995, April). *You feel like you belong: Student perspectives on becoming a community of learners.* Paper presented at the Annual Meeting of the American Educational Research Association, San Francisco.

Greeno, J. (1997). On claims that answer the wrong questions. *Educational Researcher, 26*(1), 5–18.

Greeno, J., Collins, A., & Resnick, L. (1996). Cognition and learning. In D. Berliner & R. Calfee (Eds.), *Handbook of Educational Psychology* (pp. 15–46). New York: Macmillan.

Greer, B. (1993). The mathematical modeling perspective on word problems. *Journal of Mathematical Behavior, 12,* 239–250.

Gregg, V., Gibbs, J., & Basinger, K. (1994). Patterns of developmental delay in moral judgment by male and female delinquents. *Merrill-Palmer Quarterly, 40,* 538–553.

Griffith, D. (1992, April). Prenatal exposure to cocaine and other drugs: Developmental and educational prognoses. *Phi Delta Kappan, 74,* 30–34.

Gronlund, N. (1993). *How to make achievement tests and assessments.* Needham Heights, MA: Allyn & Bacon.

Gronlund, N. (1995). *How to write and use instructional objectives* (5th ed.). Upper Saddle River, NJ: Merrill/Prentice Hall.

Gronlund, N., & Linn, R. (1995). *Measurement and evaluation in teaching* (7th ed.). Upper Saddle River, NJ: Prentice Hall.

Guilford, J. (1967). *The nature of human intelligence.* New York: McGraw-Hill.

Guilford, J. (1988). Some changes in the structure-of-intellect model. *Educational and Psychological Measurement, 48,* 1–4.

Guillaume, A., & Rudney, G. (1997, March). *Stories of struggles and success: Implementing portfolio assessment across the disciplines.* Paper presented at the Annual Meeting of the National Educational Research Association, Chicago.

Guthrie, E. (1952). *The psychology of learning* (Rev. ed.). Gloucester, MA: Smith.

Haan, N., Smith, M., & Block, J. (1968). Moral reasoning of young adults: Political-social behavior, family background, and personality correlates. *Journal of Personality and Social Psychology, 10,* 183–201.

Haertel, E. (1986, April). *Choosing and using classroom tests: Teachers' perspectives on assessment.* Paper presented at the Annual Meeting of the American Educational Research Association, San Francisco.

Hakuta, K., & Garcia, E. (1989). Bilingualism and education. *American Psychologist, 44*(2), 374–379.

Halford, J. (1997) Reading instruction. *Infobrief, 10,* Sept. Alexandria, VA:

Association for Supervision and Curriculum Development.

Hall, C., & Lindzey, G. (1978). *Theories of personality.* New York: Wiley.

Hall, R. J., Gerber, M. M., & Stricker, A. G. (1989). Cognitive training: Implications for spelling instruction. In J. N. Hughes & R. J. Hall (Eds.), *Cognitive-behavioral psychology in the schools: A comprehensive handbook* (pp. 347–388). New York: Guilford Press.

Hallahan, D., Hall, R., Ianno, S., Kneedler, R., Lloyd, J., Loper, A., & Reeve, R. (1983). Summary of research findings at the University of Virginia Learning Disabilities Research Institute. *Exceptional Education Quarterly, 4*(1), 95–114.

Hallahan, D., & Kauffman, J. (1994). *Exceptional children* (6th ed.). Needham Heights, MA: Allyn & Bacon.

Halle, T., Kurtz-Costes, B., & Mahoney, J. (1997). Family influences on school achievement in low-income, African American children. *Journal of Educational Psychology, 89*(3), 527–537.

Hallinan, M. (1984). Summary and implications. In P. Peterson, L. Wilkinson, & M. Hallinan (Eds.), *The social context of instruction: Group organization and group processes* (pp. 229–240). San Diego: Academic Press.

Hamachek, D. (1987). Humanistic psychology: Theory, postulates, and implications for educational processes. In J. Glover & R. Ronning (Eds.), *Historical foundations of educational psychology* (pp. 159–182). New York: Plenum Press.

Hamilton, R. (1997). Effects of three types of elaboration on learning concepts from text. *Contemporary Education Psychology, 22,* 299–318.

Hamm, J., & Coleman, H. (1997, March). *Adolescent strategies for coping with cultural diversity: Variability and youth outcomes.* Paper presented at the Annual meeting of the American Educational Research Association, Chicago.

Hamp-Lyons, L. (1992). Holistic writing assessment for L.E.P. students. In *Focus on evaluation and measurement* (Vol. 2, pp. 317–358). Washington, DC: U.S. Department of Education.

Hardiman, P., Pollatsek, A., & Weil, A. (1986). Learning to understand the balance beam. *Cognition and Instruction, 3,* 1–30.

Hardman, M., Drew, C., & Egan, W. (1996). *Human exceptionality* (5th ed.). Needham Heights, MA: Allyn & Bacon.

Harrington-Lueker, D. (1997). Technology works best when it serves clear educational goals. *The Harvard Education Letter, XIII,* pp. 1–5.

Harris, L., Kagay, M., & Ross, J. (1987). *The Metropolitan Life survey of the American teacher: Strengthening links between home and school.* New York: Louis Harris & Associates.

Harrow, A. (1972). *A taxonomy of the psychomotor domain: A guide for developing behavioral objectives.* New York: McKay.

Harry, B. (1992). An ethnographic study of cross-cultural communication with Puerto Rican American families in the special education system. *American Educational Research Journal, 29*(3), 471–488.

Harter, S. (1978). Pleasure derived from challenge and the effects of receiving grades on children's difficulty level choices. *Child Development, 49,* 788–789.

Harter, S. (1990). Causes, correlates, and the functional role of global self-worth: A life-span perspective. In J. Kolligan and R. Sternberg

(Eds.), *Competence considered: Perceptions of competence.* New Haven, CT: Yale University Press.

Harter, S., & Connell, J. (1984). A comparison of alternative models of the relationships between academic achievement and children's perceptions of competence, control, and motivational orientation. In J. Nicholls (Ed.), *Development of achievement-related cognitions and behavior.* Greenwich, CT: JAI Press.

Harter, S., & Jackson, B. (1992). Trait versus nontrait conceptualizations of intrinsic/extrinsic motivational orientation. Special issue: Perspectives on intrinsic motivation. *Motivation and Emotion, 16,* 209–230.

Hasselbring, T., Goin, L., & Bransford, J. (1988). Developing math automaticity in learning handicapped children: The role of computerized drill and practice. *Focus on Exceptional Children, 20,* 1–70.

Hayes, J. (1988). *The complete problem solver* (2nd ed.). Hillsdale, NJ: Erlbaum.

Hayes, J. (1996). A new framework for understanding cognition and affect in writing. In C. Levy & S. Ransdell, (Eds.), *The science of writing* (pp. 1–28). Mahwah, NJ: Erlbaum.

Hayes, J., & Flower, L. (1986). Writing research and the writer. *American Psychologist, 41,* 1106–1113.

Hayes, S., Rosenfarb, I., Wulfert, E., Munt, E., Korn, Z., & Zettle, R. (1985). Self-reinforcement effects: An artifact of social standard setting? *Journal of Applied Behavior Analysis, 18,* 201–214.

Haynes, N., & Comer, J. (1995, April). *The School Development Program (SDP): Lessons from the past.* Paper presented at the Annual Meeting of the American Educational Research Association, San Francisco.

Heath, S. (1982). Questioning at home and at school: A comparative study. In G. Spindler (Ed.), *Doing the ethnography of schooling.* New York: Holt, Rinehart & Winston.

Helmke, A., & Schrader, F. (1987). Interactional effects of instructional quality and teacher judgment accuracy on achievement. *Teaching and Teacher Education, 3,* 91–98.

Helms, J. (1992). Why is there no study of cultural equivalence in standardized cognitive ability testing? *American Psychologist, 47*(9), 1083–1101.

Hempenstall, K. (1997). The whole language-phonics controversy: An historical perspective. *Educational Psychology, 17,* 399–420.

Henson, K. (1988). *Methods and strategies for teaching in secondary and middle schools.* White Plains, NY: Longman.

Herman, J., & Winters, L. (1994). Portfolio research: A slim collection. *Educational Leadership, 52,* 48–55.

Herman, J., Abedi, J., & Golan, S. (1994). Assessing the effects of standardized testing on schools. *Educational and Psychological Measurement, 54*(2), 471–482.

Herman, J., Aschbacher, P., & Winters, L. (1992). *A practical guide to alternative assessment.* Alexandria, VA: Association for Supervision and Curriculum Development.

Hernandez, H. (1997). *Teaching in multilingual classrooms.* Columbus, OH: Merrill.

Herrnstein, R., & Murray, C. (1994). *The bell curve.* New York: Free Press.

Herrnstein, R., Nickerson, R., Sanchez, M., & Swets, J. (1986). Teaching thinking skills. *American Psychologist, 41,* 1279–1289.

Hess, R., Chih-Mei, C., & McDevitt, T. (1987). Cultural variations in family beliefs about children's performance in mathematics: Comparisons among People's Republic of China, Chinese-American, and Caucasian-American families. *Journal of Educational Psychology, 79,* 179–188.

Hess, R., & McDevitt, T. (1984). Some cognitive consequences of maternal intervention techniques: A longitudinal study. *Child Development, 55,* 2017–2020.

Heut, N., & Mariné, C. (1997). Metamemory assessment and memory behavior in a simulated memory professional task. *Contemporary Education Psychology, 22,* 507–520.

Heward, W. (1996). *Exceptional children* (5th ed.). Upper Saddle River, NJ: Merrill/Prentice Hall.

Hidi, S., & Anderson, V. (1986). Producing written summaries: Task demands, cognitive operations, and implications for instruction. *Review of Educational Research, 56,* 473–493.

Hiebert, E., & Raphael, T. (1996). Psychological perspectives on literacy and extensions to educational practice. In D. Berliner & R. Calfee (Eds.), *Handbook of educational psychology* (pp. 550–602). New York: Macmillan.

Higgins, K., & Boone, R. (1993). Technology as a tutor, tools, and agent for reading. *Journal of Special Education Technology, 12,* 28–37.

Hill, D. (1990). Order in the classroom. *Teacher, 1*(7), 70–77.

Hill, K., & Wigfield, A. (1984). Test anxiety: A major educational problem and what can be done about it. *Elementary School Journal, 85,* 105–126.

Hillocks, G. (1984). What works in teaching composition: A meta-analysis of experimental treatment studies. *American Journal of Education, 93,* 133–170.

Hmelo, C. (1995, April). *The effect of problem-based learning on the early development of medical expertise.* Paper presented at the Annual Meeting of the American Educational Research Association, San Francisco.

Hodgkinson, H. (1991). Reform vs. reality. *Phi Delta Kappan, 73*(1), 8–16.

Holstein, C. (1976). Irreversible, step-wise sequence in the development of moral judgment: A longitudinal study of males and females. *Child Development, 47,* 51–61.

Holt, J. (1964). *How children fail.* New York: Putnam.

Hoover-Dempsey, K., Bassler, O., & Burow, R. (1995). Parents' reported involvement in students' homework: Strategies and practices. *Elementary School Journal, 95*(5), 435–449.

Hornberger, N. (1989). Continua of biliteracy. *Review of Educational Research, 59,* 271–296.

Houten, R., & Doleys, D. (1983). Are social reprimands effective? In S. Axelrod & J. Apache (Eds.), *The effects of punishment on human behavior* (pp. 45–70). San Diego: Academic Press.

Hudley, C. (1992, April). *The reduction of peer-directed aggression among highly aggressive African American boys.* Paper presented at the Annual Meeting of the American Educational Research Association, San Francisco.

Humphrey, F. (1979). *"Shh!" A sociolinguistic study of teachers' turn-taking sanctions in primary school lessons.* Unpublished doctoral dissertation, Georgetown University, Washington, DC.

Hunter, M. (1982). *Mastery teaching.* El Sugundo, CA: TIP Publications.

Hvitfeldt, C. (1986). Traditional culture, perceptual style, and learning: The classroom behavior of Hmong adults. *Adult Education Quarterly, 36*(2), 65–77.

Isabella, R., & Belsky, J. (1991). Interactional synchrony and the ori-gins of infant-mother attachment: A replication study. *Child Development, 62,* 373, 384.

Jagacinski, C. (1997, March). *Effects of goal setting in an ego-involving context.* Paper presented at the Annual Meeting of the American Educational Research Association, Chicago.

Jensen, A. (1987). Individual differences in mental ability. In J. Glover & R. Ronning (Eds.), *Historical foundations of educational psychology.* New York: Plenum Press.

Jenson, W., Sloane, H., & Young, K. (1988). *Applied behavior analysis in education.* Upper Saddle River, NJ: Prentice Hall.

Jetton, T., & Alexander, P. (1997). Instruction importance: What teachers value and what students learn. *Reading Research Quarterly, 32,* 290–308.

Johnson, D., & Johnson, R. (1989). *Cooperation and competition: Theory and practice.* Edina, MN: Interaction Book Company.

Johnson, D., & Johnson, R. (1994). *Learning together and alone: Cooperation, competition, and individualization* (4th ed.). Needham Heights, MA: Allyn & Bacon.

Johnson, J. (1972). Punishment of human behavior. *American Psychologist, 27,* 1033–1054.

Jonassen, D. (1996). *Computers in the classroom: Mindtools for critical thinking.* Englewood Cliffs, NJ: Prentice Hall.

Jones, E. (1990). *Interpersonal perception.* New York: Freeman.

Jones, E. (1995, April). *Defining essential critical thinking skills for college students.* Paper presented at the Annual Meeting of the American Educational Research Association, San Francisco.

Jones, F. (1987). *Positive classroom discipline.* New York: McGraw-Hill.

Jones, L. (1996). A history of the national assessment of educational progress and some questions about its future. *Educational Researcher, 25*(7), 15–20.

Jussim, L. (1989). Teacher expectations: Self-fulfilling prophecies, perceptual biases, and accuracy. *Journal of Personality and Social Psychology, 57,* 469–480.

Just, M., & Carpenter, P. (1987). *The psychology of reading and language comprehension.* Boston: Allyn & Bacon.

Kagan, D. (1992a). Implications of research on teacher belief. *Educational Psychologist, 27,* 65–90.

Kagan, D. (1992b). Professional growth among preservice and beginning teachers. *Review of Educational Research, 62,* 129–169.

Kagan, S. (1994). *Cooperative learning.* San Juan Capistrano, CA: Resources for Teachers.

Kalechstein, P., Kalechstein, M., & Doctor, R. (1981). The effects of instruction on test-taking skills in second-grade black children. *Measurement and Evaluation in Guidance, 13,* 198–202.

Kaplan, R., & Saccuzzo, D. (1993). *Psychological testing* (3rd ed.). Pacific Grove, CA: Brooks/Cole.

Karplus, R., Karplus, E., Formisano, M., & Paulsen, A. (1979). Proportional reasoning and control of variables in seven countries. In J. Lockheed & M. Clements (Eds.), *Cognitive process instruction: Research on teaching thinking skills.* Philadelphia: Franklin Institute Press.

Karweit, N. (1989). Time and learning: A review. In R. Slavin (Ed.), *School and classroom organization.* Hillsdale, NJ: Erlbaum.

Kauchak, D., & Eggen, P. (1998). *Learning and teaching: Research-based methods* (3rd ed.). Needham Heights, MA: Allyn & Bacon.

Kavale, K., & Forness, S. (1995). The nature of learning disabilities: Critical elements of diagnosis and classification. Mahwah, N.J.: Erlbaum.

Keislar, E., & Shulman, L. (Eds.). (1966). *Learning by discovery: A critical appraisal*. Chicago: Rand McNally.

Kellogg, J. (1988). Forces of change. *Phi Delta Kappan, 70,* 199–204.

Kellogg, R. (1987). Effects of topic knowledge on the allocation of processing time and cognitive effort to writing processes. *Memory and Cognition, 15,* 256–266.

Kellogg, R. (1994). *The psychology of writing*. New York: Oxford Press.

Kelly, M., Moore, D., & Tuck, B. (1994). Reciprocal teaching in a regular primary school classroom. *Journal of Educational Research, 88*(1), 53–59.

Kerman, S. (1979). Teacher expectations and student achievement. *Phi Delta Kappan, 60,* 70–72.

Kher-Durlabhji, N., Lacina-Gifford, L., Jackson, L., Guillory, R., & Yandell, S. (1997, March). *Preservice teachers' knowledge of effective classroom management strategies*. Paper presented at the annual meeting of the American Educational Research Association, Chicago.

Kids of Room 14 (1979). *Our friends in the water*. Berkeley, CA: West Coast Print.

Kiewra, K. (1989). A review of notetaking: The encoding-storage paradigm and beyond. *Educational Psychology Review, 1,* 147–172.

Kika, F., McLaughlin, T., & Dixon, J. (1992). Effects of frequent testing of secondary algebra students. *Journal of Educational Research, 85,* 159–162.

Kim, D., Solomon, D., & Roberts, W. (1995, April). *Classroom practices that enhance students' sense of community*. Paper presented at the Annual Meeting of the American Educational Research Association, San Francisco.

King-Sears, M. (1997). Disability: Legalities and labels. In D. Bradley, M. King-Sears, & D. Tessier-Switlick (Eds.), Inclusive settings: From theory to practice. (pp. 21–55) Boston: Allyn & Bacon.

Kintsch, W. (1986). Learning from text. *Cognition and Instruction, 3,* 87–108.

Kirk, S., & Gallagher, J. (1989). *Educating exceptional students* (6th ed.). Boston: Houghton Mifflin.

Klausmeier, H. (1992). Concept learning and concept thinking. *Educational Psychologist, 27,* 267–286.

Kloosterman, P. (1997, March). *Assessing student motivation in high school mathematics*. Paper presented at the annual meeting of the American Educational Research Association, Chicago.

Knapp, M., Shields, P., & Turnbull, B. (1995). Academic challenge in high-poverty classrooms. *Phi Delta Kappan, 76,* 770–776.

Kneedler, P. (1985). California assesses critical thinking. In A. Costa (Ed.), *Developing minds: A resource book for teaching thinking* (pp. 276–282). Alexandria, VA: Association for Supervision and Curriculum Development.

Kochenberger-Stroeher, S. (1994). Sixteen kindergartners' gender-related views of careers. *Elementary School Journal, 95* (1), 95–103.

Kohlberg, L. (1963). The development of children's orientation toward moral order: Sequence in the development of human thought. *Vita Humana, 6,* 11–33.

Kohlberg, L. (1969). Stage and sequence: The cognitive-developmental approach to socialization. In D. Goslin (Ed.), *Handbook of socialization theory and research*. Chicago: Rand McNally.

Kohlberg, L. (1975). The cognitive-developmental approach to moral education. *Phi Delta Kappan, 56,* 670–677.

Kohlberg, L. (1981). *Philosophy of moral development*. New York: Harper & Row.

Kohlberg, L. (1984). *Essays on moral development: Vol. 2. The psychology of moral development*. New York: Harper & Row.

Kohn, A. (1992). *No contest: The case against competition*. Boston: Houghton Mifflin.

Kohn, A. (1993). Why incentive plans cannot work. *Harvard Business Review, 71,* 54–63.

Kohn, A. (1996). *Beyond discipline: From compliance to community*. Alexandria, VA: Association for Supervision and Curriculum Development.

Kohn, A. (1997). How not to teach values. *Phi Delta Kappan, 78*(6), 429–439.

Konstantopoulos, S. (1997, March). *Hispanic-white differences in central tendency and proportions of high- and low-scoring individuals*. Paper presented at the Annual meeting of the American Educational Research Association, Chicago.

Koretz, D., Stecher, B., & Diebert, E. (1993). *The reliability of scores from the 1992 Vermont Portfolio Assessment Program* (Tech. Rep. No. 355). Los Angeles: UCLA, Center for the Study of Evaluation.

Kounin, J. (1970). *Discipline and group management in classrooms*. New York: Holt, Rinehart & Winston.

Kozulin, A. (1990). *Vygotsky's psychology: A biography of ideas*. Cambridge, MA: Harvard University Press.

Krabbe, M., & Polivka, J. (1990, April). *An analysis of students' perceptions of effective teaching behaviors during discussion activity*.

Paper presented at the Annual Meeting of the American Educational Research Association, Boston.

Kramer, L., & Colvin, C. (1991, April). *Rules, responsibilities, and respect: The school lives of marginal students*. Paper presented at the Annual Meeting of the American Educational Research Association, Chicago.

Kramer-Schlosser, L. (1992). Teacher distance and student disengagement: School lives on the margin. *Journal of Teacher Education, 43*(2), 128–140.

Krapp, A., Hidi, S., & Renninger, K. (1992). Interest, learning, and development. In K. Renninger, S. Hidi, & A. Krapp (Eds.), *The role of interest in learning and development* (pp. 3–26). Hillsdale, NJ: Erlbaum.

Krathwohl, D., Bloom, B., & Masia, B. (1964). *Taxonomy of educational objectives: The classification of educational goals: Handbook 2. Affective domain*. New York: McKay.

Kreutzer, M., Leonard, C., & Flavell, J. (1975). An interview study of children's knowledge about memory. *Monographs of the Society for Research in Child Development, 40*(1, Serial No. 15).

Kroger, J. (1993). Ego identity: An overview. In J. Kroger (Ed.), *Discussions on ego identity*. Hillsdale, NJ: Erlbaum.

Kruger, A. (1992). The effect of peer and adult–child transactive discussions on moral reasoning. *Merrill-Palmer Quarterly, 38*(2), 191–211.

Kulik, J., & Kulik, C. (1984). Effects of accelerated instruction on students. *Review of Educational Research, 54*, 409–425.

Kuther, T., & Higgins-D'Alessandra M. (1997, March). *Effects of a just community on moral development and adolescent engagement in risk*. Paper presented at the Annual meeting of the American Educa-

tional Research Association, Chicago.

LaBerge, D., & Samuels, S. (1974). Toward a theory of automatic information processing in reading. *Cognitive Psychology, 6*, 293–323.

Labov, W. (1972). *Language in the inner city: Studies in the "Black" English vernacular*. Philadelphia: University of Pennsylvania Press.

Lammers, S. (1986). *Programmers at work: Interviews*. Redmond, WA: Microsoft Press.

Lampert, M. (1986). Knowing, doing, and teaching multiplication. *Cognition and Instruction, 3*, 305–342.

Lampert, M. (1989). Choosing and using mathematical tools in classroom discourse. In J. Brophy (Ed.), *Advances in research on teaching*. Vol. 1: *Teaching for meaningful understanding and self-regulated learning*. Greenwich, CT: JAI.

Lampert, M. (1990). When the problem is not the question and the solution is not the answer: Mathematical knowing and teaching. *American Educational Research Journal, 27*, 29–63.

Lampert, M. (1992). Practices and problems in teaching authentic mathematics. In F. Oser, A. Dick, & J. Patry (Eds.), *Effective and responsible teaching: The new synthesis* (pp. 295–314). San Francisco: Jossey-Bass.

Land, R. (1997). Moving up to complex assessment systems: Proceedings from the 1996 CRESST Conference. *Evaluation Comment, 7*(1), 1–21.

Langer, J., Bartolome, L., Vasquez, O., & Lucas, T. (1990). Meaning construction in school literacy tasks: A study of bilingual students. *American Educational Research Journal, 27*, 427–471.

Lappan, G., & Ferrini-Mundy, J. (1993). Knowing and doing mathe-

matics: A new vision for middle grades students. *Elementary School Journal, 93*, 625–641.

Larrivee, B., Semmel, M., & Gerber, M. (1997). Case studies of six schools varying in effectiveness for students with learning disabilities. *The Elementary School Journal, 98*(1), 27–50.

Lave, J. (1988). *Cognition in practice: Mind, mathematics, and culture in everyday life*. New York: Cambridge University Press.

Lawler-Prince, D., & Holloway, D. (1992). The family dynamics and characteristics of homeless children: Barriers to education. *National Forum of Teaching Education Journal, 2*(1), 49–53.

Lawson, A., & Snitgren, D. (1982). Teaching formal reasoning in a college biology course for preservice teachers. *Journal of Research in Science Teaching, 19*, 233–248.

Lawson, M., & Chinnappan, M. (1994). Generative activity during problem solving: Comparison of the performance of high-achieving and low-achieving high school students. *Cognition & Instruction, 12*(1), 61–93.

Leahey, T., & Harris, R. (1997). *Learning and cognition* (4th ed.). Upper Saddle River, NJ: Prentice Hall.

Lee, J., Pulvino, C., & Perrone, P. (1998). *Restoring harmony: A guide for managing conflicts in schools*. Columbus, OH: Merrill.

Lee, V., Burkam, D., & Smerdon, B. (1997, March). *Debunking the myths: Exploring common explanations for gender differences in high-school science achievement*. Paper presented at the Annual meeting of the American Educational Research Association, Chicago.

Le Fevre, J. (1988). Reading skill as a source of individual differences in the processing of instructional texts.

Journal of Educational Psychology, 80, 312–314.

Lemke, J. (1982, April). *Classroom communication of science* (Final report to NSF/RISE). Washington, DC: National Science Foundation. (ERIC Document Reproduction Service No. ED 222 346)

Leon, M., Lynn, T., McLean, P., & Perri, L. (1997, March). *Age and gender trends in adults' normative moral reasoning.* Paper presented at the Annual meeting of the American Educational Research Association, Chicago.

Lepper, M., & Hodell, M. (1989). Intrinsic motivation in the classroom. In C. Ames & R. Ames (Eds.), *Research on motivation in education* (Vol. 3, pp. 73–105). San Diego: Academic Press.

Levin, H. (1988, April). *Structuring schools for greater effectiveness with educationally disadvantaged or at-risk students.* Paper presented at the Annual Meeting of the American Educational Research Association, San Francisco.

Lickona, T. (1991). *Educating for character.* New York: Bantam.

Linn, M., & Burbules, N. (1993). Construction of knowledge and group learning. In. K. Tobin (Ed.), *The practice of construction in science education* (pp. 91–119). Washington, DC: American Association for the Advancement of Science.

Linn, M., & Hyde, J. (1989). Gender, mathematics, and science. *Educational Researcher, 18* (8), 17–19, 22–27.

Linn, M., Songer, N., & Eylon, B. (1996). Shifts and convergences in science learning and instruction. In D. Berliner & R Calfee (Eds.), *Handbook of educational psychology* (pp. 438–490). New York: Macmillan.

Linn, R. (1990). Essentials of student assessment: From accountability to

instructional aid. *Teachers College Record, 91,* 422–436.

Lipman, M., Sharp, A., & Oscanyan, F. (1980). *Philosophy in the classroom.* Philadelphia: Temple University Press.

Locke, E., & Latham, G. (1990). *A theory of goal setting and performance.* Upper Saddle River, NJ: Prentice Hall.

Loehlin, J. (1989). Partitioning environmental and genetic contributions to behavioral development. *American Psychologist, 44,* 1285–1292.

Lohman, D. (1995, April). *Intelligence as an outcome of schooling: Some prescriptions for developing and testing the fluidization of abilities.* Paper presented at the Annual Meeting of the American Educational Research Association, San Francisco.

Lomax, R. (1994, April). *On becoming assessment literate. Preservice teachers' beliefs and practices.* Paper presented at the Annual Meeting of the American Educational Research Association, New Orleans.

Lomax, R., & McGee, L. (1987). Young children's concepts about print and reading: Toward a model of word reading acquisition. *Reading Research Quarterly, 22,* 237–256.

Lovett, M., & Anderson, J. (1994). Effects of solving related proofs on memory and transfer in geometry problem solving. *Journal of Experimental Psychology, 20*(2), 366–378.

Luckasson, R., Coulter, D., Pollaway, E., Reiss, A., Shalock, R., Snell, M., Spitalnik, D., & Stark, J. (1992). *Mental retardation: Definition, classification, and systems of supports.* Washington, DC: American Association on Mental Retardation.

Lyman, H. (1991). *Test scores and what they mean* (5th ed.). Upper Saddle River, NJ: Prentice Hall.

Mace, F., Belfiore, P., & Shea, M. (1989). Operant theory and research on self-regulation. In B. Zimmerman & D. Schunk (Eds.), *Self-regulated learning and academic achievement: Theory, research, and practice.* New York: Springer-Verlag.

Maccoby, E., & Jacklin, C. (1974). *The psychology of sex differences.* Palo Alto, CA: Stanford University Press.

Mace, F., & Kratochwill, T. (1988). Self-monitoring. In J. Witt, S. Elliot, & F. Gresham (Eds.), *Handbook of behavior therapy in education.* New York: Plenum Press.

Macionis, J. (1994). *Sociology* (4th ed.). Upper Saddle River, NJ: Prentice Hall.

Maehr, M. (1976). Continuing motivation: An analysis of a seldom considered educational outcome. *Review of Educational Research, 46,* 443–462.

Maehr, M. (1992, April). *Transforming the school culture to enhance motivation.* Paper presented at the Annual Meeting of the American Educational Research Association, San Francisco.

Mager, R. (1962). *Preparing instructional objectives.* Palo Alto, CA: Fearon.

Maheady, L., Sacca, M., & Harper, G. (1987). Classwide student tutoring teams: The effects of peer-mediated instruction on the academic performance of secondary mainstreamed students. *Journal of Special Education, 21*(3), 107–121.

Maller, S. (1994, April). *Item bias in the WISC-III with deaf children.* Paper presented at the Annual Meeting of the National Educational Research Association, New Orleans.

Mansilla, V., & Gardner, H. (1997). Of kinds of disciplines and kinds of understanding. *Phi Delta Kappan, 78*(5), 381–386.

Mantzicopoulos, P. (1989, April). *Coping with school failure: The relationship of children's coping strategies to academic achievement, self-concept, behavior, and locus of control*. Paper presented at the Annual Meeting of the American Educational Research Association, San Francisco.

Marcia, J. (1980). Identity in adolescence. In J. Adelson (Ed.), *Handbook of adolescent psychology*. New York: Wiley.

Marcia, J. (1987). The identity status approach to the study of ego identity development. In T. Honess & K. Yardley (Eds.), *Self and identity: Perspectives across the life span*. London: Routledge & Kegan Paul.

Markman, E. (1979). Realizing that you don't understand: Elementary school children's awareness of inconsistencies. *Child Development, 50*, 643–655.

Markman, E., & Gorin, L. (1981). Children's ability to adjust their standards for evaluating comprehension. *Journal of Educational Psychology, 73*, 320–325.

Marsh, H. (1989). Age and sex effects in multiple dimensions of self-concept: Preadolescence to early adulthood. *Journal of Educational Psychology, 81*, 417–430.

Marsh, H. (1992). Content specificity of relations between academic achievement and academic self-concept. *Journal of Educational Psychology, 84*(1), 34–52.

Marsh, H., & Shavelson, R. (1985). Self-concept: Its multifaceted hierarchical structure. *Educational Psychologist, 20*, 107–123.

Marshall, H. (1992). Seeing, redefining, and supporting student learning. In H. Marshall (Ed.), *Redefining student learning: Roots of educational change* (pp. 1–32). Norwood, NJ: Ablex.

Marshall, H. (1997). Learner-centered psychological principles: Guidelines for teaching of educational psychology in teacher education programs. In N. Lambert & B. McCombs (Eds.), *How students learn: Reforming schools through learner-centered education*. Washington, DC: American Psychological Association.

Marso, R., & Pigge, F. (1992, April). *A summary of published research: Classroom teachers' knowledge and skills related to the development and use of teacher-made tests*. Paper presented at the Annual Meeting of the American Educational Research Association, San Francisco.

Martin, J. (1993). Episodic memory: A neglected phenomenon in the psychology of education. *Educational Psychologist, 28*(2), 169–183.

Maslow, A. (1968). *Toward a psychology of being* (2nd ed.). New York: Van Nostrand.

Maslow, A. (1970). *Motivation and personality* (2nd ed.). New York: Harper & Row.

Maslow, A. (1971). *The farther reaches of human nature*. New York: Viking.

Mason, C., & Kahle, J. (1989). Student attitudes toward science and science-related careers: A program designed to promote a stimulating gender-free learning environment. *Journal of Research in Science Teaching, 26*, 25–40.

Masten, A., Morison, P., Pelligrini, D., & Tellegen, A. (1990). Competence under stress: Risk and protective factors. In J. Rolf, A. Masten, D. Cicchetti, K. Nuechterlein, & P. Weintraub (Eds.), *Risk and protective factors in the development of psychopathology* (pp. 236–256). New York: Cambridge University Press.

Matsushashi, A. (1987). *Writing in real time: Modeling production processes*. Norwood, NJ: Ablex.

Matute-Bianchi, M. (1986). Ethnic identities and patterns of school success and failure among Mexican-descent and Japanese American students in a California high school: An ethnographic analysis. *American Journal of Education, 95*, 233–255.

Mayer, R. (1984). Aids to text comprehension. *Educational Psychologist, 19*, 30–42.

Mayer, R. (1987). *Educational psychology: A cognitive approach*. Boston: Little, Brown.

Mayer, R. (1992). *Thinking, problem solving, cognition* (2nd ed.). New York: Freeman.

Mayer, R. (1996). Learners as information processors: Legacies and limitations of educational psychology's second metaphor. *Educational Psychologist, 31*(4), 151–161.

Mayer, R. (1997). Multimedia learning: Are we asking the right questions? *Educational Psychologist, 32*(1), 1–19.

Mayer, R. (1999). *The promise of educational psychology: Learning in the content areas*. Columbus OH: Merrill.

Mayer, R., & Wittrock, M. (1996). Problem-solving transfer. In D. Berliner & R. Calfee (Eds.), *Handbook of Educational Psychology* (pp. 47–62). New York: Macmillan.

McBride-Chang, C., Wagner, R., & Chang, L. (1997). Growth modeling of phonological awareness. *Journal of Educational Psychology, 89*, 621–630.

McCall, R., Appelbaum, M., & Hogarty, P. (1973). Developmental changes in mental performance. *Monographs of the Society for Research in Child Development, 38*(3, Serial No. 150).

McCarthy, J. (1991, April). *Classroom environments which facilitate innovative strategies for teaching and learning*. Paper presented at the Annual Meeting of the American Educational Research Association, Chicago.

McCarthy, S. (1994). Authors, text, and talk: The internalization of dialogue from social interaction during writing. *Reading Research Quarterly, 29*, 201–231.

McCaslin, M., & Good, T. (1992). Compliant cognition: The misalliance of management and instructional goals in current school reform. *Educational Researcher, 21*(3), 4–17.

McClelland, D. (1985). *Human motivation*. Glenview, IL: Scott, Foresman.

McCloskey, M., Caramazza, A., & Green, B. (1980). Curvilinear motion in the absence of external forces: Naive beliefs about the motion of objects. *Science, 210*, 1139–1141.

McCombs, B. (1998). Integrating metacognition, affect, and motivation in improving teacher education. In N. Lambert & B. McCombs (Eds.), *How students learn: Reforming schools through learner-centered education* (pp. 379–408). Washington, DC: American Psychological Association.

McDaniel, E. (1994). *Understanding educational measurement*. Madison, WI: Brown & Benchmark.

McDougall, D., & Granby, C. (1996). How expectation of questioning method affects undergraduates' preparation for class. *Journal of Experimental Education, 65*, 43–54.

McKeachie, W., & Kulik, J. (1975). Effective college teaching. In F. Kerlinger (Ed.), *Review of research in education* (Vol. 3). Washington, DC: American Educational Research Association.

McLaughlin, H. J. (1994). From negation to negotiation: Moving away from the management metaphor. *Action in Teacher Education, 16*(1), 75–84.

McMann, R. (1979). In defense of lecture. *Social Studies, 70*, 270–274.

McMillen, L. (1997). Linguists find the debate over "ebonics" uninformed. *Education Week*, XLIII (19) June, 17, p. A16.

McTighe, J. (1996/97). What happens between assessments? *Educational Leadership, 54* (4), 6–12.

Means, B., & Knapp, M. (1991). Introduction: Rethinking teaching for disadvantaged students. In B. Means, C. Chelemer, & M. Knapp (Eds.), *Teaching advanced skills to at-risk students* (pp. 1–27). San Francisco: Jossey-Bass.

Meece, J., Blumenfeld, P., & Hoyle, R. (1988). Students' goal orientations and cognitive engagement in classroom activities. *Journal of Educational Psychology, 80*, 514–523.

Mehrabian, A., & Ferris, S. (1967). Inference of attitude from nonverbal behavior in two channels. *Journal of Consulting Psychology, 31*, 248–252.

Mehrens, W., & Lehmann, I. (1987). *Using standardized tests in education* (4th ed.). White Plains, NY: Longman.

Mercer, C., & Mercer, A. (1993). *Teaching students with learning problems* (3rd ed.). New York: Macmillan.

Merrill, M. (1983). Component display theory. In C. Reigeluth (Ed.), *Instructional design theories and models: An overview of their current status*. Hillsdale, NJ: Erlbaum.

Messick, S. (1989). Validity. In R. Linn (Ed.), *Educational measurement* (3rd ed., pp. 13–103). New York: Macmillan.

Messick, S. (1994). *Standards of validity and the validity of standards in performance assessment* (RM-94-17). Princeton, NJ: ETS.

Meyer, W. (1982). Indirect communications about perceived ability estimates. *Journal of Educational Psychology, 74*, 888–897.

Michaels, S., & O'Connor, M. (1990, Summer). *Literacy as reasoning within multiple discourses: Implications for policy and educational reform*. Paper presented at the Council of Chief State School Officers 1990 Summer Institute.

Middleton, M., & Midgley, C. (1997). Avoiding the demonstration of lack of ability: An underexplored aspect of goal theory. *Journal of Educational Psychology, 89*, 710–718.

Midgley, C., Arunkumar, R., & Urdan, T. (1996) "If I don't do well tomorrow, there's a reason": Predictors of adolescents' use of academic self-handicapping strategies. *Journal of Educational Psychology, 88*(3), 423–434.

Miller, D., Barbetta, P., & Heron, T. (1994). START tutoring: Designing, training, implementing, adapting, and evaluating tutoring programs for school and home settings. In R. Gardner, D. Sianato, J. Cooper, W. Heward, T. Heron, J. Eshleman, & T. Grossi (Eds.), *Behavior analysis in education: Focus on measurably superior instruction* (pp. 265–282). Pacific Grove, CA: Brooks/Cole.

Miller, G. (1956). Human memory and the storage of information. *IRE Transactions of Information Theory, 2–3*, 129–137.

Miller, G. (1990, April). *Critical factors in the design of successful self-instruction with disabled readers*. Paper presented at the Annual Meeting of the American Educational Research Association, Boston.

Miller, P. (1993). *Theories of developmental psychology* (3rd ed.). New York: Freeman.

Miller, S., Leinhardt, G., & Zigmond, N. (1988). Influencing engagement through accommodation: An ethnographic study of at-risk students. *American Educational Research Journal, 25*, 465–487.

Mishel, L., & Frankel, D. (1991). *The state of working America: 1990–1991 edition.* Armonk, NY: M. E. Sharpe.

Mitchell, M. (1993). Situational interest: its multifaceted structure in the secondary school mathematics classroom. *Journal of Educational Psychology, 85,* 424–436.

Moerk, E. (1992). *A first language taught and learned.* Baltimore, MD: Paul H. Brookes.

Moles, O. (1992, April). *Parental contacts about classroom behavior problems.* Paper presented at the Annual Meeting of the American Educational Research Association, San Francisco.

Moll, L., Amanti, C., Neff, D., & Gonzolez, N. (1992). Funds of knowledge for teaching: Using a qualitative approach to connect homes and classrooms. *Theory into Practice, 31*(2), 132–141.

Monroe, S., Goldman, P., & Smith, U. (1988). *Brothers: Black and poor—A true story of courage and survivors.* New York: Morrow.

Montague, M. (1990, April). *Mathematical problem-solving characteristics of middle school students with learning disabilities.* Paper presented at the Annual Meeting of the American Educational Research Association, Boston.

Moon, S., Zentall, S., Grskovic, J., Hall, A., & Stormont-Spurgin, M. (1997, March). Social/emotional characteristics of children with AD/HD and giftedness in school and family contexts. Paper presented at the annual meeting of the American Educational Research Association, Chicago.

Moreland, J., Dansereau, D., & Chmielewski, T. (1997). Recall of descriptive information: The roles of presentation format, annotation strategy, and individual differences. *Contemporary Educational Psychology, 22,* 521–533.

Morgan, M. (1985). Self-monitoring of attained subgoals in private study. *Journal of Educational Psychology, 77,* 623–630.

Morgan, M. (1987). Self-monitoring and goal setting in private study. *Contemporary Educational Psychology, 12,* 1–6.

Morris, C. (1988). *Psychology: An introduction* (6th ed.). Upper Saddle River, NJ: Prentice Hall.

Moshman, D. (1982). Exogenous, endogenous, and dialectical constructivism. *Developmental Review, 2,* 371–384.

Moss, P. (1992, April). *Shifting conceptions of validity in educational measurement: Implications for performance assessment.* Paper presented at the Annual Meeting of the American Educational Research Association, San Francisco.

Mousavi, S., Low, R., & Sweller, J. (1995). Reducing cognitive load by mixing auditory and visual presentation modes. *Journal of Education Psychology, 87*(2), 319–334.

Mullis, I., Dossey, J., Foertsh, M., Jones, L., & Gentile, C. (1991). *Trends in academic progress.* Washington, DC: U.S. Department of Education, National Center for Education Statistics.

Murdock, B. (1992). Serial organization in a distributed memory model. In A. Healy, S. Kosslyn, & R. Shiffrin (Eds.), *From learning theory to connectionist theory, Vol. I* (pp. 201–227). Hillsdale, NJ: Erlbaum.

Murphy, G., & Allopena, P. (1994). The locus of knowledge effects in concept learning. *Journal of Educational Psychology, 20*(4), 904–919.

Murphy, J., Weil, M., & McGreal, T. (1986). The basic practice model of instruction. *Elementary School Journal, 87,* 83–95.

Myers, C. (1970). Journal citations and scientific eminence in contemporary psychology. *American Psychologist, 25,* 1041–1048.

Myers, M., & Paris, S. (1978). Children's metacognitive knowledge about reading. *Journal of Educational Psychology, 70,* 680–690.

Nagy-Jacklin, C. (1989). Female and male: Classes of gender. *American Psychologist, 44*(2), 127–133.

Nahmias, M. (1995). Including a child who has ADHD. *Early Childhood Today, 10*(1), 21–22.

Naigles, L., & Gelman, S. (1995). Overextensions in comprehension and production revisited: Preferential looking in a study of dog, cat and cow. *Journal of Child Language, 22,* 19–46.

National Center for Educational Statistics. (1992). *Digest of education statistics.* Washington, DC: U.S. Department of Education.

National Center for Research on Teacher Learning. (1993). *Findings on learning to teach.* East Lansing: Michigan State University, National Center for Research on Teacher Learning.

National Commission on Excellence in Education. (1983). *A nation at risk: The imperative for educational reform.* Washington, DC: Government Printing Office.

National Commission on Testing and Public Policy. (1990). *From gatekeeper to gateway.* Chestnut Hill, MA: Boston College Press.

National Council of Teachers of Mathematics. (1989). *Curriculum and evaluation standards for school mathematics.* Reston, VA: Author.

National Council of Teachers of Mathematics. (1991). *Professional standards for teaching mathematics.* Reston, VA: Author.

National Joint Committee on Learning Disabilities. (1994). Learning disabilities: Issues on definition. A position paper of the National Joint Committee in Learning Disabilities. In *Collective perspectives on issues affecting learning disability: Position papers and statements*. Austin, TX: PRO-ED.

National Research Council. (1980). *Science and engineering doctorates in the United States*. Washington, DC: National Academy of Sciences.

National Research Council. (1996). *National science education standards*. Washington, DC: National Academy Press.

Needels, M., & Knapp, M. (1994). Teaching writing to children who are underserved. *Journal of Educational Psychology, 86*(3), 339–349.

Neisser, U. (1967). *Cognitive psychology*. New York: Appleton-Century-Crofts.

Newman, F., Secado, W., & Wehlage, G. (1995). *A guide to authentic instruction and assessment: Vision, standards & scoring*. Madison: University of Wisconsin Center for Education Research.

Newstead, J., Franklyn-Stokes, A., & Armstead, P. (1996) Individual differences in student cheating. *Journal of Educational Psychology, 88*(2), 229–241.

Nottelman, E., & Hill, K. (1977). Test anxiety and off-task behavior in evaluative situations. *Child Development, 48*, 225–231.

Nicholls, J. (1984). Achievement motivation: Conceptions of ability, subjective experience, task choice, and performance. *Psychological Review, 91*, 328–346.

Nicholls, J., & Miller, A. (1984). Conceptions of ability and achievement motivation. In R. Ames & C. Ames (Eds.), *Research on motivation in education: Vol. 1. Student motivation* (pp. 39–73). New York: Academic Press.

Nickerson, R. (1988). On improving thinking through instruction. In E. Rothkopf (Ed.), *Review of research in education* (pp. 3–57). Washington, DC: American Educational Research Association.

Noblit, G., Rogers, D., & McCadden, B. (1995). In the meantime: The possibilities of caring. *Phi Delta Kappan, 76*, 680–685.

Noddings, N. (1995). Teaching the themes of care. *Phi Delta Kappan, 76*, 675–679.

Nosofsky, R. (1988). Similarity, frequency, and category representations. *Journal of Experimental Psychology: Learning, Memory & Cognition, 14*, 54–65.

Nottelman, E., & Hill, K. (1977). Test anxiety and off-task behavior in evaluative situations. *Child Development, 48*, 225–231.

Novak, J., & Gowin, B. (1984). *Learning how to learn*. New York: Cambridge University Press.

Novak, J. D., & Musonda, D. (1991). A twelve-year longitudinal study of science concept learning. *American Educational Research Journal, 28*(1), 117–153.

Nowell, A. (1997, March). *Trends in gender differences in academic achievement from 1960 to 1994: An analysis of mean differences, variance ratios, and differences in extreme scores*. Paper presented at the Annual meeting of the American Educational Research Association, Chicago.

Nucci, L. (1987). Synthesis of research on moral development. *Educational Leadership, 44*(5), 86–92.

Nussbaum, J., & Novick, N. (1982). Alternative frameworks, conceptual conflict, and accommodation: Toward a principled teaching strategy. *Instructional Science, 11*, 183–200.

Nuthall, G., & Alton-Lee, A. (1993). Predicting student learning from

student experience of teaching: A theory of student knowledge in classrooms. *American Educational Research Journal, 30*, 799–840.

Nystrand, M. (1986). *The structure of written communication: Studies in reciprocity between writers and readers*. Orlando, FL: Academic Press.

Nystrand, M., Cohen, A., & Dowling, N. (1992, April). *Reliability of portfolio assessment for measuring verbal outcomes*. Paper presented at the Annual Meeting of the American Educational Research Association, San Francisco.

Nystrand, M., & Gamoran, A. (1989, March). *Instructional discourse and student engagement*. Paper presented at the Annual Meeting of the American Educational Research Association, San Francisco.

O'Donnell, A., & Dansereau, D. (1992). Scripted cooperation in student dyads: A method for analyzing and enhancing academic learning and performance. In R. Hertz-Lazarowitz & N. Miller (Eds.), *Interaction in cooperative groups: The theoretical anatomy of group learning*. Cambridge, MA: Harvard University Press.

O'Donnell, A., & O'Kelly, J. (1994). Learning from peers: Beyond the rhetoric of positive results. *Educational Psychology Review, 6*, 321–349.

O'Flahavan, J., Hartman, D., & Pearson, D. (1988). Teacher questioning and feedback practices: A twenty-year retrospective. In J. Readence, R. Baldwin, J. Konopak, & P. O'Keefe (Eds.), *Dialogues in literacy research* (pp. 183–208). Chicago: National Reading Conference.

O'Keefe, P., & Johnston, M. (1987, April). *Teachers' abilities to understand the perspectives of students: A case study of two teachers*. Paper presented at the Annual Meeting of the American Educational Research Association, Washington, DC.

Oakes, J. (1990). *Multiplying inequalities: The effects of race, social class, and tracking on opportunities to learn math and science.* Santa Monica, CA: RAND.

Oakes, J. (1992). Can tracking research inform practice? *Educational Researcher, 21*(4), 12–21.

Offer, D., Ostrov, E., & Howard, K. (1989). Adolescence: What is normal? *American Journal of Diseases of Children, 14*(3), 731–736.

Ogbu, J. (1987). Variability in minority school performance: A problem in search of an explanation. *Anthropology and Education Quarterly, 18,* 312–334.

Ogbu, J. (1992). Understanding cultural diversity and learning. *Educational Researcher, 21*(8), 5–14.

Ogle, D. (1986). A teaching model that develops active reading of expository text. *The Reading Teacher, 40,* 564–570.

Oka, E., Kolar, R., Rau, C., & Stahl, N. (1997, March). The dynamic nature of collaboration and inclusion. Paper presented at the Annual Meeting of the American Educational Research Association, Chicago.

Okolo, C. (1992). The effect of computer-assisted instruction format and initial attitude on the arithmetic facts proficiency and continuing motivation of students with learning disabilities. *Exceptionality: A Research Journal, 3,* 195–211.

Osborne, J. (1996). Beyond constructivism. *Science Education, 80,* 53–81.

Osborne, R., & Freyberg, R. (1985). *Learning science.* Portsmouth, NH: Heinemann.

Oser, F. (1986). Moral education and values education: The discourse perspective. In M. Wittrock (Ed.), *Handbook of research on teaching* (3rd ed., pp. 917–941). New York: Macmillan.

Ovando, C. (1997). Language diversity and education. In J. Banks and C. Banks (Eds) *Multicultural Education: Issues and Perspectives* (3rd ed.), 272–296. Boston: Allyn & Bacon.

Overton, F. (1984). Worldviews and their influence on psychological theory and research. In H. Reese (Ed.), *Advances in child development and behavior.* San Diego: Academic Press.

Page, E. B. (1992). Is the world an orderly place? A review of teacher comments and student achievement. *Journal of Experimental Education, 60*(2), 161–181.

Pajares, M. (1992). Teachers' beliefs and educational research: Cleaning up a messy construct. *Review of Educational Research, 62,* 307–322.

Palincsar, A. (1987, April). *Reciprocal teaching: Field evaluations in remedial and content area reading.* Paper presented at the Annual Meeting of the American Educational Research Association, Washington, DC.

Palincsar, A., & Brown, A. (1984). Reciprocal teaching of comprehension-fostering and comprehension-monitoring activities. *Cognition and Instruction, 2,* 117–175.

Palincsar, A., & Brown, A. (1986). Interactive teaching to promote individual learning from text. *Reading Teacher, 39,* 771–777.

Palincsar, A., & Brown, A. (1987). Advances in improving the cognitive performance of handicapped students. In M. Wang, M. Reynolds, & H. Walberg (Eds.), *Handbook of special education, research, and practice: Vol. 1. Learner characteristics and adaptive education* (pp. 93–112). New York: Pergamon Press.

Palincsar, A., Brown, A., & Martin, S. (1987). Peer interaction in reading comprehension instruction. *Educational Psychologist, 22,* 231–253.

Pallas, A., & Alexander, K. (1983). Sex differences in quantitative SAT performance: New evidence on the differential coursework hypothesis. *American Educational Research Journal, 20,* 165–182.

Pallas, A., Natriello, G., & McDill, E. (1989). The changing nature of the disadvantaged population: Current dimensions and future trends. *Educational Researcher, 18*(5), 16–22.

Papalia, D., & Wendkos-Olds, S. (1996). *A child's world: Infancy through adolescence* (7th ed.). New York: McGraw-Hill.

Paris, S., & Cunningham, A. (1996). Children becoming students. In D. Berliner & R. Calfee (Eds.), *Handbook of Educational Psychology* (pp. 117–147). New York: Macmillan.

Paris, S., Wasik, B., & Turner, J. (1991). The development of strategic readers. In R. Barr, M. Kamil, P. Mosenthal, & P. Pearson (Eds.), *Handbook of reading research* (Vol. 2, pp. 609–640). New York: Longman.

Park, C. (1997, March). *A comparative study of learning style preferences: Asian-American and Anglo students in secondary schools.* Paper presented at the Annual meeting of the American Educational Research Association, Chicago.

Parke, C., & Lane, S. (1996/97). Learning from performance assessments in math. *Educational Leadership, 54*(4), 26–29.

Parsons, J., Kaczala, C., & Meece, J. (1982). Socialization of achievement attitudes and beliefs: Classroom influences. *Child Development, 53,* 322–339.

Pask-McCartney, C. (1989). *A discussion about motivation*. Proceedings of Selected Research Presentations at the Annual Convention of the AECT (ERIC Document Reproduction No. ED 308816).

Paul, J. (1995). Pizza and spaghetti: Solving math problems in the primary classroom. *The Computing Teacher, 22,* 65–67.

Pavlov, I. (1928). *Lectures on conditioned reflexes* (W. Gantt, Trans.). New York: International Universities Press.

Peha, J. (1995). How K-12 teachers are using computer networks. *Educational Leadership, 53,* 18–25.

Peng, S., & Lee, R. (1992, April). *Home variables, parent-child activities, and academic achievement: A study of 1988 eighth graders.* Paper presented at the Annual Meeting of the American Educational Research Association, San Francisco.

Pennington, B., Groisser, D., & Welsh, M. (1993). Contrasting cognitive deficits in attention deficit disorder versus reading disability. *Developmental Psychology, 29,* 511–523.

Peregoy, S., & Boyle, O. (1997). *Reading, writing, and learning in ESL,* (2nd ed.). New York: Longman.

Perkins, D. (1987). Thinking frames: An integrated perspective on teaching cognitive skills. In J. Baron & R. Sternberg (Eds.), *Teaching thinking skills: Theory and practice* (pp. 41–61). New York: Freeman.

Perkins, D. (1995). *Outsmarting IQ.* New York: Free Press.

Perkins, D., & Blythe, T. (1994). Putting understanding up front. *Educational Leadership, 51,* 4–7.

Perkins, D., & Salomon, G. (1987). Transfer and teaching thinking. In D. Perkins, J. Lochhead, & J. Bishop (Eds.), *Thinking: The Second International Conference.* Hillsdale, NJ: Erlbaum.

Perkins, D., & Salomon, G. (1989). Are cognitive skills context-bound? *Educational Researcher, 18,* 16–25.

Perry, M., Vanderstoep, S., & Yu, S. (1993). Asking questions in first-grade mathematics classes: Potential influences on mathematical thought. *Journal of Educational Psychology, 85*(1), 31–40.

Perry, R. (1985). Instructor expressiveness: Implications for improving teaching. In J. Donald & A. Sullivan (Eds.), *Using research to improve teaching* (pp. 35–49). San Francisco: Jossey-Bass.

Perry, R., Magnusson, J., Parsonson, K., & Dickens, W. (1986). Perceived control in the college classroom: Limitations in instructor expressiveness due to noncontingent feedback and lecture content. *Journal of Educational Psychology, 78,* 96–107.

Pfiffer, L., Rosen, L., & O'Leary, S. (1985). The efficacy of an all-positive approach to classroom management. *Journal of Applied Behavior Analysis, 18,* 257–261.

Phillips, D. (1990, April). *Parents' beliefs and beyond: Contributions to children's academic self-perceptions.* Paper presented at the Annual Meeting of the American Educational Research Association, Boston.

Phillips, D. (1995). The good, the bad and the ugly: The many faces of constructivism. *Educational Researcher, 24*(7), 5–12.

Phillips, D. (1996). Rejoinder: Response to Ernst von Glaserfeld. *Educational Researcher, 25*(6), 20.

Phillips, S. (1983). *The invisible culture: Communication in classroom and community on the Warm Springs Indian Reservation.* White Plains, NY: Longman.

Phinney, J. (1989). Stages of ethnic identity development in minority group adolescents. *Journal of Early Adolescence, 9,* 34–39.

Phinney, J., & Alipuria, L. (1990). Ethnic identity in college students from four ethnic groups. *Journal of Adolescence, 13,* 171–183.

Piaget, J. (1926). *The language and thought of the child.* New York: Harcourt, Brace & World.

Piaget, J. (1932/1965). *The moral judgment of the child.* New York: Free Press. (Original work published 1932)

Piaget, J. (1952). *Origins of intelligence in children.* New York: International Universities Press.

Piaget, J. (1959). *Language and thought of the child* (M. Grabain, Trans.). New York: Humanities Press.

Piaget, J. (1970). *The science of education and the psychology of the child.* New York: Orion Press.

Piaget, J. (1977). Problems in equilibration. In M. Appel & L. Goldberg (Eds.), *Topics in cognitive development: Vol. 1. Equilibration: Theory, research, and application* (pp. 3–13). New York: Plenum Press.

Pichert, J., & Anderson, R. (1977). Taking different perspectives on a story. *Journal of Educational Psychology, 69,* 309–315.

Pintrich, P., & Garcia, T. (1991). Student goal orientation and self-regulation in the college classroom. In M. Maehr & P. Pintrich (Eds.), *Advances in motivation and achievement* (Vol. 7, pp. 371–402). Greenwich, CT: JAI Press.

Pintrich, P., Marx, R., & Boyle, R. (1993). Beyond cold conceptual change: The role of motivational beliefs and classroom contextual factors in the process of conceptual change. *Review of Educational Research, 63,* 167–199.

Pintrich, P., & Schunk, D. (1996). *Motivation in education: Theory, research, and applications.* Upper Saddle River, NJ: Prentice Hall.

Pittman, K., & Beth-Halachmy, S. (1997, March). *The role of prior knowledge in analogy use.* Paper presented at the Annual Meeting of the American Educational Research Association, Chicago.

Pleiss, M., & Feldhusen, J. (1995). Mentors, role models, and heroes in the lives of gifted children. *Educational Psychologist, 30*(3), 159–169.

Pogrow, S. (1990). Challenging at-risk students: Findings from the HOTS Program. *Phi Delta Kappan, 71*(5), 389–397.

Pomplun, M., Capps, L., & Sundbye, N. (1997, March). *Criteria teachers use to score performance items.* Paper presented at the Annual Meeting of the National Educational Research Association, Chicago.

Poole, M., Okeafor, K., & Sloan, E. (1989, April). *Teachers' interactions, personal efficacy, and change implementation.* Paper presented at the Annual Meeting of the American Educational Research Association, San Francisco.

Popham, W. (1995). *Classroom assessment: What teachers need to know.* Boston: Allyn and Bacon.

Poplin, M. (1988). Holistic/constructivist principles of the teaching/learning process: Implications for the field of learning disabilities. *Journal of Learning Disabilities, 21,* 401–416.

Porter, A. (1989). A curriculum out of balance. *Educational Researcher, 18*(5), 9–15.

Postman, L., & Underwood, B. (1973). Critical issues in interference theory. *Memory and Cognition, 1,* 19–40.

Pratton, J., & Hales, L. (1986). The effects of active participation on student learning. *Journal of Educational Research, 79,* 210–215.

Prawat, R. (1989). Promoting access to knowledge, strategy, and disposition in students: A research synthesis. *Review of Educational Research, 59,* 1–41.

Premack, D. (1965). Reinforcement theory. In D. Levine (Ed.), *Nebraska Symposium on Motivation* (Vol. 13, pp. 3–41). Lincoln: University of Nebraska Press.

Presidential Task Force on Psychology in Education. (1993). *Learner-centered psychological principles: Guidelines for school redesign and reform.* Washington, DC: American Psychological Association.

Presseisen, B. (1986). *Thinking skills: Research and practice.* Washington, DC: National Education Association.

Pressley, M. (1994). Commentary on the ERIC whole language debate. In C. Smith (Moderator), *Whole language: The debate* (pp. 187–217). Bloomington, IN: ERIC/REC.

Pressley, M., Borkowski, J., & Schneider, W. (1987). Cognitive strategies: Good strategies users coordinate metacognition and knowledge. In R. Vasta & G. Whitehurst (Eds.), *Annals of child development* (Vol. 5, pp. 89–129) Greenwich, CT: JAI Press.

Pressley, M., Harris, K., & Marks, M. (1992). But good strategy users are constructivists! *Educational Psychology Review, 4,* 3–31.

Pressley, M., Johnson, C., Symons, S., McGoldrick, J., & Kurita, J. (1989). Strategies that improve children's memory and comprehension of text. *Elementary School Journal, 90,* 3–31.

Pressley, M., Woloshyn, V., Lysynchuk, L., Martin, V., Wood, E., & Willoughby, T. (1990). A primer of research on cognitive strategy instruction: The important issues and how to address them. *Educational Psychology Review, 2,* 1–58.

Pugach, M., & Wesson, C. (1995). Teachers' and students' views of team teaching of general education and learning-disabled students in two fifth-grade classes. *Elementary School Journal, 95*(3), 279–295.

Purkey, S., & Smith, M. (1983). Effective schools: A review. *Elementary School Journal, 83,* 427–452.

Purkey, W., & Novak, J. (1984). *Inviting school success* (2nd ed.). Belmont, CA: Wadsworth.

Quin, Z., Johnson, D., & Johnson, R. (1995). Cooperative versus competitive efforts and problem solving. *Review of Educational Research, 65*(2), 129–143.

Radd, T. (1998). Developing an inviting classroom climate through a comprehensive behavior-management plan. *Journal of Invitational Theory and Practice, 5,* 19–30.

Raphael, T., & Pearson, D. (1985). Increasing students' awareness of sources of information for answering questions. *American Educational Research Journal, 22,* 217–236.

Ravetta, M., & Brunn, M. (1995, April). *Language learning, literacy, and cultural background: Second-language acquisition in a mainstreamed classroom.* Paper presented at the Annual Meeting of the American Educational Research Association, San Francisco.

Raviv, A., Raviv, A., & Reisel, E. (1990). Teachers and students: Two different perspectives? Measuring social climate in the classroom. *American Educational Research Journal, 27,* 141–157.

Reckase, M. (1997, March). *Constructs assessed by portfolios: How do they differ from those assessed by other educational tests?* Paper presented at the Annual Meeting of the National Educational Research Association, Chicago.

Reed, S., Willis, D., & Guarino, J. (1994). Selecting examples for solving word problems. *Journal of Educational Psychology, 86*(3), 380–388.

Reis, S. (1992, April). *The curriculum compacting study*. Paper presented at the Annual Meeting of the American Educational Research Association, San Francisco.

Reis, S., & Purcell, J. (1992). *An analysis of content elimination and strategies used by elementary classroom teachers in the curriculum compacting process*. Storrs: University of Connecticut, National Research Center on the Gifted and Talented.

Relan, A. (1992). *Motivational strategies in computer-based instruction: Some lessons from theories and models of motivation*. Proceedings of Selected Research Presentations at the Annual Convention of the AECT (ERIC Document Reproduction No. ED 348017).

Renzulli, J. (1986). The three-ring conception of giftedness: A developmental model for creative productivity. In R. Sternberg & J. Davidson (Eds.), *Conceptions of giftedness*. Cambridge, MA: Harvard University Press.

Renzulli, J., Smith, L., & Reis, S. (1982). Curriculum compacting: An essential strategy for working with gifted students. *Elementary School Journal, 82*(3), 185–194.

Resnick, L. (1987). *Education and learning to think*. Washington, DC: National Academy Press.

Resnick, L., & Klopfer, L. (1989). Toward the thinking curriculum: An overview. In L. Resnick & L. Klopfer (Eds.), *Toward the thinking curriculum: Current cognitive research* (pp. 1–18). Alexandria, VA: Association for Supervision and Curriculum Development.

Rest, J., Thoma, S., Narvaez, D., & Bebeau, M. (1997). Alchemy and beyond: Indexing the defining

issues test. *Journal of Educational Psychology, 89*(3), 498–507.

Reynolds, R., Sinatra, G., & Jetton, T. (1996). Views of knowledge acquisition and representation: A continuum from experience-centered to mind-centered. *Educational Psychologist, 31*, 93–194.

Rich, D. (1987). *Teachers and parents: An adult-to-adult approach*. Washington, DC: National Education Association.

Rickards, J., Fajen, B., Sullivan, J., & Gillespie, G. (1997). Signaling, notetaking, and field independence-dependence in text comprehension and recall. *Journal of Educational Psychology, 89*(3), 508–517.

Rickford, J. (1997). Suite for Ebony *and* phonics. *Discover, 18*(12), 82–87.

Ridley, D., McCombs, B., & Taylor, K. (1994) Walking the talk: Fostering self-regulated learning in the classroom. *Middle School Journal, 26*(2), 52–57.

Riley, M., Greeno, J., & Heller, J. (1982). The development of children's problem-solving ability in arithmetic. In H. Ginsburg (Ed.), *Development of mathematical thinking*. San Diego: Academic Press.

Ritts, V., Patterson, M., & Tubbs, M. (1992). Expectations, impressions, and judgments of physically attractive students: A review. *Review of Educational Research, 62*, 413–426.

Roberts, W., Horn, A., & Battistich, V. (1995, April). *Assessing students' and teachers' sense of the school as a caring community*. Paper presented at the Annual Meeting of the American Educational Research Association, San Francisco.

Roblyer, M., Edwards, J., & Havriluk, M. (1997). *Integrating technology into teaching*. Upper Saddle River, NJ: Prentice Hall.

Rogers, C. (1963). Actualizing tendency in relation to "motives" and

to consciousness. In M. Jones (Ed.), *Nebraska symposium on motivation* (pp. 1–24). Lincoln: University of Nebraska Press.

Rogers, C. (1967). Learning to be free. In C. Rogers & B. Stevens (Eds.), *The problem of being human*. Lafayette, CA: Real People Press.

Rogers, D. (1991, April). *Conceptions of caring in a fourth-grade classroom*. Paper presented at the Annual Meeting of the American Educational Research Association, Chicago.

Rogoff, B. (1990). *Apprenticeship in thinking: Cognitive development in social context*. New York: Oxford University Press.

Rogoff, B., & Chavajay, P. (1993). What's become of the research on the cultural basis of cognitive development? *American Psychologist, 44*, 343–348.

Rosen, L., O'Leary, S., Joyce, S., Conway, G., & Pfiffer, L. (1984). The importance of prudent negative consequences for maintaining the appropriate behavior of hyperactive students. *Journal of Abnormal Child Psychology, 12*, 581–604.

Rosenberg, M. (1989). The effects of daily homework assignments on the acquisition of basic skills by students with learning disabilities. *Journal of Learning Disabilities, 22*, 314–323.

Rosenfield, P., Lambert, S., & Black, R. (1985). Desk arrangement effects on pupil classroom behavior. *Journal of Educational Psychology, 77*, 101–108.

Rosenshine, B. (1979). Content, time, and direct instruction. In P. Peterson & H. Walberg (Eds.), *Research on teaching: Concepts, findings, and implications* (pp. 28–56). Berkeley, CA: McCutchan.

Rosenshine, B. (1983). Teaching functions in instructional programs. *Ele-*

mentary *School Journal, 83,* 335–351.

Rosenshine, B. (1986). Synthesis of research on explicit teaching. *Educational Leadership, 43*(7), 60–69.

Rosenshine, B. (1987). Explicit teaching. In D. Berliner & B. Rosenshine (Eds.), *Talks to teachers.* New York: Random House.

Rosenshine, B. (1997, March). *The case for explicit, teacher-led, cognitive strategy instruction.* Paper presented at the Annual Meeting of the American Educational Research Association, Chicago.

Rosenshine, B., & Meister, C. (1992, April). *The use of scaffolds for teaching less structured academic tasks.* Paper presented at the Annual Meeting of the American Educational Research Association, San Francisco.

Rosenshine, B., & Meister, C. (1994). Reciprocal teaching: A review of the research. *Review of Educational Research, 64,* 479–530.

Rosenshine, B., & Stevens, R. (1986). Teaching functions. In M. Wittrock (Ed.), *Handbook of research on teaching* (3rd ed.) (pp. 376–391). New York: Macmillan.

Ross, S., Smith, L., Loks, L., & McNelie, M. (1994). Math and reading instruction in tracked first-grade classes. *Elementary School Journal, 95*(2), 105–118.

Rothman, R. (1990). New study confirms income, education linked to parent involvement in schools. *Education Week, 9*(31), 10.

Rothman, R. (1991). Schools stress speeding up, not slowing down. *Education Week, 9*(1), 11, 15.

Rotter, J. (1966). Generalized expectancies for internal versus external control of reinforcement. *Psychological Monographs, 1*(609).

Rowe, M. (1986). Wait-time: Slowing down may be a way of speeding up. *Journal of Teacher Education, 37*(1), 43–50.

Rubin, R., & Balow, B. (1978). Prevalence of teacher-identified behavior problems: A longitudinal study. *Exceptional Children, 45,* 102–111.

Ruble, D. (1988). Sex-role development. In M. Bornstein & M. Lamb (Eds.), *Developmental psychology: An advanced textbook* (2nd ed., pp. 411–460). Hillsdale, NJ: Erlbaum.

Rutherford, F., & Algren, A. (1990). *Science for all Americans.* New York: Oxford University Press.

Rutter, M., Maughan, B., Mortimore, P., Ouston, J., & Smith, A. (1979). *Fifteen thousand hours.* Cambridge, MA: Harvard University Press.

Sadker, M., & Sadker, D. (1985, March). Sexism in the schoolroom of the 80's. *Psychology Today,* pp. 54–57.

Sadker, M., & Sadker, D. (1994). *Failing at fairness: How America's schools cheat girls.* New York: Scribner's.

Sadker, M., Sadker, D., & Klein, S. (1991). The issue of gender in elementary and secondary education. In G. Grant (Ed.), *Review of research in education* (Vol. 17, pp. 269–334). Washington, DC: American Educational Research Association.

Sadker, M., Sadker, D., & Long, L. (1997). Gender and educational equality. In J. Banks & C. Banks (Eds.), *Multicultural education: Issues and perspectives* (3rd ed.), 131–149. Boston: Allyn & Bacon.

Saigh, P. (1984). Unscheduled assessment: Test anxiety, academic achievement, and social validity. *Educational Research Quarterly, 9*(4), 6–11.

Salmon-Cox, L. (1981). Teachers and standardized achievement tests: What's really happening? *Phi Delta Kappan, 62,* 631-634.

Salomon, G., & Globerson, T. (1989). When teams do not function the way they ought to. *International Journal of Educational Research, 13,* 89–99.

Salvia, J., & Ysseldyke, J. (1988). *Assessment in special and remedial education* (4th ed.). Boston: Houghton Mifflin.

Samuels, S. (1979). The method of repeated readings. *The Reading Teacher, 32,* 403–408.

Samuels, S. (1988). Decoding and automaticity: Helping poor readers become automatic at word recognition. *Reading Teacher, 41*(8), 756–760.

Sanders, M., & Jordan, W. (1997, March). *Breaking Barriers to Student Success.* Paper presented at the Annual Meeting of the American Educational Research Association, Chicago.

Scarcella, R. (1990). *Teaching language-minority students in the multicultural classroom.* Upper Saddle River, NJ: Prentice Hall.

Scardamalia, M., Bereiter, C., & Goel, H. (1982). The role of production factors in writing ability. In M. Nystrand (Ed.), *What writers know.* New York: Academic Press.

Schab, F. (1991). Odors and remembrance of things past. *Journal of Experimental Psychology: Learning, Memory and Cognition, 17,* 648–655.

Schauble, L. (1990). Belief revision in children: The role of prior knowledge and strategies for generating evidence. *Journal of Experimental Child Psychology, 49,* 31–57.

Scheirer, M., & Kraut, R. (1979). Improving educational achievement via self-concept change. *Review of Educational Research, 49,* 131–150.

Schiff, M., Duyme, M., Dumaret, A., & Tomkiewicz, S. (1982). How much could we boost scholastic achievement and IQ scores? A direct answer from a French adoption agency. *Cognition, 12,* 165–192.

Schmidt, P. (1992). Gap cited in awareness of students' home languages. *Education Week, 11*(32), 11.

Schneider, W., & Shiffrin, R. (1977). Controlled and automatic human information processing: Detection, search, and attention. *Psychological Review, 84,* 1–66.

Schoenfeld, A. (1987). What's all the fuss about metacognition? In A. Schoenfeld (Ed.), *Cognitive science and mathematics education* (pp. 61–88). Hillsdale, NJ: Erlbaum.

Schoenfeld, A. (1988). When good teaching leads to bad results: The disasters of "well-taught" mathematics courses. *Educational Psychologist, 23,* 145–166.

Schoenfeld, A. (1989). Teaching mathematical thinking and problem solving. In L. Resnick & L. Klopfer (Eds.), *Toward the thinking curriculum: Current cognitive research* (pp. 83–103). Alexandria, VA: Association for Supervision and Curriculum Development.

Schoenfeld, A. (1991). On mathematics as sense-making: An informal attack on the unfortunate divorce of formal and informal mathematics. In. J. Voss, D. Perkins, & J. Segal (Eds.), *Informal reasoning and education* (pp. 311–343). Hillsdale, NJ: Erlbaum.

Schoenfeld, A. (1992a). Learning to think mathematically: Problem solving, metacognition, and sense-making in mathematics. In D. Grouws (Ed.), *Handbook of research on mathematics teaching and learning* (pp. 334–370). New York: Macmillan.

Schoenfeld, A. (1992b). On paradigms and methods: What do you do when the ones you know don't do what you want them to? Issues in the analysis of data in the form of

videotapes. *Journal of the Learning Sciences, 2,* 179–214.

Schon, D. (1983). *The reflective practitioner: How professionals think in action.* New York: Basic Books.

Schon, D. (1991). *Educating the reflective practitioner.* San Francisco: Jossey-Bass.

Schunk, D. (1983). Ability versus effort attributional feedback: Differential effects on self-efficacy and achievement. *Journal of Educational Psychology, 75,* 848–856.

Schunk, D. (1987). Peer models and children's behavioral change. *Review of Educational Research, 57,* 149–174.

Schunk, D. (1990). Introduction to the special section on motivation and efficacy. *Journal of Educational Psychology, 82,* 1–6.

Schunk, D. (1994, April). *Goal and self-evaluative influences during children's mathematical skill acquisition.* Paper presented at the Annual Meeting of the American Educational Research Association, New Orleans.

Schunk, D. (1996). *Learning theories* (2nd ed.). Englewood Cliffs, NJ: Prentice Hall.

Schunk, D. (1997, March). *Self-monitoring as a motivator during instruction with elementary school students.* Paper presented at the Annual Meeting of the American Educational Research Association, Chicago.

Schwartz, B. (1990). The creation and destruction of value. *American Psychologist, 45,* 7–15.

Schwartz, B., & Reisberg, D. (1991). *Learning and memory.* New York: Norton.

Scott, M. (1988, April). *Analysis of the rising tide of "at-risk" students from a developmental framework.* Paper presented at the Annual Meeting of the American Educational Research Association, New Orleans.

Sears, R., Maccoby, E., & Levin, H. (1957). *Patterns of child rearing.* Evanston, IL: Row, Peterson.

Seifert, T. (1993). Effects of elaborative interrogation with prose passages. *Journal of Educational Psychology, 85*(4), 642–651.

Seligman, D. (1975). *Helplessness.* San Francisco: Freeman.

Seligman, M. (1995). *The optimistic child.* Boston: Houghton Mifflin.

Shepard, L. (1993). Evaluating test validity. In L. Darling-Hammond (Ed.), *Review of research in education* (Vol. 19, pp. 405–450). Washington, DC: American Educational Research Association.

Sherman, L. (1988). A comparative study of cooperative and competitive achievement in two secondary biology classrooms: The group investigative model versus an individually competitive goal structure. *Journal of Research in Science Teaching, 26,* 55–64.

Shields, P., & Shaver, D. (1990, April). *The mismatch between the school and home cultures of academically at-risk students.* Paper presented at the Annual Meeting of the American Educational Research Association, Boston.

Shinn, M., & Hubbard, D. (1992). Curriculum-based measurement and problem-solving assessment: Basic procedures and outcomes. *Focus on Exceptional Children, 24*(5), 1–2.

Short, E., Schatschneider, C., & Friebert, S. (1993). Relationship between memory and metamemory performance: A comparison of specific and general strategy knowledge. *Journal of Educational Psychology, 85*(3), 412–423.

Short, G. (1985). Teacher expectation and West Indian underachievement. *Educational Researcher, 63,* 95–101.

Shuell, T. (1996). Teaching and learning in a classroom context. In D.

Berliner & R. Calfee (Eds.), *Handbook of educational psychology* (pp. 726–764). New York: Simon & Schuster Macmillan.

Shulman, J. (Ed.). (1992). *Case methods in teacher education.* New York: Teachers College Press.

Shulman, L. (1986). Those who understand: Knowledge growth in teaching. *Educational Researcher, 15*(2), 4–14.

Sieber, R. (1981). Socialization implications of school discipline, or how first graders are taught to "listen." In R. Sieber & A. Gordon (Eds.), *Children and their organizations: Investigations in American culture* (pp. 18–43). Boston: G. K. Hall.

Siegler, R. (1991). *Children's thinking* (2nd ed.). Upper Saddle River, NJ: Prentice Hall.

Silver, E., Leung, S., & Cai, J. (1992). Solving a nonroutine mathematics problem: An analysis of US. students' solution strategies and modes of explanation and a comparison with Japanese students. In J. Becker (Ed.), *Report of US-Japan cross-national research on students' problem-solving behaviors* (pp. 3–23). Carbondale, IL: Southern Illinois University.

Simon, H. (1978). Information-processing theory of human problem solving. In W. Estes (Ed.), *Handbook of learning and cognitive processes: Vol. 5, Human information processing.* Hillsdale, NJ: Erlbaum.

Simon, M. (1993). Prospective elementary teachers' knowledge of division. *Journal for Research in Mathematics Education, 24,* 233–254.

Simpson, E. (1972). *The classification of educational objectives: Psychomotor domain.* Urbana: University of Illinois Press.

Simpson, J., Olejnik, S., Tam, A., & Suprattathum, S. (1994). Elaborative verbal rehearsals and college students' cognitive performance. *Journal of Educational Psychology, 86*(2), 267–278.

Skiba, R., & Raison, J. (1990). Relationship between the use of timeout and academic achievement. *Exceptional Children, 57,* 36–47.

Skinner, B. (1953). *Science and human behavior.* New York: Macmillan.

Skinner, B. (1957). *Verbal behavior.* Upper Saddle River, NJ: Prentice Hall.

Skinner, E., & Belmont, M. (1993). Motivation in the classroom: Reciprocal effects of teacher behavior and student engagement across the school year. *Journal of Educational Psychology, 85,* 571–581.

Skoe, E., & Dressner, R. (1994). Ethics of care, justice, identity, and gender: An extension and replication. *Merrill-Palmer Quarterly, 40*(2), 272–289.

Slaughter-Defoe, D., Nakagawa, K., Takanashi, R., & Johnson, D. (1990). Toward cultural/ecological perspectives on schooling and achievement in African and Asian American children. *Child Development,* pp. 363–383.

Slavin, R. (1985). Team-assisted individualization: A cooperative learning solution for adaptive instruction in mathematics. In M. Wang & H. Walberg (Eds.), *Adapting instruction to individual differences.* Berkeley, CA: McCutchan.

Slavin, R. (1987). Ability grouping and student achievement in elementary schools: A best-evidence synthesis. *Review of Educational Research, 57,* 293–336.

Slavin, R. (1995). *Cooperative learning: Theory, research, and practice* (2nd ed.). Needham Heights, MA: Allyn & Bacon.

Slavin, R., & Karweit, N. (1982, April). *School organizational vs. developmental effects on attendance among young adolescents.* Paper presented at the Annual Meeting of the American Psychological Association, Washington, DC.

Slavin, R., Karweit, N., & Madden, N. (Eds.). (1989). *Effective programs for students at risk.* Needham Heights, MA: Allyn & Bacon.

Slavin, R., Madden, N., Karweit, N., Dolan, L., & Wasik, B. (1992). *Success for all: A relentless approach to prevention and early intervention in elementary schools.* Arlington, VA: Educational Research Service.

Smith, E., & Anderson, L. (1984). *The planning and teaching intermediate science study: Final report.* East Lansing: Michigan State University Institute for Research on Teaching.

Smith, L., & Cotten, M. (1980). Effect of lesson vagueness and discontinuity on student achievement and attitude. *Journal of Educational Psychology, 72,* 670–675.

Smokowski, P. (1997, March). *What personal essays tell us about resiliency and protective factors in adolescence.* Paper presented at the Annual meeting of the American Educational Research Association, Chicago.

Smylie, M. (1989). Teachers' views of the effectiveness of sources of learning to teach. *Elementary School Journal, 89,* 543–548.

Snyder, S., Bushur, L., Hoeksema, P., Olson, M., Clark, S., & Snyder, J. (1991, April). *The effect of instructional clarity and concept structure on students' achievement and perception.* Paper presented at the Annual Meeting of the American Educational Research Association, Chicago.

Snyderman, M., & Rothman, S. (1987). Survey of expert opinion on intelligence and aptitude testing. *American Psychologist, 42,* 137–144.

Sokolove, S., Garrett, S., Sadker, M., & Sadker, D. (1990). Interpersonal communication skills. In J. Cooper (Ed.), *Classroom teaching skills* (pp. 185–228). Lexington, MA: Heath.

Spaulding, C. (1992). *Motivation in the classroom*. New York: McGraw-Hill.

Spearman, C. (1927). *The abilities of man: Their nature and measurement*. New York: Macmillan.

Spector, J. (1992). Predicting progress in beginning reading: Dynamic assessment of phonemic awareness. *Journal of Educational Psychology, 84*(3), 353–363.

Spector, J. (1995). Phonemic awareness training: Application of principles of direct instruction. *Reading and Writing Quarterly, 11,* 37–51.

Speidel, G. (1987). Conversation and language learning in the classroom. In K. Nelson & A. Van Kleeck (Eds.), *Children's language* (Vol. 6, pp. 99–135). Hillsdale, NJ: Erlbaum.

Spiro, R., Feltovich, P., Jacobson, M., & Coulson, R. (1992). Knowledge representation, content specification, and the development of skill in situation-specific knowledge assembly: Some constructivist issues as they relate to cognitive flexibility theory and hypertext. In T. Duffy & D. Jonassen (Eds.), *Constructivism and the technology of instruction: A conversation* (pp. 121–127). Hillsdale, NJ: Erlbaum.

Sprigle, J., & Schoefer, L. (1985). Longitudinal evaluation of the effects of two compensatory preschool programs on fourth-through sixth-grade students. *Developmental Psychology, 21,* 702–708.

Stallard, C. (1974). An analysis of the writing behavior of good student writers. *Research in the Teaching of English, 8,* 206–218.

Stedman, L. (1997). International achievement differences: An assessment of a new perspective. *Educational Researcher, 26*(3), 4–15.

Stein, B. (1989). Memory and creativity. In J. Glover, R. Ronning, & C. Reynolds (Eds.), *Handbook of creativity*. New York: Plenum Press.

Stein, R. (1983). Hispanic parents' perspectives and participation in their children's special education program: Comparisons by program and race. *Learning Disability Quarterly, 6,* 432–439.

Steinberg, L. (1987). *Pubertal status, hormonal levels, and family relations: The distancing hypothesis*. Baltimore: Society for Research in Child Development.

Steinberg, L., Dornbusch, S., & Brown, B. (1992). Ethnic differences in adolescent achievement. *American Psychologist, 47*(6), 723–729.

Stern, D. (1997, March). *The role of values conflict in the development of professional attitudes*. Paper presented at the Annual meeting of the American Educational Research Association, Chicago.

Stern, E. (1993). What makes certain arithmetic word problems involving the comparison of sets so difficult for children? *Journal of Educational Psychology, 85*(1), 7–23.

Sternberg, R. (1986). *Intelligence applied: Understanding and increasing your intellectual skills*. Orlando, FL: Harcourt Brace.

Sternberg, R. (1988). *The triarchic mind*. New York: Viking.

Sternberg, R. (1989). Intelligence, wisdom, and creativity: Their natures and interrelationships. In R. Linn (Ed.), *Intelligence: Measurement, theory, and public policy* (pp. 119–146). Chicago: University of Illinois Press.

Sternberg, R. (1990). *Metaphors of mind: Conceptions of the nature of intelligence*. New York: Cambridge University Press.

Sternberg, R., & Frensch, P. (1993). Mechanisms of transfer. In D. Detterman & R. Sternberg (Eds.), *Transfer on trial: Intelligence, cognition, and instruction*. Norwood, NJ: Ablex.

Sternberg, R., & Lubart R. (1995). *Defying the crowd*. New York: Free Press.

Stevenson, H. (1992). Learning from Asian schools. *Scientific American, 267,* 70–76.

Stevenson, H., Chen, C., & Uttal, D. (1990). Beliefs and achievements: A study of Black, White, and Hispanic children. *Child Development, 61,* 508–523.

Stevenson, H., & Fantuzzo, J. (1986). The generality and social validity of a competency-based self-control training intervention for underachieving students. *Journal of Applied Behavior Analysis, 19,* 269–276.

Stevenson, H., Lee, S., & Stigler, J. (1986). Mathematics achievement of Chinese, Japanese, and American children. *Science, 231,* 693–699.

Stiggins, R. (1997). *Student-centered classroom assessment* (2nd ed.). Upper Saddle River, NJ: Prentice Hall.

Stiggins, R., & Conklin, N. (1992). *In teachers' hands*. Albany: State University of New York Press.

Stiggins, R., Conklin, N., & Bridgeford, N. (1986). Classroom assessment: A key to effective education. *Educational Measurement: Issues and Practice, 5*(2), 5–17.

Stigler, J., Fernandez, C., & Yoshida, M. (1992, August). *Children's thinking during mathematics instruction in Japanese and American elementary school classrooms*. Paper presented at the Seventh International Congress on Mathematical Education, Quebec City, Canada.

Stigler, J., & Stevenson, H. (1991). How Asian teachers polish each lesson to perfection. *American Educator, 15,* 12–20, 43–47.

Stipek, D. (1984). The development of achievement motivation. In R. Ames & C. Ames (Eds.), *Research on motivation in education: Vol. 1. Student motivation.* San Diego: Academic Press.

Stipek, D. (1996). Motivation and instruction. In D. Berliner & R. Calfee (Eds.), *Handbook of Educational Psychology* (pp. 85–113). New York: Macmillan.

Stipek, D. (1998). *Motivation to learn* (3rd ed.). Needham Heights, MA: Allyn & Bacon.

Stipek, D., & Gralinski, H. (1991, April). *Gender differences in children's achievement-related beliefs and emotional responses to success and failure in math.* Paper presented at the Annual Meeting of the American Educational Research Association, Boston.

Stoddart, T., Connell, M., Stofflett, R., & Peck, D. (1993). Reconstructing elementary teacher candidates' understanding of mathematics and science content. *Teaching and Teacher Education, 9,* 229–241.

Stodolsky, S. (1988). *The subject matters: Classroom activity in math and social studies.* Chicago: University of Chicago Press.

Stotsky, S. (1990). On planning and writing plans—or beware of borrowed theories. *College Composition and Communication, 41,* 3–57.

Stowe, C. (1992, April). *At-risk language-minority preschool children.* Paper presented at the Annual Meeting of the American Educational Research Association, San Francisco.

Strickland, B. B., & Turnbull, A. P. (1990). *Developing and implementing individualized education programs* (3rd ed.). New York: Macmillan.

Strom, B. (1990, April). *Teacher perceptions of talented and gifted minority children: An exploration.* Paper presented at the Annual Meeting of the American Educational Research Association, Boston.

Strom, S. (1989). The ethical dimension of teaching. In M. Reynolds (Ed.), *Knowledge base for the beginning teacher* (pp. 267–276). New York: Pergamon Press.

Subotnik, R. (1997) Teaching gifted students in a multicultural society. In J. Banks & C. Banks (Eds.), *Multicultural Education: Issues and Perspective,* 3rd ed. (pp. 361–382) Boston: Allyn & Bacon.

Suchman, R. (1966a). *Inquiry training program: Developing inquiry.* Chicago: Science Research Associates.

Sudweeks, R., Baird, J., & Petersen, G. (1990, April). *Test-wise responses of third-, fifth-, and sixth-grade students to clued and unclued multiple-choice science items.* Paper presented at the Annual Meeting of the American Educational Research Association, Boston.

Summers, J. (1990–1991). Effect of interactivity upon student achievement, completion intervals, and affective perceptions. *Journal of Educational Technology Systems, 19,* 53–57.

Sunai, C., & Haas, M. (1993). *Social studies and the elementary/middle school student.* New York, Harcourt Brace Jovanovich.

Svenson, A. (1971). *Relative achievement: School performance in relation to intelligence, sex, and home environment.* Stockholm: Almquist & Wiksell.

Swialth, M., & Benbow, C. (1991). Ten-year longitudinal follow-up of ability-match accelerated and unaccelerated gifted students. *Journal of Educational Psychology, 83*(4), 528–538.

Szafran, R. (1981). Question-pool study guides: Effects on test anxiety and learning retention. *Teaching Sociology, 9,* 31–43.

Tan, A., & Nicholson, T. (1997). Flashcards revisited: Training poor readers to read words faster improves their comprehension of text. *Journal of Educational Psychology, 89*(2), 276–288.

Taylor, B., & Beach, R. (1984). The effects of text structure instruction on middle-grade students' comprehension and production of expository text. *Reading Research Quarterly, 19,* 134–146.

Taylor, J. (1983). Influence of speech variety on teachers' evaluation of reading comprehension. *Journal of Educational Psychology, 75,* 662–667.

Taylor, R. (1987, March). *Knowledge for critical thinking.* Paper presented at the meeting of the Near East South Asia Council for Overseas Schools, Nairobi, Kenya.

Tennyson, R., & Cocchiarella, M. (1986). An empirically based instructional design theory for teaching concepts. *Review of Educational Research, 56,* 40–71.

Terman, L., Baldwin, B., & Bronson, E. (1925). Mental and physical traits of a thousand gifted children. In L. Terman (Ed.), *Genetic studies of genius* (Vol. 1). Stanford, CA: Stanford University Press.

Terman, L., & Oden, M. (1947). The gifted child grows up. In L. Terman (Ed.), *Genetic studies of genius* (Vol. 4). Stanford, CA: Stanford University Press.

Terman, L., & Oden, M. (1959). The gifted group in mid-life. In L. Terman (Ed.), *Genetic studies of genius* (Vol. 5). Stanford, CA: Stanford University Press.

Terwilliger, J. (1997). Semantics, psychometrics, and assessment reform:

A close look at "authentic assessments." *Educational Researcher, 26,* 24–27.

Tharp, R. (1989). Psychocultural variables and constants: Effects on teaching and learning in schools. *American Psychologist, 44*(2), 349–359.

Thoma, S., & Rest, J. (1996). *The relationship between moral decision-making and patterns of consolidation and transition in moral judgment development.* Paper presented at the Annual meeting of the American Educational Research Association, New York.

Thomas, E., & Robinson, H. (1972). *Improving reading in every class: A source book for teachers.* Needham Heights, MA: Allyn & Bacon.

Thompson, M., McLaughlin, C., & Smith, R. (1995). *Merrill physical science.* Westerville, OH: Glencoe.

Thorkildsen, T. (1996, April). *The way tests teach: Children's theories of how much testing is fair in school.* Paper presented at the Annual Meeting of the National Educational Research Association, New York.

Thorndike, E. (1924). Mental discipline in high school studies. *Journal of Educational Psychology, 15,* 1–2, 83–98.

Thorndike, R., Hagen, E., & Sattler, J. (1986). *The Stanford-Binet Intelligence Scale* (4th ed.). Chicago: Riverside.

Thornton, M., & Fuller, R. (1981). How do college students solve proportion problems? *Journal of Research in Science Teaching, 18,* 335–340.

Tingle, J., & Good, R. (1990). Effects of cooperative grouping on stoichiometric problem solving in high school chemistry. *Journal of Research in Science Teaching, 27,* 671–683.

Tishman, S., Perkins, D., & Jay, E. (1995). *The thinking classroom: Learning and teaching in a culture of thinking.* Needham Heights, MA: Allyn and Bacon.

Tobin, K. (1987). Role of wait-time in higher cognitive level learning. *Review of Educational Research, 57*(1), 69–95.

Tom, A. (1984). *Teaching as a moral craft.* London: Longman.

Tomlinson, C., Callahan, C., & Lelli, K. (1997). Challenging expectations: Case studies of high-potential, culturally diverse young children. *Gifted Child Quarterly, 41*(2), 5–17.

Tompkins, G. (1997). *Literacy for the twenty-first century.* Columbus, OH: Merrill.

Top, B., & Osgthorpe, R. (1987). Reverse-role tutoring: The effects of handicapped students tutoring regular class students. *Elementary School Journal, 87*(4), 413–423.

Torrance, E. (1983). Status of creative women past, present, future. *Creative Child and Adult Quarterly, 8,* 135–144.

Torrance, E. (1986). Teaching creative and gifted learners. In M. Wittrock (Ed.), *Handbook of research on teaching* (3rd ed., pp. 630–647). New York: Macmillan.

Torrance, E. (1995). Insights about creativity: Questioned, rejected, ridiculed, ignored. *Educational Psychology Review, 7*(3), 313–322.

Trentham, L. (1975). The effect of distractions on sixth-grade students in a testing situation. *Psychology in the Schools, 16,* 439–443.

Trujillo, C. (1986). A comparative examination of classroom interactions between professors and minority and non-minority college students. *American Educational Research Journal, 23,* 629–642.

Tulving, E. (1979). Relation between encoding specificity and level of processing. In L. Cermak & F. Craik (Eds.), *Levels of processing and human memory* (pp. 405–428). Hillsdale, NJ: Erlbaum.

Turiel, E. (1973). Stage transitions in moral development. In R. Travers (Ed.), *Second handbook of research on teaching* (pp. 732–758). Chicago: Rand McNally.

Turnbull, A., Turnbull, H. R., Shank, M., & Leal, D. (1995). *Exceptional lives.* Upper Saddle River, NJ: Prentice Hall.

Turner, J. (1995). The influence of classroom contexts on young children's motivation for literacy. *Reading Research Quarterly, 30,* 410–441.

Tyler, R. (1950). *Basic principles of curriculum and instruction.* Chicago: University of Chicago Press.

U.S. Bureau of the Census. (1994). *Statistics.* Washington, DC: Author.

U.S. Bureau of the Census. (1996). *Statistics.* Washington, DC: Author.

U.S. Congress. (1978). Educational Amendment of 1978, P.L. 95–561, IX(A).

U.S. Department of Education. (1988, June 20). Final research priorities establishment. *Federal Register, 23,* 192–193, 195.

U.S. Department of Education. (1993). *Fifteenth annual report to Congress on the implementation of the Individuals With Disabilities Act.* Washington, DC: Government Printing Office.

U.S. Department of Education. (1994). *Sixteenth annual report to Congress on the implementation of the Individuals With Disabilities Act.* Washington, DC: Government Printing Office.

U.S. Department of Health and Human Services (1914–1993). *Annual Vital Statistics Report.* Washington, D.C.: Author.

Urdan, T., Pajares, F., & Lapin, A. (1997, March). *Achievement goals, motivation, and performance: A closer look.* Paper presented at the annual meeting of the American Educational Research Association, Chicago.

Urdan, T., & Paris, S. (1991). Teachers' perceptions of standardized achievement tests. *Educational Policy, 8* (2) 137–156.

Vaillant, B., & Vaillant, C. (1990). Natural history of male psychological health, XII: A 45-year study of predictors of successful aging. *American Journal of Psychiatry, 147,* 31–37.

Valencia, S., Hiebert, E., & Afflerback, P. (Eds.). (1994). *Authentic reading assessment: Practices and possibilities.* Newark, DE: International Reading Association.

Valencia, S., & Place, N. (1994). Literacy portfolios for teaching, learning, and accountability: The Bellevue Literacy assessment project. In S. Valencia, E. Hiebert, P. Afflerbach (Eds.), *Authentic reading assessment: Practices and possibilities* (pp. 134–156). Newark, DE: International Reading Association.

Vanderstoep, S., & Seifert, C. (1994). Problem solving, transfer, and thinking. In P. Pintrich, D. Brown, & C. Weinstein (Eds.), *Student motivation, cognition, and learning* (pp. 27–49). Hillsdale, NJ: Erlbaum.

Van Haneghan, J., Barron, L., Young, M., Williams, S., Vye, N., & Bransford, J. (1992). The *Jasper* series: An experiment with new ways to enhance mathematical thinking. In D. Halpern (Ed.), *Enhancing thinking skills in the sciences and mathematics* (pp. 15–38). Hillsdale, NJ: Erlbaum.

Van Leuvan, P., Wang, M., & Hildebrandt, L. (1990, April). *Students' use of self-instructive processes in the first and second grade.* Paper presented at the Annual Meeting of the American Educational Research Association, Boston.

VanTassel-Baska, J., Patton, J., & Prillaman, D. (1989). Disadvantaged gifted learners at risk for educational attention. *Focus on Exceptional Children, 22*(3), 2–3.

Vaughn, S., McIntosh, R., Spencer, R., & Rowe, T. (1990, April). *Increasing peer acceptance with low-accepted LD students: An intervention model.* Paper presented at the Annual Meeting of the American Educational Research Association, Boston.

Veenman, S. (1984). Perceived problems of beginning teachers. *Review of Educational Research, 54,* 143–178.

Verschaffel, L., De Corte, E., & Lasure, S. (1994). Realistic considerations in mathematical modeling of school arithmetic word problems. *Learning and Instruction, 4,* 273–294.

Villasenor, A., & Kepner, H. (1993). Arithmetic from a problem-solving perspective: An urban implementation. *Journal of Research in Mathematics Education, 24,* 62–69.

Villegas, A. (1991). *Culturally responsive pedagogy for the 1990s and beyond.* Princeton, NJ: Educational Testing Service.

Vito, R., & Connell, J. (1988, April). *A longitudinal study of at-risk high school students: A theory-based description and intervention.* Paper presented at the Annual Meeting of the American Educational Research Association, New Orleans.

Volker, R. (1992). *Applications of constructivist theory to the use of hypermedia.* Proceedings of Selected Research Presentations at the Annual Convention of the AECT (ERIC Document Reproduction No. ED 348037).

Voss, J. (1987). Learning and transfer in subject-matter learning: A problem-solving model. *International Journal of Educational Research, 11,* 607–622.

Voss, J., & Wiley, J. (1995). Acquiring intellectual skills. *Annual Review of Psychology, 46,* 155–181.

Vygotsky, L. (1978). *Mind in society: The development of higher psychological processes* (M. Cole, V. John-Steiner, S. Scribner, & E. Souberman, Eds. & Trans.). Cambridge, MA: Harvard University Press.

Vygotsky, L. (1986). *Thought and language.* Cambridge: MIT Press.

Wade, S. (1992). How interest affects learning from text. In K. Renniger, S. Hidi, & A. Krapp (Eds.), *The role of interest in learning and development* (pp. 531–553). Hillsdale, NJ: Erlbaum.

Wade, S., Trathen, W., & Schraw, G. (1990). An analysis of spontaneous study strategies. *Reading Research Quarterly, 25,* 147–166.

Wadsworth, B. (1996). *Piaget's theory of cognitive and affective development* (5th ed.). White Plains, NY: Longman.

Wagner, R., & Sternberg, R. (1985). Practical intelligence in real-world pursuits: The role of tacit knowledge. *Journal of Personality and Social Psychology, 52,* 1236–1247.

Walberg, H. (1984). Improving the productivity of America's schools. *Educational Leadership, 41*(8), 19–27.

Walberg, H. (1991). Improving school science in advanced and developing countries. *Review of Educational Research, 61,* 25–70.

Walberg, H., Paschal, R., & Weinstein, T. (1985). Homework's powerful effects on learning. *Educational Leadership, 42*(7), 76–79.

Walker, D., Greenwood, C., Hart, B., & Carta, J. (1994). Prediction of school outcomes based on early language production and socioeconomic factors. *Child Development, 65,* 606–621.

Walker, H., & Bullis, M. (1991). Behavior disorder and the social context of regular class integration: A conceptual dilemma. In J. Lloyd, N. Singh, & A. Repp (Eds.), *The regular education initiative: Alternative perspectives on concepts, issues, and models* (pp. 75–94). Sycamore, IL: Sycamore.

Walker, J. (1996). *The psychology of learning: Principles and processes.* Upper Saddle River, NJ: Prentice Hall.

Walsh, D. (1991). Extending the discourse on developmental appropriateness: A developmental perspective. *Early Education and Development, 2*(2), 109–119.

Walton, S., & Taylor, K. (1996/97). How did you know the answer was boxcar? *Educational Leadership, 54*(4), 38–40.

Wang, M., Haertel, G., & Walberg, H. (1993). Toward a knowledge base for school learning. *Review of Educational Research, 63*(3), 249–294.

Wang, M., Haertel, G., & Walberg, H. (1995, April). *Educational resilience: An emerging construct.* Paper presented at the Annual Meeting of the American Educational Research Association, San Francisco.

Ward, T., Ward, S., Landrum, M., & Patton, J. (1992, April). *Examination of a new protocol for the identification of at-risk gifted learners.* Paper presented at the Annual Meeting of the American Educational Research Association, San Francisco.

Washington, V., & Miller-Jones, D. (1989). Teacher interactions with non-Standard-English speakers during reading instruction. *Contemporary Child Psychology, 14,* 280–312.

Wasserstein, P. (1995). What middle schoolers say about their schoolwork. *Educational Leadership, 53*(1), 41–43.

Waterman, A. (1985). Identity in the context of adolescent psychology. *New Directions for Child Development, 30,* 5–24.

Watson, B., & Konicek, R. (1990). Teaching for conceptual change: Confronting children's experience. *Phi Delta Kappan, 71,* 680–685.

Waxman, H., & Huang, S. (1996). Motivation and learning environment differences in inner-city middle school students. *Journal of Educational Research, 90*(2), 93–102.

Waxman, H., Huang, S., Anderson, L., & Weinstein, T. (1997). Classroom process differences in inner-city elementary schools. *Journal of Educational Research, 91*(1), 49–59.

Wayson, W., & Lasley, T. (1984). Climates for excellence: Schools that foster self-discipline. *Phi Delta Kappan, 65,* 419–421.

Weaver, L. & Padrón, Y. (1997, March). *Mainstream classroom teachers' observations of ESL teachers' instruction.* Paper presented at the Annual meeting of the American Educational Research Association, Chicago.

Webb, N. (1991). Task-related verbal interaction and mathematics learning in small groups. *Journal of Research in Mathematics Education, 22,* 366–389.

Webb, N., & Farivar, S. (1994). Promoting helping behavior in cooperative small groups in middle school mathematics, *American Educational Research Journal, 31*(2), 369–395.

Webb, N., & Palinscar, A. (1996). Group processes in the classroom. In D. Berliner & R. Calfee (Eds.), *Handbook of educational psychology* (pp. 841–876). New York: Macmillan.

Wechsler, D. (1991). *The Wechsler Intelligence Scale for Children—Third Edition—WISC-III.* San Antonio, TX: Psychological Corporation.

Weiland, A., & Coughlin, R. (1979). Self-identification and preferences: A comparison of White and Mexican American first and third graders. *Journal of Social Psychology, 10,* 356–365.

Weinberg, R. (1989). Intelligence and IQ. *American Psychologist, 44,* 98–104.

Weiner, B. (1990). History of motivational research in education. *Journal of Educational Psychology, 82,* 616–622.

Weiner, B. (1992). *Human motivation: Metaphors, theories, and research.* Newbury Park, CA: Sage.

Weiner, B. (1994a). Ability versus effort revisited: The moral determinants of achievement evaluation and achievement as a moral system. *Educational Psychologist, 29,* 163–172.

Weiner, B. (1994b). Integrating social and personal theories of achievement striving. *Review of Educational Research, 64,* 557–573.

Weinert, F., & Helmke, A. (1995). Interclassroom differences in instructional quality and interindividual differences in cognitive development. *Educational Psychologist, 30,* 15–20.

Weinstein, C. (1994). Strategic learning/strategic teaching: Flip sides of a coin. In P. Pintrich, D. Brown, & C. Weinstein (Eds.), *Student motivation, cognition, and learning* (pp. 257–273). Hillsdale, NJ: Erlbaum.

Weinstein, C., & Mignano, A. (1993). *Elementary classroom management.* New York: McGraw-Hill.

Weinstein, C., Woolfolk, A., Dittmeier, L., & Shankar, U. (1994). Protector or prison guard? Using metaphors and media to explore student teachers' thinking about classroom management. *Action in Teacher Education, 16*(1), 41–54.

Weinstein, R. (1998). Promoting positive expectations in schooling. In N. Lambert & B. McCombs (Eds.), *How students learn: Reforming schools through learner-centered education* (pp. 81–111). Washington, DC: American Psychological Association.

West, J. (1997, March). *Motivation and access to help: the influence of status on one child's motivation for literacy learning.* Paper presented at the annual meeting of the American Educational Research Association, Chicago.

Whimbey, A. (1980). Students can learn to be better problem solvers. *Educational Leadership, 37,* 560–565.

White, A., & Bailey, J. (1990). Reducing disruptive behaviors of elementary physical education students with sit and watch. *Journal of Applied Behavior Analysis, 23,* 353–359.

White, R. (1959). Motivation reconsidered: The concept of competence. *Psychological Review, 66,* 297–333.

Wigfield, A., & Eccles, J. (1989). Test anxiety in elementary and secondary school students. *Educational Psychologist, 24,* 159–183.

Wigfield, A., Eccles, J., & Pintrich, P. (1996). Development between the ages of 11 and 25. In D. Berliner & R. Calfee (Eds.), *Handbook of educational psychology* (pp. 148–185). New York: Macmillan.

Wiggins, G. (1996/97). Practicing what we preach in designing authentic assessment. *Educational Leadership, 54*(4), 18–25.

Wilkie, V. (1985). Richardson Study, Q's & A's. *G/C/T, 36,* 2–9.

Williams, J. (1992, April). *Effects of test anxiety and self-concept on performance across curricular areas.* Paper presented at the Annual Meeting of the American Educational Research Association, San Francisco.

Williams, J., & Snipper, G. (1990). *Literacy and bilingualism.* New York: Longman.

Williams, R. (1987). Current issues in classroom behavior management. In J. Glover & R. Ronning (Eds.), *Historical foundations of educational psychology* (pp. 297–325). New York: Plenum Press.

Williams, S., Bareiss, R., & Reiser, B. (1996, April). *ASK Jasper: A multimedia publishing and performance support environment for design.* Paper presented at the annual meeting of the American Educational Research Association, New York.

Willoughby, T., Wood, E., & Khan, M. (1994). Isolating variables that impact on or detract from the effectiveness of elaboration strategies. *Journal of Educational Psychology, 86*(2), 279–289.

Wilson, S., Shulman, L., & Richert, A. (1987). 150 different ways of knowing: Representations of knowledge in teaching. In J. Calderhead (Ed.), *Exploring teacher thinking* (pp. 104–124). London: Cassel.

Winitzky, N. (1991). Multicultural and mainstreamed classrooms. In R. Arends, *Learning to teach* (2nd ed., pp. 125–148). New York: McGraw-Hill.

Winn, J. (1992, April). *The promises and challenges of scaffolded instruction.* Paper presented at the Annual Meeting of the American Educational Research Association, San Francisco.

Winterton, W. A. (1977). The effect of extended wait-time on selected verbal response characteristics of some Pueblo Indian children (Doctoral dissertation, University of New Mexico, 1976). *Dissertation Abstracts International, 38,* 620-A. (University Microfilms No. 77–16, 130)

Wolf, L., Smith, J., & Birnbaum, M. (1997). *Measure-specific assessment of motivation and anxiety.* Paper presented at the annual meeting of the American Educational Research Association, Chicago.

Wolfram, W. (1991). *Dialects and American English.* Upper Saddle River, NJ: Prentice Hall.

Wolters, C. (1997, March). *Self-regulated learning and college students' regulation of motivation.* Paper presented at the annual meeting of the American Educational Research Association, Chicago.

Wong-Fillmore, L. (1992). When learning a second language means losing the first. *Education, 6*(2), 4–11.

Wood, D., Bruner, J., & Ross, S. (1976). The role of tutoring in problem solving. *British Journal of Psychology, 66,* 181–196.

Wood, T., Cobb, P., & Yackel, E. (1992). Change in learning mathematics: Change in teaching mathematics. In H. Marshall (Ed.), *Redefining student learning: Roots of educational change* (pp. 177–205). Norwood, NJ: Ablex.

Woodcock, R. (1995, April). *Conceptualizations of intelligence and their implications for education.* Paper presented at the Annual Meeting of the American Educational Research Association, San Francisco.

Woodward, J., Baxter, J., & Robinson, R. (1997, March). *Rules and reasons: Decimal instruction for academically low achieving students.* Paper presented at the annual meeting of the American Educational Research Association, Chicago.

Woolfolk, A., & Brooks, D. (1985). The influence of teachers' nonverbal behaviors on students' perceptions and performance. *Elementary School Journal, 85,* 514–528.

Worthen, B. (1993). Critical issues that will determine the future of alternative assessment. *Phi Delta Kappan, 74,* 444–454.

Wright, S., & Taylor, D. (1995). Identity and the language of the classroom: Investigating the impact of heritage versus second-language instruction on personal and collective self-esteem. *Journal of Educational Psychology, 87*(2), 241–252.

Wynne, E. (1997, March). *Moral education and character education: A comparison/contrast.* Paper presented at the Annual meeting of the American Educational Research Association, Chicago.

Yee, A. (1995). Evolution of the Nature–Nurture controversy: Response to J. Philipps Rushton. *Educational Psychology Review, 7*(4), 381–394.

Yopp, H. (1992). Developing phonemic awareness in young children. *The Reading Teacher, 45,* 696–703.

Young, M., & Scribner, J. (1997, March). *The synergy of parental involvement and student engagement at the secondary level: relationships of consequence in Mexican-American communities.* Paper presented at the Annual meeting of the American Educational Research Association, Chicago.

Yussen, S., & Levy, V. (1975). Developmental changes in predicting one's own span of short-term memory. *Journal of Experimental Child Psychology, 19,* 502–508.

Zahorik, J. (1996). Elementary and secondary teachers' reports of how they make learning interesting. *The Elementary School Journal, 96*(5), 551–564.

Zens, J., Curtis, M., Graden, J., & Ponti, C. (1988). *Helping students succeed in the regular classroom.* San Francisco: Jossey-Bass.

Zimmerman, B. (1990). Self-regulated academic learning and achievement: The emergence of a social cognitive perspective. *Educational Psychology Review, 2,* 173–201.

Zimmerman, B., & Blotner, R. (1979). Effects of model persistence and success on children's problem solving. *Journal of Educational Psychology, 71,* 508–513.

Ziomek, R. (1997, March). *The concurrent validity of ACT's Passport Portfolio program: Initial validity results.* Paper presented at the Annual Meeting of the National Educational Research Association, Chicago.

Zook, K. (1991). Effects of analogical processes on learning and misrepresentation. *Educational Psychology Review, 3,* 41–72.

Author Index

Scott, P., 4, 38
Scribner, J., 116
Sears, R., 206
Secado, W., 603
Seifert, T., 261
Seligman, M., 412, 413
Semb, M., 562
Semmel, M., 173
Shank, M., 154
Shankar, U., 463
Sharp, A., 330
Shavelson, R., 80
Shaver, D., 124, 125
Shea, M., 226
Shepard, L., 583, 632, 633
Sherman, L., 560
Shields, P., 124, 125, 540
Shiffrin, R., 243, 247, 257
Shinn, M., 177
Short, E., 270
Short, G., 426
Shuell, T., 227, 280, 392, 452, 456
Shulman, J., 10
Shulman, L., 5, 12, 13, 433, 501, 550
Shumaker, J., 325
Sieber, R., 481
Siefert, C., 337
Siegler, R., 4, 33, 40, 46, 258
Silver, E., 376
Silverman, R., 569
Simmons, D., 186
Simon, H., 285, 311
Simon, M., 380
Simpson, E., 506
Simpson, J., 261
Sinatra, G., 478
Sirotnik, K., 86
Skerry, S., 83
Skiba, R., 205
Skinner, B., 9, 57, 197, 205
Skinner, E., 405
Skoe, E., 92
Slaughter-Defoe, D., 438
Slavin, R., 13, 17, 111, 112, 124, 136, 187, 557, 558, 560, 561, 564
Sloan, E., 452
Sloane, H., 206
Smerdon, B., 134
Smiley, S., 357
Smith, A., 428, 454
Smith, E., 383, 384
Smith, J., 407
Smith, L., 111, 170, 455
Smith, M., 92, 462, 465
Smith, R., 279
Smith, U., 84
Smokowski, P., 119
Smylie, M., 6
Snipper, G., 372
Snitgren, D., 45
Snyder, J., 626
Snyder, S., 455
Snyderman, M., 103, 631
Soder, R., 86
Sokolove, S., 473

Solomon, D., 139
Songer, N., 369
Spaulding, C., 225
Spearman, C., 104
Spector, J., 51, 353, 546
Speidel, G., 125
Spencer, R., 186
Spiro, R., 336, 387, 545
Sprigle, J., 110
Stahl, N., 180
Staver, J., 550
Stecher, B., 603
Stedman, L., 625
Stein, B., 310, 312, 336
Stein, R., 488
Steinberg, L., 76, 438
Stern, D., 86
Stern, E., 319
Sternberg, B., 400
Sternberg, R., 103, 106, 108, 109, 167, 169, 315, 336
Stevens, D., 368
Stevens, R., 255, 456, 508, 511, 612, 613
Stevenson, D., 116
Stevenson, H., 122, 227, 375, 376, 438
Stiggins, R., 226, 581, 584, 585, 587, 590, 592, 593, 600
Stigler, J., 122, 375, 376
Stipek, D., 79, 81, 134, 209, 397, 398, 406, 414, 415, 416, 418, 424, 427, 431, 432, 614, 615
Stoddart, T., 523
Stodolsky, S., 524
Stofflett, R., 523
Stormont-Spurgin, M., 167
Stotsky, S., 364
Stowe, C., 127
Straudt, J., 45
Stricker, A. G., 308
Strickland, B. B., 178
Strom, B., 169
Strom, S., 94
Subotnik, R., 167, 169
Sudweeks, R., 586
Sullivan, J., 325
Summers, J., 565
Sunai, C., 86
Sundbye, N., 594–595
Suprattathum, S., 261
Svenson, A., 134
Swailth, M., 171
Sweller, J., 248
Swets, J., 330
Switlick, D., 173
Symons, S., 323
Szafran, R., 609

Takanashi, R., 438
Tam, A., 261
Tan, A., 354
Taylor, D., 82, 83
Taylor, J., 125
Taylor, K., 417, 608
Taylor, R., 91
Tellegen, A., 138
Tennyson, R., 299, 300

Terman, L., 167
Terwilliger, J., 603, 604
Tesch-Romer, R., 318
Tharp, R., 123, 520, 521
Thoma, S., 87, 94
Thomas, E., 327
Thompson, M., 279
Thorkildsen, T., 617
Thorndike, E., 335
Thorndike, R., 629
Thornton, M., 45
Tingle, J., 560
Tirosh, D., 380
Tishman, S., 332, 375, 451
Titus, A., 609
Tobias, S., 608
Tobin, K., 459
Tom, A., 86
Tomkiewicz, S., 110
Tomlinson, C., 169
Tompkins, G., 44, 353, 354
Top, B., 187
Torrance, E., 134, 167
Trathen, W., 324
Trentham, L., 610
Trollip, S., 567
Troutman, A., 9, 478, 479
Trujillo, C., 426
Tubbs, M., 582
Turiel, E., 89
Turnbull, A., 154, 178
Turnbull, B., 540
Turnbull, H. R., 154
Turner, J., 244, 280
Tyler, R., 501, 502

Underwood, B., 267
Urdan, T., 416, 419, 625
U.S. Bureau of the Census, 17, 117, 134
U.S. Congress, Educational Amendment of 1978 [PL 95-561, IX(A)], 167
U.S. Department of Education, 114, 117, 126, 153, 156, 159, 160
U.S. Department of Health and Human Services, 85–86
Uttal, D., 438

Vaillant, C., 73
Vaillant, G., 73
Valencia, S., 596, 603
Vanderstoep, S., 319, 337, 376
Van Haneghan, J., 380
Van Leuvan, P., 313, 331
Vasquez, O., 129
Vaughn, S., 186
Vavrus, L., 475
Veenman, S., 272, 580
Verschaffel, L., 375
Villasenor, A., 380
Villegas, A., 117, 118, 123, 520
Vito, R., 137
Volker, R., 566
Voss, J., 250, 337
Vye, N., 329, 380
Vygotsky, L., 47, 280

Subject Index

guidelines for, 590
Trust, 71–72
T-score, 640
Tyler teacher-centered planning model, 501–509

Underachievers, 137
Undergeneralization, 61
Understanding. *See also* Learning
assessing current, 546
constructing, 281
current context and, 282
depth of, 337
learner-centered discussion and, 556–557
shared, 51
teaching for, 540–542
Universal principles stage, moral reasoning, 88, 90–91
Unstructured discovery, 550

Validity, assessment, 582–583, 585–593
construct, 633
content, 632
predictive, 632
standardized tests, 631–633
table of specifications and, 605–606

Value theories, motivation and, 402–404
Variable-interval schedule, 210
Variable-ratio schedule, 210
Variety, learning experience, 336
Verbal feedback, 456–457
Verbal-nonverbal congruence, 471–472
Vicarious learning, 196, 220–221, 224, 228
Violence, managing, 483–484
Visual disabilities, 152, 164–165, 192
Voluntary minorities, 118
Vygotsky, Lev, 26, 47
cooperative learning theory and, 560
on experience and learning, 217
on knowledge construction, 53, 54
language development and thinking, 48
self-regulation, reflection and, 49
social constructivism and, 279
social interaction and, 48–49
sociocultural development theory, 26, 47–53, 56, 66

Wait-time, 459, 527
Native American students and, 521
Wechsler scales, 629–630
Well-defined problems, 311

Whole language reading instruction, 351–352
Within-class grouping, 111
Withitness, 474–475
Working backward, 316
Working memory, 242, 244, 245–248
automaticity and, 247–248
chunking and, 247
limitations on, 246–248
screening function, 245–246
Writing, 361–370
classroom application, 360
generating ideas, 362–363
goal setting, 362
planning stage, 362–364
problem solving and, 361–362
process, 362–366, 392–393
revising stage, 365–366
teaching, 366–370, 392–393
translation stage, 364–365
Written feedback, 457

Zone of proximal development, 49–53, 65
constructivism and, 56
cooperative learning and, 560
Z-score, 640